Autism Spectrum Disorders

Identification, Education, and Treatment

Fourth Edition

Edited by Dianne Zager, David F. Cihak, and Angi Stone-MacDonald

Routledge
Taylor & Francis Group

NEW YORK AND LONDON

Fourth edition published 2017
by Routledge
711 Third Avenue, New York, NY 10017

and by Routledge
2 Park Square, Milton Park, Abingdon, Oxon OX14 4RN

Routledge is an imprint of the Taylor & Francis Group, an informa business

© 2017 Taylor & Francis

First edition published by L. Erlbaum Associates, 1992
Third edition published by Routledge, 2005

Library of Congress Cataloging in Publication Data
Names: Berkell Zager, Dianne, 1948- editor. | Cihak, David F., editor. |
    Stone-MacDonald, Angela, editor.
Title: Autism spectrum disorders : identification, education, and treatment,
    fourth edition / edited by Dianne Zager, David F. Cihak, Angi Stone-
    MacDonald.
Description: Fourth editon. | New York : Routledge, 2017. | Includes
    bibliographical references and index.
Identifiers: LCCN 2016010243| ISBN 9781138015692 (hbk.) |
    ISBN 9781138015708 (pbk.) | ISBN 9781315794181 (ebk)
Subjects: LCSH: Autism in children. | Autistic children—Education. |
    Autism—Treatment.
Classification: LCC RJ506.A9 A9223 2017 | DDC 618.92/85882—dc23
LC record available at http://lccn.loc.gov/2016010243

ISBN: 978-1-138-01569-2 (hbk)
ISBN: 978-1-138-01570-8 (pbk)
ISBN: 978-1-315-79418-1 (ebk)

Typeset in Sabon
by Swales & Willis Ltd, Exeter, Devon, UK
Printed at CPI on sustainably sourced paper

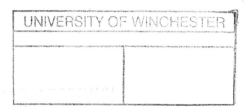

Dedication

This book is dedicated to the many knowledgeable and talented professionals who serve children and adults with autism spectrum disorders. It is our hope that you will find the information provided in the following chapters helpful in your efforts to improve the quality of life for people with autism.

Contents

Preface

Since the third edition of *Autism Spectrum Disorders: Identification, Education, and Treatment* in 2005, the incidence of autism spectrum disorders has risen steadily, with a corresponding increase in the demand for information about causes and treatment of the disorder. In the past decade, there have been changes in diagnostic criteria and nomenclature, as well as an explosion of research and development in our field. With the addition of David F. Cihak and Angi Stone-MacDonald, as co-editors, this text examines the extant knowledge base in the field of autism, with consideration of issues relevant today, providing an overview of the current state-of-the-science.

This new edition brings readers up to date on past, present, and emerging directions in education and intervention. The prior edition had been responsive to the astounding increases in diagnosis through its broadened focus across the spectrum and incorporation of advances to the field. In this edition, advances in education and treatment are considered in relation to needs of individuals on the spectrum through the continuum of developmental stages. Chapter authors examine historical perspectives, evidence-based best practices, and emerging trends.

The text is divided into three sections. The first section sets the stage for the following chapters with an overview of the field, beginning with diagnostic criteria changes for Autism Spectrum Disorders (ASD) in the Fifth Edition of the *Diagnostic and Statistical Manual* (DSM-5; American Psychiatry Association, 2012). In Chapter 1, Carter, Maye, and Kiss describe the new clinical diagnosis criteria for ASD and the impact on educational services. In Chapter 2, Smith, Schaefer, and Mrla provide an historical overview of ASD. They describe clinical cases since the 1700s and how ASD has been defined and redefined over time as a result of advocacy, litigation, and legislation. Legislation, program development, and service delivery for people with ASD are presented in Chapter 3. Murdick and Gartin describe the impact of IDEA and other key legislation on people with ASD, as well as service delivery models and the Universal Design for Learning framework for meeting children's instructional needs. In Chapter 4, Umbarger discusses advances in neurobiological research. Over the past decade, considerable progress has been made in the identification of biological risk factors that define specific neuroanatomy and pathways underlying the associated characteristics related to ASD. This section concludes with a global perspective of autism in Chapter 5. Stone-MacDonald and Cousik examine the role of the World Health Organization (WHO) and the challenges faced by families. Educational opportunities and treatments in African countries, China, India, and the Middle East are highlighted.

The second section focuses on evidence-based practices for children from birth through elementary school across developmental domains. Each chapter highlights the most current research and examples of evidence-based practices for children with autism spectrum disorder. In the first chapter in this section, Fettig and Fleury discuss issues of diagnosis and early treatment for children in the early intervention system. Denning and Moody describe placement challenges and service delivery as children transition to preschool and kindergarten settings, focusing on play-based interventions in Chapter 7. Whitby, Lorah, Love, and Lawless describe interventions for young children to address speech and language issues and improve communication skills to increase access to the curriculum in Chapter 8. In Chapter 9, Boutot, Ramey, and Pullen discuss functional behavior assessment and current intervention strategies for addressing challenging behaviors and provide detailed descriptions and examples of behavior management strategies for children in elementary and middle school. Wood, Thompson, and Root delve into academic interventions for Science, Math, and English/Language Arts at the elementary level and provide strategies to engage students in the curriculum with their peers in Chapter 10. The final chapter in this section by Cihak and Smith brings together communication and behavior to provide examples of evidence-based interventions to support children's social skills, self-regulation, and independence.

The third section of the text addresses the needs of adolescents and young adults. The section begins by addressing self-determination for school and community in Chapter 12 by Wehmeyer and Shogren, who present information on self-determination and student involvement in transition planning. Self-determination competence has been shown to be causally related to more positive school and transition outcomes and to be predictive of positive quality of life and life satisfaction outcomes. An introduction to Universal Design for Transition (UDT) is presented in Chapter 13. Thoma, Cain, Wojcik, Best, and Scott describe UDT, introducing a new framework for educational planning/instructional design, and assessment that promotes successful transitional outcomes by combining academic and transition education. Chapter 14 by Cote and Sparks focuses on individualized behavioral supports, behavioral management strategies, positive learning environments, cognitive behavioral modification strategies, and intervention strategies for students with ASD in middle and high school. Stansberry-Brusnahan, Ellison, and Hafner examine the secondary to postsecondary transition in Chapter 15, by presenting a variety of higher education models and programs and highlighting economic and employment benefits of higher education. In Chapter 16, Zager and Dreyfus delve into integrated employment and community living. Components of secondary and postsecondary education programs are covered, with a focus on collaborative models that include personnel from varied disciplines, family involvement, and experiences and supports needed to enhance the likelihood of successful outcomes. The culminating chapter deals with the field as a whole from the early years through young adulthood. In this closing chapter, Bouck and Weng discuss the critical issue of collaboration among professionals across disciplines.

This new edition describes up-to-date, evidence-based practices and service delivery models to educate and treat people with ASD from the early years and diagnosis to adulthood. The text addresses advocacy, legislation, and current issues that resulted in improved services and opportunities in the United States. Scientific advances are occurring rapidly and this edition describes current research to inform practices to ensure all people with ASD are self-determined to actively and fully participate in their education, community, and society.

The fourth edition of *Autism Spectrum Disorders: Identification, Education, and Treatment* is the product of the collective and cumulative efforts of many leaders in the field of ASD. Because of their efforts, readers of this edition will be introduced to topics by scholars whose research has helped to define and develop current practices in the education and treatment of people with ASD with a global perspective. We would like to thank the authors for their seminal work and outstanding contributions to this new edition of *Autism Spectrum Disorders: Identification, Education, and Treatment*.

Dianne Zager, David Cihak, and
Angi Stone-MacDonald

Contributors

Kathryn Best, M.A., Doctoral Candidate, Special Education & Disability Policy, School of Education, Virginia Commonwealth University.

Emily C. Bouck, Ph.D., Associate Professor, Department of Counseling, Special Education, and Educational Psychology, College of Education, Michigan State University.

E. Amanda Boutot, Ph.D., BCBA-D, Associate Professor, Department of Curriculum and Instruction, College of Education, Texas State University.

Irina Cain, M.Ed., Doctoral Candidate, Chair of Department of Special Education & Disability Policy, Virginia Commonwealth University.

Alice S. Carter, Ph.D., Professor of Psychology, Department of Clinical Psychology, University of Massachusetts Boston.

David F. Cihak, Ph.D., Associate Professor, Special Education Program Coordinator, Department of Theory & Practice in Teacher Education, College of Education, Health & Human Sciences, University of Tennessee.

Debra L. Cote, Ph.D., Associate Professor, Department of Special Education, College of Education, California State University, Fullerton.

Rama Cousik, Ph.D., Assistant Professor, Special Education, Indiana University – Purdue University, Fort Wayne.

Christopher B. Denning, Ph.D., Assistant Professor, College of Education and Human Development, University of Massachusetts Boston.

Francine L. Dreyfus, Ed.D., Adjunct Assistant Professor, Department of Special Education, Hunter College, City University of New York.

Marc Ellison, Ed.D., Executive Director, LPC, West Virginia Autism Training Center, The College Program for Students with Autism Spectrum Disorder, Marshall University, West Virginia.

Angel Fettig, Ph.D., Assistant Professor of Early Childhood Education, University of Massachusetts Boston.

Veronica P. Fleury, Ph.D., Assistant Professor of Special Education, Department of Educational Psychology, College of Education and Human Development, University of Minnesota.

Barbara C. Gartin, Ed.D., Professor, Special Education, School of Education, Department of CIED/Special Education, University of Arkansas.

Ivy Giserman Kiss, M.A., Doctoral Candidate, Clinical Psychology, University of Massachusetts Boston.

Dedra Hafner, Ed.D., Assistant Professor, Director of Cutting-Edge, Edgewood College, School of Education, Madison, Wisconsin.

Gauri S. Joshi, Ph.D., Volunteer Research Assistant, Department of Special Education, Portland State University, Oregon.

Hollie Lawless, M.Ed., Research Assistant, Department of Curriculum and Instruction, College of Education and Health Professions, University of Arkansas.

Elizabeth Lorah, Ph.D., BCBA-D, Assistant Professor of Curriculum and Instruction College of Education and Health Professions, University of Arkansas.

Jessica Love, Ph.D. BCBA-D, Center for Autism Spectrum Disorders, Project and Research Coordinator, University of Nevada, Las Vegas.

L. Lynn Stansberry-Brusnahan, Ph.D., Associate Professor, Autism Spectrum Disorder Programming, University of St. Thomas, Minnesota.

Melissa P. Maye, M.A., Doctoral Candidate, Clinical Psychology, University of Massachusetts Boston.

Amelia K. Moody, Ph.D., Associate Professor, Watson College of Education, Department of Early Childhood, Elementary, Middle Grades, Literacy and Special Education, University of North Carolina at Wilmington.

Tiffany Mrla, MAT, BCBA, Doctoral Student, College of Education & Health Professions, University of Arkansas.

Nikki L. Murdick, Ph.D., Professor, Disability Education, School of Education, Saint Louis University, Missouri.

Nathan Pullen, Austin Independent School District, Austin, Texas.

Devon Ramey, M.Ed., BCBA, Doctoral Student, School of Psychology, Trinity University, Dublin.

Jenny Root, M.Ed., BCBA, Graduate Research Assistant, Department of Special Education and Child Development, College of Education, University of North Carolina at Charlotte.

Peggy Schaefer-Whitby, Ph.D., BCBA-D, Associate Professor, Special Education Program Coordinator, Department of Curriculum and Instruction, College of Education and Health Professions, University of Arkansas.

LaRon A. Scott, Ed.D., Assistant Professor, Department of Special Education & Disability Policy, Virginia Commonwealth University.

Karrie A. Shogren, Ph.D., Associate Professor, Department of Special Education; Co-director, Kansas University Center on Developmental Disabilities; Associate Director and Associate Scientist, Beach Center on Disability, University of Kansas.

Cate C. Smith, Ph.D., Assistant Professor, Department of Reading Education and Special Education, Appalachian State University, North Carolina.

Tom E.C. Smith, Ed.D., Dean, College of Education and Health Professions, University of Arkansas.

Shannon L. Sparks, Ph.D., Visiting Faculty, Las Vegas College of Education, University of Nevada, Las Vegas.

Angi Stone-MacDonald, Ph.D., Assistant Professor, Curriculum and Instruction, University of Massachusetts Boston.

Colleen A. Thoma, Ph.D., Professor and Chair of Department of Special Education & Disability Policy, Virginia Commonwealth University.

Julie L. Thompson, Ph.D., BCBA-D, Research Associate, Counseling, Educational Psychology, and Special Education, Michigan State University.

Gardner T. Umbarger, III, Ph.D., Associate Professor, Special Education, Saginaw Valley State University, Michigan.

Michael L. Wehmeyer, Ph.D., Professor, Department of Special Education, Director, Kansas University Center on Developmental Disabilities, and Senior Scientist, Beach Center on Disability, University of Kansas.

Pei-Lin Weng, Ph.D., Assistant Professor, Department of Special Education and Professional Counseling, College of Education, William Patterson University, New Jersey.

Andrew J. Wojcik, M.Ed., Doctoral Candidate, Department of Special Education & Disability Policy, Virginia Commonwealth University & Adaptive and General Education Curriculum Specialist, Albemarle County Public Schools, Richmond, Virginia.

Leah Wood, Ph.D., BCBA-D, Assistant Professor of Special Education, School of Education, California Polytechnic State University.

Dianne Zager, Ph.D., Michael C. Koffler Professor in Autism, Dyson College of Arts and Sciences, Pace University, New York.

Chapter 1

Definitions and Classification of Autism Spectrum Disorders

Melissa P. Maye, Ivy Giserman Kiss, and Alice S. Carter

Autism Spectrum Disorder, a new diagnosis in the fifth edition of the Diagnostic and Statistical Manual (DSM-5), was developed to classify individuals with impairments due to difficulties with social communication and social interaction, as well as the presence of restrictive and repetitive behaviors, interests, or activities (American Psychiatric Association, 2013). Autism Spectrum Disorder (ASD) replaces a set of diagnoses that were included in the fourth edition of the Diagnostic and Statistical Manual (DSM-IV), including Autistic Disorder, Pervasive Developmental Disorder (PDD) – Not Otherwise Specified, and Asperger's Disorder (APA, 2000). These diagnoses were previously grouped together within a category labeled Pervasive Developmental Disorders. At present, it is estimated that one in 68 children (one in 42 boys; one in 189 girls) have an ASD diagnosis (Center for Disease Control, 2014).

In this chapter, the ways in which the conceptualization of the construct *autism* has changed over the last century are explored, and modifications made to the diagnostic criteria in each edition of the DSM are described. Special emphasis is placed on the most recent changes introduced in the DSM-5 in 2013. Symptom criteria that are used to diagnose Autism Spectrum Disorder in the DSM-5 are described in detail.

A number of screening tools and diagnostic measures have been developed to aid clinicians and researchers in making earlier and more accurate diagnoses of the previous diagnosis of PDD and the current diagnosis of ASD (e.g., Lord et al., 2012; Lord, Rutter, & Le Couteur et al., 1994; Luyster et al., 2009; Robins et al., 2014; Rutter, Bailey, Lord, Cianchetti, & Fancello, 2007; Schopler, Van Bourgondien, Wellman, & Love, 2010; Stone, Coonrod, & Turner; 2004; Stone, McMahon, & Henderson, 2008). In addition to reviewing historical shifts in diagnostic criteria and conceptualizations, this chapter presents three diagnostic measures that are widely used in diagnostic assessment and have strong evidentiary bases. It is important to note that while these diagnostic measures are extremely useful as aids in clinical decision-making, they are not considered diagnostic instruments. They should be used to inform, rather than to replace, clinical judgment.

Historical Changes in Diagnosis and DSM Criteria

The conceptualization of ASD has changed over time to accommodate our evolving understanding of the disorder. In 1911, Eugen Bleuler, a Swiss psychiatrist, coined the terms *autism* and *autistic*, which were developed from the root Greek word *autos*, meaning *self*. Bleuler used the term *autism* to describe a symptom of Schizophrenia, in which individuals actively withdrew from the external world and into themselves, "rejecting reality" (Moskowitz & Heim, 2011). Regarding this *autistic* behavioral pattern, Bleuler (1951) wrote, "the most severe cases withdraw completely and live in a dream world; the milder cases withdraw to a lesser degree" (p. 399). Rather than referring to individuals now understood to have ASD, Bleuler intended for his term *autism* to refer to the "isolated self" observed in individuals with psychosis. Thus, in DSM-I, published in 1952, the term *autism* was used to describe psychotic reactions observed in children with childhood-onset Schizophrenia (American Psychiatric Association, 1952). DSM-II (American Psychiatric Association, 1968) also mentioned autism only within the context of childhood Schizophrenia.

Between the 1940s and 1960s, the symptom of autism continued to be widely regarded as an early indicator of childhood Schizophrenia (Baker, 2013). Moreover, causing significant stigma, pain, and suffering to families, this symptom was often erroneously attributed to distant parenting (Bettelheim, 1967). During this time, Leo Kanner, an American psychiatrist, sought to distinguish autism as its own disorder, characterized by a unique set of behaviors, independent of childhood Schizophrenia. Kanner's 1943 publication, entitled "Autistic disturbances of affective contact," presented 11 comprehensive case histories of children with characteristics similar to those by which ASD is defined today. Their shared symptoms included social withdrawal, echolalia, the need for sameness/resistance to change, atypical sensory responses, and repetitive behaviors such as spinning and rocking. Kanner rejected the commonly held belief that autism was a product of "cold" child-rearing environments, and instead came to believe that autism was congenital in nature (Baker, 2013; Kanner, 1943). Kanner's documentation of the common behavioral profiles of this group of patients broadened the definition and understanding of autism as a behavioral disorder.

Interestingly, at the same time that Kanner was completing his work in the United States, Hans Asperger, an Austrian pediatrician, used the term *autistic* to describe a group of four boys who had traits similar to Kanner's cohort of patients but who were higher-functioning in terms of cognitive capacities. In his classic "Autistic psychopathology" article published in 1944, Asperger described deficits that were slightly more social in nature in the four boys whom he characterized as "little professors," a term that was often applied to describe children who met criteria for the later defined Asperger's Syndrome, which was included in DSM-IV, but is considered part of ASD in DSM-5.

The works of Kanner, Asperger, and Rimland suggested that autism was based in biology and not caused by distant or cold parenting. These early writings laid the groundwork for the emergence of infantile autism as its own disorder in the DSM-III in 1980. Infantile autism in the DSM-III, consisted of the following three major symptom clusters, each of which had to emerge before 30 months of age: lack of responsiveness to others, severe impairments in language development, and "bizarre responses" to aspects of the environment. Additionally, to distinguish infantile autism from childhood Schizophrenia, the authors of the DSM-III included a requirement of an absence of delusions and hallucinations. DSM-III applied a monothetic approach (i.e. an individual had to meet all three diagnostic criteria), and therefore focused on what might now be considered classic autism, as manifested in more severely affected individuals.

The conceptualization of the disorder changed significantly from DSM-III to DSM-III-R (APA, 1987). This version introduced a more developmental emphasis and polythetic criteria (i.e. an individual had to meet a certain minimal number of defining characteristics, but not all symptoms of the diagnostic criteria) in which individuals had to meet only eight of 16 defined criteria. Additionally, the requirement for an age of onset prior to 30 months was removed. The descriptions of the 16 possible symptoms in the DSM-III-R reflected an attempt to enhance diagnostic precision based on the prevailing understandings of the disorder, which were rooted in both the extant research and clinical practice. To meet criteria for the diagnosis, an individual needed to show at least two of five symptoms that reflected evidence of impaired reciprocal social interaction, one of six symptoms that reflected evidence of impaired verbal and nonverbal communication, and one of five symptoms that reflected the presence of restricted and/or repetitive behavior. Further, the authors of the DSM-III-R created an additional category called Pervasive Developmental Disorder – Not Otherwise Specified (PDD-NOS) for children who displayed some of these symptoms but did not meet the full criteria for a diagnosis of autistic disorder. While the given list of symptoms provided a more structured organization of the criteria for the disorder, the addition of PDD-NOS increased the overall flexibility of the application of the diagnosis and increased the number of individuals who met criteria for these disorders (Hansen, Schendel, & Par, 2015).

While DSM-III-R included the addition of PDD-NOS, it was not until the 1990s that Lorna Wing, an English psychiatrist, and Uta Frith, an

English psychologist, popularized the term *Asperger's Syndrome*. The work of Wing and Frith contributed to another shift in the conceptualization of autism when Asperger's Syndrome was officially recognized as a distinct subtype of the disorder in the publication of DSM-IV in 1994. The diagnostic criteria for Asperger's Syndrome were similar to that of autistic disorder, but required typical language development, average cognitive abilities, and average adaptive behavior abilities (other than in social interaction). At this point, clinicians and researchers began to conceptualize autism along a broad continuum or spectrum of functioning levels and abilities (Baker, 2013).

Similar to DSM-III-R, DSM-IV relied on a polythetic approach, such that a diagnosis of autistic disorder required at least six of 12 listed criteria. To receive the diagnosis, an individual was required to evidence at least two of four symptoms of "qualitatively" impaired social interaction, one of four symptoms of "qualitatively" impaired communication, and one of four restricted or repetitive behaviors or interests. Moreover, the age of onset criteria was reinstated: at least one of the behaviors needed to be evident prior to three years of age. The criteria for autistic disorder, PDD-NOS and Asperger's Syndrome did not change in DSM-IV-TR, published in 2000.

The publication of the DSM-5 (APA, 2013) sparked a great deal of controversy among family members, clinicians, and researchers. It also captured the attention of the general public, as marked changes were made to the criteria and manner in which disorders would be classified. Specifically, multiple disorders are now subsumed within a single autism spectrum disorder classification, a major change from the manner in which disorders were grouped in DSM-IV. In addition, where appropriate, in DSM-5 clinicians are required to provide a qualifier to the ASD diagnosis, which is quantified along a continuum of severity. The qualifier is used to designate the degree of support the individual with ASD requires, ranging from individuals who require minimal support to those who require very substantial support. Additionally, the qualifier helps to describe an individual's current symptomatology with the recognition that severity may vary by context. The revision committee eliminated the subtypes of Asperger's Syndrome and PDD-NOS as well as the overarching category of Pervasive Developmental Disorders, replacing these classifications with a single classification termed Autism Spectrum Disorder (Ozonoff, 2012).

This decision created a powerful discourse regarding the loss of an entire group's identity. For example, Giles (2013) discussed how a culture developed around the diagnosis of Asperger's Syndrome, and thus meeting criteria for this disorder shaped a "blueprint for social identity" (p. 3). The committee justified their decision of creating a single "autism spectrum disorder" (ASD) diagnosis based on a body of evidence supporting that differentiation of ASD from typical development and other childhood disorders was done reliably and validly, while the distinction between the three subtypes was found to be inconsistent and varied across research sites (Gibbs et al., 2012).

Moreover, in DSM-5 the traditional triad of symptom domains (i.e. social, communication, and atypical/repetitive behaviors) was reduced to a dyad of symptoms by combining social and communication symptoms into a single domain (social communication deficits) to emphasize the social nature of communication symptoms relevant in ASD. In addition, sensory abnormalities were added to the second domain of restricted, repetitive behaviors, interests, or activities (RRBI). Sensory abnormalities were not included in the DSM-IV-TR RRBI criteria. In contrast to the polythetic criteria in the third and fourth editions of the manual, the DSM-5 re-adopted a mixed monothetic and polythetic approach that requires meeting all of the listed social-communicative criteria (i.e., monothetic) that is contrasted with a polythetic approach for RRBI criteria, for which only two of the four defined symptoms must be present to assign a diagnosis. Finally, the specific age of onset was removed so that symptoms of the disorder must be present in infancy or early childhood, recognizing that the full disorder may become apparent in later years as the social demands of interpersonal relations increase.

The development of the new DSM-5 diagnosis of ASD leaves some questions unanswered. Although the majority of individuals who would have met DSM-IV criteria are likely to also meet DSM-5 criteria, there will not be 100 percent concordance. It remains unclear who will gain and who will lose a diagnosis with the revised DSM-5 diagnostic criteria, and what the long-term effects will be on access to services. Revising the organization, criteria, and nomenclature for describing the individuals first identified by Kanner and Asperger as having a unique set of symptoms associated with impairment associated autism is not a new phenomena. The conceptualization of ASD has undergone several shifts over time to accommodate new understandings of the etiology and developmental course of the disorder.

Symptoms

ASD is currently characterized by impairments in an individual's social communication as well as the presence of RRBIs. Both retrospective and prospective research has informed the current conceptualization of the diagnosis (Ozonoff, 2012). Below, the defining symptoms of ASD, as described in the DSM-5, are explained in detail. The symptoms are divided into two domains: (1) impaired social communication skills (including impaired social-emotional reciprocity, impaired nonverbal communication, and atypical social relationships) and (2) restrictive and repetitive behaviors and interests. See Table 1.1 for DSM-5 descriptions of social communication and social interaction symptoms and restricted, repetitive patterns of behavior, interests, or activities symptoms (APA, 2013).

Table 1.1 Autism Spectrum Disorder DSM-5 Criteria for Social Communication and Restricted and Repetitive Patterns of Behavior, Interests, or Activities

A. *Persistent deficits in social communication and social interaction across multiple contexts, as manifested by the following, currently or by history (examples are illustrative, not exhaustive; see text):*

1 Deficits in social-emotional reciprocity	*Examples:* abnormal social approach and failure of normal back-and-forth conversation, reduced sharing of interests, emotions, or affect, failure to initiate or respond to social interactions
2 Deficits in nonverbal communicative behaviors used for social interaction	*Examples:* poorly integrated verbal and nonverbal communication, abnormalities in eye contact and body language or deficits in understanding and use of gestures, a lack of facial expressions and nonverbal communication
3 Deficits in developing, maintaining, and understanding relationships	*Examples:* difficulties adjusting behavior to suit various social contexts, difficulties in sharing imaginative play or in making friends, absence of interest in peers

B *Restricted, repetitive patterns of behavior, interests, or activities, as manifested by at least two of the following, currently or by history (examples are illustrative, not exhaustive; see text):*

1 Stereotyped or repetitive motor movements, use of objects, or speech	*Examples:* simple motor stereotypies, lining up toys or flipping objects, echolalia, idiosyncratic phrases
2 Insistence on sameness, inflexible adherence to routines, or ritualized patterns or verbal nonverbal behavior	*Examples:* extreme distress at small changes, difficulties with transitions, rigid thinking patterns, greeting rituals, need to take same route or eat food every day
3 Highly restricted, fixated interests that are abnormal in intensity or focus	*Examples:* strong attachment to or preoccupation with unusual objects, excessively circumscribed or perseverative interest
4 Hyper- or hyporeactivity to sensory input or unusual interests in sensory aspects of the environment	*Examples:* apparent indifference to pain/temperature, adverse response to specific sounds or textures, excessive smelling or touching of objects, visual fascination with lights or movement

A. Impaired Social Communication Domain

1. Impaired Social-emotional Reciprocity

Starting from a very early age, children with ASD show abnormal social-emotional responses (De Giacomo & Fombonne, 1998; Gillberg et al., 1999; Guinchat et al., 2012; Osterling & Dawson, 1994; Webb & Jones,

2009; Werner, Dawson, Osterling, & Dinno, 2000; Wimpory, Hobson, Williams, & Nash, 2000; Young, Brewer, & Pattison, 2003), including the presence of some or all of the following symptoms: lack of and/or abnormal eye contact or gaze; decreased frequency of looking at others' faces; lack of interest in playing with other children; preference for playing alone; absence of pointing, giving, and showing objects; and lack of response to social stimuli, such as the child's own name being called. Such impaired social-emotional responses have been documented as early as within the first six months of life (Maestro et al., 2002). However, prospective studies of high-risk infants (infant-siblings of older children diagnosed with ASD) have revealed that most infants who go on to later receive an ASD diagnosis do not show significant differences in social-emotional responses until the second year of life (Ozonoff et al., 2010). By 12 months of age, some infants later diagnosed with ASD can be differentiated from those who remain unaffected by the absence of social-communication competencies and/or atypical social-communication behaviors, including limited or unusual eye contact (Zwaigenbaum et al., 2005) and failure to orient to their name being called (Frohna, 2007). However, other children become asymptomatic and do not meet diagnostic criteria until 18, 24, 30, or even 36 months of age (Ozonoff et al., 2010). In preschool and older-aged children, adolescents, and adults, impaired social-emotional reciprocity can also include a limited ability to engage in a back-and-forth conversation, reduced sharing of interests and emotions, and an absence of initiation of/response to social interactions.

2. Impaired Nonverbal Communication

Nonverbal communication includes facial expressions, body postures, and gestures, and is used to communicate needs, wants, and desires directly (e.g. pointing to direct attention, reaching to be picked up, shrugging shoulders to indicate lack of knowledge). Nonverbal communication may also be used to add nuance or punctuation to verbal communication (e.g. winking during or following a statement, nodding the head and/or using hand gestures while speaking) and to supplement language to help engage and connect with listeners and emphasize messages. Children and adults with ASD show deficits in nonverbal communication that is used for social purposes. It is common for individuals with ASD to demonstrate a lack of or atypical use of eye contact, facial expressions, and body language, as well as a reduced use and understanding of gestures. Additionally, children and adults with ASD oftentimes show atypical prosody, or changes in intonation and rhythm in speech. Instead of modulating his or her tone of voice, a child or adult with ASD will babble or speak in an abnormal or flat/monotonous tone that lacks appropriate stress or emphasis (Jones, Gliga, Bedford, Charman, & Johnson, 2014).

3. Atypical Social Relationships

Across the lifespan, individuals with ASD have difficulties relating to others. In early childhood, infants and toddlers with ASD often demonstrate a reduced interest in people, and show a decreased frequency of looking at faces as well as a lack of interest in playing with other children. Children with ASD have difficulty initiating and sharing in imaginative play; they tend to struggle to engage in pretend play, especially with regard to the frequency, complexity, spontaneity, and playfulness of the activity (Porter, 2012). As they grow older, children with ASD continue to have difficulty maintaining and understanding social relationships. For example, children with the disorder frequently show a limited ability to pick up social cues to appropriately adjust their behavior to various social contexts (Jing & Fang, 2014).

B. Repetitive and Restricted Behaviors and Interests Domain

1. Stereotyped or Repetitive Motor and Vocal Mannerisms

Because repetitive motor mannerisms are commonly seen in typical development, some of the behaviors that are characteristic of older children with ASD may be hard to distinguish from typical behaviors (Jones et al., 2014). However, well-documented stereotypies in young children include repetitive hand and body movements, lining up toys, repeating idiosyncratic words or phrases, and spinning, rotating, and/or exploring objects visually in an unusual manner sometimes described as peering (Ozonoff et al., 2008). A recent review of stereotypic behavior in ASD (DiGennaro Reed, Hirst, & Hyman, 2012) found that commonly reported forms of stereotypic behaviors in ASD included body/head rocking/swaying, unrecognizable vocalizations, and hand flapping/waving, along with 25 additional categories of stereotypies.

2. Inflexible Adherence to Routines or Rituals

Starting in toddlerhood, individuals with ASD frequently begin to show a desire for, or insistence on, sameness (Leekam et al., 2007), which can also manifest as distress when rituals and/or routines are disrupted. Across childhood, this desire can take the form of the following behaviors: extreme distress at small changes, challenges with transitions, or the need to follow the same routine every day (American Psychiatric Association, 2013). Additionally, rigid thinking patterns and cognitive inflexibility often emerge as children with ASD grow older; these frequently lead to behavioral and social impairments (Memari, 2013).

3. Preoccupations and Restricted Interests

Children and adults with ASD often have highly narrow interests. The term *restricted interest* is frequently interchanged with the terms *circumscribed interest* and *special interest*. Examples of restricted interests for children with ASD are particular machines, train schedules, and dinosaurs (Porter, 2012). The intensive and extensive knowledge gained about a restricted interest may or may not have any utility (e.g. an interest in train schedules for a specific city in another country or in the past, or a preoccupation with memorizing and updating the map of the NYC subway). Individuals with ASD become hyper-focused on or preoccupied with restricted interests, and therefore become cognitively "stuck" (Charman, 2008). Early intervention services for children with ASD often focus on the ability to be redirected and the skill of flexibility.

4. Sensory Behaviors

Many children and adults with ASD respond differently than individuals with typical development to sensory stimuli. Prior to the DSM-5, sensory behaviors were not included in the diagnostic criteria for the disorder. A recent review by Hazen, Stornelli, O'Rourke, Koesterer, and McDougle (2014) describes the three most common categories of impaired sensory modulation. The first category is *sensory overresponsivity*, where an individual experiences distress or a strong negative reaction to sensory input, often leading to avoidance (e.g. a child having an intense negative reaction to the noise of sirens, leading her to cover her ears or run away from police cars and fire trucks). The second category is *sensory underresponsivity*, in which an individual may seem to be unaware of, or display a delayed reaction to, a sensory stimulus that would normally lead to a response (e.g. a toddler repeatedly banging his or her head on the bottom of a table as if nothing happened, a teenager not reacting when he puts his hand on a hot stove). The final category of impaired sensory modulation is *sensory-seeking behavior*, also referred to as *craving*, in which an individual demonstrates a preoccupation with certain sensory experiences (e.g. a child repetitively staring at things that move or emit light, or a child licking walls or the floor).

Current Assessment Tools for Diagnosis

Researchers have completed extensive research over the last several decades in an effort to both define the construct of autism and to identify those at risk for an ASD. At present, autism screening and diagnostic research has made it possible to identify children at high risk for ASD based on elevated ASD symptoms, and to diagnose ASD in children as young as 12 months of age (Luyster et al., 2009; Osterling, Dawson, & Munson, 2002; Ozonoff et al., 2008; Ozonoff et al., 2010; Zwaigenbaum et al., 2005). A number of empirically validated screening tools exist to help professionals identify children who are in need of a more thorough ASD evaluation in research and clinical settings (e.g. pediatric offices). These measures include brief screening instruments such as the (a) Modified Checklist for Autism in Toddlers, (age range: 16 to 30 months) (Robins et al., 2014); (b) longer questionnaires to capture variability in normative and atypical expressions of symptoms such as the Social Communication Questionnaire (48 months of age and older) (Rutter et al., 2008); (c) observational, play-based assessments that can supplement screening questionnaires or be used independently for screening, such as the Screening Tool for Autism in Toddlers and Young Children (18 to 36 months of age) (Stone et al., 2004; Stone et al., 2008); (d) Autism Observation Scale for Infants, (6 to 18 months of age) (Bryson, Zwaigenbaum, McDermott, Rombough, & Brian, 2008); and (e) Communication and Symbolic Behavior Scales – Developmental Profile, (9 to 24 months of age) (Wetherby, 2001). Screening tools are used in a number of settings, most prominently in pediatric offices. Families are often given screeners at well-child visits, beginning at 18 months of age. If a child performs poorly on a screening questionnaire, pediatricians should discuss the findings with parents and, when appropriate, refer children for a developmental and diagnostic evaluation by a psychologist, psychiatrist, or developmental pediatrician.

Once referred, children suspected to be at risk of having ASD should ideally receive an evidence-based assessment of their current behaviors and interactions. The Autism Diagnostic Observation Schedule – Second Edition (ADOS-2; Lord et al., 2012) is considered the gold standard empirically validated observational assessment of ASD and is widely used in research on individuals with ASD. A second empirically validated tool is the Childhood Autism Rating Scales, Second Edition (CARS2; Schopler et al., 2010). These two empirically validated observational measures allow clinicians to directly assess an individual's behaviors and interactions. Both the ADOS-2 and CARS2 are appropriate for very young children through adulthood; the CARS2 is recommended for children 24 months of age and older and the ADOS-2 has a specific Toddler Module (Luyster et al., 2009) that is appropriate for children as young as 12 months of age.

The *Autism Diagnostic Interview – Revised* (ADI-R; Lord et al., 1994) is an empirically validated, semi-structured caregiver interview that provides information about the identified individual's social, communication, and restricted and repetitive behaviors. The ADI-R allows comprehensive data to be gathered regarding both the individual's current and past functioning and is suitable for use in children 3.5 years old and older. In the following sections, each measure is described in relation to the population for which it was designed, how the measure is administered, and what psychometric data are available; including where appropriate, internal consistency, sensitivity, and specificity. These measures can be used in combination in clinical diagnostic practice.

The *Autism Diagnostic Observation Schedule-2* (ADOS-2; Lord et al., 2012) is an observational assessment that trained clinicians can use as one part of their diagnostic battery to assess for the presence of ASD. The ADOS-2 takes approximately 45 minutes to one hour to complete and consists of five modules, which are appropriate for individuals across the lifespan and across different levels of linguistic and developmental functioning. The newest module, the Toddler Module, is appropriate for young children between 12 and 30 months of age, who have not yet obtained phrase speech but have a nonverbal mental age of at least 12 months, and are walking independently (Luyster et al., 2009). An administration of the ADOS-2 consists of a series of semi-structured, play-based tasks that elicit social communication behaviors and skills that are rated on a variety of dimensions to acquire a score in the Social Affective Domain (SA Domain), as well as ratings of observed restricted interests, repetitive behaviors, and sensory interests in the Restrictive Repetitive Behavior domain (RRB domain). Throughout the administration, the clinician takes detailed observational notes regarding the participant's verbalizations and behaviors in the SA, and RRB domains.

The Toddler Module is comprised of 11 semi-structured tasks that elicit behaviors that are used to assess a toddler's social communication abilities as well as the presence or absence of sensory interests and RRBIs. Some of these tasks include: a free play interaction, a bubble play task where the examiner blows bubbles without explicitly calling the toddler's attention to them and then pauses to see whether or how the child requests more bubbles, a bath time routine with a doll to assess the presence or quality of functional and pretend play, and anticipatory social routines where the examiner engages the toddler in an interaction and observes his or her responses.

During these different tasks, the examiner observes how the toddler responds and notes behaviors and verbalizations relevant for considering social communication skills and presence of RRBI. For example, during the bubble-blowing task, the examiner notes the toddler's reaction to the bubbles being blown around the room. We might expect a typical toddler to look up, make eye contact with the examiner, and smile. The toddler also might notice the bubbles and direct his or her caregiver's attention to them by pointing at the bubbles, smiling, using eye contact, and looking back and forth between the bubbles and the caregiver. However, it is likely that toddlers with an ASD would use few of these joint attention strategies when noticing the bubbles. Additionally, sensory interests and

RRBIs may be noted during this task. For example, a child may explore the bubble toy in a sensory-seeking manner by visually inspecting the toy bubble blower while looking at it and watching the propellers spin out of the corner of his/her eyes. Or, the toddler may demonstrate a restricted interest in colors by labeling all of the colors on the toy bubble blower as well as most of the colors of other objects throughout the assessment.

Modules 1 and 2 of the ADOS-2 are for individuals older than 30 months of age who have not yet attained fluent speech. Module 1 is appropriate for individuals who are either non-verbal or use single words only and is comprised of 10 semi-structured tasks. Module 2 is appropriate for individuals who are using phrase speech and is comprised of 14 semi-structured tasks, with many tasks overlapping from Module 1.

Modules 1 and 2 both have tasks that overlap with the Toddler Module, such as a free play interaction, a task testing the child's response to his or her name, a task assessing the child's response to joint attention, and anticipation of a social routine with the examiner. Different from Module 1, Module 2 includes tasks that require a higher level of language ability. Some examples of these tasks are making up a story using a picture book that has few words, having a simple conversation with the examiner, and demonstrating make-believe play using a variety of toys and figures.

A birthday party routine task is present in both Modules 1 and 2. The birthday party interaction follows a simple script where children are given multiple opportunities to imitate play, expand on the prompts the examiner provides, and create their own make-believe play interaction. During this interaction, examiners can note any relevant social communication skills, sensory interests, or RRBIs. However, the specific aim of this task is to draw out functional play, creative behaviors, and social reciprocity while observing how the child responds to the social interaction with the examiner.

Modules 3 and 4 of the ADOS-2 are designed for individuals with fluent speech. This is estimated at approximately a four-year-old expressive language level and includes presence of complex sentences. Module 3 is comprised of 14 different semi-structured tasks and is appropriate for children and adolescents with adequate language. Module 4 is comprised of 15 semi-structured tasks and is appropriate for individuals over the age of 16 who have a higher level of responsibility. Modules 3 and 4 include tasks similar to Module 2 such as a puzzle making task, a make-believe task, and a story-telling task with a book that is primarily pictures. However, Modules 3 and 4 also include activities that require fluent speech and a higher level of social communication development. For instance, there is a series of questions that explore topics such as social difficulties, friends, and relationships that require the individual to reflect on his/her experiences and describe those to the examiner. During these tasks, the examiner is able to observe social communication behaviors such as reciprocal conversation, sharing of interests with others, sharing of emotions or affect, and presence of friendships or romantic relationships.

At the end of the assessment, the behaviors and verbalizations that the examiner noted are coded using a standardized protocol, and algorithm scores for both the SA and RRB domains are calculated. Examiners can then use these scores to determine whether an individual is at risk for an ASD (the Toddler Module only assesses risk) or has met the cut-off for a classification of ASD on the ADOS-2 (Modules 1–4). These scores are used to determine a clinical diagnosis of ASD, but should not be used as an independent determination of diagnosis; all diagnostic measures are limited by their individual psychometric properties of sensitivity (i.e. the probability of a positive test among people with ASD) and specificity (i.e. the probability of a negative test among people without ASD).

The ADOS-2, Modules 1–4 and the Toddler Module demonstrate strong psychometric properties. All five modules of the ADOS-2 demonstrate strong internal consistency within the SA domain. However, internal consistency is reduced for the RRB domain across all five modules (Gotham, Risi, Pickles, & Lord, 2007; Luyster et al., 2009). The variability within the RRB domain is a limitation of the measure; however, it was to be expected due to the heterogeneous nature of the symptoms within this category.

Sensitivity and specificity ratings exceed 85 percent for almost all individuals studied across the five modules (Gotham et al., 2007; Luyster et al., 2009). However, for nonverbal toddlers between 21 and 30 months of age on the Toddler Module, and for individuals with nonverbal mental ages of less than 15 months on Modules 1–4, specificity, but not sensitivity, is reduced (Gotham et al., 2007; Gotham et al., 2008; Lord et al., 2000; Luyster *et al.*, 2009). Despite this one shortcoming, the ADOS-2 as a whole provides clinicians with an excellent tool to use as part of a comprehensive evaluation.

The *Autism* Diagnostic Interview – Revised (ADI-R; Lord et al., 1994) is a standardized interview that trained interviewers can use as one part of a diagnostic battery to assess for ASD. The ADI-R is administered to caregivers of individuals with ASD and is appropriate for individuals who are at least 3.5 years old, and have a mental age of at least two years old, through adulthood. Caregivers are asked questions based on their child's age and verbal abilities. For example, caregivers of individuals without spoken language are not asked questions regarding their child's ability to carry a conversation, and caregivers of individuals who are three years old are not asked questions about the period of time between their child's fourth and fifth birthday (a series of questions focuses on this time period).

Interview questions primarily focus on social communication and the presence of restricted interests and repetitive behaviors. Throughout the administration, the interviewer codes caregiver responses based on their report of the individual's behavior as opposed to asking caregivers to choose a rating. When the interview is complete, the interviewer calculates a total score using one of three algorithms based on the child's age, nonverbal and verbal mental age, and reported language abilities. The ADI-R adjusts for expressive language levels with different algorithms and total score cut-offs and is available for children who use daily, functional, use of language (i.e. three-word phrases that sometimes include a verb) and those with very limited language abilities (i.e. mostly single words, or no words at all).

The ADI-R takes approximately 1.5 hours to complete for caregivers who are reporting on a child approximately 3.5–4 years old. However, the interview could take substantially longer for an older child. Though the interview is lengthy, Lord et al. (1994) report that parents found the interview to be relatively comfortable, and felt as though the interviewers cared about their perspective of their child and were able to gain more information about their child than they would in an observational assessment.

The ADI-R has shown strong psychometric properties for individuals regardless of chronological or mental age. The ADI-R demonstrates strong internal consistency for the social domain and good internal consistency for the RRB domain (Lord et al., 1994). Further, sensitivity for all individuals studied was over 90 percent. Specificity was over 85 percent for all verbal groups. Specificity for nonverbal groups was measured as 79 percent (Lord et al., 1997). Overall, the ADI-R complements the ADOS-2 in terms of gathering information for a clinical diagnosis. However, it is rarely used in clinical settings due to the length of time the interview takes to complete.

The Childhood Autism Rating Scale, Second Edition (CARS2; Schopler et al., 2010) consists of three forms: the Childhood Autism Rating Scale, Second Edition-Standard Version (CARS2-ST), the Childhood Autism Rating Scale, Second Edition-High Functioning Version (CARS2-HF), and the Childhood Autism Rating Scale, Second Edition-Questionnaire for Parents or Caregivers (CARS2-QPC).

Trained examiners in a variety of settings, including psychologists, psychiatrists, pediatricians, and special educators, may administer the CARS2-ST and CARS2-HF. Different from the ADOS-2, there are no specific prompts, tasks, or interactions that examiners employ when making their ratings of the child. In contrast to the semi-structured standardized activities included in the ADOS modules, the CARS2-HF and CARS2-ST are flexible, in that examiners can make observations in any way that is convenient for the individual and their support system so long as adequate observational data are collected.

Prior to beginning the assessment, examiners complete a language sample to determine the most appropriate version of the CARS2. Individuals who are verbally fluent with full-scale IQ scores over 80 are administered the CARS2-HF and those who are not fluent with full-scale IQ scores below 80 are administered the CARS2-ST. Children under six years of age are administered the CARS2-ST regardless of cognitive ability or verbal fluency. These measures evaluate individuals who have been referred for an ASD evaluation and should not be used within the general population. The CARS2-ST and CARS2-HF were developed to provide quantitative data obtained through a comprehensive evaluation within a referred population.

During an administration of the CARS2-ST and CARS2-HF, examiners take detailed notes on behaviors, verbalizations, and interactions, and then use a standardized form to rate an individual across 15 different functional areas. Examiners should be very familiar with the 15 different functional areas and scoring system of the CARS2-ST and CARS-HF prior to rating an individual's behaviors. The CARS2-HF has been adapted to adjust for differences in cognitive development. Thus, while many of the functional areas are similar across both the CARS2-ST and the CARS2-HF, there are key differences of which examiners should be aware.

For example, relating to people is a functional area on both the CARS2-ST and the CARS2-HF. Both functional areas require the examiner to assess the individual's behavior in a variety of situations while interacting with other people. However, the expectations for a level of social complexity are higher for individuals being examined with the CARS2-HF. Additionally, though the functional areas are similar in definition, and both are scored on a four-point scale, the CARS-ST and CARS-HF have different scoring criteria.

The CARS2-QPC is an optional parent interview that can be used in conjunction with the CARS2-ST or CARS2-HF to supplement information that was not collected during the observational period. The CARS2-QPC collects data from each of the 15 areas of the CARS2-ST/CARS2-HF. It was organized in a way that is most meaningful for caregivers and thus does not directly map onto the rating form for the CARS-ST or CARS2-HF. Following the data collection period (i.e. the CARS2-ST, CARS2-HF, and possibly the CARS2-QPC), a trained clinician codes the data across the 15 different categories and generates a total score that is used to assess the likelihood that an individual meets criteria for ASD. It is suggested that the CARS2-QPC be administered after the CARS2-ST/CARS2-HF, and used as supplementary data to fill in gaps that may have been overlooked during the observational data collection period.

The CARS and CARS2 demonstrate strong psychometric properties. Several studies have reported strong total score internal consistency reliability for the CARS and CARS2 (Chlebowski, Green, Barton, & Fein,

2010; Schopler, Reichler, DeVellis, & Daly, 1980; Schopler et al., 2010). Further, the CARS and CARS2 has consistently demonstrated excellent sensitivity and specificity, with percentages over 85 percent for each (Chlebowski et al., 2010; Perry, Caondillac, Freeman, Dunn-Geir, & Belair, 2005; Schopler et al., 2010).

The ADOS-2, ADI-R, and CARS2 are three diagnostic measures that are clinically useful and have strong psychometric properties. Individually, they can stand alone as good measures to aid clinical judgment in making an ASD diagnosis, with all three demonstrating strong levels of sensitivity and specificity (Chlebowski et al., 2010; Gotham et al., 2008; Gotham et al., 2007; Lord et al., 1997; Lord et al., 2000; Lord et al., 2012; Lord et al., 1994; Luyster et al., 2009; Perry et al., 2005; Schopler et al., 1980; Schopler et al., 2010).

The use of several diagnostic measures increases the likelihood of making an accurate diagnosis. For example, it has been well documented that using both the ADOS-2 and ADI-R together in a comprehensive ASD assessment increases the likelihood that an accurate diagnosis is made (De Bildt et al., 2004; Kim & Lord, 2012; Le Couteur, Haden, Hammeal & McConachie, 2008; Risi et al., 2006). Though administering at least two diagnostic measures is time-consuming, each measure brings unique, as well as overlapping, information about the individual, providing a more comprehensive assessment (Kim & Lord, 2012). For example, the ADI-R asks about both past and current skills and behaviors whereas all versions of the ADOS-2 only consider current and past skills and behaviors. The CARS has not been considered in terms of increased sensitivity or specificity when combined with other instruments. Researchers have demonstrated a high degree of diagnostic agreement (85 percent) between the CARS and the ADI-R (Pilowsky, Yirmiya, Shulman, & Dover, 1998). The authors hypothesized that the disagreement between the two measures was related, in part, to the method in which data were collected – observational (CARS) versus an interview comprised of both past and present information (ADI-R).

In summary, the ADOS-2, ADI-R, and CARS2 consistently provide diagnoses high in specificity and sensitivity when administered individually. Additional diagnostic certainty can be obtained by administering at least two diagnostic measures, preferably a direct observational measure (i.e. ADOS-2 or CARS2) and a caregiver interview (i.e. ADI-R, CARS-QPC) or one of the more thorough parent/caregiver screeners such as the SCQ (Rutter et al., 2008) or the SRS (Constantino et al., 2003).

Summary and Conclusions

The construct of *autism,* which was coined over 100 years ago, has been evolving as scientists work toward understanding and refining a diagnostic entity that reflects a constellation of social communication, RRBIs, and sensory-interest symptoms. At present, we have moved towards a spectrum approach to understanding and studying autism (ASD) and have broken away from categorical diagnoses (i.e. Autistic Disorder, Asperger's disorder, and PDD-NOS). While we continue to make progress in understanding how to best conceptualize the disorder, deficits in social communication and presence of RRBIs have been anchors of this diagnosis since the DSM-III was published in 1980.

At this time, many screening tools and diagnostic measures have been developed to identify autism (Bryson et al., 2008; Lord et al., 2012; Lord et al., 1994; Robins et al., 2014; Rutter et al., 2008; Schopler et al., 1980; Schopler et al., 2010; Stone et al., 2004; Stone et al., 2008; Wetherby, 2001). These measures focus on the core symptoms of ASD, social communication difficulties, and presence of RRBIs and sensory interests, and have enabled examiners to make earlier and more accurate diagnoses (Zwaigenbaum et al., 2009). In particular, the diagnostic measures discussed in this chapter boast high levels of sensitivity and specificity for most individuals (Chlebowski et al., 2010; Gotham et al., 2007; Gotham et al., 2008; Lord et al., 1997; Lord et al., 2000; Luyster et al., 2009; Perry et al., 2005; Schopler et al., 2010).

Diagnosticians are still limited in their ability to make accurate and reliable diagnoses for individuals who are minimally verbal and have very low cognitive abilities. Continued research in refining our understanding of the presentation of symptoms of ASD among cognitively lower functioning individuals needs to be continued to provide earlier and accurate diagnoses among individuals of varying cognitive abilities.

References

American Psychiatric Association. (1952). *Diagnostic and statistical manual of mental disorders* (1st ed.). Washington, DC: Author.

American Psychiatric Association. (1968). *Diagnostic and statistical manual of mental disorders* (2nd ed.). Washington, DC: Author.

American Psychiatric Association.(1987). *Diagnostic and statistical manual of mental disorders* (3rd ed., text rev.). Washington, DC: Author.

American Psychiatric Association. (1994). *Diagnostic and statistical manual of mental disorders* (4th ed.). Washington, DC: Author.

American Psychiatric Association. (2000). *Diagnostic and statistical manual of mental disorders* (4th ed., text rev.). Washington, DC: Author.

American Psychiatric Association. (2013). *Diagnostic and statistical manual of mental disorders* (5th ed.). Washington, DC: Author.

Asperger H. (1944) Die "AutistichenPsychopathen" imKindesalter. *Archivfür Psychiatrie und Nervenkrankheiten*, 117: 76–136.

Baker, J. P. (2013). Autism at 70—Redrawing the boundaries. *The New England Journal Of Medicine*, 369(12), 1089–1091. doi:10.1056/NEJMp1306380

Bettelheim, B. (1967). *The empty fortress. Infantile autism and the birth of the self.* New York: The Free Press.

Bleuler, E. (1951). Autistic thinking. In, *Organization and pathology of thought: Selected sources* (pp. 399–437). New York: Columbia University Press. doi:10.1037/10584-020

Bryson, S.E., Zwaigenbaum, L., McDermott, C., Rombough, V., & Brian, J. (2008). The autism observational scale for infants: Scale development and reliability data. *Journal of Autism and Developmental Disorders. 38*(4), 737–738. doi: 10.1007/s10803-007-0440-y

Charman, T. (2008). Autism spectrum disorders. *Psychiatry, 7*(8) 331–334.

Center for Disease Control and Prevention. *Prevalence of autism spectrum disorders aged 8 years-autism and developmental disabilities monitoring network, 11 Sites, United States, 2010.* MMWR 2014; 62(SS02): 1–21.

Chlebowski, C., Green, J. A., Barton, M. L., & Fein, D. (2010). Using the childhood autism rating scale to diagnose autism spectrum disorders. *Journal of Autism and Developmental Disorders, 40*(7), 787–799. doi: 10.1007/s10803-009-0926-x

Constantino, J. N., Davis, S. A., Todd, R. D., Schindler, M. K., Gross, M. M., Brophy, S. L., . . . Reich, W. (2003). Validation of a brief quantitative measure of autistic traits: Comparison of the social responsiveness scale with the autism diagnostic interview-revised. *Journal of Autism and Developmental Disorders, 33*(4), 427–433. doi:10.1023/A:1025014929212

De Bildt, A., Sytema, S., Ketelaars, C., Kraijer, D., Mulder, E., Volkmar, F., & Minderaa, R. (2004). Interrelationship between autism diagnostic observation schedule-generic (ADOS-G), autism diagnostic interview-revised (ADI-R), and the diagnostic and statistical manual of mental disorders (DSM-IV-TR) classification in children and adolescents with mental retardation. *Journal of Autism and Developmental Disorders, 34*(2), 129–137. doi: 0162-3257/04/0400-0129/0

De Giacomo, A. A., & Fombonne, E. E. (1998). Parental recognition of developmental abnormalities in autism. *European Child & Adolescent Psychiatry, 7*(3), 131–136. doi:10.1007/s007870050058

Frohna, J. G. (2007). Failure to respond to name is indicator of possible autism spectrum disorder. *The Journal of Pediatrics, 151*(3), 327–328. doi:10.1016/j.jpeds.2007.07.023

Gibbs, V., Aldridge, F., Chandler, F., Witzlsperger, E., & Smith, K. (2012). An exploratory study comparing diagnostic outcomes for autism spectrum disorders under DSM-IV-TR with the proposed DSM-5 revision. *Journal of Autism and Developmental Disorders, 42*(8), 1750–1756. doi:10.1007/s10803-012-1560-6

Giles, D. C. (2013). "DSM-V is taking away our identity": The reaction of the online community to the proposed changes in the diagnosis of Asperger's disorder. *Health (London), 0*(0) 1–13.

Gillberg, C., Ehlers, S., Schaumann, H., Jakobsson, G., Dalgren, S.O., Lindblom, R., ... Blidner, E. (1999). Autism under 3 years: A clinical study of 28 cases referred for autism symptoms in infancy. *Journal of Child Psychology and Psychiatry, 31*(6), 921–934.

Gotham, K., Risi, S., Pickles, A., & Lord, C. (2007). The Autism diagnostic observation schedule: Revised algorithms for improved diagnostic validity.

Journal of Autism and Developmental Disorders, 37(4), 613–627. doi: 10.1007/ s10803-006-0280-1

Gotham, K., Risi, S., Dawson, G., Tager-Flusberg, H., Joseph, R., Carter, A., . . . Lord, C. (2008). A replication of the Autism diagnostic observation schedule (ADOS) revised algorithms. *Journal of the American Academy of Child & Adolescent Psychiatry, 47*(6), 642–651. doi:10.1097/CHI.0b013e31816bffb7

Guinchat, V., Chamak, B., Bonniau, B., Bodeau, N., Perisse, D., Cohen, D., & Danion, A. (2012). Very early signs of autism reported by parents include many concerns not specific to autism criteria. *Research in Autism Spectrum Disorders, 6*(2), 589–601. doi:10.1016/j.rasd.2011.10.005

Hansen, S. N., Schendel, D. E., & Parner, E. T. (2015). Explaining the increase in the prevalence of autism spectrum disorders: The proportion attributable to changes in reporting practices. *JAMA Pediatrics, 169*(1), 56–62. doi:10.1001/ jamapediatrics.2014.1893

Hazen, E. P., Stornelli, J. L., O'Rourke, J. A., Koesterer, K., & McDougle, C. J. (2014). Sensory symptoms in autism spectrum disorders. *Harvard Review of Psychiatry, 22*(2), 112–124. doi:10.1097/01.HRP.0000445143.08773.58

Jing, W. & Fang, J. (2014). Brief report: Do children with autism gather information from social contexts to aid their word learning? *Journal of Autism and Developmental Disorders, 44*(6), 1478–1482. doi:10.1007/s10803-013-1994-5

Jones, E. H., Gliga, T., Bedford, R., Charman, T., & Johnson, M. H. (2014). Developmental pathways to autism: A review of prospective studies of infants at risk. *Neuroscience and Biobehavioral Reviews, 391*–33. doi:10.1016/j. neubiorev.2013.12.001

Kanner L. (1943). Autistic disturbances of affective contact. *The Nervous Child,* 2: 217–250.

Kim, S. H., & Lord, C. (2012). Combining information from multiple sources for the diagnosis of autism spectrum disorders for toddlers and young preschoolers from 12 to 47 months of age. *Journal of Child Psychology and Psychiatry, 53*(2), 143–151. doi: 10.1111/j.1469-7610.2011.02458.x

Kuhn, T. S. (1962). *The structure of scientific revolutions.* Chicago: University of Chicago Press.

Le Couteur, A., Haden, G., Hammal, D., & McConachie, H. (2008). Diagnosing autism spectrum disorders in pre-school children using two standardised assessment instruments: The ADI-R and the ADOS. *Journal of Autism and Developmental Disorders, 38*(2), 362–372. doi: 10.1007/s10803-007-0403-3

Lord, C., Pickles, A., McLennan, J., Rutter, M., Bregman, J., Folstein, S., . . . Minshew, N. (1997). Diagnosing autism: Analyses of data from the Autism Diagnostic Interview. *Journal of Autism and Developmental Disorders, 27*(5), 501–517. doi: 10.1023/A:1025873925661

Lord, C., Risi, S., Lambrecht, L., Cook Jr., E. H., Leventhal, B. L., DiLavore, P. C., . . . Rutter, M. (2000). The Autism Diagnostic Observation Schedule— Generic: A standard measure of social and communication deficits associated with the spectrum of autism. *Journal of Autism and Developmental Disorders, 30*(3), 205–223. doi: 10.1023/A:1005592401947

Lord, C., Rutter, M., DiLavore, P. C., Risi, S., Gotham, K., & Bishop, S. (2012). *Autism diagnostic observation schedule: ADOS-2.* Los Angeles, CA: Western Psychological Services.

Lord, C., Rutter, M., & Le Couteur, A. (1994). Autism Diagnostic Interview-Revised: A revised version of a diagnostic interview for caregivers of individuals with possible pervasive developmental disorders. *Journal of Autism and Developmental Disorders, 24*(5), 659–685. doi:0162-3257/94/1000-0659507.00/0

Leekam, S., Tandos, J., McConachie, H., Meins, E., Parkinson, K., Wright, C., . . . Le Couteur, A. (2007). Repetitive behaviours in typically developing 2-year-olds. *Journal of Child Psychology and Psychiatry, 48*(11), 1131–1138. doi: 10.1111/j.1469-7610.2007.01778.x

Luyster, R., Gotham, K., Guthrie, W., Coffing, M., Petrak, R., Pierce, K., . . . Lord, C. (2009). The Autism Diagnostic Observation Schedule—Toddler Module: A new module of a standardized diagnostic measure for autism spectrum disorders. *Journal of Autism and Developmental Disorders, 39*(9), 1305–1320. doi: 10.1007/s10803-009-0746-z

Maestro, S., Muratori, F., Cavallaro, M., Pei, F., Stern, D., Golse, B., & Palacio-Espasa, F. (2002). Attentional skills during the first 6 months of age in autism spectrum disorder. *Journal of the American Academy of Child & Adolescent Psychiatry, 41*(10), 1239–1245. doi:10.1097/00004583-200210000-00014

Memari, A. H., Ziaee, V., Shayestehfar, M., Ghanouni, P., Mansournia, M. A., & Moshayedi, P. (2013). Cognitive flexibility impairments in children with autism spectrum disorders: Links to age, gender and child outcomes. *Research in Developmental Disabilities, 34*(10), 3218–3225. doi:10.1016/j.ridd.2013.06.033

Moskowitz, A. & Heim, G. (2011). Eugen Bleuler's dementia praecox or the group of schizophrenias (1911): A centenary appreciation and reconsideration. *Schizophrenia Bulletin, 37*(3), 471–479. doi:10.1093/schbul/sbr016

Osterling, J., & Dawson, G. (1994). Early recognition of children with autism: A study of first birthday home videotapes. *Journal of Autism and Developmental Disorders, 24*(3), 247–257. doi:10.1007/BF02172225

Osterling, J. A., Dawson, G., & Munson, J. A. (2002). Early recognition of 1-year-old infants with autism spectrum disorder versus mental retardation. *Development and Psychopathology, 14*(2), 239–251. doi:10.1017/S0954579402002031

Ozonoff, S. (2012). Editorial perspective: Autism spectrum disorders in DSM-5—An historical perspective and the need for change. *Journal Of Child Psychology And Psychiatry, 53*(10), 1092–1094. doi:10.1111/j.1469-7610.2012.02614.x

Ozonoff, S., Iosif, A.-M., Baguio, F., Cook, I. C., Hill, M. M., Hutman, T., . . . Sigman, M. (2010). A prospective study of the emergence of early behavioral signs of autism. *Journal of the American Academy of Child & Adolescent Psychiatry, 49*(3), 256–266.

Ozonoff, S., Macari, S., Young, G. S., Goldring, S., Thompson, M., & Rogers, S. J. (2008). Atypical object exploration at 12 months of age is associated with autism in a prospective sample. *Autism, 12*(5), 457–472. doi: 10.1177/1362361308096402

Perry, A., Condillac, R. A., Freeman, N. L., Dunn-Geier, J., & Belair, J. (2005). Multi-site study of the Childhood Autism Rating Scale (CARS) in five clinical groups of young children. *Journal of Autism and Developmental Disorders, 35*(5), 625–634. doi: 10.1007/s10803-005-0006-9

Pilowsky, T., Yirmiya, N., Shulman, C., & Dover, R. (1998). The Autism Diagnostic Interview-Revised and the Childhood Autism Rating Scale: Differences between diagnostic systems and comparison between genders. *Journal of autism and developmental disorders, 28*(2), 143–151. doi: 0162-3257/98/0400-0143$15.00/0

Porter, N. (2012). Promotion of pretend play for children with high-functioning autism through the use of circumscribed interests. *Early Childhood Education Journal, 40*(3), 161–167. doi:10.1007/s10643-012-0505-1

Risi, S., Lord, C., Gotham, K., Corsello, C., Chrysler, C., Szatmari, P., . . . Pickles, A. (2006). Combining information from multiple sources in the diagnosis of autism spectrum disorders. *Journal of the American Academy of Child & Adolescent Psychiatry, 45*(9), 1094–1103. doi: 10.1007/s10803-006-0280-1

Robins, D. L., Casagrande, K., Barton, M., Chen, C. M. A., Dumont-Mathieu, T., & Fein, D. (2014). Validation of the modified checklist for autism in toddlers, revised with follow-up (M-CHAT-R/F). *Pediatrics, 133*(1), 37–45. doi: 10.1542/peds.2013-1813

Rutter, M., Bailey, A., Lord, C., Cianchetti, C., & Fancello, G. S. (2007). *SCQ: Social Communication Questionnaire: manuale.* Giunti OS.

Schopler, E., Reichler, R. J., DeVellis, R. F., & Daly, K. (1980). Toward objective classification of childhood autism: Childhood Autism Rating Scale (CARS). *Journal of Autism and Developmental Disorders, 10*(1), 91–103. doi:0162-3257/80/0300-0091$03.00/0

Schopler, E., Van Bourgondien, M., Wellman, J., & Love, S. (2010). *Childhood Autism Rating Scale—Second edition (CARS2): Manual.* Los Angeles: Western Psychological Services.

Stone, W. L., Coonrod, E. E., Turner, L. M., & Pozdol, S. L. (2004). Psychometric properties of the STAT for early autism screening. *Journal of Autism and Developmental Disorders, 34*(6), 691–701. doi:10.1007/s10803-004-5289-8

Stone, W. L., McMahon, C. R., & Henderson, L. M. (2008). Use of the Screening Tool for Autism in Two-Year-Olds (STAT) for children under 24 months: An exploratory study. *Autism, 12*(5), 557–573. doi:10.1177/1362361308096403

Webb, S., & Jones, E. H. (2009). Early identification of autism: Early characteristics, onset of symptoms, and diagnostic stability. *Infants & Young Children, 22*(2), 100–118. doi:10.1097/IYC.0b013e3181a02f7f

Werner, E., Dawson, G., Osterling, J., & Dinno, N. (2000). Brief report: Recognition of autism spectrum disorder before one year of age: A retrospective study based on home videotapes. *Journal of Autism and Developmental Disorders, 30*(2), 157–162. doi:10.1023/A:1005463707029

Wetherby, A. (2001). *Communication and symbolic behavior scales developmental profile, Preliminary normed edition.* Baltimore, MD: Paul H. Brookes.

Wimpory, D. C., Hobson, R., Williams, J. G., & Nash, S. (2000). Are infants with autism socially engaged? A study of recent retrospective parental reports. *Journal of Autism and Developmental Disorders, 30*(6), 525–536. doi:10.1023/A:1005683209438

Wing, L. (1981). Asperger's syndrome: A clinical account. *Psychological Medicine* 11: 115–130.

Young, R. L., Brewer, N., & Pattison, C. (2003). Parental identification of early behavioural abnormalities in children with autistic disorder. *Autism, 7*(2), 125–143. doi:10.1177/1362361303007002002

Zwaigenbaum, L., Bryson, S., Carter, A. S., Lord, C., Rogers, S., Chawarska, K., Constantino, J., Dawson, G., Dobkins, K., Fein, D., Iverson, J., Klin, A., Landa, R., Sigman, M., Messinger, D., Ozonoff, S., Stone, W. ... Yirmiya, N. (2009). Clinical assessment and management of toddlers with suspected ASD: Insights from studies of high-risk infants. *Pediatrics, 123:* 1383–1391. doi: 10.1542/peds.2008-1606

Zwaigenbaum L., Bryson S., Rogers T., Roberts W., Brian J., & Szatmari, P. (2005). Behavioral manifestations of autism in the first year of life. *International Journal of Developmental Neuroscience, 23:* 143–152. doi:10.1016/j.ijdevneu.2004.05.001

Chapter 2

Historical Overview of the Education and Treatment of Persons with Autism

Tom E.C. Smith, Peggy Schaefer-Whitby, and Tiffany Mrla

Autism spectrum disorder (ASD) is a relatively new term used to describe individuals with a variety of characteristics primarily affecting social language and social interaction, and with the display of restricted, repetitive behaviors or interests. These language, social interaction, and communication deficits are pervasive, sustained, and affect social functioning (American Psychiatric Association, 2013; Goldstein, Naglieri, & Ozonoff, 2009). While intellectual disabilities have been described in the literature for centuries, the characteristics of autism have become a focused area of research within the past six decades.

Leo Kanner, an American child psychiatrist, first introduced the term *autism* in 1943. His description and subsequent diagnostic criteria correlate to what is often termed *classic autism*. Through time, this spectrum disorder has been referred to as Kanner's autism, infantile autism, nuclear autism, and autistic disorder ("Childhood autism and related conditions," 1980; Eyal, 2013; Goldstein et al., 2009; Hill, 2003; Newschaffer & Curran 2003). While Kanner's research was developing, Hans Asperger, an Austrian pediatrician, began identifying characteristics of what is commonly referred to as Asperger syndrome or high-functioning autism. His work in this area was first published in 1944, although not translated into English for several decades (Frith, 1991; Goldstein et al., 2009; Wing, 1991; Zager, 2004).

Autistic disorder was not differentiated for diagnostic purposes until the 1940s, despite suspected cases of a similar nature having been documented since the late 1700s. Jean Itard's adoption of Victor was one of the first known of such cases (Goldstein et al., 2009). Myths surrounding people with autism are fueled by historical perspectives, cultural distinctions, and psychosocial influences across time. Many of these misperceptions are still present today. By reviewing the history of autism as a developmental disability, teachers, professionals, and families will develop an improved paradigm of autism as it is appreciated in its current practice. Understanding the past helps drive the future. The purpose of this chapter is to discuss the history of autism in society, the criteria for diagnosis of autism spectrum disorder, and policy that supports the education of people with autism.

Early Accounts of Children with Autism

A well-known account of suspected autism, documented prior to the conceptualization of ASD, occurred in 1798. Dr. Jean Itard adopted and educated Victor, a 12-year-old feral boy, through a purposefully designed behavioral program of instruction. Itard's clinical descriptions of Victor describe the characteristics of ASD as classified in modern times, to include: a distant, absent gaze; persistent rocking; deficient imitation skills; vocalizations limited to guttural sounds; restricted food interests, although gluttonous towards preferred items; and dysfunctional sensory integration and processing. Given the accounts of Dr. Itard, a French physician, it is unknown whether Victor was abandoned in the woods due to his disability or if his developmental delay resulted from the absence of stimulation needed to acquire language and social develop-ment. Regardless, while Victor made significant progress under Itard's care, to include the acquisition of several words and the development of attachment behaviors displayed towards Itard and his nanny, he contin-ued to display indications of developmental disability (Goldstein et al., 2009; Malson, 1972; Wolff, 2004). These indications resemble what is now referred to as ASD.

Uta Frith, a leader in the field of autism research over the past several decades, identified a historical account of a Scottish landowner, Hugh Blair, in the late 1700s (Wolffe, 2004). According to Wolffe, Frith's review of legal documents referencing Blair's mental capacities identified several descriptions now aligned with the identification of ASD. According to the court records, Blair's mental capacity was in question. Respondents indi-cated that he displayed multiple language delays, to include echolalia and processing delays; repetitive behaviors and insistence on sameness; collect-ing unusual objects or items; difficulty with social interaction displayed through an absent gaze; limited connections with others; and insensitive, tactless, interactions.

Additional accounts of suspected autism have been documented in the psychiatric literature, as well as in cultural accounts of fictional and non-fictional characters throughout history. Henry Maudsley, a lead-ing author in the field of psychiatry during the late 1800s in England, authored a text titled *The physiology and pathology of the mind*, in 1867. In this text, he described the characteristics of insanity as mani-fested in children, to include sensory-motor responses to environmental stimuli, ineffective communication skills, aggressive outbursts, and rigid movements or actions. Maudsley's accounts appear to be consistent with modern day descriptions of ASD (Goldstein et al., 2009; Wolffe, 2004).

Haslam described cases of "insane children" in 1809, in which one case describes a child with possible autism (Wolff, 2004). Through extensive record and literature reviews, researchers have identified many cases, such as the aforementioned, and have ascertained that the authors are describing ASD as we conceptualize it in modern times (Frith, 2000; Frith, 2003; Wing, 1976).

In 1908, Theodore Heller, a pioneer in special education from Vienna, documented a regressive pattern of behavior in children after two years of age. His accounts identify the loss of skills in the areas of language and social interaction, as well as adaptive behaviors, following a period of typical development. In addition, these children displayed rigid patterns of behavior, with repetitive, stereotypical interests. The skill-regression deficits were noted to be pervasive and severe (Westphal, Schelinski, Volkmar, & Pelphrey, 2013). This disorder was initially coined *Heller syndrome*, and later referred to as dementia infantilis, or childhood psychosis. The terms dementia and psychosis were aligned with initial theories that autism was a psychotic disorder and not a developmental disability. These regressive deficits were later identified as childhood disintegrative disorder in *The diagnostic and statistical manual of mental disorders, fourth edition* (DSM-IV), (American Psychiatric Association, 1994). In more recent revisions of the DSM, childhood disintegrated disorder is removed and the regressive deficits are captured in the broader category of autism spectrum disorder (American Psychiatric Association, 2013). Regressive patterns of skill loss in children with ASD are still reported today.

In 1911, the term translated as *autism* was introduced by Eugene Bleuler (Fitzgerald, 2014). Bleuler was a Swiss psychiatrist known for his work in the area of schizophrenic disorders. The origin of the term coined by Bleuler, *autismus*, is derived from two Greek terms translated as *self* (*autos*) with the suffix (*ismos*) translated as an action or state. When introducing the term, *autismus*, Blueler was not referring to autism as we know it today. Instead, he was referring to a condition of schizophrenic disorder manifesting as difficulty in interpersonal relations due to detachment or affective incongruence.

It should be noted that prior to 1980, autism was more closely aligned with schizophrenia in psychiatric literature. In 1967, autism was classified as a type of schizophrenia, a personality disorder meeting criteria similar to ASD. It was not until 1980, with the publication of the *Diagnostic and statistical manual of mental disorders, third edition* (DSM-III), that autism was introduced as a developmental disorder classified outside of schizophrenia (American Psychological Association, 1980; Baker, 2013). In fact, autism was no longer considered a psychotic disorder, and schizophrenia had to be ruled out to receive an autism diagnosis.

In the 1940s, two pioneers in the field of ASD published research findings documenting the characteristics of ASD. In 1943, Leo Kanner described a group of children with deficits in language development and use, social interaction, and communication, as well as the display of repetitive behaviors/restricted interests. This profile is aligned with the current paradigm of ASD. Specifically, Kanner described the individuals under study as isolated and detached; displaying echolalia, reversal, and literal use of language; and monotonous behaviors displayed in repetitive manners. Kanner's extensive body of work suggested that autism was an emotional disorder with biological etiology and implications of genetic predisposition with symptoms present since birth. Kanner, incongruent to theories of mental illness of the time, did not imply that parental lack of warmth was a factor. However, the myth of parental blame in the manifestation of autism continued to prevail for decades (Wolff, 2004; Zager, 2004).

For decades the theory of poor parenting as the cause of autism prevailed. This theory was promoted in the 1960s by Freudian psychologists. Bruno Bettleheim coined the term "refrigerator mothers" and published extensively on therapeutic interventions. He believed that autism was caused by the coldness of mothers and unapproachable parenting. During this time period, children with autism were removed from the home and placed in therapeutic hospitals to address the attachment to their mother issues. Therapeutic interventions included holding the children to a woman's chest, extensive psychoanalysis, and explicit instruction in language development and use.

During the same era, Bernard Rimland, a psychiatrist, had a son who was diagnosed with infantile autism. It was at this time that Rimland set out to learn more about autism. In 1964, he published *Infantile autism: the syndrome and its implications for a neural theory of behavior*. His work suggested that autism was a neurodevelopmental disability with genetic predispositions similar to Kanner's original ideas on the neurological basis for autism (Wolff, 2004). The theory of autism as a brain-based neurodevelopmental disability holds true today.

Across the globe, around the same time as the publication of Kanner's initial research findings, a German psychiatrist by the name of Hans Asperger was studying a similar group of children. He described this group as "little professors." These children were very similar to the children Kanner described, although no cognitive delay was noted and the children displayed typical patterns of language development in the early developmental years. Asperger's work, however, was overlooked at the time by Western researchers. It was not until the 1980s, when Lorna Wing reintroduced Asperger's work, that this subpopulation of individuals with symptoms related to ASD began to be included in the research and development of practices for the identification and treatment of ASD (Wolff, 2004).

Dr. Lorna Wing and Dr. Judy Gould extensively explored the work of both Kanner and Asperger as part of their research at the National

Autism Society in Great Britain. These researchers found similarities in the early cases of autism across both Kanner's and Asperger's work. The similarities noted included impairments in social interaction, communication, and restricted interests/repetitive behaviors. They coined these three areas the "triad of impairments" in autism spectrum disorders. They further suggested that Asperger syndrome was a form of high-functioning autism (Wolff, 2004). As a result of their work, autism began to be viewed as a spectrum disorder. By referring to autism as a spectrum disorder, a continuum of severity levels for the varying characteristics could be included within the category, allowing for unification of research, treatment, resources, and services.

In the 1990s, Uta Frith translated the writings of Asperger. At that time, the debate regarding the differentiation of Asperger syndrome as a distinct disorder, apart from ASD, was initiated. Asperger believed it was separate; however, Wing suggested it was more aptly identified as a form of high-functioning autism. Initial inclusion of Asperger syndrome in the *Diagnostic and statistical manual for mental health disorders* occurred in the third, revised edition (American Psychiatry Association, 1987). At this time, Asperger syndrome was listed as a separate diagnostic criterium under the umbrella of pervasive developmental disorder. Recent revisions to the DSM, following extended controversy and debate, merged Asperger syndrome, autistic disorder, and pervasive developmental disorder, not otherwise specified (PPD-NOS) into one disorder: autism spectrum disorder (American Psychiatric Association, 2013).

Wing later referred to her original work discussing Asperger's clinical discussions as opening Pandora's box. She understood there would be great controversy surrounding the issue of Asperger syndrome and high-functioning autism. Prior to Asperger's death, she discussed the diagnosis of Asperger syndrome and high-functioning autism with Asperger. They agreed to disagree. While Asperger syndrome has been removed from the current DSM-5, many in the field continue to agree to disagree. Those given the diagnosis of Asperger's prior to the DSM-5 are able to continue to carry that label (Reichenberg, 2013).

Over time, the evolution of theories related to autism continues to drive changes in the concept and definition of autism. Kanner presented a very narrow concept of autism. In the 1950s, Rimland's findings helped broaden the concept of autism. Wing's work broadened the concept of autism even further and subsequently helped drive the most recent revisions in both the DSM-IV-TR and the DSM-5.

The History of the Diagnoses of Autism

The American Psychiatric Association is the governing body for the *Diagnostic and statistical manual of mental disorders-V* (DSM-5). Beginning approximately 60 years ago, the Association developed the manual in an effort to assist practitioners, clinicians, researchers, and students from a variety of fields to ensure fidelity and consistency in the diagnosis and treatment of mental health disorders across organizations. The manual is now in its fifth revision and remains an objective measure used by psychiatrists, psychologists, counselors, social workers, physicians, and other health professionals in the diagnosis and treatment of mental health diseases. Table 2.1 provides an overview of the changes in the DSM over time.

The diagnostic and statistical manual of mental health disorders, third edition, included the first categorical diagnostic criteria for pervasive developmental disorders (PDD). It was under this new class that infantile autism made an entry as a developmental disorder, separate from a precursor to schizophrenia (Volkmar, Bregman, Cohen, & Cicchetti, 1988). In addition to infantile autism, additional related disorders were included within this class. These disorders were childhood-onset pervasive developmental disorder, residual infantile autism, and residual childhood-onset pervasive developmental disorder. The criteria for infantile autism were based on the work of Kanner and Rutter, and included onset prior to 30 months of age, pervasive lack of social relationships, deficits of language/communication, and the absence of delusions or hallucinations. The revisions to DSM-III amended this class of disorders due to findings related to the developmental approach to classification, thus broadening the class and modifying the categories. Specifically for autistic disorder, a developmental approach was emphasized and the term "infantile" was removed to capture both the developmental and age-related variables. There were 16 possible criteria for diagnosis under this category, of which eight had to be met for diagnosis with a minimum of three in each sub-category to include social and communicative deficits, as well as restrictive/repetitive behaviors (Volkmar et al., 1988).

Asperger syndrome was officially added as a category under the classification of PDD in the fourth revision of the DSM, published in 1994 (American Psychiatric Association, 1994). The DSM-IV identified five potential categorical placements within the classification of PDD. These included autistic disorder, PDD-NOS, Asperger disorder, Rett's syndrome, and childhood disintegrative disorder. The DSM-IV-TR continues the placement of autism under the category of PDD. Twelve symptoms are outlined with criteria under three areas of impairment: social interaction, communication, and restricted/repetitive behaviors or activities. There are three possible classifications of autism spectrum disorders identified under the category of PDD: autistic disorder, PDD-NOS, and Asperger's syndrome, with autistic disorder requiring the identification of six characteristics, to include two from the area of social interaction, one from the area of communication, and one from the area of restricted behaviors or activities (American Psychiatric Association, 1994, 2000).

Table 2.1 Changes in the DSM for Autism Diagnostic Criteria

DSM-III (APA, 1980)	DSM-III-R (APA, 1987)	DSM-IV (APA, 1994)	DSM-IV-TR	DSM-5 (APA, 2013)
New classification of PDD	Developmental approach to classification	Inclusion of Asperger's disorder		Autism spectrum disorder is now the identifying class under neuro-developmental disorders
Categories of PDD: • infantile autism • childhood-onset pervasive developmental disorder, • residual infantile autism, and • residual childhood-onset pervasive developmental disorder	Specifier "infantile" removed Criteria expanded: • 16 possible criteria • 8 required diagnosis minimum of 3 in each sub-category of social and communicative deficits, as well as restrictive/repetitive behaviors • Removed criteria for age of onset	Categories expanded: • autistic disorder • asperger's disorder • pervasive developmental delay- not otherwise specified • childhood disintegrative disorder • Rett's disorder		Impairments in two categories: • social interaction • repetitive interests and activities
3 essential features: • pervasive lack of social relationships, • deficits of language and/or communication, • absence of delusions or hallucinations	Added PDD-NOS	Complex criteria for autistic disorder: • identification of six characteristics • two from the area of social interaction, • one from the area of communication, • one from the area of restricted behaviors or activities		Differentiation based on level of impairment with language and intellectual ability Dimensional versus categorical approach
Manifesting within the first 30 months of life Distinctive from schizophrenia				Inclusion of comorbid conditions: • ADHD • anxiety • depression

Asperger syndrome was maintained on the spectrum of disorders, with distinct differences from autism. Autistic disorder must be ruled out prior to a diagnosis of Asperger syndrome. The primary differences between the two lie in the age of initial onset, with a diagnosis of Asperger syndrome not reliant on identification prior to age two. Additional differences are noted in the impact the disorder has on functional communication, language, and the display of restricted or repetitive interests, with no requirement of characteristics identified within the area of communication. Additionally, there must be no notable differences in adaptive behaviors or cognitive impairment (Gibbs, Aldridge, Chandler, Witzlsperger & Smith 2012).

In the most recent revision of the DSM, the organization has been restructured to reflect a focus on the dimensional aspects of mental health, maintaining a categorical approach but also reflecting the continuum and commonality between disorders. In addition, the manual is organized in a manner similar to the manual developed by the World Health Organization, the *International classification of diseases*, in an effort to more closely align research and practice across boundaries. The philosophy behind this reorganization reflects a representation of developmental issues, advances in genetics and neuroimaging, neuroscience, and neuropsychology, a streamlined classification of disorders, and the conceptualization of personality disorders.

Among these changes, a significant reclassification of autism spectrum disorders emerged. The changes reflect the work of leading researchers, public commentary, and a peer review process with the intention of highlighting the symptoms of the disorder within the continuum to more efficiently identify severity of symptoms for coordination of treatment and services. The DSM-5 replaces the previous category of pervasive development disorders, used in DSM-IV, with the broad continuum of autism spectrum disorders which is then specified by severity level, accompanying intellectual disability, language impairment, known medical or genetic conditions, environmental factors, neurodevelopmental, mental, or behavior disorders.

Autism as a Spectrum Disorder

The most significant change to the class of disorders related to autism in the DSM-5 eliminates the overall class of PDD and replaces it with autism spectrum disorder. Within this category, specific classes are eliminated, to include the differentiation between autistic disorder, Asperger syndrome and PDD-NOS. Viewing autism as a multifaceted spectrum with varying dimensions allows for clarification when diagnosing, identifying resources, and completing research. The specific nuances between the various labels are dismissed, allowing for the focus to remain on identifying the impact of the disorder on overall functioning, to include language and intellectual ability (Szatmari, 2011).

This new system of classification has raised some controversy, with advocates stating that the reduction of subtypes improves diagnosis across categories, capturing individuals once missed in the previous categorical discriminations. Furthermore, advocates promote the improvements possible in research and the allocation of resources, where once individuals with particular categories of ASD may have been denied services due to the language of governmental and agency rules. The new classification system focuses on the severity of impact the spectrum disorder has on language and intellectual ability, as well as identifying the appearance of comorbid conditions (i.e. anxiety, depression, ADHD, childhood disintegrative disorder, and catatonia).

Disadvantages of the new system of classification include the possibility that diagnosticians will fail to see the subtle nuances related to the identification of Asperger syndrome and PDD-NOS given the higher levels of overall functioning typically present. This raises concern that individuals may be less likely to be identified due to perceived narrowness in the classification system. Additionally, supporters of a separate category for Asperger syndrome indicate that there are significant differences in the manifestation and treatment of Asperger syndrome versus autism. According to Szmarti (2011) and Huerta et al. (2012), the majority of individuals classified under PDD-NOS and Asperger syndrome will retain their classification under autism spectrum.

The history of autism diagnosis and treatment is based upon the psychosocial culture of the times. As a result, there are ideas that are no longer valid. Poor parenting as an etiology is no longer accepted. While poor parenting certainly does not help a child with autism, it does not cause autism. Autism is not schizophrenia. Indeed, schizophrenia must be ruled out in order for a person to receive an autism diagnosis. Research does not support a link between immunizations and autism. However, the cause of the increase in prevalence remains a concern. Autism is a neurodevelopmental disability of genetic etiology. There are many genetic indicators of autism, however, the variations are too great to guide diagnosis or treatment at this time.

History of Legislation and Litigation

Individuals with autism spectrum disorders have been impacted by a host of legislation and litigation that has shaped services and treatment for this group. Since the field of autism has only become an area of study and concern over the past 30 years, legislation and litigation related to this disability category is relatively new. For the most part, legislation focusing on the general population of individuals with disabilities, such as the *Individuals with Disabilities Education Act* (IDEA), has been applied to children and adults with autism spectrum disorders. These general legislative acts will be described later. There are however, in addition to these general acts, several specific pieces of legislation directly related to individuals with autism spectrum disorders.

In 2000, Congress passed the *Children's Health Act*. This piece of legislation authorized the establishment of Centers of Excellence with the purpose of encouraging research into autism. The act also called for the Centers for Disease Control (CDC) and the National Institutes of Health (NIH) to monitor the etiology, diagnosis, early detection, prevention, and treatment of autism. At the federal level in the United States, the most important legislation has been the *Combatting Autism Act* passed in 2006 and signed into law by President George W. Bush on December 19. This act, which was an amendment to the *Public Health Service Act*, focused on addressing the growing number of individuals with autism spectrum disorders through research, screening, intervention, and education. To make these efforts possible, the Act authorized approximately $950 million over a five-year period.

The *Combating Autism Act* provided money for the Centers for Disease Control (CDC) to conduct programs to determine the prevalence of autism spectrums, and to coordinate with the Department of Health and Human Services and the National Institutes of Health (NIH). There are several specific actions required by the act, including:

- Develop and implement a strategic plan.
- Provide grants for screening, diagnosis, and intervention programs.
- Create the position of an autism czar who would provide coordination and oversight for research.
- Increase the number of Centers of Excellence on Autism to ten.
- Provide technical assistance and data management to states.
- Assist in the development of statewide screening systems.
- Fund the surveillance program overseen by the CDC.

In 2011, Congress passed the *Combating Autism Reauthorization Act*. This act authorized $231 million per year for five years to continue the provisions of the original act. On August 8, 2014, President Obama, reauthorized the act a second time by signing the *Autism Collaboration, Accountability, Research, Education and Support Act* (CARES). This act dedicated $1.3 billion in federal funding for autism over five years, primarily focused on research, and continues prevalence monitoring, training medical professionals in identification of ASD, and efforts to develop treatments of medical conditions associated with ASD. An important component of CARES requires the federal government to review services for adults with ASD. With many children identified with ASD becoming adults, this addition to the act comes at a very critical time.

One area related to autism spectrum disorders and legislation deals with insurance coverage. In 2012 the National Conference of State Legislatures reported that 37 states and the District of Columbia had passed legislation related to autism and insurance coverage. Thirty-one of those states actually required insurance companies to provide coverage for costs related to treating autism. Most of the state legislation related to coverage for individuals with autism has been passed since 2007. Table 2.2 lists states and the dates when legislation was passed.

Table 2.2 States with Legislation Related to Insurance and Individuals with Autism

State	Year passed	Provisions
Arizona	2007–2008	Required coverage for autism
Connecticut	2007–2008	Required only for some services
Florida	2007–2008	Required coverage for autism
Illinois	2007–2008	Required coverage for autism
Louisiana	2007–2008	Required coverage for autism
Pennsylvania	2007–2008	Required coverage for autism
South Carolina	2007–2008	Required coverage for autism
Texas	2007–2008	Required coverage for autism
Colorado	2009	Required coverage for autism
Connecticut	2009	Required coverage for autism
Montana	2009	Required coverage for autism
Nevada	2009	Required coverage for autism
New Jersey	2009	Required coverage for autism
New Mexico	2009	Required coverage for autism
Wisconsin	2009	Required coverage for autism
Iowa	2010	Required coverage for autism
Kansas	2010	Required coverage for autism
Kentucky	2010	Required coverage for autism
Maine	2010	Required coverage for autism
Massachusetts	2010	Required coverage for autism
Missouri	2010	Required coverage for autism
New Hampshire	2010	Required coverage for autism
Oklahoma	2010	Same coverage as other children
Vermont	2010	Required coverage for autism
Arkansas	2011	Required coverage for autism
California	2011	Required coverage for autism
New York	2011	Required coverage for autism
Rhode Island	2011	Required coverage for autism
Virginia	2011	Required coverage for autism
West Virginia	2011	Required coverage for autism
Alabama	2012	Required to *offer* coverage
Alaska	2012	Required coverage for autism
Michigan	2012	Required coverage for autism

Source: National Conference of State Legislatures (2012). *Insurance Coverage for Autism*. Retrieved April 1, 2015 from www.ncsl.org/research/health/autism-and-insurance-coverage-state-laws.aspx.

In addition to federal legislation specifically targeting individuals with autism spectrum disorders, there are three laws mandating services and protections for a wide variety of individuals with disabilities, including those with autism. These include the *Individuals with Disabilities Education Act* (IDEA), Section 504 of the *Rehabilitation Act of 1973*, and the *Americans with Disabilities Act* (ADA).

Public Law 94-142/IDEA. The law that has had the greatest impact on the education of students with autism spectrum disorders is the *Individuals with Disabilities Education Act (IDEA)*. Originally passed in 1975 as Public Law 94-142, the law requires schools to provide a free, appropriate public education (FAPE) for all school-age children, in the least restrictive environment (Smith, Polloway, Doughty, Patton, & Dowdy, 2016). Prior to the passage of this law there were numerous other federal acts that impacted services to individuals with disabilities. Some of these laws included the following (Smith, 1987):

- Public Law 19-8, passed in 1832, provided federal land to establish a residential school for the deaf in Kentucky.
- Public Law 45-186, passed in 1879, provided $10,000 for the production of Braille materials.
- Public Law 66-236, passed in 1920, opened vocational rehabilitation services to civilians.
- Public Law 80-617, passed in 1948, prevented employment discrimination for individuals with physical impairments.
- Public Law 83-531, passed in 1954, provided funding for research into intellectual disabilities.
- Public Law 85-926, passed in 1958, provided funding for teacher preparation in the area of intellectual disabilities.
- Public Law 88-164, passed in 1963, provided funding for teacher preparation in all disability areas.
- Public Law 89-10, the *Elementary and Secondary Education Act*, passed in 1965, provided funding to implement programs for disadvantaged students and students with disabilities.
- Public Law 89-36, passed in 1965, created the National Institute for the Deaf.
- Public Law 89-750, passed in 1966, created the Bureau of Education for the Handicapped, currently the Office of Special Education Programs.
- Public Law 91-61, passed in 1969, created the Center for Educational Media and Materials for individuals with disabilities.
- Public Law 91-205, passed in 1970, mandated that buildings constructed with federal funds be accessible for individuals with disabilities.
- Public Law 93-112, passed in 1973, prohibited discrimination against individuals with disabilities; this law is now referred to as Section 504.

- Public Law 93-380, passed in 1974, was the precursor to Public Law 94-142, mandating many of the provisions later found in Public Law 94-142.

While these laws did not directly refer to individuals with autism spectrum disorders, they did provide the foundation for future legislation impacting students with all disabilities, including those with autism spectrum disorders.

The law that has had the greatest impact on individuals with disabilities, including those with autism spectrum disorders, is Public Law 94-142. Originally, autism spectrum disorders were not included as a specific disability covered, meaning that for students with ASD to be eligible for services under PL 94-142 they had to be identified as having one of the approved disability categories. The result was that some children with autism spectrum disorders were identified as having intellectual disabilities or even serious emotional disturbance in order to be eligible for services (Smith et al., 2016).

Since its original passage, PL 94-142 has been reauthorized several times. The 1990 reauthorization changed the name of the legislation to the *Individuals with Disabilities Education Act* (IDEA) but, more importantly, included autism as one of the specific disabilities resulting in eligibility for IDEA services. Therefore, since 1990, children with autism, who need special education, have been eligible for IDEA services. IDEA is a very comprehensive, very prescriptive law. There are numerous specific requirements schools must follow when identifying and providing services to students. These will be described in another chapter in the book, but they include areas such as nondiscriminatory assessment, eligibility criteria, mandatory individual education programs, least-restrictive-environment mandate, and due process rights. The law also requires schools to involve parents of students in the entire educational process.

In addition to IDEA, the second law currently affecting schools is Section 504 of the *Rehabilitation Act of 1973*, which is civil rights legislation for persons with disabilities. The law prohibits discrimination against any *otherwise qualified* individual with a disability in entities that receive federal funds. Since school districts are recipients of federal funds, they must comply with Section 504. The criteria for eligibility under Section 504 differ from eligibility requirements for IDEA. Students are eligible under IDEA if they have one of the specified disabilities and need special education. Eligibility under Section 504 is based on an individual having a physical or mental impairment that substantially limits a major life activity. Unlike IDEA, Section 504 does not provide a list of disabilities; rather it requires that a student have a physical or mental impairment. It also does not require that an individual needs special education, but that the physical or mental impairment substantially limits a major life activity. The provides a non-exhaustive list of major life activities, including learning, walking, talking, breathing, sitting, standing, seeing, and hearing (Smith, & Patton, 2016).

While autism, or any other disability, is not specifically listed in Section 504, it is definitely a physical or mental impairment, and it is highly likely to result in substantial limitation of a major life activity: learning. Therefore, children and adults with autism are very likely eligible for services and protections under Section 504. Since Section 504 is a civil rights law, the focus of interventions is the prevention of discrimination. Therefore, as long as individuals with autism have equal opportunities to be successful as individuals without disabilities, the intent of the law is achieved. This could require schools and employers to provide accommodations and modifications.

The *Americans with Disabilities Act* (ADA) was passed in 1990. It is also a civil rights act for individuals with disabilities. The reason the ADA was passed, after Section 504 had already been in place for 17 years, was that Section 504 only applies to entities that receive federal funds. Department stores, entertainment venues, hotels, restaurants, and many other establishments do not receive federal funds, meaning that Section 504 did not provide any protections to individuals in these establishments. The ADA is not restricted to entities that receive federal funds, but applies to virtually everything except churches and private clubs. The result is that individuals with disabilities cannot be discriminated against in hotels, restaurants, and other public accommodations, or by government entities.

Eligibility for the ADA is the same as for Section 504, meaning that individuals with autism are likely protected under the ADA because they have a physical or mental impairment that results in substantial limitations to a major life activity. Therefore, children and adults with autism cannot be discriminated against in virtually any business or venue.

Legislation affecting individuals with autism has also been passed outside the United States. In 1996, the European Parliament adopted a written declaration called the *Charter of Rights of Persons with Autism*. This declaration, calling for individuals with autism to enjoy the same rights and privileges as all other individuals in Europe, included the following rights (Feinstein, 2010):

- The right to live independent and full lives to the limit of their potential.
- The right to an accessible, unbiased, and accurate clinical diagnosis and assessment.
- The right to accessible and appropriate education.
- The right to an income or wage sufficient to provide adequate food, clothing, accommodation, and the other necessities of life.

- The right to meaningful employment and vocational training without discrimination or stereotype.
- The right to freedom from fear or threat of unwarranted incarceration in psychiatric hospitals or any other restrictive institution.
- The right to freedom from pharmaceutical abuse or misuse.

Litigation

In addition to legislation laying out basic rights for individuals with autism spectrum disorders, numerous court cases have focused on this group of individuals and resulted in significant opportunities. The number of due process hearings and court cases related to students with autism has been increasing parallel to the number of students identified as having autism (Hill, Martin, & Nelson-Head, 2011). Issues in these cases have ranged from the right to education, educational placement, applied behavior analysis and Lovaas interventions, and employment. Gorn (1999) noted that the majority of court cases dealing with students with autism have focused on educational methodology, quantum of benefit, or generalization. The following provides an overview of several court cases dealing with students with autism:

- *Delaware IU v. Martin K. (1993).* The parents of a three-year-old boy with pervasive developmental disabilities requested reimbursement from the school district for their use of a private Lovaas instructor. The school had told the parents that they would develop an IEP for the student in November but did not produce the IEP until January, at which time they were proposing using the TEACCH method. The court ruled in favor of the parents based on procedural errors in developing the IEP, and for not providing educational programming that would result in an educational benefit.
- *Gill ex rel. Gill v. Columbia 93 School District* (2000). In this case, parents were requesting the school pay for private Lovaas services for their seven-year-old child with autism. The Eighth Circuit, U.S. Court Appeals, ruled in favor of the district. The court found that the intervention techniques used by the district were sufficient and that decisions regarding methodology should be left to experts in the schools (Hulett, 2009).
- *Hartmann v. Loudoun County Board of Education* (1997). In this case, parents of an 11-year-old boy diagnosed with autism wanted the student to remain in the general classroom with an aide. The district wanted to move the student to a more restricted setting because he was not making academic progress in the general classroom and he was disruptive to other students. The Fourth Circuit, U.S. Court of Appeals, ruled in favor of the school, noting that including students

in general classroom settings is not required when the student would not receive educational benefit, the student is disruptive, and any benefits of inclusion would be outweighed by benefits received in a more restrictive setting (Hill & Hill, 2012).

While the courts have routinely ruled that educational methodology should be the decision of the school district, many parents have prevailed in court cases dealing with the Lovaas method by portraying it as an alternative to programs provided by the schools that were not producing educational benefit, the hallmark of the *Rowley* case in determining FAPE. Yell and Drasgow (2000) reviewed 45 cases dealing with students with autism and the Lovaas method and found that parents prevailed in 34 of the cases, or 76 percent of the time. In the majority of these decisions, schools lost by either violating procedural safeguards or not showing that their programs provided meaningful benefit to the student.

Conclusion

Despite historical references to the specific characteristics of autism dating back to the 1700s, focused research did not begin until the 1940s with the work of Kanner and Asperger. In the time since, the classification of autism spectrum disorders has undergone significant change. Once thought of as a manifestation of early-onset schizophrenia, autism is now identified as a neurodevelopmental disorder with genetic and environmental factors influencing manifestation. There are still many unknown variables in the cause of the disorder; however, research continues to identify factors influencing symptoms and response to treatment. The most recent research indicates the manifestation of autism spectrum disorders falls on a continuum with a range of severity levels and comorbid conditions. Primary predictors for improvement include level of language impairment and intellectual ability. In the community and school settings, advancements have been fueled by litigation and legislation, leading to improved educational opportunities, improved opportunities for inclusion in society, and, more importantly, improved outcomes in treatment and management of the symptoms related to autism spectrum disorders.

References

American Psychiatric Association. (1980). *Diagnostic and statistical manual of mental disorders*. Washington, D.C: American Psychiatric Association.
American Psychiatric Association. (1987). *Diagnostic and statistical manual of mental disorders: DSM-III-R*. Washington, D.C.: American Psychiatric Association.

American Psychiatric Association. (1994). *Diagnostic and statistical manual of mental diseases: DSM-IV. 4th ed.* Washington, D.C.: American Psychiatric Association.

American Psychiatric Association. (2000). *Diagnostic and statistical manual of mental disorders, text revision (DSM-IV-TR).* Washington, D.C: American Psychiatric Association.

American Psychiatric Association. (2013). *Diagnostic and statistical manual of mental disorders, (DSM-5®).* American Psychiatric Association.

Baker, J. P. (2013). Autism at 70–Redrawing the boundaries. *The New England Journal of Medicine, 369*(12), 1089–1091.

Childhood autism and related conditions. (1980). *British Medical Journal, 281*(6243), 761–762, Retrieved July 19, 2016 from http://www.ncbi.nlm.nih.gov/pmc/articles/PMC1714009/pdf/brmedj00039-0005.pdf

Eyal, G. (2013). For a sociology of expertise: The social origins of the autism epidemic. *American Journal of Sociology, 118*(4), 863–907.

Feinstein, A. (2010) *A history of autism: conversations with the pioneers.* Oxford: Wiley-Blackwell.

Fitzgerald, M. (2014). Overlap between autism and schizophrenia: History and current status. *Advances in Mental Health and Intellectual Disabilities, 8*(1), 15–23.

Frith, U. (1991). *Autism and Asperger syndrome.* New York: Cambridge University Press.

Frith C. D. (2000). The role of the dorsolateral prefrontal cortex in the selection of action. In S. Monsell & J. Driver (Eds.), *Control of cognitive processes. Attention and performance XVIII* (pp. 549–565). Cambridge MA: MIT Press.

Frith, C. D. (2003). What do imaging studies tell us about the neural basis of autism? In G. Bock & J. Goode (Eds.), *Autism: Neural Basis and Treatment Possibilities, Novartis Symposium 251.* Chichester, UK: Wiley.

Gibbs, V., Aldridge, F., Chandler, F., Witzlsperger, E., & Smith, K. (2012). Brief report: An exploratory study comparing diagnostic outcomes for autism spectrum disorders under DSM-IV-TR with the proposed DSM-5 revision. *Journal Of Autism And Developmental Disorders, 42*(8), 1750–1756.

Goldstein, S., Naglieri, J. A., & Ozonoff, S. (2009). *Assessment of autism spectrum disorders.* New York: Guilford Press.

Gorn, D. (1999). *What do I do when. . . . The answer book on special education law.* Horsham, P.A.: LRP Publications.

Hill, E. L., & Frith, U. (2003). Understanding autism: Insights from mind and brain. *Philosophical Transactions of the Royal Society B: Biological Sciences, 358*(1430), 281–289.

Hill, D. A., & Hill, S. J. (2012). Autism spectrum disorder, Individuals with Disabilities Education Act, and case law: Who really wins? *Preventing School Failure, 56,* 157–164.

Hill, D. A., Martin, E. D., & Nelson-Head, C. (2011). Examination of case law (2007–2008) regarding autism spectrum disorder and violations of the Individuals with Disabilities Education Act. *Preventing School Failure, 55,* 214–225.

Hulett, K. E. (2009). *Legal aspects of special education.* Upper Saddle River, N.J.: Pearson.

Malson, L. (1972). *Wolf children and the problem of human nature*; and *Jean Itard the wild boy of Aveyron* (trsl. by E. Fawcett, P. Ayton and J. White). London: NLB.

Maudsley, H. (1867). *The physiology and pathology of the mind.* New York: Appleton.

National Conference of State Legislatures (2012). *Insurance coverage for autism.* www.ncsl.org/research/health/autism-and-insurance-coverage-state-laws. aspx. Downloaded 4/1/2015.

Newschaffer, C. J., & Curran, L. K. (2003). Autism: an emerging public health problem. *Public Health Reports, 118*(5), 393.

Reichenberg, M. *(2013)*. "I liked the text about the little bird." Five intellectually disabled persons talk about texts. *Scandinavian Journal of Disability Research, 15(2),* 108–124.

Smith, T. E. C. (1987). *Introduction to education.* St. Paul, M.N.: West Publishing.

Smith, T. E. C. & Patton, J. R. (2016). *Section 504 and public schools.* 3rd ed. Austin: Pro-Ed Publishing.

Smith, T. E. C., Polloway, E. A., Doughty, T. A., Patton, J. R., & Dowdy, C. A. (2016). *Teaching students with special needs in inclusive settings*, 7th ed. Upper Saddle River, N.J.: Pearson.

Szatmari, P. (2011). *A mind apart: understanding children with autism and Asperger syndrome.* New York: Guilford Press.

Volkmar, F. R., Bregman, J., Cohen, D. J., & Cicchetti, D. V. (1988). DSM-III and DSM-III-R diagnoses of autism. *The American Journal of Psychiatry, 145*(11), 1404–1408.

Wing, J. K. (1976). Kanner's syndrome: a Historical introduction. In L. Wing (Ed.), *Early childhood autism: Clinical, educational and social aspects (2nd ed.).* Oxford: Pergamon.

Wing, L. (1991). The relationship between Asperger syndrom and Kanner's autism. *Autism and Asperger Syndrome*, 93–121.

Westphal, A., Schelinski, S., Volkmar, F., & Pelphrey, K. (2013). Revisiting regression in autism: Heller's dementia infantilis. *Journal of Autism and Developmental Disorders, 43*(2), 265–271.

Wolff, S. (2004). The history of autism. *European Child & Adolescent Psychiatry, 13*(4), 201–208.

Yell, M. L., & Drasgow, E. (2000). Litigating a free appropriate public education: The Lovaas hearing and cases. *The Journal of Special Education, 33*, 205–214.

Zager, D. (Ed.). (2004). *Autism spectrum disorders: identification, education, and treatment.* Mahwah, N.J.: Lawrence Erlbaum Publishers.

Chapter 3

Legislation, Program Development, and Service Delivery

Nikki L. Murdick and Barbara C. Gartin

Although autism was recognized and identified in the early 1960s, education and treatment programs at that time were scarce. Nevertheless, parents were organizing and initiating programs for their children with autism. The history of autism legislation reflects the same confusion that education and health professions encountered when trying to provide services to children with autism and their families. Unarguably, the most important legislation for children and youth with disabilities was IDEA (Individuals with Disabilities Education Act). However, bowing to political demands, autism was not listed as a category under IDEA until 1990. Still, individuals with autism were eligible for some services under other disability legislation. A dramatic increase in numbers of persons identified with autism burst into the public consciousness through personal accounts from movies, books, and advocacy groups and changes in legislation, program development, and service delivery expanded at the same time. This chapter provides information on legislation that helped define the programs and service delivery systems designed to meet the growing need.

Legislation Impacting Individuals with Autism

Over the decades, as information concerning autism has expanded, the "growing prevalence of ASD is shaping current law and policy relating to all disabilities and will have a profound impact on children with disabilities, particularly concerning special education" (Dicker & Bennett, 2011, p. 416). Table 3.1 lists key legislation related to Autism Spectrum Disorders (ASD).

Autism originally was known as a low incidence category, inferring that the numbers of children with this type of disability were few. As a result, prior to 1975, children with autism were routinely excluded from attending schools because of the belief that they could not learn or that they would interfere with the learning of other students in the class (Dicker & Bennett, 2011; Hass, 2008). Thus, many children who would

Table 3.1 ASD Legislation

ASD Legislation

Achieving a Better Life Experience Act (ABLE) of 2014, Public Law 113–297, 26 U.S.C. § 529

Autism CARES Act of 2014, Public Law 113–157, 42 U.S.C. 201 *et seq.*

Children's Health Act of 2000, Public Law 106–301, 42 U.S.C. 201 *et seq.*

Combatting Autism Act of 2006, Public Law 109–416, 42 U.S.C. 201 *et seq.*

Combatting Autism Reauthorization Act of 2011, Public Law 112-32, 42 U.S.C. 201 *et seq.*

Developmental Disabilities Assistance and Bill of Rights Act 2000. Public Law 106–402, 42 U.S.C. § 6000 *et seq.*

Education for All Handicapped Children Act of 1975, Public Law 94–142, 20 U.S.C. § 1471 *et seq.*

Education of the Handicapped Act of 1970, Public Law 91-230, §§ 601–662, 84 Stat. 175. of 1986, 20 U.S.C. § 1401 *et seq.*

Education of the Handicapped Act of 1974, Public Law 93-380, 20 U.S.C. § 1232 *et seq.*

Elementary and Secondary Education Act (ESEA) of 1965, Public Law 89–10, 20 U.S.C. § 16301 *et seq.*

Elementary and Secondary Education Act, amended by Public Law 89–750. 20 U.S.C. § 161 [Title VI], 80 stat. 1204 (1966).

Handicapped Children's Protection Act of 1986, Public Law 99–372, 20 U.S.C § 1401 *et seq.*

Higher Education Opportunity Act of 2008, Public Law 110–315, 20 U.S.C.§ 1001 *et seq.*

Individuals with Disabilities Education Act of 1990, Public Law 101–476, 20 U.S.C. § 1400 *et seq.*

Individuals with Disabilities Education Act Amendments of 1997, Public Law 105–17, 20 U.S.C. § 1400 *et seq.*

Individuals with Disabilities Education Improvement Act of 2004, Public Law 108–446, 20 U.S.C. § 1400 *et seq.*

No Child Left Behind Act of 2001. Public Law 107–110, 20 U.S.C. 70 § 6301 *et. seq.*

Patient Protection and Affordable Care Act of 2010, Public Law 111–148, 42 U.S.C. § 18001 *et seq.*

Rehabilitation Act of 1973, Section 504, Public Law 93–112, 29 U.S.C. § 794 *et seq.*

now be considered as having autism were labeled under the category of mental retardation or emotional disturbance, spending the majority of their lives in an institutional setting. As a result, much of the pre-1990 legislation did not include autism specifically as a category of disability. A brief description of legislation that was important in the provision of services for children with autism and other disabilities follows.

Rehabilitation Act (Section 504) (Public Law 93–112)

Public Law 93-112, known as the Rehabilitation Act, was enacted in 1973. It was an expansion of several earlier acts beginning in the early

1900s with the Soldier's Rehabilitation Act (1918). One part of the Act, Section 504, is considered to be the part of this legislation that focuses on nondiscrimination of individuals with a disability. Specific categories of disability are not included in the Rehabilitation Act as it used a functional definition focusing entirely on the existence of a disability and its impact on the individual's chances for success. The Rehabilitation Act is basically civil rights legislation for persons with disabilities and, as such, is more inclusive in its outlook than other education-focused pieces of legislation, such as the Individuals with Disabilities Education Act.

Developmental Disabilities Assistance and Bill of Rights Act (Public Law 106–402)

There has been ongoing controversy over the classification of persons with mental retardation and other disabilities and how should they be identified. As a result of this moral question, in 1975 a new more global category was invented—developmental disabilities (Eyal, Hart, Onculer, Oren, & Rossi, 2010). This piece of legislation was an amendment of a 1963 act known as the Mental Health Centers Construction Act. The act included a variety of changes including a functional, as opposed to a categorical, definition of disability, i.e. developmental disabilities (DD), and an expansion of state involvement through state plans, state grants and State Developmental Disabilities Councils.

In addition, it included a Bill of Rights for Persons with Disabilities. Because it includes a functional definition, autism was not named specially, although individuals could be served under the eligibility rubric of DD. This piece of legislation was most recently reauthorized in 2000 to continue its focus on programs for individuals with developmental disabilities (Title I), family support (Title II), and programs for direct support workers who assist individuals with developmental disabilities (Title III).

Education for All Handicapped Children Act (Public Law 94–142)

In 1975, a piece of legislation considered to be the most important in this century for persons with disabilities was enacted. The Education for All Handicapped Children Act (EAHCA) essentially included a Bill of Rights for Children with Disabilities with the assurance that all children with disabilities receive a free, appropriate, public education, abbreviated as FAPE (Murdick, Gartin, & Fowler, 2014). Thirteen specific categories of disability were listed and explicitly covered by this legislation. Autism was not included as one of these, as it still was considered to be a rare disability. As such, autism was subsumed within the disability category of *seriously emotionally disturbed (SED)* and later in 1981 moved to the *other health impaired (OHI)* category (Zager, Wehmeyer, & Simpson, 2012). The EAHCA was amended once more before the new decade began. The Education of the Handicapped Amendments (EHA) of 1986 included two new programs addressing the needs of infants and toddlers with disabilities and also pre-school children ages three to five years old. Although the law was expanded, still autism was not included as a separate category in the legislation.

As the country moved into the 1990s, autism finally was recognized as a separate category. It was believed that by specifically naming autism as a category, more appropriate research, education, and legislation could be provided for individuals with autism and their families. Subsequently, during the past 25 years, the number of pieces of legislation that have included or focused on children with autism has increased, as has research on ASD.

Individuals with Disabilities Education Act and its Reauthorizations (Public Laws 101–476, 105–17, and 108–446)

In 1990, a more extensive reauthorization of the EAHCA occurred, including a name change to reflect the field's move to focus on people first language. Thus, the new law was entitled the Individuals with Disabilities Education Act (IDEA) of 1990. Additional changes included expansion of service delivery to students with disabilities ages 18–21 years old, inclusion of transition services and assistive technology as approved special education services, and rehabilitation counseling and social work services under the list of related services. But to the field of autism, the most important aspect was the inclusion of autism as a specific, free-standing category for the first time (Murdick et al., 2014). The law has been reauthorized and revised three more times since. The first reauthorization was in 1991, titled the Individuals with Disabilities Education Act Amendments (IDEAA) with changes in the Part H program for infants and toddlers and the inclusion of an Individualized Family Service Plan (IFSP) instead of an Individualized Education Plan (IEP) for children ages three to five. Again, the law was reauthorized in 1997, with changes focusing on school safety, parental participation, and finance.

In 2004, a major revision of IDEA was completed. This reauthorization, known as the Individuals with Disabilities Education Improvement Act (IDEIA), included a definition of highly qualified special education teachers, a provision for reducing paperwork, appropriate education for homeless or migrant children, changes in procedural safeguards, and a revision of state performance goals and requirements to bring IDEIA into compliance with the reauthorization of Elementary and Secondary Education Act (ESEA) of 1965, now known as No Child Left Behind Act

(NCLB). In addition, this reauthorization addressed the programmatic needs of children with autism by calling for the development and expansion of programs to train teachers for this group of students (Dicker & Bennett, 2011) and to increase the use of research-based teaching methodologies (Zager et al., 2012). According to Murdick et al. (2014, p. 30), "the changes to IDEA may be seen as an attempt to reduce the conflict between IDEA and the No Child Left Behind Act (NCLB) of 2001 (P.L. 107–110)," that is, the individual focus of IDEA and the group focus of NCLB have led to concerns over the appropriateness of programming and assessment of student progress.

Children's Health Act (Public Law 106–310)

The Children's Health Act of 2000 was signed by President Clinton to increase research and treatment in a variety of health issues including autism. There are five sections of the law that focus on the issues related to autism. Section 101 focuses on the "expansion, intensification, and coordination of activities of National Institutes of Health with respect to research on autism" (U.S. GPO, 2000). Section 102 focuses on developmental disabilities surveillance and research programs for individuals with autism, including the National Autism and Pervasive Developmental Disabilities Surveillance Program, the Centers of Excellence in Autism and Pervasive Developmental Disabilities Epidemiology, and a Clearinghouse at the CDC for storage of data generated under this section. Section 103 expands and implements a program to provide information and education in the field of autism to professionals and the general public. Section 104 of this law mandates the establishment of a group to oversee and coordinate research in the field of autism known as the Interagency Autism Coordinating Committee (IACC). The IACC's mission is to "facilitate the effective and efficient exchange of information on autism activities among the member agencies and to coordinate autism-related activities" (U.S. Department of Health and Human Services, 2003). And the final section, 105, requires a yearly report to Congress on the progress of these sections of the legislation.

No Child Left Behind Act (Public Law 107–110)

The No Child Left Behind Act of 2001, or NCLB, is a reauthorization of the ESEA and is considered to be one of the most sweeping pieces of legislation since IDEA was first enacted in 1975. According to the Office of the Under Secretary of the U.S. Department of Education "[t]his historic reform gives states and school districts unprecedented flexibility in how they spend their education dollars, in return for setting standards for student achievement and holding students and educators accountable for results" (2002, p. 3). Thus, the purpose of the act is to "close the achievement gap by holding states, local school districts, and schools accountable for improving the academic achievement of children" (Wright, Wright, & Heath, 2004, p. 21). This focus on academic accountability through the use of state-developed tests becomes one of the most controversial, as there are concerns that the focus on testing as the means to identify progress may impact negatively on students with disabilities and those from minority or poverty-stricken areas of the country.

Combatting Autism Act and Reauthorizations
(Public Laws 109–416, 112–32, and 113–157)

The Combatting Autism Act (CAA) was enacted in 2006 by President Bush "in recognition of the rapid growth in the number of children diagnosed with autism" (White, Smith, Smith, & Stodden, 2012, p. 8). This Act provides federal funding for research, screening, intervention, and education for individuals with autism. The CAA was reauthorized by President Obama in 2011 as the Combatting Autism Reauthorization Act (CARA) in order to ensure the continuation of the research, early identification, and professional training that had begun under CAA. Again, CARA was reauthorized by Congress and signed by President Obama in 2014. It became law and was retitled as the Autism Collaboration, Accountability, Research, Education and Support Act, or Autism CARES Act. This Act reauthorizes the Combating Autism Act and continues funding for research in the identification of risk factors, treatments and interventions, services, and data collection for both children and adults on the autism spectrum for five years (the White House Blog, 2014).

Higher Education Opportunity Act
(Public Law 110–315)

The Higher Education Opportunity Act of 2008 is usually considered to focus on students with intellectually disabilities. The Act was the latest of many reauthorizations of the Higher Education Act of 1965, enacted to improve access to college or career schools for students with intellectual disabilities (ID) (Center for Autism Research, 2014; Lee, 2009). This Act provided increased access for these students to Pell grants and other financial aid opportunities for those students with intellectual disabilities who "are enrolled or accepted for enrollment in a comprehensive transition and postsecondary program at specific institutions of higher education (IHE) and maintain satisfactory progress in the program" (Lee, 2009). Although this act focuses on students with intellectual disabilities (ID), there is increasing evidence that many students with ID also have autism. According to the Center for Disease Control's (CDC) latest prevalence study of records since 2008, 10 percent of those individuals whose primary diagnosis is ID also have a secondary diagnosis of Autism Spectrum Disorder (ASD), and 38 percent of those individuals whose primary diagnosis is ASD have a secondary diagnosis of ASD (Center for Autism Research, 2014). As a result, professionals and parents addressing the programmatic needs and future plans for students with ASD should be cognizant of the provisions of this Act.

Affordable Care Act (Public Law 111–148)

The Patient Protection and Affordable Care Act of 2010, commonly called the Affordable Care Act and signed by President Obama, includes a significant section for children with autism as individuals with ASD can face complex health needs throughout their lifespan (Autism Speaks, 2015a). For most families of children with autism, it is critical that they have some type of financial support to manage the variety of medical, behavioral, and developmental health services required for their child. According to Autism Speaks (2015a), this can require a complex navigation of multiple medical professionals and insurance reimbursement rules that may not cover all the needed services. As a result of this problem, many reported that they had to pay much of the medical costs themselves. With the enactment of the Affordable Care Act, insurance companies are prohibited from denying coverage to children with pre-existing conditions that include autism. The act also includes behavioral health treatments on its list of essential benefits. Even with this change, there continues to be concern that parents with fewer resources still will be unable to access appropriate services for their child with autism.

Achieving a Better Life Experience Act (Public Law 113–295)

As noted previously, many individuals with disabilities (and their families) have had difficulty paying for their disability related services (Autism Speaks, 2015b). To address part of this issue the Achieving a Better Life Experience Act, or the ABLE Act of 2014, an amendment to the Internal Revenue Code of 1986, was signed by President Obama. Its purpose is to:

> (1) encourage and assist individuals and families in saving private funds for the purpose of supporting individuals with disabilities to maintain health, independence, and quality of life; and (2) provide secure funding for disability-related expenses of beneficiaries with disabilities that will supplement, but not supplant, benefits provided through private insurance, Title XVI (Supplemental Security Income)

and Title XIX (Medicaid) of the Social Security Act, the beneficiary's employment, and other sources to allow parents to set up a special tax-free savings account for disability-related expenses.

(Library of Congress, 2015)

Although major changes and legislative support expanded the options for individuals with ASD, problems still continue to arise. Most noteworthy is that children with autism who are high functioning may not be eligible to receive needed special education and related services because of the manner in which the regulations are written. In addition, the NCLB's focus on alternative testing for those with a disability may hamper the educational future of these students because these tests may be unable to adequately measure ability. Also, legislation is occurring across the states, which holds promise for children with autism and their families but also leaves concern that consistency of educational programming will not occur since all states could pass legislation with differing requirements.

Program Development for Individuals with Autism

Developing an appropriate educational program for children and adolescents with autism is an essential, although sometimes difficult, task. Both IDEA and educational research agree that all programs should be based on an assessment of the individual's unique needs as well as his/her strengths. The focus of this assessment and subsequent program development has changed over time, moving from a deficit approach to a more child-focused, classroom approach.

Deficit Approach to Program Development

According to Harry and Klingner (2007), special education service delivery, that is program development for educational programs, was based originally on the deficit model. This model views children with unique needs through the lens of difference and developmental limitations. Thus, teachers and other educators often see disability as something inherent in the child that needs to be remediated or eliminated. Unfortunately, those performing the individualized assessments did not consider other reasons for why the child might be unsuccessful in school or on assessment items. Disability in the view of the deficit model is difference, and differences need to be eradicated. According to Pfeiffer (2002, p. 3):

there are three variations of the deficit model: the medical model, the rehabilitation model related to employment, and the special education model. Each model specifies a deficit (health condition, employment condition, learning condition) which must be corrected in order to make the person with a disability "normal."

The research and philosophy of special education originally was focused on this deficit model, with most children viewed from the perspective of the medical model which focuses on the health issues of the child. Thus, the diagnostic emphasis for a child with autism would focus on qualitative impairments in social reciprocity, atypical communication, and atypical behavior (Hyman & Towbin, 2007).

During the 1970s, a number of individuals began to question the use of the deficit model as the focus for decisions concerning eligibility for special education services (see Deno, 1970 and Blatt, Biklen, & Bogdan, 1977 for an early discussion of this issue). This discussion continues over the next 40 years with many espousing an entirely different viewpoint that moves completely away from this model to embrace the disability studies philosophy (Ware, 2011), while others continue using the deficit model because they are unwilling to totally discard the research and methodology developed under the earlier special education rubric. As Banks (2014, pp. 510–511) states in support of the change:

> Special education provides service and access to students and families who have varied life experiences that manifest as variations in development, learning, and behavior. If the initial statement is true and we, as a field, understand that the children and youth we serve are different, why is special education couched in a deficit service provision model?

Program Development for Children and Youth with Autism

Program development for children and youth with autism and other disabilities has been the major focus since the early days of special education. As said previously, the issue often has arisen as to what type of programming is needed and where the program should be implemented. Today, most educators agree that, "at first glance, there may appear to be multiple goals of education. However, there is one absolute target for all students, including those with ASD: Preparation for Adulthood" (VA DOE, 2011, p. 8). What was and continues to be needed is a framework on which to base the development of an appropriate program. The appropriate education framework was initiated with the enactment of IDEA in 1975. Although initially IDEA was based on the medical model, reauthorizations provided significant movement toward a more inclusive, non-deficit view of identification and program development. As Banks (2014, p. 517) noted:

focusing on human variation as opposed to pathology has been argued as a viable option for moving special education from a deficit model to a model that embraces divergence, keeping in mind that difference is not unique but is the one variable that resonates in all people, including children and youth.

Early Intervention Program Development

Recent research has long shown that by providing children with appropriate services and supports early in their life, significant gains in language, behavior, social skills, and eventually education can be made (ASGRC, 2011). With the IDEA reauthorization in 1986, service requirements were expanded to include children from ages three through five years old who were eligible under the law. This free, appropriate public education (FAPE) program was to be provided in the least restrictive environment (LRE) and to include both academic and behavioral goals that addressed the student's unique strengths and needs. In addition, a new section of the law was added to address the provision of early intervention services for young children with special needs, those from birth to age three years old who are experiencing a developmental delay: "The centerpiece of the infants and toddlers section of the law was the individualized family service plan (IFSP)" (Yell, 2014, p. 43). The IFSP should be developed by a multidisciplinary, interagency team that includes the parents as essential members. The IFSP is different from an IEP, as it focuses on the child as a member of a family system and looks at the unique needs of the child in his/her natural environment, his/her home. Between the ages of three and five years old, the child can be served by the school district by continuing use of the IFSP or transferring the child's educational planning to an IEP.

When the child transitions into the education-focused planning, then the program will be based on an assessment of the child's not the family's unique needs. This assessment must be a multidisciplinary assessment which has a twofold focus: to determine the child's eligibility for special education services under IDEA and to develop the educational program that will meet the child's needs. This multidisciplinary assessment is to be completed by the members of the multidisciplinary team. According to IDEA, the team should include the parents of the child with a disability, at least one regular education teacher of the child, at least one special education teacher, a representative of the local educational agency who is knowledgeable about curriculum and available resources and can provide or supervise such, an individual who can interpret the evaluation results, related service personnel as needed, and the child when appropriate (IDEA, 20 U.S.C. § 1414[d][B]).

Both the assessment and the program development should focus on the child's specific unique needs. Once these needs have been identified and the child has been declared eligible for services then the setting where this education program should be provided is identified. This service delivery should be considered on the basis of where the child's educational and social needs can best be met, not according to the eligibility label. The other requirement for the setting of the service delivery is that it be in the LRE for the particular child. As has been noted earlier, there is no specific "least restrictive environment," instead it is based on where the child can receive the most appropriate services as close to his/her peers in the general education classroom as possible.

Classroom-based approach

For most children with autism, the general education classroom is the least restrictive environment where students have more opportunities to "learn from typically developing peers in naturalistic settings" (ASGRC, 2011, p. 102). Any programs in the general education, inclusive classroom will need adaptations for successful learning to occur. There are a number of research-based programs that focus on the education of students with autism. Three of these programs (TEACCH, ABA, and BI/FAB) will be briefly described.

Treatment and Education of Autistic and related Communication Handicapped Children (TEACCH)

The TEACCH program is one of the earlier programs that were developed to address the specific needs of children with autism. Eric Schopler developed the TEACCH program in the 1960s. TEACCH focuses on the needs of children with autism "for an intensive and coordinated approach to skill building and developing communication abilities" (Hyman & Towbin, 2007, p. 335). TEACCH uses parents as co-therapists who teach new skills to their child with autism. The importance of teaching as a structured activity is also stressed, meaning that the adult plans the activity, secures the materials for use, determines the length of time for the session, and communicates the information clearly to the student (Mesibov, Shea, & McCaskill, 2012). As a result of this general view of program planning, TEACCH is considered to use an eclectic program format, which incorporates a number of different behavioral methods including applied behavior analysis (ABA).

Applied Behavior Analysis (ABA)

ABA "is science devoted to the understanding and improvement of human behavior" (Cooper, Heron, & Heward, 2007, p. 3). ABA is based on the pioneering work on the science of behavior by Watson and his

Stimulus-Response Behaviorism of the early 1900s and Skinner's Radical Behaviorism of the mid to late 1900s. From this foundation come studies that employed behaviorist principles to humans. Baer, Wolf, and Risley's 1968 seminal paper describes applied behavior analysis and explains that it "should be *applied, behavioral, analytic, technological, conceptually systematic, effective,* and capable of appropriately *generalized outcomes*" (Cooper et al., 2007, p. 16, emphasis added). Those who use this method believe that many student behaviors are learned; thus, students can learn new behaviors (Vaughan & Bos, 2012). Programs based on Applied Behavior Analysis incorporate intensive, early intervention and employ discrete trial training, prompting, and reinforcement of appropriate behaviors. Discrete trial training, or DTT, is a specific ABA method that has been shown to be effective in teaching children with autism. This method is used effectively in Lovaas' 1987 seminal work on using behavioral treatment with children with autism (Scott & Bennett, 2012) and in many classrooms today.

Behavior Intervention and Functional Analysis of Behavior (FBA)

Behavior interventions are based on the belief that "behavior carries meaning and should not be presumed to be a random act" (Hyman & Towbin, 2007, p. 337). This presumption leads the way to a more effective assessment of the child's behavior and how it is related to the scenario in which it is occurring. From there, the multidisciplinary team can develop a behavior plan to address behaviors that may be hindering the success of the individual in his/her home, school, or community environment.

The process using functional analysis of behavior is also known as functional behavioral assessment or FBA. FBA is included in IDEA 1997 as a required step in the assessment and program development process. An FBA is "the process of gathering information about a learner's behaviors in order to determine the purpose of a problem behavior in addition to its antecedents and consequences" (Raymond, 2012, p. 42). This process allows the team to identify the behaviors of concern as well as the setting and context of the behavior and, more importantly, the possible function that the behavior serves for the individual (Cooper et al., 2007). Essentially the FBA is an attempt to identify the cause-and-effect relationship between the individual's behaviors, the environment in which the behavior occurs including the setting and the individuals present in the setting, and the presence of precursors of the behavior (i.e. antecedents, individual's responses, and reinforcement of the behavior). As Hyman and Towbin (2007, p. 337) explain, "If the origin of the behavior is considered, it may be possible to teach more effective ways to achieve a similar result (e.g., comfort, communication) and to expand behaviors that increase social adaptability."

Universal Design for Learning (UDL) Approach

There is a continuing debate as to whether the most appropriate educational setting for students with autism is the general education classroom or not. For many parents and educators, education in the least restrictive environment, wherever that may be on the continuum of alternative placements, is the most appropriate site. For others, the most appropriate placement is the inclusive classroom. Inclusion is considered to be both a philosophy of education and an educational placement type. Those who consider inclusion as a philosophy believe that all children should have access to a quality education in the same setting as their neighborhood age peers. For an inclusive environment to be a successful placement for students with autism, teachers must develop accommodations and/or modifications in both curriculum and physical environments for use in addressing the child's unique needs (Clair, Church, & Batshaw, 2007). For teachers to do this successfully, many turn to the concept known as Universal Design for Learning (UDL), also known as Universal Design for Instruction (UDI). This concept is adapted from the concept of Universal Design in architecture and engineering, which focuses on developing designs that increase accessibility for persons with disabilities, but are useful for all (Hackman, 2008). According to the CAST website (2015), "Universal Design for Learning (UDL) is a research-based set of principles to guide the design of learning environments that are accessible and effective for all." In operation, UDL typically includes curriculum, curricular materials, instructional activities and procedures, and evaluation procedures and materials designed to meet the needs of *all* students in the classroom. Thus, the teacher reviews his/her classroom environment, curriculum and instruction, and materials and methods in order to identify which ones could be designed to meet the multiple needs and skills of all students in the classroom. Lessons and the classroom environment are revised so that they promote "access, participation, and progress in the general education curriculum for all learners by proactively embedding accommodations into instruction to meet learning needs of all students" (Heflin & Isbell, 2012, p. 192). The proactive behavior is in opposition to the retroactive identification and implementation of accommodations after the curriculum, lessons, activities, and settings are planned. Therefore, an educational program for a child with autism, or another disability, might include both placements in an inclusive classroom where UDL approaches are used and in classrooms where educational approaches and accommodations are designed specific to the child's unique needs.

Parent Involvement

When one reviews the issues inherent in the provision of educational services for children with autism, the involvement of parents and families in the child's educational program is a principle present in all approaches (Hecimovic, Powell, & Christensen, 1999). The inclusion of parents is a significant change from earlier times, when parents often were blamed for their child's disability and seldom notified or included in any of the program developments or their implementation. Today, parent and family involvement is a requirement when the child with autism is receiving infant and toddler services. Parents are an essential part of the development of the IFSP and also in the implementation of the program delivery. As the child transitions into school-based services, family involvement continues. This involvement may be support in the home for the school-based program, or it may be involvement with interventionists who are providing behavioral treatment in the home. Parent involvement is best described by ten principles suggested by Hecimovic, Powell, and Christensen in 1999. These are: (1) children grow best in families; (2) family members are interdependent; (3) parents are the best judges of their children's needs; (4) the family is the best advocate; (5) families want involvement; (6) professionals need to support families; (7) parents should question professionals; (8) autism need not be negative; (9) concern is for the long term; and (10) there is more than autism (p. 265–266).

The family-centered approach described by the previous list and encapsulated in the IDEA legislation sees professionals and families as supporters of each other in the education of the child with autism. According to Dunst, Johanson, Trivette, and Hamby (1991), family- centered support promotes the family in learning to make decisions, in focusing on the capabilities and competencies of the family members, and in choosing resources and support to assist them in building a network to strengthen their capacity to work with their child. This collaborative approach requires that the professional be the ally of the family as the child moves through the educational system to reach his/her goal of life in the community (VA DOE, 2011). As a supportive family-centered ally, professionals assist families in addressing problems that may arise, such as lack of support within the community, individual and family member stress including that of siblings and extended family members, financial issues, marital stress, concerns over conflicting professional advice, and questions about professionals' knowledge base (Agosta & Melda, 1995; Hecimovic et al., 1999).

Evidence-based Practices: The National Standards Project

In this chapter, the legislative background for program development and service delivery have been examined. Along with this discussion, program development and changes in educational philosophy have been examined as they relate to the placement of students and the involvement of parents. One area that has not been considered is the evidence base for practices and methods being used by professionals who work with students with autism. Some states have developed their own guides to assist the members of the multidisciplinary team on appropriate selection of evidenced-based practices for use with children with autism. For state examples, review Virginia's *Models of Best Practice* (2011), Ohio's *Autism Reaching for a Brighter Future* (2011), and Missouri's *Autism Spectrum Disorders: A Guide to Evidence-Based Interventions* (2012). On the national arena, one can access the National Standards Project Report (2009, 2015) for information about effective practices. According to the National Autism Center (2015), *The National Standards Report* answers the question of how to effectively treat individuals with autism spectrum disorder (ASD). This project was begun in 2005 by the National Autism Center in collaboration with an expert panel of scholars, researchers, and other national leaders. It is considered to be the most comprehensive analysis of evidence-based interventions for children and adolescents with autism (National Autism Center, 2015). The project was completed in two phases: Phase 1 from 2005 through 2009 and Phase 2 from 2009 through 2015. Phase 1 includes an examination and quantification of the level of research that support interventions targeted toward children, adolescents, and young adults with autism. Phase 2 provides an updated examination for this age group and extends the research base to adults over age 22.

According to the National Autism Center (2015), the National Research Project is an expansion of a 2001 report by the National Research Council (NRC). That report identifies effective practices such as early intervention, instructional programming, parent involvement, utilization of deliberate teaching, small group or one-to-one instruction, and a communication-rich environment (NRC, 2001). Even with the publication of that report, families, educators, and service providers were still confused with the myriad and sometimes conflicting information about available treatments. Thus, the 2015 report is seen as a much-needed step in "helping to reduce the resulting turmoil and uncertainty by addressing the need for evidence-based practice standards and providing guidelines for how to make choices about interventions" (National Autism Center, 2015, p. 1).

Services for persons with autism have developed quickly, but through research data educators and medical professionals learned some important principles. First, early intervention leads to better outcomes. Parent involvement is not only important, but it leads to better outcomes for both the child and the family. Autism spans all ages, but its impact differs according to the age of the person with autism. Thus, services must develop a lifespan approach. Finally, the National Standards Project report identified effective practices such as early intervention, instructional programming, parent involvement, utilization of deliberate teaching, small group or one-to-one instruction, and a communication-rich environment as a result of a thorough examination of research data. The next section provides information on the strategies used for the delivery of services to the children with autism and their families.

Service Delivery

In earlier times, the diagnosis of autism was the pivotal point for a decision as to where the student would receive his/her services. The diagnosis driven decision-making changed during the past 40 years, so that now "educational placement decisions must be based on the assessed strengths, challenges, and educational needs of the student rather than on the label of autism" (VA DOE, 2011, p. 26). In other words, the disability label of autism moved from a unitary label to one that is more heterogenic, thus a spectrum of disorders that requires the understanding that individuals with autism have different needs and that their needs will change with their age and level of schooling. A brief discussion of the early service delivery models existing before the enactment of IDEA follows. The discussion includes those models most often used with children and youth identified with the autism label. To complete the chapter, a description of the changes that have occurred since the enactment of IDEA is provided.

Early Service Delivery Models (Pre-IDEA)

Raymond (2012) notes that pre-IDEA, "early public special education efforts operated on a selective basis" (p. 30). Children identified with autism most often displayed significant intellectual and behavioral issues; thus, in many instances, they were educated with children demonstrating severe intellectual disability and/or serious emotional disturbance. Routinely, public schools denied access to children with autism, stating that schools did not have the capacity to meet the child's needs. Typically, the only educational options available for parents were to arrange for home schooling or to place the child in a state or private institutional setting. The result of this denial of services was that the child with autism was being educated in an inappropriate educational program in a highly restrictive residential setting with persons labelled as having severe/profound mental retardation or severe mental health issues. The denial of services by public schools is one of the injustices that Congress sought to rectify by passing IDEA in 1975.

Institutional Placement

Early institutions were seen as facilities to house individuals who had mental retardation (now intellectual disability) and/or those who were considered insane (now mental illness). In fact, when Howe and his colleagues originally planned institutions, they were called schools and were considered to be places for habilitation (Noll, Smith, & Wehmeyer, 2013). Two types of institutions were most prevalent: (1) large imposing buildings that housed numerous individuals or (2) groups of smaller buildings known as cottages. At their conception, institutions were developed to meet the needs of the patients and to allow healing or training to occur; later institutions became storehouses for persons whose disability or behaviors were unacceptable to society. Wolfensberger (1975) notes that institutions are places where inmates are isolated from family and society, where they are crowded into spaces built for fewer patients than their current population, and where higher functioning inmates are exploited as free labor to support the institution and care for those who are less able.

Self-contained Schools

Post World War II, many parents of children with intellectual disability and/or autism began to question the placement of their children in institutions. Parent advocacy groups began a twofold campaign, one focus being the development of private, self-contained day schools for their children and the other a movement to expand services in the public schools so that their children could be educated with their peers. It was at this time that educational programs for students with autism began to appear, although most of these programs were not in public school settings (White et al., 2012). During these years, parents and researchers often agreed that self-contained schools would be the best option for those individuals whose "need for specialized instruction is considered so significant that a special school or other facility is considered necessary" (Mastropieri & Scruggs, 2014, p. 18). One of the most influential alliances at this time was The National Association of Parents and Friends of Mentally Retarded Children, which was founded in 1950 by a collection of parent groups and interested professionals. The organization grew and is now known as The Arc, which continues to support children and adults with intellectual disability. With the enactment of IDEA in 1975, the numbers of special day schools and other private or public facilities has declined. Mostly, the decline has been the result of the parent advocacy movement and the legislative mandate for the expansion of service options within the public school programs.

Self-contained Classrooms

The first step toward moving students with disabilities into the public schools was the development of specialized classes. Students placed in self-contained classrooms, at that time, did not participate in the general education class with their peers. All content as well as support classes such as art, music, and physical education were taught separately from grade-level peers.

According to Kavale and Forness (2000), "the special class was seen as the best means for avoiding conflicts while providing universal education" (p. 280).

Although this was movement forward, many parents of children with disabilities want their children to have opportunities for interaction with their peers.

Later Service Delivery Models (Post-IDEA)

Following the enactment of IDEA, the shift in service delivery is from "historical placement in large, isolated residential institutions to the more common practice in recent years of placing children in the neighborhood schools they would be attending if they had no disabilities" (Raymond, 2012, p. 30). This shift is a monumental change in the method in which students with disabilities receive services and is seen in the number of students with autism who are now being educated in general education classrooms. Heward (2009) states that now "Approximately 3 in 10 students with ASD are educated in general education classrooms, about 18% of students with ASD are served in resource rooms, 40% in separate classrooms, and 10% in separate schools or residential facilities" (p. 282).

Continuum of Alternative Placements (CAP)

With the enactment of IDEA in 1975, there came a change in educational service delivery. The primary goal according to Kavale (2002) was "to ensure educational equity and eliminate the miseducation and chronic exclusion experienced by children with disabilities" (p. 201). To do this, schools districts were required to provide a full continuum of placement options, also known as a continuum of alternative placements (CAP). The CAP model is based on a model developed by Deno in 1970, called the Cascade Model. Deno's model features an up-ended pyramid divided into seven horizontal sections, representing by size the number of students who should be provided with each type of services. The service options ranged from total immersion in the general education setting with no additional supports, to a setting in a residential or hospital setting where extensive supports are provided (Hong, Schulte, & Ivy, 2015). As the Virginia Department of Education (2011) states "using the continuum concept makes it more likely that each student will be placed appropriately in an environment that is specifically suited for him or her" (p. 26).

In later IDEA authorizations, a similar form was included in the legislation and labeled as a Continuum of Alternative Placements (CAP). The legislation mandates that all children, regardless of disability or not, be provided a free, appropriate public education (FAPE) in the least restrictive environment (LRE). The environment is to be selected from this continuum of placements or alternative settings where appropriate education programs could be designed to meet the unique needs of each child (Kavale & Forness, 2000). CAP contains placement options similar to those proposed by Deno, ranging from the most integrated, that is, general education with the student's peers, to the most segregated, that is, hospital or homebound education. However, the degree of restrictiveness of the placement is based on the needs of the individual student and not on an established view of what would be the most restrictive.

Pull-out Services (Self-contained and Resource Rooms)

The first steps down on the CAP, after the general education classrooms, were two sites where students would receive some or all of their educational services: resource room and self-contained classroom. Typically, the amount of time when services are delivered outside the regular (general) classroom denotes whether the placement is considered to be a resource room or a self-contained classroom. According to Heward (2009, p. 283):

> Many students with autism spend a portion of each school day in the general education classroom with same-age peers and part of the day in a resource room where they receive intensive, specialized instruction focused on their individualized education program (IEP) goals and objectives.

When students are assigned to a resource room service delivery model, they will spend a portion of the day in the general education classroom with their peers and a designated amount of time in the resource room receiving specialized instruction in content areas or social skill development (Mastropieri & Scruggs, 2014). Those students whose needs indicate more time is required for instruction may be assigned to a self-contained class. Although the name seems to indicate that the student will spend all his/her time in the classroom away from the general education class, usually this is not the case. It typically does indicate, though, that the student will spend most of his/her time away from his/her general education peers. Even at this level of the CAP, however, students with disabilities usually "interact with their nondisabled peers during art, music, physical education, recess, lunch, and assemblies" (Mastropieri & Scruggs, 2014, p. 18).

Push-in Programs (Mainstreaming)

In conjunction with the introduction of legislation such as IDEA and differing service delivery options was the introduction of a process known as "mainstreaming." Mainstreaming focused on moving students from their self-contained classes into the general education classroom. Kavale (1979, 2002) suggested that the concept of mainstreaming, or the push-in programs, was actually a reaction against the exclusive use of the special class where students continued to be segregated from their peers. That is, they were included in the school but still excluded from full participation with their peers. On the positive side, Mastropieri and Scruggs (2014) stated that advocates of mainstreaming believed that students, both those with disabilities and those without, would benefit if they all had some time in the classroom together. General education teachers espoused concerns that these students with a disability were just "visiting" the classroom at specific times during the day and that the teacher did not have full responsibility for the programming. An additional concern was the conviction by many that the student should not be allowed to participate in the general education classroom until he/she reached an "adequate" skill level; that is to say the student with autism must have earned the right to attend the general education class. In this model, a student with disabilities begins his/her educational cycle in the special classroom and if he/she progresses enough, he/she might be allowed to participate in the general education classroom; hence, the student is moved to that setting. Consequently, as Kavale (2002) states, the process of trying to gain access to the general education classroom from a special education classroom "resulted in special education becoming a place rather than a process" (p. 205).

Inclusive Programming

From the opposite point of view, those who espouse inclusion, or inclusive programming, believe that all students should begin their education career in the general education classroom. Students are separated only if their unique needs are significant enough that they could not be addressed appropriately in the general education classroom. Only then would they receive some, or most, of their education outside of the general education class. According to Batten (as cited in VA DOE, 2011), "the extent of inclusion should be driven by the student's needs as determined by the educational team, not by the district's convenience" (p. 28). There continues to be an expanding view that students with autism should receive their education in the general education classroom as much as possible. The result is that data show a substantial increase in the numbers of students with autism receiving an inclusive education. According to Sansosti and Sansosti (2013, p. 229):

data from the U.S. Department of Education reveal that participation of students with ASD in the general education curriculum for more than 80% of the day increased from 9% in 1992 to 31% in 2006, representing an increase of 244%.

But still there is controversy as to the most appropriate service delivery option for students with autism and whether general education placements should be recommended for students with autism at all (Simpson, de Boer, & Smith-Myles, 2003).

Early Intervention Models

Early intervention center-based programs and family centered, home-based programs are two types of programs encouraged and supported since the 1986 IDEA reauthorization, which includes education for infants, toddlers and young children and their families in its requirements for service provision. Both program types continue to be included in the IDEA legislation. An expansion of the legislation now requires a specific family-based program plan known as the Individualized Family Service Plan (IFSP) to indicate that the focus in the child's earlier years should be family centered, not individual child or school centered. The past two decades of research indicate that "appropriately structured educational programs and management in the early years can play a significant role in enhancing functioning in later life" (Dahle, 2003, p. 66). Parents and educators focus on early intervention with the belief that it can reduce the future need for more restrictive placement and expand the probability of a successful educational future for their child (Peacock et al., 2013). The requirement for early intervention has been verified by research, so that focus continues.

IDEA also requires that the child's placement should be in the LRE. For most young children, the natural setting is the home with his/her family. Thus, according to Dahle (2003), family-centered home programs for young children with autism, or any disability, should include (a) the recognition that the child is an integral part of a family system, (b) that the family's needs, concerns, and priorities must guide any educational program, and (c) that the family must be given the opportunity to participate in their child's programming. Accordingly, Handleman and Harris (2001) state, "it is well known that parental and family involvement is critical for establishing and maintaining behavior changes by students with autism" (p. 9). In fact, parental involvement and the subsequent training as providers for their child's educational and behavioral program has been emphasized since the early 1970s, when Lovaas and his colleagues trained parents of children in their study to be co-teachers (Ingersoll & Dvortcsak, 2006). The results found that the children's success continued if they lived at home with their parents and decreased if they went to an institutional

setting. Therefore, parent training to participate in the program development and implementation for children with autism continues to increase.

When looking at the history of services for children with disabilities in
general and autism in particular, there has been:

> [A] steady press toward greater integration of students with disabilities.
> The law demands education in the LRE, but difficulties have resulted
> from this provision coming to be interpreted as solely the general edu-
> cation classroom, particularly for all students regardless of type and
> level of disability.
>
> (Kavale & Forness, 2000, p. 290)

This steady progress began even before the original enactment of IDEA,
with its focus on the LRE (Simpson *et al.*, 2003). As we look toward the
future of educational services for children with autism, it is imperative that
we focus educational program and service delivery planning on the unique
needs of each child and where he or she is most likely to have educational,
behavioral and, eventually, life success.

Where Do We Go From Here?

As the number of new cases of autism continues to rise, families and professionals agree that there are questions that need answers. What is, or
are, the underlying cause or causes of autism? What are the most appropriate evidenced-based interventions? Which educational and behavioral
programs are the most effective in addressing the unique needs of individuals with autism? What service delivery options should be we identify for
future educational service delivery? How can parents and family members
be more involved with their children with autism as they transition into
adulthood? What we do know is that research is slowly revealing answers
to these questions. For example, we know now that early intervention is
critical and that some persons with autism will need support long beyond
high school. Of course, the journey that began in the early 1960s with
our search for how to address these intense, diverse, and sometimes overwhelming needs of the individual with autism is not over yet. The following chapters provide information to guide the provision of services from
birth to adulthood, ending with the need for collaboration and teamwork.

References

Agosta, J., & Melda, K. (1995). Supporting families who provide care at home
for children with disabilities. *Exceptional Children*, 62(3), 271–282.
Autism Service Guidelines Revision Committee (ASGRC). (2011). *Autism: Reaching
for a brighter future*. Columbus, OH: Author.

Autism Speaks. (2015a). *The affordable care act and autism*. Retrieved June 1, 2016 from http://autismspeaks.org.

Autism Speaks. (2015b). *Federal initiatives*. Retrieved June 1, 2016 from http://autismspeaks.org.

Banks, T. (2014). From deficit to divergence: Integrating theory to inform the selection of interventions in special education. *Creative Education, 5*, 510–518.

Blatt, B., Biklen, D., & Bogdan, R. (Eds.). (1977). *An alternative textbook in special education, people, schools and other institutions*. Denver, CO: Love.

Center for Applied Special Technology (CAST). (2015). About Universal Design for Learning. Retrieved June 1, 2016 from http://cast.org.

Center for Autism Research. (2014). Higher Education Opportunity Act of 2008. *The Children's Hospital of Philadelphia Research Institute*. Retrieved June 1, 2016 from http://carautismroadmap.org/.

Center for Autism Research. (2014). Intellectual Disability and ASD. *The Children's Hospital of Philadelphia Research Institute*. Retrieved June 1, 2016 from http://carautismroadmap.org/.

Clair, E. B., Church, R. P., & Batshaw, M. L. (2007). Special education services. In M. L. Batshaw, L. Pellegrino, & N. J. Roizen, *Children with disabilities* (6th ed., pp. 523–538). Baltimore, MO: Paul H. Brookes.

Cooper, J. O., Heron, T. E., & Heward, W. L. (2007). *Applied behavior analysis* (2nd ed.). Upper Saddle River, NJ: Pearson.

Dahle, K. B. (2003). Services to include young children with autism in the general classroom. *Early Childhood Education Journal, 31*(1), 65–70.

Deno, E. (1970). Special education as developmental capital. *Exceptional Children, 37*(3), 237–239.

Dicker, S., & Bennett, E. (2011). Engulfed by the spectrum: The impact of Autism Spectrum Disorders on law and policy. *Valparaiso University Law Review, 45*(2), 415–455.

Dunst, C. J., Johanson, C., Trivette, C. M., & Hamby, D. (1991). Family oriented family intervention policies and practices: Family-centered or not? *Exceptional Children, 58*(2), 115–126.

Eyal, G., Hart, B., Onculer, E., Oren, N., & Rossi, N. (2010). *The autism matrix: The social origins of the autism epidemic*. Malden, MA: Polity.

Hackman, H. W. (2008). Broadening the pathway to academic success: The critical intersections of social justice education, critical multicultural education, and universal instructional design. In J. L. Higbee & E. Goff (Eds.), *Pedagogy and student services for institutional transformation: Implementing universal design in higher education* (pp. 25–48). Minneapolis, MN: Regents of the University of Minnesota, Center for Research on Developmental Education and Urban Literacy, College of Education and Human Development, University of Minnesota.

Harry, B., & Klingner, J. (2007). Discarding the deficit model. *Educational Leadership, 64*(5), 16–21.

Hass, T. (2008). School-based services. In G. R. Buckendorf (Ed.), *Autism: A guide for educators, clinicians, and parents* (pp. 139–152). Greenville, SC: Thinking Publications.

Handleman, J. S., & Harris, S. L. (2001). *Preschool education programs for children with autism* (2nd ed.). Austin, TX: Pro-Ed.

Hecimovic, A., Powell, T. H., & Christensen, L. (1999). Supporting families in meeting their needs. In D. Zager (Ed.), *Autism: Identification, Education, and Treatment* (2nd ed., pp. 261–299). Mahwah, NJ: Lawrence Erlbaum.

Heflin, L. J., & Isbell, J. S. (2012). Education through the developmental stages: School-age children and adolescents. In D. Zager, M. L. Wehmeyer, & R. L. Simpson, *Educating students with autism spectrum disorders: Research-based principles and practices* (pp. 179–206). New York: Routledge.

Heward, W. L. (2009). *Exceptional children: An introduction to special education* (9th ed.). Upper Saddle River, NJ: Pearson.

Hong, B., Schulte, D., & Ivy, F. (2015). A multidimensional approach for educating all children: Empowering stakeholders to make appropriate decisions. Retrieved June 1, 2016 from http://oercommons.org.

Hyman, S. L., & Towbin, K. E. (2007). Autism Spectrum Disorders. In M. L. Batshaw, L. Pellegrino, & N. J. Roizen (Eds.), *Children with disabilities* (6th ed., pp. 325–343). Baltimore, MD: Paul H. Brookes.

Ingersoll, B., & Dvortcsak, A. (2006). Including parent training in the early childhood special education curriculum for children with autism spectrum disorders. *Journal of Positive Behavior Interventions*, 8(2), 79–87.

Kavale, K. A. (1979). Mainstreaming: The genesis of an idea. *The Exceptional Child*, 26, 3–21.

Kavale, K. A. (2002). Mainstreaming to full inclusion: From orthogenesis to pathogenesis of an idea. *International Journal of Disability, Development and Education*, 49(2), 201–214.

Kavale, K., & Forness, S. (2000). History, rhetoric, and reality: Analysis of the inclusion debate. *Remedial and Special Education*, 21(5), 279–296.

Lee, S. S. (2009). Overview of the Federal Higher Education Opportunity Act Reauthorization. *Insight*, 1. Retrieved June 1, 2016 from http://www.think college.net.

Library of Congress. (2015). *Summary: H.R. 647—ABLE Act of 2014*. Retrieved June 1, 2016 from http://congress.gov.

Mastropieri, M. A., & Scruggs, T. E. (2014). *The inclusive classroom: Strategies for effective differentiated instruction* (5th ed.). Boston, MA: Pearson.

Mesibov, G. B., Shea, V., & McCaskill, S. (2012). Structured teaching and the TEACCH program. In D. Zager, M. L. Wehmeyer, & R. L. Simpson, *Educating students with autism spectrum disorders: Research-based principles and practices* (pp. 99–112). New York: Routledge.

Murdick, N., Gartin, B. C., & Fowler, G. (2014). *Special education law* (3rd ed.). Boston, MA: Pearson.

National Autism Center. (2015). *The National Standards Report*. Randolph, MA: Author.

National Research Council. (2001). *Educating children with autism*. Washington, DC: National Academy Press.

Noll, S., Smith, J. D., & Wehmeyer, M. (2013). In search of a science: Intellectual disability in late model times (1900 CE to 1930 CE). In M. L. Wehmeyer (Ed.). *The story of intellectual disability: An evolution of meaning, understanding, and perception*. Baltimore, MO: Paul H. Brookes.

Peacock, G., Lin, S., Bogin, J., Rhodes, C., & Wolf, R. B. (2013). Learn the signs. Act early: The public health approach to the early identification of children at risk for autism spectrum disorder and other developmental disabilities (pp. 231–247). In P. Doehring, *Autism services across America: Road maps for improving state and national education, research and training programs.* Baltimore, MO: Paul H. Brookes.

Pfeiffer, D. (2002). The philosophical foundations of disability studies. *Disability Studies Quarterly, 22*(2), 3–23.

Raymond, E. B. (2012). *Learners with mild disabilities: A characteristics approach* (4th ed.). Boston, MA: Pearson.

Sansosti, F. J., & Sansosti, J. M. (2013). Effective school based delivery for students with autism spectrum disorders: Where we are and where we need to go. *Psychology in the Schools, 50*(3), 229–244.

Scott, J., & Bennett, K. (2012). Applied behavior analysis and learners with autism spectrum disorders. In D. Zager, M. L. Wehmeyer, & R. L. Simpson, *Educating students with autism spectrum disorders: Research-based principles and practices* (pp. 63–81). New York: Routledge.

Simpson, R. L., de Boer-Ott, S. R., & Smith-Myles, B. (2003). Inclusion of learners with autism spectrum disorders in general education settings. *Topics in Language Disorders, 23*(2), 116–133.

U.S. Department of Health and Human Services, Interagency Autism Coordinating Committee. (2003). *Report to Congress on autism activities under the Children's Health Act of 2000 (Fiscal Year 2002).* Retrieved June 1, 2016 from http://iacc.hhs.gov.

U.S. Government Printing Office (GPO). (2000). *Public Law 106-310.* Retrieved June 1, 2016 from http://gpo.gov.

Vaughan, S., & Bos, C. S. (2012). *Strategies for teaching students with learning and behavior problems* (8th ed.). Boston, MA: Pearson.

Virginia Department of Education (VA DOE). (2011). *Models of best practice in the education of students with autism spectrum disorders.* Richmond, VA: Author.

Ware, L. (2011). Disability studies in education. In S. Tozer, B. P. Gallegos, A. Henry, M. B. Greiner, & P. G. Price (Eds.), *Handbook of research in the social foundations of education* (pp. 244–260). New York: Routledge.

White, M. L., Smith, J. D., Smith, T. E. C., & Stodden, R. (2012). Autism Spectrum Disorders: Historical, legislative, and current perspectives. In D. Zager, M. L. Wehmeyer, & R. L. Simpson (Eds.), *Educating students with Autism Spectrum Disorders: Research-based principles and practices* (pp. 3–12). New York: Routledge.

White House Blog. (2014, Aug. 11). President Obama signs bill to support the needs of people with autism. Retrieved June 1, 2016 from http://whitehouse. gov.

Wolfensberger, W. (1975). *The origin and nature of our institutional models.* Syracuse, NY: Human Policy Press.

Wright, P. W. D., Wright, P. D., & Heath, S. W. (2004). *No Child Left Behind.* Hartfield, VA: Harbor House Law Press.

Yell, M. L. (2014). *The law and special education* (4th ed.). Boston, MA: Pearson.

Zager, D., Wehmeyer, M. L., & Simpson, R. L. (2012). *Educating students with autism spectrum disorders: Research-based principles and practices.* New York: Routledge.

Chapter 4

Advances in Neurobiological and Medical Research

Gardner T. Umbarger, III

The management of autism by medical practitioners has been slow to evolve due to the nature of autism spectrum disorders (ASD). As this chapter will discuss, the lack of specific medical causes for autism spectrum disorders complicates the ability of health professionals to provide meaningful interventions that have been shown to be effective in treating children with ASD. Most treatments focus on the affective characteristics of ASD, even as their underlying reason for their expression is poorly articulated, meaning the treatments often fail to live up to their expectations. This explains, in part, why complementary and alternative interventions have been so popular with families who have children with ASD.

The American Academy of Pediatrics (AAP) and its Council on Children with Disabilities has developed and published clinical practice guidelines on the management of children with ASD (Myers & Johnson, 2007). The purpose of these guidelines was to acknowledge the role pediatricians have in the evaluation and diagnosis of ASD and management of the chronic conditions associated with it. It recognizes that the ultimate goal of coordination of care is to maximize the child's ability to become an independent adult through the development of communication, socialization, cognitive, and motor skills necessary for that independence. These services are best accomplished through medical management, intervening to manage behavioral challenges, and, when necessary, collaborating with practitioners across the various disciplines that serve these children. This chapter discusses the nature of ASD, current medical understanding of autism based on genetics and etiological risk factors; and finally the identification, management, and treatment of autism and its related disabilities.

Autism Spectrum Disorders

The *Diagnostic and statistical manual of mental disorders*, 5th Revision (DSM-5) (American Psychiatric Association, 2013) and the International Statistical Classification of Diseases and Related Health Problems,

10th Edition (ICD-10) (World Health Organization, 1992) recognize autism spectrum disorders as a form of developmental delay. Under these classification systems, it is associated with conditions that are usually diagnosed during early childhood, including delays in cognitive development, learning, motor skills, communication, and other skills acquired and refined during the period from birth to age 21 (American Psychiatric Association, 2013; World Health Organization, 1992).

Current medical identification of ASD involves the same observational techniques used in mental health and education to identify the presence of symptomology, followed by specialized testing to evaluate the severity of specific limitations in the areas of concern. This is because medicine has failed to identify specific markers, either genetic or physiological, that are unique to individuals with ASD due to the belief that a number of genes are responsible for ASD (Chaste & Leboyer, 2012). The sequencing of the human genome has provided insight into the genetic qualities of humanity, and studies on twins suggest a strong genetic role in the etiology of autism.

Autism spectrum disorders also lack a specific phenotype, or visual expression, that would provide a clarifying or definitive diagnosis. However, there are characteristics that are specific to individuals with ASD, which have a strong association with specific genetic markers. For example, multiple studies have implicated chromosomal region 7q35 and associated gene CNTNAP2, as being strongly associated with language impairment (Veatch et al., 2014) and for which prior research (Alarcon et al., 2008; El-Fishawy & State 2010; Peter et al., 2011; Vernes et al., 2008; Whitehouse, Bishop, Ang, Pennell, & Fisher, 2011) had indicated a genetic link.

The Human Genome and Disability

An effort to sequence and identify the location of all the genes in the human genome commenced in 1990, with the final sequencing completed in 2000 and published in *Nature* in February 2001 (Wolfsberg, McEntyre, & Schuler, 2001). It published a continuous sequencing of all 24 chromosomes to identify the location of all genes. Building on the success of this project, a consortium of researchers launched the Autism Genome Project (Hu-Lince, Craig, Huentelman, & Stephan, 2005) with the goal to identify genes strongly associated with ASD and mutations that make individuals susceptible to the characteristics associated with the condition. The hope is for early identification and intervention that result in better and more targeted treatments.

Phase I of this project identified several genes that share common locations on specific chromosomes. Genes located on chromosome 7 have been identified with individuals displaying severe language delays, a core characteristic found in individuals who have autism (Lai, Fisher,

Hurst, Vargh-Khadems & Monaco, 2001; Schumann et al., 2011). Another group of genes on chromosome 15 has been found to be associated with a number of chromosomal abnormalities in individuals with ASD. They are also associated with some syndromes often co-morbid with ASD. However, these markers themselves do not indicate the presence of autism in all individuals with these genes, and the variability is such that they alone fail to provide a definitive indicator of ASD and its associated characteristics.

Phase II focused on identifying specific nucleotide changes that predispose individuals to autism that were associated with the locations identified in Phase I. This phase involved comparing the mutations found at specific chromosomal locations in people with autism to determine if there is a functional significance that could explain the presence of autism in that individual. An additional goal is to use this information to develop a potential newborn screening and specific therapeutic interventions for treating autism (Hu-Lince et al., 2005). This is complicated by a lack of understanding of the specific neurogenic processes resulting from the expression of these genes.

Co-Morbidity with ASD

Autism has a strong co-morbidity with a range of genetic disorders such as Fragile X, tuberous sclerosis, Prader-Willi syndrome, and Rett's disorder, among others (Caglayan, 2010; Gillberg & Billstedt, 2000). These co-morbidities also include the presence of other conditions such as intellectual disability (Rutter, 1983; Wing, 1996), epilepsy (Gillberg, 1992), and Tourette syndrome (Gillberg & Billstedt, 2000). Often much attention is given to the prevalence rates for this co-morbidity without acknowledging that individuals with autism are subject to the same range of medical conditions as the general public, and as such exhibit great variability across severity levels. What becomes interesting is when these conditions occur at rates that far exceed the rates found in the general population and become strongly associated with ASD. Such is the case with these genetic disorders, as well as those with a wide range of causes.

Many of these syndromes are caused by genetic changes associated with the genes identified in the Phase I of the Autism Genome Project. William's syndrome, a condition that shares many similarities with ASD, is caused by multiple deletions on chromosome 5 but does not show the same negative impact on language and communication as found in ASD. Angelman and Prader-Willi syndromes share a common loci of influence from chromosome 15, with the differences determined by which parent's chromosome 15 was impacted. A number of syndromes are associated with errors on chromosome 17, including Neurofibromatosis type 1, Smith-Magenis syndrome, and Sanfillippo syndrome (Caglayan, 2010). This would suggest that some chromosomes, and certainly the genes contained on that loci, are influenced by environmental as well as genetic factors.

Brain Development and ASD

One of the more persistent lines of research into the causes of ASD has focused on differences between the brains of children with ASD and those who are typically developing, and the impact of genetic and neurotropic factors on brain development. Distinctive features have been noted in individuals with ASD that suggest a unique development of brain structures, but there has yet to be a definitive cause for these structural differences. Some of these changes are thought to take place during fetal development, while others appear to take place after birth. Head circumference is one of the most noticeable conditions of brain development found in individuals with ASD.

One of Kanner's initial observations in his patients with autism was that five of the 11 children had relatively large heads (Kanner, 1943). Macrocephaly, a condition characterized by head circumferences greater than the 98th percentile, has been examined by a number of researchers in recent years, with rates varying from 11 percent (van Daalen, Swinkels, Dietz, Van Engeland, & Buitelaar, 2008) to 29.7 percent (Woodhouse et al., 1996). This macrocephaly is a symptom of abnormal brain growth in early childhood and not a characteristic found at birth. This suggests a period of rapid brain growth early in life that later slows as the child approaches adolescence (Courchesne, 2004; Herbert, 2005).

While there is no definitive explanation for this rapid perinatal brain development, it has been noted that this process leads to the development of a number of atypical structures in the brain (Nickl-Jockschate & Michel, 2011), specifically in the proportion of gray and white matter. Imaging techniques have identified increased gray matter in the areas of the brain that govern social processing and learning (Ashtari et al., 2007). Grey matter contains most of the brain's neuronal cell bodies and includes regions of the brain involved in muscle control, sensory perception, memory, emotions, speech, decision making, and self-control (Miller & Alston, 2008). White matter modulates the distribution of neural activity, acting as a relay and coordinating communication between different brain regions (Marner, Nyengaard, Tang, & Pakkenberg, 2003). This could explain some of the affective characteristics exhibited by individuals with ASD. It should be noted that men have more white matter than females both in volume and in length of myelinated axons, which may explain some of the observed differences between men and women with autism. The significance of this will become more apparent in the discussion on some of the clinical findings from functional MRI investigations.

Advances in Neuroimaging

There have been tremendous advances over the past decade in the use of neuroimaging to better understand the brain structure and functions unique to individuals with ASD. While it is premature to consider it a useful tool for screening and diagnosis of ASD due to the heterogeneity of the population, neuroimaging has provided researchers with a better understanding of some of the salient characteristics found in people with ASD. What it does offer is a unique view of how the brain of a person with autism responds to the same sensory inputs experienced by those without autism. One of the most valuable tools for viewing these response differences is through the use of the functional magnetic resonance imaging, or fMRI. The pairing of research using fMRI, coupled with a better understanding of brain typology, may ultimately help researchers better understand some of the core deficits seen in individuals who have ASD.

Functional Magnetic Resonance Imaging

Functional magnetic resonance imaging (fMRI) is an imaging process that uses specialized pulse sequences to highlight areas of the brain associated with specific cognitive functions (Dichter, 2012). It is non-invasive, requires no radiotracers like other advanced imaging systems, and has the ability to observe the brain in a range of tasks that exhibit the detailed functioning of specific sections of the brain. Researchers use fMRI to identify differences between identical regions of the brains in two different individuals performing the same task. For example, the researcher might ask a person with autism to look at a picture during an fMRI session and record the areas of the brain stimulated by that picture. The same picture is then viewed by a person without autism, and the differences between the regions of the brain stimulated tells us what regions of the brain are stimulated by viewing the picture. Thus, we can see into the brain and better understand how and to what it responds.

This use of fMRI has been adopted as a way of trying to measure how the brains of people with autism respond to environmental stimuli in an attempt to gain more insight into social communication. This research has centered on how people with autism respond to the following three cognitive tasks: social intelligence, cognitive control, and communication. These represent the primary cognitive processes associated with core deficits associated with ASD.

Social Intelligence

It has long been recognized that individuals with ASD struggle with understanding social cues and process social information very differently from those without ASD. Tasks related to fMRI studies on the areas of the brain associated with social cognition have examined the temporoparetial junction, that mediates mentalizing; the posterior superior temporal sulcus, that is activated by biological motion; the interior frontal gyrus, involved in emotional judgments; the interparietal sulcus, which is responsible for determining how we gauge our personal space; the amygdala, which helps in facial emotional recognition; the fusiform gyrus, that is used for face processing; and the anterior insula, which guides our response to social expressions in others (Dichter, 2012). They have provided researchers with new information on three of the distinctive characteristics associated with individuals who have ASD.

Face Processing

It has long been recognized that individuals with ASD frequently are challenged with interpreting the emotional state of others due to deficits in face processing. Typically developing infants attend to faces from infancy (Johnson, Dziurawiec, Ellis, & Morton, 1991), while young children with ASD often struggle with joint attention, eye contact, and facial recognition and discrimination, which in turn leads to impaired social emotional recognition and facial perception, as well as abnormal scanning of the faces of others (Klin, *et al.*, 1999; Klin, Jones, Schultz, Volkmar, & Cohen, 2002). A person with autism experiences hypoactivity in those regions activated in response to faces and facial expressions (Dichter, 2012), although it should be noted that other research has found no differences in response to familiar faces (Pierce, Haist, Sedaghat, & Courcesne, 2004), strangers' faces (Hadjikhani et al., 2004), and inverted facial recognition (Bookheimer, Wang, Scott, Sigman, & Dapretto, 2008).

Much of the attention in this area has focused on the role the amygdala plays in face processing, since prior studies (Ashwin, Baron-Cohen, Wheelwright, O'Riordan, & Bullmore, 2007; Dapretto et al., 2006) found that individuals with ASD display decreased amygdala activation when compared to their typically developing peers when required to view faces and facial expressions associated with certain emotional states. This hypoactivity is then expressed as a lack of attention or interest in face processing. This, in turn, offers some explanation for the inability of many individuals with autism to identify the emotional state of others, which often leads to difficulties in social situations.

Findings from these studies suggest that individuals with ASD may experience this hypoactivity for a number of reasons. Functional MRI studies have indicated increased activation of white matter in the brain of individuals with ASD. Since white matter acts as a relay and coordinating communication between different brain regions (Marner et al., 2003), this could explain the hypo-arousal of the amygdala and why men have higher rates of ASD than women.

Environmental Influences on ASD

Environmental influences have been suggested as a possible trigger for autism in susceptible individuals due to established association between certain substances in the environment (Kalkbrenner, Schmidt, & Penlesky, 2014). The reason this hypothesis is compelling is that it offers a possible explanation for the wide variability of symptomology seen in the ASD population. This is one reason why monozygotic twins, who are genetically identical in every way, may not always share the same autistic characteristics even though they share a common history of environmental exposures. This suggests that multiple genes and multiple environmental factors interact to influence the development of autism.

Some environmental factors appear to have a minimal impact on an increase in the incidence of ASD. For example, tobacco exposure, both through the mother smoking and second-hand smoke, appears to have little influence on increasing rates of autism (Kalkbrenner et al., 2014). One of the surprising finds in their review was that maternal smoking during pregnancy was associated with higher-functioning autism when compared to lower-functioning autism. While no definitive explanation was offered for this observation, it was suggested that nicotine might cause a different response in individuals predisposed to ASD that is not present in children who might later be diagnosed with attention-deficit or intellectual disability, which is strongly influenced by tobacco use.

It is thought that many of the symptoms seen in individuals with ASD are the result of oxidative stress, which is one of the results of repeated and constant exposure to environmental toxins (Sunyer, 2008). The oxidative stress results from chronic inflammation of lung tissue that is thought to alter the production of inflammatory mediating substances in the blood stream. Air pollution also contains a mixture of heavy metals and carbon, both of which have been shown to be responsible for oxidative stress in humans and in animal models. Complementary and alternative medical interventions have been proposed as treatments for this oxidative stress, although the role of oxidative stress is still not well understood (Balachandar et al., 2015).

Prenatal Risk Factors

It is suspected that some processes occur during fetal development, which are later seen in children who are subsequently identified as a having ASD. Prenatal exposure to certain environmental factors has long been recognized as having an impact on brain development (Kolevzon, Gross, & Reichenberg, 2007), although the exact processes may not be completely understood. Kolevzon, Gross, and Reichenberg conducted a systematic review to identify, from epidemiological studies, the most common pre- and perinatal influences that were most strongly associated with a later diagnosis of ASD. Of particular concern to them were the characteristics of the parents, because there is a strong association between older parents and their children having autism and obstetric conditions, specifically duration of pregnancy and intrapartum hypoxia. Prenatal exposure to alcohol, for example, has been demonstrated to have consistent and recognized effects, as does prenatal exposure to certain medications such a valproic acid and thalidomide (Landrigan, 2010). It is suspected that a similar process may be involved with autism, although efforts to identify specific substances and dosage rates have proven challenging.

Parental Age

Given the strong role genetics plays in autism, there is particular interest in what role parental age and other associative reproductive factors have on the increase in incidence rates for ASD. The role of parental age has garnered interest by researchers due to the increasing age at time of birth in the developing countries, which corresponds to increases in identification rates for ASD. Prior research has been mixed and may be a reflection of the data sets and methodologies used in these studies, one thing that Kolevzon et al. (2007) sought to avoid in their systematic review of prenatal risk factors.

Hultman, Sandin, Levine, Lichtenstein, and Reichenberg (2011) conducted a review of Swedish registries of birth cohorts to identify factors associated in cases where children were later diagnosed with ASD. They examined familial factors such as parental education, place of birth, and prior psychiatric hospitalization, as well as perinatal infant characteristics such as birth weight, size for gestational age, and the presence of fetal distress during birth. With regard to paternal age, the results found that risk began to increase at the age of 30, stabilized in the 40s, and peaked in the 50s and held for both mothers and fathers across all age bands. The risk of autism due to parental age was consistent for families that included children with and without ASD. Children who were affected with autism were born to older parents, while those children without autism were born to parents of younger ages. There were a number of possible causal factors concluded from these results.

One explanation, consistent with our current knowledge of genetics, is that increased parental age increases the chances that spontaneous genetic alterations may be taking place. The repeated cellular divisions that take place in spermatozoa are thought to be a source of increased spontaneous genomic changes, resulting in higher rates of mutations and changes in the sperm of older men (Buwe, Guttenbach, & Schmid, 2005). This phenomenon is not limited to fathers who had their first child at a later age, but might also explain why younger children in families have a higher risk of being identified as having ASD. Advanced maternal age also has been identified by Kolevzon et al. (2007) as a significant risk factor for autism. Of the seven articles reviewed in their systematic review, six found that mothers of advanced age were up to four times as likely to have a child diagnosed with autism as younger mothers.

One potential explanation may lie in use of certain forms of medication during pregnancy by the mother and their impact on fetal brain development. Maimburg and Vaeth (2006) found a 50% increase in risk of autism associated with medication use, with the majority of cases associated with mothers who had used psychoactive drugs, although the medications themselves may not be responsible for the effects. Rather, it may instead be a result of the underlying condition being treated affecting fetal brain development or genetic influences related to the psychiatric condition.

Assisted Reproduction

Researchers (Fountain et al., 2015) have observed that families using in vitro fertilization (IVF) or some other form of assistive reproduction have been observed to have greater rates of children born with ASD than those who did not. This is interesting to researchers because of the expanded use of IVF and other forms of assistive reproduction since the first IVF birth in 1978 (CDC, 2012). This has created a temporal association, where the number of families using IVF has increased at the same time that we have seen an increase in number of children identified as having ASD.

Results from a review of California birth registries from 1997 to 2007 found that the incidence of autism diagnosis was twice as high for families who used assisted reproductive technologies when compared to families who conceived naturally, although even after adjustment for demographic factors and birth outcomes there was still a statistically significant difference in outcomes for younger women aged 20 to 34 (Fountain et al., 2015). Another study, this one using a smaller sample of individuals with an ASD diagnosis, found that assistive reproduction was strongly associated with ASD, despite other important factors such as parental age, low birth weight, and family history of ASD being important factors (Zachor & Itzchak, 2011). A population-based study in Denmark found no risk for ASD in children born after assisted conception, although their research suggests that further study needs to be done to ascertain the role that the use of follicle stimulating hormone has on increased rates of ASD (Hvidtjorn et al., 2011). All three studies suggested the need for further research to better understand this phenomenon.

Valproic Acid

One maternal medication that has been shown to have a strong association with later cases of autism is valproic acid (Moore et al., 2002; Rasalam et al., 2005; Bromley, Mawer, Clayton-Smith, & Baker, 2008), a common antiepileptic medication used to treat seizures and manic episodes associated with bipolar disorder (American Society of Health-System Pharmacists, Inc., 2015). It is also used to treat migraine headaches and has various off-label applications for treating behavioral disorders (Guzman, 2015). Children diagnosed with fetal anti-convulsant syndrome, the result of maternal use of valproic acid, were found in a population-based study in Denmark to be up to four times more likely to have autism than children without prenatal exposure.

Peri- and Post-natal Risk Factors

Not all autism risks are prenatal in nature. The constant exposure to environmental pollutants is thought to be a contributing factor to many of the developmental challenges experienced by children eventually diagnosed with autism or another developmental disability. Common sources of pollution in the environment include contaminated water sources such as river, lakes, and aquifers; air pollution caused by automobiles, factories, and petrochemical plants; as well as the presence of naturally occurring toxins in the environment. At the present time there is limited knowledge of the physiological mechanism that causes autism in some individuals but not others, even when exposed to the same total dosage.

Air and Water Pollution

One set of environmental factors that have been suggested as a possible cause for ASD is regulated and traffic air pollution due to systematic inflammation to the brain (Calderón-Gardidueñas, et al., 2011). This air pollution includes a variety of chemicals in varying levels of concentration, including particulates, liquids, and gases. Exposure is largely a result of inhalation, but ingestion in water, food pollution, and skin exposure offer a range of other exposure options. Concentrations of these pollutants vary based on locale, from urban areas with high concentrations to rural areas where concentrations are much lower. These chemicals can cause a variety of responses that have a negative impact on neurodevelopment.

Epidemiologists often use time and space clusters to identify the introduction of an etiological factor for a condition (Lilienfeld & Stolley, 1994), and this has proven a challenge to interpret with any degree of accuracy when it comes to its role in autism. Palmer, Blanchard, Stein,

Mandell, and Miller (2006) looked at the impact of environmental mercury release and special education rates for autism in Texas. Much of the mercury exposure that children receive comes directly from coal-fired power plants and, along with fish consumption, represents the vast majority of exposure for most children. It can impact a large area surrounding its source, and calculating actual exposure is challenging. It is also complicated by the inability to control for other possible sources of mercury in the diet or environment, or other chemicals that could as easily prove to be the toxic source.

A broader application of this model was used in conjunction with the Harvard Nursing Health Study II (NHS II), which used a nested, case-control analysis to look at the role of particulate matter of air pollution before, during, and after pregnancy and the rates of autism spectrum disorder in that cohort. This study looked at the children of the participants who had been diagnosed with an ASD. Exposure was assessed based on mailing addresses, and other variables were identified and collected including birth month and year, sex, maternal age at birth, and socio-economic levels for their census tract. Odds ratios were calculated using a logistic regression model based on exposure nine months prior to and following pregnancy. The study found that particulate matter concentrations were strongly associated with a child identified with ASD, and especially when the exposure occurred during pregnancy. Weaker associations were identified if the exposure occurred prior to or following the pregnancy, suggesting a strong prenatal exposure risk, especially when it occurs in the third trimester (Raz et al., 2015).

Vaccine Ingredients

It would be irresponsible to not clarify the role of supposed toxic chemicals found in childhood immunizations. This issue came about as a result of the publication in 1998 of a theory by a British gastroenterologist suggesting that the MMR vaccine (measles, mumps, and rubella) was responsible for the autism identified in a subset of young men in Great Britain. Even though this theory was found to be based on falsified data (Rao & Andrade, 2011), it brought into question a possible role for vaccines in the increase of children being diagnosed with autism. Several substances commonly found in vaccines have been identified as possible culprits, with thimerosal and aluminum being the most likely candidates.

Thimerosal is a commonly used preservative for liquids prone to adulteration by bacteria, and is a compound used in multi-dosed vaccines. It is a 50 percent solution of ethyl mercury. Mercury has been recognized for years as a neurotoxin, leading to suggestions that it could be responsible for some of the neurological damage associated with ASD. As a result of concerns over its safety in vaccines for children, it was removed from vaccines included in the childhood immunization schedule supported by the American Academy of Pediatrics. At the present time, children receive approximately 125 micrograms of thimerosal from multi-dosed flu vaccines, although thimerosal-free vaccines are available. What is important to remember is that most children are exposed to greater amounts of mercury in their daily interaction with their environment and this form of mercury, methyl mercury, is more dangerous and more difficult to excrete from the body (Pichichero et al., 2009). Subsequent research on mercury toxicity and its role in autism has involved a number of *in situ* studies among populations exposed to dangerous levels of mercury due to industrial accidents (Minamata) and those who consume large quantities of fish containing mercury (Faeroe and Seychelles islanders). In both cases, the prevalence rates for ASD were no greater than those who consumed less fish, and the symptoms of mercury poisoning bear little relation to those seen in individuals with ASD (Baker, 2008). It should be noted that these studies examined the role of methyl mercury, which is far more toxic and plentiful in the environment and not found in any vaccines.

The presence of aluminum in vaccines has spawned a number of claims that it contributes to the development of autism in a specific subgroup of children. Aluminum is used in vaccines to enhance and increase the development of an immune response because of aluminum's strong immuno-response mechanism. Aluminum has already been suggested as a contributing factor in a number of autoimmune disorders (Tomljenovic & Shaw, 2011) and may play a role in Alzheimer's disease (Ferreira, Piai, Takayanagui, & Segura-Muñoz, 2008), and since autism shares features with these conditions it has been suggested that it also may contribute in some way to autism. While there may be a strong correlation between increases in required vaccines and increases in the incidence rate for ASD (Tomljenovic & Shaw), the causal association is much more difficult to ascertain.

What is important to remember about these environmental risk factors is that like any toxic substance, their effects increase as total dosage rates increase. Children who grow up in urban areas or in places with multiple toxic risks will likely display a wider range of symptoms related to these exposures, and some will mimic those found in children with autism. Until the underlying causes of ASD are better understood it is premature to attribute any case of autism to any one specific environmental cause. There are many other factors that may prove to be more responsible for autism and its related characteristics than simply environmental ones.

Medical Management of Children with ASD

Pediatricians and other primary care physicians (PCPs) play a crucial role in the diagnosis and management of chronic health conditions found in children with ASD and their co-morbid conditions. It is important to remember that while children with ASD may seem to have elevated risks for various medical conditions, they also are subject to the same types of medical conditions seen in all children and benefit from the same system of health promotion and disease prevention required of other children (Myers & Johnson, 2007). In addition, they often have co-morbidities that create a unique set of health needs not commonly seen in their typically developing peers. Many of these also pose a risk of future permanent disability. Therefore, when it is said that children with ASD report higher rates of certain medical conditions, what it really means is that they have been observed and reported in higher rates.

Surveillance and Screening

Primary care physicians have a responsibility to conduct active surveillance and screening of their patients to identify developmental delays associated with a particular health condition. Surveillance involves monitoring the child's development to identify developmental concerns with attention to specific characteristics, such as joint attention, that are known signs of a potential diagnosis of ASD. The other is to conduct specific screenings using standardized instruments to create baselines to monitor future delays and to identify when the child is responding to treatment. This is best managed in a setting that allows the primary care physician (PCP) to coordinate care and act as a conduit for screenings and evaluations conducted by specialists (Johnson & Myers, 2007).

Among the areas suggested for active surveillance (Johnson & Myers, 2007) are possible genetic causes, frequently identified by their association with known genetic syndromes. Another is potential exposure to environmental toxins, either pre-, peri-, or post-natally. This is where a thorough family and child-specific medical history is especially useful. One of the most valuable tools is the clinical screening that includes collecting information on social skills development, and examination of communication deficits, skill regression, play skills, and restrictive and repetitive patterns of behavior. Children who meet clinical levels of delay can then receive the specialize screenings that offer a more definitive diagnosis and better understanding of necessary treatments.

Management of Chronic Conditions

Children and adults with ASD are at increased risk for some specific chronic conditions that require constant, and in many cases, life-long management to treat effectively. It is often thought that these conditions are unique to those with ASD, but they are more frequently the result of the same co-morbidities found in the general population. It is important to remember that these are separate from the core deficits of ASD. Some of the most common co-morbidities associated with ASD are the presence of epilepsy or other seizure conditions, gastrointestinal disorders, and food allergies or sensitivities.

Seizure Disorders

Seizure conditions are found in up to 40 percent of children with ASD (Ballaban-Gill & Tuchman, 2000), with the higher prevalence rates found in children who had more significant cognitive and motor delays. Seizures are managed using anti-convulsant medications using the same criteria used for children without ASD (Myers & Johnson, 2007). This includes an accurate diagnosis on the specific type of seizure, and involves the use of electroencephalography (EEG) to determine the presence of abnormal brain patterns indicative of epilepsy. Because of the strong association between seizures and ASD, it is recommended that physicians and families be especially vigilant in their observations of potential seizures. The use of EEGs should be considered when there are indications of seizure activity.

Gastrointestinal Disorders

It has been reported that children with ASD suffer higher rates of gastro-intestinal (GI) problems than the rest of the population. This has helped support a continued belief that vaccines and related damage to the small intestines are a causal factor for ASD, even though over 20 epidemiological studies have failed to support this hypothesis. It has also led to the belief that specialty diets, specifically those that restrict intake of gluten and casein, or that involve supplements such as secretin, can improve behavioral challenges often associated with ASD (Horvath & Perman, 2002). Understanding of the prevalence of GI disorders is currently limited by a small number of studies that lack the statistical power to determine the actual prevalence of these conditions and their causes.

What we do know is that children with ASD appear to have higher rates of reported symptoms such as diarrhea and constipation than their siblings. They also appear to suffer much higher rates of gastritis and gastroesophageal reflux disease (GERD) than the general population. A record review of individuals in Sweden who were diagnosed with various forms of GI disorders was conducted to better understand the association between ASD and celiac disease. They found that children with ASD do not have higher rates of celiac disease (CD) than the general population, although they do seem to have higher rates of positive celiac disease serologic test with no intestinal damage (Ludvigsson, Reichenberg, Hultman, & Murray, 2013). It should be noted this study did not control for diet, which would be reflected in the percentage of individuals having positive CD serology results.

Food Allergies and Sensitivities

There is insufficient evidence to suggest that individuals with ASD have higher rates of food allergies and sensitivities than the general population (Lydall, Van de Water, Ashwood, & Hertz-Picciotto, 2015), even though anecdotal evidence suggests otherwise. The most common treatment for food allergies and sensitivity is an elimination diet that removes those items causing a reaction from the diet. Gluten-free and casein-free diets (GFCF) have become popular with parents who have observed episodes of diarrhea, constipation, gas, and intestinal bloating in their child and attributed it to a gluten or casein sensitivity. This diet reflects a long-held belief among some practitioners that malabsorption of casein (a milk protein) and gluten (a wheat protein) might alter neurotransmitter function, which in turn is responsible for the symptoms associated with ASD (Panskepp, 1979). Celiac disease is an autoimmune disorder thought to affect about 1 percent of the population (Rubio-Tapia, Ludvigsson, Brantner, Murray, & Everhart, 2012). It is caused by the ingestion of gluten and causes damage to the small intestine. As previously stated, children with ASD do not appear to suffer from higher rates of celiac disease compared to the general population (Ludvigsson et al., 2013), although it is unclear if they react differently to these products than others.

Advances in Medical Treatments for ASD

The nature of ASD as a condition characterized by specific behaviors complicates the development of specific treatments for ASD. This has led parents and practitioners to make use of "off-label" applications of FDA-approved treatments for other conditions. The FDA permits the off-label use of medications that have been found safe for use to treat other conditions. However, because these off-label uses are not subjected to the types of clinical trials required for FDA approval, there is often little quality research conducted on these interventions. As such, their use as primary interventions is not recommended at the present time.

Understanding Benefits and Risks

All interventions carry some form of risk, although for the vast majority those risks may be outweighed by their benefits to the individual. This includes relatively innocuous treatments like vitamin supplements that are used by millions as part of their daily routine. However, one of the challenges faced in the medical treatment of ASD is the lack of knowledge for the risks presented to any single individual when they are subjected to multiple interventions simultaneously. This also applies to the benefits. When it is said that studies found poor methodology and treatment fidelity, what we often mean is the impact of each individual intervention cannot be determined due to multiple treatments with non-specific outcomes. That means we cannot attribute the outcomes to any one intervention nor determine which ones might be responsible for the outcomes. As such, families and practitioners need to be vigilant when identifying, selecting, and monitoring outcomes when using multiple interventions concurrently.

Off-label Uses

There are few medical treatments for ASD that have been approved by the FDA, but a large number have never been subjected to any form of clinical trial to ascertain their effectiveness for treating the core deficits associated with ASD. This is especially problematic for families who have legitimate concerns for possible side effects, and also for practitioners who may have legitimate concerns about using treatments that have not been subjected to the scrutiny required of treatments approved by the FDA. This lack of FDA-approved pharmacological intervention for treating psychiatric problems in children has allowed the proliferation of complementary and alternative medical treatments, which have not received FDA approval for these applications.

These off-label uses come with their own benefits and risks. Typically, they involve either the unique use of a treatment of novel clinical application or the use of that treatment for an unapproved population (Stafford, 2008). These off-label uses provide physicians with an opportunity to create innovative treatments in the absence of beneficial alternatives. At the same time, the failure to collect information on their efficacy injects additional risks to those receiving the treatment. This should be a concern to consumers of these treatments, since these treatments account for up to 20 percent of all prescriptions and up to 70 percent for anti-convulsants. Perhaps most disturbing is that it was the antipsychotics and anti-convulsants that had the least evidence for their efficacy. Some of the most commonly accessed classes of treatments prescribed off-label are those associated with complementary and alternative medical treatments.

Complementary and Alternative Medical Treatments (CAM)

Complementary and Alternative Treatments (CAMs) encompass treatments outside of allopathic medicine, which we would characterize as "Western medicine." The term *complementary* generally refers to using a non-mainstream approach together with conventional medicine, while the term *alternative* refers to using a non-mainstream approach in place of conventional medicine (National Center for Complementary and Alternative Medicine [NCCAM], 2014). There are a number of CAMs that are used to enhance the desirability of treatments or to improve the physiological statement of the patient during treatment. However, all CAMs should be expected to meet minimal standards of safety and efficacy, and many of them fail to meet this threshold, while yet others are dangerous and should be avoided.

If CAMs fail to meet minimal standards of efficacy and safety, then why do they remain popular with parents and individuals with ASD? The first reason for their use is to complement and enhance the effectiveness of conventional treatments. Treatments such as massage therapy help individuals relax, minimize pain and discomfort, and otherwise make better use of the other treatments they are receiving. A second reason is that conventional treatments have not worked, a common concern for individuals with ASD since we lack a good understanding of the physiological factors associated with the condition and frequently lack better alternatives. In some cases they are suggested by professionals who may have been exposed to them through professional literature, or by other practitioners who have seen them benefit their patients. Yet another reason is that conventional treatments are often too expensive and their costs far exceed their benefits (Levy & Hyman, 2005).

Use of CAMs by Families of Children with ASD

The use of CAMs has expanded as families have become frustrated with the perceived lack of benefits from traditional treatments for ASD and the suggestion by some physicians that the core deficits of ASD can be reversed and an individual cured of autism. While much of this is a result of Internet anecdotes and marketing by Defeat Autism Now (DAN) practitioners and service providers, there is an increasing number of physicians who are willing to recommend less risky treatments with more generalized outcomes.

Global studies report rates of CAM use for ASD ranging from 32 percent to 87 percent in the US and 52 percent in Canada (Lofthouse, Hendren, Hurt, Arnold & Butter, 2012), even though most families expected and received minimal benefits from the use of CAM (Christon, Mackintosh, & Myers, 2010). The most common referral sources for families were physicians, other parents, and the Internet (Christon et al., 2010), although physicians report providing families with guidance on access to services and use. The use of CAMs based on physician referral tends to reflect the relative benefits and risks of the individual treatment. For example, Golnick and Ireland (2009) found that a small percentage of physicians (fewer than 25 percent) were fine with their patients taking essential fatty acids for brain function, melatonin to help with sleep, and probiotics for digestion. At the same time, over half discouraged their patients from treatments that were considered potentially dangerous (use of chelation and delaying/withholding immunizations) to those that are simply based on a poor understanding of the underlying causes of ASD (anti-infectives for treating *candida albicans*). These low-risk treatments present little in the way of harm, little in the way of benefits, and as such do not provoke undue risks to those using them. On the other hand, high-risk treatments pose significant risks to patients who use them. Chelation, used to treat heavy metal poisoning and toxicity, was proposed as a treatment for exposure to thimerosal until one patient died during treatment. Subsequently, no academic institutional review boards were willing to sign off on these trials given the risks associated with the treatment and the fact that research has indicated that thimerosal does not cause autism.

The National Center for Complementary and Alternative Medicine (NCCAM) separates CAMs into five distinct classes, although an easier way to conceptualize them is as biological or non-biological treatments. Biologically based therapies use substances found in nature, such as herbs, foods, and vitamins, with the belief that individuals with autism suffer from nutritional deficiencies that are replaced by these supplements. Many of us use these supplements for much the same reason, and they are generally safe when used as recommended. Non-biological interventions are thought to interfere with the underlying causes of autism with the hope of changing brain function. They tend to be based on alternative theories of brain functions. Examples of these interventions include auditory integration training, craniosacral manipulation, and facilitated communication.

What CAMs Work?

Complementary and alternative treatments can be most effectively categorized by their proposed action on routine bodily functions strongly associated with ASD. These include treatments that are thought to have a positive impact on neurotransmitters, gastrointestinal (GI) function, the immune system, and some form of detoxification (Copeland, 2007). However, these are based on models that are either unproven or fail to meet scientific standards or based on poor research methods and measurements. It is the poor history of medical effectiveness that haunts the use of CAMs for treating ASD, and this reflects the relative benefits and risks associated with the treatment and reflects their frequent off-label uses that have not been held to standards of therapeutic efficacy. The issue of off-label use will be discussed later in this chapter.

The next section will discuss the general classes of CAMs in greater detail and discuss some of the existing research on the efficacies of these interventions. This list is not meant to be exhaustive and instead is provided as a cautionary tale for parents and practitioners considering the use of CAMs for treating autism. The majority of examples represent off-label applications, and even those that have been researched frequently suffer from a lack of evidence to support their use. As such, it is in the best interests of all parties to seek out the counsel of informed practitioners who are not selling their own services or alternative interventions that are not considered to be evidence-based.

Biologically-based Therapies

The proliferation of biomedical interventions claiming to improve the key symptomology of ASD ranges from simple supplements and dietary changes, to hyperbaric oxygen therapy to decrease inflammation in the brain, to dangerous treatments such as chelation for removing heavy metals from the body. Proponents of each therapy claim their therapies reverse one or more of the underlying causes of autism, at least based on their theory of what causes autism, and whether or not these causes can be reversed by a specific regimen of treatments. The data do not seem to support the effectiveness of these treatments, and efforts to offer supporting research suffer from too many methodological and selection bias issues to form a legitimate evidence-based support.

There is a wide range of common biologically based therapies used to treat children with autism that include modified diets (e.g. additive-free, Feingold diet, sugar-free, wheat-free, vegan, etc.), vitamin and mineral supplements (e.g. Vitamin B6, Vitamin C, zinc etc.), and food supplements (e.g., blue green algae, evening primrose oil, fish oil, omega 3 fatty acids, etc.) that are used as complementary treatments for autism, even though many have little evidence to support their use. For example, there is little in the way of scientific evidence to support the use of omega 3 fatty acids to improve the neurological functioning in individuals with ASD (Bent, Bertoglio, & Hendren, 2009). As for dietary restrictions, there is concern that GFCF (gluten-free, casein-free) diets put children at risk of nutritional deficiencies and as such should only be used if evidence supports true GI problems (Mulloy et al., 2009). Other common interventions suffer from insufficient evidence of effectiveness, and the theoretical basis for its effectiveness is still not supported by the clinical evidence.

Many of these biomedical interventions present little in the way of harm to the individual as long as the dosage does not exceed recommended guidelines for their use. Vitamins and supplements, for example, do not require FDA approval for their use, only that they meet pure food and drug standards. The quantity of active ingredients often varies between manufacturers, and there is no way to verify the potency of the compounds. Excess water-soluble vitamins are excreted through urination and it is the fat-soluble vitamins that carry the greatest risk of over-use. Most vitamins and supplements present little in the way of harm, yet they also present little in the way of benefits beyond their value as a supplement, since there is little to no credible evidence that they improve the core deficits found in individuals with ASD. The following is a representative sample of some of the more common biologically based interventions.

Vitamin B6

Vitamin B6 contains various forms of pyridoxine, which are involved in the formation of several neurotransmitters (Gualtitieri, Golden, & Fahs, 1983) such as serotonin (5-HT), gamma-aminobutyric acid (GABA), dopamine (DA), norepinephrine (NE), and epinephrine (E) (Pfieffer, Norton, Nelson, & Schott, 1995), and it was believed that supplementing the diet with B6 would enhance the function of these neurotransmitters. Unfortunately, multiple studies found a number of methodological shortcomings that make it impossible to measure the benefits of this treatment regimen when compared to the risks associated with their abuse. Vitamin B6 is in a class of fat-soluble vitamins that can be toxic in megadoses (> 500 mg/day) (Merck Manual, 2008) and is a leading cause of childhood poisoning (Copeland, 2007). There is scant evidence to support Vitamin B6 as a beneficial supplement for ASD (Nye & Brice, 2005), and the lack of strong dependent variable measures on their use makes it difficult to accurately measure benefits. Fortunately, as long as dosages are kept below the maximum daily dosage rates, there is little serious risk of permanent damage to health.

Gluten-free and Casein-free Diets

One of the more popular biologically based diets frequently used by families who have children with autism is one that contains no gluten or casein products. Gluten is a grain protein found primarily in wheat and barley products, while casein is a protein found in dairy products. This elimination diet is based on the theory that peptides found in gluten and casein are not properly metabolized by individuals with autism and are subsequently absorbed into the brain as opioids responsible for some of the behaviors associated with ASD (Panskepp, 1979).

Systematic reviews on the effectiveness of GFCF diets have not provided conclusive proof of their efficacy for improving the symptomology. A review by Mulloy et al. (2009) reviewed 14 different studies on the effectiveness of GFCF diets. Their conclusions were that the existing research on these diets was limited with regard to the scope of their study and that the quality of the research designs was such that they lacked support for the use of GFCF diets in treating students with ASD. Similarly, Zhang, Mayton, and Wheeler (2013) reviewed a total of 23 different articles and found similar problems with methodology, lack of conclusive data to support the effectiveness of GFCF diets, and their failure to control for other treatment variables. Based on our current understanding of GI disorders and the underlying theories for their cause in individuals with ASD, the use of a GFCF diet should be made solely on an individualized basis that reflects the presence of symptoms associated with gluten and casein sensitivities.

Non-Biological Interventions

Individuals with ASD frequently exhibit deficits in self-regulation and are challenged to increase their ability to identify and respond appropriately to physiological changes to their bodies. Mind–body interventions used as CAMs include actions such as prayer and meditation, Tai Chi, biofeedback, cognitive behavioral therapy, and hypnosis. A study by Sanders *et al.* (2003) found prayer to be the most widely used intervention in their study of mind–body intervention practices in Southern Arizona. Cognitive behavioral therapy was found to be effective for reducing anxiety in children with ASD (Lang, Regester, Lauderdale, Ashbaugh, & Haring, 2010), and neurofeedback techniques are considered beneficial for improving many of the affective characteristics associated with ASD (Coben, Linden, & Myers, 2010), such as executive function and social behavior (Kouijzer, de Moor, Gerrits, Buitelaar, & van Schie, 2009). Yoga and other mind–body interventions are considered "novel and emerging" (Rossignol, 2009) and lack sufficient study to determine their status as an effective intervention at the present time.

Example of manipulation and body-based methods include cranial-sacral therapy, auditory integration training (AIT), sensory integration training (SIT), facilitated communication (FC), valgus nerve stimulation, and hyperbaric oxygen therapy (HBOT). Unfortunately, the majority of these methods are based on poorly articulated science and fail to meet the minimal standards of science necessary to establish them as an evidence-based practice or to be recommended by professional organizations and the clinical guidelines they develop. The American Speech and Hearing Association (ASHA) recommends against the use of AIT (2003) because of potential damage to a patient's hearing, and also against the use of FC (1994) as the sole alternative or augmentative communication system. There is insufficient evidence to support the use of cranial-sacral therapy (Green, Martin, Bassett, & Kazanjian, 1999), and the quantity of research regarding the effectiveness of sensory integration therapy is limited and inconclusive (AAP, 2012). The use of HBOT for treating ASD is inconclusive and portable units are insufficient to produce beneficial effects (Ghanizadeh, 2012; Schechtman, 2007) because they are only capable of providing oxygen at atmospheric pressures and concentrations.

Some forms of energy therapies used to treat individuals with ASD include healing touch/laying on of hands and Reiki, a Japanese form of massage. Very little has been done in the study of the use of Energies Therapies for treating ASD, although a systematic review on the use of Reiki found insufficient evidence to determine efficacy of it as a therapeutic treatment (vanderVaart, Gijsen, de Wildt, & Koren, 2009).

Alternative Medical Systems

Families also seek out alternative medical systems to treat their family member with ASD that include the use of homeopathy, a medical system for treating illnesses that uses very small amounts of substances that would in larger amounts produce symptoms of the illnesses in healthy people. Chiropractice is a system based on the diagnosis and manipulative treatment of misalignments of the joints, which are held to cause other disorders by affecting the nerves, muscles, and organs. Chinese Medicine uses herbal medicines and various mind and body practices, such as *acupuncture* and Tai Chi, to treat or prevent health problems. Studies provide mixed evidence of acupuncture's effectiveness as a treatment for ASD symptoms (Nye & Brice, 2011; Lee, Choi, Shin, & Ernst, 2012). Robinson (2001) found that homeopathic treatment with secretin actually worsens symptoms of ASD, while a systematic review by Ernst (2002) failed to provide strong evidence in favor of homeopathy and its effects were indistinguishable from placebos. The research base on the use of chiropractice is limited.

Pharmacological Interventions

The Food and Drug Administration (n.d) has approved two medications for use in treating the symptoms associated with ASD. The first is risperidone, trade named Risperdal®, and the other is aripiprazole, known by the brand name Abilify®. Both were prescribed off-label prior to their recent FDA approval for treating children under the age of 17 who have ASD. It is important to remember that all medications carry specific risks to certain patients, and both medications have significant side effects that must be considered with their administration. There may be individuals whose behavioral issues are so severe that the risk of side effects is outweighed by the medication's ability to better manage behaviors, leading to enhanced quality of life. These decisions require careful and thoughtful discussions between the family and their physician to determine if the benefits outweigh these risks.

Conclusion

The role of the physician and other health providers who are involved in the delivery of medical and health services to children and adults with ASD is evolving as our understanding of the causes of autism has evolved. We now understand that autism is a condition that is strongly genetic in nature, and that it is influenced by a number of physiological factors that we are only beginning to identify and understand. Yet at the same time we know very little about the way in which autism develops in children who will ultimately be diagnosed with the condition. The American Academy of Pediatrics has recognized the role of pediatric providers in the surveillance and screening of ASD, the importance of both medical and educational interventions for enhancing the quality of life for the child and his/her family, and the need for further research into the causes and long-term treatment of ASD.

Physicians play an essential role in the identification, selection, and delivery of medical interventions for treating the affective symptoms associated with ASD. They have an ethical obligation to families to provide them with information on the benefits and risks of all treatment options, especially since most medical and CAM treatments used with patients who have ASD are not FDA approved and represent off-label uses for these treatments. It is essential that they inform families of the potential outcomes, cost of treatment, and any financial interests they may have with these services, and, perhaps most importantly, help the family develop a long-term care plan that enhances the quality of life of the individual with ASD.

References

Alarcon, M., Abrahams, B. S., Stone, J. L., Duvall, J. A., Perederiy, J. V., Bomar, J. M., . . . Geschwind, D. H. (2008). Linkage, association, and gene-expression analyses identify CNTNAP2 as an autism-susceptibility gene. *American Journal of Human Genetics, 82,* 150–159.

American Academy of Pediatrics [AAP], Section on Complementary and Integrative Medicine, Council on Children with Disabilities (2012). Sensory integration therapies for children with developmental and behavioral disorders, *Pediatrics, 129*(6), 1186–1189.

American Psychiatric Association [APA]. (2013). *Diagnostic and statistical manual of mental disorders* (5th ed.). Washington, DC: Author.

American Society of Health-System Pharmacists, Inc.: AHFS Consumer Medication Information [Internet]. Bethesda (MD). (2015). Valproic acid [revised 07/15/2014]. Retrieved June 2, 2016 from www.nlm.nih.gov/medlineplus/druginfo/meds/a682412.html.

American Speech-Language-Hearing Association [ASHA]. (1995). *Facilitated communication* [Position Statement]. Retrieved June 2, 2016 from www.asha.org/policy.

American Speech-Language-Hearing Association [ASHA]. (2004). *Auditory integration training* [Position Statement]. Retrieved June 2, 2016 from www.asha. org/policy.

Ashtari, M., Nichols, S., McIlree, M. S., Spritzer, B. S., Adesman, A., & Ardekani, B. (2007, November). *Novel imaging technique shows gray matter increase in brains of autistic children.* Annual Meeting of the Radiological Society of North America (RSNA), Chicago.

Ashwin, C., Baron-Cohen, S., Wheelwright, S., O'Riordan, M., & Bullmore, E. T. (2007). Differential activation of the amygdala and the "social brain" during fearful face processing in Asperger Syndrome. *Neuropsychologia, 45*, 2–14.

Bailey, A., Le Couteur, A., Gottesman, I., Bolton, P., Simonoff, E., Yuzda, E., & Rutter, M. (1995). Autism as a strongly genetic disorder: Evidence from a British twin study. *Psychology & Medicine, 25*, 63–77.

Baker, J. P. (2008). Mercury, vaccines, and autism: One controversy, three histories. *American Journal of Public Health, 98*(2), 244–253.

Balachandar, V., Sureshkumar, S., Mohanadevi, S., Balamuralikrishnan, B., Sankar, K., Arun, M., Dharwadkar, S. N., & Sasikala, K. (2015). Peripheral blood markers of homocysteine, paraoxonase1 (PON1) activity and oxidative stress in autism, *International Journal of Developmental Neuroscience 47A*(December), 82–83.http://dx.doi.org/10.1016/j.ijdevneu.2015.04.226

Ballaban-Gil, K., & Tuchman, R. (2000). Epilepsy and epileptiform EEG: Association with autism and language disorders. *Mental Retardation and Developmental Disabilities Research Reviews, 6*(4), 300–308.

Bazzano, A. T. F., Mangione-Smith, R., Schonlau, M., Suttorp, M. J., & Brook, R. H. (2009). Off-label prescribing to children in the United States outpatient setting. *Academic Pediatrics, 9*(2), 81–88.

Beers, M. H., & Merck Research Laboratories. (2006).*The Merck manual of diagnosis and therapy.* Whitehouse Station, NJ: Merck Research Laboratories.

Bent, S., Bertoglio, K., & Hendren, R. L. (2009). Omega-3 fatty acids for autistic spectrum disorder: A systematic review. *Journal of Autism and Developmental Disorders, 39*(8), 1145–1154. http://doi.org/10.1007/s10803-009-0724-5

Bookheimer, S. Y., Wang, A. T., Scott, A., Sigman, M., & Dapretto, M. (2008). Frontal contributions to face processing differences in autism: Evidence from fMRI of inverted face processing. *Journal of the International Neuropsychological Society: JINS, 14*, 922–932. http://doi.org/10.1017/S13556177 0808140X

Bromley, R. L., Mawer, G., Clayton-Smith, J., & Baker, G. A. (2008). Autism spectrum disorders following in utero exposure to antiepileptic drugs. *Neurology, 71*, 1923–1924.

Buwe, A., Guttenbach, M., & Schmid, M. (2005). Effect of paternal age on the frequency of cytogenetic abnormalities in human spermatozoa. *Cytogenet Genome Research, 111*, 213–228.

Caglayan, A. O. (2010). Genetic causes of syndromic and non-syndromic autism. *Developmental Medicine & Child Neurology, 52*, 130–138. doi: 10.1111/j.1469-8749.2009.03523.x

Calderón-Garcidueñas, L., Engle, R., Mora-Tiscareño, A., Styner, M., Gómez-Garza, G., Zhu, H., Jewells, V., . . . D'Angiulli, A. (2011). Exposure to severe urban air pollution influences cognitive outcomes, brain volume and systemic inflammation in clinically healthy children. *Brain and Cognition, 77*(3), 345–355.

Centers for Disease Control and Prevention; American Society for Reproductive Medicine; Society for Assisted Reproductive Technology (2009). *Assisted reproductive technology success rates: National summary and fertility clinic reports.* Atlanta, GA: Centers for Disease Control and Prevention.

Centers for Disease Control and Prevention (2012). Assistive reproductive technology surveillance – United States, 2009. *Morbidity and Mortality Weekly Report Surveillance, 61*(7), 1–23.

Chaste, P., & Leboyer, M. (2012). Autism risk factors: Genes, environment, and gene-environment interactions. *Dialogues in Clinical Neuroscience, 14*(3), 281–292.

Christon, L. M., Mackintosh, V. H., & Myers, B. J. (2010). Use of complementary and alternative medicine (CAM) treatments by parents of children with autism spectrum disorders. *Research in Autism Spectrum Disorders, 4*(2), 249–259.

Coben, R., Linden, M., & Myers, T. E. (2010). Neurofeedback for autistic spectrum disorder: A review of the literature. Applied Psychophysiological Biofeedback, 35(1), 83–105. doi: 10.1007/s10484-009-9117-y

Copeland, L. (2007). *The evidence on complementary and alternative medical interventions for autism.* PowerPoint retrieved June 2, 2016 from www.dcc-cde.ca.gov/.

Courchesne, E. (2004). Brain development in autism: Early growth followed by premature arrest of growth. *Mental Retardation and Developmental Disabilities Research Reviews, 10*(2), 106–111.

Courchesne, E., Carper, R., & Akshoomoff, N. (2003). Evidence of brain overgrowth in the first year of life in autism. *JAMA, the Journal of the American Medical Association, 290*(3), 337–344. doi:10.1001/jama.290.3.337

Dapretto, M., Davies, M. S., Pfeifer, J. H., Scott, A., Sigman, M., Bookheimer, S. Y., & Iacoboni, M. (2006). Understanding emotions in others: Mirror neuron dysfunction in children with autism spectrum disorders. *Nature Neuroscience, 9*, 28–30.

Dichter, G. S. (2012). Functional magnetic resonance imaging of autism spectrum disorders. *Dialogs in Clinical Neuroscience, 14*, 319–351.

Ecker, C., Ronan, L., Feng, Y., Daly, E., Murphy, C., Ginestet, C. E., . . . Williams, S. C. (2013). Intrinsic gray-matter connectivity of the brain in adults with autism spectrum disorder. *Proceedings of the National Academy of Sciences of the United States of America, 110*(32), 13222–13227. http://doi.org/10.1073/pnas.1221880110

El-Fishawy, P., & State, M. W. (2010). The genetics of autism: Key issues, recent findings, and clinical implications. *Psychiatric Clinics of North America, 33*, 83–105.

Ernst, E. (2002). A systematic review of systematic reviews of homeopathy. *British Journal of Clinical Pharmacology, 54*(6), 577–582. http://doi.org/10.1046/j.1365-2125.2002.01699.x

Ferreira, P. C., Piai, K. A., Takayanagui, A. M. M., & Segura-Muñoz, S. I. (2008). Aluminum as a risk factor for Alzheimer's disease. *Review Latino-am Enfermagem, 16*(1), 151–157.

Food and Drug Administration (n.d.). Retrieved June 2, 2016 from www.fda.gov/Drugs/DrugSafety/PostmarketDrugSafetyInformationforPatientsandProviders/ucm192645.htm.

Fountain, C., Zhang, Y., Kissin, D. M., Schieve, L. A., Jamieson, D. J., Rice, C., & Bearman, P. (2015). Association between assisted reproduction technology conception and autism in California, 1997–2007. *American Journal of Public Health, 105*(5), 963–971.

Ghanizadeh, A. (2012). Hyperbaric oxygen therapy for treatment of children with autism: A systematic review of randomized trials. *Medical Gas Research, 2*, 13–20. doi.org/10.1186/2045-9912-2-13

Gillberg, C. (1992). The Emmanuel Miller Memorial Lecture 1991. Autism and autistic-like conditions: Subclasses among disorders of empathy. *Journal of Child Psychology and Psychiatry, 33*, 813–842.

Gillberg, C. & Bilstedt, E. (2000). Autism and Asperger syndrome: Coexistence with other clinical disorders. *Acta Psychiatrica Scandinavica, 102*, 321–330.

Golnik, A. E., & Ireland M. (2009). Complementary alternative medicine for children with autism: A physician survey. *Journal of Autism and Developmental Disorders, 39*(7), 996–1005. doi: 10.1007/s10803-009-0714-7

Green, C., Martin, C. W., Bassett, K., & Kazanjian, A. (1999). A systematic review of craniosacral therapy: Biological plausibility, assessment reliability and clinical effectiveness. *Complementary and Therapeutic Medicine, 7*(4), 201–207.

Gualtieri, C., Golden, R., & Fahs, J. (1983). New developments in pediatric psychopharmacology. *Developmental and Behavioral Pediatrics, 3*, 202–209.

Guzman, F. (2015). *Valproate in psychiatry: Approved indications and off-label uses.* Retrieved June 2, 2016 from http://psychopharmacologyinstitute.com/mood-stabilizers/valproate-in-psychiatry-approved-indications-and-off-label-uses/.

Hadjikhani, N., Joseph, R. M., Snyder, J., Chabris, C. F., Clark, J., Steele, S., . . . Tager-Flusberg, H. (2004). Activation of the fusiform gyrus when individuals with autism spectrum disorder view faces. *NeuroImage, 22*(3), 1141–1150.

Herbert, M. R. (2005). Large brains in autism: The challenge of pervasive abnormality. *The Neuroscientist: A Review Journal Bringing Neurobiology, Neurology and Psychiatry, 11*(5), 417–440. doi:10.1177/0091270005278866

Horvath, K., & Perman, J. A. (2002). Autistic disorder and gastrointestinal disease. *Current Opinions in Pediatrics, 14*, 583–587.

Hu-Lince, D., Craig, D. W., Huentelman, M. J., & Stephan, D. A. (2005). The autism genome project: Goals and strategies. *American Journal of Pharagogenomics, 5*, 233–246.

Hultman, C. M., Sandin, S., Levine, S. Z., Lichenstein, P., & Reichenberg, A. (2011). Advancing parental age and risk of autism: New evidence from a population-based study and a meta-analysis of epidemiological studies. *Molecular Psychiatry, 16*(12), 1203–1212.

Hvidtjorn, D., Grove, J., Schendel, D., Schieve, L. A., Svaerke, C., Ernst, E., & Thorsen, P. (2011). Risk of autism spectrum disorders in children born after assisted contraception: A population-based follow-up study. *Journal of Epidemiology and Community Health, 65*, 497–502.

Johnson, C. P. & Myers, S. M. (2007). Identification and evaluation of children with autism spectrum disorders. *Pediatrics, 120*, 1183–1215.

Johnson, L. E. (2014). Vitamin B6. *Merck Manual Professional Edition*. Retrieved June 2, 2016 from www.merckmanuals.com/professional/nutritional-disorders/vitamin-deficiency-dependency-and-toxicity/vitamin-b-sub-6-sub.

Johnson, M. H., Dziurawiec, S., Ellis, H., & Morton, J., (1991). Newborn's preferential tracking of face-like stimuli and its subsequent decline. *Cognition*, *40*, 1–19.

Kalkbrenner, A. E., Schmidt, R. J., & Penlesky, A. C. (2014). Environmental chemical exposures and autism spectrum disorders: A review of the epidemiological evidence. *Current Problems in Pediatric and Adolescent Health Care*, *44*(10), 277–318.

Kanner, L. (1943). Autistic disturbances of affective contact. *Nervous Child*, 2(21), 217–250.

Klin, A., Jones, W., Schultz, R., Volkmar, F., & Cohen, D. (2002). Visual fixation patterns during viewing of naturalistic social situations as predictors of social competence in individuals with autism. *Archives of General Psychiatry*, *59*, 809–816.

Klin, A., Sparrow, S. S., de Bildt, A., Cicchetti, D. V., Cohen, D. J., & Volkmar, F., (1999). A normed study of face recognition in autism and related disorders. *Journal of Autism and Developmental Disorders*, *29*, 499–508.

Kolevson, A., Gross, R., & Reichenberg, A. (2007). Prenatal and perinatal risk factors for autism: A review and integration of findings. *Archives of Pediatric and Adolescent Medicine*, *161*, 326–333.

Kouijzer, M., de Moor, J. M. H., Gerrits, B., Buitelaar, J., & van Schie, H. T. (2009). Long-term effects of neurofeedback treatment in autism. *Research in Autism Spectrum Disorders*, *3*(2), 496–501. doi: 10.1016/j.rasd.2008.10.003

Lai, C. S. L., Fisher, S. E., Hurst, J. A., Vargha-Khadem, F., & Monaco, A. P., (2001). A forkhead-domain gene is mutated in severe speech and language disorder. *Nature*, *413*, 519–523.

Landrigan, P. J. (2010). What causes autism? Exploring the environmental contribution. *Current Opinions in Pediatrics*, *22*, 219–225. Retrieved June 2, 2016 from http://faculty.washington.edu/rab2/Site/AUT501_files/Landrigan%20env%20factors%202010.pdf.

Lang, R. B., Regester, A., Lauderdale, S., Ashbaugh, K., & Haring, A. (2010). Treatment of anxiety in autism spectrum disorders using cognitive behavior therapy: A systematic review. *Developmental Neurorehabilitation*, *13*, 53–63.

Lee, M. S., Choi, T.-Y., Shin, B.-C., & Ernst, E. (2012). Acupuncture for children with autism spectrum disorders: A systematic review of randomized clinical trials. *Journal of Autism and Developmental Disorders*, *42*, 1671–1683.

Levy, S. E., & Hyman, S. L. (2005). Novel treatments for autistic spectrum disorders. *Mental Retardation and Developmental Disabilities Research Reviews*, *11*(2), 131–142.

Lilienfeld, D. E., & Stolley, P. D. (1994). *Foundations of epidemiology* (3rd ed.). Oxford: Oxford University Press.

Lofthouse, N., Hendren, R., Hurt, E., Arnold, L. E., & Butter, E. (2012). A review of complementary and alternative treatments for autism spectrum disorders. *Autism Research and Treatment*, Article ID 870391, 21 pages, doi:10.1155/2012/870391

Ludvigsson, J. F., Reichenberg, A., Hultman, C., & Murray, J. A. (2013). A nationwide study of small intestinal histopathology and risk of autistic spectrum disorders. *JAMA Psychiatry*, *70*(11), 1224–1230. doi.org/10.1001/jamapsychiatry.2013.2048

Lydall, K., Van de Water, J., Ashwood, P., & Hertz-Picciotto, I. (2015). Asthma and allergies in children with autism spectrum disorders: Results from CHARGE study. *Autism Research*, *8*, 567–574.

Maimburg, R. D., & Vaeth, M. (2006). Prenatal risk factors and infantile autism. *Acta Psychiatrica Scandinavica*, *114*, 257–264.

Marner, L., Nyengaard, J. R., Tang, Y., & Pakkenberg, B. (2003). Marked loss of myelinated nerve fibers in the human brain with age. *The Journal of Comparative Neurology*, *462*(2), 144–152. doi:10.1002/cne.10714. PMID 12794739

Miller, A. K. H. & Alston, C. (2008). Variation with age in the volumes of grey and white matter in the cerebral hemispheres of man: Measurements with an image analyzer. *Neuropathology and Applied Neurobiology*, *6*(2): 119–132. doi:10.1111/j.1365-2990.1980.tb00283.x. PMID 7374914

Moore, S. J., Turnpenny P., Quinn A., Glover S., Lloyd D. J., Montgomery T., & Dean J. C. S. (2002). A clinical study of 57 children with fetal anticonvulsant syndromes. *Journal of Medical Genetics*, *37*, 489–497.

Mulloy, A., Lang, R., O'Reilly, M., Sigaffos, J., Lancioni. G., & Rispoli, M. (2009). Gluten-free and casein-free diets in the treatment of autism spectrum disorders: A systematic review. *Research in Autism Spectrum Disorders*, *4*(3), 328–339.

Myers, S. M., & Johnson, C. P. (2007). Management of children with autism spectrum disorders. *Pediatrics*, *120*(5), 1162–1182.

National Center for Complementary and Alternative Medicine [NCCAM], (2014). Complementary, alternative, or integrative health: What's in a name? Retrieved June 2, 2016 from https://nccih.nih.gov/health/integrative-health.

Nickl-Jockschat, T., & Michel, T. M. (2011). The role of neurotropic factors in autism. *Molecular Psychiatry*, *16*, 478–490.

Nye C., & Brice A. (2005). Combined vitamin B6-magnesium treatment in autism spectrum disorder. *Cochrane Database of Systematic Reviews*, *19* (4), CD003497.

Palmer, R. F., Blanchard, S., Stein, Z., Mandell, D., & Miller, C. (2006). Environmental mercury release, special education rates, and autism disorder: An ecological study of Texas. *Health & Place*, *12*, 203–209.

Panskepp, J. A. (1979). A neurochemical theory of autism. *Trends in Neuroscience*, *2*, 174–177.

Peter, B., Raskind, W. H., Matsushita, M., Lisowski, M., Vu, T., Berninger, V. W., … Brkanac, Z. (2011). Replication of CNTNAP2 association with non-word repetition and support for FOXP2 association with timed reading and motor activities in a dyslexia family sample. *Journal of Neurodevelopmental Disorders*, *39*(1), 39–49.

Pfeiffer, S. I., Norton, J., Nelson, L., & Shott, S. (1995). Efficacy of Vitamin B6 and magnesium in the treatment of autism: A methodology review and summary of outcomes, *Journal of Autism and Developmental Disorders*, *25*(5), 481–493.

Pichichero, M. E., Gentile, A., Giglio, N., Alonso, M. M., Fernandez Mentaberri, M. V., Zareba, G., . . . Treanor, J. (2009). Mercury levels in premature and low birth weight newborns after receipt of thimerosal-containing vaccines. *The Journal of Pediatrics*, *155*(4), 495–499. http://doi.org/10.1016/j.jpeds.2009.04.011

Pierce, K., Haist, F., Sedaghat, F., & Courchesne, E. (2004). The brain response to personally familiar faces in autism: Findings of fusiform activity and beyond. *Brain*, *127*, 2703–2716.

Rao, T. S. S., & Andrade, C. (2011). The MMR vaccine and autism: Sensation, refutation, retraction, and fraud. *Indian Journal of Psychiatry*, *53*(2), 95–96. http://doi.org/10.4103/0019-5545.82529

Rasalam, A. D., Hailey, H., Williams, J. H. G., Moore, S. J., Turnpenny, P. D., Lloyd, D. J., & Dean, J. C. S. (2005). Characteristics of fetal anticonvulsant syndrome associated autistic disorder. *Developmental Medicine and Child Neurology*, *47*(8), 551–555. Retrieved June 2, 2016 from http://search.proquest.com.library.svsu.edu/docview/195591714?accountid=960.

Raz, R., Roberts, A. L., Lyall, K, Hart, J. E., Just, A. C., Laden, F., & Weisskopf, M. G. (2015). Autism spectrum disorder and particulate matter air pollution before, during, and after pregnancy: A nested case-control analysis within the Nurses' Health Study II cohort. *Environmental Health Perspectives*, *123*, 264–230.

Robinson, T. W. (2001). Homeopathic secretin in autism: A clinical pilot study. *British Homeopathic Journal*, *90*(2), 86–91.

Rossignol, D. A. (2009). Novel and emerging treatments for autism spectrum disorders: A systematic review. *Annals of Clinical Psychiatry*, *21*(4), 213–236.

Rubio-Tapia, A., Ludvigsson, J. F., Brantner, T. L., Murray, J. A., & Everhart, J. E. (2012). The prevalence of celiac disease in the United States. *The American Journal of Gastroenterology*, *107*, 1538–1544 doi:10.1038/ajg.2012.219

Rutter, M. (1983). Cognitive deficits in the pathogenesis of autism. *Journal of Child Psychology and Psychiatry*, *24*, 513–531.

Sanders, H., Davis, M. F., Duncan, B., Meaney, F. J., Haynes, J., & Barton, L. L. (2003). Use of complementary and alternative medical therapies among children with special health care needs in southern Arizona. *Pediatrics*, *111*(3), 584–587.

Schumann, G., Coin, L. J., Lourdusamy, A., Charoen, P., Berger, K. A., Stacey, D., . . . Elliott, P. (2011). Genome-wide association and genetic functional studies identify susceptibility candidate 2 gene (AUTS2) in the regulation of alcohol consumption. *Proceedings of the National Academy of Science*, *108*, 7119–7124.

Schechtman, M. A. (2007). Scientifically unsupported therapies in the treatment of young children with autism spectrum disorders. *Pediatric Annals*, *36*(8), 497–505.

Stafford, R. S. (2008). Regulating off-label drug use: Rethinking the role of the FDA. *New England Journal of Medicine*, *358*, 1427–1429.

Sunyer, J. (2008). The neurological effects of air pollution in children. *European Respiratory Journal*, *32*, 535–537.

Tomljenovic, L., & Shaw, C. A. (2011). Do aluminum vaccine adjuvants contribute to the rising prevalence of autism? *Journal of Inorganic Biochemistry*, *105*, 1489–1499.

van Daalen, E., Swinkels, S. H., Dietz, C., van Engeland, H., & Buitelaar, J. K. (2007). Body length and head growth in the first year of life in autism. *Pediatric Neurology, 37*(5), 324–330. doi:10.1016/j.pediatrneurol.2007.06.006

Van Engeland, H. & Buitelaar, J. K. (2008). Autism spectrum disorders. In M. Rutter et al. *Rutter's child and adolescent psychiatry: fifth edition* (5th ed., pp. 759–781). Hoboken, New Jersey: Wiley-Blackwell.

vanderVaart, S., Gijsen, V. M., de Wildt, S. N., & Koren, G. (2009). A systematic review of the therapeutic effects of Reiki. *Journal of Alternative and Complementary Medicine, 15*, 1157–1169. doi: 10.1089/acm.2009.0036

Veatch, O. J., Veenstra-VanderWeele, J., Potter, M., Pericak-Vance, M. A., & Haines, J. L. (2014). Genetically meaningful phenotypic subgroups in autism spectrum disorders. *Genes, Brains, and Behavior, 13*, 276–288.

Vernes, S. C., Newbury, D. F., Abrahams, B. S., Winchester, L., Nicod, J., Groszer, M., . . . Fisher, S. E. (2008). A functional genetic link between distinct developmental language disorders. *New England Journal of Medicine, 359*, 2337–2345.

Whitehouse, A. J., Bishop, D. V., Ang, Q. W., Pennell, C. E., & Fisher, S. E. (2011). CNTNAP2 variants affect early language development in the general population. *Genes, Brain, Behavior, 10*, 451–456.

Wing, L. (1996). Autism spectrum disorder (Editorial). *British Medical Journal, 312*, 327–328.

Wolfsberg, T. G., McEntyre, J., & Schuler, G. D. (2001). Analysis: Guide to the human draft genome. *Nature, 405*, 824–826.

Woodhouse, W., Bailey, A., Rutter, M., Bolton, P., Baird, G., & LeCouteur, A. (1996). Head circumference in autism and other pervasive developmental disorders. *Journal of Child Psychology and Psychiatry and Allied Disciplines, 37*(6), 665–671.

World Health Organization [WHO]. (1992). *The ICD-10 classification of mental and behavioural disorders: Clinical descriptions and diagnostic guidelines.* Geneva: World Health Organization.

Zachor, D. A., & Itzchak, E. B. (2011). Assisted reproductive technology and risk for autism spectrum disorder. *Research in Developmental Disabilities, 32*, 2950–2956.

Zhang, J., Mayton, M. R., & Wheeler, J. J. (2013). Effectiveness of gluten-free and casein-free diets for individuals with autism spectrum disorders: An evidence-based research synthesis. *Education and Training in Autism and Developmental Disabilities, 48*(2), 276–287.

Chapter 5

Global Perspectives

Autism Education and Treatment in Other Nations

Angi Stone-MacDonald and Rama Cousik

While autism was first written about in Europe in the 1940s, there have been stories of suspected cases of autism documented as early as 1724 (Feinstein, 2010). Autism exists all over the world. On World Autism Awareness Day in 2013, UN Secretary General Ban Ki-Moon stated, "Autism is not limited to a single region or country; it is a worldwide challenge that requires global action. This international attention is essential to address stigma, lack of awareness and inadequate support structures" (Smith, 2014). Autism exists in all cultures, but the neurobiological expression of autism spectrum disorder can look different in different cultures. Autism is truly a spectrum disorder, not just in the level of severity, but also in the symptoms that are most commonly observed in different cultures. Until recently, the importance of culture was generally ignored in relation to autism, both in diagnosis and treatment (Daley, 2002). At the same time, there was a misconception in some countries outside of North America and Europe that autism was the result of modernization and it did not exist outside of "Western" countries (Daley & Sigman, 2002; Hudec, 2012). This belief is still present amongst some people in African and Asian countries. The general diagnosis of ASD around the world is based on whether behavior deviates from what is considered typical in that culture, but there is less consensus among research where the line between behavior differences lies and the diagnosis of an autism spectrum disorder (Freeth, Milne, Sheppard, & Ramachandran, 2014; Grinker, 2008).

In Chapter 1 of this volume, Maye, Kiss, and Carter discussed the formal DSM definition and the characteristics and symptoms of autism used to identify and diagnose autism. In low- and middle-income countries, it is more common for doctors and rehabilitation staff to use the WHO definition. According the World Health Organization, ASD comprises a group of complex, lifelong, neurodevelopmental disorders usually noticeable prior to three years of age. The conditions are characterized by qualitative impairments in reciprocal social interaction, impairments in verbal and nonverbal communication skills, and a restricted pattern of interest or behavior (World Health Organization, 1992; American Psychiatric Association, 2013). ASD is found in every race, ethnic group, and socio-economic class. Despite the universality, relatively less research and resources have been used to address people with ASD in low- and middle-income countries. Dyches, Wilder, Sudweeks, Obiakor, and Algozzine, B. (2004) found that "students with multicultural backgrounds and autism are challenged on at least four dimensions: communication, social skills, behavioral repertoires, and culture. The professional literature continues to address the first three; it is imperative to now consider the third: multicultural issues" (p. 221).

While the DSM and WHO have clear definitions based on characteristics and symptomology, often children in countries without standardized assessment protocols are diagnosed with autism because they meet the core criteria of autism, but their presentation of symptoms looks different from some more classic cases of autism in the US. For example, in studies in African countries, hand flapping is a very rare symptom and is rarely reported (Bakare & Munir, 2011). In African countries, spinning, hand flapping and object spinning were less common than in a US sample, whereas more children with ASD were non-verbal and possessed poor non-verbal communication skills as well (Bello-Mojeed, Bakare, & Munir, 2014). In addition, some behaviors assessed by standardized screening and assessment tools, such as the M-CHAT and ADOS, may not be viewed as deviant in certain cultures, so they are not seen as concerns for autism by parents and caregivers (Daly, 2004; Freeth et al., 2014). For example, in some Asian countries eye contact with adults is not normal, so it is not considered deviant to not make eye contact with parents and caregivers. Behaviors exhibited by children with autism may look different in different cultures. In studies in several African countries, over half of children diagnosed with autism were also non-verbal in one study and over 70 percent were non-verbal in the other study (Belhadj, Mrad, & Halayem, 2006; Mankoski et al., 2006). In addition, over 60 percent of children were also diagnosed with intellectual disability (Bakare & Munir, 2011). Observational measures and functional skill assessments are most commonly used in low- and middle-income countries, because there are no appropriate measures and/or health care workers do not have training in standardized assessments. There is a complex relationship between culture and all developmental disabilities, including autism, which needs to be addressed through more research. In India, Daley (2004) found that some pediatricians and psychiatrists used the terms autism, autistic traits, and PDD interchangeably and did not use standardized tools or a systematic process for diagnosis.

In working with families and conducting research on autism, it is critical to focus assessment and treatment on the child's or adult's ability to function in society and community within their culture and not use Western models of assessment and diagnosis, because this introduces systematic bias (Freeth et al., 2014). That is not to say that certain assessment tools cannot be used as a guide, but it is necessary to assess their validity within the language and cultural context and make any needed adjustments for language and culture before they are used as a standardized method of assessment. Health care professionals and educators working with families should focus on helping the individual increase their ability to function in society and work on building skills most relevant to their community and successful community membership (Stone-MacDonald, 2014).

Labels and Stigma around ASD and Developmental Disabilities

Labeling ASD can be a daunting task because it can be difficult for health care professionals and educators to determine if in fact a child has ASD based on diagnostic criteria due to lack of training, lack of standardized assessment tools, and cultural differences in the expression of symptoms in different countries. In addition, a diagnosis does not always lead to services or an understanding by parents and caregivers about the ramifications of the diagnosis and how that will impact a child and a family's life. In India, parents are often not given the specific diagnosis of autism because the label itself does not provide additional services. Children need a label of intellectual disability to receive additional mental health and educational services (Daley 2004). In South Korea, mothers often reject any label because of the intense stigma associated with it and the desire to continue to see their child as normal (Grinker & Cho, 2013). South Korean mothers refer to their children as "border children," where they view their children as living with a temporary deficit in the single domain of social impairment (Grinker & Cho, 2013, p. 46). Furthermore, if children are able to attend a general education school and do well in some school subjects, then the label is incompatible with their child having a pervasive developmental disorder such as ASD.

Labels can also be linked to beliefs about the causes of the disability. Cultural factors influence acceptance and understanding of intervention strategies (Mandell & Novak, 2005). In several African countries, people hold both biological and spiritual beliefs about the causes of disability (Ametepe & Chiyito, 2009; Stone-MacDonald & Butera, 2012). Mankoski et al. (2006) found that it was believed that severe cases of malaria or a Vitamin D deficiency in the first two years of life caused ASD. In Tanzania, while it is recognized that children with disabilities, especially children with developmental disabilities such as ASD or ID, should be cared for and families should meet their needs, it is not necessary to educate children with disabilities and some people do not believe that these children can learn and participate in society (Stone-MacDonald, 2014). Historically, children with disabilities were hidden due to stigma (Bello-Mojeed et al., 2014; Butera & Stone-MacDonald, 2012). These attitudes are slowly changing and children are given educational opportunities, but often—in African countries—children with autism are taught in separate classrooms or separate schools that can provide more intensive interventions.

In African and Middle Eastern countries, stigma is attached to labels of disability (Bello-Mojeed et al., 2014). Families experience shame because often they feel that a family member or family member's action is to blame for the disability (Holroyd, 2003). Samadi, McConkey, and Kelly (2013) found in Iran that there was a great deal of stigma for the family of an individual with ID or ASD.

> Having a child who has a disability is considered by many religious Iranians to be a result of a sin and hence disability is a source of shame for the broader family, with negative effects on the marriage prospects of siblings, for example.
>
> (Samadi et al., 2013, p. 4)

In Chinese culture, mental health conditions and disabilities attract social shame, and denial may be preferable to seeking advice (Mak & Kwok, 2010). Often families also still feel stigma over having a child with autism because there is still a belief that a family member (often the mother) did something wrong to cause the disability (Holroyd, 2003). Previous research found negative attitudes and feelings of shame regarding epilepsy (Fong & Hung, 2002) and mental illness (Tsang, Tam, Chan, & Cheung, 2003; Yang & Pearson, 2002). McCabe (2007) interviewed 38 families about their perceptions on having a child with autism. She found a high level of concern amongst caregivers about stigma and discrimination:

> . . . caregivers' perceptions of the existence of beliefs and practices that discriminate against individuals with disabilities and their families, due to a low awareness and acceptance of disability and difference. Almost every family interviewed for this study mentioned their fear of being discriminated against if others found out that their child had autism (or was in some way "different" from typically developing children). This meant that it was often difficult for them to take the steps necessary to seek assistance.
>
> (McCabe, 2007, p. 43)

Yan (2005) found that slowly the population is acknowledging that people with disabilities have a right to a high quality of life, and traditional cultural beliefs that they are "useless burdens on society" (Yan, 2005, p. 43) are slowly changing (McCabe, 2008a). While parents in several studies conducted by McCabe sought support and interventions, parents talked of others they knew with children with autism or other developmental disabilities who did not seek support out of a fear of stigma from friends and family (McCabe, 2007).

Treatment, Education, and Parental Perspectives around the World

In this chapter, we have chosen to focus on issues around identification and awareness about autism, treatment and education of individuals with autism, and parental perspectives using four countries or regions as examples. Because we cannot talk about all countries in this short chapter, we wanted to focus on low- and middle-income countries where less research is done and disseminated worldwide. We will focus on the following areas: (1) African countries; (2) China; (3) India; and (4) the Middle East. We chose these areas because they represent both low- and middle-income countries and the literature available was in English. We were unable to include research on Central or South America because most of the research is published in Spanish. To begin, we will look at overall prevalence and identification in each region/country.

Prevalence and Identification

African Countries

Although there has been extensive research on the assessment and diagnosis of ASD in North America, Europe, and Asia, people in many low- and middle-income regions, such as many African countries, still do not have access to ASD assessment and diagnostic services (Elsabbagh et al., 2012). Prevalence in African countries is difficult to establish due to the lack of research and the lack of health care or educational professionals with the knowledge and expertise required to identify ASD in children. At present there are no ASD diagnostic instruments validated for use in Swahili, a language that is spoken by millions of people in Kenya, Tanzania, and Uganda. In other African countries, there are also no validated measures for use in the local language. However, there remain noteworthy disparities in the age of onset and identification of ASD with a prominent problem of late identification among affected children in Africa (Mandel, Ittenbach, Levy, & Pinto-Martin, 2007; Bello-Mojeed et al., 2011; Bakare & Munir 2011).

In South Africa, there are an estimated 135,000 children with autism (Smith, 2014). However, three published meta-analyses found that there are no population-based studies or reports on the specific prevalence of ASD or PDD in African countries and more research is needed (Ametepee & Chiyito, 2009; Bakare & Munir, 2011; Elsabbagh et al., 2012). Nevertheless, studies have documented the existence of autism in African countries since 1978 (Lotter, 1978; Ampetee & Chiyito, 2009). A higher male-to-female ratio was consistent across studies in African countries and consistent with studies from the United States and Europe (Khan & Hombarume, 1996; Lotter, 1978; Mankoski et al., 2006). Studies also showed an over-representation of higher socioeconomic backgrounds and higher frequency of cases co-morbid with intellectual difficulties. Most children who were identified as having both ID and autism were non-verbal.

Among health care workers in Nigeria, Bakare, Ebigbo, Agomoh, and Menkiti (2008) Bakare et al. (2009) and Igwe, Ahanotu, Bakare, Achor, and Igwe (2011) found a low level of knowledge and awareness of ASD among health care workers, with the highest level observed among those in working psychiatric facilities in Nigeria. Amongst the general population, they found a very low level of knowledge and understanding of ASD. Furthermore, psychiatrists, who often diagnose children with autism are rare in many African countries. In Nigeria and Ghana, each country has only one psychiatrist to serve over one million people in each country, respectively; and Liberia has one psychiatrist for over 3.4 million people (Smith, 2014).

India

Similar to the situation in African countries, there are no systematic epidemiological studies on the specific prevalence of autism in India. However, Krishnamurthy (2008) estimated that there are 2.3 million children with autistic spectrum disorder in India, based on worldwide prevalence estimates. Children usually get a diagnosis of intellectual disability and autism is added as a co-morbid condition. For example, Silberg et al. (2014) examined the prevalence of Neuro Development Disorders (NDD) including autism across urban, rural, and hilly regions of India and estimated that 10–18 percent of children between the ages of two and nine had NDD.

Current estimates of prevalence rates in India based on population studies are not yet available. There is a possibility that prevalence rates may be underestimated in countries like India, and scholars and stakeholders present diverse viewpoints as to the reasons. One reason is that the majority of the population (70 percent) lives in rural areas where access to services is scarce. Advocacy groups argued that some doctors did not see it as a benefit to offer a diagnosis if there were no services to treat the diagnosis of autism, particularly in the rural areas (Daley, 2004).

Thus, autism is possibly seen as an urban phenomenon, with more people in the higher economic strata affected than those in the low Social Economic Stauts (SES) bracket. Daley argues that the lack of education among the rural poor prevents them from recognizing the signs and seeking support and remediation. Another reason for the lower prevalence rates is that autism is not usually the primary diagnosis or considered a disability by most diagnosticians in India. Children are often initially given the diagnosis of intellectual disability, but not autism because children and families can receive additional services for a diagnosis of ID but no additional services for a diagnosis of autism. In Daley's study, health care professionals attributed a higher proportion of children with autism from higher-income families to a "greater awareness of norms for children" (2004, p.1331).

Standardized assessments are just starting to be validated and used in India for the diagnosis of autism. In a recent study by Rudra et al. (2014), researchers tested the usability of a translated version of four widely used assessments: SDT (Social Communication Disorder Checklist, Autism Spectrum Quotient, Social Communication Questionnaire, and Autism Diagnostic Observation Schedule) in Bengali and Hindi, two local regional languages. Initial results indicated that the assessments were effective in identifying children with autism. Manohari, Raman, & Ashok (2013) used the Vineland Adaptive Behavior Scales to assess the skills of children with autism. While their use was more informative about the children's skills than diagnostic, the Vineland scale provided meaningful information for working with children with autism.

China

There have been several recent studies on the prevalence of autism in China, where more data are available in comparison to India and Africa countries. In a meta-analysis of prevalence studies, Sun et al. (2013) found that a pooled prevalence of childhood autism was 11.8 per 10,000 individuals in mainland China and a pooled prevalence of ASC was 26.6 per 10,000 for China, Hong Kong, and Taiwan. There was considerable variability in prevalence statistics that the research team attributed to differences in the selected screening tool. They noted that the focus for screening is on childhood autism and not on the entire ASD spectrum, which would result in under-diagnosis of children with ASD. In addition, newer screening tools provided a higher prevalence. Prevalence numbers for ASD varied substantially by gender, location of residence, date of publication, and source of the sample (Wan et al., 2013). As in India and African countries, the lack of qualified professionals to diagnose ASD was stated as a reason for the low prevalence rates. Health care providers in China have limited knowledge about children with ASD and lack systematic training on evaluation of and interventions for ASD (Xiong et al., 2011). Li, Chen, Song, Du, and Zheng (2011) found a prevalence rate of ASD in China as low as 2.38 per 10,000, based on a national disability survey. Feng et al. (2013) described an increase in the urban ASD population, but also noted that children in rural areas may be under-diagnosed due to a lack of resources and personnel.

Similar to the situation in India, autism was not considered a disability in China until 2006 under the China Disability Law (Gu, 2007). Until then, all disabilities and learning difficulties were referred to broadly as a disability. Without specific criteria, diagnostic procedures, and classification, services for children with autism can be difficult to develop and implement (McCabe, 2003). Currently, there have been several studies looking at how to serve children and families, from identification to service provision as well as some of the methodological problems that exist in diagnosis and intervention implementation (Clark & Zhou, 2005; McCabe & McCabe, 2013; Yu & Takahashi, 2009; Zhang & Spencer, 2015). While China has started to validate and use standardized diagnostic assessment measures such as a Mandarin M-CHAT screening tool, the Childhood Autism Behavior Scale (CABS), and the Autism Behavior Checklist (ABC), more research is needed to validate these measures and test for cultural validity, as well (Gadow, Schwartz, Devincent, Strong, & Cuva, 2008; Kawamura Takahashi, & Ishii, 2008; Miranda-Linne, Fredrika, & Melin, 2002; Xuerong Li & Jinmei Chen, 2004; Wong et al., 2004). The screening and diagnostic tools used in mainland China are often old versions of questionnaires that were adopted from the West in the 1980s, such as the Autism Behaviours Checklist (ABC) (Krug, Arick, & Almond, 1980; Yang, Huang, Jia, & Chen, 1993), the Clancy Autism Behaviour Scale (CABS) (Rendle-Short, Clancy, & Dugdale, 1969; Wang, Wang, & Wang, 2003), and the Childhood Autism Rating Scale (CARS) (Schopler, Reichler, DeVellis, & Daly, 1980), which need to be updated. The Autism Diagnostic Observation Schedule (ADOS) (Lord et al., 2000) and the Autism Diagnostic Interview-Revised (ADI-R) (Lord, Storoschuk, Rutter, & Pickles, 1993) have not been well adapted in clinical or research settings in mainland China (Sun et al., 2013).

The Middle East

In the Middle East, there are various prevalence estimates for several countries, but it is still suspected that autism is undiagnosed for the same reasons as in other low- and middle-income countries, namely lack of qualified personnel and resources and lack of knowledge and awareness about ASD. It has been estimated that 14 per 10,000 children of Omani children (aged 0–14 years) have ASD (Al-Farsi et al., 2011), 29 per 10,000 in the United Arab Emirates (Eapen, Mabrouk, Zoubeidi, &

Yunis, 2007) and 6.3 cases per 10,000 in Iran (Samadi, Mahmoodizadeh, & McConkey, 2012). The low prevalence in the Omani and Iranian studies was attributed to prevalence caused by under-diagnosis and the under-reporting of cases based on limited access to educational and medical services (Al-Farsi et al., 2011). In a study of ASD among children with developmental disabilities, Seif Eldin et al. (2008) used the M-CHAT to screen for young children with ASD in a multinational Arab population in Tunisia and Egypt, two Northern African countries. Seif Eldin et al. (2008) reported the prevalence of ASD to be 11.5–33.6 percent among children with developmental disabilities in Tunisia and Egypt, respectively.

In Iran, preschool children with ASD are usually diagnosed by private medical doctors or at a non-profit clinic. Before children start school, they are screened for special needs. The Social Communication Questionnaire (SCQ) was recently added the screening process to help screen for autism. Suspected cases are referred to trained educational assessors for diagnosis using a translated version of the Autism Diagnostic Interview-Revised (ADI-R) (Samadi et al., 2013). In Oman, clinical information was collected and a validated, Arabic CARS was administered for diagnosis in multiple studies (Al-Shomari & Al-Saratwai, 2002; Al Farsi et al., 2011). More Middle Eastern countries are using standardized assessments that have been validated in Arabic and align with the DSM-V criteria for ASD. Sief Eldin et al. (2008) studied the use of the M-CHAT as an early screening tool for autism in nine Arabic-speaking countries, using an Arabic version. The team felt this was a good screening tool because you did not need to be a trained medical professional to use it, and it could be used as training in the tool. The team argued for expanded usage to gather additional clinical data about children and their families.

Treatment and Education

African Countries

In many African countries, children with ASD attend special schools or are in segregated classes, if they have the opportunity to attend school. The provision of special education and rehabilitation services are impeded in sub-Saharan Africa by several factors, including lack of resources, teachers, and teacher training facilities. Kalabula (2000) pinpoints a number of these factors, including wide gaps between knowledge and expectations of national education officials and classroom teachers close to the problem; a lack of understanding of specific needs of individual children with ASD and other disabilities by administrators of the education system at different levels of service delivery; negative attitudes of regular education teachers, other children, and other school staff toward the services and children with special educational needs; and lack of advocacy. In

Tanzania, the special education needs of children with ASD have received very little attention from society. Most educational efforts for children with ASD exist within non-governmental organizations and children with autism are often turned away from public primary schools (Stone-MacDonald, 2014). The government has put little effort into establishing schools or services for children with ASD and other developmental disabilities. Mbwilo, Smide, and Aarts (2010) noted that many families expressed concerns that their children were not benefiting from schooling because the children were not receiving the specialized instruction they needed and often received very little attention in the crowded classroom.

In Ghana, those children attending school (86 percent) were in private school settings. Children received group educational instruction, speech therapy, behavioral therapy, and recreation. The majority of children had a paraprofessional to help them work throughout the day on individual goals. Interviewees were asked to list the services that are needed to help their children with autism. The most frequently reported service needs were speech therapy (36 percent), teacher education (36 percent), parent/family training (32 percent), and behavior management (28 percent) (Dixon, Badoe, & Owusu, 2015). This list is fairly typical for African countries. With the exception of South Africa, many countries have only a few or no speech therapists.

Specifically, Ghana is an exception where there are a larger number of inclusion programs. In Ghana, the majority of children with disabilities are schooled in general education classrooms rather than segregated special education classrooms solely for children with disabilities (Dixon et al., 2015). At the same time, the results suggested that children with ASD did not have access to needed special education services and they experienced ostracism and discrimination resulting from the social stigma of having an ASD. While children with disabilities are generally included, Ghana uses a mainstreaming model and like many African countries does not have personnel with adequate training to provide specialized interventions for children with ASD. A primary factor in the lack of diagnostic educational services is the lack of health professionals' knowledge of ASD and ID, particularly in rural areas (Dixon et al., 2015). Grinker et al. (2012) studied a community-based project to implement a culturally relevant early intervention program for children with ASD in South Africa. This project was a model for researchers and community organizations working together to provide services to the community with the participation and input of stakeholders and families of children with ASD.

India

Children with autism usually attend special schools for children with developmental disabilities, but recently there has been an increase in the number of centers and special schools that provide education exclusively for children with autism. A publication by the National Institute for the Mentally Handicapped (NIMH), one of the four national institutes run by the Ministry of Social Justice and Empowerment, lists 36 such organizations, but the problem is that all these centers or schools are located in large, urban cities such as Delhi, Bangalore, Chennai, and Mumbai. Narayan, Chakravarti, David and Kanniappan (2005) found there were four models of education practiced in India, including special schools, home-based training, inclusive schools and parent-run centers. In the 2000s in India, the National Trust for Welfare of Persons with Autism, Cerebral Palsy, Mental Retardation and Multiple Disabilities Act (1999) covered people with autism with regard to guardianship and welfare. On the other hand, the legislation concerning persons with disabilities for education and employment (Equal Opportunities, Protection of Rights and Full Participation Act, 1995) did not list autism as a disability, and therefore, those individuals are not included in the law (Krishnamurthy, 2008). Narayan et al. (2005) proposed that including autism as a disability category under the EOPRFP Act (1995) might enhance educational opportunities for children with autism in mainstream schools. Recently, Action for Autism, a parent advocacy organization, has begun to offer a two-year teacher training program called the Diploma in Special Education—Autism Spectrum Disorders. The program is recognized by the Rehabilitation Council of India, which is an organization that provides certification for various training programs in the field of disability rehabilitation.

According to the Autism Information and Resource Center, an initiative of the National Trust, a comprehensive evaluation of the child that includes educational and psychological tests is done before deciding on the educational placement. The Center has published a book titled *Inclusion of children with Autism: A handbook for teachers*, which contains information about the characteristics of autism and how they affect children's learning (Singh, 2008). The book also has guidelines for teachers on how to include children with autism in the regular school setting. Strategies include the structuring of the environment, social skills training, and the education of peers on the condition.

Around India, different models have been developed through a variety of government and non-governmental organizations. ADAPT India, formerly known as the Spastics Society of India, strives to provide models of inclusive education for children with autism in rural and tribal regions (Alur, 2014). The Spastics Society of Karnataka, formerly an offshoot of ADAPT, provides a two-year "Diploma in Education Special Education— Autism Spectrum Disorders" (D.Ed. S.E-ASD), and also provides direct services that include sensory integration training. Kalyanpur (2008) found that children with multiple or severe disabilities, such as autism, had very limited access to education because of the limited resources for children with disabilities in general in the typical school.

A look at the approaches used across organizations reveals that centers practice a combination of therapeutic approaches. Although most of these are practices that originated in the West such as Lovaas, Sensory Integration Therapy, Option Method, TEACCH, and Higashi from Japan, they are now widely used in centers in India. Another institute, The Open Door Day School, stated that it used a combination of teaching methodologies including Structured Teaching, ABA and Verbal Behavior Analysis (National Center for Autism India, 2015). A center in Mumbai, The Support for Autistic Individuals, uses Relationship Development Training (RDI), which was developed by Dr. Steven Gutstein to treat children with autism. The center advertises the provision of educational services and parent training as important components of the services offered. However, RDI also has a very limited evidence base. Several of the methods used are not considered to be evidence-based in the United States or in India, such as Sensory Integration Therapy and Hyperbaric Oxygen Therapy, which are still practiced in some institutions (IRIS, 2010). The Autism Information and Resource Center (AIRC) lists several developmental interventions for autism that seem to be a compilation of approaches used across the world, from Floortime to ABA, TEACCH and PECS, some of which are evidence based in the United States and some of which are not (Autism Information and Resource Centre, 2011).

Another organization, the Behavior Momentum India, provides exclusive services using Applied Behavior Analysis (ABA). The center is guided by a team of experts in ABA from Canada, Australia, and Northern Ireland. The organization also provides certification in ABA, which is approved by the BACB (Behavior Momentum, 2014). The Special Child Trust is another organization that provides ABA under the guidance of two ABA specialists from Massachusetts, USA. The Institute for Child Development in Delhi provides center-based therapies and also coordinates with local schools to assist teachers in mainstreaming children with autism (Institute for Child Development, 2014). It also offers certification in Neurodevelopmental Therapy and Sensory Integration Therapy and an orientation course for parents on supporting young children with autism at home.

China

According to scholars, ancient Chinese texts declared that "handicapped people" should be supported and posited that formal special education for children with disabilities in China began around the 19th century (Kritzer, 2011; Chen, 1996; Yang & Wang, 1994). However, researchers and educators agree that providing special education to children with more challenging disabilities such as autism and severe, multiple disabilities is still problematic and often these children are excluded from the mainstream education system (Huang & Wheeler, 2007). According to Ellsworth and Zhang (2007), China made efforts to build the special education system for students with disabilities when it opened its doors to the world in 1979. Contact with other countries led to major social and economic reforms and children with disabilities were now also afforded nine years of free education from the state (Chen, 1996). However, there was a considerable delay until the late 1980s, when the policy became a reality for children and families (Pang & Richey, 2006).

Many families have been proactive in seeking services and advocating for their children (McCabe, 2007), but because of a lack of support and resources, families who have a child with a disability are often forced to leave the child at home because they find there are no services in their area, or even bring their children to orphanages, known as welfare institutes (McCabe, 2013; Shang, 2002).

For school age children, there are four educational settings available in China: home, special education schools, rehabilitation centers, and mainstream primary schools (Sun et al., 2013). No data were available for the percentage of children with ASC attending compulsory education. Two papers listed available intervention methods for autism and intellectual disabilities (Lu, Zhang, & Liu, 2008; Zhang & Ji, 2005). These included hospital treatment options such as medication, surgical operations, and physical therapy; family treatment such as in home intervention and training by parents, educators, or therapists; treatment options in a clinic such as special therapy and training in a rehabilitation center; and, finally, educational services in a nursery or a kindergarten or a mainstream primary school. Another study, based on interviews with parents of children with autism from rural areas in China, found that rehabilitation and education services for autism in rural areas were less available compared with urban areas due to financial constraints and the lack of community support (Liu & Wen, 2006). Sun et al. (2013, p. 445) found that

> although children with autism have been given more attention than in previous years, the system of service support from the government and society is still under-developed with limited resources that cannot fulfil the needs of these children and their families.

In reviewing data from individual centers in China, some used the Applied Behavior Analysis theory (ABA) (Hilton & Seal, 2007), Treatment and Education of Autistic and Communication Handicapped Children (TEACCH) (Panerai, Ferrante, & Caputo, 1997), and Relationship Development Intervention (RDI) (Gutstein, Burgess, & Montfort, 2007) as the theoretical basis for the training, which was adopted from the United States. While ABA and TEACCH have an evidence base, as noted in the India treatment options, RDI does not. Because the government offers minimal services, children and families often have to seek private services for a fee or from a non-governmental organization offering a low-cost or no-cost option. Because there is not national autism policy or strategy for providing services for families, various local entities offer more or less support based on local resources and available expertise (Sun et al., 2013).

The Middle East

In several Middle Eastern countries, the systems addressing children with impairment, disability, and handicaps are rudimentary (Eapen et al., 2007; Profanter 2009). As a result, the family caring for a child with a disability has to take the initiative (Read & Schofield, 2010). In the Middle East, educational services vary significantly for children in both general and special education. For example, in Oman, the government has invested a lot of money in improving the education and health care systems. In Jordan and several countries, special education schools and centers are more common options for children with ASD, but the educational system is moving towards inclusion of students in general education settings (Al-Rossan, 2012). In a study of perceptions of inclusion among teachers in Jordan, young teachers with bachelor's degrees had a more favorable view of inclusion for children with autism because the philosophy of inclusion was taught in pre-service education and demonstrated a willingness to differentiate and support children with ASD in the classroom (Abu-Hamour & Muhaidat, 2013). Because there are no standard educational options or settings for children with ASD, children tend to end up in a variety of settings based on parental input and resources (Seif Eldin et al., 2008). This often results in families resorting to "doctor shopping," where parents with more means and more flexible employment options are able to secure more services for their child (Al Farsi et al., 2013; Chakrabarti, 2009).

One of the key societal responses to children with developmental disabilities, such as those with ASD, is to provide special education services. Oman has led the region in advocating for the integration of children with special needs (Al-Lamki & Ohlin, 1992). Initially, the modern Omani education system focused on increasing literacy rates and this effort has been successful (Al-Adawi, 2006). However, education and services for children with special needs have been lagging behind other developments in the country. It is still unclear what the impact is for children and families who are trying to access relevant intervention, rehabilitation, and special education services in the country (Al Farsi et al., 2013).

In Iran, state-funded special schools are part of the Iranian public school system, but many parents choose to enroll their children in private schools or engage private therapists for their children with ASD. Children with severe and multiple disabilities can participate in state-funded day treatment programs. However, these services are available only in larger cities and often only for more affluent families (Samadi et al., 2013). More formalized services are available to families who can afford private settings and private therapists, but there is limited evidence that children who use public systems are receiving specific services for children with ASD. In the literature from Middle Eastern countries, the focus is on general services and assessment that are available, but studies were not available on the effectiveness of specific interventions for children with ASD. This is an area in need of future research.

Parental Perspectives

In low- and middle-income countries, three common themes arose after reviewing the literature from the selected areas for families with a child with ASD: (1) having a child can cause emotional and financial stress on the family due to lack of resources and information and the effort required to find and utilize services; (2) parents generally want to care for their children, but can face considerable discrimination from people in their countries due to a lack of information about ASD and characteristics and capabilities of an individual with ASD; and (3) families wanted and benefited from the comradery of support groups, parent-to-parent groups, and professional support, but these resources were hard to find and maintain based on cost, distance, and time constraints.

African Countries

In African countries, services are often rare and are run by local non-governmental organizations. While several countries on the continent have implemented disability policies and inclusive school policies, children with ASD and other developmental disabilities are often still turned away from public schools because typical primary and secondary teachers do not have any training in working with children with disabilities and have little or no knowledge of autism (African Decade of Disabled Persons, 2009; Fakolade, & Adeniyi, 2009; Stone-MacDonald, 2014). In 2014, 14 African nations participated in an Autism Speaks conference in Ghana, where leaders from Ghana and Tanzania pledged to enact change for children and families with autism, but this commitment will take time and money to trickle down to communities (United States House, & Committee on Foreign Affairs, 2014). Miles and Kaplan (2005) found that in Africa, children with disabilities might belong to any number of marginalized groups and "tend to be disproportionately represented in the out-of-school population" (p. 78).

In a Ghanaian study, parents stated that they wanted training, support groups, and behavior management training and support for their children with ASD. In addition, parents wanted their children's health care workers and educators to have more training and support to work with their child and their unique needs based on the ASD diagnosis areas (Dixon et al., 2015). Specifically, parents stated that "behavior management in public places was cited as a particular concern, particularly with regard to difficulties with public transportation and negotiating busy open markets" (Dixon et al., 2015, Discussion section, para. 3). Parent education and support services are needed across the continent.

In Tanzania, two studies found similar results to the Ghanaian study discussed above. McNally and Meenan (2013) found that the parents also experienced financial burdens and emotional stress, but most critically a lack of money for daily living supplies. Parents were positive about their children and used coping mechanisms such as spirituality and support from the community and neighbors. At the same time, three new findings emerged from the data:

> Although the demands of care are high, parents do not feel burdened or overwhelmed by their children. The parents do not see the child as the problem. It is the inability to provide for the child that creates the most stress. Carers have a clear idea of what they need in the present and the future to care for their child. Parents do not doubt their parenting abilities.
>
> (McNally & Meenan, 2013, pp. 7–8)

The second study, by Mbwilo, Smide, and Aarts (2010), came to similar conclusions, but parents focused more on the hardships faced, the lack of educational support, and the financial burdens of caring for a child with a disability. In reviewing the literature from African countries, many studies include families caring for a child with autism, but often include family perspectives based on children with a variety of developmental disabilities (Mbwilo, Smide, & Aarts, 2010; McNally & Meenan, 2013; Stone-MacDonald, 2014).

India

Though a growing number of studies have explored the impact of other developmental disabilities on Indian families and the accompanying social ostracism and stigma that they face (Dhar, 2009; Edwardraj, Mumtaj, Prasad, Kuruvilla, & Jacob, 2010; Gupta & Singhal, 2004; Kembhavi, 2009), there is comparatively little work which has explored the impact of ASD on families. The two main studies were done by Desai, Divan, Wertz, and Patel (2012) and Divan, Vajaratkar, Desai, Strik-Lievers, and Patel (2012).

When Indian parents first hear the term "autism," they have nothing to connect it to and it does not mean anything to them. Parents did not see how it applied to them because of lack of familiarity with the word or because their child was able to function well in most areas of academic and life skills. One family in the first study said:

> That first time when we were told autism, we had taken it carelessly. We had never heard about it. (F2) And he was okay in other things (M2). . . . His only problem was that he was not communicating. He was not communicating but other things he was doing. He used to understand us if we told him anything. (F2)
>
> (Desai et al., 2012, p. 620)

Because families could not connect knowledge of autism to their child, it also meant that parents had a hard time understanding the implications of an autism diagnosis for the future and their child's life outcomes, in terms of both successes and challenges (Desai et al., 2012).

Divan et al. (2012) had four major findings: (1) raising a child with ASD puts a tremendous social and financial strain on families, leading to initial social withdrawal with subsequent reintegration into social networks; (2) the impact is complex and spread into the wider community, with negative experiences of discrimination; (3) parents actively respond to challenges, seeking a range of supports through social and health networks; (4) health care professionals, educators, and religious leaders have a limited awareness for the unique needs of families living with ASD, which can lead to considerable economic and emotional burdens on families; and (5), due to the various challenges, families are increasingly isolated and have limited access to available services for ASD.

China

There is still a lack of awareness in China about autism spectrum disorder and its symptoms and impact. However, in an earlier study (McCabe, 2004), only one of 43 parents had even heard of autism before her child was diagnosed. Lack of knowledge by parents and professionals also leads to delayed diagnosis and intervention because parents do not know where to look and often continue to seek out second opinions or alternative therapies, which has been shown to occur with other disabilities in China as well (Callaway, 2000; McCabe, 2008). Furthermore, the need to spend money on seeking services and paying for services puts great stress on Chinese families (Su, Long, Chen, & Fang, 2013).

Chinese parents participating in programs for their children with autism repeatedly emphasized the importance of learning from other parents, and learning by being with other families who also had children with autism (McCabe, 2004; 2008). Parents offered specific examples where they learned from mistakes other parents made and shared ideas that had worked well in their family. Families felt a bond in talking to other families with a child with autism and found sharing experiences with parents of children without autism difficult (McCabe, 2008). Prior to participating in autism intervention programs, many parents found a lack of services for their children and despite the law in China that all children receive nine years of compulsory schooling regardless of a disability, many parents did not pursue services because of a fear of rejection (McCabe, 2007). Parents in the study wanted their children to learn verbal expression and receptive language skills because these skills were often required in order to be accepted on educational programs.

The Middle East

Parents in the Middle East experience many of the same joys and concerns as parents in the other regions. Studies from this region focused heavily on the impact that lack of knowledge by parents and caregivers had on families and family functioning. In Iran, Samadi et al. (2012) surveyed Iranian parents about their knowledge of ASD and the impact it had on their lives. Families faced stress and health problems similar to those of parents in other countries, with a tendency to rely on emotionally focused coping, and experienced more difficulties in family functioning. However, many families lacked accurate information about ASD and its causes and they had few opportunities to gather information, advice, and support for themselves as parents, either informally or from professional services (Dunst, Trivette, & Hamby, 2007).

Beresford (1995) argued that a lack of information for parents of children with ASD further contributes to their stress and anxiety. Turkish mothers, for example, reported that a lack of knowledge of ASD contributed to their stress and negative feelings about the child (Bilgin & Kucuk, 2010). One significant benefit of increased knowledge about ASD and its causes is that families were more able to counter the stigma they experienced from others, including professionals (Farrugia, 2009), which in itself can be another source of stress for parents (Mak & Kwok, 2010).

For example, Khoshabi (2003) found that Iranian mothers of children with ASD had poorer mental health than mothers of typically developing children. Sabih and Sajid (2008) reported higher levels of stress among Pakistani mothers compared with fathers.

In the Middle East, religion played a large role in parents' perception and positive feelings about their child. Their religion urged them to maintain a positive attitude and to do everything they could to help their child. This is consistent with the discussion of Islam and disability provided by Morad, Nasri, and Merrick (2001, p. 66):

> The society according to Islam is obliged to assess, assist and respect the person with intellectual disability and give the person an equal life chance. . . . In Islamic tradition, it has been stated that the best therapy is the one directed to enhance the health of the person, his psyche and spirit, in order for him to fight illness. His environment should be beautiful, filled with music and people he likes.

Muslim families believed that they had been chosen to care for the child with autism and this child was special and given to the family as a gift from Allah; their child was part of their fate (Jegatheesan, Miller & Fowler, 2010).

Internationally, there is a clear need for families of children with ASD to be better informed about this disorder and to be supported to cope with the stresses that most experience in raising their children. However, in low- and middle-income countries, where access to services provided by experts and professionals is limited, greater reliance will need to be placed on individual families and training will need to be adapted to the cultural context and sensitivities. Moreover, establishing the feasibility and effectiveness of these culturally relevant, methodologically sound interventions should encourage their implementation (Samadi, McConkey, & Kelly, 2013).

Discussion and Future Research

Each of these regions faces many of the same challenges: resources; lack of awareness and education of service providers, doctors, and educators; lack of knowledge of parents; stigma and discrimination; and lack of culturally relevant and validated assessment tools and interventions. While many of these countries are moving toward inclusive policies in their education systems for children with ASD, the implementation of those inclusive practices is still fragmented. At the same time, individuals with ASD are also not receiving the intensive and specialized interventions that they may need to support their development and to grow into productive members of their communities.

In countries like Costa Rica, China, and Tanzania, the concept of inclusion naturally reflects the collective attitudes of society and natural tendencies to care for children with disabilities. In Costa Rica, this relationship between societal attitudes and inclusion seems to have advanced inclusion's development. However, in China and Tanzania, other factors such as a lack of resources, a competitive educational system, and a huge number of children to serve seem to have overshadowed the positive societal attitudes toward inclusion and have hindered the progress toward inclusion for children with autism and other disabilities (Hippensteel, 2008).

When determining research priorities, it is important to look at issues that will improve the lives of individuals with autism and their families. Vitally important, research and interventions should be "rigorous, empirical, family-centered, culturally grounded, and methodologically sound" (Freeth et al., 2014, p. 999). There are several areas of future research that need to be addressed. Certainly more work needs to be done in creating and implementing culturally relevant—but also valid—measures of assessment of ASD in many different languages. Interventions need to be adapted and researched in the local context. In many of these countries, parents do not receive definitive diagnoses, but still need education and support for the needs of their child, wherever they are on the autism spectrum, or if their child has intellectual disabilities. In the higher-income countries, the world of ASD and special education in general can involve many acronyms, jargon, and complex terminology that needs to be broken down and demystified for both providers and families. Furthermore, in low- and middle-income countries, biological parents may not be the primary caregivers or the daily caregivers. Primary caregivers could be other relatives, such as grandparents, aunts, neighbors, or friends. Providers need to respect and work with the family unit presented to them with the child. While interventions, assessments, and educational systems from the United States and Europe can inform policy and practice for children and families with ASD in other countries, those policies and practices should not be used without adaptation. Most critically, researchers, providers, and policy makers need to remember the important role of the cultural and local context in every step of diagnosis, intervention, education, and research to support families in ways that are meaningful and create systems that can be sustainable in the local context because they are built on local values, knowledge, and buy-in. While ASD is a worldwide phenomenon, the sustainable programs to help children and families participate actively in their communities will need to be based in those local context and cultures.

References

Abu-Hamour, B., & Muhaidat, M. (2013). Special education teachers & apos; Attitudes towards inclusion of students with autism in Jordan. *Journal of the International Association of Special Education*, 14(1), 34–40.

African Decade of Disabled Persons. (2009). Declaration of the African decade. Retrieved March 25, 2009, from www.africa-union.org/africandecade/declaration.htm

Al-Adawi, S. (2006). Adolescence in Oman. In J. J. Arnett (Ed.), *International encyclopedia of adolescence: A historical and cultural survey of young people around the world*. New York: Routledge.

Al-Farsi, Y. M., Al-Sharbati, M. M., Al-Farsi, O. A., Al-Shafaee, M. S., Brooks, D. R., & Waly, M. I. (2011). Brief report: prevalence of autistic spectrum disorders in the sultanate of Oman. *Journal of autism and developmental disorders*, 41(6), 821–825.

Al-Farsi, Y. M., Waly, M. I., Al-Sharbati, M. M., Al-Shafaee, M., Al-Farsi, O., Al-Fahdi, S., . . . Al-Adawi, S. (2013). Variation in socio-economic burden for caring of children with autism spectrum disorder in Oman: Caregiver perspectives. *Journal of Autism and Developmental Disorders*, 43(5), 1214–1221.

Al-Lamki, Z., & Ohlin, C. (1992). A Community-based study of childhood handicap in Oman. *Journal of Tropical Pediatrics*, 38(6), 314–316.

Al-Rossan, F. (2012). *Introduction to special education*. Dar Al-fker, Amman, Jordan.

Al-Shomari, T., & Al-Saratwai, Z. (2002). The Saudi and Kuwaiti standards of childhood autism rating scale (CARS): Standardization and validation. *Journal of Special Education Academy*, 1, 1–39. Arabic.

Alur, M. (2014). *ADAPT (formerly The Spastics Society of India)*. Retrieved from www.adaptssi.org/home.html. Accessed June 2, 2014.

American Psychiatric Association [APA]. (2013). *Diagnostic and statistical manual of mental disorders* (5th ed.). Washington, DC: Author.

Ametepee, L. K., & Chitiyo, M. (2009). What we know about autism in Africa: A brief research synthesis. *The Journal of the International Association of Special Education*, 10(1),11–13.

Bakare, M. O., Ebigbo, P. O., Agomoh, A. O., Eaton, J., Onyeama, G. M., Okonkwo, K. O., . . . Aguocha, C. M. (2009). Knowledge about childhood autism and opinion among healthcare workers on availability of facilities and law caring for the needs and rights of children with childhood autism and other developmental disorders in Nigeria. *BMC pediatrics*, 9(1), 1.

Bakare, M. O., Ebigbo, P. O., Agomoh, A. O., & Menkiti, N. C. (2008). Knowledge about childhood autism among health workers (KCAHW) questionnaire: Description, reliability and internal consistency. *Clinical Practice and Epidemiology in Mental Health*, 4(1), 17.

Bakare, M. O., & Munir, K. M. (2011). Autism spectrum disorders (ASD) in Africa: a perspective. *African Journal of Psychiatry*, 14(3), 208–210.

Behavior Momentum. (2014). Behavior Momentum India. Retrieved March 15, 2015 from http://behaviormomentum.com/. Accessed March 15, 2015.

Belhadj, A., Mrad, R., & Halayem, M. B. (2006). A clinic and a paraclinic study of Tunisian population of children with autism. About 63 cases. *La Tunisie medicale*, 84(12), 763–767.

Bello-Mojeed, M. A., Bakare, M. O., & Munir, K. (2014). Identification of autism spectrum disorders (ASD) in Africa: Need for shifting research and public health focus. In *Comprehensive Guide to Autism* (pp. 2437–2453). New York: Springer.

Bello-Mojeed, M. A., Ogun, O. C., Omigbodun, O. O., Adewuya, A. O., & Ladapo, H. T. O. (2011). Late identification of autistic disorder in Nigeria: An illustration with 2 case reports. *Nigerian Journal of Psychiatry*, 9(2).

Beresford B (1995) Resources and strategies: How parents cope with the care of a disabled child. *Journal of Child Psychology and Psychiatry* 35(1): 171–209.

Bilgin H. & Kucuk L. (2010) Raising an autistic child: Perspectives from Turkish mothers. *Journal of Child and Adolescent Psychiatric Nursing* 23, 92–99.

Callaway, A. (2000). *Deaf children in China*. Washington, DC: Gallaudet University.

Chakrabarti, S. (2009). Early identification of autism. *Indian Pediatrics*, 46, 412–414.

Chen, Y. (1996). Making special education compulsory and inclusive in China. *Cambridge Journal of Education*, 26(1), 47–58.

Clark, E. & Zhou, Z. (2005). Autism in China: From acupuncture to applied behavior analysis. *Psychology in School*, 42(3), 285–295.

Daley, B. J. (2002). Context: Implications for learning in professional practices. In M.V. Alfred (ed.), Learning and sociocultural contexts: Implications for adults, community, and workplace education (pp. 79-88). San Francisco: Jossey Bass. (New Directions for Adult and Continuing Education, No. 96).

Daly, M. (2004) *Families and family life in Ireland. Challenges for the future, report of public consultation for a*. Department of Social & Family Affairs. Retrieved from www.welfare.ie/en/downloads/iyf2004.pdf. Accessed June 2, 2015.

Daley, T. C., & Sigman, M. D. (2002). Diagnostic conceptualization of autism among Indian psychiatrists, psychologists, and pediatricians. *Journal of Autism and Developmental Disorders*, 32,12–23.

Desai, M. U., Divan, G., Wertz, F. J., & Patel, V. (2012). The discovery of autism: Indian parents' experiences of caring for their child with an autism spectrum disorder. *Transcultural Psychiatry*, 49(3–4), 613–637.

Dhar, R. (2009). Living with a developmentally disabled child: Attitude of family members in India. *The Social Science Journal*, 46, 738–755.

Dixon, P., Badoe, E. V., & Owusu, N. A. V. (2015). Family Perspectives of Autism Spectrum Disorders in Urban Ghana. *JICNA*, 1(1).

Divan, G., Vajaratkar, V., Desai, M. U., Strik-Lievers, L., & Patel, V. (2012). Challenges, coping strategies, and unmet needs of families with a child with autism spectrum disorder in Goa, India. *Autism Research*, 5(3), 190–200.

Dunst, C. J., Trivette, C. M., & Hamby, D. W. (2007). Meta-analysis of family-centered help giving practices research. *Mental Retardation and Developmental Disabilities Research Reviews*, 13(4), 370–378.

Dyches, T. T., Wilder, L. K., Sudweeks, R. R., Obiakor, F. E., & Algozzine, B. (2004). Multicultural issues in autism. *Journal of autism and developmental disorders*, 34(2), 211–222.

Eapen, V., Mabrouk, A. A., Zoubeidi, T., & Yunis, F. (2007). Prevalence of pervasive developmental disorders in preschool children in the UAE. *Journal of Tropical Pediatrics*, 53(3), 202–205.

Edwardraj, S., Mumtaj, K., Prasad, J. H., Kuruvilla, A., & Jacob, K. S. (2010). Perceptions about intellectual disability: A qualitative study from Vellore, South India. *Journal of Intellectual Disability Research*, 54, 736–748.

Ellsworth, N. J., & Zhang, C. (2007). Progress and Challenges in China's Special Education Development Observations, Reflections, and Recommendations. *Remedial and Special Education*, 28(1), 58–64.

Elsabbagh, M., Divan, G., Koh, Y. J., Kim, Y. S., Kauchali, S., Marcín, C., ...
Yasamy, M. T. (2012). Global prevalence of autism and other pervasive developmental disorders. *Autism Research*, 5(3), 160–179.

Fakolade, O. A., & Adeniyi, S. O. (2009). Attitude of teachers toward the inclusion of children with special needs in the general education classroom: The
case of teachers in selected schools in Nigeria. *The Journal of the International
Association of Special Education,* 10(1), 60–64.

Farrugia, D. (2009) Exploring stigma: Medical knowledge and the stigmatisation
of parents of children diagnosed with autism spectrum disorder. *Sociology of
Health & Illness*, 31: 1011–1027.

Feinstein, M. M. (2010). *Holocaust survivors in postwar Germany, 1945–1957.*
Cambridge: Cambridge University Press.

Feng, L., Li, C., Chiu, H., Lee, T. S., Spencer, M. D., & Wong, J. C. (2013).
Autism spectrum disorder in Chinese populations: A brief review. *Asia-Pacific
Psychiatry*, 5, 54–60.

Fong, C. Y. G., & Hung, A. (2002). Public awareness, attitude, and understanding of epilepsy in Hong Kong Special Administrative Region, China. *Epilepsia*,
43(3), 311–316.

Freeth, M., Milne, E., Sheppard, E., & Ramachandran, R. (2014). Autism
across cultures: Perspectives from non-Western cultures and implications
for research. *Handbook of Autism and Pervasive Developmental Disorders,
Fourth Edition.*

Gadow, K. D., Schwartz, J., DeVincent, C., Strong, G., & Cuva, S. (2008).
Clinical utility of autism spectrum disorder scoring algorithms for the child
symptom inventory-4. *Journal of Autism and Developmental Disorders*, 38(3),
419–427.

Grinker, R. R. (2008). *Unstrange minds: Remapping the world of autism.* Cambridge,
MA: Da Capo Press.

Grinker, R. R., Chambers, N., Njongwe, N., Lagman, A. E., Guthrie, W.,
Stronach, S., ... Yucel, F. (2012). "Communities" in community engagement:
Lessons learned from autism research in South Korea and South Africa. *Autism
Research*, 5(3), 201–210.

Grinker, R. R., & Cho, K. (2013). Border children: Interpreting autism spectrum
disorder in South Korea. *Ethos*, 41(1), 46–74.

Gu, Y. (2007, January 11). Gudu zheng ertong qidai geng duo guanzhu [Children
with autism look forward to more attention]. *Xinwen Shijie (News World)*.

Gupta A., & Singhal, N. (2004). Positive perceptions in parents of children with
disabiilties. *Asia Pacific Disability Rehabilitation Journal*, 15, 22–35.

Gutstein, S. E., Burgess, A. F., & Montfort, K. (2007). Evaluation of the relationship development intervention program. *Autism*, 11(5), 397–411.

Hippensteel, L. F. (2008). *Comparative study: Educating a student with autism
in Tanzania and the United States.* University of Tennessee Honors Thesis.
Projects. Retrieved from http://trace.tennessee.edu/utk_chanhonoproj/1192.
Accessed March 12, 2015.

Holroyd, R. A. (2003). *Fields of experience: Young people's constructions of
embodied identities.* Unpublished dissertation, Loughborough University,
Loughborough.

Huang, A. X., & Wheeler, J. J. (2007). Including children with autism in general education in China. *Childhood Education, 83*(6), 356–360.

Hudec, T. (2012). *The attitudes of social workers in Kerala to complementary and alternative interventions for children with autism spectrum disorders* (Doctoral dissertation, Doctoral thesis). Masarkova University, Czech Republic. Retrieved from http://is.muni.cz/th/365957/fss_m/Attitudes-Kerala. pdf). Accessed March 12, 2015.

Igwe, M. N., Ahanotu, A. C., Bakare, M. O., Achor, J. U., & Igwe, C. (2011). Assessment of knowledge about childhood autism among paediatric and psychiatric nurses in Ebonyi state, Nigeria. *Child & Adolescent Psychiatry & Mental Health, 5*, 1–8.

Institute for Child Development. (2015). ICD-Treatment. Retrieved from www.icddelhi.org/index.html. Accessed March 12, 2015.

IRIS. (2010). Institute for Remedial Intervention Services (IRIS). Retrieved February 15, 2015, from www.autismindia.com/index.php. Accessed March 12, 2015.

Jegatheesan, B., Miller, P. J., & Fowler, S. A. (2010). Autism from a religious perspective: A study of parental beliefs in South Asian Muslim immigrant families. *Focus on Autism and Other Developmental Disabilities, 25*(2), 98–109.

Kalabula, M. D. (2000). Inclusive education in Africa: A myth or reality? A Zambian case. Retrieved May 1, 2005, from www.isec2000.org.uk/abstracts/papers_k/ kkalabula_1.htm.

Kalyanpur, M. (2008). The paradox of majority underrepresentation in special education in India: Constructions of difference in a developing country. *The Journal of Special Education, 42*, 55–64. doi:10.1177/0022466907313610

Kawamura, Y., Takahashi, O., & Ishii, T. (2008). Reevaluating the incidence of pervasive developmental disorders: Impact of elevated rates of detection through implementation of an integrated system of screening in Toyota, Japan. *Psychiatry and Clinical Neurosciences, 62*(2), 152–159.

Kembhavi, G. (2009). *Perceptions of participation and inclusion among adolescents with disabilities: Experiences from South India.* London: London Publishers.

Khan, N., & Hombarume, J. (1996). Levels of autistic behaviour among the mentally handicapped children in Zimbabwe. *The Central African journal of medicine, 42*(2), 36–39.

Khoshabi, K. (2003). The Adjustment Mechanisms in Parents with Autistic Child. The 5th National Conference on Children Intellectual Disability. Homepage of University of Social Welfare and Rehabilitation. Retrieved from www.rehabiran.net/ViewMqlh.aspx?&cd=759. Accessed March 12, 2015.

Krishnamurthy, V. (2008). A clinical experience of autism in India. *Journal of Developmental & Behavioral Pediatrics, 29*(4), 331–333.

Kritzer, J. B. (2011). Special education in China. *Eastern Education Journal, 40*(1), 57–63.

Krug, D. A., Arick, J., & Almond, P. (1980). Behaviour checklist for identifying severely handicapped individuals with high levels of autistic behaviour. *Journal of Child Psychology and Psychiatry, 21*, 221–229.

Li, N., Chen, G., Song, X., Du, W., & Zheng, X. (2011). Prevalence of autism-caused disability among Chinese children: A national population-based survey. *Epilepsy & Behavior, 22*(4), 786–789.

Li, X., & Chen, J. (2004). *Diagnosis of Autism*. Changsha, China: Central South University Press.

Liu, Y., & Wen, J. (2006). The investigation of the current situation on the education of autistic children in rural areas in Jiangxi Province. *Agricultural Archaeology*, 6, 32–33.

Lord, C., Risi, S., Lambrecht, L., Cook Jr., E. H., Leventhal, B. L., DiLavore, P. C., . . . Rutter, M. (2000). The Autism Diagnostic Observation Schedule—Generic: A standard measure of social and communication deficits associated with the spectrum of autism. *Journal of autism and developmental disorders*, 30(3), 205–223.

Lord, C., Storoschuk, S., Rutter, M., & Pickles, A. (1993). Using the ADI-R to diagnose autism in preschool children. *Infant Mental Health Journal*, 14, 234–252.

Lotter, V. (1978). Childhood autism in Africa. *Journal of Child Psychology and Psychiatry*, 19(3), 231–244.

Lu, C., Zhang, X., & Liu, H. (2008). The investigation of the current situation on hospital referral and rehabilitation of autistic children in Tianjin city. *Chinese Journal of Rehabilitation Medicine*, 23, 79–80.

McCabe, H. (2003). The beginnings of inclusion in the People's Republic of China. *Research and Practice for Persons with Severe Disabilities*, 28(1), 16–22.

Mak, W. W., & Kwok, Y. T. (2010). Internalization of stigma for parents of children with autism spectrum disorder in Hong Kong. *Social Science & Medicine*, 70(12), 2045–2051.

Mandell, D. S., & Novak, M. (2005). The role of culture in families' treatment decisions for children with autism spectrum disorders. *Mental Retardation and Developmental Disabilities Research Reviews*, 11(2), 110–115.

Mankoski, R. E., Collins, M., Ndosi, N. K., Mgalla, E. H., Sarwatt, V. V., & Folstein, S. E. (2006). Etiologies of autism in a case-series from Tanzania. *Journal of Autism and Developmental Disorders*, 36(8), 1039–1051.

Manohari, S., Raman, V., & Ashok, M. (2013). Use of Vineland Adaptive Behavior Scales-II in children with autism—an Indian experience. *Journal of Indian Association for Child and Adolescent Mental Health*, 9(1), 5–12.

Mbwilo, G., Smide, B., & Aarts, C. (2010). Family perceptions in caring for children and adolescents with mental disabilities: A qualitative study from Tanzania. *Tanzania Journal of Health Research*, 12(2), 129–137.

McCabe, H. (2004). *State, society and disability: Supporting families of children with autism in the People's Republic of China*. Unpublished dissertation, Indiana University.

McCabe, H. (2007). Parent advocacy in the face of adversity autism and families in the People's Republic of China. *Focus on Autism and Other Developmental Disabilities*, 22(1), 39–50.

McCabe, H. (2008a). Autism and family in the People's Republic of China: Learning from parents' perspectives. *Research & Practice for Persons with Severe Disabilities*, 33(1/2), 37–47.

McCabe, H. (2008b). The importance of parent-to-parent support among families of children with autism in the People's Republic of China. *International Journal of Disability, Development and Education*, 55(4), 303–314.

McCabe, H. (2013). Bamboo shoots after the rain: Development and challenges of autism intervention in China. *Autism: The International Journal of Research and Practice*, 17(5), 510–526.

McCabe, H., & McCabe, K. (2013). Disability and family in the People's Republic of China: Implementation, benefits, and comparison of two mutual support groups. *Journal of Intellectual & Developmental Disability*, 38(1), 12–22. doi: 10.3109/13668250.2012.756462

McNally, A., & Mannan, H. (2013). Perceptions of caring for children with disabilities: Experiences from Moshi, Tanzania. *African Journal of Disability*, 2(1), 1–10.

Miles, S., & Kaplan, I. (2005). Using images to promote reflection: An action research study in Zambia and Tanzania. *Journal of Research in Special Educational Needs*, 5(2), 77–83.

Miranda-Linne, F. M., & Melin, L. (2002). A factor analytic study of the Autism Behavior Checklist. *Journal of Autism and Developmental Disorders*, 32(3), 181–188.

Morad, M., Nasri, Y., & Merrick, J. (2001). Islam and the person with intellectual disability. *Journal of Religion, Disability and Health*, 5, 65–71.

Narayan, J., Chakravarti, S. N., David, J., & Kanniappan, M. (2005). Analysis of educational support systems for children with mental retardation and autism spectrum disorders. *International Journal of Rehabilitation Research*, 28(4), 365–368.

National Center for Autism India. (2015). Open Door Programme. Retrieved from www.autism-india.org/open-door-day-programme. Accessed March 12, 2015.

Panerai, S., Ferrante, L., & Caputo, V. (1997). The TEACCH strategy in mentally retarded children with autism: A multidimensional assessment. Pilot study. Treatment and education of autistic and communication handicapped children. *Journal of Autism and Developmental Disorders*, 27, 345–347.

Pang, Y., & Richey, D. (2006). The development of special education in China. *International Journal of Special Education*, 21(1), 77–86.

Profanter A (2009) Facing the challenges of children and youth with special abilities and needs on the fringes of Omani society. *Children and Youth Services Review*, 31, 8–15.

Read, N., & Schofield, A. (2010). Autism: Are mental health services failing children and parents? *Journal of Family Health Care*, 20, 120–124.

Rendle-Short, J., Clancy, H., & Dugdale, A. (1969). The diagnosis of infantile autism. *Developmental Medicine and Child Neurology*, 11, 432–442.

Rudra, A., Banerjee, S., Singhal, N., Barua, M., Mukerji, S., & Chakrabarti, B. (2014). Translation and usability of autism screening and diagnostic tools for autism spectrum conditions in India. *Autism Research*, 7(5), 598–607.

Sabih, S., & Sajid, W.B. (2008). There is a significant stress among parents having children with autism. *Rawalpindi Medical Journal*, 33, 2, 214–216.

Samadi, S. A., McConkey, R., & Kelly, G. (2013). Enhancing parental well-being and coping through a family-centered short course for Iranian parents of children with an autism spectrum disorder. *Autism: The International Journal of Research And Practice*, 17(1), 27–43.

Samadi, S. A., Mahmoodizadeh, A., & McConkey, R. (2012). A national study of the prevalence of autism among five-year-old children in Iran. *Autism*, 16(1), 5–14.

Schopler, E., Reichler, R. J., DeVellis, R. F., & Daly, K. (1980). Toward objective classification of childhood autism: Childhood Autism Rating Scale (CARS). *Journal of Autism and Developmental Disorders*, 10(1), 91–103.

Seif Eldin, A., Habib, D., Noufal, A., Farrag, S., Bazaid, K., Al-Sharbati, M., . . . Gaddour, N. (2008). Use of M-CHAT for a multinational screening of young children with autism in the Arab countries. *International Review of Psychiatry*, 20(3), 281–289.

Shang, X . (2002). Looking for a better way to care for children: Cooperation between the state and civil society in China. *Social Service Review*, 76, 203–228. doi:10.1086/339671

Silberberg, D., Arora, N., Bhutani, V., Durkin, M., Gulati, S., Nair, M., & Pinto-Martin, J. (2014). Neuro-Developmental Disorders in India-From Epidemiology to Public Policy (P.7.324). *Neurology*, 82(10 Supplement), P7. 324.

Singh, K. (2008). *Inclusion of Children with Autism Handbook for Teachers*. Retrieved fromwww.thenationaltrust.co.in/nt/images/stories/Other_ Publication/handbook_for_teachers.pdf. Accessed March 12, 2015.

Smith, C. (2014). The global challenge of autism. *House Hearing of the Subcommittee on Africa, Global Health, Global Human Rights and International Organizations*. Retrieved from http://chrissmith.house.gov/uploadedfiles/ 2014-07-23_global_autism_hearing.pdf. Accessed June 2, 2015.

Stone-MacDonald, A. (2014). *Community-based education for students with developmental disabilities in Tanzania*. Dordrecht, Netherlands: Springer.

Stone-MacDonald, A., & Butera, G. (2012). Cultural beliefs and attitudes about disability in Sub-Saharan Africa. *Review of Disability Studies*, 8, 62–77.

Su, X., Long, T., Chen, L., & Fang, J. (2013). Early intervention for children with autism spectrum disorders in China: A family perspective. *Infants and Young Children*, 26(2), 111–125.

Sun, X., Allison, C., Auyeung, B., Matthews, F. E., Baron-Cohen, S., & Brayne, C. (2013). Service provision for autism in mainland China: Preliminary mapping of service pathways. *Social Science & Medicine*, 98, 87–94. doi: 10.1016/j. socscimed.2013.08.016

The Autism Information and Resource Center (2011). *Interventions of Autism*. Retrieved from http://autismresourcecenter.in/Interventions.aspx. Accessed June 2, 2016.

The Global Call for Autism: Hearing Before Subcommittee on Africa, Global Health, Global Human Rights, And International Organizations of the Committee on Foreign Affairs of *the House of Representatives*.113th Cong. 1 (2014).

Tsang, H. W. H., Tam, P. K. C., Chan, F., & Cheung, W. M. (2003). Stigmatizing attitudes towards individuals with mental illness in Hong Kong: Implications for their recovery. *Journal of Community Psychology*, 31, 383–396.

United States House, & Committee on Foreign Affairs, S. o. A., Global Health Global Human Rights and International, Organizations. (2014). The global challenge of autism: Hearing before the Subcommittee on Africa, Global Health, Global Human Rights, and International Organizations of the Committee on Foreign Affairs, House of Representatives, One Hundred Thirteenth Congress, second session, July 24, 2014.

Wan, M. W., Green, J., Elsabbagh, M., Johnson, M., Charman, T., & Plummer, F. (2013). Quality of interaction between at-risk infants and caregiver at 12–15 months is associated with 3-year autism outcome. *Journal of Child Psychology and Psychiatry*, 54(7), 763–771.

Wang, Y., Wang, G., & Wang, Y. (2003). Analysis of childhood autism by using Clancy autism behaviour scale and autism behaviour checklist. *Journal of Shandong University (Health Sciences)*, 41, 213–214.

Wong, S. Y., Wong, T. K.S., Martinson, I., Lai, A. C., Chen, W.J., & He, Y.S. (2004) Needs of Chinese parents of children with developmental disability. *Journal of Intellectual Disabilities*, 8, 141–158.

World Health Organization *(1992), ICD-10 Classification of mental and behavioral disorders, clinical description and diagnostic guidelines.* Geneva: World Health Organization.

Xiong, C., Jiang, Q.-J., Li, D., Liu, N., Yang, C., Zheng, X., & Zhang, J. (2011). Analysis on the detection's diagnosis and treatment times of children with autism. *Maternal and Child Health Care of China*, 26, 4688–4690.

Yan, Y. B. (2005). Wo guo ruozhi renshi shehui fuwu xianzhuang [The current situation of social services for individuals with mental retardation in China]. *Shehui fuli [China Social Welfare]*, 4, 43–45.

Yang, H., & Wang, H. (1994). Special education in China. *The Journal of Special Education*, 28(1), 93–105.

Yang, L. H., & Pearson, V. J . (2002). Understanding families in their own context: Schizophrenia and structural family therapy in Beijing. *Journal of Family Therapy*, 24, 233–257. doi:10.1111/1467-6427.00214

Yang, X., Huang, Y., Jia, M., & Chen, S. (1993). Analysis of Autism Behavior Checklist. *Chinese Mental Health Journal*, 7(6), 279–280, 275.

Yu, X., & Takahashi, S. (2009). Problems of establishing an early diagnosis and detecting system for autism in China: A survey of doctors at medical institutions. *Journal of Japanese Special Education*, 46(6), 489–502.

Zhang, D., & Spencer, V. G. (2015). Addressing the needs of students with autism and other disabilities in China: Perspectives from the field. *International Journal of Disability, Development & Education*, 62(2), 168–181. doi: 10.1080/1034912X.2014.998175

Zhang, X., & Ji, C. Y. (2005). Autism and mental retardation of young children in China. *Biomedical and Environmental Sciences*, 18, 334–340.

Chapter 6

Early Intervention Services for Children with Autism

Angel Fettig and Veronica P. Fleury

Introduction

The rising prevalence of Autism Spectrum Disorder (ASD) has increasingly become an important public health concern with significant impact on early intervention systems, schools, and communities. Children's caregivers and other close family members often notice some early behavioral indicators associated with ASD before the age of two years, although the child may not receive a medical diagnosis until later. National efforts by government and private organizations are focused towards improving public awareness of early behavioral indicators facilitating accurate and earlier diagnosis, which enables children to access critical early intervention services. It is well documented that early intervention services play a critical role in maximizing outcomes and reducing debilitating impact for children with ASD (Hume, Bellini, Pratt, 2005; National Research Council, 2001; Rogers, 1999; Woods & Wetherby, 2003). This chapter provides an overview of the purpose of early intervention services, specific interventions available for children with ASD, and issues and factors to consider when examining early intervention services for children with ASD.

Purpose of Early Intervention

Early intervention services for infants and toddlers with special needs from birth to age three have been a part of the Individuals with Disabilities Education Act (IDEA) since 1986. This section of the law is commonly known as *Part C of IDEA*. Early intervention focuses on providing family centered services for children from birth to age three who have disabilities or are at risk for developmental delays. Eligibility for these services is determined by evaluating the child to see if a delay in development or a disability exists. Children who meet these criteria can receive early intervention services from birth through their third birthday, and sometimes beyond if further services are warranted. Sometimes caregivers and professionals know from the moment a child is born that early intervention services will be essential in helping the child grow and develop. This is often the case for children who are diagnosed at birth with a specific condition or who experience significant prematurity, very low birth weight, illness, or surgery soon after being born. Even before heading home from the hospital, these children's parents may be given a referral to their local early intervention office to facilitate the start of the process into early intervention services. Some children, like those with ASD, have a relatively routine entry into the world, but may develop more slowly than others, experience setbacks, or be diagnosed with a specific disability in the first few years of their lives. For these children, a visit with a developmental pediatrician and a thorough evaluation may lead to an early intervention referral.

The IDEA provides states with federal grants to institute early intervention programs. Any child younger than age three who is experiencing significant delays in his or her development, or has a physical or mental condition likely to result in a developmental delay, is eligible to receive early intervention services through these programs. Early intervention services can vary from state to state and region to region. However, the services should address the child's unique needs and should not be limited to what is currently available or customary in the region where the child is being served. Based on a comprehensive evaluation by a team of developmental experts, an Individual Family Service Program (IFSP) is created, which documents the child's needs, goals, and services that will be provided to the child and his/her family. Additional information about legislation and service delivery is covered in an earlier chapter in this text (see Chapter 3).

Early Detection of ASD

Our knowledge regarding early behavioral manifestations of ASD has grown tremendously over the past decade. Many behavioral symptoms often can be detected in children as young as 18 months of age. Although experienced professionals can provide reliable diagnoses by the age of two, many children do not receive a final diagnosis until they are much older. This is due to a number of factors, particularly limited access to high-quality healthcare providers who are knowledgeable about ASD and a prevailing stigma associated with pursuing a diagnosis in some cultural groups (Lord et al., 2006). National public efforts by the American Academy of Pediatrics (AAP, 2007) in concert with professional organizations such as the Center for Disease Control's Learn the Signs Campaign, Autism Speaks, and First Signs (http://firstsigns.org/) have improved both procedures for detection and public awareness about early behaviors that may indicate a risk for ASD. These early behaviors, oftentimes referred to as *red flags*, reflect the core difficulties and characteristics of ASD, namely problems with social interaction, communication, and the *red*

Table 6.1 Early Red Flags for ASD

Behavior of Concern	Description
Impairment in Social Interaction	
Lack of appropriate eye gaze	Child does not consistently make eye contact with people or looks at objects from unusual angles.
Lack of joyful expressions with gaze	Child does not direct smiles or laughs to another person
Lack of response to name	Child does not immediately look or attend when his/her name is called
Lack of sharing interest or enjoyment	Child does not show, draw attention to objects of interests for the purpose of sharing enjoyment
Impairment in Communication	
Limited use of showing gestures	Child does not hold an object out towards others in order to bring another's attention to the object
Lack of coordination of nonverbal communication	No back and forth sharing of enjoyment. Non-verbal communicative attempts are not well integrated (i.e. child may point to an object, but does not pair it with eye contact)
Unusual prosody of verbal language	Child's cries/speech has little variation in pitch, odd intonation, irregular rhythm, and/or unusual voice quality
Repetitive behaviors and restricted interests	
Repetitive movements of objects	Child plays with objects the same way repeatedly in a stereotyped or repeated fashion (taps, spins, lines up, etc.)
Repetitive movements or posturing of body, arms, hands, or fingers	Repetitive movements or posturing of body, arms, hands, or fingers

Note: This table summarizes potential early behaviors commonly exhibited by two-year-old children based on research conducted by Wetherby, A., Woods, J., Allen, L., Cleary, J., Dickinson, H., & Lord, C. (2004). Early indicators of autism spectrum disorders in the second year of life, *Journal of Autism and Developmental Disorders*, 34, 473–493.

flags. Caregivers of infants who show two or more of these behaviors are encouraged to talk to their child's pediatric healthcare provider (AAP 2006; Wetherby et al., 2004).

The AAP recommends that pediatricians screen all children specifically for ASD during the 18-month and 24-month regular well-child visits in addition to general developmental surveillance and screening during regular well-child visits. Many screening instruments rely solely on parents' responses to a questionnaire, while others involve a combination of parent report and direct observation. Screening tools are designed to be quick to administer and enable practitioners to focus on key *red flags* of ASD to guide their decision about whether further evaluation

Table 6.2 Autism Screening Tools

Screening Tool	Description	Admin Time	Who Completes
Autism Behavior Checklist (ABC) (Krug, Arick, & Almonmd, 1980)	ABC is used to assess behaviors and symptoms of autism in the categories of sensory, relating, body and object use, language, and social and self-help for children aged three and older.	10–20 mins	Parents or teachers; scored by professionals
Ages & Stages Questionnaire: Social- Emotional (ASQ-SE 2) (Squires, Bricker, & Twombly, 2009)	ASQ-SE focuses on identifying social emotional behavior for children ages 1–72 months.	10–15 mins	Parents and caregivers
Brief Infant Toddler Social Emotional Assessment (BITSEA) (Briggs-Gowen, J. & Carter, A., 2002)	BITSEA is a brief comprehensive screening instrument to evaluate social and emotional behavior for children ages 12–36 months.	7–10 mins	Parents and childcare providers
Communication and Symbolic Behavior Scales Developmental Profile Infant/Toddler Checklist (CSBS-DP) (Wetherby & Prizant, 2002)	CSBS-DP is a screening tool used to identify children ages 6–24 months in need of further evaluation for autism and other developmental delays.	5–10 mins	Parents and caregivers
Modified Checklist for Autism in Toddlers (MCHAT) Checklist for Autism in Toddlers (CHAT) (Robins, Fein, & Barton, 2009)	M-CHAT is designed for children of 16–30 months of age and assesses risk for autism spectrum disorder.	5–10 mins	Parents and caregivers
Screening Tool for Autism in Two-Year-Olds (STAT) (Stone, McMahon, & Henderson, 2008)	STAT is designed to screen for autism in children between 24 and 36 months of age.	20 mins	Service providers and clinicians

is needed. A list of ASD-specific screening tools is outlined in Table 6.2. By having procedures to identify children at risk for ASD combined with overall improved awareness of *red flags* means that children are being diagnosed at earlier ages, which ultimately translates to earlier opportunities to access important intervention.

Young children with ASD often have difficulty participating in appropriate play, meeting developmental milestones, communicating effectively with others, developing friendships, and conforming to expected behavioral norms. It is important that children with ASD start receiving services to address these concerns as soon as ASD is suspected. The effectiveness of early intervention has been clearly demonstrated by research (National Research Council, 2001). The question is no longer *Does early intervention work?* Rather, it is *How early can we intervene?* Some researchers believe that treatment will be most effective if intervention services begin before a child's second birthday. Accordingly, many professionals advocate for treatment to begin as soon as any early behavioral *red flags* are detected rather than waiting for a formal clinical diagnosis. The rationale behind this thinking is that the early behavioral characteristics of ASD prevent a young child from interacting with their environment, and people within their environment, in meaningful ways that are believed to promote healthy development. Interventions that enable young children at risk for ASD to become more socially engaged and interactive can change a child's developmental trajectory, and even prevent these early symptoms from exacerbating to a point where they would no longer reach the clinical threshold for ASD (Dawson, 2008).

Approaches to Intervention

Over the years, treatments have been developed for children with ASD to address the core symptoms associated with ASD: social-communication and behavioral difficulties; however, children with ASD may also benefit from additional services to address any broader developmental needs. Accordingly, early intervention services for children with ASD vary depending on a child's individual needs and may include, but are not limited to, early intensive behavioral intervention speech and language therapy, occupational therapy, and physical therapy. In this section, we will first describe common services that children with ASD may receive as part of their early intervention programming. Although each of these services may differ in their focus, service providers should incorporate instructional strategies (referred to as *Focused Intervention Strategies*) that have strong evidentiary support as the basis for their instruction. Recommended focused intervention strategies for children with ASD are discussed later in this section.

Early Intensive Behavioral Intervention (EIBI)

Some families with children with ASD may choose to participate in EIBI programming in an effort to improve overall developmental outcomes for their affected child. Sometimes referred to as *Comprehensive Treatment Models* (CTM), these programs consist of a set of practices designed to achieve a broad learning or developmental impact on the core deficits of ASD (CTM; Odom, Boyd, Hall, & Hume, 2010). Specific instructional approaches vary across programming, as do the amount of time children spend receiving services (range: 12–40 hours per week). The National Academy of Science Committee on Educational Interventions for Children with Autism (National Research Council, 2001) identified 10 CTMs. Examples include the UCLA Young Autism Program by Lovaas and colleagues (Smith, Groen, & Winn, 2000), the TEACCH program developed by Schopler and colleagues (Marcus, Schopler, & Lord, 2000), the LEAP model (Strain & Hoyson, 2000), and the Denver model, designed by Rogers and colleagues (Rogers, Hall, Osaki, Reaven, & Herbison, 2000). It should be noted that most of the research that has been conducted with these models focuses on preschool-age or older children.

Speech and Language Therapy

Children with ASD vary widely in their speech and communication needs. Some children never develop functional speech and will learn to communicate using augmentative and alternative communication. Licensed speech language pathologists (SLP) can work with young children to teach them an effective means of communicating. Options range from low-technology systems, such as using pictures to communicate (i.e. Picture Exchange Communication System; Bondy and Frost, 2001) to high-technology systems that include voice-output devices once children are older. Children with ASD who develop speech may continue to face difficulty with pragmatics of language, or the social application of using speech. For these children, SLP services will consist of teaching children to appropriately engage in conversations with others.

Occupational Therapy (OT)

OT focuses on helping children to be as independent as possible in all areas of their daily goals and routines. According to the American Therapy Association (2010) for young children with ASD, the scope of OT services generally focuses on self-management skills (e.g. dressing, feeding, hygiene, and sleep), regulation of emotional and behavioral responses, processing of sensory information to ensure participation in natural settings, and development of social and interpersonal skills and peer relationships.

Physical Therapy (PT)

Children with ASD often have challenges with motor skills such as sitting, walking, running, or jumping. PT focuses on addressing poor muscle tone, balance, and coordination to improve the motor skills for these children so their developmental and functional obstacles are reduced and they are able to participate in their natural routines and environments. Early intervention services are designed to meet the specific needs of the children with ASD and their families, therefore no two children will have the exact same learning goals or services. Children with ASD may receive early intervention services to address global developmental delays as well as symptoms specific to ASD. These services should occur in children's natural environments, that is, settings that are typical for children. During early childhood, these settings can include, but are not limited to, the family's home, childcare programs, and other community settings.

Focused Intervention Strategies

The intervention literature for children with ASD has grown dramatically over the past decade. Practitioners and parents are bombarded with conflicting information regarding treatment options, some of which are ineffective or potentially harmful. Fortunately, there are resources that are publicly available to assist practitioners and parents in selecting strategies that are supported by research. Researchers with the National Professional Development Center on ASD (NPDC) published a technical report in which they summarized the results of a systematic review of the intervention research for individuals with ASD from birth to age 21 (Wong et al., 2014). In this review, the researchers identified 27 evidence-based practices (EBP) that address a number of different outcomes for individuals with ASD. Out of a total of 446 studies included in the NPDC review, only 30 studies included a child under the age of three (Wong, Fleury, & Fettig, 2013). Because this review only included research that targeted individuals who were identified as having ASD, this small number of studies is not surprising given that the average age of diagnosis is age three or later (Lord et al., 2006). There is clearly a need to continue to conduct research to identify and validate strategies that are effective for infants and toddlers at risk for ASD.

Parent-implemented Interventions

In nearly half of all of the studies targeting young children with ASD in the NPDC report, parents were trained to deliver interventions with their toddler. Family-centered practices are the cornerstones of early intervention services. One of the key missions of early intervention is to build on and support the families' and caregivers' confidence and competence as they nurture their children's development (Workgroup on Principles and Practices in Natural Environments, 2008). The family-centered approach highlights that family contexts and experiences are critical to a child's development and early intervention service providers must recognize that the family is the constant unit in the child's life and development (Bruder, 2000). Families know their children best and can provide an important source of information to ensure that early intervention services are meeting the needs of the child and their families. Early interventionists focus on preparing families and caregivers with skills they need to support the use of intervention skills in their daily lives. Involving families and caregivers in implementing intervention strategies allows the maximization of intervention provided in early intervention practices because families and caregivers can continue to support their child in using the learned skills throughout their daily routines.

In parent-implemented intervention (PII) programs, a toddler's caregiver is responsible for carrying out some or all of the components of the intervention. Caregivers are typically trained by the professional or member of the research team in either their homes or in community settings. The methods used to train caregivers vary across programs, but often will include didactic instruction, discussion, modeling, coaching, and feedback about the caregiver's performance (Schultz, 2013). Common toddler behaviors that are targeted in these programs also vary, but typically focus on improving communication, play, and self-help skills and/or decreasing challenging behavior. A major benefit of PII programs is that caregivers are empowered to interact with their children in a meaningful way, which can have major benefits in the child's development as well as improve overall family functioning. A description of different PII research that was included in the NPDC review can be found in Table 6.3.

Other Focused Intervention Approaches used with Toddlers

Interventions implemented by parents are the most commonly researched intervention practice for children under the age of three; however, researchers have begun to explore the use of other strategies to improve social-communication skills and reduce challenging behaviors for toddlers with ASD. The following list of intervention strategies did not have sufficient research to qualify as evidence-based practices for toddlers according to NPDC criteria; however, they have some preliminary research that included at least one child with ASD under the age of three:

- *Prompting*. Prompting procedures involve an adult providing additional assistance so that the toddler successfully demonstrates a target skill. Prompts can take different forms depending on the skill being taught and the toddler's learning style. Common forms of prompting

Table 6.3 Parent Implemented Interventions that Included Toddlers with ASD

Study	Intervention	Outcomes
Aldred, Green, & Adams (2004)	Parents were trained to use adapted communication tailored to their child's individual competencies.	Significant improvements made in children's total ADOS scores, particularly in the areas of social interaction, expressive language, social initiations, and parent–child interactions.
Green, et al. (2010)	Preschool Autism Communication Trial [PACT]. Parents were taught to increase their sensitivity and responsiveness to children's communicative attempts.	Improvements in children's overall autism severity as measured by the ADOS, parent–child interaction, expressive language skills, and adaptive skills.
Jocelyn, Casiro, Beattie, Bow, & Kneisz (1998)	12-week intervention consisting of lectures and on-site day care consultations to help caregivers to predict behavior, improve communication, and enhance mutual enjoyment in activities. Caregivers were taught to use functional analysis to understand problem behaviors and facilitate language and social development.	Improvements in children's language ability, caregivers' knowledge about ASD, greater perception of control on the part of mothers, and greater parent satisfaction.
Kasari, Gulsrud, Wong, Kwon, & Locke (2010)	8-week intervention that used developmental procedures of responsive and facilitative interaction methods as well as aspects of applied behavior analysis. Parents were taught the following skills: following the child's lead and interest in activities, imitating child actions, talking about what the child was doing, repeating back what the child said, expanding on what the child said, giving corrective feedback, sitting close to the child and making eye contact, and making environmental adjustments to engage the child.	Improvements in joint engagement, responsiveness to joint attention, and diversity of functional play acts.

Stahmer, & Gist (2001)	Assessed the effectiveness of a parent education support group in addition to an accelerated parent-education program.	Parents who participated in the parent education support group showed increased learning of teaching techniques, which led to improvement in children's language skills.
Kashinath, Woods, & Goldstein (2006)	Parents were taught to use 2 different teaching strategies. Researchers systematically selected strategies that could be embedded across different routine activities.	Parents demonstrated proficient use of teaching strategies and generalized their use across routines. The intervention had positive effects on child communication outcomes. All parents perceived the intervention to be beneficial.
Najdowski, et al. (2010)	Mothers were trained to implement differential reinforcement of alternative behavior (DRA) combined with non-removal of the spoon and demand fading for the treatment of their children's food selectivity.	Improvements in children's tolerance to different foods.
Reagon & Higbee (2009)	Three mothers of children with autism were taught to create, implement, and systematically fade scripts to promote vocal initiations during play.	Parents successfully implemented script-fading procedures in their homes and these procedures were effective in increasing children's vocal initiations during play.
Rocha, Schreibman, & Stahmer (2007)	Parents were trained to increase their joint attention bids using behavior analytic techniques to facilitate appropriate responding.	As parent joint attention bids increased, children's responses increased. Children's joint attention initiations also increased, even though this was not a direct target of the intervention.

(continued)

Table 6.3 *(continued)*

Study	Intervention	Outcomes
Schertz & Odom (2007)	Parents were taught to promote joint attention in their children. The intervention consisted of four phases: focusing on faces, turn-taking, responding to joint attention, and initiating joint attention.	All children showed improvements in engagement and joint attention.
Symon (2005)	Parents attended a week-long parent education program focused on the use of a pivotal response training intervention to improve children's social-communication skills.	Parents successfully learned the strategies and were able to train others to implement the techniques presented during the program. Additionally, the children's social communication and behaviors improved during interactions with caregivers.
Kaiser, Hancock, & Nietfeld (2000)	Parents were trained to use a naturalistic teaching strategy, called Enhanced Milieu Teaching (EMT), to improve children's social-communication skills.	Positive effects were observed on the use of communication targets for all children and on the complexity and diversity of productive language for most children.

Source: Data extracted from Wong, et al. (2014) *Evidence-based practice for children, youth, and young adults with autism spectrum disorder.* Chapel Hill, NC: Frank Porter Graham Child Development Institute.

include a physical assistance (i.e. hand-over-hand guidance), verbal (i.e. telling the child more information to demonstrate the behavior), visual (i.e. using picture cues), and gestural (i.e. pointing).

- *Reinforcement.* The consequences that occur after a toddler engages in a desired behavior can increase the likelihood that the behavior will re-occur in the future. These consequences may be purposefully manipulated by an adult, but can also occur naturally in the environment. Positive reinforcement involves the application of something pleasurable (i.e. praise, tickles, access to preferred toys) following a behavior. Negative reinforcement involves the removal of something that the toddler does not like when a child engages in the target behavior (i.e. the toddler is hot so he takes off his coat. By taking off his coat, the toddler *removes* the uncomfortable feeling of being too hot).

- *Naturalistic Intervention.* Naturalistic interventions occur within typical settings (i.e. home, childcare), activities, and routines in which toddlers participate. Naturalistic interventions may include a variety of practices such as environmental arrangements, techniques to facilitate parent–child interactions, and other strategies based on applied behavior analysis. The adult takes advantage of the toddler's interests and uses these strategies to improve the complexity of the skills, while relying on naturally reinforcing contingencies to maintain the behavior.

- *Pivotal Response Training.* Pivotal Response Training (PRT) is a type of naturalistic intervention based on principles of applied behavior analysis that is particularly effective in improving communication, play, and social behaviors in young children. PRT specifically targets behaviors that are believed to be "pivotal learning variables," specifically, motivation, responding to multiple cues, and initiating social interactions. These are believed to be pivotal skills for toddlers because they provide a foundation upon which toddlers can make generalized improvements in other areas of development.

- *Functional Behavior Assessment.* Challenging behaviors are believed to have a communicative function. Toddlers may engage in challenging behaviors in order to obtain something (e.g. parent's attention; access to a desired item) or escape undesired activities or parental demands. Functional behavior assessment (FBA) provides a systematic way for professionals to determine the underlying communicative function of a challenging behavior. The FBA process involves collecting data through a variety of methods (i.e. observation, parent report) in order to describe events that may trigger the behavior and consequences that may reinforce or maintain the behavior. Based on this data, professionals create a hypothesis about why the toddler engages in the challenging behavior. This data is used to develop a behavior intervention plan to decrease or eliminate the challenging behavior.

- *Video Modeling.* Some research has used video technology to teach toddlers a new skill. An adult shows the toddler a video of someone performing the target behavior. The toddler is then given an opportunity to practice the skill he or she watched in the video. Video modeling has been used in isolation, but is commonly combined with other intervention strategies, such as prompting and reinforcement.
- *Modeling.* Modeling is a procedure that involves somebody correctly performing a target behavior. The learner observes the performance and is then given an opportunity to imitate the modeled behavior. Typically, the desired behavior is modeled *before* the child is expected to demonstrate the behavior (as a *primer*). Modeling has also been used as a prompt in order to provide extra support to the child *after* the direction has been given as the child attempts to use the skill.
- *Antecedent-Based Interventions.* Antecedent-based interventions (ABI) involve an adult modifying environmental conditions that are believed to elicit a toddler's challenging behavior, which are commonly identified through a functional behavior assessment. Once these environmental factors are determined, ABI are implemented to modify those factors so that they no longer elicit the challenging behavior. The types of modifications used in ABI for toddlers may include: incorporating choices in undesired activities, modifying the child's schedule, enriching the environment to provide additional cues for appropriate behavior (i.e. visual supports) or access to additional materials.

These *focused intervention strategies* can be used by practitioners to create an eclectic treatment program for young children that can be individualized to align with child and family goals. A new project funded by Autism Speaks, called the ASD Toddler Initiative, has expanded the work conducted by the NPDC to develop training materials to assist practitioners and families who want to learn more about using these strategies with toddlers in home and/or childcare settings. This resource is free to the public and can be located at http://asdtoddler.fpg.unc.edu.

Challenges for Accessing Early Intervention Services

Prior to receiving early intervention services, children need to be diagnosed with a disability or identified as having a delay in order to access the services available. The American Academy of Pediatrics recommends that young children are screened twice for autism before the age of 24 months, at the 9–18 and 24–30 month well-baby check visits (Johnson & Myers, 2007). Over the past decade, researchers have made significant advances in developing reliable screening measures to detect ASD in children as young as 14 months (Dumont-Mathieu & Fein, 2005; Stone *et al.*, 2008). Yet, despite the greater availability of reliable ASD-specific and broader developmental delay screening measures, ASD diagnosis is often delayed until children are at preschool age (Mandell, Novak, & Zubritsky, 2005; Shattuck et al., 2009; Wiggins, Baio, & Rice, 2006). Various studies have noted that parents' concerns about their children almost always arise before or around the second year of age (Chawarska et al., 2007; Hess & Landa, 2012; Ozonoff et al., 2009). Nonetheless, the gap between initial parental concern and receipt of diagnosis continues to be wide (Kozlowski, Matson, Horovitz, Worley, & Neal, 2011; Young, Brewer, & Pattison, 2003). Delay in diagnosis hinders young children from benefiting from critical opportunities for early intervention, which not only fosters optimal development but also decreases lifelong care costs (Peters-Scheffer, Didden, Korzilius, & Matson, 2012; Warren & Stone, 2011).

As methods for earlier detection become available, infants diagnosed with ASD or flagged as at risk for ASD may likewise benefit from early intervention. Because of the complex etiology of ASD and multiple areas of developmental needs, intensive early intervention is required to ensure that children's development is maximized. While the need for intensive early intervention is documented, there is often a long wait for these interventions due to the demands of these services. Some families might choose to pay out of pocket or seek insurance coverage for private services, which can be costly. Many resort to waiting until services become available.

It is important to highlight the need for interdisciplinary efforts when providing support for young children. Children with ASD often require services from speech and language therapists, occupational therapists, physical therapists, as well as early developmental pediatricians and psychologists. It is critical that providers from the necessary disciplines work together to create the best intervention approach for the child. However, the importance of interdisciplinary intervention to ensure children with ASD are receiving services required and communication among the key contributors to the intervention plan are often lacking. Additionally, the field of early intervention needs to train task forces to be competent in serving families from diverse linguistic and cultural backgrounds. Early intervention providers who are culturally competent actively reflect on how individual families' backgrounds affect children's development and behavior as well as how their own values and beliefs impact their service delivery. To the extent possible, a match between the provider and a family should be targeted. This match in cultural and linguistic compatibility will allow professionals to maximize families' strengths when identifying and delivering early intervention services.

One of the major challenges of early intervention services for children with ASD is the extent to which families and caregivers actively participate in the intervention services provided. While family-centered practices are the key to ensure successful and effective early intervention services, many barriers are present that make family-centered intervention practices difficult. Families may see the service delivery time as a respite time for them, thus removing themselves from full participation in intervention sessions. Additionally, families often carry the belief that the professionals know what is best for their children, thus minimizing the importance of their own expertise in their children during service delivery. Early intervention professionals must acknowledge families' strength and role in these services and empower families to fully participate in planning and delivery of early intervention services.

Conclusion

As the fields of early intervention and early childhood special education advance in their techniques to enhance screening practices and early identification of children with ASD, intervention professionals increasingly are being tasked with the responsibility of providing practices that are beneficial in supporting children's development and reducing the impact of symptoms on later years. Early intervention professionals should capitalize on family strength and benefits of professional collaboration to create intervention plans that best meet the needs of families and children with ASD.

References

Aldred, C., Green, J., & Adams, C. (2004). A new social communication intervention for children with autism: Pilot randomized controlled treatment study suggesting effectiveness. *Journal of Child Psychology and Psychiatry, 45*(8), 1420–1430.

American Academy of Pediatrics (2006). Understanding autism spectrum disorders. Elk Grove, IL: Author.

American Academy of Pediatrics (2007, October 29). New AAP reports help pediatricians identify and manage autism earlier. Retrieved June 5, 2016 from www.aap.org.

American Occupational Therapy Association. (2010). The scope of occupational therapy services for individuals with an autism spectrum disorder across the life course. *American Journal of Occupational Therapy, 64*, 125–136.

Bondy, A., & Frost, L. (2001). The picture exchange communication system. *Behavior Modification, 25*(5), 725–744.

Briggs-Gowan, M. J., & Carter, A. S. (2002). *Brief-Infant-Toddler Social and Emotional Assessment (BITSEA): Manual. Version 2.0.* New Haven, CT: Yale University.

Bruder, M. B. (2000). Family-centered early intervention: Clarifying our values for the new millennium. *Topics in Early Childhood Special Education, 20*(2), 105–115.

Chawarska, K., Paul, R., Klin, A., Hannigen, S., Dichtel, L., & Volkmar, F. (2007). Parental recognition of developmental problems in toddlers with autism spectrum disorders. *Journal of Autism and Developmental Disorders, 37*(1), 62–72.

Dawson, G. (2008). Early behavioral intervention, brain plasticity, and the prevention of autism spectrum disorder. *Development and Psychopathology, 20*(03), 775–803.

Dumont-Mathieu, T., & Fein, D. (2005). Screening for autism in young children: The modified checklist for Autism in toddlers (M-CHAT) and other measures. *Mental Retardation and Developmental Disabilities Research Reviews, 11*(3), 253–262.

Green, J., Charman, T., McConachie, H., Aldred, C., Slonims, V., Howlin, P., . . . Pickles, A. (2010). Parent- mediated communication- focused treatment in children with autism (PACT): A randomized controlled trial. *The Lancet, 375*(9732), 2152–2160.

Hess, C., & Landa, R. (2012). Predictive and concurrent validity of parent concern about young children at risk for autism. *Journal of Autism & Developmental Disorders, 42*(4), 575–584.

Hume, K., Bellini, S., & Pratt, C. (2005). The usage and perceived outcomes of early intervention and early childhood programs for young children with autism spectrum disorder. *Topics in Early Childhood Special Education, 25*(4), 195–207.

Jocelyn, L. J., Casiro, O. G., Beattie, D., Bow, J., & Kneisz, J. (1998). Treatment of children with autism: A randomized controlled trial to evaluate a caregiver-based intervention program in community day-care centers. *Journal of Developmental and Behavioral Pediatrics, 19*(5), 326–334.

Johnson, C. P., & Myers, S. M. (2007). Identification and evaluation of children with autism spectrum disorders. *Pediatrics, 120*(5), 1183–1215.

Kaiser, A. P., Hancock, T. B., & Nietfeld, J. P. (2000). The effects of parent-implemented enhanced milieu teaching on the social communication of children who have autism. *Early Education & Development, 11*(4), 423–446.

Kasari, C., Gulsrud, A. C., Wong, C., Kwon, S., & Locke, J. (2010). Randomized controlled caregiver mediated joint engagement intervention for toddlers with autism. *Journal of Autism and Developmental Disorders, 40*(9), 1045–1056.

Kashinath, S., Woods, J., & Goldstein, H. (2006). Enhancing generalized teaching strategy use in daily routines by parents of children with autism. *Journal of Speech, Language, and Hearing Research, 49*(3), 466–485.

Kozlowski, A. M., Matson, J. L., Horovitz, M., Worley, J. A., & Neal, D. (2011). Parents' first concerns of their child's development in toddlers with autism spectrum disorders. *Developmental Neurorehabilitation, 14*(2), 72–78.

Krug, D. A., Arick, J. R., & Almond, P. J. (1980). Behavior checklist for identifying severely handicapped individuals with high levels of autistic behavior. *Journal of Child Psychology and Psychiatry, 21*, 221–229.

Lord, C., Risi, S., DiLavore, P. S., Shulman, C., Thurm, A., & Pickles, A. (2006). Autism from 2 to 9 years of age. *Arch Gen Psychiatry, 63*(6), 694–701.

Mandell, D., Novak, M., & Zubritsky, C. (2005). Factors associated with age of diagnosis among children with autism spectrum disorders. *Pediatrics, 116*(6), 1480–1486.

Marcus, L., Schopler, L., & Lord, C. (2000). TEACCH services for preschool children. In J. Handleman & S. Harris (Eds.), *Preschool education programs for children with autism* (2nd ed., pp. 215–232). Austin, TX: PRO-ED.

Najdowski, A. C., Wallace, M. D., Reagon, K., Penrod, B., Higbee, T. S., & Tarbox, J. (2010). Utilizing a home- based parent training approach in the treatment of food selectivity. *Behavioral Interventions*, *25*(2), 89–107.

National Research Council. (2001). *Educating children with autism*. Committee on Educational Interventions for Children with Autism. C. Lord & J. P. McGee (Eds.). Washington, DC: National Academy Press, Division of Behavioral and Social Sciences and Education.

Odom, S. L., Boyd, B., Hall, L., & Hume, K. (2010). Evaluation of comprehensive treatment models for individuals with autism spectrum disorders. *Journal of Autism and Developmental Disorders*, *40*, 425–436.

Ozonoff, S., Young, G. S., Steinfeld, M., Hill, M. M., Cook, I., Hutman, T., & . . . Sigman, M. (2009). How early do parent concerns predict later autism diagnosis?. *Journal of Developmental and Behavioral Pediatrics*, *30*(5), 367–375.

Peters-Scheffer, N., Didden, R., Korzilius, H., & Matson, J. (2012). Cost comparison of early intensive behavioral intervention and treatment as usual for children with autism spectrum disorder in The Netherlands. *Research In Developmental Disabilities*, *33*(6), 1763–1772.

Reagon, K. A., & Higbee, T. S. (2009). Parent- implemented script fading to promote play- based verbal initiations in children with autism. *Journal of Applied Behavior Analysis*, *42*(3), 659–664.

Robins, D. L., Fein, D., & Barton, M. (2009). Modified Checklist for Autism in Toddlers, Revised, with Follow-Up (M-CHAT-R/F). Retrieved June 5, 2016 from www.autismspeaks.org/sites/default/files/docs/sciencedocs/m-chat/m-chat-r_f.pdf?v=1.

Rocha, M. L., Schreibman, L., & Stahmer, A. C. (2007). Effectiveness of training parents to teach joint attention in children with autism. *Journal of Early Intervention*, *29*(2), 154–173.

Rogers, S. J. (1999). Intervention for young children with autism: From research to practice. *Infants & Young Children*, *12*(2), 1–16.

Rogers, S. J., Hall, T., Osaki, D., Reaven, J., & Herbison, J. (2000). The Denver Model: A comprehensive, integrated educational approach to young children with autism and their families. In J. Handleman & S. Harris (Eds.), *Preschool education programs for children with autism* (2nd ed., pp. 95–135). Austin, TX: PRO-ED.

Schertz, H. H., & Odom, S. L. (2007). Promoting joint attention in toddlers with autism: A parent-mediated developmental model. *Journal of Autism and Developmental Disorders*, *37*(8), 1562–1575.

Schultz, T. R. (2013). *Parent-implemented intervention (PII) fact sheet*. Chapel Hill: The University of North Carolina, Frank Porter Graham Child Development Institute, The National Professional Development Center on Autism Spectrum Disorders. Retrieved June 5, 2016 from http://autismpdc.fpg.unc.edu/sites/autismpdc.fpg.unc.edu/files/Parent_Implemented_factsheet.pdf.

Shattuck, P. T., Durkin, M., Maenner, M., Newschaffer, C., Mandell, D. S., Wiggins, L., . . . Cuniff, C. (2009). Timing of identification among children with an autism spectrum disorder: Findings from a population-based surveillance study. *Journal of the American Academy of Child & Adolescent Psychiatry*, *48*(5), 474–483.

Smith, T., Groen, A. D., & Wynn, J. W. (2000). Randomized trial of intensive early intervention for children with pervasive developmental disorders. *American Journal on Mental Retardation*, *105*, 269–285.

Squires, J., Bricker, D. D., & Twombly, E. (2009). *Ages & stages questionnaires: A parent-completed child monitoring system.* Baltimore, MD: Paul H. Brookes Publishing Company.

Stahmer, A. C., & Gist, K. (2001). The effects of an accelerated parent education program on technique mastery and child outcome. *Journal of Positive Behavior Interventions, 3*(2), 75.

Stone, W. L., McMahon, C. R., & Henderson, L. M. (2008). Use of the screening tool for autism in two-year-olds (STAT) for children under 24 months: An exploratory study. *Autism, 12*(5), 557–573.

Strain, P. S., & Hoyson, M. (2000). On the need for longitudinal, intensive social skill intervention: LEAP follow-up outcomes for children with autism as a case-in-point. *Topics in Early Childhood Special Education, 20*(2), 116–122.

Symon, J. B. (2005). Expanding interventions for children with autism: Parents as trainers. *Journal of Positive Behavior Interventions, 7*(3), 159–173.

Warren, Z., & Stone, W. L. (2011). Why is early intervention important in ASC? In S. Bölte, & J. Hallmayer (Eds.), *Autism spectrum conditions: FAQs on autism, Asperger syndrome, and atypical autism answered by international experts* (pp. 167–169). Cambridge, MA: Hogrefe Publishing.

Wetherby, A. M., & Prizant, B. M. (2002). *Communication and symbolic behavior scales: Developmental profile.* Baltimore, MD: Paul H Brookes Publishing.

Wetherby, A., Woods, J., Allen, L., Cleary, J., Dickinson, H., & Lord, C. (2004). Early indicators of autism spectrum disorders in the second year of life. *Journal of Autism and Developmental Disorders, 34,* 473–493. Based on research at the Florida State University FIRST WORDS® Project.

Wiggins, L. D., Baio, J., & Rice, C. (2006). Examination of the time between first evaluation and first autism spectrum diagnosis in a population-based sample. *Journal of Developmental and Behavioral Pediatrics, 27*(Suppl2), S79–S87.

Wong, C., Fleury, V.P., & Fettig, A. (2013, October). *Evidence-based practices for young children with Autism Spectrum Disorders.* Paper presented at the meeting of Division for Early Childhood Annual International Conference on Young Children with Special Needs and their Families; San Francisco, CA.

Wong, C., Odom, S.L., Hume, K., Cox, A.W., Fettig, A., Kucharczyk, S., . . . Schultz, T.R. (2014). *Evidence-based practice for children, youth, and young adults with autism spectrum disorder.* Chapel Hill, NC: Frank Porter Graham Child Development Institute.

Woods, J. J., & Wetherby, A. M. (2003). Early identification of and intervention for infants and toddlers who are at risk for autism spectrum disorder. *Language, Speech, and Hearing Services in Schools, 34*(3), 180–193.

Workgroup on Principles and Practices in Natural Environments, OSEP TA Community of Practice: Part C Settings. (2008, March). *Agreed upon mission and key principles for providing early intervention services in natural environments.* Retrieved June 5, 2016 from http://ectacenter.org/~pdfs/topics/families/Finalmissionandprinciples3_11_08.pdf.

Young, R. L., Brewer, N., & Pattison, C. (2003). Parental identification of early behavioral abnormalities in children with autistic disorder. *Autism, 7*(2), 125–143.

Chapter 7

Preschool Years

Christopher B. Denning and Amelia K. Moody

Changes in diagnosis, programming, and an increased focus upon research-based interventions have affected classroom services for young children with ASD. The effects of increased numbers of diagnoses continue to strain support systems, and the new definition of ASD in the DSM-5 (APA, 2013) may have an impact on treatment and placement decisions, as school districts and families strive to put students in inclusive settings to the greatest extent possible. Such considerations have the potential to influence how researchers evaluate program quality and play a role in determining future directions for preschool programs.

Effects of Increased Diagnoses

There has been a consistent increase in the number of individuals diagnosed with ASD in recent years. The CDC (2014) reported an overall prevalence rate of one out of 68 children diagnosed with ASD in 2010, which denoted a 60 percent increase from 2006 and a 120 percent increase from 2002. These increases affect teacher preparation as programs focus upon services and interventions for young children with ASD (Hendricks, 2010). These practices include research on behavioral interventions (Peters-Scheffer, Didden, Korzilius, & Sturmey, 2011), including Applied Behavioral Analysis, Positive Behavioral Intervention Supports (PBIS), and language and social skills interventions such as the Picture Exchange Communication System (PECS: Bondy & Frost, 2001). As diagnostic changes are made to meet the needs of a growing population of children with autism, costs are impacted as well. Although evidence-based practices may increase costs for families and school districts in the short term, effective treatment may ultimately reduce costs by as much as 65 percent across a child's lifetime (National Autism Center, 2009).

Preschool programs are widespread. Effective programs that meet the communication, social, and behavioral needs of young children with ASD can be costly. Data suggest that Americans spend $61–$66 billion dollars on services for children with ASD across their lifespan (Buescher, Cidav,

Knapp, & Madell, 2014). The expense rates for educating children with ASD are estimated at $12,000 per year (NCES, 2014) and researchers estimate that expenses for this population are approximately $8,600 more than their typically developing peers (Buescher *et al.*, 2014). Programs can be costly; however, using evidence-based practices can enhance developmental gains and later academic achievement (Dawson *et al.*, 2010; Strain, Schwartz, & Barton, 2011).

IDEA and NCLB require that practitioners use evidence-based practices in the classroom. Although researchers and administrators are promoting programs that support the use of evidence-based interventions, the quality of preschool programs for children with ASD are variable. Evidence-based programs and practices are those supported by an accumulation of rigorous and systematic scientific research (Vaughn & Damann, 2001; West, McCollow, Umbarger, Kidwell, & Cote, 2013). Programs and interventions require a broad literature base, quality data collection and analysis, explanations of disconfirming data, and interpretation and dissemination of significant findings to inform practice to be considered evidence-based (Vaughn & Damann, 2001). West *et al.* (2013) suggest that encouraging practitioners to utilize their professional judgment and experience when selecting interventions and accounting for family preferences may strengthen the utilization of evidence-based practices. Vaughn and Damann (2001) also encourage researchers in special education to use designs that are meaningful in the classroom context, influence education, and are accessible to teachers to create positive change. The increased focus on evidence-based practices should increase student achievement.

Potential Impacts of New Definition

The Diagnostic and Statistical Manual of Mental Disorders made considerable changes to the definition of ASD in the most recent edition (DSM-5: APA, 2013). These changes may affect the preschool classroom in multiple ways. First, the new definition allows clinicians to focus on a child's overall profile, rather than their diagnosis. This may support the development and implementation of more targeted interventions (Vivanti et al., 2013). Second, the new definition provides an increased focus on how a child uses language to initiate and maintain social interactions, rather than a focus on the timeline of their language development. This may support earlier diagnoses for children who do not have delays in language development (Vivanti *et al.*, 2013). Third, little evidence exists that diagnostic category impacts intervention selection (Vivanti *et al.*, 2013). Rather, clinicians should base interventions on the child's characteristics. Therefore, the new definition may have limited impact on intervention and strategy use. Lastly, it is unclear how the new definition will impact funding from state legislatures and insurance companies. One possibility is that funding will be tied to the severity rating and it may, therefore, be more difficult to fund services for children with a rating of one (i.e. requiring support) than for children with a rating a three (i.e. requiring very substantial support: Vivanti *et al.*, 2013). Over time, clinicians will have a better idea of how the new definition impacts services for young children.

The new definition of ASD and criteria for the disorder may also influence how the Center for Disease Control (CDC) monitors prevalence rates. A recent study by the CDC (2014) reported that prevalence rates will likely decrease due to the changes in the DSM-5. In response, the CDC reported efforts to expand national monitoring to include four-year-old children receiving diagnoses and interventions for ASD. This is important to consider as incidence rates rise, because an increase could result in changes regarding services for preschool populations.

Placement Decisions

Practitioners debate where young children with ASD are adequately educated under provisions of providing a free appropriate public education (FAPE: IDEA, 2004). Placements can vary from inclusive to self-contained settings, and across the service continuum. According to IDEA (2004), placement options should be decided by the IEP team and should be in the least restrictive environment (LRE). Kurth (2014) analyzed data from the U.S. Department of Education to examine placement of individuals with ASD in schools. Her findings specified that from 1998 to 2008, the rates of inclusion varied greatly across states from 8 percent to 62 percent with an average of 37 percent of children spending 80 percent or more of their day in inclusive settings. This research seems to highlight that states and school districts may interpret placement decisions quite differently. While some children spend the majority of their day in an inclusive setting, most do not. Bitterman, Daley, Mirsa, Carolson, & Markowitz (2008) completed a five-year examination to determine parent satisfaction with their children's preschool experiences in a subset of 186 preschoolers from across the United States. The study indicated that children with ASD spend less time in inclusive environments during the school day than their peers with other similar disabilities. This separation from typically developing children caused increased dissatisfaction in parents. Parents also noted that they were satisfied with services, but sought more inclusive interventions that could be delivered in the general education setting so their children would not be separated from their typically developing peers. Thus, placement remains a controversial issue.

Delmolino and Harris (2011) determined that children's needs should be assessed, prioritized, and agreed upon by parents and professionals of children with ASD. When considering placements, they recommended that teams consider the following factors: setting, instructional variables, treatments, evaluation methods, and family involvement. This research provides evidence that placements are highly complex and should be individualized based on the needs of children and families. Similarly, Callahan, Henson, & Cowan (2008) asked parents of children with ASD to identify values attached to educational placements and found that individualized instruction, data collection, evidence-based instruction, and effective collaboration all contributed to ensuring that children reached their academic goals.

Multiple factors may affect the placement of young children with ASD. For example, time spent in inclusive classrooms increased for older children, children with higher daily living skills, and families from higher socio-economic levels (Yianni-Coudurier et al., 2008). In a national, longitudinal study of 421 preschoolers diagnosed with ASD, researchers studied adaptive skills and autism symptom severity in children ages 2–4 years old. Results suggested a need for differentiated interventions for children due to varying developmental trajectories, as measured by the Vineland Adaptive Scale and ASD Severity Scale (Szatmari et al., 2015). This study demonstrated a critical need for young children with ASD to receive individualized interventions that are evidence based. Research by Klin, Danovitch, Merz, and Volkmar (2007) showed that children with high-functioning autism tended not to make similar gains over time compared to typically developing peers. This may be due to the fact that the socialization skills of children with ASD were the most impaired (Perry, Flanagan, Geier, & Freeman, 2009). Inclusive settings can offer positive role modeling, language and socialization, and social skills development if individualized interventions can be easily embedded into the classroom (Kohler & Strain, 1999).

In order for instructional methods to be effective, they must be easy to embed into the daily classroom routine and be accessible for classroom teachers (McLeskey & Waldron, 2007). Schwartz, Billingsley, and McBride (1998) suggested five key elements to promote successful inclusion of preschoolers: (a) developing a strong classroom community, (b) enhancing opportunities for individualization and independence, (c) sponsoring easily integrated interventions, (d) providing instructional strategies that fit the classroom, and (e) teaching communicative and social competence.

Parent and Family Collaborations

Friend and Cook (2010) define collaboration as the interaction between two equal individuals working towards a common goal. Since children with ASD are educated in a variety of settings and have multiple personnel assisting with their educational development, collaborative relationships are especially important. Collaboration occurs both on a school level and amongst team members. Teams can include regular and special educators; physical, occupation, and/or speech language therapists; and others. Important partnerships also exist between families and schools.

Transitions

Family collaborations are an essential component of the preschool experience because children continue to require a strong family support system as they develop independence. Correa, Jones, Thomas and Morsink (2005) suggested that families are a crucial part of the educational team and remain strong contributors to a child's education. However, transitions are a high source of stress for families in the early years (Buescher *et al.*, 2014). The complexity of issues dealt with during transitions requires effective collaboration efforts over time (Friend & Cook, 2010). Families and schools can be more effective when they build relationships, share goals and decision making, and promote active communication (Friend & Cook, 2010).

Transitions in education are defined as movement through groups (i.e. different play groups) or schools (i.e. pre-K to kindergarten; Fabian & Dunlop, 2002). Examples of transitions that young children with ASD experience include movement into EI, preK (preschool), and kindergarten. Researchers suggest that transitions are non-static and multifaceted (Rosenkoetter *et al.*, 2009). Relationships can play an integral role in how a child handles a transition.

Rous (2009) identified several relevant themes related to transitions and found evidence that effective support services and activities can decrease family stress. They determined that parental involvement with schools during transitions could increase academic outcomes. They reported that high quality programs, ecological factors (e.g. SES, family psychosocial factors; Mantzicopoulos, 2005), and positive teacher–child relationships (Peisner-Feinberg *et al.*, 2001) all increased academic and social outcomes during transitions.

In studies examining collaboration between schools and families, researchers found that children at risk for school failure and those with disabilities show better adjustment and more positive academic and social outcomes when both educational entities are involved in the transition to the next environment (Kemp, 2003). One reason for this is that collaborative approaches offer opportunities for educational team members to discuss challenges, strengths, and needs for support (Early, Pianta & Cox, 1999). This is critical, since transitions are defining moments for young children, especially children with ASD who naturally struggle with changes in routines. Evidence suggests that transitions may be even more difficult for families who support children with disabilities (Rice & O'Brien, 1990). Educators and family members experience a high level of tension and worry during transitions (Harbin, McWilliam, & Gallagher, 2000). Families with the most pervasive needs (e.g. low SES, minority, disability) are at the greatest risk for poor academic and social outcomes when they fail to receive effective supports. Policies and practices that provide supports for families with varying needs are essential (Knapp, 1995).

Collaboration sets the tone for ensuring the academic success of children diagnosed with ASD and develops through stages over time (Friend & Cook, 2010; Snell & Janney, 2005). Collaborations expand relationships into service delivery opportunities including coaching, mentoring, and feedback. For example, a teacher may watch a therapist complete an intervention, implement the intervention in the classroom, and teach a family member the intervention for the home setting. Each member is dependent on the other, but may offer a new perspective regarding how to adapt the instruction to fit their setting, child, and needs. Relationships are a key aspect of effective collaborations between school and home. It is critical to keep all parties informed. Effective communication and shared goals and partnerships influence relationships (Decker & Decker, 2003). Open and honest communication offers members opportunities to build trust and respectful relationships. When these relationships are strong, problem solving is more fluid and teams can better influence a child's academic progress (Epstein, 2001).

Family members play an integral part in the collaborative process for children as they enter, attend, and exit preschool. Two major transitions take place as children diagnosed with ASD exit early intervention services and later move onto kindergarten. Family members often play a significant role in delivering interventions, and may have extensive opportunities to learn and communicate with service providers assisting their children. As families transition away from EI services and move into pre-K settings, collaboration and communication are essential components to ensure everyone is involved. Roles and responsibilities of family members and educators may shift and require negotiation to make sure families remain an integral part of these considerable changes. Many children enter more formalized programs for longer periods throughout the day. Communication and collaboration with family members are necessary to develop a shared vision (Friend & Cook, 2010).

Transition from EI through Kindergarten

The Importance of Early Intervention

Transition support is a crucial area of focus for early childhood educators. Early intervention is driven, in part, by the requirements of IDEA (2004). Although IDEA stipulates that transition services must be included in the

IEP when students reach 16 years of age, there are no expectations for preschool-age children. It is important, however, for early educators to focus upon the transition into and out of preschool programs.

Early intervention is one cost-effective method for increasing future academic and social development for young children with ASD by providing children with interactional opportunities and a wealth of new experiences. Preschools can assist children in developing foundational skills that translate into later school success (Burchinal, Peisner-Feinberg, Pianta, & Howes, 2002). When early intervention is not provided, valuable instructional time is lost. Furthermore, if children fail to gain needed skills, additional and more extensive services may be required in later years. Thus, the cost-effectiveness of early intervention is a benefit as government agencies save money over time by providing early assistance (Barnett, 1998). In addition, parent involvement in instruction can focus upon effective strategies to use in the home setting. Delmolino, Harris, Ferraioli, & Hansford (2009) noted that parents showed greater ability to generalize behavioral and academic interventions outside of school when their children received early intervention services. Given these benefits, efforts are being made to identify children with ASD and increase access to service delivery programs.

Individuals with Disabilities Education Act (IDEA)

The Individuals with Disabilities Education Act (IDEA) was passed to ensure that individuals with disabilities are provided access to a free and appropriate public education and services that meet their individualized needs. It was reenacted as the Individuals with Disabilities Improvement Education Act (Public Law 108-446) in 2004. The new legislation updated the law in efforts to provide individuals with disabilities access to NCLB benefits while continuing to provide unique programs and services to people with disabilities. Part C of IDEA offers assistance to infants and toddlers with disabilities from birth through two years old and their families. Part B of IDEA continues preschool services for children ages three to five years old, based upon eligibility, and can extend through the age of 21. Part D supports the use of evidence-based practices by service providers with training, service, and assistance to promote child outcomes in individuals with disabilities (IDEA, 2004).

Supports within the Individualized Family Service Plan (IFSP) focus upon the family's and the child's needs in order to teach family members how to best care for their children (IDEA, 2004). Once children age-out of early intervention, they receive school-age services under Part C of the law (IDEA, 2004). This constitutes a major transition because families are no longer the focus of the intervention and services alongside the child. Although family members remain a critical part of the educational team, the preschool environment focuses on the child. Transition procedures are in place to support families and their children as long as they remain eligible for continued services (Early Childhood Technical Assistance Center, 2011).

Research on transitioning out of early intervention (EI) is limited, but the findings seem to specify that factors influencing transitions include preferred school districts, teacher expectations, parent knowledge and teacher experience (e.g. Daley, Munk, & Carolson, 2010). Daley *et al.* (2010) analyzed data from the Pre-Elementary Education Longitudinal Study (PEELS; Carlson *et al.*, 2009) that focused on three- to five-year-old children receiving special education services. Analysis of a subset of children with ASD suggested that their families received more high intensity transition supports (e.g. home visits, phone calls) compared to their peers with other developmental delays. The highest reported transition services were categorized as low intensity and included attaining school records (85 percent), meeting school personnel (84 percent), sending introductory information (81 percent), visiting the classroom (77 percent), and providing letters from teachers (71 percent). It was noted that large districts provided fewer supports than smaller districts, and children from high poverty areas received fewer supports, possibly due to parent knowledge of programs and services.

Transitions from Preschool to Kindergarten

Children with disabilities may require specific interventions that are unique to the child (e.g. social, behavioral, and medical). Specialized instruction is at the cornerstone of IDEA (2004). In efforts to promote individualized services in the LRE a new birth through six years option was developed. IDEA (Section 619) now offers options for children already identified through Part C to receive continued early intervention services until eligible for kindergarten in efforts help them reach school readiness including the development of language, literacy, and math skills (Walsh & LaRocco, 2005).

A diagnosis of ASD can influence transition practices. Quintero and McIntyre (2010) examined teacher and parent practices to compare children with ASD ($n=19$) to children diagnosed with developmental delays (DD: $n=76$) during transitions to Kindergarten. Pre-scores revealed no significant differences between the cognitive skills of the children in both groups. However, when they responded to qualitative measures, teachers were more concerned about the transition of children with ASD than about their peers with DD. Teachers were also more likely to recommend Kindergarten classroom visits, meeting with the kindergarten teacher, and increasing collaboration between preschool and Kindergarten personnel (Lin, Lawrence, & Gorrell, 2003). This is in agreement with research on collaboration that suggests that increased communication, common goal settings, and effective problem solving can be helpful for school teams (Snell & Janney, 2005).

Play-based Interventions

Definitions of play vary depending on the social contexts (e.g. group, solitary), setting (e.g. naturalistic, laboratory), and age of the child (Garner & Bergen, 2006). Rubin, Fein, and Vandenberg (1983) offered a broad set of criteria that define play. These included: (a) personally motivated, (b) concerned with activities more than goals, (c) spontaneous, (d) occurs with familiar objects or the exploration of unfamiliar objects, (e) can be non-literal, (f) has rules that players can modify, and (g) requires active engagement. Definitions, though varying, seem to contain common traits that include: pleasure, flexibility, and active engagement.

Two key areas for practitioners of young children with ASD to consider are the zone of proximal development (Vygotsky, 1967) and theory of mind (Lillard, 2001). Vygotsky (1967) viewed play as the leading source of cognitive development in the preschool years. He believed play's distinguishing feature is that a child creates an imaginary situation, often based upon real events that contain rules of expected behavior. The zone of proximal development (ZPD) was defined as the distance between what a child can do independently and what a child can master with the support of adults or more capable peers (Vygotsky, 1978). Learning should be matched with a child's developmental level, and can be facilitated through play as peers or adults build upon previously learned skills. More recently, Lillard (2001) examined the relationship between pretend play and theory of mind.

Theory of mind refers to an individual's ability to understand what other people are thinking or the ability to take another person's perspective, and to understand that another person's beliefs can differ from their own (e.g. Baron-Cohen, 1989). Theory of mind and pretend play both share early skills that include: (a) joint attention, (b) social referencing, and (c) reading intentions. Children with ASD may be delayed in their development of theory of mind (Baron-Cohen, 1989).

Researchers have noted differences in the play skills of children with ASD (Anderson, Moore, Godfrey, & Fletcher-Finn, 2004; Jarrold, 2003; Rutherford, Young, Hepburn, & Rogers, 2007). Children with ASD demonstrate difficulties developing play skills in a meaningful context to build friendships and interact with their peers. They have been observed to have difficulty conceiving of non-literal situations (e.g. imaginative play, pretend play) and using objects in pretend play (Jarrold, 2003). Anderson *et al.* (2004) found that children with ASD interacted more frequently with adults than with peers. Rutherford *et al.* (2007) found that young children with ASD had significantly less spontaneous and pretend play than children with developmental disabilities or typically developing peers. Restricted interests and stereotypic or repetitive patterns of behavior may impede play (Jung & Sainato, 2013). Direct and systematic instruction is often needed to address these concerns and increase play skills.

Interventions to Support Play Development

Jung and Sainato (2013) stress that play should be viewed as a critical development area so children can develop friendships and effectively interact with others. The preschool environment offers a natural setting where adults and peers can support play development and provide socialization opportunities in a fun and social environment. Barton and Pavilanis (2012) noted that play is a crucial intervention goal for children with ASD in inclusive settings, because it creates natural opportunities for children to engage in social interactions with peers, caregivers, and teachers. Positive changes in play skills have been associated with improvements in socialization, language, cognition, functional use of objects, motor skills, and exercise (Brown & Murray, 2001). Overall, play-based interventions can create a natural setting for developmental growth to occur.

Systematic Literature Reviews

Recent reviews of peer-mediated interventions that target play skills for children with ASD have found varying results. Lang and colleagues (2009) updated older reviews to examine research targeting functional and symbolic play in children with ASD. Modeling, prompting with contingent reinforcement, and child directed or *naturalistic* instruction appeared related to successful interventions. Modeling of appropriate play was the most common feature of interventions that targeted both functional and symbolic play. In general, outcomes improved when interventions focused on: increased dosages, intervention setting, matching instruction with skill deficit (Bellini, Peters, Benner, & Hopf, 2007), peer modeling, and targeting social responses (Zhang & Wheeler, 2011). Zhang and Wheeler (2011) noted that interventions were more effective when they took place in the home, and when collaboration occurred across school staff and involved parents or siblings. Interventions should examine interaction quality and complexity to ensure that changes will affect naturally occurring events.

Brown and Murray (2001) highlighted specific strategies to consider when developing a play intervention. First, practitioners should assess children through observation in natural contexts. This could also include a play observation scale, such as Wolfberg (1995). Second, goals should be set. Potential targets include: socialization, language or communication, cognitive skills, appropriate use of free time, imitation skills, functional use of objects or toys, motor skills, and exercise (Brown & Murray, 2001), how to share, give compliments, and take turns (Ostrosky & Chatham, 2005), initiations, name use, responding to peer initiations, and turn-taking. Third, the program should support and teach play.

Early stage support should include engaging children and supporting interactions with peers or adults. Play partners can follow the child's lead and encourage target children to join activities initiated by their play partner. Intermediate stage support includes turn-taking through playing with shared objects. One key element to consider is planned variation, such as altering routines to help children with ASD learn to adapt to the flexibility of play situations. Teachers should provide brief instructions, model what you want them to say and do, have them practice what you want them to say and do, and provide feedback on their practice (Ostrosky & Chatham, 2005). Finally, children are supported in early cooperative play by establishing play partners. It may be necessary to teach some skills with an adult or peer partner and then help support generalization to other peers. In addition, several strategies support success during an intervention. These include: create structured sessions for play, find an area with few distractions, carefully select materials, have a clear beginning and end to sessions, end on a positive note, use visual supports, such as a play organizer (Brown and Murray, 2001), prompt children's social skill use in the classroom, reinforce children's use of social skills, and teach social skills within a context that captivates their attention (Ostrosky & Chatham, 2005).

Sociodramatic Script Training

Sociodramatic play scripts have been used effectively with preschoolers to support play or teach specific skills during free play. Targeted skills included increased interactions toward peers (Goldstein & Cisar, 1992) and adults, requests for attention, responses to questions (e.g. Charlop-Christy & Kelso, 2003), and conversational statements (Sarokoff, Taylor, & Poulson, 2001). Prompting also has appeared to increase social interactions, but generalization and maintenance data have been inconsistent (e.g. Goldstein & Cisar, 1992).

Discrete Skill Instruction

Interventions have attempted to teach specific social skills to children with a range of disabilities (e.g. ASD, developmental delay, language impairment). Three studies have focused on children with ASD in kindergarten through

2nd grade (Jahr, Eldevik, & Eikseth, 2000; Liber, Frea, & Symon, 2008; Licciardello, Harchik, & Luiselli, 2008). Jahr et al. (2008) intervened with six children, three of whom were under eight years old. Participants were taught to (a) initiate and sustain play episodes, (b) take turns, (c) vary their play within and between play episodes, and (d) transfer skills across partners, settings, and time. Two methods were used. In the first, participants observed two models engaged in a play episode before taking the place of one of the models. The second was the same as the first, except that participants had to verbally describe the play episode before they entered. Results showed that describing the play episode was necessary for participants to improve their cooperative play. Liber *et al.* (2008) used a time-delay prompt procedure with two children under the age of eight. Participants were taught to (a) use their peer's name, (b) turn shoulder and face toward their peer, and (c) make a statement, request, or ask a question. Generalization probes used the same play activity toys with different peers. Results showed that participants had increased peer interactions with fewer prompts, and one of the two participants was able to generalize the skills learned to new peers.

Licciardello *et al.* (2008) taught three children to initiate and respond to peers. Participants were taught through (a) preteaching (e.g. instruction, demonstration and behavioral rehearsal about how to play with peers), (b) prompting, and (c) praise and rewards. Children were able to select their play partner and toys. Results showed that social responses and social initiations increased for all three participants. The specific level of play, however, was not reported as an outcome measure.

Video Modeling

Interventions use a video model of a specific skill and children are asked to imitate the model's behavior. Models could be provided by adults, peers, self, a viewpoint that shows the behavior but not the person performing it, or a combination of all of them (Jung & Sainato, 2013). The video models have the advantage of relying on visual strengths and interests of children with ASD, and provide repeated practice and multiple exemplars (McCoy & Hermansen, 2007). D'Ateno and colleagues (2003) used videotaped play sequences, such as having a tea party or shopping, modeled by adults with a preschool girl with ASD. The child was provided with the same play materials from the demonstrations. Results suggested that the subject was able to appropriately play with the toys without additional reinforcement or prompting.

Pivotal Response Training

Pivotal Response Training (PRT) includes child-initiated naturalistic interventions that target *pivotal* areas of development, such as motivation, response to multiple cues, self-management and initiations. Improvements in the pivotal areas are intended to affect broader areas, such as sociability, communication, behavior and academic skill building (Koegel & Koegel, 2006). PRT may be more effective for children with some object manipulation and imitation skills (Stahmer, 1999). Studies focused on symbolic play and reported improvements through generalization and maintenance to different toys, settings, and people (Jung & Sainato, 2013).

Social Stories™

Barry and Burlew (2004) taught choice making and appropriate play skills to children with ASD using Social Stories™. Stories included photographs demonstrating appropriate behavior and new skills, such as choice making, expectations and appropriate play with children and materials. Improvements were noted in independent choice making, appropriate play with material, independent play and interactive play with peers. Daily review, corrective feedback and prompts may also improve results (Barry & Burlew, 2004).

Effective Academic Components

Young children with ASD have a number of unique needs related to effectively engaging with the classroom environment (Keen, 2009). Specific challenges include deficits in attention related to filtering information, selective attention or shifts in focus, and difficulty attending to meaningful aspects of the learning environment, especially when it is not explicitly stated (e.g. Klin, 2000). Challenges with task completion may be related to executive functioning deficits in young children with ASD (Ozonoff & Strayer, 2001). Executive functioning relates to the ability for individuals to coordinate goal-directed behavior and includes: (a) inhibition, (b) set shifting, (c) planning, (d) working memory, and (e) self-monitoring. Additional support and reliance on their strengths can improve classroom performance. For example, children with ASD have shown strengths in rote memory. Therefore, children with ASD can improve in these areas if teachers provide supports within the classroom.

Teachers face a number of challenges in educating young children with ASD. In order to accomplish this efficiently and effectively, Strain et al. (2011) suggest that teachers need to be able to identify the instructional needs of students, develop plans to support identified needs, match interventions to instructional needs, evaluate progress and adjust programs to ensure success. The last phase is crucial, as it supports ongoing needs and monitors progress. Potential areas to consider for change include ensuring that the intervention is implemented with fidelity, exploring varying types of reinforcement, adjusting the intensity of the intervention or changing the intervention or strategy being used.

Structuring the Environment

Activity Schedules

Activity schedules can help children organize their day, plan for changes in their routine, support transitions, and complete tasks by supporting expressive and receptive language abilities (e.g. Dettmer, Simpson, Myles, & Ganz, 2000; Kimball, Kinney, Taylor, & Stromer, 2003). Schedules provide a visual warning prior to transitions and help students plan for the day's events. By letting students know what will happen in advance, teachers can help reduce anxiety and allow students time to prepare for an activity. These supports help to promote children's functional independence and decrease their disruptive behaviors (Kimball *et al.*, 2003). For example, Dettmer *et al.* (2000) utilized a visual schedule, a sub-schedule that consisted of a finished box routine, and a Time Timer™ to support appropriate behavior and work completion. The finished box was used during independent work sessions. It consisted of 3×5 inch note cards that described instructions and a coffee can with a slot in the top that was large enough for the card to slide through when the task was completed. Results showed that transition times decreased and the intervention reduced the need for physical and verbal prompts. The target child's mother reported starting visual schedules at home after noting the success in school.

Priming

Priming helps prepare students for the day or for a specific activity by reducing surprises. Essentially, priming involves letting the child know what will happen during the day or during a specific activity in advance. This can be done the day before or when the children first arrive at school. Teachers or parents (if items are sent home) can prime children by providing background knowledge, preparing them for the expectations, and providing examples (Koegel, Koegel, Frea, & Green-Hopkins, 2003). Strategies include providing access to visual material that discusses the day's topics, providing books on tape or in digital format for students to review at home, or briefly discussing the day's plan when the day starts. Koegel *et al.* (2003) used daily priming sessions that were implemented at home and were reported to last for one hour. Results confirmed that priming positively impacted academic responding and decreased problem behaviors.

Components of Effective Instruction

Choice

Choice can be highly motivating, increase the likelihood of task completion, and reduce disruptions for young children with ASD (e.g. Carter, 2001; Koegel, Singh, & Koegel, 2010; Moses, 1998). Choice may be effective for multiple reasons. Choice may (a) provide access to preferred materials, (b) create opportunities for new responses, and (c) provide children with some level of control over the environment (Carter, 2001). Moses (1998) found that providing young children with choices in work assignments increased work completion, improved accuracy, and reduced disruptive behaviors. Choices included the order of activities, the order of the items within the activities, and the materials used (e.g. type of pen, color of pen or pencil, glue, scissors). Koegel et al. (2010) utilized choice, embedding reinforcers within tasks, and interspersing maintenance tasks to increase motivation and assignment completion. Choice included materials (e.g. type of pen, color) and setting (i.e. where would you like to sit?). Embedding reinforcement included activities such as having a child write about playing outside and then playing outside when the task was completed or completing math problems using Cheerios and then eating the Cheerios when the problems were completed. Researchers found decreases in latency to begin tasks, increases in task completion, and decreases in disruptive behavior. Choice has also been used to increase language use. Koegel et al. (2003) used choice to teach morpheme usage and demonstrated that the intervention supported generalization to other words, question forms, and settings.

Finally, choice has been used to support social interactions. Carter (2001) utilized a choice procedure whereby children were able to self-select games for a treatment session. Results signified that play initiations increased and disruptive behaviors decreased during sessions when children selected the games. Choice increased motivation to participate and supported generalization of learned skills to other settings.

Self-monitoring

Self-monitoring has been used effectively with young children to increase behaviors such as peer interactions (Shearer, Kohler, Buchan, & McCullough, 1996), and independence (Massey & Wheeler, 200). Shearer and colleagues (1996) utilized self-monitoring as the second phase of an intervention focused upon increasing social interactions with peers. The self-monitoring procedure maintained peer interactions as adult prompts were removed. Morrison, Sainato, Benchaaban, and Endo (2002) used correspondence training and activity schedules to increase play skills and keep children engaged in the classroom during free play. Children were taught to develop a play schedule using pictures from around the classroom and were instructed to follow their schedule. Teachers then used a least-to-most prompting procedure to help children complete the schedule. This included a play review session at the end. Prompts were gradually decreased for all children during subsequent play sessions. The children's on-task and play correspondence behaviors increased and adult prompts decreased.

Special Interests

Teachers can use a child's special interest to create engagement in multiple ways (e.g. Mancil & Pearl, 2008). Special interests can be blended naturally into the classroom activities either by occasionally individualizing work or by creating opportunities for children to choose some of their own topics. Baker, Koegel, and Koegel (1998) modified playground games based upon children's special interests in order to increase the amount of time target children engaged with an activity and to increase their positive affect. Games included an outside tag game on a giant map and a follow the leader game that used a Disney™ character theme. Results indicated that all children engaged with their peers more frequently and had a more positive affect. Behavioral improvements also generalized to non-special interest themed games. The researchers noted that the children seemed to really enjoy the games and that the children with ASD were viewed as more socially competent by peers due to their knowledge of the special interest theme (e.g. child knew the locations of all the states). They hypothesized that this may have related to the high levels of social play observed following the intervention and to the generalization to non-special interest themes. Vismara and Lyons (2007) combined pivotal response training (PRT) with materials (e.g. objects, toys, activities) related to the child's special interests to examine effects on joint attention as a collateral effect. Joint attention increased during sessions using preferred materials. In addition, improvements were noted in the quality of interactions with caregivers and improved joint attention when non-preferred objects were used. Changes during interactions with non-preferred items led the authors to hypothesize that the intervention may have positively impacted the children's desire to engage in social sharing with their caregivers. Massey and Wheeler (2000) used an individualized picture activity schedule along with graduated physical guidance to support task engagement in an integrated preschool classroom. The schedule included both leisure and work activities. Results showed that task engagement increased across both work and leisure activities. Challenging behaviors decreased during work and lunch, but increased during leisure time suggesting the need for additional supports in leisure skills.

Summary

Early intervention is critical for children with ASD because they are at risk for behavioral, social, and communication delays. Interventions that are naturalistic and easily embedded into the classroom environment are especially beneficial during the preschool years. Play-based interventions include sociodramatic script training, discrete trial instruction, video modeling, pivotal response training, and social stories in a child's zone of proximal development (Vygotsky, 1967). When choosing interventions, it is important to consider factors such as ease of implementation, cost, effectiveness, and generalizability. Decisions should be made collaboratively between families and educators based on the child's individualized needs.

Classroom supports are also necessary for children with ASD. Environmental structure can offer children greater success at navigating their environment, completing tasks, and staying motivated. Activity schedules, priming, choice, self-monitoring, and special interests have been shown to enhance productivity, independence, and comfort within the classroom and home. Streamlining home and school interventions and supports provides greater opportunities for success during preschool years.

References

American Psychiatric Association (2013). *Diagnostic and statistical manual of mental disorders (5th ed.)*. Washington, DC: Author.

Anderson, A., Moore, D. W., Godfrey, R., & Fletcher-Flinn, C. M. (2004). Social skills assessment of children with ASD in free-play situations. *Autism, 8*(4), 369–385.

Baker M., Koegel R., & Koegel L. (1998). Increasing the social behavior of young children with ASD using their obsessive behaviors. *Journal of the Association of Persons with Severe Handicaps, 23*, 300–308.

Barnett, W. S. (1998). Long-term cognitive and academic effects of early childhood education on children in poverty. *Preventive Medicine, 27*, 204–207.

Baron-Cohen, S. (1989). The autistic child's theory of mind: A case of specific developmental delay. *Journal of Child Psychology and Psychiatry, 30*(2), 285–297.

Barry, L. M., & Burlew, S. B. (2004). Using Social Stories to teach choice and play skills to children with Autism. *Focus on Autism and Other Developmental Disabilities, 19*, 45–51.

Barton, E. E. & Pavilanis, R. L. (2012). Teaching pretend play to young children with autism. *Young Exceptional Children, 15*, 5–17.

Bellini, S., Peters, J. K., Benner, L., & Hopf, A. (2007). A meta-analysis of school-based social skills interventions for children with autism spectrum disorders. *Remedial and Special Education, 28*, 153–162.

Bitterman, A., Daley, T., Mirsa, S., Carolson, E., & Markowitz, J. (2008). A national sample of preschoolers with autism spectrum disorders: Special education services and parent satisfaction. *Journal of Autism and Developmental Disorders, 38*, 1509–1517.

Bondy, A., & Frost, L. (2001). The picture exchange communication system. *Behavior Modification, 25*(4), 725–744.

Brown, J., & Murray, D. (2001). Strategies for enhancing play skills for children with autism spectrum disorders. *Education and Training in Mental Retardation and Developmental Disabilities, 36*, 312–317.

Buescher, A., Cidav, C., Knapp, M. & Madell, D. (2014). Costs of autism spectrum disorders in the United Kingdom and the United States. *JAMA Pediatrics, 168*(8), 721–728.

Burchinal, M. R., Peisner-Feinberg, E., Bryant, D. M., & Clifford, R. (2000). Children's social and cognitive development and child care quality: Testing for different associations related to poverty, gender, or ethnicity. *Journal of Applied Developmental Sciences, 4*, 149–165.

Burchinal, M. R., Peisner-Feinberg, E. S., Pianta, R., & Howes, C. (2002). Development of academic skills from preschool through second grade: Family and classroom predictors of developmental trajectories. *Journal of School Psychology, 40*(5), 415–436.

Callahan, K., Henson, R., & Cowan, A. (2008). Social validation of evidence-based practices in autism by parents, teachers, and administrators. *Journal of Autism and Developmental Disorders, 38*, 678–692.

Carlson, E., Daley, T., Bitterman, A., Heinzen, H., Keller, B., Markowitz, J., & Riley, J. (2009). *Early school transitions and the social behavior of children with disabilities: Selected findings from the pre-elementary education longitudinal study*. Rockville, MD: Westat.

Carter, C. M. (2001). Using choice with game play to increase language skills and interactive behaviors in children with autism. *Journal of Positive Behavior Interventions, 3*(3), 131–151.

Centers for Disease Control and Prevention (2014). Prevalence of autism spectrum disorder among children aged 8 years—Autism and Developmental Disabilities Monitoring Network, 11 Sites, United States, 2010. *MMWR Surveillance Summary, 63*, 1–21.

Charlop-Christy, M. H., & Kelso, S. E., (2003). Teaching children with ASD conversational speech using a cue card/written script program. *Education and Treatment of Children, 26,* 108–127.

Correa, V. I., Jones, H. A., Thomas, C. C., & Morsink, C. V. (2005). *Interactive teaming: Enhancing programs for students with special needs* (4th ed.). Upper Saddle River, NJ: Merrill Prentice Hall.

Daley, T. C., Munk, T., & Carlson, E. (2010). A national study of kindergarten transition practices for children with disabilities. *Early Childhood Research Quarterly, 26*(4), 409–419.

D'Ateno P, Mangiapanello K, & Taylor B. (2003). Using video modeling to teach complex play sequences to a preschooler with autism. *Journal of Positive Behavior Interventions, 5*, 5–11.

Dawson, G., Rogers, S. J., Munson, J., Smith, M., Winter, J., Greenson, J., . . . Varley, J. (2010). Randomized, controlled trial of an intervention for toddlers with autism: The early start Denver model. *Pediatrics, 125*, e17–e23.

Decker, L. E., & Decker, V. A. (2003). *Home, school, and community partnerships.* Lanham, MD: Scarecrow.

Delmolino, L., Harris, S. L., Ferraioli, S. J., & Hansford, A. (2009). Living with autism: How families cope. *Mensa Research Journal, 40*(3), 8–18

Delmolino, L., & Harris, S. (2011). Matching children on the autism spectrum to classrooms: A guide for parents and professionals. *Journal of Autism and Developmental Disorders, 42*(6), 1197–1204. DOI 10.1007/s10803-011-1298-6

Dettmer, S., Simpson, R. L., Myles, B. S., & Ganz, J. B. (2000). The use of visual supports to facilitate transitions of students with autism. *Focus on Autism and Other Developmental Disabilities, 15*(3), 163–169.

Early Childhood Technical Assistance Center (2011). Defining, understanding, and implementing evidence-based practice. Retrieved June 5, 2016 from http:/ectacenter.org/topics/evbased/evbased.asp.

Early, D., Pianta, R., & M. Cox. 1999. Kindergarten teachers and classrooms: A transition context. *Early Education and Development, 10*(1), 25–46.

Epstein, J. (2001). *School, family, and community partnerships: Preparing educators and improving schools.* Boulder, CO: Westview.

Fabian, H. and Dunlop, A. (2002). *Inter-conneXions. Early years matter.* Dundee: Learning and Teaching: Scotland.

Friend, M. & Cook, L. (2010). *Interactions: Collaboration skills for school professionals* (6th ed.). Columbus, OH: Merrill.

Garner, B. P., & Bergen, D. (2006). Play development from birth to age four. In D. P. Fromberg & D. Bergen (Eds.), *Play from birth to twelve: Contexts, perspectives, and meanings* (2nd ed., pp. 3–12). New York: Routledge.

Goldstein, H., & Cisar, C. L. (1992). Promoting interaction during sociodramatic play: Teaching scripts to typical preschoolers and classmates with disabilities. *Journal of Applied Behavior Analysis, 25,* 265–280.

Harbin, G. L., McWilliam, R. A., & Gallagher, J. J. (2000). Services for young children with disabilities and their families. In J. P. Shonkoff & S. J. Meisels (Eds.), *Handbook of early childhood intervention* (2nd ed., pp. 387–415). New York: Cambridge University Press.

Hendricks, D. (2010). Employment and adults with autism spectrum disorders: Challenges and strategies for success. *Journal of Vocational Rehabilitation, 32,* 125–134.

Individuals With Disabilities Education Act, 20 U.S.C. § 1400 (2004).

Jahr, E., Eldevik, S., & Eikeseth, S. (2000). Teaching children with autism to initiate and sustain cooperative play. *Research in Developmental Disabilities, 21*(2), 151–169.

Jarrold, C. (2003). A review of research into pretend play in autism. *Autism, 7,* 379–390.

Jung, S., & Sainato, D. M. (2013). Teaching play skills to young children with autism. *Journal of Intellectual & Developmental Disability, 38,* 74–90.

Keen, D. (2009). Engagement in children with ASD in learning. *Australian Journal of Special Education, 33*(2), 130–140.

Kemp, C. (2003). Investigating the transition of young children with intellectual disabilities to mainstream classes: An Australian perspective. *International Journal of Disability, Development and Education, 50,* 403–433.

Kimball, J., Kinney, E., Taylor, B., & Stromer, R. (2004). Video enhanced activity schedules for children with autism: A promising package for teaching social skills. *Education and Treatment of Children*, *27*, 280–298.

Klin, A. (2000). Attributing social meaning to ambiguous visual stimuli in higher functioning autism and Asperger syndrome: The social attribution task. *Journal of Child Psychology, Psychiatry and Allied Disciplines*, *33*, 763–769.

Klin, A., Danovitch, J. H., Merz, A. B., & Volkmar, F. R. (2007). Circumscribed interests in higher functioning individuals with autism spectrum disorders: An exploratory study. *Research & Practice for Persons with Severe Disabilities*, *32*(2), 89–100.

Knapp, M. S. (1995). How shall we study comprehensive collaborative services for children and families? *Educational Researcher*, *24*, 5–16.

Koegel, L., Koegel, R. L., Frea, W., & Green-Hopkins, I. (2003). Priming as a method of coordinating educational services for students with autism. *Language, Speech, and Hearing Services in Schools*, *34*(3), 228–235. DOI: 10.1044/0161-1461(2003/019)

Koegel, L. K., Carter, C. M., & Koegel, R. L. (2003). Teaching children with autism self-initiations as a pivotal response. *Topics in Language Disorders*, *23*(2), 134–145.

Koegel, L. K., Singh, A. K., & Koegel, R. L. (2010). Improving motivation for academics in children with autism. *Journal of Autism and Developmental Disorders*, *40*, 1057–1066.

Koegel, R. L., & Koegel, L. K. (2006). *Pivotal response treatments for autism: Communication, social, & academic development*. Baltimore, MD: Brookes.

Kohler, F. W., & Strain, P. S. (1999). Maximizing peer-mediated resources in integrated preschool classrooms. *Topics in Early Childhood Special Education*, *19*(2), 92–102.

Kurth, J. (2014). Educational placement of students with autism: The impact of state of residence. *Focus on Autism and Developmental Disabilities*, *1–8*. DOI: 10.1177/1088357614547891

Lang, R., O'Reilley, M., Rispoli, M., Shogren, K., Machalicek, W., Sigafoos, J., & Regester, A. (2009). Review of interventions to increase functional and symbolic play in children with autism. *Education and Training in Developmental Disabilities*, *44*, 481–492.

Liber, D. B., Frea, W. D., & Symon, J. B. G. (2008). Using time-delay to improve social play skills with peers for children with autism. *Journal of Autism and Developmental Disorders*, *38*(2), 312–313.

Licciardello, C. C., Harchik, A. E., & Luiselli, J. K. (2008). Social skills intervention for children with autism during interactive play at a public elementary school. *Education and Treatment of Children*, *31*(1), 27–37.

Lillard, A. S. (2001). Pretend play as twin earth: A social-cognitive analysis. *Developmental Review*, *21*(4), 495–531.

Lin, H., Lawrence, F., & Gorrell, J. (2003). Kindergarten teachers' views of children's readiness for school. *Early Childhood Research Quarterly*, *18*, 225–237.

McCoy, K., & Hermansen, E. (2007). Video modeling for individuals with autism: A review of model types and effects. *Education and Treatment of Children*, *30*, 183–213.

McLeskey, J., & Waldron, N. (2007). *Inclusive education in action: Making differences ordinary.* Alexandria, VA: Association for Supervision and Curriculum Development.

Mancil, G. R., & Pearl, C. E. (2008). Restricted interests as motivators: Improving academic engagement and outcomes of children on the autism spectrum. *Teaching Exceptional Children Plus,* 4(6) Article 7.

Mantzicopoulos, P. (2005). Conflictual relationships between kindergarten children and their teachers: Associations with child and classroom context variables. *Journal of Social Psychology, 43,* 425–442.

Massey, N. G., & Wheeler, J. J. (2000). Acquisition and generalization of activity schedules and their effects on task engagement in a young child with ASD in an inclusive preschool. *Education and Training in Mental Retardation and Developmental Disabilities, 35,* 326–335.

Morrison, R. S., Sainato, D. M., Benchaaban D., & Endo, S. (2002). Increasing play skills of children with autism using activity schedules and correspondence training. *Journal of Early Intervention, 25,* 58–72.

Moses, D. R. (1998). Integrating choice-making opportunities within teacher-assigned academic tasks to facilitate the performance of children with autism. *Journal of the Association for Persons with Severe Handicaps, 23*(4), 319–328.

National Autism Center (2009). *National standards project: Addressing the need for evidence-based practice guidelines for autism spectrum disorders.* Randolph, MA: National Autism Center.

Ostrosky, M. M. & Cheatham, G. A. (2005). Teaching the use of a problem-solving process to early educators. *Young Exceptional Children, 9,* 12–19.

Ozonoff, S., & Strayer, D. L. (2001). Further evidence of intact working memory in autism. *Journal of Autism and Developmental Disorders, 31,* 257–263.

Peisner-Feinberg, E., Burchinal, M. R., Clifford, R. M., Culkin, M. L., Howes, C., Kagan, S. L., & Yazejian, N. (2001). The relation of preschool child-care quality to children's cognitive and social developmental trajectories through second grade. *Child Development, 72,* 1534–1553.

Perry A., Flanagan, H. E., Geier, J. D., & Freeman, N. L. (2009). Brief report: The Vineland Adaptive Behavior Scales in young children with autism spectrum disorders at different cognitive levels. *Journal of Autism and Developmental Disorders, 39,* 1066–1078.

Peters-Scheffer, N., Didden, R., Korzilius, H., & Sturmey, P. (2011). A meta-analytic study on the effectiveness of comprehensive ABA-based early intervention programs for children with autism spectrum disorders. *Research in Autism Spectrum Disorders, 5*(1), 60–69.

Quintero, N. & McIntyre, L (2001). Kindergarten transition: A comparison of teacher and parent practices for children with autism and other developmental disabilities. *Early Childhood Education Journal, 38,* 411–420. DOI 10.1007/s10643-010-0427-8

Rice, M. L., & O'Brien, M. (1990). Transitions: Times of change and accommodation. *Topics in Early Childhood Special Education, 9*(4), 1–14.

Rosenkoetter, S., Schroeder, C., Rous, B., Hains, A., Shaw, J., & McCormick, K. (2009). *A review of research in early childhood transition: Child and family studies. Technical Report #5.* Lexington, KY: National Early Childhood Transition Center.

Rous, B. (2009, April). *Review of transition research*. Transition Alert. National Early Childhood Transition Center. Retrieved June 5, 2016 from http://www. hdi.uky.edu/NECTC/Publications/transalterts.aspx.

Rubin, K. H., Fein, G. G., & Vandenberg, B. (1983). Play. In E. M. Hetherignton (Ed.), P. H. Mussen (Series Ed.), *Handbook of Child Psychology: Vol. 4. Socialization, personality, and social development* (pp. 693–741). New York: Wiley.

Rutherford, M. D., Young, G. S., Hepburn, S., & Rogers, S. J. (2007). A longitudinal study of pretend play in ASD. *Journal of Autism & Developmental Disorders*, *37*(6), 1024–1039.

Sarokoff, R. A., Taylor, B. A., & Poulson, C. L. (2001). Teaching children with autism to engage in conversational exchanges: Script fading with embedded textual stimuli. *Journal of Applied Behavior Analysis*, *34*, 81–84.

Schwartz, I. S., Billingsley, F. F., & McBride, B. M. (1998). Including children with autism in inclusive preschools: Strategies that work. *Young Exceptional Children*, *1*, 19–26, DOI:10.1177/109625069800100204

Shearer, D. D., Kohler, F. W., Buchan, K. A., & McCullough, K. M. (1996). Promoting independent interactions between preschoolers with autism and their nondisabled peers: An analysis of self-monitoring. *Early Education and Development*, *7*, 205–220.

Snell, M. E., & Janney, R. E. (2005). *Practices for inclusive schools: Collaborative teaming* (2nd ed.). Baltimore, MD: Paul H. Brookes.

Stahmer, A. C. (1999). Using pivotal response training to training to facilitate appropriate play in children with autistic spectrum disorders. *Child Language Teaching and Therapy*, *15*, 29–40.

Strain, P. S., Schwartz, I. S., & Barton, E. E. (2011). Providing interventions for young children with autism spectrum disorders: What we still need to accomplish. *Journal of Early Intervention*, *33*, 321–332. DOI: 10.1177/10 53815111429970

Szatmari, P., Georgiades, S., Duku, E., Bennett, T., Bryson, S., Fombonne, E., . . . Thompson, A. (2015). Developmental trajectories of symptom severity and adaptive functioning in an inception cohort of preschool children with autism spectrum disorder. *JAMA Psychiatry*, *72*(3), 276–283. DOI: 10.1001/jamaspy chiatry.2014.2463.

U. S. Department of Education, National Center for Education Statistics. (2014). *The Condition of Education* (NCES 2014-083). Retrieved June 5, 2016 from http://nces.ed.gov/fastfacts/display.asp?id=66.

Vaughn, S., & Damann, J. D. (2001). Science and sanity in special education. *Behavioral Disorders*, *27*, 21–29.

Vismara, L. A., & Lyons, G. L. (2007). Using perseverative interests to elicit joint attention behaviors in young children with autism: Theoretical and clinical implications for understanding motivation. *Journal of Positive Behavior Interventions*, *9*, 214–228.

Vivanti, G., Hudry, K., Trembath, D., Barbaro, J., Richdale, A., & Dissanayake, C. (2013). Towards the DSM-5 criteria for ASD: Clinical, cultural, and research implications. *Australian Psychologist*, *48*, 258–261.

Vygotsky, L. S. (1967). Play and its role in the mental development of the child. *Soviet Psychology*, *5*(3), 6–18.

Vygotsky, L. S. (1978). *Mind in society: The development of higher psychological processes*. Cambridge, MA: Harvard University Press.

Walsh, S., & LaRocco, D. J. (2005, June). IDEA. Presentation at NAEYC's 14th National Institute for Early Childhood Professional Development, Miami Beach, FL.

West, E. A., McCollow, M., Umbarger, G., Kidwell, J., & Cote, D. L. (2013). Current status of evidence-based practice for students with intellectual disability and ASD spectrum disorders. *Education and Training in Autism and Developmental Disorders, 48*, 443–455.

Wolfberg, P. (1995). Enhancing children's play. In K. Quill (Ed.), *Teaching children with autism* (pp. 193–218). New York: Delmar.

Yianni-Coudurier, C., Darrou, C., Lenoir, P., Verrecchia, B., Assouline, B., Ledesert, B., . . . Baghdadli, A. (2008). What clinical characteristics of children with autism influence their inclusion in regular classrooms? *Journal of Intellectual Disability Research, 52*(10), 855–863.

Zhang, J., & Wheeler, J. J. (2011). A meta-analysis of peer-mediated interventions for young children with autism spectrum disorders. *Education and Training in Autism and Developmental Disorders, 46*(1), 62–77.

Chapter 8

Enhancing Communication and Language Development

Peggy Schaefer-Whitby, Elizabeth Lorah, Jessica Love, and Hollie Lawless

One of the most basic human rights is to communicate one's needs and wants. It is the responsibility of educators to provide learners with a system with which they can communicate. For children with ASD, teaching communication is critical because gains in communication and language skills are predictors for student outcomes (Gillberg, 1991; Lord & Paul, 1997; Szatmari et al., 2003) and are necessary for learning. This chapter provides an overview of the communication and language impairments and excesses seen in ASD, introduces assessments that drive communication interventions, presents evidence-based practices in teaching communication skills to children with ASD, and discusses the use of technology as a promising practice.

Understanding Communication and Language

Communication is the ability to receive, send, process, and comprehend concepts of verbal, nonverbal, and graphic symbols (Heflin & Alaimo, 2007). Communication occurs when one person sends a message to another and the message is understood (Butterfield & Arthur, 1995). Communication only occurs when the listener acts upon the message of the speaker. Therefore, communicative behaviors differ from other behaviors, as they are mediated by a listener (Skinner, 1957). Language is a symbolic abstract system with formalized rules for word representation, production, and use (Heflin & Alaimo, 2007). Key communication developmental milestones include: eye gaze, babbling, imitation, pointing, gestures, responding to requests, joint attention, using words, following directions, naming objects, articulation, and using pronouns and other language-based rules (CDC, 2015).

Not every child develops language typically. Speech/language delays are a red flag for developmental delays. For many children, communication delays are the first sign of a problem reported by parents. Delays in communication can affect a child's ability to interact with others and negatively influence many areas of development.

Communication and Language Issues in ASD

Communicative ability varies greatly across children with ASD, from those without vocal communication skills to those with a high level of vocal ability who yet struggle with social communication. Social communication is the ability to use conventional and socially appropriate verbal and nonverbal means to communicate based on social setting (Aspy & Grossman, 2014). Social communication requires the ability to change behavior based on factors in an environment, and self-monitor behavior in relation to others. Children with ASD have such varied ability that teaching communication and language skills requires extensive professional training and skill.

Communication and language skills have been determined to be a predictor of outcome, with children with ASD who develop communication and language skills by the age of five showing optimal outcomes (Szatmari et al., 2003). For many individuals with ASD, early intervention targeting communication is effective, and there are evidence-based strategies to support the communication of those who do not develop functional speech. Understanding the strengths and weaknesses of the individual learner through assessment helps to lead to the selection of evidence-based practices to systematically teach communication skills.

Assessing Communication

The process of acquiring both speaker and listener repertoires can be lengthy, complex, and full of detours. Having an organized and clear understanding of both a learner's skill level and a future teaching pathway is vital to producing a language-rich future. Two assessments that accomplish both of these objectives are the *Verbal Behavior Milestones and Placement Program* (VB-MAPP; Sundberg, 2014), and the *Assessment of Basic Language and Learning Skills—Revised* (ABLLS-R; Partington, 2015). Both are useful tools derived from a behavior analytic approach to teaching and learning, and are used by behavior analysts, speech/language pathologists, occupational therapists, and teachers who work with language-acquisition needs. The VB-MAPP and ABLLS-R have similarities and differences. Both will be discussed in the context of the information they provide and the implications of information they do not provide.

Verbal Behavior Milestones and Placement Program

The Verbal Behavior Milestones and Placement Program (VB-MAPP) is based on the analysis of verbal behavior as conceptualized by Skinner in his work *Verbal Behavior* (1957). The VB-MAPP uses the same terminology as Skinner in its differentiation of the distinct repertoires of speaker and listener, as well as in the terminology of speaker behavior. Additionally, learning and school readiness skills such as matching-to-sample, imitation, reading, writing, and math are included within the assessment. The VB-MAPP was developed by Sundberg, and comprehensively provides assessment, curriculum planning, and skill monitoring (Sundberg, 2013).

Assessment and curriculum of the VB-MAPPP is based on typical developmental milestones up to 48 months (Sundberg, 2013). It contains up to 900 skills that comprise the milestones and serve as targets within goals for a learner's individualized education program. In addition to the assessment of current repertoires, the VB-MAPP's strength is its assessment of barriers to language acquisition. It is praised for providing assessment of language according to the source of control of the language response, versus only the topography; i.e. what the response looks or sounds like (Esch, LaLonde, & Esch, 2010). It is not only important to know a learner's current language development, but possibly more important to understand the faulty sources of control, competing contingencies, or other variables in the environment or learner's history that affect acquisition challenges. For example, self-stimulatory behavior may compete with other items or activities during mand training, blocking other potential sources of motivating operation control and serving as a barrier to mand acquisition. Finally, the VB-MAPP also includes a self-care checklist of skills based on developmental milestones. See Table 8.1 for a list of the domains included in the VB-MAPP.

The Assessment of Basic Language and Living Skills

Similar to the VB-MAPP, the Assessment of Basic Language and Living Skills—Revised (ABLLS-R) provides assessment, curriculum guidance, and a method for skill tracking based on developmental milestones. However, it provides the information on a slightly broader range of skill types, and domains are based on criterion references for children slightly older than with the VB-MAPP (kindergarten age vs. 48 months).

The ABLLS-R can assess and plan for 500 skills across language, social, motor, self-help, and academic domains (Partington, 2015). See Table 8.1 for a side-by-side comparison of skill domains between the VB-MAPP and ABLLS-R. Like the VB-MAPP, the ABLLS-R provides differentiation of expressive language according to Skinner's analysis of verbal behavior. For example, it assesses and tracks mands, tacts, intraverbals, etc. Notable skill targets also include other precursor skills to language such as joint attention (Partington, 2015). The ABLLS-R does not provide assessment of possible learning barriers, but does provide guidance on goal creation for individualized education programs. Table 8.1 provides an overview of both the ABLLS-R and the VB-MAPP.

Table 8.1 Comparison of Domains Between VB-MAPP and ABLLS-R

VB-MAPP Domains (Sundberg, 2014)	ABLLS-R Domains (Livingston & Young, 2004)
• Basic verbal operants (e.g. echoic, mand, tact, intraverbal) • Listener skills • Vocal output • Independent play • Social skills and social play • Visual perceptual skills and matching-to-sample • Grammatical and syntactical skills • Group and classroom skills • Beginning academic skills	• Cooperation & reinforcer Effectiveness • Visual performance • Receptive language • Imitation • Vocal imitation • Requests (mands) • Labeling (tacts) • Intraverbals • Spontaneous vocalizations • Syntax & grammar • Play & leisure • Social interaction • Group instruction • Classroom routines • Generalized responding • Reading • Math

The main weakness of both assessments is that although they provide information about current skill levels and future plans for acquisition, they do not identify teaching procedures that may result in the most efficient acquisition of skill targets. Neither assessment provides methods for identifying the types of specific prompting and error-correction procedures that work best for an individual, as an individual's prompting or error-correction history may influence skill acquisition (e.g. Coon & Miguel, 2012; McGhan & Lerman, 2013). Conducting an additional initial assessment to identify prompts and error-correction procedures that best suit an individual's needs, and choosing an evidence-based intervention to implement the curriculum is advised.

Generally, when a child completes the milestones of the ABLLS-R or the VB-MAPP, it is thought they have the skills necessary to learn social communication from their natural environment. Many times that is not necessarily the case for children with ASD, as children with high-functioning autism may continue to struggle with social communication.

While the ABLLS-R and the VB-MAPP are useful tools to guide programming for young children and beginning level communicators, there is a continued need to address advanced skills for those who acquire the skills on the ABLLS-R or VB-MAPP and for those with more advanced communication needs, such as those with high-functioning ASD. These learners may need assessment and programming in pragmatics and social communication aligned closely with social skill instruction.

Teaching Communication and Language

Once the assessment is complete and teaching targets have been identified, it is critical that practitioners, teachers, and families have access to evidence-based interventions to teach the targets. The National Autism Center (2015) and the National Professional Development Center on autism (Wong et al., 2014) have developed practitioner and family guides on evidence-based practices for teaching children diagnosed with ASD. The following practices have been identified as evidence-based for teaching communication skills, and should be a part of intervention programs. Table 8.2 provides an overview of the evidence-based practices identified to teach communication skills to people who have autism. Resources on learning more about the intervention are also provided.

Both the National Autism Center Guide for Evidence-based Practices (NAC, 2015) and the National Professional Development Center (NPDC) National Standards Report (Wong et al., 2014) recognize applied behavior analytic (ABA) teaching strategies as evidence-based. The NAC identifies ABA as a treatment package, along with ABA naturalistic interventions. The NPDC identifies specific ABA teaching techniques as evidenced based. It should be noted that the specific teaching techniques are consistent with the teaching practices embedded in a behavior-treatment package. Table 8.3 provides an overview of ABA teaching strategies that are considered evidence based.

ABA is the systematic application of interventions based on the principles of learning to improve socially significant behavior and demonstrating that the intervention was responsible for the behavior change (functional relationship) (Baer, Wolfe, & Risley, 1968). It should be noted that ABA is not one teaching strategy, such as Discrete Trial Instruction (DTI), but a technology of interventions based on learning theory (Ghezzi, 2007). DTI is one strategy for teaching and has a strong evidence base for teaching communication.

DTI is appropriate for teaching communication skills for those who present with little or no spoken language (Burggraff & Anderson, 2011). The characteristics of autism in the area of social communication and social interaction may influence the motivation of a child to interact with others. By using tangible motivators (positive reinforcers), the learning environment can be arranged to increase motivation for the learner. DTI uses a *stimulus-response-consequence* teaching format (Ghezzi, 2007). In this teaching sequence, a stimulus is presented, the child responds or the response is prompted, and a consequence, positive reinforcement, is provided. Tangible reinforcers are paired with naturally occurring social reinforcers. Skills to be taught are broken into small, attainable tasks so that the child can obtain success and receive reinforcement often. When a skill is reinforced, it is more likely to occur in the future. Often, the

Table 8.2 Evidence-based Interventions for Teaching Communication

Intervention	Age range	Resource(s)
Antecedent-based intervention**	0–22	Antecedent-based interventions for children and youth with autism spectrum disorders: Online training module (Neitzel, 2010)
Behavioral interventions*	3–21	Applying Behavior Analysis Across the Autism Spectrum (Sulzer-Azaroff, 2007)
Cognitive behavioral interventions**	6–14	CBT for Children and Adolescents with High-Functioning Autism Spectrum Disorders (Scarpa, White & Atwood, 2013)
Differential reinforcement**	6–14	Applied Behavior Analysis (Cooper, Heron, & Heward, 2007)
Discrete trial training**	0–14	Teach Me Language: A Language Manual for children with autism, Asperger's syndrome and related developmental disorders (Freeman & Dake, 1997)
		Teaching developmentally disabled children: The me book (Lovaas, 1981).
Functional communication training**	0–22	Functional communication training for children and youth with autism spectrum disorders: Online Training Module (Franzone, 2010)
Language training*	3–9	Treatment of autism spectrum disorders: evidence-based intervention strategies for communication and social interactions (Prelock & McCauley, 2012).
Modeling and video modeling**	0–22	Video modeling for young children with autism spectrum disorder: A practical guide for parents and professionals (Murray & Nolan, 2013)
Naturalistic interventions**	0–14	How to Do Incidental Teaching (Charlop-Christy, 2008)
Peer training package**	3–14	Peer support strategies for improving all students' social lives and learning (Carter, Cushing, & Kennedy, 2008)
Picture exchange communication system	0–14	PECS Manual Training 2nd Edition (Bondy & Frost, 2002)
Pivotal response training**	3–9	The PRT pocket guide: Pivotal response treatment for autism spectrum disorders (Koegel & Koegel, 2012)
Scripting**	3–14	Teach me with pictures: 40 fun picture scripts to develop play and communication skills in children on the autism spectrum (Griffin, Harris, & Hodgdon, 2013)
Technology aided instruction and intervention*	0–22	A systematic review of tablet based computers and portable media players as speech generating deices for individuals with autism spectrum disorder (Lorah, E. R., Parnell, A., Schaefer-Whitby, P., & Hantula, D., 2014).
Visual supports**	0–14	Visual strategies for improving communication: Practical supports for school and home (Hodgdon, 2011)

Notes:

* National Autism Center. (2015). Findings and conclusions: National standards project, phase 2. Randolph, MA: Author.

** Wong, C., Odom, S. L., Hume, K. Cox, A. W., Fettig, A., Kucharczyk, S., ... Schultz, T. R. (2014). Evidence-based practices for children, youth, and young adults with Autism Spectrum Disorder. Chapel Hill: The University of North Carolina, Frank Porter Graham Child Development Institute, Autism Evidence-Based Practice Review Group.

Table 8.3 ABA Teaching Technologies Considered Evidence Based by NPDC on ASD (Cooper, Heron, & Heward, 1987; Newman, Reeve, Reeve, & Ryan, 2003)

Strategy	Definition
Prompting	Antecedent stimulus that brings about a specific behavior to occur. Prompting includes verbal, visual, and physical prompts.
Antecedent-based intervention	A behavior change strategy that manipulates the motivating operations and precedes the behavior.
Time delay	Designed to teach a behavior by allowing a brief delay between instruction and additional supporting prompts.
Reinforcement	Providing consequences for a behavior that increases the frequency with which behavior will occur again.
Task analysis	A sequence of complex behaviors or skills broken down into smaller units. Task analyses are constructed and individualized based on the need of the individual.
Discrete trial instruction	DTI is composed of a three-term contingency A-B-C that is applied to teach new skills. A discrete response only exists when given the opportunity to respond.
Functional communication training	An antecedent-based procedure where interfering behaviors are replaced by an alternative and appropriate way to communicate (e.g. pointing, picture exchange, signing, verbalizations).
Differential reinforcement	Reinforcement is contingent on specific responses that meet criterion. All other responses on placed on extinction.
Extinction	Discontinuing the reinforcement of a previously reinforced behavior in order to decrease the frequency of the behavior.

reinforcer is related to the task (i.e. manding for a preferred item), but it does not have to be explicitly linked to the task (point to a picture and immediately receives a reinforcer). Learners acquire skills more quickly when they are highly motivated. Many times children with ASD need the repetition of the *stimulus-response-consequences* to learn a skill (Burgraff & Anderson, 2011). The format of DTI is fast paced and highly reinforcing, allowing for high repetition and fast learning. Figure 8.2 provides a graphic overview of the DTI teaching sequence.

When teaching communication, ABA is applied to verbal operants, i.e. verbal behavior. Verbal behavior differs from other behavior analysis in that verbal behavior operates across a four-term contingency in which it is reinforced through the mediation of a listener.

Within verbal behavior, both form and function are analyzed. Form refers to what people say or write. Function refers to the source of control or the contingency that maintains the behavior. Verbal behavior (Skinner, 1957) is behavior exhibited by a speaker and mediated (or reinforced) by a listener. Within the framework of verbal behavior, it is not the topography (e.g. vocal output, sign language), but rather the function of the behavior that is of interest. We use ABA teaching techniques to teach verbal operants based on the function of the communicative attempt in the environment.

Table 8.4 presents an overview of Skinner's verbal operants (1957).

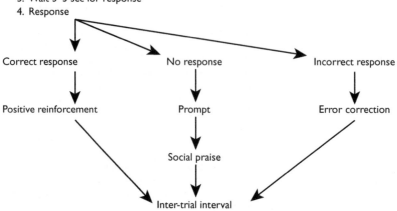

Figure 8.1 The Discrete Trial Instruction Sequence

Figure 8.2 Verbal Behavior Four-term Contingency

Table 8.4 Skinner's Verbal Operants (1957)

Verbal Operant	Definition
Mand	Verbal operant that requests the "speaker" to do something. There is a unique relationship between the response and the reinforcement.
Tact	Verbal operant that elicits an evoked response and makes contact with the environment.
Echoic	Verbal operant that occasions a corresponding vocal verbal response and response is an exact replica of the original verbal stimulus.
Intraverbal	Verbal response occasioned by a verbal stimulus. It is not an exact replica of the original verbal stimulus (e.g. reciting the alphabet).
Textual	Verbal operant regulated by verbal stimuli that includes a correspondence between the stimulus and response.
Transcription	Verbal operant that includes a verbal stimulus that evokes a written response, which includes a correspondence between the stimulus and response.

To program for generalization in teaching communication skills (Cowen & Allen, 2007), teachers should consider Applied Behavior Analysis naturalistic environment teaching (NET). When teaching using NET, the same *stimulus-response-consequence* teaching pattern is followed, except that it is embedded into daily activities and the child's interests are used to guide the interventions (Cowen & Allen, 2007). NET was developed out of incidental teaching and milieu language intervention. Pivotal Response Training (PRT) is an evidence-based NET intervention based on the theoretical components of incidental teaching and mileau therapy.

Pivotal response training emerged from the ABA field when researchers Koegel and Frea (1993) identified pivotal skills that differentiated successful learners from unsuccessful learners after receiving ABA therapy. When children learn these pivotal skills, other skills emerge without being explicitly taught. The pivotal skills include motivation, initiation, responsiveness to multiple cues, and self-management.

When teaching children to communicate, a form of communication is determined based on the student's strengths and preferences. No matter which form is chosen, the principles of learning are applied systematically. Examples of different forms for communication are spoken language, pictures, or sign language. Augmentative Assistive Communication (AAC) uses different forms for communication depending upon the learner's needs.

One distinction between ABA and other language intervention approaches is the focus on mand training as the first skill to target. *Mands* are expressions of need, motivated by an individual wanting or needing something. Mand training utilizes naturally occurring reinforcers (items the child desires) as well as establishing and motivating operants, thereby increasing the likelihood of success. When learners are able to request items they desire and their wants and needs are met, maladaptive behaviors may be reduced. Generally, variants of a mand-model procedure are used. In the mand-model procedure, the therapist controls access to what

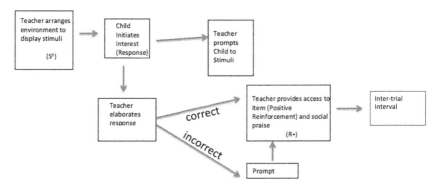

Figure 8.3 Naturalistic Environment Teaching Sequence

the child wants. As soon as the child directs attention to the item they want (grabbing, eye gaze), the therapist models the request (i.e. says the word "bubbles" for bubbles). If the child imitates the word, the item is immediately provided to the child. If not, a prompting hierarchy is used to provide increased support so that the child is successful in manding for the item they want. During initial mand training, it is important to honor all requests across environments so that positive reinforcement is received and the skill will generalize. The mand-model procedure is the first skill taught when using augmentative and alternative communication, as well as functional communication training.

After a child has mastered the basic skills (ABLLS-R and VB-MAPP), it is important to continue to address advanced communication skills. Social skills instruction is an evidence-based practice to address communication. However, good teaching of social skills includes the use of applied behavior analysis across the three-term contingency (*antecedent-behavior-consequence*) to insure skills are maintained over time. Table 8.5 provides an overview of strategies to teach social skills and social communication skills aligned with the ABA teaching technique that supports the efficacy.

Augmentative and Alternative Communication

Given the impairments demonstrated by individuals with ASD, coupled with individuals who fail to develop vocal output capabilities, it is often necessary to incorporate the use of an augmentative and alternative communication (AAC) system when establishing a verbal behavior for individuals with ASD (Schlosser, 2006). There are several modes of communication, both aided and unaided (Mirenda, 2003).

Manual Sign

Manual signs and gestures are an unaided form of AAC, as signing does not require aids or devices. The use of gestures is, developmentally, one

Table 8.5 Evidence-based Interventions for Teaching Social Communication and Aligned with ABA Teaching Technique across the Three-term Contingency

Three-term Contingency	ABA Technique	Evidence-based Intervention
Antecedent-based intervention	Priming	Social stories
		Social scripts
	Modeling	Video modeling
		Peer mentoring
Behavioral teaching interventions	Prompting	Social scripts
		Script fading
		CBT/Self-management
Consequence-based intervention	Reinforcement	Contrived reinforcement
		Natural reinforcement

of the earliest forms of non-vocal communication. Typically developing children generally develop gesturing prior to the development of spoken language. When teaching communication using manual sign, many times the sign is paired with the spoken word or in combination with speech. This is referred to as simultaneous communication. Research supports the use of manual signs in teaching children with ASD. Sundberg & Parrington (1998) suggest that manual sign may be successful for children with ASD, as it is an easier option than vocal word production (i.e. for children with ASD sign takes less effort than speech). Furthermore, these children may have better motor imitation than vocal imitation, making learning quicker. Motor imitation is easier to teach when physical prompting is utilized. Signs have an iconic relationship to the object supporting comprehension. However, given the high demands placed on the communicative partner (who must also understand the sign or gesture), aided communication systems may be a better option. Aided communication systems include picture exchange and computer devices.

Picture Exchange

Picture exchange is the use of graphic symbols to teach communication skills (Schlosser & Sigafoos, 2002). The theory behind the use of pictures or graphic symbols is that they benefit learners because they are not transient in nature. Once a word is spoken it is gone, but a picture remains as long as the learner needs it. Picture exchange, icon-based communication systems, or the use of graphic symbols are different than Picture Exchange Communication Systems, as they do not use the same teaching phases that PECS requires. Picture exchange as an AAC has been empirically validated for teaching requesting.

PICTURE EXCHANGE COMMUNICATION SYSTEM

The Picture Exchange Communication System (PECS) is a manualized intervention for teaching communication (Bondy & Frost, 1994). PECS uses picture symbols for the exchange in a six-phase teaching format. Progress through the phases progresses to complex verbal operants. In phase one, learners are taught to exchange a picture for a desired item (mand training). Phase two involves teaching the learner to expand spontaneity and persistence to communicate, as the learner is required to exchange the picture with a communication partner across the room. Phase three requires the student to discriminate between two or more picture symbols. Phase four begins teaching a sentence structure with manding ("I want . . ."). Phase five teaches the learner how to respond to direct questions ("What do you want?"). Finally, phase six teaches the learner to respond and spontaneously comment. There is empirical support for the use of PECS to teach requesting, commenting, and expansion of language.

Voice Output Technology

Speech-generating devices (SGD) or voice output communication aids (VOCA) are a form of AAC. A SGD is an electronic device that relies on the speaker's pressing of a picture, word, or symbol with sufficient force to evoke a digitized output, which typically occurs in the form of synthesis speech. For example, if a child wants a cookie, he or she can press the picture, word or symbol that represents *cookie* and a digitized output of *cookie* will be produced by the device. There is empirical research to support the use of SGDs (e.g. Lorah, Crouser, Gilroy, Tincani, & Hantula, 2014); however, further research on the impact of SGDs on the augmentation of speech production is needed.

Families are often hesitant to use AAC as a form of communication for their child as they want their child to *talk*. To date, no studies suggest a decrease in vocal output based on the use of AAC. On the contrary, it has been suggested that AAC supplements vocal output, and in some cases increased vocal output has been noted (Tincani, Crozier, & Alazetta, 2006). More research is needed in this area. However, the use of AAC as a functional communication system has been linked to a decrease in problem behaviors (Carr & Durand, 1985; Durand & Carr, 1991).

Functional Communication Training

Often, problem behaviors are used to communicate. When individuals with challenging behaviors learn communication skills that serve the same function of the behavior, the challenging behaviors tend to decrease (Carr & Durand, 1985; Durand & Carr, 1991). Functional communication training (FCT) is an evidence-based practice for teaching replacement behaviors for communicating needs and wants. The first step in FCT is conducting an assessment to determine the function of the challenging behavior. Once the function is determined, a replacement behavior is identified that is functionally equivalent, requires less response effort, and is understood by communicative partners. The replacement behavior is then taught to the learner explicitly and in context. It is important that the challenging behavior be placed on extinction and the new replacement is reinforced. The replacement behavior may have to be prompted at first, with the prompts later faded. Common replacement behaviors are the use of a break card, picture exchange systems, or requesting help by raising a hand.

Precautions of Pseudoscience

Unfortunately, the treatment of autism is rife with pseudoscience and many times families are desperate to find a solution. In order to support learners with ASD and their families, practitioners and educators need to be aware of pseudoscience in teaching.

The history of teaching communication skills to children with ASD provides ample evidence of the need to use science to guide intervention choices. Many times, anecdotal information is presented as science. Families are exploited as they try to navigate services and find help for their children. Facilitated communication—the use of a facilitator to provide physical assistance with spelling out responses—is an example. In this system, the facilitator uses his or her hand to guide the individual with disabilities' efforts to push keys on a keyboard. After each stroke, the facilitator moves the learner's arm back to avoid errors.

In 1993, a report on the use of facilitated communication in cases of abuse in which individuals with disabilities were removed from a home prompted extensive research on the practice (Schreibman, 2005). In subsequent research the practice has been discredited (Schreibman, 2005; Simpson, 2005: NAC, 2015; Wong et al., 2014). Even with ample support discrediting the intervention, facilitated communication and similar interventions, such as rapid prompting method, are still in use today. The accusations of abuse reported via facilitated communication were false, and research has discredited the practice.

When choosing interventions for individuals with ASD, professionals and families should select evidence-based practices that meet the needs of the learner and the context of the family. A way to assess communication strategies is to keep in mind that communication with or by the learner does not occur until all prompts are faded. If the communication is prompted, there is no way to ascertain if the learner or the facilitator is communicating. Travers, Tincani, and Lang (2015) provide a thorough overview of pseudoscience in communication interventions, highlighting the difference between facilitated communication and assistive augmentative communication.

Technology as a Promising Intervention

Access to relatively low-cost devices has increased the use of technology as a tool for communication. As the media report stories of people using technology to communicate, parents as well as professionals hope that technology is an answer for their children. It is important to understand that technology alone is not an intervention; it is simply the mechanism used to teach the learner to use a device. Speech-generating devices or voice output communication aids have been successfully used as an alternative means to vocal speech.

Speech-generating Devices

As mentioned above, speech-generating devices (SGD) and voice output communication aids (VOCA) are electronic devices that rely on the speaker pressing on a picture, word, or other symbol depicting an item, activity, response, or statement on an electronic screen with enough force to evoke a synthetic speech output (Lancioni et al., 2007). For example, if a child needs help, he or she would press the picture that depicts help and the device would produce the audible output help. Dozens of SGD devices exist and vary greatly in cost and technological capabilities (Lancioni et al., 2007). For example, the GoTalk Express 32 is a SGD that contains 32 pre-programmed digitized outputs. The GoTalk Express 32, produced by Mayer-Johnson, costs $241.95 U.S. at the time of this writing (www. mayer-johnson.com/gotalk-express-32/). The DynaVox Maestro has Wi-Fi capabilities, allowing the individual to reprogram the device at any time. Including new items requires wireless Internet access. The DynaVox Maestro costs approximately $8,000 U.S. Additional information may be accessed at (www.dynavoxtech.com/products/maestro/interaact/).

SGD differ from other methods of aided AAC (such as picture-based communication), and unaided AA (such as sign language), in several ways. First, because SGD generate intelligible audio output, the speaker is not required to gain the attention of the listener, and the listener can interpret the speaker's message even if he or she is not looking at the speaker. Second, SGD produce audible speech more similar to natural speech production than picture-based communication systems or manual sign. Third, in using SGD, the speaker only needs to demonstrate one-response topography (i.e. pressing a button). This is not the case with manual sign, which requires multiple response topographies, or with picture-based communication, which commonly requires the speaker to remove and exchange a picture card with the listener. Finally, as a speaker acquires a larger vocabulary, the use of a picture-based communication system may become cumbersome in terms of storing and transporting picture cards. SGD, on the other hand, can store thousands of electronic picture cards in a compact manner (Lorah et al., 2014).

In terms of effectiveness, the use of SGD as an AAC has undergone more than 20 years of research on communication acquisition, teaching strategies, and comparisons to other methods (e.g. Dicarlo & Banajee, 2000; Thunberg, Ahlsén, & Dahlgren Sandberg, 2007; Sigafoos, Didden, & O'Reilly, 2003; Schepis & Reid, 2003; Beck, Stoner, Bock, & Parton, 2008). The results have been generally favorable and the use of SGD for communication training is considered effective. Studies comparing SGD with other methods of AAC (e.g. PECS, manual sign, picture-based communication) have been largely inconclusive and/or have produced mixed results. This indicates that either method of aided AAC may be a viable option for communication training.

Advances in Mobile Technology

Since teachers, practitioners, and caregivers must often choose between AAC systems, and given the exorbitant costs associated with SGD that possess substantial technological capabilities such as immediate customization options, stakeholders (e.g. clinicians, teachers, parents) are often left with few alternatives beyond low- or no-technology AAC. But given recent technological advances in the development of powerful, portable, off-the-shelf handheld devices such as tablet computers (e.g. the iPad®; Galaxy®), portable media players (i.e. the iPod®), and applications such as Proloqu2Go™, stakeholders now have affordable alternatives. For example, at the time of this writing, an iPad® or Galaxy® tablet costs $150–$400 U.S. Such consumer products are available to more individuals than traditional SGD. Additionally, the use of tablet computers and/or portable multimedia players may be less stigmatizing than traditional SGD or picture-based communication. Another potential benefit of handheld computing devices and portable media players as SGD is that such devices can be used for additional functions, such as learning or leisure activities (Lorah et al., 2014).

An additional consideration in terms of the selection of an AAC system, specifically in the selection of an SGD, is durability. Durability refers to the reliability of the device and is essential in any communication tool. The literature on the use of traditional SGD notes durability issues of high-capability SGD, citing untimely repairs and costly services as potential limitations (Shepherd, Campbell, Renzoni, & Sloan, 2009). Since handheld computing devices (e.g. iPad®) are available off-the-shelf at most electronic and department stores, and these devices can be serviced where they are sold, the issue of durability is somewhat rectified.

The availability and reliability of handheld computing devices, such as the iPad®, coupled with applications such as Proloqu2Go™, which presents an interface similar to that of traditional SGD, has resulted in an increase in research investigating the use of such devices as SGD in terms of the acquisition of communicative repertoires with individuals with developmental disabilities, including autism (e.g. Kagohara et al., 2010; van der Meer et al., 2011; Lorah et al., 2014; Strasberger & Ferreri, 2013). There have been studies comparing acquisition between and across other methods of AAC, including participant device preference (e.g. Flores et al., 2012; Lorah et al., 2013; van der Meer et al., 2012a; van der Meer, Sutherland, O'Reilly, Lancioni, & Sigafoos, 2012b).

In general, the results of such investigations are positive. In a 2014 review of the literature, the authors concluded that 93 percent of participants involved in such research demonstrated an increased ability to communicate when using a handheld computing device or portable multimedia player as an SGD (Lorah et al., 2014). Given the heterogeneous nature of the population with developmental disabilities, these data are compelling. Furthermore, in terms of comparison studies, it was generally found that iPad® and SGD were as effective in terms of mand (requesting) training as picture-based communication methods, and were often more effective than manual sign. Regarding participant device preference, the research indicates that the majority of participants preferred the use of the iPad® and SGD compared to manual sign or picture-based communication systems, with 84 percent of participants demonstrating such a preference (Lorah et al., 2014).

A handheld SGD can also be used for communication training that goes beyond the basic mand (requesting) repertoire. For example Lorah et al. (2014) taught three preschool children with developmental disabilities to tact (label) environmental stimuli in complete sentences, such as "I see dog." Additionally, it has been shown that such devices can be used to teach children to accurately respond to questions such as, "What is it?" (Karagohara et al., 2013). Finally, these devices have been demonstrated to effectively teach children with a diagnosis of autism to respond accurately to questions about personal information such as, "What is your name?" (Strasberger & Ferreri, 2014).

Considerations for Practice

We know that handheld computing devices (e.g. iPad®) and portable multimedia players (e.g. iPod®) can be adapted to function as SGD with applications such as Proloqu2Go™. We also know that these devices are as effective as other methods of AAC, and present distinct benefits. However, when it comes to using such devices, there are some considerations to take into account. The first is also a benefit of using handheld computing devices as an AAC: flexibility in terms of additional functions including learning and leisure activities. While most handheld computing devices can be loaded with fun and educational applications, when using the device as an SGD it is important that learners, especially young learners, only use it as an SGD, at least initially. This is because it is often difficult for learners to discriminate between the device as a communication tool versus a fun gadget, and continual switching between the two functions may evoke problem behavior. After a learner uses the device as an SGD independently and appropriately, it is possible to teach them to use it as a leisure activity. Devices such as the iPad® actually provide users with a *guided* access setting that prevents leaving a specific application. This function is helpful for the initial training on the device as an SGD.

A secondary consideration has to do with the actual teaching strategies used to establish communication with handheld devices. A variety of behaviorally based teaching strategies are effective for communication training. Strategies such as prompting (Lorah et al., 2013), chaining (Achamadi et al., 2012), fading (Lorah et al., 2014), and reinforcement (Strasberger & Ferreri, 2013) are required for instructional purposes. Thus, it is necessary to combine handheld devices with evidenced-based teaching strategies, and not simply provide the learner with the device and expect communication acquisition. It is the device plus teaching that allows learners to acquire the ability to communicate using handheld computing devices and portable multimedia players.

Conclusion

The ability to communicate is a basic human right. Communication competence enables people's need to engage in the environment to access needs and wants, share information with others, and develop meaningful relationships to the greatest extent possible.

Teaching communication skills to children with ASD begins with assessment to build a treatment plan. Based upon assessment findings that identify the needs of the learner, an evidence-based strategy for teaching can be selected. Once teaching begins, it is important to collect data on the progress of each objective being addressed. If a child is not progressing, the educator needs to adapt the instruction to facilitate learning. Using a transdisciplinary approach to teaching communicative skills allows a team to teach across settings and communicative partners to foster generalization. In order for a child to be a successful communicator, the skill must be reinforced in all settings. Otherwise, more maladaptive communicative behaviors (e.g. crying, pulling, tantrums) may be utilized by the learner. If a behavior is not reinforced, the learner is likely to stop using it.

The ability to communicate is a basic human right. All people have the right to engage in the environment to access needs and wants, share information with others, and develop meaningful relationships to the greatest extent possible.

Communication delays are a core deficit area for people with ASD. Gains in communication make a significant difference in quality of life, not only for the learner with ASD but for family members and others supporting the learner.

References

Achamadi, D., Kagohara, D. M., van der Meer, L., O'Reilly, M., Lancioni, G., & Sutherland, D (2012). Teaching advanced operation of an iPod-based speech-generating device to two students with autism spectrum disorders. *Research in Autism Spectrum Disorders*, 6, 1258–1264.

Aspy, R., & Grossman, B. G. (2014, February 17). Autism Internet Modules | Welcome. *Autism Internet Modules | Welcome*. Retrieved June 5, 2016 from www.autisminternetmodules.org/.

Baer, D. M., Wolf, M. M., & Risley, T. R. (1968). Some current dimensions of applied behavior analysis. *Journal of Applied Behavior Analysis*, 1, 91–97.

Beck, A. R., Stoner, J. B., Bock, S. J., & Parton, T. (2008). Comparison of PECS and the use of a VOCA: A replication. *Education and Training in Developmental Disabilities*, 43, 198–216.

Bondy, A., & Frost, L. (1994). The picture exchange communication system. *Focus on Autistic Behavior*, 9(3), 1–19.

Bondy, A., & Frost, L. (2002). *A picture's worth: PECS and other visual communication strategies in autism. Topics in Autism*. Woodbine House, 6510 Bells Mill Rd., Bethesda, MD 20817.

Burggraff, B. & Anderson, C. A. (2011) Discrete trial intervention for children with limited social and language skills and intellectual delays. In T. Thompson, *Individualized Autism Intervention for Young Children* (pp. 73–98). Baltimore, MO: Brookes Publishing.

Butterfield, N. & Arthur, M. (1995). Shifting the focus: Emerging priorities in communication programming for students with a severe intellectual disability, *Education and Training in Mental Retardation and Developmental Disabilities*, 30 (1), 41–50.

Carr, E. G., & Durand, V. M. (1985). Reducing behavior problems through functional communication training. *Journal of Applied Behavior Analysis*, 18, 111–126.

Carter, E. W., Cushing, L. S., & Kennedy, C. H. (2008). *Peer support strategies for improving all students' social lives and learning*. Baltimore, MD: Paul H. Brooks.

Centers for Disease Control and Prevention (2015). Developmental Disabilities Homepage. Retrieved June 5, 2016 from: www.cdc.gov/ncbddd/developmental disabilities/specificconditions.html.

Charlop-Christy, M. H. (2008). *How to do incidental teaching*. Austin, TX: PRO-ED.

Coon, J. T., & Miguel, C. F. (2012). The role of increased exposure to transfer-of-stimulus-control procedures on the acquisition of intraverbal behavior. *Journal of Applied Behavior Analysis*, 45, 657–666.

Cooper, J. O., Heron, T. E., & Heward, W. L. (2007). *Applied Behavior Analysis* (2nd ed.). Columbus, Ohio: Pearson Merrill Prentice Hall.

Cowan, R. J. & Allen, K. D. (2007). Using naturalistic procedures to enhance learning in individuals with ASD: A focus on generalized teaching in the classroom setting, *Psychology in the Schools*, (44) 7, 701–715.

Dicarlo, C. F., & Banajee, M. (2000). Using voice output devices to increase initiations of young children with disabilities. *Journal of Early Intervention*, 23, 191–199.

Durand, V. M., & Carr, E. G. (1991). Functional communication training to reduce challenging behavior: Maintenance and application in new settings. *Journal of Applied Behavior Analysis*, 24, 251–264.

Esch, B. E., LaLonde, K. B., & Esch, J. W. (2010). Speech and language assessment: A verbal behavior analysis. *The Journal of Speech and Language Pathology-Applied Behavior Analysis*, 5 (2), 166–191.

Flores, M., Musgrove, K., Renner, S., Hinton, V., Strozier, S., & Franklin, S. (2012). A comparison of communication using the Apple iPad and a picture-based communication system. *Augmentative and Alternative Communication*, 28, 74–84.

Franzone, E. (2010). *Naturalistic intervention for children and youth with autism spectrum disorders: Online training module*. (Madison, WI: National Professional Development Center on Autism Spectrum Disorders, Waisman

Center, University of Wisconsin). Retrieved June 5, 2016 from Ohio Center for Autism and Low Incidence (OCALI), Autism Internet Modules, www. autism internetmodules.org.

Ghezzi, P. (2007). Discrete trials teaching. *Psychology in the Schools*, 44(7), 667–679.

Gillberg, C. (1991). Clinical and neurobiological aspects of Asperger syndrome in six family studies. In U. Frith (Ed.), *Autism and Asperger syndrome* (pp. 122–146). Cambridge: Cambridge University Press.

Griffin, S., Harris, R., & Hogdon, L. (2013). *Teach me with pictures: 40 fun picture scripts to develop play and communication skills in children on the autism spectrum*. London: Jessica Kingsley Publishers.

Heflin, J. L., & Alaimo, D. (2007). *Students with autism spectrum disorder: Effective instructional practices*. Upper Saddle River, NJ: Pearson.

Hodgdon, L. A. (2011). *Visual strategies for improving communication: Practical supports for autism spectrum disorders*. Troy, MI: Quirk Roberts Publishing.

Kagohara, D. M., van der Meer, L., Achmadi, D., Green, V. A., O'Reilly, & M., Mulloy, A. (2010). Behavioral intervention promotes successful use of an iPod-based communication device by an adolescent with ASD. *Clinical Case Studies*, 9, 328–338.

Kagohara, D. M., van der Meer, L., Ramdoss, S., O'Reilly, M. F., Lancioni, G. E., Davis, T. N., . . . & Green, V. A. (2013). Using iPods® and iPads® in teaching programs for individuals with developmental disabilities: A systematic review. *Research in developmental disabilities*, 34(1), 147–156.

Koegel, R. L., & Frea, W. D. (1993). Treatment of social behavior in autism through the modification of pivotal social skills. *Journal of Applied Behavior Analysis*, 26, 369–377.

Koegel, R. L., & Koegel, L. K. (2012). *The PRT pocket guide: Pivotal response treatment for autism spectrum disorders*. Baltimore, MD: Paul H. Brookes.

Lancioni, G. E., O'Reilly, M. F., Cuvo, A. J., Singh, N. N., Sigafoos, J., & Didden, R. (2007). PECS and VOCAs to enable students with developmental disabilities to make requests: An overview of the literature. *Research in Developmental Disabilities*, 28, 468–488.

Livingston, T. J., & Young, B. (2004). The assessment of basic language and learning skills (ABLLS). Presented at the Midwest Symposium for Behavior Disorders. Retrieved June 5, 2016 from http://poac.net/download/resources/What%20is%20the%20ABLLS.pdf.

Lorah, E. R., Crouser, J., Gilroy, S. P., Tincani, M., & Hantula, D. (2014). Within stimulus prompting to teach symbol discrimination using an iPad® speech generating device. *Journal of Developmental and Physical Disabilities*, 26(3), 335–346. DOI: 10.1007/s10882-014-9369-1 1-12

Lorah, E. R., & Parnell, A. (2014). The acquisition of letter writing using portable multimedia players in young children with developmental disabilities. *Journal of Developmental and Physical Disabilities*, 26(6), 655–666. DOI: 10.1007/ s10882-014-9386-0

Lorah, E. R., Parnell, A., Schaefer-Whitby, P., & Hantula, D. (2014). A systematic review of tablet based computers and portable media players as speech generating deices for individuals with ASD spectrum disorder. *Journal of*

Autism and Developmental Disorders, 45(12), 3792–3804. DOI: 10.1007/ s10803-014-2314-4

Lorah, E. R., Parnell, A., & Speight, D. R. (2014). Acquisition of sentence frame discrimination using the iPad as a speech generating device in young children with developmental disabilities. *Research in Autism Spectrum Disorders, 8,* 1734–1740.

Lorah, E. R., Tincani, M., Dodge, J., Gilroy, S., Hickey, A., & Hantula, D. (2013). Evaluating picture exchange and the iPad as a speech generating device to teach communication to young children with ASD. *Journal of Developmental and Physical Disabilities, 25*(6), 637–649. DOI 10.1007/ s10882-013-9337-1

Lord, C., & Paul, R. (1997). Language and communication in autism. In D. J. Cohen & F. R. Volkmar (Eds.), *Handbook of autism and pervasive development disorders* (2nd ed.). New York: Wiley.

Lovaas, O.I. (1981). *Teaching developmentally disabled children: The me book.* Austin, TX: PRO-ED, Inc.

McGhan, A. C., & Lerman, D. C. (2013). An assessment of error correction procedures for learners with ASD. *Journal of Applied Behavior Analysis, 46,* 626–639.

Mirenda, P. (2003). Toward functional augmentative and alternative communication for students with ASD: Manual signs, graphic symbols, and voice output communication aids. *Language, Speech, and Hearing Services in Schools, 34,* 203–216.

Murray, S. & Nolan, B. (2013). *Video modeling for young children with ASD spectrum disorder: A practical guide for parents and professionals.* London: Jessica Kingsley Publishers.

National Autism Center. (2015). *Findings and conclusions: National standards project, phase 2.* Randolph, MA: Author

Neitzel, J. (2010). Positive behavior supports for children and youth with autism spectrum disorders. *Preventing School Failure, 54,* 247–255.

Newman, B., Reeve, K. F., Reeve, S. A., & Ryan, C. S. (2003). *Behavior speak: glossary of terms in applied behavior analysis (ABA).* New York: Dove and Orca.

Partington (2015). The Assessment of Basic Language and Learning Skills – Revised (ABLLS-R). Retrieved June 5, 2016 from www.partingtonbehavior analysts.com/page/ablls-r-25.html.

Prelock, P. A., & McCauley, R. J. (Eds.) (2012). *Treatment of autism spectrum disorders: Evidence-based intervention strategies for communication and social interactions.* Baltimore, MD: Paul H. Brookes Publishing Company.

Scarpa, A., White, S. W., & Attwood, T. (Eds.) (2013). *CBT for children and adolescents with high-functioning autism spectrum disorders.* New York: Guilford Press.

Schepis, M., & Reid, D. (2003). Issues affecting staff enhancement of speech-generating device use among people with severe cognitive disabilities. *Augmentative and Alternative Communication, 19,* 59–65.

Schlosser, R., & Sigafoos, J. (2002). Selecting graphic symbols for an initial request lexicon: Integrative review. *Augmentative and Alternative Communication, 18*(2), 102–123.

Schlosser, R. W. (2006). Evidence-based practice for AAC practitioners. *Perspectives on Augmentative and Alternative Communication*, 15(3), 8–9. doi:10.1044/aac17.3.113

Schreibman L. (2005). *The science and fiction of autism*. Cambridge, MA: Harvard University Press.

Simpson, R. (2005). Evidence-based practices and students with autism spectrum disorders. *Focus on Autism and Other Developmental Disabilities*, 20 (3), 140–149.

Shepherd, T. A., Campbell, K. A., Renzoni, A. & Sloan, N. (2009). Reliability of speech Generating devices: A 5-year review. *Augmentative and Alternative Communication*, 25, 145–153.

Sigafoos, J., Didden, R., & O'Reilly, M. (2003). Effects of speech output on maintenance of requesting and frequency of vocalizations in three children with developmental disabilities. *Augmentative and Alternative Communication*, 19, 37–47.

Skinner, B. F. (1957). *Verbal Behavior*. Acton, MA: Copley Publishing Group.

Strasberger, S. K., & Ferreri, S. J. (2013). The effects of peer assisted communication application training on the communicative and social behaviors of children with ASD. *Journal of Developmental and Physical Disabilities*, 1–14.

Strasberger, S. K., & Ferreri, S. J. (2014). The effects of peer assisted communication application training on the communicative and social behaviors of children with autism. *Journal of Developmental and Physical Disabilities*, 26 (5), 513–526.

Sulzer-Azaroff, B. (2007). *Applying behavior analysis across the autism spectrum: A guide for practitioners*. Cornwall-on-Hudson, NY: Sloan Publishing.

Sundberg, M. L. (2013). A functional analysis of language. In Bill L. Heward (Ed.) *Exceptional children (10th Ed.)*. Upper Saddle River, NJ: Pearson.

Sundberg, M. L. (2014). The VB-MAPP: Conducting the assessment and identifying intervention priorities. Retrieved June 5, 2016 from http://autism.outreach.psu.edu/sites/omcphplive.outreach.psu.edu.drpms.autismconference/files/18and30Presentation_0.pdf.

Sundberg, M.L. and Parrington, J. W. (1998). *Teaching language to children with autism or other developmental disabilities*. Behavioral Analysts, Inc.

Szatmari, P., Bryson, S. E., Boyle, M. H., Streiner, D. L., & Duku, E. (2003). Predictors of outcome among high functioning children with ASD and Asperger syndrome. *Journal of Child Psychology and Psychiatry*, 44, 520–528.

Thunberg, G., Ahlsén, E., & Dahlgren Sandberg, A. (2007). Children with autistic spectrum disorders and speech-generating devices: Communication in different activities at home. *Clinical linguistics & phonetics*, 21, 457–479.

Tincani, M., Crozier, S. E., & Alazetta, L. (2006). The picture exchange communication system: Effects on manding and speech development for school-aged children with autism. *Education and Training in Developmental Disabilities*, 41 (2), 177–184.

Travers, J. T., Tincani, M., & Lang R. (2014). Facilitated communication denies people with disabilities their voices. *Research and Practice for People with Severe Disabilities*, 39 (3), 195–202.

van der Meer, L., Kagohara, D. M., Achmadi, D., Green, V. A., O'Reilly, M. F., & Lancioni, G. E. (2011). Teaching functional use of an iPod-based speech-generating device to individuals with developmental disabilities. *Journal of Special Education Technology*, 26, 1–11.

van der Meer, L., Kagohara, D. M., Achmadi, D., O'Reilly, M. F., Lancioni, G. E., & Sutherland, D. (2012a). Speech-generating devices versus manual signing for children with developmental disabilities. *Research in Developmental Disabilities*, 33, 1658–1669.

van der Meer, L., Sutherland, D., O'Reilly, M. F., Lancioni, G. E., & Sigafoos, J. (2012b). A further comparison of manual signing, picture exchange, and speech-generating devices as communication modes for children with ASD spectrum disorders. *Research in Autism Spectrum Disorders*, 6, 1247–1257.

Wong, C., Odom, S. L., Hume, K., Cox, A. W., Fettig, A., Kucharczyk, S., . . . Schultz, T. R. (2014). *Evidence-based practices for children, youth, and young ddults with ASD Spectrum Disorder*. Chapel Hill: The University of North Carolina, Frank Porter Graham Child Development Institute, Autism Evidence-Based Practice Review Group.

Chapter 9

Building and Managing Appropriate Behaviors

E. Amanda Boutot, Devon Ramey, and Nathan Pullen

Introduction

Along with behavioral deficits (e.g. communication, social skills), individuals with autism spectrum disorder (ASD) often present with various behavioral excesses, which may inhibit their ability to be successful in a school, home, or community environment. We refer to behavioral excesses as "challenging behaviors" because they challenge the person's ability to achieve success (Olive, Boutot, & Tarvox, 2011). Examples of behavioral excesses, or challenging behaviors that may be seen in students with autism are stereotypical/self-stimulatory behaviors (such as hand flapping or making loud noises), self-injurious behaviors (such as head hitting or self biting), aggression (i.e. pinching, kicking), eloping (running away), noncompliance, work refusal, off task, and out of seat, among others. A key factor associated with challenging behaviors is often the level of communication the individual has, as well as the degree of structure and behavioral training of the adults working with him or her. The purpose of this chapter is to discuss some of the major considerations when addressing challenging behaviors of students with ASD. We will begin with a rationale behind identification of the *function* of the behavior, because *function-based decision making* is the first step in identifying and resolving the behavior. Next, we will list and describe some *antecedent-based strategies* that can be used to create necessary structure and prevent challenging behaviors. We will complete the chapter with a discussion of *consequence-based strategies*, paying particular attention to the difference between reinforcement and punishment and the guidelines for the use of each of these.

Function-based Decision Making

Rationale for Functional Behavioral Assessments

Identifying the function of the challenging behavior is the necessary first step in the process of decreasing and/or stopping that behavior. Often, as teachers, we may find ourselves trying to "treat" a challenging behavior in the absence of an appropriate assessment. However, this is ill advised. Reading specialists and math specialists would not attempt to "treat" a reading or a math difficulty without completing an appropriate assessment first to understand the problem; therefore, teachers treating behavioral challenges must also conduct an assessment before beginning treatment. The appropriate assessment for challenging behavior is a functional behavioral assessment, or FBA.

FBA Procedures

A functional behavioral assessment is designed to provide as much information as possible about a specific behavior or behaviors and the environment in which it occurs. An FBA makes it possible for professionals to form a hypothesis about the function a particular behavior may serve for an individual. The steps to complete an FBA include: (1) forming a multidisciplinary team (this may include teachers, parents, related service personnel, teaching assistants), (2) identifying the behavior(s) of concern and writing an operational definition, (3) collecting baseline data on the behavior(s) of concern, (4) forming a hypothesis that involves the antecedents, consequences, and function of the behavior, (5) developing interventions based off of the tested hypothesis, and (6) monitoring interventions for effectiveness. In the first step, a team of individuals who know the student well and/or who are familiar with the challenging behavior should be assembled as the "team." Often this is the child's IEP (Individualized Education Program) team. Occasionally, outside experts or specialists may be called in to assist with an FBA, such as a Board Certified Behavior Analyst (BCBA). In the second step, the goal is to identify the behavior or behaviors you wish to target for both assessment and intervention and to describe them in the most observable and measurable terms. For example, rather than saying "Jason gets upset" you would describe his behavior as "Jason throws his lunch box across the room." In the third step, team members collect data that can be used to identify a possible function (these types of data collection methods appear in the next section). The fourth step involves using the data previously collected to form a hypothesis as to behavioral function. Because we can never truly know what a behavioral function is, we always use hypothesis statements when discussing function. The fifth and final step in the process is to develop an intervention plan that is based on this hypothesized function. If our plan works, our hypothesis as to function was most likely correct.

Functions of Behavior

Identifying the hypothesized, or possible, function of a challenging behavior is the goal of an FBA, however, what do we mean by "function"?

Another way to describe the process is to say that an FBA allows us to determine the source of reinforcement that may be maintaining a behavior or, in other words, it enables staff to determine why an individual is exhibiting a particular behavior. According to behavioral theory, all behavior serves a purpose—to either gain something of value or avoid/escape something aversive or unpleasant. In operant conditioning, we refer to reinforcement and punishment. These terms will be discussed in more detail elsewhere in this chapter, but the critical distinction between them is that reinforcement increases behavior, while punishment decreases it. Thus, if a challenging behavior is continuing to occur despite efforts to decrease or stop it, something must be serving as a reinforcer for that behavior. Thus, in an FBA, one of the critical areas of examination is the consequence that follows the behavior, in an attempt to discern the possible function. Other variables also influence the behavior, such as how motivated the individual is to exhibit that behavior (e.g. the individual is hungry), if the individual believes that reinforcement will be available to them (e.g. mom is in the room and she usually provides food), and the person's history of reinforcement for that behavior (e.g. crying has usually resulted in mom providing a snack in the past). Here we will look further into the functions that may be responsible for maintaining behavior.

Socially Mediated Functions of Behavior

Functions of behavior can very generally be grouped into either socially mediated or automatic functions. A behavior that has a socially mediated function requires the presence and action of somebody other than the person exhibiting the behavior. In other words, reinforcement is delivered by another person. Behaviors with socially mediated functions can be further divided into socially mediated positive and socially mediated negative functions. In this case, positive and negative do not mean "good" and "bad," but more along the lines of "addition" and "subtraction." A behavior with a function that is *socially mediated positive* would involve the actions of another in the individual's environment who provides, or *adds*, something. An example of a socially mediated positive challenging behavior would be a child banging fists on a table in order to have their mother bring them a preferred food. The behavior would not be reinforced unless the mother was present and providing food to the individual. A behavior with *a socially-mediated negative* function is that which requires another to *remove* something from the environment. An example of a socially-mediated negative behavior would be a child throwing his math paper on the ground and the teacher sending her to time out; if math is aversive for the child, time out would be reinforcing because it would get her out of math.

Automatic Functions of Behavior

A behavior with an automatic function is one that does not require the presence or action of another person in order to obtain reinforcement. Behaviors with automatic functions can further be divided into automatic positive and automatic negative. An example of a behavior with an automatic positive function would be an individual eating a sandwich to relieve their hunger. An example of a behavior with an automatic negative function would be somebody chewing their fingernails in order to remove an uncomfortable sensation from a hangnail.

FBA Data Collection Procedures

Screening Tools

Screening tools are useful to provide professionals and the family of a child with challenging behaviors to identify the perceived function of each of these individuals. Several commercially available screening tools can be found on the Internet. The Functional Assessment Screening Tool (FAST) consists of 27 questions (O'Neill, Horner, Albin, Storey, & Sprague, 1997). The questions assess for functions of social positive reinforcement, social negative reinforcement, automatic positive reinforcement, and automatic negative reinforcement. Another screening tool, the Questions About Behavioral Function (QABF) is a 25-item indirect assessment tool that can help professionals develop a hypothesis about the functions of maladaptive behaviors and plan interventions that decrease these behaviors while increasing more functional skills as replacement behavior. The factors measured in the QABF are social attention, escape, tangible reinforcement, physical discomfort, and nonsocial reinforcement. Matson, Bamburg, Cherry, & Paclawskyj (1999) investigated the validity of treatments derived from QABFs and found that the QABF was beneficial in planning treatments to match functions and provide appropriate replacement behaviors. The QABF is an effective indirect assessment tool that should be used in conjunction with direct assessment methods, and a functional analysis, if possible. The QABF and FAST may be graphed to more easily compare the ratings of the different scorers (e.g. mother, father, teacher, babysitter, etc.).

Other screening tools include the Motivation Assessment Scale (MAS), the Functional Assessment Interview (FAI), and the Problem Behavior Questionnaire (PBQ). The MAS includes 16 items that are rated on a seven-point Likert scale, which scores to four factors and includes escape from aversive events, access to social attention, access to tangible rewards, and sensory reinforcement. The FAI includes questions about the events that predict the behavior, possible functions, and a summary statement that hypothesizes the function of the behavior. The PBQ includes 15 items and indicates the frequency with which the behavior of concern is observed.

ABC Charts

One of the most useful tools to use during an FBA is the Antecedent Behavior Consequence chart, commonly referred to as ABC chart. This a manner of recording each behavioral incident right when it occurs, documenting what occurs immediately prior to a behavior, the behavior itself, and the consequence that immediately follows this behavior. This type of data collection is useful in determining possible correlations between behavior and some environmental events. A sample of an ABC chart is provided in Figure 9.1.

Scatterplot

A scatterplot is a type of data recording system that enables the person recording and analyzing the data to determine when and where the behavior(s) of interest occurred, and at what frequency. Scatterplots require dividing the observation period into time intervals and recording whether or not a behavior occurred during the time interval. This method of recording can help narrow down environmental events that may trigger and reinforce the behavior of interest. An example of a completed scatterplot data sheet is provided. The data in this scatterplot is indicative of the student having recurring challenging behavior during the first class of the day (Social Studies) and the last class of the day (Math). An example of a completed scatterplot is provided in Figure 9.2.

In summary, assessment data—in particular the ABC chart—provides information on the variables (antecedents and consequences) that may help determine a hypothesis for behavioral function. In analyzing the data, professionals conducting FBAs examine patterns in the data that suggest one or more possible functions. Once a function has been hypothesized, an intervention plan that directly considers the function, as well as other data derived from the FBA, can be developed.

Behavioral Intervention Planning

The FBA is only the first part of addressing a challenging behavior. Behavioral intervention planning involves addressing the variables identified through the FBA as either occurring as antecedents or as reinforcing consequences for the challenging behavior. There are two basic types of intervention strategies that may be used. First, professionals often use what are known as antecedent-based strategies to effectively prevent the occurrence of the challenging behavior. The second type, consequence-based strategies, involves the use of reinforcement and punishment procedures. This section will describe each of these broad types in more detail and provide specific examples of each.

Student: Shawn M.
Observer: Ms. Janner, Teaching Assistant

Date/Setting	Time	Antecedent	Behavior	Consequence	Hypothesized function(s)
11/15/15—3rd Period Reading class in group circle	11:13 a.m.	Teacher asked group to answer what the main idea of the story was.	Loudly yelled out incorrect answer.	Teacher stated "remember to raise your hand" and called on another student.	Attention
11/29/15— 2nd period Science class	10:09 a.m.	Working independently —and heard another student sharpen pencil on electric sharpener.	Covered ears with hands and screamed loudly.	Teacher said student's name and raised finger to mouth, making "shhh" sound.	Attention

Figure 9.1 ABC Chart

Student Name: **David**						
Behavior (operational definition):						
Verbal disruption—crying, with or without tears, screaming/yelling at a volume above that which is appropriate for the environment that David is currently in, cursing or threatening language.						
Time ↓	**Activity/Class** ↓	3/12/15	3/13/15	3/14/15	3/15/15	3/16/15
9:00	Social Studies	IIIII	IIIII	IIIII	IIII	III
10:15	Reading	I	I	I		I
11:15	Science			I		I
12:30	Lunch					
1:15	P.E.		II	I		I
2:00	Math	IIII	IIII	III	IIIIII	IIIII

Figure 9.2 Scatterplot

Antecedent-based Strategies

Antecedent-based strategies are designed to prevent the challenging behavior from occurring in the first place. For example, the child who threw her reading paper because she wanted to escape reading found reading aversive in some way (socially mediated negative reinforcement). A goal would be to identify *why* she finds reading aversive. It could be too many questions, too little support, or she does not feel she is a good reader. By identifying and addressing why she finds reading aversive, the team can create a situation in which she is less likely to *need* to throw her paper. Following are some other examples that are particularly useful for students with ASD. These supports provided structure and predictability to these students, the lack of which is often a trigger for challenging behaviors.

Visual Schedules

Visual schedules are supports that accommodate the need for predictability by making it clear to the individual with ASD when activities or tasks are to occur. They can present a wide range of information to individuals with autism, such as a daily schedule, activities to be completed during a class period, a series of steps to be completed in a task, among others. Information that is listed in a visual schedule varies according to the age and functioning level of the learner, and may include written words, objects, photographs, line drawings, symbols, or a combination of these. The format of the information presented and the location of presentation of the visual schedule are determined by the learner and the goal for which the visual is being used. Several studies have demonstrated beneficial effects of visual schedules in learners with Autism Spectrum Disorder (Carlile, Reeve, Reeve, & DeBar, 2013; Lequia, Machalicek, & Rispoli, 2012; Machalicek et al., 2009; Pierce, Spriggs, Gast, & Luscre, 2013). In their review of the literature, Banda and Grimmett found that several studies of visual schedules decreased challenging behaviors (2008), including off-task behavior, disruptive behavior, and tantrums. In the following section, examples (e.g., social narratives, social scripts, cartooning, power cards, social autopsies, and vide modeling) of visual schedules for a student with ASD in a public elementary school are presented.

Social Narratives

The National Professional Development Committee (NPDC, 2014) has identified social narratives as an evidence-based practice for students with autism. Social narratives are pictorial or written "stories" that depict a situation or a skill with which the individual is unfamiliar or currently unsuccessful, in a manner that is most easily understood, including relevant cues and expected responses (Test, Richter, Knight, & Spooner, 2011). According to a recent review of social narratives, several challenging behaviors have been found to decrease as a result of using social narratives, with or without additional procedures, including aggression, inappropriate vocalizations, shouting/yelling, crying, talking out, disruptive behavior, and stereotypical behavior (Test et al., 2011). When combined with other procedures such as prompting, focusing on student interest, and reinforcement, social narratives are also found to be effective (Test et al., 2011). Social narratives may take on many forms and may address many skills, but typically involve the use of visual cues and simple sentences and phrases that address a deficit in social behavior. Below are some social narrative forms that may be of benefit to individuals with autism.

Social Scripts

Social scripts include written or audio sentences or paragraphs that individuals with autism may use across settings and situations to enhance social interactions with peers and adults. Social scripts take into account the reading or listening ability of the learner, and aim to provide information and instruction for appropriate social behavior to the individual with autism. Social scripts are typically employed with a systematic script fading procedure to effectively remove the script and have the individual produce unprompted responses. This procedure has produced positive results in numerous studies with learners of a large age range (Parker & Kamps, 2011; Wichnic, Vener, Keating, & Pouson, 2009; Wichnick, Vener, Pyrtek, & Poulson, 2010).

Cartooning

Cartooning is a method of enhancing social understanding through the use of simple illustrations. The basic premise for cartooning is that individuals with autism are considered to do well with information presented visually. Cartooning frequently involves the drawing of thought and speech bubbles, which may enable an individual with autism to better understand nuances of social interaction, as well as what other people might be thinking during social interactions (Kerr & Durkin, 2004). Information that should typically be included for effective cartooning includes: where the student is, who else is with them, what the student is doing, what others are doing, what happened, what the student said, what the other people said, what the student was thinking, what the other people were thinking. Studies have shown positive outcomes from cartooning in elementary through high school-age individuals in areas of social behavior (Hutchins & Prelock, 2013; Kerr & Durkin, 2004; Li & Huang, 2012; Pierson & Glaeser, 2007, Thiemann & Goldstein, 2004; Rogers & Myles, 2001).

Power Cards

Power cards utilize the perseverative interests, which are characteristic of those with ASD as a means of motivation. The strategy was developed by Gagnon (2001) and consists of a brief scenario with a visual cue, typically aiding students with learning appropriate social behaviors. Power cards are explained in more detail in Chapter 11. The effectiveness of Power cards as an intervention for individuals with autism has been investigated in a small number of studies which demonstrated positive outcomes for most individuals (Angell, Nicholson, Watts & Blum, 2011; Campbell & Tincani, 2011; Davis, Boon, Cihak, & Fore III, 2010; Keeling, Myles, Gagnon, & Simpson, 2003).

Social Autopsies

A social autopsy is a problem-solving strategy designed to support social skills. Social autopsies can help students understand social interactions by analyzing any social errors committed in order to correct these errors in the future. Social autopsies can include any area where a person with a disability makes a social error. Some examples of social autopsy topics include responding to others' greetings, asking questions in class without raising a hand, continuing to talk about a topic others are not interested in, as well as many others. After a social error occurs, an adult works in a one-to-one session with the individual with a disability who committed the social error to ask and answer questions related to the social interaction where the error occurred. Social autopsies are not an evidence-based intervention for individuals with disabilities due to a lack of published research, although their use has anecdotally been reported to be beneficial to individuals with autism.

Video Modeling

Video modeling is an evidence-based practice for individuals with autism that combines the concept of modeling and visual learning, both of which are effective practices for those with autism. The basic steps for the implementation of video modeling related to behavior issues include: (1) identify a target behavior, (2) decide who should demonstrate the behavior on video (self, adult, peer, point-of-view), (3) create a script for the video, (4) collect baseline data, (5) record the video, (6) identify when and where to watch the video, (7) show the video to the learner, (8) monitor for effectiveness, (9) fade the video and prompt to correct errors. Video modeling has been used for a wide age range in individuals with autism across skills such as social communication, eye contact, toilet training, task engagement, purchasing skills, vocational skills, pretend play skills, cooking skills, among others.

In summary, antecedent-based strategies can be useful in both preventing challenging behaviors and in teaching appropriate behaviors so that the challenging behaviors are no longer necessary. The next sections of this chapter focus on two broad procedures often used in behavior intervention planning: reinforcement and punishment. Each will be discussed, along with specific information about types. We will give particular attention to the ethical use of punishment.

Reinforcement-based Strategies

What is Reinforcement?

Reinforcement is considered to be the most important principle of behavior and the key element of most behavior change programs (Northup, Vollmer, & Serrett, 1993). From the child receiving praise for a job well done, to the teenager skipping class to avoid concepts he does not understand, reinforcement contingencies can be seen all around us in everyday situations. Reinforcement is considered a naturally occurring phenomenon, and a person does not need to be aware of the contingencies taking place for reinforcement to work (Alberto & Troutman, 2012).

When most people think of reinforcement, they think of a person receiving something perceived as "good" (e.g., candy, high fives, praise). However, reinforcement is not about the perceived *quality* of the consequence provided; rather, it is concerned with how that consequence *affects* the future frequency of a behavior. For example, a consequence that one might find aversive (e.g., scolding, loud noises, painful stimulation) may actually be a reinforcer for someone else depending on the situation. What makes a consequence a reinforcer is its ability to increase the future frequency of the behavior it follows (Alberto & Troutman, 2012). There are two different types of reinforcement: positive reinforcement and negative reinforcement, and they are described in more detail below.

Types of Reinforcement

There are two types of reinforcement: positive reinforcement and negative reinforcement. It is a common misconception for individuals unfamiliar with behavioral terminology to assume that "positive" means "good" and "negative" means "bad," but these terms are not synonyms. "Reinforcement" always means an *increase* in the response rate of a target behavior, and the modifiers "positive" and "negative" only refer to the type of stimulus change occurring (Cooper, Heron, & Heward, 2007).

Positive Reinforcement

Positive reinforcement is what most people think of when asked to describe reinforcement, and it involves the introduction (or increase) of a stimulus following a behavior of interest. When a target behavior is followed by the presentation (or increase) of a stimulus, and as a result, the behavior occurs more frequently in the future, positive reinforcement has taken place (Alberto & Troutman, 2012). Everyday examples would include giving a student a sticker for correctly completing a worksheet (in which the sticker is the introduced stimulus or reinforcer); or telling a stranger "thank you" for holding the door open for you (in which the acknowledgement is the reinforcer). However, it is important to note that these examples would only be considered reinforcement if the student were to correctly complete more worksheets in the future, or the stranger were to open more doors in the future. A reinforcer does not (and cannot) affect the behavior it follows because that behavior has already occurred; a reinforcer can only affect the future frequency of that response in similar circumstances (Cooper et al., 2007). Therefore, one cannot assume a stimulus acted as a reinforcer unless the rate of the behavior of interest increases in the future.

Negative Reinforcement

Negative reinforcement is a less well-understood principle of behavior. It is characterized by escape or avoidance contingencies, in which a person engages in a target behavior in order to escape or avoid an aversive stimulus (Alberto & Troutman, 2012). When the target behavior is followed by the removal, termination, reduction, or postponement of an aversive stimulus, and as a result the behavior occurs more often in the future, negative reinforcement has taken place (Cooper et al., 2007). Examples of negative reinforcement would include taking a different route to work to avoid traffic (in which traffic is the aversive stimulus) or putting earplugs in your ears to escape, or reduce, a loud noise (in which the loud noise is the aversive stimulus). Just like with the examples of positive reinforcement, these instances could only be considered examples of reinforcement if the behaviors of taking a different route to work and using earplugs increased in the future.

Not surprisingly, many people tend to confuse negative reinforcement with punishment because they mistakenly think "negative" is synonymous for "bad" or because aversive stimuli are involved in both negative reinforcement and punishment (specifically positive punishment). However, in a negative reinforcement contingency, an *already present* aversive stimulus is terminated (or reduced) by the target behavior which then *increases* the future frequency of the behavior; and in a punishment contingency, an *absent* aversive stimulus is introduced (or increased) following the target behavior, which then *decreases* the future frequency of the behavior (Cooper et al., 2007).

Differential Reinforcement

Differential reinforcement is a reinforcement-based procedure that involves reinforcing one behavior while withholding reinforcement for another behavior. There are four different types of differential reinforcement commonly used in applied settings: differential reinforcement of alternative behavior (DRA), differential reinforcement of incompatible behavior (DRI), differential reinforcement of other behavior (DRO), and differential reinforcement of low rates of responding (DRL).

DIFFERENTIAL REINFORCEMENT OF ALTERNATIVE BEHAVIOR (DRA)

When using DRA, a practitioner is reinforcing a desirable alternative behavior while withholding reinforcement for the problem behavior (Vollmer, Roane, Ringdahl, & Marcus, 1999). Usually, the alternative behavior selected for a DRA program will be functionally equivalent to the problem behavior. This means that the alternative behavior will still be gaining the type of reinforcement that was once provided for the problem behavior, but in a manner that is more appropriate (i.e. a child raising his hand instead of shouting out to get the teacher's attention). An example of DRA commonly used in communication programs is functional communication training (FCT), in which a more appropriate communicative response is reinforced while the problem behavior (which served as communication) is placed on extinction (Vollmer et al., 1999).

DIFFERENTIAL REINFORCEMENT OF INCOMPATIBLE BEHAVIOR (DRI)

DRI is very similar to DRA, except that the alternative behavior reinforced is incompatible with the problem behavior (Alberto & Troutman, 2012). It is impossible for the incompatible alternative behavior to be performed simultaneously with the problem behavior because they are of different topographies. If the DRI program is implemented correctly, it is more likely for the incompatible, alternative behavior to occur than the problem behavior. An example of DRI procedure for use with a student with ASD who engages in motor stereotypy (i.e. hand flapping) while walking in the hallways might involve having the student carry books or other items that prevent him from engaging in the stereotypy.

DIFFERENTIAL REINFORCEMENT OF OTHER BEHAVIOR (DRO)

During a DRO, reinforcement is "delivered following a period of time during which the target behavior does not occur" (Nuernberger, Vargo, & Ringdahl, 2013, p. 106). If the problem behavior does occur during a set interval, reinforcement is withheld and the interval is reset. DRO programs provide reinforcement for not engaging in the problem behavior rather than providing reinforcement for engaging in an alternative behavior. For example, a teacher may set the class timer for 10-minute intervals, and reinforce those students who remain on task for the entire interval. The DRO procedure has been used successfully for both individual students and groups.

DIFFERENTIAL REINFORCEMENT OF LOW RATES OF RESPONDING (DRL)

The DRL procedure, reserved for those behaviors that are problematic in their frequency or duration, but for which complete removal of the behavior from the individual's repertoire is not the goal, involves the systematic reinforcement of progressively less (lower rates) incidence of a challenging behavior over time (Alberto & Troutman, 2012). For example, when teaching social skills to a student with ASD, one may wish to decrease a student's talk about their favorite topic (e.g. roller coasters) yet not wish to eliminate the student's talking altogether. The teacher may note that before intervention, the student on average talked about roller coasters for ten minutes, while talking about other topics with others for only two minutes.

Choose Effective Reinforcers   Reinforcement programs will be unsuccessful if an effective reinforcer is not used. Reinforcer preferences will often change because they are dependent on factors such as age, time of day, social interactions, and interest level, among others. Identifying reinforcers for most learners is relatively easy, although it can be difficult with learners having more severe disabilities (Cooper et al., 2007). This is why it is important to conduct preference assessments prior to beginning any reinforcement program.

Vary Reinforcers to Minimize Satiation Effects   When a practitioner uses a variety of reinforcers, it is less likely for the individual to become satiated with one particular reinforcer.

Provide Reinforcement Immediately   Reinforcement should always be provided immediately following the target behavior. If reinforcement is delayed, the direct effects of reinforcement will lose their effectiveness.

Reinforcement Must be Contingent   Reinforcement should be provided contingent upon the target behavior only. If reinforcement is not provided contingently upon the target behavior there is a risk of reinforcing other unwanted behaviors.

Set an Easily Achieved Initial Criterion for Reinforcement   Reinforcement should be easily achieved during the early stages of a reinforcement program so that the individual can come into contact with the reinforcement contingency quickly. In general, the initial criterion will be set slightly above baseline responding so that reinforcement is easily available yet teaching can still occur.

Shift from Contrived Reinforcement to Natural Reinforcement   It is preferable to use natural reinforcement, such as social praise, over contrived reinforcement because natural reinforcement is more likely to occur in everyday environments and the individual is more likely to come across these contingencies in day-to-day life (see Table 9.1).

Ethical Use of Punishment

What is Punishment?

Punishment is frequently used in disciplinary procedures within the school and justice system, as well as in the workplace and home environment.

Table 9.1 Advantages and Disadvantages of Reinforcement

Advantages of Reinforcement	Disadvantages of Reinforcement
• can be used to teach new skills • can be used to maintain already taught skills • can be used to shape behaviors • can be used to manage behavior • can increase motivation for learning • simple to use	• can lead to dependency on unnatural reinforcers for responding to occur • reinforcement "breaks" can take away from learning time • inadvertent use of negative reinforcement, DRO to reinforce problem behaviors • ethical considerations with negative reinforcement (i.e. using aversive stimuli to evoke a response) • loss of intrinsic motivation

Although it is commonly thought of as a bad thing, punishment is just as important to learning as reinforcement because it teaches us not to repeat behaviors that can cause us harm (Cooper et al., 2007). Like reinforcement, punishment is a naturally occurring phenomenon.

Punishment is the opposite of reinforcement in that it is used to *decrease* behavior rather than increase it. Specifically, when a stimulus change immediately follows a response and then decreases the future frequency of that response in similar conditions, it is said that punishment has taken place (Cooper et al., 2007). Just because a child is scolded at for coloring on the walls, you cannot say punishment has taken place. This would only qualify as punishment if the child decreased the amount of times he colored on the walls in the future or discontinued coloring on the walls altogether (Alberto & Troutman, 2012).

Although punishment is one of the basic principles of behavior, it is poorly understood, frequently misused, and is often the source of controversy (Cooper et al., 2007). This section will help to clarify some common misunderstandings with punishment, explain ways in which it can be used ethically, and some guidelines to keep in mind when using punishment-based interventions.

Types of Punishment

As with reinforcement, there are two forms of punishment: positive and negative punishment. Furthermore, just like with reinforcement, the terms "positive" and "negative" refer to the type of stimulus change taking place. Positive punishment involves the presentation or increase of a stimulus, and negative punishment involves the withdrawal or decrease of a stimulus. It is a common misconception to think that "positive" is synonymous with "good" and "negative" with "bad," but that is not the case. The term "punishment" will always mean that there is a *decrease* in the rate of a target behavior.

Positive Punishment

Positive punishment, also known as Type I punishment, occurs when a behavior is followed by the presentation (or increase in intensity) of an aversive stimulus that decreases the future frequency of the behavior (Cooper et al., 2007). An aversive stimulus would be considered any noxious or unpleasant stimulus whose introduction acts as a punisher. An example of positive punishment would be a child receiving a reprimand from her teacher for talking during a test, or a chef burning himself for holding his hand too close to a hot stove.

Negative Punishment

Negative punishment is also known as Type II punishment. With a negative punishment contingency, a target behavior is followed by the removal (or decrease in intensity) of an already present stimulus that decreases the future frequency of the behavior (Cooper et al., 2007). An example of negative punishment would be a child losing a point in class for getting out of his seat without permission. If the child decreases his rate of out-of-seat behavior in the future, then the loss of a point has acted as a punishment. For negative punishment to be effective, the stimulus that is removed (or decreased in intensity) must be considered to be a reinforcer for the individual.

Response Blocking

Response blocking involves the practitioner physically intervening as soon as an individual begins an undesired behavior to prevent or block the completion of the behavior (Langone, Luiselli, & Hamill, 2013). It is important to implement response blocking for every attempt to engage in the behavior. Response blocking can also lead to side effects such as aggression or resistance to the blocking procedure—this can be avoided by providing prompts and reinforcement for an alternative behavior (Cooper et al., 2007).

Overcorrection

Overcorrection requires the individual to engage in effortful behavior directly or logically related to the target behavior (Cooper et al., 2007). There are two types of overcorrection: restitutional overcorrection and positive practice overcorrection.

RESTITUTIONAL OVERCORRECTION

Restitutional overcorrection requires the individual to repair the damage caused by his or her misbehavior by returning the environment to its original state, and then engaging in additional behavior to bring the environment to a better condition than it was prior to the problem behavior (Miltenberger & Fuqua, 1981). An example would be a student throwing his box of crayons—he is required to pick up all of the crayons and put them away in his cubby and then he is asked to pick up all of the toys in the play area. Restitutional overcorrection cannot be used with behaviors which cause an irreversible effect or if the corrective behavior is not in the person's repertoire (Cooper et al., 2007).

POSITIVE PRACTICE OVERCORRECTION

Positive practice overcorrection "involves the interruption of problem behavior followed by a period of physically guided practice of an appropriate alternative response" (Peters & Thompson, 2013, p. 613). Positive practice overcorrection is useful in that it teaches the individual what is expected instead of the problem behavior. An example of positive practice overcorrection would be to require a student to walk around the perimeter of the pool following an instance of running.

Research has demonstrated that positive practice overcorrection can be effective at decreasing challenging behaviors for children with autism. Anderson and Le (2011) successfully decreased vocal stereotypy and increased engaged time for a seven year old with autism by instituting a positive practice overcorrection procedure for the vocal stereotypy. In their study, the researchers compared the effectiveness of the positive practice overcorrection procedure to differential reinforcement of other behaviors and response cost, finding that the overcorrection had greater success (Anderson & Le, 2011).

Examples of Negative Punishment Interventions

Time-out from Positive Reinforcement (Time-out)

Time-out is a well-known form of punishment. Time-out is implemented in both the educational and home environment as a go-to disciplinary procedure but, unfortunately, it is often misused and misunderstood by practitioners and parents. Time-out is defined as the contingent withdrawal of the opportunity to earn positive reinforcement or the loss of access to positive reinforcers following a problem behavior (Everett, 2010). This does not necessarily mean an individual is being moved to an isolated setting—it only means that the individual is losing reinforcement for an amount of time following the problem behavior. In other words, a child can physically remain in the time-in setting but not have access reinforcement. It is a common misunderstanding that time-out must involve the removal of the individual from the environment. Although there are time-out procedures that do involve a removal of the individual, they are not always more effective and are considered to be more restrictive.

There are three important aspects to time-out: there must be a discrepancy between the time-in and time-out environment, there must be a response-contingent loss of reinforcement, and the procedure must result in a decrease in the future frequency of the problem behavior. The distinction between the time-in and time-out environment is very important because the more reinforcing the time-in environment is, the more effective time-out will be as a punisher (Cooper et al., 2007).

Response Cost

A response cost procedure is similar to the withdrawal of a specific positive reinforcer, but response cost usually involves the removal of generalized conditioned reinforcers (e.g. money, tokens), tangibles (e.g. stickers, toys), or time from activities (e.g. minutes from recess or play time). Response cost is defined as a form of punishment in which the loss of a specific amount of reinforcement occurs following the problem behavior and results in a decrease in the future frequency of the problem behavior (Watkins, Paananen, Rudrud, & Rapp, 2011). Response cost can be used in tandem with positive reinforcement contingencies as well as with group contingencies (where a group of individuals earn reinforcers for certain behaviors).

A common way to implement response cost is to combine it with a token reinforcement system—where the individual can earn tokens for appropriate behaviors and lose tokens contingent upon problem behaviors. Response cost is implemented as a *fine*. A fine is when an individual is "fined" a specific amount of positive reinforcers contingent upon misbehavior.

Response cost is a fairly simple punishment procedure to implement as long as a practitioner determines in advance when and how it will be implemented, which behaviors result in a fine, and how many reinforcers can be taken at one time. If used appropriately, response cost can be effective in reducing a variety of problem behaviors without the undesirable side effects usually associated with punishment (Alberto & Troutman, 2012).

Effective Use of Punishment

When using behavioral interventions to decrease challenging behaviors, it is the ethical responsibility of the practitioner to implement the least-restrictive procedure. This means that reinforcement-based strategies—such as differential reinforcement and extinction—should always be implemented prior to a punishment-based intervention being attempted. If, however, reinforcement-based strategies have not been effective in reducing the problem behavior, and all the least restrictive options have been ruled out, then a punishment-based procedure may be considered.

Ethical Considerations for Punishment

Various professional organizations—including the Council for Exceptional Children (CEC), the Association of Professional Behavior Analysts (APBA), the Council for Children with Behavior Disorders (CCBD), and the Behavior Analyst Certification Board (BACB)—have developed guidelines and standards related to the use of punishment to address challenging behaviors. These guidelines and standards can help guide a practitioner in making ethical decisions when deciding on whether or not to use punishment as an intervention. There are several ethical considerations that a practitioner must look at, and three of the major issues regarding the use of punishment include the client's right to safe and humane treatment, the professional's responsibility to use the least restrictive intervention, and the client's right to effective treatment (Bailey & Burch, 2011).

Right to Safe and Humane Treatment

The main responsibility of any practitioner is to do no harm, which means the intervention itself must be physically safe for all involved and contain no elements of degradation or disrespect for the client (Bailey & Burch, 2011). The dignity, health, and safety of the client must be protected at all times for a punishment procedure to be considered humane. Although there is not a universal definition for "humane treatment," Cooper et al. (2007) suggest that a treatment can generally be considered humane if it is designed for therapeutic effectiveness, delivered in a compassionate manner, assessed frequently to determine effectiveness, terminated for ineffectiveness, and sensitive to the overall physical, psychological, and social needs of a client.

Least Restrictive Alternative

The more an intervention affects an individual's personal independence, the more restrictive it is. The *doctrine of the least restrictive alternative* holds that less intrusive procedures should always be tried and found to be ineffective before more intrusive procedures are implemented (Bailey & Burch, 2011). It is the responsibility of the practitioner to ensure that the least intrusive but *effective* treatment is used. In other words, if it comes down to a less intrusive, but ineffective intervention and a more intrusive, but effective intervention, the latter should always be chosen.

Professional organizations such as the BACB promote the use of reinforcement over punishment because reinforcement is considered to be less restrictive and more humane for the client. For a punishment-based intervention to be implemented, it is presumed that all positive approaches have been deemed ineffective. Although reinforcement-based interventions are considered to be less restrictive than punishment-based interventions, the restrictiveness of an intervention cannot be determined by the principles of behavior alone (Cooper et al., 2007). An intervention's level of restrictiveness depends on several factors, including the effects on a person's life and independence, procedural details, the amount of time required until clinical results are obtained, and the consequences associated with delaying the intervention.

Right to Effective Treatment

The Association for Behavior Analysis (1989/1990) has published two position papers on the effective treatment of clients. These two statements outline the client's rights during treatment and emphasize the importance of only choosing an intervention that is likely to be effective, based on both empirical evidence and assessment results (Bailey & Burch, 2011). In addition to these two statements, the BACB also emphasizes the client's right to effective treatment and recommends scientifically supported procedures during intervention (Behavior Analyst Certification Board, 2010). The right to effective treatment raises an important issue when considering the treatment for chronic, life-threatening problem behaviors. Although punishment may be considered a more restrictive intervention, it may be the most effective treatment for some individuals who have chronic, life-threatening challenging behaviors.

State and Federal Laws on Restraint and Seclusion

Two of the most controversial procedures used in the educational setting are restraint and seclusion. Seclusion is different from a time-out room in that it involves the student being confined to a locked room or space where he or she is physically prevented from leaving (in contrast to a time-out room in which the room is not locked). The United States Department of Education (USDE) released a document in 2012 that addresses the use of restraint and seclusion in public schools. This document outlines 15 principles that must be considered when developing and implementing restraint or seclusion procedures and specific restrictions in the use of these procedures.

In this document, the USDE emphasizes that,

> physical restraint or seclusion should not be used except in situations where the child's behavior poses imminent danger of serious physical harm to self or others and restraint and seclusion should be avoided to the greatest extent possible without endangering the safety of students and staff.

(USDE, 2012, p. 2)

Furthermore, the document states that:

> in cases where a student has a history of dangerous behavior for which restraint or seclusion was considered or used, a school should have a plan for: (1) teaching and supporting more appropriate behavior; and (2) determining positive methods to prevent behavioral escalations that have previously resulted in the use of restraint or seclusion.
>
> (USDE, 2012, p. 6)

Conclusion

Students with ASD do, from time to time, exhibit challenging behaviors: excesses that challenge their ability to be successful academically, socially, or functionally; as well as behavioral deficits. In this chapter we highlighted the first, and arguably one of the most important steps in addressing challenging behaviors, the functional behavioral assessment (FBA). The importance of the FBA is akin to the importance of an academic assessment when a student exhibits difficulties in math or reading. With behavior, however, the goal is to identify patterns of antecedents and consequences that point to a possible function, or maintaining reinforcer, for the behavior. Teachers and other professionals are part of a multi-disciplinary team that conducts the FBA, develops the Behavior Intervention Plan, and monitors the student's progress. When the student makes progress, the plan can be called successful and the hypothesized function may have been correct. If the student fails to make progress, however, there are numerous possible reasons. First and foremost among these is the possibility that the hypothesis as to function was incorrect. Professionals are urged in such cases to complete the FBA again to determine if another function may have been the issue. Other possible reasons for failure to make progress include human error (someone on the team fails to implement the intervention correctly or consistently), poor or inconsistent data collection to monitor progress, or lack of buy-in from professionals or family. Practitioners are encouraged to seek out specialists in their schools, districts, and communities for behaviors that are severe or threaten the safety of the student, staff, or peers.

References

Alberto, P. A., & Troutman, A. C. (2012). Applied behavior analysis for teachers (9th ed.). Upper Saddle River, NJ: Pearson.

Anderson, J., & Le, D.D. (2011). Abatement of intractable vocal stereotypy using an overcorrection procedure. *Behavioral Interventions*, 26(1), 134–146.

Angell, M. E., Nicholson, J. K., Watts, E. H., & Blum, C. (2011). Using a multi-component adapted power card strategy to decrease latency during interactivity transitions for three children with developmental disabilities. *Focus on Autism and Other Developmental Disabilities, 26*(4), 206–217.

Association for Behavior Analysis. (1989). *The right to effective behavioral treatment.* Kalamazoo, MI: Author. Retrieved March 25, 2015, from www.abainternational.org/about-us/policies-and-positions/right-to-effective-behavioral-treatment,-1989.aspx.

Association for Behavior Analysis. (1990). *Students' right to effective education.* Kalamazoo, MI: Author. Retrieved March 25, 2015, from www.abainternational.org/about-us/policies-and-positions/students-rights-to-effective-education,-1990.aspx.

Bailey, J. & Burch, M. (2011). *Ethics for Behavior Analysts* (2nd ed.). New York: Routledge, Taylor & Francis Group LLC.

Banda, D. R. & Grimmett, E. (2008). Enhancing social and transition behaviors of persons with autism through activity schedules: A review. *Education and †raining in Developmental Disabilities, 43*(3), 324–333.

Behavior Analyst Certification Board. (2010). *Guidelines for responsible conduct for behavior analysts.* Tallahassee, F.L.: Author. Retrieved March 25, 2015, from http://www.bacb.com/index.php?page=57.

Boesch, M. C., Wendt, O., Subramanian, A., & Hsu, N. (2013). Comparative efficacy of the Picture Exchange Communication System (PECS) versus a speech-generating device: effects on requesting skills. *Research in Autism Spectrum Disorders, 7*(3), 480–493.

Campbell, A., & Tincani, M. (2011). The Power Card strategy: Strength-based intervention to increase direction following of children with autism spectrum disorder. *Journal of Positive Behavior Interventions, 13*(4), 240–249.

Carlile, K., Reeve, S., Reeve, K., & DeBar, R. (2013). Using activity schedules on the iPod touch to teach leisure skills to children with autism. *Education and Treatment of Children, 36*(2), 33–57.

Cooper, J. O., Heron, T. E., & Heward, W. L. (2007). Applied behavior analysis (2nd ed.). Upper Saddle River, N.J.: Pearson.

Davis, K. M., Boon, R. T., Cihak, D. F., & Fore III, C. (2010). Power Cards to improve conversational skills in adolescents with Asperger syndrome. *Focus on Autism and Other Developmental Disabilities, 25*(1), 12–22.

Everett, G. E. (2010). Time-out in special education settings: The parameters of previuos implementation. *North American Journal of Psychology, 12*(1), 159–170.

Gagnon, E. (2001*). Power Cards: Using special interests to motivate children and youth with Asperger Syndrome and autism.* Shawnee Mission, KS: Autism Asperger Publishing Company.

Hutchins, T., & Prelock, P. (2013). Parents' perceptions of their children's social behavior: The social validity of social stories™ and comic strip conversations. *Journal of Positive Behavior Interventions, 15*(156), 156–168.

Keeling, K., Myles, B. S., Gagnon, E., & Simpson, R. L. (2003). Using the Power Card Strategy to teach sportsmanship skills to a child with autism. *Focus on Autism and Other Developmental Disabilities, 18*, 105–111.

Kerr, S., & Durkin, K. (2004). Understanding of thought bubbles as mental representation in children with autism: Implications for theory of mind. *Journal of Autism and Developmental Disorders, 34*, 637–648.

Lancioni, G. E., Singh, N. N., O'Reilly, M. F., Sigafoos, J., & Didden, R. (2012). Function of challenging behaviors. *Autism and Child Psychopathology Series.* doi:10.1007/978-1-4614-3037-7_4.

Langone, S. R., Luiselli, J. K., & Hamill, J. (2013). Effects of response blocking and programmed stimulus control on motor stereotypy: A pilot study. *Child and Family Behavior Therapy*, 35(2) 249–255).

Lequia, J., Machalicek, W., & Rispoli, M. J. (2012). Effects of activity schedules on challenging behavior exhibited in children with autism spectrum disorders: A systematic review. *Research in Autism Spectrum Disorders*, 6(1), 480–492.

Li, X., & Huang, Y. (2012). The Intervenient Strategy to develop autistic children's social understanding ability. *Qingdao Daxue Shifanxueyuan Xuebao/Journal of Teachers College Qingdao University*, 29(1), 49–54.

Machalicek, W., Shogren, K., Lang, R., Rispoli, M., O'Reilly, M. F., Franco, J. H., & Sigafoos, J. (2009). Increasing play and decreasing the challenging behavior of children with autism during recess with activity schedules and task correspondence training. *Research in Autism Spectrum Disorders*, 3, 547–555.

Matson, J. L., Bamburg, J. W., Cherry, K. E., & Paclawskyj, T. R. (1999). A validity study on the Questions About Behavioral Function (QABF) scale: Predicting treatment success for self-injury, aggression, and stereotypies. *Research in Developmental Disabilities*, 20(2), 163–175. doi:10.1016/S0891-4222(98)00039-0

Miltenberger, R. G. & Fuqua, R. W. (1981). Overcorrection: A review and critical analysis. *The Behavior Analyst*, 4(2), 123–141.

National Professional Development Center on Autism Spectrum Disorders. (2014). Retrieved June 5, 2016 from http://autismpdc.fpg.unc.edu/.

Northup, J., Vollmer, T. R., & Serrett, K. (1993). Publication trends in 25 years of the *Journal of Applied Behavior Analysis. Journal of Applied Behavior Analysis*, 26, 527–537.

Nuernberger, J. E., Vargo, K. K., & Ringdahl, J. E. (2013). An application of differential reinforcement of other behavior and self-monitoring to address repetitive behavior. *Journal of Developmental and Physical Disabilities*, 25(1), 105–117.

Olive, M. L., Boutot, E. A., & Tarbox, J. (2011). Teaching students with autism using the principles of applied behavior analysis. In E. A. Boutot, & B. S. Myles (Eds.) *Autism education and practice.* Boston, MA: Pearson.

O'Neill, R. E., Horner, R. H., Albin, R. W., Storey, K., & Sprague, J. R. (1997). *Functional assessment and program development: A practical handbook.* Pacific Grove, CA: Brookes/Cole Publishing Company.

Parker, D., & Kamps, D. (2011). Effects of task analysis and self-monitoring for children with autism in multiple social settings. *Focus on Autism and Other Developmental Disabilities*, 26(3), 131–142.

Peters, L. C. & Thompson, R. H. (2013). Some indirect effects of positive practice overcorrection. *Journal of Applied Behavior Analysis*, 46(3), 613–625.

Pierce, J., Spriggs, A., Gast, D., & Luscre, D. (2013). Effects of visual activity schedules on independent classroom transitions for students with autism. *Journal of Disability, Development, and Education*, 60(3), 253–269.

Pierson, M. R., & Glaeser, B. C. (2007). Using comic strip conversations to increase social satisfaction and decrease loneliness in students with autism spectrum disorder. *Education and Training in Developmental Disabilities*, 42, 460–466.

Rogers, M. F., & Myles, B. S. (2001). Using social stories and comic strip conversations to interpret social situations for an adolescent with Asperger Syndrome. *Intervention in School and Clinic, 36*, 310–313.

Test, D. W., Richter, S., Knight, V., & Spooner, F. (2011). A comprehensive review and meta-analysis of the social stories literature. *Focus on Autism and Other Developmental Disabilities, 26*(1), 49–62.

Thiemann, K., & Goldstein, H. (2004). Effects of peer training and written text cuing on social communication of school age children with pervasive developmental disorder. *Journal of Speech, Language, and Hearing Research, 47*, 126–144.

United States Department of Education. (2012). *Restraint and seclusion: resource document.* Washington, D.C.

Vollmer, T. R., Roane, H. S., Bingdahl, J. E., & Marcus, B. A. (1999). Evaluating treatment challenges with differential reinforcement of alternative behavior. *Journal of Applied Behavior Analysis, 32*(1), 9–23.

Watkins, N., Paananen, L., Rudrud, E., & Rapp, J. T. (2011). Treating vocal stereotypy with environmental enrichment and response cost. *Clinical Case Studies, 10*(6), 440–448.

Wichnick, A. M., Vener, S. M., Keating, C., & Pouson, C. L. (2009). The effect of a script-fading procedure on unscripted social initiations and novel utterances of young children with autism. *Research in Autism Spectrum Disorders, 4*, 51–64.

Wichnick, A. M., Vener, S. M., Pyrtek, M., & Poulson, C. L. (2010). The effect of a script-fading procedure on responses to peer initiations among young children with autism. *Research in Autism Spectrum Disorders, 4*, 290–299.

Chapter 10

Development of Academic Skills in Childhood

Leah Wood, Julie L. Thompson, and Jenny Root

Access to high-quality academic instruction provides students with autism spectrum disorder (ASD) the skills needed to be successful in life after school. Further, academic instruction can add richness, variety, and high-interest content into the lives of students with ASD. Given that individuals with autism demonstrate difficulties with social interaction, social communication, and restricted, repetitive interests that may lead to problem behaviors such as aggression and/or withdrawal, it is no wonder that the majority of interventions for individuals with ASD target language, social, and/or behavioral interventions.

Often academic instruction is a secondary or even tertiary concern, if a concern at all. Yet, public schools are federally mandated to align instruction for individuals with disabilities, including those with ASD, to the general curriculum (which for most states is the Common Core State Standards (CCSS); Common Core Standards Initiative, 2012a, 2012b; and the Next Generation Science Standards; NGSS, 2013). While not all individuals with ASD have intellectual disability (ID), the severity of ASD characteristics in some individuals, regardless of cognitive ability, may cause practitioners to call into question the priority of academic instruction for this population (e.g. Ayres, Lowrey, Douglas, & Sievers, 2011).

There is inherent value in providing academic instruction to all individuals with ASD. Dynamic, explicit instruction in academic skills can lead to improved post-school outcomes for students with a variety of support needs (Fleury et al., 2014). Martha Snell, an expert in the field of special education, urged professionals to evaluate the effectiveness of current practices and continuously seek out practices that are *even more* effective (Snell, 1983). Currently, there is a shift toward academics, with an emphasis on higher expectations for growth and achievement for all students (Courtade, Spooner, Browder, & Jimenez, 2012). This shift provides an opportunity for the field to seek out and evaluate academic practices that could improve the overall quality of life for individuals with ASD. Emerging research indicates that through appropriate academic instruction, students with ASD may experience a reduction in problem behaviors, an increase in engagement, and an increase in vocabulary and communication exchanges with others (e.g. Reutebuch, Zein, Kim, Weinberg, & Vaughn, 2015).

Adapting Instruction for Students with ASD

Undoubtedly, the challenge in providing effective instruction is modifying teaching to meet the unique profiles of individuals with ASD. This is a complex process due to the broad range of abilities and needs demonstrated by this population of students. The DSM-V describes students with ASD according to their level of support needs. Throughout this chapter, students with ASD are discussed according to the type of academic content standards they access. Students with ASD who need extensive academic supports typically access alternate assessments based on alternate achievement standards (AA-AAS). Students with ASD who need less extensive academic support typically access the unaltered CCSS. Research-based and evidence-based strategies are presented for supporting the specific needs of all students with ASD (those who access either format of the CCSS).

When selecting or modifying academic instruction, practitioners should consider how cognitive deficits experienced by individuals with ASD might impact academic performance. First, a deficit in joint attention (i.e. using eye gaze or gesture to attend to an item or event of interest; Mundy, Sigman, & Kasari, 1990) may interfere with a student's ability to detect when a teacher is emphasizing salient information. Second, limited perspective taking (i.e. Theory of Mind; Baron-Cohen, Leslie, & Frith, 1985) may impair a student's ability to write a persuasive argument, decipher the author or character's intent, and interpret complex mathematical situations. Third, individuals with weak central coherence (i.e. a strong bias towards details affecting focus on the whole task) will need explicit instruction on examining the whole of a concept or task and understanding how details situate themselves within this whole. Finally, difficulties with executive functioning (e.g. skills related to problem solving, planning, flexibility; Rajendran & Mitchell, 2007) can result in problems with organizing an outline to develop an expository text, planning an inquiry-based process to answer a science question, or setting up an equation based on a word problem (Loveland & Tunali-Kotoski, 2005).

In addition to taking into consideration the cognitive profiles of individuals with ASD, it is also important to understand the academic achievement profiles of this population. Whitby and Mancil (2009) conducted a literature review on the academic achievement of individuals identified with high-functioning autism or Asperger Syndrome across the ages of 3–17 years. Participants demonstrated average abilities in reading, decoding, and mathematics computation; they displayed deficits in comprehension, written expression, and complex problem-solving skills. Subsequently, Estes, Rivera, Bryan, Cali, and Dawson (2011) conducted a review of predicted academic achievement based on IQ scores and observed the academic achievement of children with ASD and IQ scores of 70 or above. Results were mixed. A number of students demonstrated strength in one academic area with simultaneous weakness in another. Some students performed significantly higher than grade level in mathematics and significantly lower in reading, while others performed significantly higher in reading and lower in mathematics.

Other studies (e.g. Brown, Oram-Cardy, & Johnson, 2013; Jacobs & Richdale, 2013; Nation, Clark, Write, & Williams, 2006) have assessed skill profiles of individuals with ASD specifically in the area of reading comprehension. From these investigations, two themes have emerged. First, oral language significantly impacts the reading comprehension of students with ASD (Ricketts, Jones, Happé, & Charman, 2012). There is a positive correlation between oral language skills and reading comprehension; the more skilled an individual with ASD is in communicating verbally, the more skilled this individual will be in comprehending written text (Brown et al., 2013). In general, individuals with ASD may have difficulty with the following comprehension processes: combining salient information, understanding references to previous ideas in the text, applying prior knowledge to reading, and self-monitoring text comprehension (Nation et al., 2006). Second, studies investigating the predictors of reading comprehension overwhelmingly included individuals with ASD who were vocal-verbal with IQs above 70. In effect, this provides little to no information for the approximately 50 percent of individuals with ASD who are served in public schools and have Iqs below 70 (Anderson et al., 2007). Fortunately, while there may be little research regarding the academic profile of this population, there is growing academic intervention research for individuals with ASD who are minimally vocal. This is encouraging because reading comprehension is a pivotal skill that provides access to all other content areas as well as leisure, daily living, and employment activities (Mastropieri & Scruggs, 1997; Spooner & Browder, 2015).

Recently, Wong et al. (2014) conducted a comprehensive literature review and identified 27 evidence-based practices (EBPs; Odom et al., 2005) for individuals with ASD. An EBP is an intervention that has been demonstrated successfully through a number of rigorous research investigations, has been carefully scrutinized through a systematic review using quality indicators, and is identified as meeting a high criterion of evidence and efficacy (Cook et al., 2015). The report from the National Professional Development Center (Wong et al., 2014) identified 13 EBPs supporting academic outcomes for elementary-aged students with ASD:

antecedent-based interventions, differential reinforcement of alternate/ incompatible/other behaviors, discrete-trial training, functional behavior assessment, peer-mediated instruction and intervention, prompting, reinforcement, social narrative, task analysis, technology-aided instruction and intervention, time delay, video modeling, and visual supports. For detailed description of these practices, readers are directed to pages 20–23 of the Wong et al. report. Classroom teachers can integrate these practices into instructional design to teach a range of academic skills to students with ASD who access the general curriculum or who access AA-AAS.

The following section of the chapter includes brief descriptions of the big ideas of mathematics, English language arts (ELA), and science. The section includes specific examples of instructional strategies derived from the research literature that can be applied to teach this content. The chapter concludes with suggestions for promoting maintenance and generalization of academic skills.

Teaching Mathematics, ELA, and Science to Students with ASD

This section examines big ideas across the core content areas for students in grades K-8 with ASD who access the general curriculum and students who access AA-AAS. The big ideas identified in this section are derived from the CCSS and the NGSS. Currently, the CCSS and the NGSS are the most commonly used academic standards in public schools. Additionally, the historical foundations of the CCSS and NGSS are rooted in research from the National Assessment of Education Progress (NAEP) frameworks (for reading and writing), the Trends in International Mathematics and Science Study (TIMSS; for mathematics), and the National Research Council (of the National Academy of Sciences; for science).

Mathematics

Mathematics standards in the elementary grades (K-5) within most states align with the domains outlined in the CCSS: counting and cardinality, numbers and operations/fractions, numbers and operations in base ten, operations and algebraic thinking, geometry, and measurement and data. The content of mathematics instruction for all students with ASD, including those who access AA-AAS, should align with the standards used in general education mathematics. The content should be prioritized so that it (a) focuses on pinpointed skills that represent key ideas within the domains and (b) supports the individual's ability to achieve personal life goals (Hunt, McDonnell, & Crocket, 2012).

Counting and Cardinality

Early numeracy, or number sense, is a key component to meaningful participation and access to mathematics for all students (NCTM, 2000). Number sense, and the foundation it lays for understanding operations, prepares students for making mathematical judgments and solving complex problems (McIntosh, Reys, & Reys, 1992). In the CCSS, early numeracy skills are directly addressed within the domain of counting and cardinality. Early numeracy skills include: rote counting, number identification, one-to-one correspondence, and orders of magnitude (e.g. "Show me *more*").

The domain of counting and cardinality is only addressed in kindergarten in the CCSS, however it is a vital prerequisite skill for the remaining domains. It is known that early mathematical understanding strongly influences later success in mathematics, and students who struggle in mathematics have often lacked opportunities to learn critical early numeracy skills (Berch & Mazzocco, 2007). If students with ASD who access the CCSS progress to later grades and struggle in mathematics, teachers should assess their early numeracy skills and consider whether the students received adequate opportunities to practice these skills in the past. Students who have difficulty with one-step addition word problems may not have the conceptual understanding of part-part whole relationships.

Saunders, Lo, and Polly (2014) described two tasks that teach students to decompose (subtract) and compose (add) to teach part-part whole relationships. In one task, students are provided with an initial and final set of a number sentence and are taught to find the medial set. This can be displayed visually or presented in the context of a word problem. In another task, teachers give students the final set (or "whole") and have students identify the initial and middle sets (or "parts").

Early numeracy skills within the domain of counting and cardinality can be taught to students with ASD who access AA-AAS during grade-aligned mathematics lessons using embedded instruction. For example, early numeracy skills can be embedded in a task analysis for solving grade-aligned mathematics problems across CCSS domains. (Jimenez & Kemmery, 2013; Jimenez & Staples, 2015). Students can be given instruction on the targeted early numeracy skills (i.e. making and combining sets), however they can be applied within the grade-aligned problem without additional instruction (i.e. use operations with whole numbers to solve a problem). If students with ASD are provided with intensive instruction on early numeracy skills, such as one-to-one correspondence, making sets, and identifying patterns, they can apply those skills within grade-aligned activities. For example, when measuring perimeter students can place one-inch tiles around the perimeter and use one-to-one correspondence to count the perimeter in inches.

Numbers and Operations

Two domains within the CCSS address numbers and operations; the skills are divided between base ten and fractions. Standards within numbers and operations in base ten build upon standards in the domain of counting and cardinality. Place value is heavily emphasized from first through fifth grade, as it is used for problem solving with single and multi-digit numbers across the four operations. Comparing magnitude and quantities is an early numeracy skill that is needed as comparisons are made between multi-digit numbers based on their place value. The early numeracy skill of patterning is built upon in this domain, as concepts of multiplication and scientific notation are introduced. The application of numbers and operations to fractions is introduced in the later elementary grades by first recognizing and representing fractions and then understanding equivalence and orders of magnitude. The relationship between fractions, decimals, and percent is a foundational skill for algebra and requires fluency with solving calculation and word problems requiring all four operations.

Mastropieri, Bakken, and Scruggs (1991) identified a continuum of research-based strategies for teaching computational skills, which ranges from concrete (manipulative) to abstract (numeral) approaches. Representational strategies lie between the concrete and abstract approaches. The use of a number line is one abstract approach that is emphasized in the CCSS throughout elementary and secondary grades. A number line is a graphic organizer; it provides a concrete representation of the relationship between numbers and can provide a support for students to complete computation problems.

Another abstract approach is dot notation, first introduced by Kramer and Krug (1973). Popularly referred to as "Touch Math" or "Touch Points," stimulus cues are embedded within each numeral and students are taught to count each touch point within the numerals in a forward or backward motion to complete addition or subtraction operations. In an investigation of the differential effectiveness of number lines and dot notation, Cihak and Foust (2008) taught elementary students with autism who accessed AA-AAS single-digit addition problems with each of the methods and found students had an increased rate of learning and success with the dot notation strategy compared to when they used the number lines. Both abstract strategies of number lines and dot notations are portable and generalizable strategies to teach elementary students with ASD who have the fine motor and working memory prerequisite computational skills.

Manipulatives can be used to teach students numbers and operations in base ten. Virtual manipulatives in mathematics for general education students have had positive results (Reimer & Moyer, 2005; Suh, Moyer, & Heo, 2005) and initial investigations show that it is a promising practice for elementary students with ASD as well. Emerging research has shown that virtual manipulatives may be more effective for and preferred by students with ASD (Bouck, Satsangi, Doughty, & Courtney, 2013; Root, Browder, Saunders, & Lo, 2015). Virtual manipulatives can be accessed using free online resources such as the National Library of Virtual Manipulatives (http://nlvm.usu.edu) or created using software programs such as SMARTboard®.

Operations and Algebraic Thinking

Foundations for algebraic thinking are laid in the beginning years of mathematics instruction. Those early reasoning skills are applied throughout the domains of the CCSS as well as in real-world contexts. Real-world problems involve recognizing and analyzing relationships between quantities. Without conceptual understanding of operations and their relationship to algebra, students are limited to computational skills without real-world application.

According to the information processing theory (Sternberg, 1985), executive functioning processes influence an individual's learning ability and are crucial for planning, monitoring, and evaluating academic tasks (Montague, 1997). Mathematics problem solving requires the allocation of mental resources to lower order processes for carrying out problem solving and higher-order executive functioning processes to monitor and evaluate task performance (Kolligan & Sternberg, 1987). Cognitive strategy instruction utilizes key features of explicit instruction (Montague & Dietz, 2009) and cognitive and metacognitive strategies for solving word problems. Cognitive strategy instruction, such as the use of the commercial *Solve it!* program, has been shown to be effective for teaching students who access the CCSS to solve math word problems (Whitby, 2012). For students with ASD who access the CCSS, cognitive strategy instruction provides a systematic method for solving problems. For those students with ASD who access AA-AAS, a more explicit problem-solving strategy may be needed.

Research is emerging on the efficacy of modified schema-based instruction (SBI) to teach problem solving to students with ASD who access AA-AAS. When students do not have the computational skills to solve problems, conceptual strategy instruction needs to be supplemented with procedural strategy instruction. In order to effectively support students with ASD in learning word problem-solving skills, modifying the traditional approach to SBI and taking into consideration the learning challenges of this population shows promise (Root et al., 2015; Saunders et al., 2014). Modified SBI incorporates (a) a task analysis paired with pictures in each step as a heuristic for solving the problem, which replaces the mnemonics (e.g. "RUNS") in other SBI interventions; (b) a color-coded graphic organizer for each problem type to represent concrete schemas, with manipulatives to enhance the salient features of each problem type; and (c) explicit and systematic prompting to teach each step of the task analysis, addressing both conceptual and procedural knowledge of word problem solving.

Geometry, Measurement, and Data

The sequence of skills within the elementary CCSS domain of geometry progresses from the identification of shapes and solving problems related to their properties to using the coordinate plane. The domain of measurement and data is present across the elementary grades in the mathematics CCSS. Skills build from recognizing and describing attributes to solving problems using standard and non-standard measurements in kindergarten through second grade. Later elementary grades apply previous knowledge to describing attributes of and solving problems with shapes and figures. Finally, students are expected to know how to display and interpret data using various methods.

The literature base on teaching skills that fall within the domain of measurement to students with ASD is extensive. Based on the comprehensive mathematics literature review conducted by Browder, Spooner, Ahlgrim-Delzell, Harris, and Wakeman (2008), 36 out of the 79 empirical design studies published between 1975 and 2005 that taught mathematics to individuals with severe disabilities, including students with autism who accessed alternate achievement standards, fell under the domain of measurement. On the other hand, there were only two studies that met inclusion criteria that targeted data analysis. Since 2005, an additional 13 studies have been published targeting measurement skills, one of which also taught data analysis to high school students with autism and moderate ID (Browder et al., 2012). Across the published high-quality studies teaching measurement and data analysis, systematic instruction with multiple exemplars is a common feature of instructional packages, which promotes generalization.

Prompting has been identified as an EBP for teaching academic content to students with ASD (Wong *et al.*, 2014). One research-based prompting procedure for teaching concepts to students with ASD is explicit instruction. Explicit instruction is characterized by conspicuous sequences of instruction (Dixon, Carnine, & Kame'enui, 1992). Multiple exemplar training is one explicit instruction strategy. In multiple exemplar training, the instructor presents both examples and non-examples (e.g. items that are same and items that are different). First, the instructor models with rapid succession, pointing to an example and stating the concept (e.g. "These are the same") and then pointing to a non-example and stating that it is not the concept (e.g. "This is not same"). Massed trials are conducted with instructor models. After sufficient modeling, the instructor may test for either expressive or receptive understanding. To test expressive understanding, the instructor may say: "What is this?" and require the student to say "same" or "not same." To test receptive understanding, the instructor may say: "Touch same" or "Touch not same." A rule would be set for the number of errors a student can make before the instructor resumes modeling (i.e. two consecutive errors results in five additional modeling rounds). Only once mastery is met on the first concept (same) would the instructor introduce the opposite concept (different).

English Language Arts

In response to the need to determine the most effective and efficient ways to teach students to read, congress appointed a National Reading Panel (NRP, 2000) comprised of literacy experts, educators, and parents to conduct a comprehensive review of research on reading instruction. They submitted a report delineating five fundamental skill areas crucial to developing highly effective reading abilities: phonemic awareness, phonics, reading fluency, vocabulary, and reading comprehension (NRP, 2000), which are embedded within the CCSS ELA anchor standards in reading, writing, speaking and listening, language, and foundational skills. This section describes research and strategies for these five key areas of reading instruction that have been effectively used with students with ASD who access either the CCSS or AA-AAS. Additionally, research and strategies related to writing are included, as this is an important cross-cutting skill, with both academic and functional utility.

Phonemic Awareness

Phonemic awareness is the ability to hear the smallest units of sounds in words. Students with proficient phonemic awareness skills can identify all the separate sounds in a word they hear (i.e. segment the sounds in words). They can also put sounds together to say the word as a whole (i.e. blend the sounds; NRP, 2000). Phonemic awareness is addressed in kindergarten and first grade in the CCSS within the Reading Standards: Foundational Skills. While not directly addressed in subsequent grades, due to the importance of this skill, students continue to benefit from consistent practice, which can be easily embedded into daily instruction (Bursuck & Damer, 2011). Students in upper elementary who have not mastered letter sound identification can practice identifying and producing the first sound they hear in grade-level science vocabulary. Explicit instruction in phonemic awareness is demonstrated to result in significant long-term gains in reading and comprehension for children without disabilities (Kjeldsen, Kärnä, Niemi, Olofsson, & Witting, 2014).

Table 10.1 Research-based Practices and Examples for Teaching Math

Math Domain	Examples for Students who Access the General Curriculum	Examples for Students who Access AA-AAS
Counting and cardinality	Using model-lead-test and *visual supports* of a numbers chart, students learn to orally skip count by 10s, 5s, and 2s. For example, a teacher first points to the number 5 and says "My turn. I am going to point to the numbers and skip count by 5s to 30. 5, 10, 15, 20, 25, 30. Now let's count together." The teacher and student(s) count together (lead). Finally, the teacher provides the student with an opportunity to practice the skill independently. As the student demonstrates fluency and mastery, the *visual support* of the hundreds chart should be faded.	Using *time delay*, teachers teach number identification. In a 0-s round, the teacher holds up a flash card with the number 3 and provides the instructional cue "What number?" immediately followed by the controlling prompt "3." After the student responds "3," the teacher provides praise and moves on to another number. Following several 0-s rounds, a delay of 4s is inserted between the instructional cue ("What number") and the controlling prompt ("3"). If the student makes an error, the teacher states, "If you are unsure, wait and I will help you." Students are taught to demonstrate mastery of both receptive and expressive number identification.
Numbers and operations	Students solve a double-digit addition problem with the use of *technology-aided instruction and intervention*, which is used to display virtual manipulatives for students to use in solving double-digit addition problems that require regrouping. The teacher will use the *least-to-most prompting* by following a hierarchy of verbal, specific verbal, and model prompts when the student demonstrates an incorrect or no response.	Using *discrete-trial training and explicit instruction*, the teacher first identifies examples (e.g. "This is more") and non-examples (e.g. "This is not more") before asking students to identify "more" and "not more" using multiple exemplars.
Operations and algebraic thinking	Students use a *task analysis* containing the steps of solving a word problem in both words and pictures as a *visual support*.	During *peer-mediated instruction*, one solving word problems, peers use model-lead-test to help students use manipulatives to create sets representing the situation posed in the word problem.
Measurement and data	A classmate uses *peer-mediated instruction* to teach the definition of obtuse, acute, right, reflex, and straight angles using *time delay*.	The teacher constructs a pictograph of the student's favorite animals as an *antecedent-based intervention*. The student compares the number of dogs and cats using the *visual support* of a number line.
Geometry	*Technology-aided instruction and interventions* is used by students as they use virtual measurement devices and calculators to find the area and perimeter of real-world quadrilaterals.	The teacher creates a PowerPoint slide depicting examples and non-examples of ABAB patterns using multiple exemplars as *technology-aided instruction and intervention*. When the student selects the ABAB pattern, music plays briefly as *reinforcement* for the correct answer before moving on to the next slide.

Phonemic awareness has been typically taught to individuals with ASD as a component of larger comprehensive reading programs (e.g. Early Literacy Skill Builder©, HeadSprout© Early Learning; Browder, Ahlgrim-Delzell, Courtade, Gibbs, & Flowers, 2007; Grindle, Hughes, Saville, Huxley, & Hastings, 2013). Students with ASD who access the general curriculum are likely to successfully learn phonemic awareness via traditional instructional activities, such as learning to "stretch" the sounds in words and then say the words "fast." Instruction for students who access AA-AAS and/or are minimally vocal can be taught by the teacher modeling how to segment sounds by slowly saying each sound (phoneme) in a word while simultaneously tapping once for each syllable (e.g. "sh"/tap, "u"/tap, "t"/tap). Then, using a hierarchy of prompts from least intrusive (e.g. verbal prompt) to most intrusive (e.g. model prompt) as needed, teachers can teach students to tap simultaneously while the teacher slowly says each sound in the word (Browder et al., 2007).

Phonics

Phonics is the ability to connect a spoken sound to a written letter or sounds to groups of letters (NRP, 2000). Phonics is best taught through explicit instruction for all students including those with ASD (NRP, 2000). Understanding the letter–sound relationship enables individuals to read novel words; this is called decoding. Phonics instruction is addressed in kindergarten through fifth grade in the CCSS within the Reading Standards: Foundational Skills. Initially, children learn basic one-to-one correspondence of letter to sound and build towards combined knowledge of roots, prefixes, and suffixes to access unfamiliar words. Many children with autism demonstrate the ability to sight read orally at a young age, yet they are unable to decode nonwords (e.g. bep, snad, dop). Unfortunately, this ability to sight read has tempted teachers to neglect decoding instruction for individuals with ASD; however, strength in decoding is a significant predictor of reading comprehension and should be taught to auditory-intact students with ASD even those who can fluently read most whole words (Brown et al. 2013; Nation et al., 2006). Phonics instruction has typically been taught using discrete-trial training or time delay, via teacher-led and/or technology assisted instruction, to students with ASD across all support levels (Ahlgrim-Delzell, Browder, & Wood, 2014; Bailey, Angell, & Stoner, 2011; Browder et al., 2007; Grindle et al., 2013; Houglum, Mclaughlin, Weber, Neyman, & Gould, 2013; Nopprapun & Holloway, 2014). However, students with ASD who do not use functional vocal speech have not typically been able to access decoding programs that require the independent production of speech sounds. Technology-assisted instruction (TAI) allows students to produce phoneme sounds through technology-based platforms, such as iPads. For example, programs that pair systematic instruction procedures (e.g. constant time delay) with TAI can teach students with ASD to segment and blend sounds and read connected text (Early Reading Skills Builder©; Ahlgrim-Delzell et al., 2014; Whalen et al., 2010)

Fluency

Reading fluency involves reading connected text at a proficient rate and with accuracy and expression (NRP, 2000). Once students are able to decode words, it is important that they learn to read fluently so that they can focus on deriving meaning from text (Fuchs, Fuchs, Hosp, & Jenkins, 2001). Fluency instruction is addressed in kindergarten through fifth grade in the CCSS within the Reading Standards: Foundational Skills. Initially children learn to read emergent texts with accuracy and build towards expressive well-paced reading, demonstrating comprehension of text (e.g. voice increasing pitch to indicate a question). One promising approach to support fluency of students with ASD, for both those who access the general curriculum and those accessing AAA-AS, is through the use of repeated reading (i.e. students read a passage 2–4 times in a row; Hua et al., 2012; Kamps, Barbetta, Leonard, & Delquqndri, 1994; Reisener, Lancaster, McMullin, & Ho, 2014). Repeated reading conducted during peer-mediated instruction has been demonstrated to be beneficial to both individuals with ASD and their typically developing peers (Kamps et al., 1994). Peers can take turns with one student reading a brief passage aloud at least twice while the other peer provides positive feedback and points on a score card for correctly read sentences (Kamps et al., 1994).

Vocabulary

Vocabulary skills include (a) understanding the meaning of words that are heard and read and (b) using words accurately in speaking and writing (NRP, 2000). Vocabulary instruction is taught from kindergarten through fifth grade in the CCSS within the Language Standards. Across all grade levels students learn unknown and multiple-meaning words and explore the nuances of word meanings. Moreover, students learn to embed acquired words in spoken and written products. Vocabulary words increase in complexity over the years. In addition, students in upper grades are taught the concept of figurative language. Vocabulary is also often embedded into comprehensive literacy programs such as Corrective Reading©, Early Literacy Skill Builder©, Early Reading Skill Builder©, HeadSprout© Early Reading, and Language for Learning©, all of which have research demonstrating successful effects on vocabulary acquisition by students with autism who access either CCSS or AA-AAS

(Ahlgrim-Delzell et al., 2014; Browder et al., 2008; Flores et al., 2013; Grindle et al., 2013). These programs, as well as other independent interventions, use time delay, explicit instruction, within stimulus prompting, Direct Instruction, and/or TAI to teach vocabulary. For example, students who access AA-AAS can be taught sight words using time delay instruction by superimposing the text over corresponding photographs depicting the meaning of the text and slowly fading the picture in the background until only the sight word is shown (Birkan, McClannahan, & Kranz, 2007).

Another effective approach for teaching novel vocabulary to students with ASD, including those who are linguistically diverse, is the use of shared stories with embedded discrete trial instruction on contextual vocabulary words (Spooner, Rivera, Browder, Baker, & Salas, 2009). Teachers can select culturally relevant texts for interactive read-alouds. While reading the text aloud to students, teachers can embed instructional trials to teach literacy concepts such as target text vocabulary using systematic prompting strategies like constant time delay. After introducing the story, teachers can *warm up vocabulary* by first modeling how to pair each target word with a definition (picture or word) using 0-s time delay procedures, and then by repeating the trials with an embedded 4-s delay prior to the delivery of the model prompt (e.g. "Show me *colony*"). Then the teacher can read the story aloud and test for recognition and understanding of the vocabulary words as they appear throughout the story.

It is important that students with ASD be taught to understand figurative language and words with multiple meanings (i.e. homophones). Students with ASD who access the CCSS can be taught to increase their understanding of metaphors, idioms, and homophones, by modeling and then prompting students to use a visual support, such as thinking maps (i.e. graphic organizer student fills in to develop visual representations of the relationships between words). For example, students can use thinking maps to identify the individual meanings of the parts in words and then find common or connecting meanings between the words using the graphic organizer (Marshal & Kasirer, 2011).

Comprehension

Reading comprehension involves deriving meaning from connected text, which can be demonstrated by answering questions about a text, following written instructions, retelling a story or passage, and making predictions regarding future events in a text (NRP, 2000). Comprehending text is often difficult for students with ASD, even when they have proficient decoding skills (Asberg & Sandberg, 2010). There has been limited research on teaching comprehension to this population of students (Chiang & Lin, 2007). The use of shared stories (or interactive read-alouds) is an EBP for teaching literacy skills to students with moderate and severe disabilities, including some students with ASD. Prompting and visual supports in the form of graphic organizers have been used in this research to promote the listening comprehension of texts read aloud to students. Students who access the AA-AAS can be taught to answer questions about grade-level literature read aloud to them by using a modified system of least prompts to explicitly teach the process of answering comprehension questions (Mims, Hudson, & Browder, 2012). The least intrusive prompt is a verbal or visual reminder to the students of the "rule" for answering WH questions (e.g. "When you hear *where*, find a word that is a *place*"). The next level of prompting includes a repeated reading of the target text containing the answer (e.g. the teacher says, "I heard the answer in the text. Listen," and then rereads the sentence or sentences that contain the correct answer). For the final prompt, the instructor shows the student the answer in the text and states the answer out loud. Essential elements of these procedures include explicitly and systematically teaching students with ASD to identify the meaning of the question words and strategies for locating the answer in the text. This system of least prompts can also be modified to support students in answering inferential questions using a system of least prompts with a think aloud procedure (e.g. "I can think of a time that happened to me. Can you think of a time that happened to you?"; Hudson, Browder, & Jimenez, 2014). Another approach to support comprehension is by explicitly teaching story grammar to students with ASD who access AA-AAS. Students can listen to grade-aligned narrative texts read aloud. Then teachers can provide an electronic story map presented on an iPad and students can identify and record elements of the story (e.g. character, plot, setting). Students use the map to answer comprehension questions about the story (Browder, Root, Wood, & Allison, 2015).

Comprehension instruction for individuals with autism who access the general curriculum mirrors strategies used in general education or with individuals with learning disabilities including using story maps, anaphoric cueing, and peer-mediated instruction. Anaphoric cuing involves cuing students to underline all the pronouns in a passage and identify the person, place, or thing to which the pronoun is referring (O'Conner & Klein, 2004). Additionally, teachers can use examples and non-examples to teach students to complete a story map (a graphic organizer with blanks for characters, time, place, beginning, middle, and end) about a text (Stringfield, Luscre, & Gast, 2011). Finally, students with ASD can participate in collaborative strategic reading (CSR), a specific type of peer-mediated instruction, which includes making predictions, generating questions, summarizing, and problem-solving tricky vocabulary (Reutebuch *et al.*, 2015).

Writing

Writing, another element of ELA, can be used as a tool for promoting communication and assessing students' comprehension of texts. Writing is any permanent product that students produce, ranging from a written essay to a graphic organizer with picture symbols students paste in boxes to represent key details from a story. Despite the importance of writing, research on teaching writing is sparse (Pennington, Collins, Stenhoff, Turner, & Gunselman, 2014). The majority of this small body of research has focused on teaching spelling skills (e.g. Schlosser & Blischak, 2004) and sentence writing (e.g. Basil & Reyes, 2003). Only a few studies have examined strategies for teaching more sophisticated writing, including narrative writing (e.g. Pennington, Ault, Schuster, & Sanders, 2011; Pennington, *et al.*, 2014). One approach is to combine simultaneous prompting procedures (i.e. starting with a testing round to assess if a student can perform a skill independently, and following with a 0-s delay instructional round if needed; Morse & Schuster, 2004) with computer-assisted instruction to teach story writing skills to elementary aged students with ASD who access AA-AAS. Specifically, using TAI software (e.g. Pixwriter™) and simultaneous prompting procedures, students can learn to construct stories using a bank of preselected words (Pennington *et al.*, 2014).

Science

To address the need for improved outcomes for all students, the Committee on a Conceptual Framework for New K-12 Science Education Standards formulated a guide for teaching science to school-aged students. This framework includes the skills and processes students need to develop appreciation for science, gain employment skills based on scientific principles, acquire knowledge of scientific content, and hone the life-long skill of thinking critically about scientific information (NGSS Lead States, 2013). Collectively, the practices, concepts, and core ideas of this framework form the basis for the Next Generation Science Standards (NGSS), a set of performance standards intended to promote deep understanding and application of science.

Only a small amount of research has been done on teaching science to students with developmental disabilities. Within this body of research, an even smaller amount has focused on outcomes for students with ASD. Even so, the findings and implications within the emerging body of research suggest students with ASD can learn core vocabulary and concepts, comprehension, and an inquiry-based process for scientific understanding. The overall implication has potential to pique interest in scientific content, increase the capacity of students to communicate about scientific phenomena, and teach students problem-solving skills

Table 10.2 Research-based Practices and Examples for Teaching ELA

Reading Domain	Examples for Students who Access the General Curriculum	Examples for Students who Access AA-AAS
Phonemic awareness	Using *visual supports*, students learn to orally segment and blend during choral responding activities (e.g. teacher holds up one finger per phoneme as he says the sounds slowly and then closes his hand into a fist when he says the sounds "fast" as the word. When students are given the turn to chorally respond, the teacher continues to use his hand signal as a *visual support* to assist the students in segmenting and blending).	Using distributed *discrete-trial training* via *technology-aided instruction* students select pictures that correspond with segmented sounds (e.g. student hears /c/ /a/ /t/ and selects picture of a cat) and when given a picture selects the animated character who said the word (e.g. student shown picture of "bed," then three characters say three "stretched" words and the student selects the one that says /b/ / eeeee/ /d/.)
Phonics	Using model-lead-test and *reinforcement*, such as a token economy system for accurate responding, students name letter sounds corresponding with letters shown. For example, teachers shows letter M and says, "My turn: M," say it with me "M" (student says "M"). "Your turn" (student says "M") teacher provides student a token. After student earns preset number of tokens, session is briefly suspended while student gains access to preferred item. This *reinforcement* strategy can also be used with *discrete trial training* where the teacher first includes a series of teaching trials using letter cards and saying: "This says 'T' what sound?" (student says "T"), and this is repeated for several letter sounds. Then the teacher reintroduces the set and says: "What sound?" and provides *prompting* (e.g. teacher forms her mouth in shape to say to say sound) or error correction as needed.	Using *discrete-trial training* interspersed in a repetitive story lesson students point to correct letters from an array of four to indicate initial or final letter sounds of pictures shown in stories. For example, if "t" were the target letter sound, the teacher would read the story page then point to the cat and say, "This is a cat. Cat. /t/ Cat ends in /t/." The teacher gestures to letter cards on the table and says: "Can you show me /t/?" and provides *prompting* as needed.

Fluency	Using *technology-aided instruction* and a *task analysis* students listen to an e-book, practice reading the e-book aloud twice, record themselves reading the e-book, and email the recording to their teacher, family, or a friend.	Using *peer-mediated instruction* students follow along as their peer reads connected text aloud, then students practice reading aloud while peer provides *prompting* and *reinforcement* as needed. For students who are minimally vocal, *technology-aided instruction, prompting,* and *reinforcement* can be used to build fluency. For example, a student shown a sentence is given an interval of time to select the picture and is *prompted* if needed. In successive sessions, the teacher shortens the interval and only reinforces answers that "beat the timer," encouraging the student to build fluency.
Vocabulary	Teacher models reading, illustrating, and using a word in a sentence. Then, using *prompting* and *reinforcement* the teacher asks a student to formulate a new sentence with the word.	Using *time delay* teachers display a photo and direct the student to select the correct word in print from an array of four. This can also be taught using technology-aided instruction.
Comprehension	A teachers uses *prompting* with a think aloud procedure to teach and model how to answer inferential questions about the novel the student is reading.	Using *time delay*, the teacher pre-teaches the definition of story elements. After reading an adapted text aloud to the students, the teacher *prompts* students as needed using a system of least prompts to guide them to construct a story map using *technology-aided instruction*. Students use story maps to answer comprehension questions about the text.

that could possibly promote independence and quality of life outcomes. The small body of research on science for students with ASD is embedded primarily in research for students with severe disabilities, or students with moderate to severe ID. For this reason, the majority of research reviewed in this section includes science practices that were developed for students who access AA-AAS.

Spooner, Knight, Browder, Jimenez, and DiBiase (2011) conducted a review of literature in which science skills were taught to students with severe disabilities (including students with ASD). The findings from this review indicated this population of students was most typically taught science content or skills related to recall of science vocabulary terms, cooking, or health and safety. Spooner et al. (2011) identified 17 studies meeting inclusion criteria, and only one of these studies (Agran, Cavin, Wehmeyer, & Palmer, 2006) included instruction in the inquiry process. Based on the outcomes of these studies, Spooner et al. (2011) identified systematic instruction as an EBP for teaching science to students with severe disabilities.

Since the 2011 review by Spooner and his colleagues, several studies have been conducted in which science has been taught to students with ASD or other developmental disabilities. Instructional methods used in these studies all included explicit or systematic instruction. Targeted learning outcomes ranged from knowledge of core content to scientific practices, including inquiry-based approaches. The following instructional methods have emerged from this body of research.

Teaching Science Vocabulary

First, there are several examples from recent research for teaching science vocabulary and core concepts to students with ASD. Teaching science vocabulary, including scientific academic language (e.g. cause, effect) scientific descriptors (e.g. cold, hot) and scientific concepts (e.g. force, velocity) can be used to support comprehension of scientific content, including that presented through texts, video examples, and dialogue during in-class experiments and demonstrations. Equipping students with ASD with the vocabulary necessary to receptively understand content and expressively communicate ideas related to the content is a prerequisite to engaging in scientific activities and experiences. Explicit and systematic instruction can be used to teach science vocabulary. For example, science descriptors (e.g. cold, wet, heavy) can be embedded in inquiry lessons and taught explicitly to students with ASD through multiple exemplar training using a model-lead-test format (e.g. "This is cold, this is cold, this is *not* cold"; Knight, Smith, Spooner & Browder, 2012). Additionally, to promote generalization, novel objects can be embedded in the inquiry lesson as well.

Explicit instruction can also be used to teach understanding of scientific concepts. Knight, Spooner, Browder, Smith, and Wood (2013) taught the comprehension of science concepts through time delay and multiple exemplar training using a model-lead-test approach and a graphic organizer to students with ASD and ID. Through these procedures, students learned to sort pictures as examples or non-examples on a T chart (a two-column chart with the word "yes" on the left and "no" on the right). Smith, Spooner, and Wood (2013) taught students with ASD and ID to identify key science concepts through embedded computer-assisted instruction (CAI) delivered on an iPad. The researchers taught students using model-test explicit instruction procedures to teach both the recognition and application of science vocabulary terms (e.g. mitosis).

Teaching Comprehension of Science Texts

As mentioned in the section on English-Language Arts, there is a research base for teaching listening comprehension to students with ASD using systematic instructional procedures. Among the research on teaching listening comprehension of expository texts read aloud to students with developmental disabilities are two studies with a specific emphasis on science texts (Hudson et al., 2014; Wood et al., 2015). Hudson et al. (2014) taught peers in an upper-elementary school classroom to read adapted science texts aloud and ask questions to students with developmental disability. The peers were also taught to deliver a system of least prompts procedure as needed, using prompting procedures adapted from Mims et al. (2012). Wood et al. (2015) taught elementary-aged students with developmental disabilities to ask and answer questions to science texts through technology-aided instruction (e-texts) and systematic instruction (task analytic instruction, time delay, least-to-most prompting, and reinforcement). Specifically, through constant time delay procedures and a template on an iPad, students were taught to form a question that they could reference and replay using text-to-speech capabilities throughout the session. Students learned to locate answers to their questions in the e-text through least intrusive prompting procedures.

Inquiry-based Instruction

Another research-based instructional method for teaching science to students with ASD includes teaching the process of inquiry through task analytic instruction. Courtade, Browder, Spooner, and DiBiase (2010) trained special education teachers to follow the steps of a task analysis for teaching an inquiry-based lesson to students with moderate and severe disabilities in a middle school classroom. A recommendation from this research is to develop a task analysis across four phases:

(a) promote engagement, (b) investigate and describe relationships, (c) construct explanation, and (d) report. During the engagement phase, teachers can pique student interest by presenting related pictures or objects, prompting students to access prior knowledge or personal experiences, and asking students what else they would like to know about the specific topic. During the investigation phase, teachers can give students choice in the materials they would use to examine the investigative questions. Teachers can ask students to identify patterns and observe characteristics. In the construct explanation phase, teachers can teach students to use pictures, symbols, or words to explain, justify, and test their explanations. In the report phase, teachers can give students opportunities to share their discoveries and answer questions to test their knowledge.

The strategies and procedures developed by Courtade et al. (2010) have been applied in settings with students with ASD, as well. Jimenez, Lo, and Saunders (2014) taught three students in grades 3 and 4 with ASD and moderate to severe ID to participate in inquiry lessons spanning the topics of rock cycle, life cycle, and senses. A recommendation from this research is to develop instruction with nine essential elements: (a) teacher reads a *wonder story*, a brief science text intended to pique interest and link topics to personal experiences; (b) teacher uses constant time delay procedures to pre-teach core vocabulary; (c) students make a prediction about the outcome of the experiment or demonstration; (d) teacher uses multiple exemplar training (i.e. examples and non-examples) to teach the key scientific concept; (e) teacher guides the student through a demonstration or experiment; (f) student records observations on a KWHL chart; (g) student reexamines the original prediction and makes changes if necessary; (h) teacher uses a model-lead-test approach to teach students to use observation data to complete the concept statement and record what was learned on the "L" of the KWHL chart; (i) students independently complete science quizzes about the target concept.

Teachers can also use technology-aided instruction to deliver inquiry-based lessons to students with ASD. Task analyzed science lessons with embedded prompting and error correction procedures can be presented electronically. For example, Smith, Spooner, Jimenez, and Browder (2013) presented the wonder story, KWHL chart, and response options electronically, allowing for students to record predictions and observation data and select comprehension question responses all from the SMARTboard.

Putting it All Together

If EBPs are used to teach not only academic content, but also academic processes; students with ASD can apply these processes across instructional

Table 10.3 Research-based Practices and Examples for Teaching Science

Research-based Practice	Examples for Students who Access the General Curriculum	Examples for Students who Access AA-AAS
Science vocabulary	Prior to a lesson on landforms, in a 1:1 format, the teacher uses *prompting* to teach the concept of different landforms (e.g. glacier, sand dune) and forces that change the shape of landforms (e.g. gravity, ice, wind).	Prior to a lesson on ecosystems, a teacher uses *time delay procedures* to teach recognition of five core vocabulary words (e.g. habitat, terrain, animal, plant, climate). The teacher also teaches definitions of the words using multiple exemplar training (e.g. this is a habitat, this is NOT a habitat).
Listening comprehension of science texts	The teacher gives a student a science e-text *(technology-aided instruction)* on solar systems to read independently. The text is at the student's readability level (fourth grade), and the student has been *prompted* to use the supported features to replay any text he struggles to read independently. The student records questions and answers to his questions in a science journal.	A teacher notices that his students are fascinated by rain. The teacher selects a book about the water cycle that is written at a second-grade listening comprehension level. The teacher uses a system of least prompts procedure and a graphic organizer as a *visual support* to help students ask and answer questions about the water cycle before and during reading.
Inquiry-based instruction	A student and his group of two peers *(peer mediated instruction)* pick a unit to explore given a choice of three. They choose to learn about electricity. With the help of *verbal prompts* from his partner and a *task analysis* for completing the steps of the experiment, the student and his partner formulate questions about electricity, conduct an experiment, record observation notes in a science journal, and report findings to the class.	A teacher shows *pictures and objects (visual supports)* related to reptiles, and the students record facts they already know about reptiles on a KWHL chart *(visual supports)*. Peers in the students' groups *model* how to ask questions. Using a *template (visual supports)* on an iPad *(technology aided instruction)*, the students select a question word and a question stem to form the question, "What do reptiles eat?" One group discusses how to investigate this question, and they decide to observe the class lizard. They record observations on the *KWHL chart*, and the student with ASD selects *pictures* from examples and non-examples to represent evidence.

units and content areas. The application of content area skills using natural supports in generalized settings is what makes the content functional. Without the cognitive processes of critical thinking (including self-questioning, problem solving, critical thinking, and inquiry) the functional application of content area knowledge is limited. Graphic organizers and technology are supports that can be applied to academic instruction across content areas to help promote generalization of skills and processes.

Graphic Organizers

Supports such as graphic organizers can facilitate critical thinking for students with ASD. Graphic organizers are visual displays that show the relationship between units of information (Fischer & Schumaker, 1995). For students with ASD, they are tools that provide concrete visual representations of abstract concepts, providing a visual representation for reasoning and critical thinking. Two important steps must be taken before students are expected to be able to use a graphic organizer: (1) the graphic organizer must be deliberately selected or created, and (2) the student must be taught how to use it (for a decision making process for selecting or creating graphic organizers, see Root & Wood, 2015). In the case of reading comprehension, a graphic organizer could be used to teach students with ASD to identify and record story elements, following the steps outlined in the studies conducted by Browder et al. (in press). Graphic organizers can also be used to support mathematical problem solving for students with ASD. For students who know their math facts, graphic organizers are used to represent the problem types and "story grammar" of what is happening in math word problems. A student with ASD who accesses the general curriculum could be taught to use a graphic organizer to discriminate between when to add and subtract in word problems based on his conceptual understanding instead of false reliance on key words (for an example, see Rockwell, Griffin, & Jones, 2011). A student with ASD who accesses AA-AAS could use manipulatives in combination with a graphic organizer to control for math fact knowledge and a variety of fine motor abilities. Recording background knowledge, questions, and outcomes on a KWHL chart during an inquiry-based science lesson has been shown to be instructionally beneficial.

Technological Supports

As technology has rapidly changed in formats and capabilities, the field of special education has followed with empirical evaluations on how this may enhance the lives of individuals with disabilities (Kagahora et al., 2013; Knight, McKissick, & Saunders, 2013; Pennington, 2010). Technology-assisted instruction (TAI) has been identified as an EBP for individuals with ASD (Wong et al., 2014). In an analysis of the types of skills addressed through TAI interventions for individuals with moderate and severe disabilities, including ASD, Browder et al. (2015) reported that many studies focused only on discrete skills, such as picture, object, and symbol identification (e.g., Bossler & Massaro, 2003; Chen & Bernard-Opitz, 1993). While these studies were successful, Browder et al. (2015) point out that little empirical evidence is available to support the use of TAI to teach complex skills to students with ASD, and that existing evidence varies across content areas. More evidence is available for TAI targeting literacy skills than mathematics or science standards.

Benefits of TAI include its ability to alleviate the burden of modeling tasks in the setting by staff (Ayers, Mechling, & Sansosti, 2013), reinforcement (Moore & Calvert, 2000), and the removal of social demands (Higgins & Boone, 2006). TAI has been shown to be not only effective in increasing academic skills of students with ASD, but in decreasing challenging behaviors (Chen & Bernard-Opitz, 1993, Moore & Calvert, 2000), and increasing appropriate behaviors (Bosseler & Massaro, 2003; Heimann, Nelson, Tjus, & Gillberg, 1995). When TAI is used for group instruction, students with ASD can learn non-target information through observational learning (Mechling, Gast, & Krupa 2007). This increases the efficiency of teacher instruction by targeting multiple student objectives within one lesson. Practitioners can also use the embedded features within TAI to make modifications to learning materials based on individual student needs (McKissick, Spooner, Wood, & Diegelmann, 2013). For example, although one PowerPoint or SMARTboard lesson may be created to address a common learning objective, it can be individualized to address students' interest topics, prerequisite skills, or to adjust for low or high ability learners. In addition, the electronic format of many TAI interventions allows for easy sharing among educators and families, allowing for continuity of interventions across classrooms, school years, and between home and school.

Conclusion

The true test of mastery and generalization is when individuals with disabilities are able to apply skills they have learned in naturally occurring situations. Three major takeaways from research reviewed in this chapter include: (1) education of students with ASD must include instruction in foundational academic skills with academic language; (2) using EBPs and research-based methods, students with ASD can learn standards-based academic skills; and (3) students with ASD can learn not only academic content, but also academic processes.

Through academic processes, such as asking questions, solving problems, understanding text, and seeking information, students can learn skills to support and promote post-school outcomes and overall quality of life. Students may use these skills in their home, job and community. Through use of high-quality supports like graphic organizers and TAI, and multiple opportunities to practice skills across people, settings, and materials, students with ASD have the potential to benefit greatly from well-designed instruction in academic skills.

References

Agran, M., Cavin, M., Wehmeyer, M., & Palmer, S. (2006). Participation of students with moderate to severe disabilities in the general curriculum: The effects of the Self-Determined Learning Model of Instruction. *Research and Practice for Persons with Severe Disabilities, 31*, 230–241.

Ahlgrim-Delzell, L., Browder, D., & Wood, L. (2014). Effects of systematic instruction and an augmentative communication device on phonics skills acquisition for students with moderate intellectual disability who are non-verbal. *Education and Training in Autism and Developmental Disabilities, 49*, 517–532.

Anderson, D. K., Lord, C., Risi, S., DiLavore, P. S., Shulman, C., Thurm, A., . . . Pickles, A. (2007). Patterns of growth in verbal abilities among children with autism spectrum disorder. *Journal of Consulting and Clinical Psychology, 75*(4), 594–604.

Asberg, J., & Sandberg, A. D. (2010). Discourse comprehension intervention for high-functioning students with autism spectrum disorders: Preliminary findings from a school-based study. *Journal of Research in Special Educational Needs, 10*(2), 91–98.

Ayres, K. M., Lowrey, K. A., Douglas, K. H., & Sievers, C. (2011). I can identify Saturn but I can't brush my teeth: What happens when the curricular focus for students with severe disabilities shifts. *Education and Training in Autism and Developmental Disabilities*, 11–21.

Ayres, K. M., Lowrey, K. A., Douglas, K. H., & Sievers, C. (2012). The question still remains: What happens when the curricular focus for students with severe disabilities shifts? A reply to Courtade, Spooner, Browder, and Jimenez (2012). *Education and Training in Autism and Developmental Disabilities, 47*, 14–22.

Ayres, K. M., Mechling, L., & Sansosti, F. J. (2013). The use of mobile technologies to assist with life skills/independence of students with moderate/severe intellectual disability and/or autism spectrum disorders: Considerations for the future of school psychology. *Psychology in the Schools, 50*, 259–271.

Bailey, R. L., Angell, M. E., & Stoner, J. B. (2011). Improving literacy skills in students with complex communication needs who use augmentative/alternative communication systems. *Education and Training in Autism and Developmental Disabilities, 46,* 352–368.

Baron-Cohen, S., Leslie, A. M., & Frith, U. (1985). Does the autistic child have a "theory of mind"? *Cognition, 21*, 37–46.

Basil, C., & Reyes, S. (2003). Acquisition of literacy skills by children with severe disability. *Child Language Teaching and Therapy, 19*, 27–48.

Berch, D. B., & Mazzocco, M. M. (2007). *Why is math so hard for some children? The nature and origins of mathematical learning difficulties and disabilities.* Baltimore, MD: Brookes.

Birkan, B., McClannahan, L. E., & Krantz, P. J. (2007). Effects of superimposition and background fading on the sight-word reading of a boy with autism. *Research in Autism Spectrum Disorders, 1,* 117–125.

Bossler, A. & Massaro, D. W. (2003). Development and evaluation of a computer-animated tutor for vocabulary and language learning in children with autism. *Journal of Autism and Developmental Disorders, 33,* 653–672.

Bouck, E. C., Satsangi, R., Doughty, T. T., & Courtney, W. T. (2013). Virtual and concrete manipulatives: A comparison of approaches for solving mathematics problems for students with autism spectrum disorder. *Journal of Autism and Developmental Disorders, 44,* 180–193.

Browder, D. M., Ahlgrim-Delzell, L., Courtade, G., Gibbs, S. L., & Flowers, C. (2008). Evaluation of the effectiveness of an early literacy program for students with significant developmental disabilities. *Exceptional Children, 75,* 33–52.

Browder, D. M., Gibbs, S., Courtade, G., Ahlgrim-Delzell, L., & Lee, A. (2007). *Early literacy skills builder.* Verona, WI: Attainment Co.

Browder, D. M., Root, J. R., Wood, L., & Allison, C. (2015). Effects of a story-mapping procedure using the iPad on the comprehension of narrative texts by students with autism spectrum disorder. *Focus on Autism and Other Developmental Disabilities.* DOI: 1088357615611387. Retrieved June 5, 2016 from http://foa.sagepub.com/content/early/2015/10/12/1088357615611387.full.pdf+html.

Browder, D. M., Saunders, A. F., & Root, J. R. (in press). Technology-assisted learning and assessment for students with moderate and severe developmental disabilities In S. Ferrara, Y. Rosen, & M. Tager (Eds.). *Handbook of research on computational tools for real-world skill development.* Hershey, PA: IGI Global.

Browder, D. M., Spooner, F., Ahlgrim-Delzell, L., & Harris, A., Wakeman, S. Y. (2008). A meta-analysis for teaching mathematics to individuals with significant cognitive disabilities. *Exceptional Children, 74,* 404–432.

Browder, D. M., Trela, K., Courtade, G. R., Jimenez, B. A., Knight, V., & Flowers, C. (2012). Teaching mathematics and science standards to students with moderate and severe developmental disabilities. *The Journal of Special Education, 46,* 26–35.

Brown, H. M., Oram-Cardy, J., & Johnson, A. (2013). A meta-analysis of the reading comprehension skills of individuals on the autism spectrum. *Journal of Autism and Developmental Disorders, 43,* 932–955.

Bursuck, W. D., & Damer, M. (2011). *Teaching reading to students who are at risk or have disabilities: A multi-tier approach.* Pearson. Upper Saddle River, NJ.

Chen, S. H. A., & Bernard-Opitz, V. (1993). Comparison of personal and computer-assisted instruction for children with autism. *Mental retardation, 31,* 368–376.

Chiang, H. M., & Lin, Y. H. (2007). Reading comprehension instruction for students with autism spectrum disorders a review of the literature. *Focus on Autism and Other Developmental Disabilities, 22,* 259–267.

Cihak, D. F., & Foust, J. L. (2008). Comparing number lines and touch points to teach addition facts to students with autism. *Focus on Autism and Other Developmental Disabilities, 23*, 131–137.

Common Core State Standards Initiative. (2012a). *Common core state standards for English language arts & literacy in history/social studies, science, and technical subjects.* Common Core Standards Initiative.

Common Core State Standards Initiative. (2012b). *Common core state standards for mathematics.* Common Core State Standards Initiative.

Cook, B. G., Buysse, V., Klingner, J., Landrum, T. J., McWilliam, R. A., Tankersley, M., & Test, D. W. (2015). CEC's standards for classifying the evidence base of practices in special education. *Remedial and Special Education, 36*, 220–234. DOI.org/10.1177/0741932514557271.

Courtade, G., Browder, D. M., Spooner, F., & DiBiase, W. (2010). Training teachers to use an inquiry-based task analysis to teach science to students with moderate and severe disabilities. *Education and Training in Developmental Disabilities, 45*, 378–399.

Courtade, G., Spooner, F., Browder, D., & Jimenez, B. (2012). Seven reasons to promote standards-based instruction for students with severe disabilities: A reply to Ayres, Lowrey, Douglas, & Sievers (2011). *Education and Training in Autism and Developmental Disabilities, 47*, 3–13.

Dixon, R., Carnine, D., & Kame'enui, E. J. (1992). Math curriculum guidelines for diverse learners. *Curriculum/Technology Quarterly, 3*(3), 1–3.

Estes, A., Rivera, V., Bryan, M., Cali, P., & Dawson, G. (2011). Discrepancies between academic achievement and intellectual ability in higher-functioning school-aged children with autism spectrum disorder. *Journal of Autism and Developmental Disorders, 41*, 1044–1052.

Fleury, V. P., Hedges, S., Hume, K., Browder, D. M., Thompson, J. L., Fallin, K., . . . Vaughn, S. (2014). Addressing the academic needs of adolescents with autism spectrum disorder in secondary education. *Remedial and Special Education, 35*(2), 68–79.

Flores, M. M., Nelson, C., Hinton, V., Franklin, T. M., Strozier, S. D., Terry, L., & Franklin, S. (2013). Teaching reading comprehension and language skills to students with autism spectrum disorders and developmental disabilities using direct instruction. *Education and Training in Autism and Developmental Disabilities, 48*, 41–48.

Fischer, J. B., & Schumaker, J. B. (1995). Searching for validated inclusive practices: A review of the literature. *Focus on Exceptional Children, 28*(4), 1–20.

Fuchs, L. S., Fuchs, D., Hosp, M. K., & Jenkins, J. R. (2001). Oral reading fluency as an indicator of reading competence: A theoretical, empirical, and historical analysis. *Scientific Studies of Reading, 5*, 239–256.

Grindle, C. F., Carl Hughes, J., Saville, M., Huxley, K., & Hastings, R. P. (2013). Teaching early reading skills to children with autism using MimioSprout early reading. *Behavioral Interventions, 28*, 203–224. DOI.org/10.1002/bin.1364

Heimann, M., Nelson, K. E., Tjus, T., & Gillberg, C. (1995). Increasing reading and communication skills in children with autism through an interactive multimedia computer program. *Journal of Autism and Developmental Disorders, 25*, 459–480.

Higgins, K., & Boone, R. (1996). Creating individualized computer-assisted instruction for students with autism using multimedia authoring software. *Focus on Autism and Other Developmental Disabilities, 11,* 69–78.

Houglum, R., McLaughlin, T. F., Weber, K. P., Neyman, J., & Gould, C. (2013). The effectiveness of direct instruction flashcards with guided practice activities to instruct two elementary students diagnosed with autism spectrum disorder and delays in pre-academics and communication. *International Journal of Basic and Applied Science, 2,* 11–37.

Hua, Y., Therrien, W. J., Hendrickson, J. M., Woods-Groves, S., Ries, P. S., & Shaw, J. W. (2012). Effects of combined repeated reading and question generation intervention on young adults with cognitive disabilities. *Education and Training in Autism and Developmental Disabilities, 47,* 72–83.

Hudson, M. E., Browder, D. M., & Jimenez, B. (2014). Effects of a peer-delivered system of least prompts intervention and adapted science read-alouds on listening comprehension for participants with moderate intellectual disability. *Education and Training in Autism and Developmental Disabilities, 49,* 60–77.

Hunt, P., McDonnell, J., & Crockett, M. A. (2012). Reconciling an ecological curricular framework focusing on quality of life outcomes with the development and instruction of standards-based academic goals. *Research and Practice for Persons with Severe Disabilities, 37,* 139–152.

Jacobs, D. W., & Richdale, A. L. (2013). Predicting literacy in children with a high-functioning autism spectrum disorder. *Research in Developmental Disabilities, 34,* 2379–2390.

Jimenez, B. A., & Kemmery, M. (2013). Building early numeracy skills in students with moderate intellectual disability. *Education and Training in Autism and Developmental Disabilities, 48,* 479–490.

Jimenez, B. A., Lo, Y., & Saunders, A. F. (2014). The additive effects of scripted lessons plus guided notes on science quiz scores of students with intellectual disability and autism. *The Journal of Special Education, 47,* 231–244.

Jimenez, B. A., & Staples, K. (2015). Access to the Common Core State Standards in mathematics through early numeracy skill building for students with moderate intellectual disability. *Education and Training in Autism and Developmental Disabilities, 50,* 17–30.

Kagohara, D. M., van der Meer, L., Ramdoss, S., O'Reilly, M. F., Lancioni, G. E., Davis, T. N., & . . . Sigafoos, J. (2013). Using iPods and iPads in teaching programs for individuals with developmental disabilities: A systematic review. *Research In Developmental Disabilities: A Multidisciplinary Journal, 34,* 147–156.

Kamps, D. M., Barbetta, P. M., Leonard, B. R., & Delquadri, J. (1994). Classwide peer tutoring: An integration strategy to improve reading skills and promote peer interactions among students with autism and general education peers. *Journal of Applied Behavior Analysis, 27,* 49–61.

Kjeldsen, A. C., Kärnä, A., Niemi, P., Olofsson, Å., & Witting, K. (2014). Gains from training in phonological awareness in kindergarten predict reading comprehension in grade 9. *Scientific Studies of Reading, 18,* 452–467.

Knight, V., McKissick, B. R., & Saunders, A. (2013). A review of technology-based interventions to teach academic skills to students with autism spectrum disorder. *Journal of Autism and Developmental Disorders, 43,* 2628–2648.

Knight, V. F., Smith, B. R., Spooner, F., & Browder, D. M. (2012). Using explicit instruction to teach science descriptors to students with autism spectrum disorders. *Journal of Autism and Developmental Disorders, 42,* 378–389.

Knight, V., Spooner, F., Browder, D. M., Smith, B. R., & Wood, C. L. (2013). Using systematic instruction and graphic organizers to teach science to students with autism spectrum disorders and intellectual disability. *Focus on Autism and Other Developmental Disabilities, 28,* 115–126.

Kolligian, J., & Sternberg, R. J. (1987). Intelligence, information processing, and specific learning disabilities: A triarchic synthesis. *Journal of Learning Disabilities, 20,* 8–17.

Kramer, T., & Krug, D. A. (1973). A rationale and procedure for teaching addition. *Education and Training of the Mentally Retarded, 8,* 140–145.

Loveland, K. A., & Tunali-Kotoski, B. (2005). The school-age child with an autistic spectrum disorder. In F. R. Volkmar, R. Paul, A. Kim, & D. J. Cohen (Eds.) *Handbook of Autism and Pervasive Developmental Disorders* (Vol 1, 3rd ed., pp. 247–287). Hoboken, NJ: John Wiley & Sons.

McIntosh, A., Reys, B. J., & Reys, R. E. (1992). A proposed framework for examining basic number sense. *For the Learning of Mathematics,* 2–44.

McKissick, B. R., Spooner, F., Wood, C. L., & Diegelmann, K. M. (2013). Effects of computer-assisted explicit instruction on map-reading skills for students with autism. *Research in Autism Spectrum Disorders, 7,* 1653–1662.

Marshal, N., & Kasirer, A. (2011). Thinking maps enhance metaphoric competence in children with autism and learning disabilities. *Research in Developmental Disabilities: A Multidisciplinary Journal, 32*(6), 2045–2054.

Mastropieri, M. A., Bakken, J. P., & Scruggs, T. E. (1991). Mathematics instruction for individuals with mental retardation: A perspective and research synthesis. *Education and Training in Mental Retardation, 26,* 115–129.

Mastropieri, M. A., & Scruggs, T. E. (1997). Best practices in promoting reading comprehension in students with learning disabilities 1976 to 1996. *Remedial and Special Education, 18,* 198–213.

Mechling, L. C., Gast, D. L., & Krupa, K. (2007). Impact of SMARTboard technology: An investigation of sight word reading and observational learning. *Journal of Autism and Developmental Disorders, 37,* 1869–1882.

Mims, P., Hudson, M., & Browder, D. M. (2012). Using read alouds of grade-level biographies and systematic prompting to promote comprehension for students with moderate and severe developmental disabilities. *Focus on Autism and Developmental Disabilities, 27,* 65–78.

Montague, M. (1997). Cognitive strategy instruction in mathematics for students with learning disabilities. *Journal of Learning Disabilities, 30,* 164–177.

Montague, M., & Dietz, S. (2009). Evaluating the evidence base for cognitive strategy instruction and mathematical problem solving. *Exceptional Children, 75,* 285–302.

Moore, M. & Calvert, S. (2000). Vocabulary acquisition for children with autism: Teacher or computer instruction. *Journal of Autism and Developmental Disorders, 30,* 359–362.

Morse, T. E., & Schuster, J. W. (2004). Simultaneous prompting: A review of the literature. *Education and Training in Developmental Disabilities, 39,* 153–168.

Mundy, P., Sigman, M., & Kasari, C. (1990). A longitudinal study of joint attention and language development in autistic children. *Journal of Autism and Developmental Disorders, 20*, 115–128.

Nation, K., Clarke, P., Wright, B., & Williams, C. (2006). Patterns of reading ability in children with autism spectrum disorder. *Journal of Autism and Developmental Disorders, 36*, 911–919.

National Council of Teachers of Mathematics. (2000) *Principles and standards for school mathematics*. Reston, VA: NCTM.

National Reading Panel. (2000). *Report of the National Reading Panel: Teaching children to read* [Online]. Retreived June 5, 2016 from www.nichd.nih.gov/research/supported/Pages/nrp.aspx.

NGSS Lead States. (2013). *Next Generation Science Standards: For states, by state*s. Washington, DC: The National Academies Press.

Nopprapun, M., & Holloway, J. (2014). A comparison of fluency training and discrete trial instruction to teach letter sounds to children with ASD: Acquisition and learning outcomes. *Research in Autism Spectrum Disorders, 8*, 788–802.

O'Connor, I. M., & Kline, P. D. (2004). Exploration of strategies for facilitating the reading comprehension of high-functioning students with autism spectrum disorders. *Journal of Autism and Developmental Disorders, 34*, 115–127.

Odom, S. L., Brantlinger, E., Gersten, R., Horner, R. H., Thompson, B., & Harris, K. R. (2005). Research in special education: Scientific methods and evidence-based practices. *Exceptional children, 71*, 137–148.

Pennington, R. C. (2010). Computer-assisted instruction for teaching academic skills to students with autism spectrum disorders: A review of literature. *Focus on Autism and Other Developmental Disabilities, 25*, 239–248.

Pennington, R. C., Ault, M. J., Schuster, J. W., & Sanders, A. (2011). Using simultaneous prompting and computer-assisted instruction to teach story writing to students with autism. *Assistive Technology Outcomes and Benefits, 7*, 24–38.

Pennington, R. C., Collins, B. C., Stenhoff, D. M., Turner, K., & Gunselman, K. (2014). Using simultaneous prompting and computer-assisted instruction to teach narrative writing skills to students with autism. *Education and Training in Autism and Developmental Disabilities, 49*, 396–414.

Ricketts, J., Jones, C. R., Happé, F., & Charman, T. (2013). Reading comprehension in autism spectrum disorders: The role of oral language and social functioning. *Journal of Autism and Developmental Disorders, 43*, 807–816.

Reimer, K., & Moyer, P. S. (2005). Third-graders learn about fractions using virtual manipulatives: A classroom study. *Journal of Computers in Mathematics and Science Teaching, 24*, 5–25.

Reisener, C. D., Lancaster, A. L., McMullin, W. A., & Ho, T. (2014). A preliminary investigation of evidence-based interventions to increase oral reading fluency in children with autism. *Journal of Applied School Psychology, 30*, 50–67.

Reutebuch, C. K., El Zein, F., Kim, M. K., Weinberg, A. N., & Vaughn, S. (2015). Investigating a reading comprehension intervention for high school students with autism spectrum disorder: A pilot study. *Research in Autism Spectrum Disorders, 9*, 96–111.

Rajendran, G., & Mitchell, P. (2007). Cognitive theories of autism. *Developmental Review, 27,* 224–260.

Root, J. R., Browder, D. M., Saunders, A.F., & Lo, Y.-y. (2015). Effects of modified schema based instruction with concrete and virtual manipulatives on word problem solving skills for students with autism spectrum disorder and moderate intellectual disability. *Manuscript in preparation.*

Root, J. R., & Wood, L. (2015). A decision-making framework for teaching students with developmental disability to use graphic organizers. *Manuscript in preparation.*

Rockwell, S. B., Griffin, C. C., & Jones, H. A. (2011). Schema-based strategy instruction in mathematics and the word problem-solving performance of a student with autism. *Focus on Autism and Other Developmental Disabilities, 26,* 87–95.

Saunders, A. F., Lo, Y.-y., & Polly, D. (2014). Beginning numeracy skills. In D.M. Browder & F. Spooner (Eds.) *More language arts, math, and science for students with severe disabilities* (pp. 149–168). Baltimore, MD: Brookes.

Schlosser, R. W., & Blischak, D. M. (2004). Effects of speech and print feedback on spelling by children with autism. *Journal of Speech, Language, and Hearing Research, 47,* 848–862.

Smith, B. R., Spooner, F., Jimenez, B., & Browder, D. M. (2013). Using an early science curriculum to teach science vocabulary and concepts to students with severe developmental disabilities. *Education & Treatment of Children, 36,* 1–31.

Smith, B. R., Spooner, F., & Wood, C. L. (2013). Using embedded computer-assisted explicit instruction to teach science to students with autism spectrum disorder. *Research in Autism Spectrum Disorders, 7,* 433–443.

Snell, M. E. (Ed.) (1983). *Systematic instruction of the moderately and severely handicapped* (2nd ed.). Columbus, OH: Charles E. Merrill.

Spooner, F., & Browder, D. M. (2015). Raising the bar: Significant advances and future needs for promoting learning for students with severe disabilities. *Remedial and Special Education, 36,* 28–32. DOI.org/10.1177/074193251 4555022

Spooner, F., Knight, V., Browder, D. M., Jimenez, B., & DiBiase, W. (2011). Evaluating evidence-based practice in teaching science content to students with severe developmental disabilities. *Research and Practice in Severe Disabilities, 36,* 62–75.

Spooner, F., Rivera, C. J., Browder, D. M., Baker, J. N., & Salas, S. (2009). Teaching emergent literacy skills using cultural contextual story-based lessons. *Research and Practice for Persons with Severe Disabilities, 34,* 102–112.

Sternberg, R. J. (1985). *Beyond IQ: A triarchic theory of human intelligence.* Cambridge, UK: Cambridge University Press.

Stringfield, S. G., Luscre, D., & Gast, D. L. (2011). Effects of a story map on accelerated reader postreading test scores in students with high-functioning autism. *Focus on Autism and Other Developmental Disabilities, 26,* 218–229.

Suh, J., Moyer, P. S., & Heo, H. (2005). Examining technology uses in the classroom: Developing fraction sense using virtual manipulative concept tutorials. *Journal of Interactive Online Learning, 3*(4), 1–21.

Whalen, C., Moss, D., Ilan, A. B., Vaupel, M., Fielding, P., MacDonald, K., & . . . Symon, J. (2010). Efficacy of Teachtown: Basics computer-assisted intervention for the intensive comprehensive autism program in Los Angeles Unified School District. *Autism: The International Journal of Research and Practice, 14,* 179–197.

Whitby, P. (2012). The effects of "Solve It!" on the mathematical word problem solving ability of adolescents with autism spectrum disorders. *Focus on Autism And Other Developmental Disabilities, 28,* 78–88.

Whitby, P. J. S., & Mancil, G. R. (2009). Academic achievement profiles of children with high functioning autism and Asperger syndrome: A review of the literature. *Education and Training in Developmental Disabilities, 44,* 551–560.

Wong, C., Odom, S. L., Hume, K., Cox, A. W., Fettig, A., Kucharczyk, S, . . . Schultz, T. R. (2014). *Evidence-based practices for children, youth, and young adults with autism spectrum disorder.* Chapel Hill: The University of North Carolina, Frank Pottery Graham Child Development Institute, Autism Evidence-Based Practice Review Group.

Wood, L. Browder, D. M., & Spooner, F. (2015). Teaching students with moderate intellectual disability to use a self-questioning strategy and iPad to comprehend science e-text. *Manuscript in preparation.*

Chapter 11

Developing Social Interaction Competence

David F. Cihak and Cate C. Smith

This chapter will cover topics related to the challenges individuals with ASD have that are related to developing social interaction skills and evidence-based practices for becoming socially competent. The chapter will begin with social-communicative difficulties described by the DSM-5 Diagnostic Criteria. Then, essential social skills and evidence-based teaching methods will be presented to develop social interaction competencies.

DSM-5: Social Communication

The DSM-5 represents ASD symptoms across two domains: (a) social communication deficits and (b) restricted, repetitive behaviors. The text of DSM-5 offers more detail on the topography of core symptoms of ASD at different ages; characteristics are described for toddlers, school-aged children, and adults. Social communication criteria provide examples of how symptoms may manifest in mildly affected individuals without language or cognitive deficits and in individuals with impairments in these areas. Examples relevant for different ages are also provided. For example, a possible symptom within the social relationships criterion is an apparent lack of interest in peers. This would be an irrelevant characteristic in toddlers for whom establishing and maintaining friendships is not yet developmentally expected.

While DSM-IV social interaction and communication domains were collapsed and reorganized in DSM-5, individual symptoms are largely retained. Constantino et al.'s (2004) landmark factor analytic study revealed that symptoms representing the DSM-IV clusters, Social Interaction and Communication, were best represented by a single "social communication" factor. Furthermore, stereotyped speech related more to the repetitive behaviors factor rather than social communication. The DSM-5 version identifies a smaller number of more general principles in social communication that are expected to be present in all individuals with ASD regardless of age or developmental level, but that can be manifested in many different ways (Mahjouri & Lord, 2012). Additionally, social communication symptoms have been reconfigured as a dimensional continuum of behaviors representing social-emotional reciprocity, coordination of verbal and nonverbal communication, and establishing, maintaining, and understanding social relationships.

The DSM-5 includes modifications to the descriptions of social interaction contained in the DSM-IV. Specifically, the DSM-5 requires that all social communication criteria have been met, either currently or by history, for a diagnosis of ASD. These changes were made to improve diagnostic specificity.

Severity is rated separately for social communication. Because a diagnosis requires that symptoms impair functioning, even the lowest level of severity indicates the presence of noticeable impairments or interference with functioning. Three levels of severity are available: Level 1, requiring support; Level 2, requiring substantial support; and Level 3, requiring very substantial support. Each level provides descriptions of the extent to which social communication and repetitive behavior deficits affect an individual's functioning. The DSM-5 severity ratings are designed to provide information on the extent to which ASD impacts daily functioning. The DSM-5 attempts to provide objective information for clinicians to use in choosing a rating. For example, a Level 2 repetitive behavior should appear frequently enough to be noticed by the "casual observer" (APA, 2013, p. 52). Although severity ratings are based on current behavior, the DSM-5 recognizes that a child's level of impairment may be fluid over time or vary by context.

Severity ratings in the DSM-5 may provide a useful structure for summarizing information from observation and interview measures in evaluation reports, to lead to service and support decisions. For example, social communication severity ratings describe a child's ability to interact with general education peers and teachers without supports. A child with mild social communication severity may do well with coaching and instruction given within inclusive settings, while a child with severe social communication deficits may need a service plan that includes assistive/augmentative communication supports.

Social Differences

Both Leo Kanner (1943) and Hans Asperger (1944) described children and youth with ASD as having a marked difference in their abilities to interact socially. For many individuals with ASD, their strong preferences for and attachment to objects are in sharp contrast to the absence of relatedness to other people (Dawson, Meltzoff, Osterling, Rinaldi, & Brown, 1998). By three to five years of age, children with ASD may show preferences for their caregivers over strangers (Sigman, Dijamco,

Gratier, & Rozga, 2004), but the way they show these preferences may be unusual (Rogers, Ozonoff, & Masline-Cole, 1993). From an early age, most individuals with ASD initiate less (verbally and nonverbally), make fewer spontaneous requests, perseverate on specific topics, and usually remain on the periphery or totally isolated, resulting in fewer occasions for social reciprocity (Yang, Wolfberg, Wu, & Hwu, 2003).

Problems with socialization for individuals with ASD result from their difficulty with interpersonal communication, their ability to be flexible, their need to be literal, their tendency to be disorganized, and their difficulty to generalize or transfer social skills to novel circumstances (Terpstra, Higgins, & Pierce, 2002). Social competency of some individuals with ASD may be further impeded by their failure to express and understand emotions and perceptions (Myles & Adreon, 2001), which may result in undesirable behaviors (Prizant, Wetherby, Rubin, Laurent, & Rydell, 2002) as well as stereotypical behaviors (Schopler & Mesibov, 1985). As breakdowns occur in the ability to communicate and the regulation of emotions, individuals with ASD have fewer opportunities to develop and maintain friendships (Boucher, 1999) and the chances of being included in a peer group are weighted against them (Kohler, Strain, & Shearer, 1992). As individuals with ASD engage less with peers, fewer attempts are made by peers to initiate with them, which then provides fewer opportunities for individuals with ASD to interact socially, resulting in more time away from their peers.

Some individuals with ASD do not understand social conventions and expectations. Typically developing individuals learn relatively quickly how to behave around certain people and what behaviors to demonstrate or to avoid in order to stay out of trouble or appear different. Since these skills are not taught directly or explicitly, but must be inferred and learned by trial and error, they are referred to as the "hidden social curriculum" (Myles & Simpson, 2001). Most individuals with ASD do not have the ability to access the hidden social curriculum due to their neurological differences. Therefore, individuals with ASD may not have any concept of how people are expected to behave in different contexts and appear to have no behavioral inhibitions.

Individuals functioning on the higher end of the ASD spectrum may be successful in storing the specific words or rules that apply to social situations, but are unable to recall, use, and apply them when appropriate in other situations (Wolery & Garfinkle, 2002). Unfortunately, since many individuals with ASD can repeat social rules, teachers assume they should be able to apply the skills at any time. For example, an individual may be able to recall and repeat that it is not appropriate to barge into the middle of a group of people and begin talking about foreign currency, but may fail to recognize when a break in the conversation occurs or how to initiate a discussion (Myles & Adreon, 2001). It may be difficult to recognize that telling others how to follow the rules may be perceived as rude or bossy. These misperceptions may result in some individuals with ASD being disciplined unnecessarily and subject to peer and adult rejection. Myles and Simpson (2001) noted that children and youth with ASD might be unaware of this hidden curriculum and misunderstand figurative expressions.

Demonstrating poor social inhibitions, engaging in behaviors others consider aberrant, and misinterpreting others' social behaviors can result in individuals with ASD being ignored, teased, and/or bullied (Heerey, Capps, Keltner, & Kring, 2005). Being disciplined for failure to identify and engage in correct social behaviors, as well as being rejected by peers can lead to individuals with ASD becoming anxious and depressed (Bellini, 2006). Students who demonstrate social challenges may experience future problems, such as fewer friends and attendance at fewer social activities (Barkley, Anastopolous, Goevremont, & Fletcher, 1991); poor school performance and poor self-esteem into adulthood (Heflin & Alaimo, 2007).

Nonverbal Communication

Developing and understanding nonverbal communication is a common barrier for students with ASD. Nonverbal communication includes a variety of gestures, facial expressions, and body postures that can be difficult to comprehend. Additionally, the inability to determine how these unspoken forms of communication work together to convey an implicit meaning may contribute to feelings of frustration.

A lack of understanding facial expressions also leads to poor social communication for those with ASD. Instead of reading facial features as a whole and piecing them together mentally to derive a global emotion (e.g. mom's eyebrows are raised, her cheeks are red, and her jaw is clenched; therefore she must be angry), children with ASD often focus on one facial feature and miss constructing the entire understanding (Reichow & Volkmar, 2010). This lack of understanding also leads to misused or unused facial expressions on the part of the child. Children with ASD may appear to have a flat affect or to be detached from the conversation. If the child is unable to gain information from the faces of those around him, he is unlikely to use his own face to convey information to others. Or, the child may engage in inappropriate facial expressions as he is unsure which expression matches the current situation.

Deficits in understanding nonverbal communication lead to difficulty structuring and maintaining conversations with others. Children with ASD often engage in atypical eye contact (e.g. holding the gaze of others for too long, or not long enough) (Paul, Orlovski, Marcinko, & Volkmar, 2009). This increased eye contact or lack thereof can be uncomfortable for a communicative partner. Children with ASD may also infringe upon the personal space of others without understanding the social ramifications.

Poorly integrated verbal and nonverbal communication skills contribute to misunderstandings or missed opportunities to engage with others socially. Rather than avoiding interactions with others on purpose, a child with ASD may be unaware of the attempt to socialize and inadvertently ignore the other child. Additionally, many children with ASD do not understand the use of gestures to indicate meaning and will ignore these attempts to communicate (e.g. pointing, waving). They may also ignore facial expressions such as smiling and miss opportunities to develop relationships with others.

Many children with ASD have a variety of social language impairments. These deficits include difficulty making inferences and understanding implicit information (Reichow & Volkmar, 2010). Additionally, nonliteral and ambiguous meanings of language can be difficult. This difficulty is referred to as a deficit in pragmatic language (Martin & McDonald, 2004). Examples of nonliteral and ambiguous language include idioms ("she put her foot in her mouth"), humor, irony (a large dog named "Tiny"), sarcasm, and metaphors ("the test was a breeze"). Understanding abstract concepts that are not presented visually is difficult for those with autism (Reichow & Volkmar, 2010). When teaching and interacting with children who have autism, it is best to limit the use of nonliteral or ambiguous language.

Understanding Relationships

Social impairments also lead to problems engaging in and understanding relationships with others. Children with ASD have the same social and psychological needs as other children (White, Keonig, Scahill, 2007). Many long to have friendships and share connections with others. However, difficulty processing social information leads to problems in making, keeping, and understanding relationships with others. Relating to others and engaging in relationships requires emotional reciprocity, which is difficult for students with ASD.

One of the difficulties faced by children with ASD is an inability to engage in symbolic or pretend play. Pretend play involves creativity, flexibility, and nonliteral uses of toys (Kasari, Chang, & Patterson, 2013). Children engaged in pretend play may gather rocks to make "dinner" or use a banana as a phone. In contrast, a child with ASD may stack building blocks in size order or categorize them by shape and color (i.e. using the toys for their literal purpose). Children with ASD may play with toys inappropriately (e.g. flipping cars over to spin the wheels repeatedly, or lining up toys around the perimeter of the room) (Heflin & Alaimo, 2007).

The unspoken rules of communicating with others include: matching the context and needs of the listener, using appropriate tone and language (both verbal and nonverbal), and avoiding the use of overly formal language (Paul et al., 2009). Conversation rules also include the need to adjust behavior to meet social contexts. For example, when speaking in a library, it is appropriate to whisper or speak softly; however, a conversation at a party would be loud and energetic. Understanding embedded environment cues (e.g. a "no talking" sign in the library) helps one to use the appropriate volume, gestures, and body language.

Other social skill deficits contribute to problems relating to others. Many people with ASD lack the ability to be flexible and may become rigid in the need for order and structure (Heflin & Alaimo, 2007). Rigidity can lead to distress over changes in routine and possibly an inability to relate to others. Children with ASD also have difficulty expressing and regulating their emotions (White et al., 2007). Problem behaviors caused by difficulty regulating emotions, such as acting aggressively toward others, may lead to isolation in both school and home settings. Other atypical behaviors such as unusual language (e.g. overly formal), fixations with favorite objects, and a lack of understanding social norms can lead to a higher incidence of bullying. Research indicates that children with ASD are more likely to be bullied than their peers without disabilities (Humphrey & Symes, 2010). In turn, bullying can lead to low self-esteem and higher rates of depression and anxiety (Bellini, 2006; Tse, Strulvitch, Tagalakis, Meng, & Fombonne, 2007; Zablotsky, Bradshaw, Anderson, Law, 2013).

As children with ASD become adolescents, they may choose to engage in friendships and dating relationships. However, social and communication deficits often lead to trouble connecting appropriately with others. Adolescents and young adults with ASD often have difficulty understanding the unspoken rules of dating (Volkmar, Rogers, Paul, & Pelphrey, 2014). For example, calling or texting someone repeatedly is considered rude or even stalking behavior. However, to a teen with ASD this may be a demonstration of sincere interest in the other person. Limited awareness of nonverbal cues such as body language may also lead to unwanted physical advances such as hugging without permission. Social media is another outlet in which unspoken rules of common courtesy apply. Technology and social media are embedded in every facet of our lives. Misunderstanding the needs, desires, and intentions of others often leads to inappropriate behaviors such as contact that is too frequent or unwanted (Stokes, Newton, Kaur, 2007).

Social Communicative Assessments

Many children and youth with ASD exhibit social skills deficits including impaired communication, limited interactions, and inappropriate behaviors toward others. The first step in teaching any new skill, including social skills, is to measure the area of deficit in order to understand present levels of functioning and subsequently plan for appropriate interventions. Researchers refer to behaviors that serve as a threshold to other, more advanced behaviors as *behavioral cusps* (Rosales-Ruiz, & Baer, 1997). An example of a behavioral cusp is teaching a child to push a button on a switch. By learning to press the button, the child has unlocked the potential to indicate choices, identify objects, and communicate via the device in the future. Similarly, social skills and behaviors should be assessed to identify the target behavioral cusps that will lead to long-term positive outcomes. For example, will the social skill lead to increased friendships and reduced isolation for the individual? Or, does the target skill have the potential to be generalizable (used in more than one setting with a variety of people)? Once these questions are answered, the social skill deficits should be assessed and prioritized for intervention (Bosch & Fuqua, 2001).

There are both formal and informal assessments available for social skills. Both formal and informal assessments involve gathering information about the present level of skills, interpreting this data, and taking action based on the results of the assessment. Formal assessments are standardized measures designed to assess student knowledge, whereas informal assessments generate evidence of skills learned over time through informal day-to-day interactions and observations (Ruiz-Primo & Furtak, 2006). Formal assessments include standardized and norm-referenced measures such as an intelligence or IQ test, where students are compared to other students. Informal assessments include direct observations, interviews, and portfolio assessments.

There are many commercially available formal assessments for the purpose of assessing social skill deficits. For young children, the Social Skills Checklist (Quill, 2000) allows parents and teachers to assess play and group skills in a yes/no format. For older children and adolescents, the Social Skills Rating System (SSRS; Gresham & Elliot, 1990) measures social skills, problem behaviors, and academic competency. Using parent, teacher, and student questionnaires, the SSRS assesses skills including cooperation, empathy and self-control. Similarly, the Social Responsiveness Scale-Second Edition (SRS-2; Constantino & Gruber, 2012) uses feedback from parents and teachers to assess social skills. Used in screening and diagnosis of ASD, the SRS-2 measures skills including social awareness, social cognition, social communication, social motivation, and restricted interests and behaviors. To assess initial deficits and progress post-intervention, the Autism Social Skills Profile (ASSP; Bellini, 2006) uses a Likert scale to measure social reciprocity, social participation/avoidance, and detrimental social behaviors. The ASSP also provides a total score of social functioning. These assessment tools must be given by qualified personnel, usually a school or clinical psychologist.

Table 11.1 Examples of Informal Assessments for Social Skills

Assessment Strategy	Description
Observation	Observing child engaging with others in natural settings.
Interview	Engaging child in discussion through questions.
Anecdotal record	Record notes of observed behaviors during interactions with peers.
Event sampling	Record data of target behavior occurrence during a specific period (e.g. hitting others at lunchtime or talking out during reading group).
Time sampling	Record target behavior occurrence or nonoccurrence at the end of specific time intervals (e.g. five minutes, ten minutes).
Checklist	A list of target or ideal behaviors which allows teachers to check off behaviors that are present or absent.
Work Sample	This may be a drawing or writing sample chosen by the child.
Portfolio	A collection of the child's work samples and other products such as videos and test scores.

Informal assessments also yield valuable information about the present levels and social skills deficits of children with ASD. Information is gained by observing the student in various academic or social experiences. The experiences may occur naturally or be created by the observer. Often, informal assessments are teacher-created checklists or tests, making them inexpensive and easy to obtain. A variety of individuals may gather data for informal assessments. Teachers, parents, or other professionals who work with the child may conduct informal assessments. See Table 11.1 for examples of informal assessments.

An individual's social competence is typically defined by the perceptions of others (Dodge, Petit, McClaskey, & Brown, 1986). That is, people are socially competent if others view their behavior as appropriate. Social competence implies that the individual has the knowledge and skills to successfully navigate the constantly changing social landscape. Crick and Dodge (1994) identified three predictors for social competence in students: (1) the extent to which students are accepted by their peers, (2) the degree to which students are aggressive towards their peers, and (3) the degree to which students withdraw from peer interactions. Crick and Dodge also determined that the inability to understand others' emotions and solve problems, academic failure, social rejection, and the inability to get along in a group to form friendships are major risk factors that interfere with the performance of social skills.

Teaching Social Skills

Once social skills are assessed, the results should be discussed with the child and family in order to bring awareness to the areas of deficit. Social skills should be targeted for instruction based on priority of importance for long-term success of the child (Bosch & Fuqua, 2001). There are specific social skills that can be taught to increase the chances of acceptance by others. These skills may be categorized as: (1) nonverbal behaviors, (2) social interactions, and (3) relationship skills.

The first category of skills to teach is nonverbal behaviors. These include eye contact, gestures, joint attention, proximity, and understanding the body language of others. Eye contact is difficult for those with autism for a variety of reasons (Paul et al., 2009). When eye contact lasts too long or not long enough, it is necessary to teach this skill. Effective practices to teach the use of eye contact include direct instruction, modeling, and role-play. Understanding that gestures indicate meaning or add to the content of the discussion is also necessary to develop nonverbal behavior skills. Joint attention involves orienting and attending to the peer or adult conversation partner (Lovass & Smith, 1989). Taking the time to share attention on an object or conversation topic is helpful in teaching this skill. Proximity and personal space are other nonverbal behaviors to teach children with ASD. Understanding the concept of "my space" and "your space" is crucial to establishing conversations and, ultimately relationships with others. Finally, awareness of the meanings of body language and facial expressions in others is a critical skill.

The second category of skills to teach is social interaction skills. Social interaction skills include recognizing social cues, conversational and emotional reciprocity, empathy, and perspective taking (Stichter et al., 2010). Teaching children with ASD to recognize and respond to cues such as facial expressions, tone, and body language enables them to establish conversations with others. Social and emotional reciprocity instruction should also be incorporated. Social reciprocity involves maintaining the conversation by taking turns and continuing the back and forth pattern of conversing. Emotional reciprocity entails recognizing emotions and demonstrating empathy and understanding toward others. Finally, perspective taking requires the use of environmental cues, emotional cues from others, and the understanding that the beliefs and perspectives of others may differ from our own (Stichter et. al, 2010). When combined, social interaction skills enable individuals to participate in meaningful conversations and relationships with others.

Finally, the third category of social skills for target instruction is relationship skills. Relationship skills include intrapersonal skills (e.g. self-esteem, self-regulation) and interpersonal skills (e.g. friendships, group interactions, dating, and digital social skills). It is important to establish positive self-esteem for children with ASD. Self-regulation involves awareness of one's own emotions and using coping strategies to deal with difficult situations. Establishing these two intrapersonal skills enables a child with an ASD to develop interpersonal skills with others. Friendship skills include developing relationships and interacting with friends. In a related skillset, group skills include sharing, turn taking, listening, and following directions. Teaching group skills enables children with ASD to benefit from positive social interactions with their peers.

For teens and young adults with ASD, navigating relationships with others can be especially difficult. Understanding appropriate social contact is one of the first dating skills to develop (Stokes et al., 2007). This begins with an awareness of one's own body and the difference in appropriate and inappropriate touching. Communicating with a partner is another crucial dating skill. Knowing the acceptable forms of communication (e.g. texting once per day or sending one message via a social networking platform) versus unacceptable communication (e.g. calling or messaging repeatedly) are important differentiations. Digital social skills and networking skills must also be established. From creating an email account to using "netiquette" online, digital platforms are readily available and helpful in establishing and maintaining connections with others. Table 11.2 lists social skills categories to develop for children and youth.

Teaching social skills to individuals with ASD can be one of the most challenging and rewarding tasks to carry out. Often communication skills carry little influence if social skills are not developed to provide the ability to communicate. Social difficulties for people with autism are diverse. Some are mild, while others may involve severe antisocial behavior. All involve problems with social understanding and may be affected by difficulties with attention, communication, problem solving, cognition, sensory processing, and motor problems. According to the National Professional Development Center on Autism Spectrum Disorder, evidence-based

Table 11.2 Social Skills to Teach Children with Autism Spectrum Disorders

Category	Social Skills
Nonverbal behaviors	Eye contact
	Gestures
	Joint attention
	Proximity
	Body language
Social interaction skills	Social cues
	Conversational reciprocity
	Emotional reciprocity
	Empathy
	Perspective taking
Intrapersonal relationship skills	Self-regulation
	Self-esteem
Interpersonal relationship skills	Friendships
	Group interactions
	Dating
	Digital social skills

practices (EBPs) are techniques and interventions shown to be effective for teaching skills to children with ASD (Wong et al., 2012).

Positive Reinforcement describes a relation between learner behavior and a consequence that follows the behavior. Reinforcement is an evidence-based practice used to increase appropriate behavior and teach new skills (e.g. replacement behavior in place of an interfering behavior) that was described in Chapter 9. For example, children learn to ask for something politely if they want to receive it in return. The ultimate goal of reinforcement is to help learners with ASD learn new skills and maintain their use over time in a variety of settings with many different individuals.

Priming may be used to provide a person with information and answers before they are presented with an activity or before they enter a social situation. The positive effects of priming to facilitate social behavior are supported by researchers, who used priming to increase the social initiations of children with ASD (Sancho, Sidener, Reeve, & Sidner, 2010) and to decrease problem behaviors (Koegel, Koegel, Frea, & Green-Hopkins, 2003). Social behaviors (e.g. greeting others) can be primed by presenting behavioral primes just prior to performance of the skill or behavior in the natural environment.

Prompts are highly effective in facilitating child–adult and child–child interactions in children with ASD (McConnell, 2002). Prompts are supports that provide assistances to the child to successfully perform behaviors. Prompts may be used to teach new social skills and to enhance performance of previously acquired skills. A limitation of prompting strategies is that the child with ASD may limit social interactions to only instances in which prompting is provided. As such, a prompt-fading plan needs to be implemented to systematically fade prompts from most-to-least assistances. Types of prompts (from least-to-most supportive) include:

- natural: saying or doing what would typically happen before a behavior
- gestural: pointing to, looking at, moving, or touching an item or area to indicate a correct response
- verbal: providing a verbal instruction, cue, or model
- modeling: the acting out of a target behavior with the hope the child will imitate
- physical: moving the child through the behavior; can be full, which is doing the whole behavior, or partial, such as just touching the hand.

Antecedent-Based Interventions (ABI) is an evidence-based practice used to address both interfering and on-task behaviors (e.g. Ahearn, Clark, DeBar, & Florentino, 2005; Schilling & Schwartz, 2004). This practice is most often used after a functional behavior assessment (FBA) has been conducted to identify the function of the interfering behavior. Many interfering behaviors continue to occur because the environmental conditions in a particular setting have become linked to the behavior over time. The kinds of behavioral interventions that are widely used when antecedent factors are identified as the precipitating factors in challenging behavior are often described as *prevention-focused interventions*. Reszka, Odom, and Hume (2012) indicated increased social engagement of preschool children with ASD with their peers when they were in a classroom book area. Books may provide a more concrete basis for initiating and sustaining interactions (e.g. showing pictures or discussing topics from a book) than materials requiring more imaginative play. In addition, children may select books that relate to their interest areas; interest areas of children with ASD are related to joint attention and engagement with others (Adamson, Deckner, & Bakeman, 2010). Research has indicated that large motor activities can assist in increasing appropriate play behaviors in children with ASD (Schlelen, Heyne, & Berken, 1988) and often are preferred activities for them (Case-Smith & Kuhaneck, 2008).

Visual Supports are any tools presented visually that support individual access and/or communicate information (Cohen & Sloan, 2007; Mesibov, Shea, & Schopler, 2005; Massey & Wheeler, 2000; Morrison, Sainato, BenChaaban, & Endo, 2002). Visual supports might include, but are not limited to, pictures, written words, objects within the environment, arrangement of the environment or visual boundaries, schedules, maps, labels, organization systems, timelines, and scripts. They are used across settings (e.g. school, home, community) to encourage social interaction (National Research Council, 2001). Many students with ASD have difficulty thinking about abstract concepts, and respond better to visual information (Heflin & Alaimo, 2007). Visual supports have been proven effective in increasing play skills, social interaction skills, and social initiation (Johnston, Nelson, Evans, & Palazolo, 2003; O'Reilly, Sigafoos, Lancioni, Edrisinha, & Andrews, 2005; Tissot, & Evans, 2003). Visual supports meet the evidence-based practice criteria within the early childhood, elementary, and middle school-age groups.

Video Modeling is an evidence-based practice that uses video recording and display equipment to provide a visual model of the targeted behavior or skill (Cihak, Kildare, Smith, McMahon, & Quinn-Brown, 2012; Cihak, Fahrenkrog, Ayres, & Smith, 2010; Kroeger, Schultz, & Newsom, 2007; Nikopoulos & Keenan, 2004; Bellini, Akullian, & Hopf, 2007). *Basic video modeling* involves recording a model (e.g. teacher, parent, or peer) engaging in the target behavior or skill and the learner watches the video at a later time. *Video self-modeling* is used to record the learner displaying the target skill or behavior and is reviewed later. *Point-of-view video modeling* is when the target behavior or skill is recorded from the perspective of the learner. *Video prompting* involves breaking the behavior skill into steps and recording each step with incorporated pauses during which the learner may attempt the step before viewing subsequent steps. Video prompting may be done with either the learner or another person acting as a model.

Social Narratives are interventions that describe social situations in some detail by highlighting relevant cues and offering examples of appropriate responding. In general, social stories are read to the child before they enter the difficult situation being described in the story. Their purpose is to support learners in adjusting to changes in routine and adapting their behaviors based on the social and physical cues of a situation, or in teaching specific social skills or behaviors. Social narratives may be individualized according to learner needs and typically are quite short, often incorporating illustrations, pictures or other visual aids, and songs. Social narratives encompass a variety of interventions that function to introduce and teach appropriate behavior through written story form, such as Social Stories, Power Cards, and other written story-based prompts.

The most common of these are Social Stories, developed by Carol Gray (Gray, 1995; 2004; 2005; Gray & Garand, 1993). A Social Story describes a situation, skill, or concept in terms of relevant social cues, perspectives, and common responses. Specific sentence types that are often used when constructing Social Stories include: descriptive, directive, perspective, affirmative, control, and cooperative. Evidence-based research suggests that social narratives can be used effectively with learners with ASD, especially when positive reinforcement is applied (Agosta, Graetz, Mastropieri, & Scruggs, 2004; Barry & Burlew, 2004; Crozier, & Tincani, 2005; 2007; Delano & Snell, 2006). Another type of social narrative is Power Cards. The primary difference between Social Stories and Power Cards is that Power Cards incorporate the child's special interest area (Gagnon, 2001). Power Cards have demonstrated effectiveness in developing social behaviors, such as increasing the percentage of time that adolescents engaged in conversation outside of their preferred topic (Davis, Boon, Fore, & Cihak, 2010).

A recent meta-analysis on the effectiveness of Social Stories (Kokina & Kern 2010) resulted in low to questionable effects. This low to questionable effect is surprising given the popularity of Social Stories. However, the authors concluded that most of the studies reviewed either resulted in a high degree of effectiveness or were not effective at all, suggesting that not all youth may benefit equally from this intervention. Social Story effects were greater when children were their own agent of the intervention, as opposed to having the story read by a parent, teacher, or researcher, and when it was read just before the situation described. In addition, simple stories presented within a brief time frame resulted in better outcomes.

Peer-Mediated Intervention (PMI) has been identified as a versatile and potentially effective intervention approach to teach a variety of skills to individuals with ASD (Chan *et al.* 2009; Odom & Strain 1984;

Odom et al. 2003; Reichow & Volkmar, 2010). PMI components include training peers to implement pivotal response training techniques (Harper, Symon, & Frea, 2008), training participants to use scripted phrases related to different play themes (Ganz & Flores 2008), and implementing high-probability request sequences with embedded peer modeling during play sessions (Jung, Sainato, & Davis, 2008). Developing peer modeling of social skills, have been successfully applied in inclusive environments and can be used to promote social interaction between students with ASD and their peers (Chan et al., 2009; Koegel, Matos-Freden, Lang, & Koegel, 2012). PMI offers unique advantages that are particularly beneficial in inclusive settings. Peers acting as intervention agents may increase the amount of intervention access for the individual with ASD while also potentially placing fewer demands on teachers to serve as the sole intervention provider (Chan et al., 2009). Furthermore, PMI potentially creates opportunities for students with ASD to interact and practice social skills with a variety of communication partners, thus possibly increasing the likelihood that these acquired skills will generalize across settings and individuals. Finally, PMI can be incorporated into the natural context of daily activities, making it particularly well suited to inclusive settings (Hemmeter, 2000).

Cognitive Behavioral Therapy (CBI) is a method that focuses on targeting positive and negative thought processes to change behavior. Some researchers have posited that social skill deficits occur as a function of avoidance due to increased social anxiety (Bellini, 2006). It is used primarily with those who experience anxiety or difficulty controlling expressions of anger and aggressive behavior. White and colleagues (2010) suggest that CBI alleviates anxiety experienced by youth with ASD and increases social competence. It is effective with youth from elementary school age to high school (Brock, 2013). Individuals using CBI are taught to identify their feelings and the thoughts associated with those feelings and then use strategies to express their behavior in a more appropriate manner. CBI requires students to self-evaluate the social situation and determine an appropriate plan of action. Therefore, the student learns to function in a more socially appropriate manner by addressing the thoughts and feelings associated with social anxiety. Additionally, other studies reported that the use of CBI was effective in increasing executive functioning skills, facial recognition, problem solving, Theory of Mind, reading nonverbal cues, and accurately describing how to respond in a social situation (Koning, Magill-Evans, Volden, & Dick., 2011; Stitcher et al., 2010).

Becoming Socially Competent

Social competence can be defined as independently and successfully engaging with others, understanding social situations, and establishing and maintaining relationships (Stichter et al., 2010). Social competency also involves taking the perspective of others, learning from social interactions, and applying this knowledge to future interactions. Socially competent individuals enjoy relationships with others, have increased levels of self-esteem and self-confidence, and are adaptable to a variety of environments. At each stage of development, the goals for social competence will vary.

For young children, social competency focuses on getting along with others. Goals at this stage of development include increasing communicative attempts, learning to respect the boundaries of others, and interacting with peers in play and group settings. Many early skills are learned through play, specifically pretend play. Pretend play contributes to cognitive as well as social development. Play also encourages perspective-taking and empathy. Families play a critical role in encouraging the development of these skills (Carter et al., 2014). Research indicates that peers without disabilities can be useful in supporting social skill development in children with ASD through the use of prompting and visual supports (Delano & Snell, 2006). As children mature and develop these skills, they can expand upon the basics by adding conversation skills, practicing empathy for others, and developing friendships with peers. Children in elementary and middle school should begin to develop self-regulation skills, including identifying their own emotions and using self-control.

Adolescents with ASD face increased expectations to act in socially competent ways, along with a desire to develop relationships with others. Social demands become more complex, requiring an expanding skill set and increasing awareness for social success. Middle and high school students often engage in social banter, including joking, teasing, and conversing about popular music or events. For adolescents with ASD, it is crucial to understand the context to engage in these socially fluid interactions. The adolescent period is full of both physical and emotional changes for all teenagers. From evolving relationships with parents and peers, to shifting school and leisure environments, youth with ASD are forced to confront change. Adding to the complexities of adolescence, many teens with ASD report feeling lonely, isolated, or bullied by peers (Humphrey & Symes, 2010).

As adolescents become young adults, the focus on achieving social competence shifts to a need for developing relationships with others, pursuing employment or higher education, and engaging in community recreation and leisure activities. Teaching students to become socially competent is especially critical during the transition from school to adulthood period (Carter & Draper, 2010). In addition to giving students the skills to be successful during high school and in higher education settings, educators must give students with ASD the tools to be socially successful in everyday life (Carter et al., 2014).

Overall, the desired outcome for students with ASD is to achieve high levels of social functioning, engage in fulfilling relationships with others, and develop self-esteem. Social functioning is a global term encompassing employment, friendships, and independence (Gillespie-Lynch et al., 2011). Social skills including communication, self-regulation, and understanding the social expectations of new settings are critical skills to obtain and maintain employment and pursue an independent adult life.

Conclusion

Differences in communication and social skills can contribute to problems relating to others. Gaining social competence through the teaching of social skills and the application of interventions gives individuals with autism spectrum disorders a better chance at getting along with others, making friends, and being able to obtain and sustain a job. Learning how to initiate, reciprocate, and think about social interactions is key to decreasing the challenges persons with ASD experience. People on the spectrum need to be assessed and have individualized programs developed to help them move toward higher levels of social competence. Several varied interventions are described in this chapter to assist with teaching social interaction competence.

References

Adamson, L. B., Deckner, D. F., & Bakeman, R. (2010). Early interests and joint engagement in typical development, autism, and Down syndrome. *Journal of Autism and Developmental Disorders*, 40, 665–676.

Agosta, E., Graetz, J. E., Mastropieri, M., & Scruggs, T. E. (2004). Teacher–researcher partnerships to improve social behavior through social stories. *Intervention in School & Clinic*, 39(5), 276–287.

Ahearn, W. H., Clark, K. M., DeBar, R., & Florentino, C. (2005). On the role of preference in response competition. *Journal of Applied Behavior Analysis*, 38(2), 247–250.

American Psychiatric Association (2013). *Diagnostic and statistical manual of mental disorders, fifth edition (DSM-5)*. Arlington, VA: American Psychiatric Publishing.

Asperger, H. (1944). Die Autistischen Psychopathen im Kindesalter. *European Archives of Psychiatry and Clinical Neuroscience*, 117(1), 76–136.

Barkley, R. A., Anastopoulos, A. D., Guevremont, D. C., & Fletcher, K. E. (1991). Adolescents with ADHD: Patterns of behavioral adjustment, academic functioning, and treatment utilization. *Journal of the American Academy of Child & Adolescent Psychiatry*, 30(5), 752–761.

Barry, L. M., & Burlew, S. B. (2004). Using social stories to teach choice and play skills to children with autism. *Focus on Autism and Other Developmental Disabilities*, 19(1), 45–51.

Bellini, S. (2006). The development of social anxiety in adolescents with autism spectrum disorders. *Focus on Autism and Other Developmental Disabilities, 21*(3), 138–145.

Bellini, S., Akullian, J., & Hopf, A. (2007). Increasing social engagement in young children with autism spectrum disorders using video self modeling. *School Psychology Review, 36*(1), 80–90.

Bosch, S., & Fuqua, R. W. (2001). Behavioral cusps: A model for selecting target behaviors. *Journal of Applied Behavioral Analysis, 34*(1), 123–125.

Boucher, J. (1999). Editorial: Interventions with children with autism-methods based on play. *Child language teaching and therapy, 15*(1), 1–5.

Brock, M. E. (2013). *Cognitive behavioral intervention (CBI) fact sheet.* Chapel Hill (NC): The University of North Carolina; Frank Porter Graham Child Development Institute; The National Professional Development Center on Autism Spectrum.

Carter, E. W., Common, E. A., Sreckovic, M. A., Heartley, B. H., Bottema-Beutel, K., Gustafson, J. R., . . . Hume, K. (2014). Promoting social competence and peer relationships for adolescents with autism spectrum disorders. *Remedial and Special Education, 35*(2), 91–101.

Carter, E. W., & Draper, J. (2010). Making school matter: Supporting meaningful secondary experiences for adolescents who use AAC. In D. B. McNaughton & D. R. Buekelman (Eds.), *Transition strategies for adolescents and young adults who use augmentative and alternative communication* (pp. 69–90.) Baltimore, MD: Brookes.

Case-Smith, J., & Kuhaneck, H. M. (2008). Play preferences of typically developing children and children with developmental delays between ages 3 and 7 years. *OTJR: Occupation, Participation and Health, 28*, 19–29.

Chan, J. M., Lang, R., Rispoli, M., O'Reilly, M., Sigafoos, J., & Cole, H. (2009). Use of peer-mediated interventions in the treatment of autism spectrum disorders: A systematic review. *Research in Autism Spectrum Disorders, 3*(4), 876–889.

Cihak, D. F., Fahrenkrog, C. D., Ayres, K. M., & Smith, C. (2010). The use of video modeling via a video iPod® and a system of least prompts to improve transitional behaviors for students with autism spectrum disorders in the general education classroom. *Journal of Positive Behavior Interventions, 12*, 103–115.

Cihak, D. F., Kildare, L., Smith, C., McMahon, D. D., & Quinn-Brown, L. (2012). Using video Social Stories™ to increase task engagement for middle schools students with autism spectrum disorders. *Behavior Modification, 36*, 399–425.

Cohen, M. J., & Sloan, D. L. (2007). *Visual supports for people with autism: A guide for parents and professionals.* Bethesda, MD: Woodbine House.

Constantino, J. N., & Gruber, C. P. (2012). *Social Responsiveness Scale, second edition.* Los Angeles: Western Psychological Services.

Constantino, J. N., Gruber, C. P., Davis, S., Hayes, S., Passanante, N., & Przybeck, T. (2004). The factor structure of autistic traits. *Journal of Child Psychology and Psychiatry and Allied Disciplines, 45*(4), 718–726.

Crick, N. R., & Dodge, K. A. (1994). A review and reformulation of social-information-processing mechanisms in children's social adjustment. *Psychological Bulletin, 115*, 74– 101.

Crozier, S., & Tincani, M. J. (2005). Using a modified social story to decrease disruptive behavior of a child with autism. *Focus on Autism and Other Developmental Disabilities, 20*(3), 150–157.

Crozier, S., & Tincani, M. J. (2007). Effects of social stories on prosocial behavior of preschool children with autism spectrum disorders. *Journal of Autism & Developmental Disorders, 37*(9), 1803–1814.

Davis, K. T., Boon, R. T., Fore, C., & Cihak, D. F. (2010). Improving the conversational skills among adolescents with Asperger's syndrome via the use of power cards. *Focus on Autism and Other Developmental Disabilities, 25*, 12–22.

Dawson, G., Meltzoff, A. N., Osterling, J., Rinaldi, J., & Brown, E. (1998). Children with autism fail to orient to naturally occurring social stimuli. *Journal of autism and developmental disorders, 28*(6), 479–485.

Delano, M., & Snell, M. (2006). The effects of social stories on the social engagement of children with autism. *Journal of Positive Behavior Interventions, 8*(1), 29–42.

Dodge K. A., Pettit G. S., McClaskey C. L., Brown M. M. (1986). Social competence in children. *Monographs of the Society for Research in Child Development*. 51: Ser. No. 213.

Gagnon E. (2001). *Power cards: using special interests to motivate children and youth with Asperger syndrome and autism.* Shawnee Mission, KS: Autism Asperger Publishing.

Ganz, J. B., & Flores, M. M. (2008). Effects of the use of visual strategies in play groups for children with autism spectrum disorders and their peers. *Journal of Autism and Developmental Disorders, 38*(5), 926–940.

Gillespie-Lynch, K., Sepeta, L., Wang, Y., Marshall, S., Gomez, L., Sigman, M., & Hutman, T. (2011). Early childhood predictors of the social competence of adults with autism. *Journal of Autism and Developmental Disorders, 42*, 161–174.

Gray, C. (1995). Teaching children with autism to "read" social situations. In K. Quill (Ed.), *Teaching Children with Autism: Strategies to Enhance Communication and Socialization* (pp. 219–241). Albany, NY: Delmar.

Gray, C. (2004) Social Stories 10.0. *Jenison Autism Journal, 15*(4), 2–21.

Gray, C. (2005) Social Stories. Retrieved March 15, 2015 from www.thegraycenter.org/.

Gray, C. A., & Garand, J. D. (1993). Social stories: Improving responses of students with autism with accurate social information. *Focus on Autistic Behavior, 8*, 1–10.

Gresham, F. M., & Elliot, S. N. (1990). *Social Skills Rating System Manual.* Circle Pines, MN: American Guidance Service.

Harper, C. B., Symon, J. B. G., & Frea, W. D. (2008). Recess is time-in: Using peers to improve social skills of children with autism. *Journal of Autism and Developmental Disorders, 38*, 815–826.

Hemmeter, M. L. (2000). Classroom-based interventions evaluating the past and looking toward the future. *Topics in Early Childhood Special Education, 20*(1), 56–61.

Heerey, E. A., Capps, L. M., Keltner, D., & Kring, A. M. (2005). Understanding teasing: Lessons from children with autism. *Journal of Abnormal Child Psychology, 33*(1), 55–68.

Heflin, J., & Alaimo, D. (2007). *Students with autism spectrum disorders: Effective instructional practices.* Upper Saddle River, NJ: Pearson and Merrill/Prentice Hall.

Humphrey, N., & Symes, W. (2010). Perceptions of social support and experience of bullying among pupils with autism spectrum disorders in mainstream secondary schools. *European Journal of Special Needs Education, 25,* 77–91.

Johnston, S., Nelson, C., Evans, J., & Palazolo, K. (2003). The use of visual supports in teaching young children with autism spectrum disorder to initiate interactions. *AAC: Augmentative & Alternative Communication, 19,* 86–104.

Jung, S., Sainato, D. M., & Davis, C. A. (2008). Using high-probability request sequences to increase social interactions in young children with autism. *Journal of Early Intervention, 30*(3), 163–187.

Kanner, L. (1943). Autistic disturbances of affective contact. *Nervous Child, 2,* 217–250.

Kasari, C., Chang, Y., & Patterson, S. (2013). Pretending to play or playing to pretend: The case of autism. *American Journal of Play, 6*(1), 124–135.

Kohler, F. W., Strain, P. S., & Shearer, D. D. (1992). The overtures of preschool social skill intervention agents differential rates, forms, and functions. *Behavior modification, 16*(4), 525–542.

Kokina, A., & Kern, L. (2010). Social story interventions for students with autism spectrum disorders: a meta-analysis. *Journal of Autism and Developmental Disorders, 40,* 812–826.

Koning, C., Magill-Evans, J., Volden, J., & Dick, B. (2011). Efficacy of cognitive behavior therapy-based social skills intervention for school-aged boys with autism spectrum disorders. *Research in Autism Spectrum Disorders, 7,* 1280–1290.

Koegel, L. K., Koegel, R. L., Frea, W., & Green-Hopkins, I. (2003). Priming as a method of coordinating educational services for students with autism. *Language, Speech, and Hearing Services in the Schools, 34*(3), 228–235.

Koegel, L., Matos-Freden, R., Lang, R., & Koegel, R. (2012). Interventions for children with autism spectrum disorders in inclusive school settings. *Cognitive and Behavioral Practice, 19,* 401–412.

Kroeger, K. A., Schultz, J. R., & Newsom, C. (2007). A comparison of two group-delivered social skills programs for young children with autism. *Journal of Autism and Developmental Disorders, 37*(5), 808–817.

Lovaas, O. I., & Smith, T. (1989). A comprehensive behavioral theory of autistic children: Paradigm for research and treatment. *Journal of behavior therapy and experimental psychiatry, 20*(1), 17–29.

McConnell, S. R. (2002). Interventions to facilitate social interaction for young children with autism: Review of available research and recommendations for educational intervention and future research. *Journal of autism and developmental disorders, 32*(5), 351–372.

Mahjouri, S., & Lord, C. E. (2012). What the DSM-5 portends for research, diagnosis, and treatment of autism spectrum disorders. *Current Psychiatry Reports, 14*(6), 739–747.

Martin, I., & McDonald, S. (2004). An exploration of causes of non-literal language problems in individuals with Asperger Syndrome. *Journal of Autism and Developmental Disorders, 34*(3), 311–328.

Massey, G., & Wheeler, J. (2000). Acquisition and generalization of activity schedules and their effects on task engagement in a young child with autism in an inclusive preschool classroom. *Education and Training in Mental Retardation and Developmental Disabilities, 35*, 326–335.

Mesibov, G., Shea, V., & Schopler, E. (2005). *The TEACCH approach to autism spectrum disorders.* New York: Plenum Press.

Morrison, R., Sainato, D., Benchaaban, D., & Endo, S. (2002). Increasing play skills of children with autism using activity schedules and correspondence training. *Journal of Early Intervention, 25*, 58–72.

Myles, B. S., & Adreon, D. (2001). *Asperger syndrome and adolescence: Practical solutions for school success.* AAPC Publishing.

Myles, B. S., & Simpson, R. L. (2001). Understanding the hidden curriculum: An essential social skill for children and youth with asperger syndrome. *Intervention in School and Clinic, 36*(5), 279–286.

National Research Council. (2001). *Educating children with autism.* Washington, DC: National Academy Press.

Nikopoulos, C. K., & Keenan, M. (2004). Effects of video modeling on social initiations by children with autism. *Journal of Applied Behavior Analysis, 37*(1), 93–96.

Odom, S. L., Brown, W. H., Frey, T., Karasu, N., Smith-Canter, L. L., & Strain, P. S. (2003). Evidence-based practices for young children with autism contributions for single-subject design research. *Focus on Autism and Other Developmental Disabilities, 18*(3), 166–175.

Odom, S. L., & Strain, P. S. (1984). Peer mediated approaches to promoting children's social interaction: A review. *American Journal of Orthopsychiatry, 54*, 544–557.

O'Reilly, M., Sigafoos, J., Lancioni, G., Edrisinha, C., & Andrews, A. (2005). An examination of the effects of a classroom activity schedule on levels of self-injury and engagement for a child with severe autism. *Journal of Autism and Developmental Disorders, 35*, 305–311.

Paul, R., Orlovski, S. M., Marcinko, H. C., & Volkmar, F. (2009). Conversational behaviors in youth with high-functioning ASD and Asperger syndrome. *Journal of Autism and Developmental Disorders, 39*(1), 115–125.

Prizant, B., Wetherby, A., Rubin, E., Laurent, A., & Rydell, P. (2002). The SCERTS model: Enhancing communication and socioemotional abilities of children with Autism Spectrum Disorders. *Jenison Autism Journal, 14* (4), 2–19. Retrieved on February 15, 2015.

Quill, K. (2000). *DO-WATCH-LISTEN-SAY: Social and communication intervention for children with autism.* Baltimore, New York: Brookes Publishing.

Reichow, B. & Vokmar, F. R. (2010). Social skills interventions for individuals with autism: Evaluation for evidence-based practices within a best evidence synthesis framework, *Journal of Autism and Developmental Disorders, 40*, 149–166.

Reszka, S. S., Odom, S. L., & Hume, K. A. (2012). Ecological features of preschools and the social engagement of children with autism. *Journal of Early Intervention, 34*, 40–56.

Rogers, S., Ozonoff, S., & Masline-Cole, C. (1993). Developmental aspects of attachment behavior in young children with pervasive developmental disorder.

Journal of American Academy of Child and Adolescence Psychiatry, 32, 1274–1282.

Rosales-Ruiz, J., & Baer, D. M. (1997). Behavioral cusps: A developmental and pragmatic concept for behavior analysis. *Journal of Applied Behavioral Analysis, 30*(3), 533–544.

Ruiz-Primo, M. A., & Furtak, E. M. (2006). Informal formative assessment and scientific inquiry: Exploring teachers' practices and student learning. *Educational Assessment, 11*(3), 205–235.

Sancho, K. Sidener, T. M., Reeve, S. A., & Sidener, D. W. (2010). Two variations of video modeling interventions for teaching play skills to children with autism. *Education and Treatment of Children, 33,* 421–442.

Schilling, D. L., & Schwartz, I. S. (2004). Alternative seating for young children with autism spectrum disorder: Effects on classroom behavior. *Journal of Autism & -Developmental Disorders, 34*(4), 423–432.

Schlelen, S., Heyne, L., & Berken, S. B. (1988). Integrating physical education to teach appropriate play skills to learners with autism: A pilot study. *Adapted Physical Activity Quarterly, 5,* 182–192.

Schopler, E., & Mesibov, G. B. (1985). *Communication problems in autism.* Springer Science & Business Media.

Sigman, M., Dijamco, A., Gratier, M., & Rozga, A. (2004). Early detection of core deficits in autism. *Mental Retardation and Developmental Disabilities Research Reviews, 10*(4), 221–233.

Stichter, J. P., Herzog, M. J., Visovsky, K., Schmidt, C., Randolph, J., Schultz, T., & Gage, N. (2010). Social competence intervention for youth with Asperger syndrome and high-functioning autism: An initial investigation. *Journal of Autism and Developmental Disorders, 40,* 1067–1079.

Stokes, M., Newton, N., & Kaur, A. (2007). Stalking, and social and romantic functioning among adolescents and adults with autism spectrum disorder. *Journal of Autism and Developmental Disorders, 37*(10), 1969–1986.

Terpstra, J. E., Higgins, K., & Pierce, T. (2002). Can I play? Classroom-based interventions for teaching play skills to children with autism. *Focus on Autism and Other Developmental Disabilities, 17*(2), 119–127.

Tissot, C., & Evans, R. (2003). Visual teaching strategies for children with autism. *Early Child Development and Care, 174*(4), 425–433.

Tse, J., Strulovitch, J., Tagalakis, V., Meng, L., Fombonne, E. (2007) Social skills training for adolescents with Asperger Syndrome and high-functioning autism. *Journal of Autism and Developmental Disorders, 37*(10), 1960–1968.

Volkmar, Rogers, S., Paul, R., & Pelphrey, K.A. (2014). *Handbook of autism and pervasive developmental disorders. 4th ed.* Hoboken, NJ: John Wiley & Sons, Inc.

White, S. W., Keonig, K., Scahill, L. (2007). Social skills development in children with autism spectrum disorders: A review of the intervention research. *Journal of Autism and Developmental Disorders, 37,* 1858–1868.

Wong, C., Odom, S. L., Hume, K., Cox, A. W., Brock, M. E., Plavnick, J. B., . . . Kucharczyk, S. (2012). *Evidence-based practices update: Reviewer training.* Chapel Hill: The University of North Carolina, Frank Porter Graham Child Development Institute, Autism Evidence-Based Practice Review Group.

Wolery, M., & Garfinkle, A. N. (2002). Measures in intervention research with young children who have autism. *Journal of Autism and Developmental Disorders*, *32*(5), 463–478.

Yang, T. R., Wolfberg, P. J., Wu, S. C., & Hwu, P. Y. (2003). Supporting children on the autism spectrum in peer play at home and school piloting the integrated play groups model in Taiwan. *Autism*, *7*(4), 437–453.

Zablotsky, B., Bradshaw, C. P., Anderson, C., & Law, P. A. (2013). The association between bullying and the psychological functioning of children with autism spectrum disorders. *Journal of Developmental and Behavioral Pediatrics*, *34*(1), 1–8.

Chapter 12

Self-determination for School and Community

Michael L. Wehmeyer and
Karrie A. Shogren

The transition from school to community has been a focus of special education since the mid-1980s and transition planning has been mandated in the Individuals with Disabilities Education Act since 1992. Much of the nation's progress toward achieving the goal of ensuring that youth and young adults receiving special education services transition to meaningful post-school outcomes—from independent living to meaningful employment and community inclusion—has been documented by a series of national longitudinal studies, the most recent of which (National Longitudinal Transition Study 2, or NLTS2) completed data collection in 2010. Among the areas of progress tracked by NLTS2 was the degree to which students receiving special education services become more self-determined over time. Discussed in more detail subsequently, this is because promoting self-determination and student involvement in transition planning has been shown to be causally related to more positive school and transition outcomes for youth and young adults (Shogren, Palmer, Wehmeyer, Williams-Diehm, & Little, 2012; Shogren, Wehmeyer, Palmer, Rifenbark, & Little, 2015) and to be predictive of more positive quality of life and life satisfaction outcomes (Nota, Ferrari, Soresi, & Wehmeyer, 2007; Shogren, Lopez, Wehmeyer, Little, & Pressgrove, 2006).

So, what does the NLTS2 tell us about the current state of transition outcomes for youth with Autism Spectrum Disorders (ASD)? Shogren and Plotner (2012) examined the transition planning experiences of students with intellectual disability, autism, or other disabilities (e.g. all other disability groups in NLTS2 combined, including learning disabilities, emotional behavior disorders, speech and language disorders, etc.) as reported in the NLTS2. Students with ASD were no different from their peers with intellectual disability or other disabilities in the percent of students ages 14 and over (the age at the time of data collection at which federally-mandated transition planning was to occur) for whom planning for transition had occurred, although at 86.3 percent of students receiving such planning, that means there are roughly 14 percent of students who are not receiving any such planning, despite the federal mandate. There were significant differences as to whether students with ASD received instruction driven by transition planning (70.6 percent of students with ASD compared to 75.8 percent of students with intellectual disability), and the focus of goals related to transition outcomes.

As can be seen in Figure 12.1, there were differences by disability category in the primary goal focus for students' education programs. Students with ASD had significantly different percentages compared to the other disability group on every goal focus area. Youth with ASD were less likely to have goals pertaining to college attendance, postsecondary vocational training, competitive employment, and independent living than students with other disabilities, and more likely to have goals pertaining to sheltered employment, supported employment, functional independence, and social/interpersonal relationships that the other disabilities group. The intellectual disability group showed similar differences with the other disability group. Youth with ASD had statistically significant differences from students with intellectual disability in five primary goal areas. Youth with intellectual disability were more likely than students with ASD to have a primary focus on competitive employment and independent living and were less likely to have (when compared to students with ASD) a primary goal focus on college, sheltered employment,

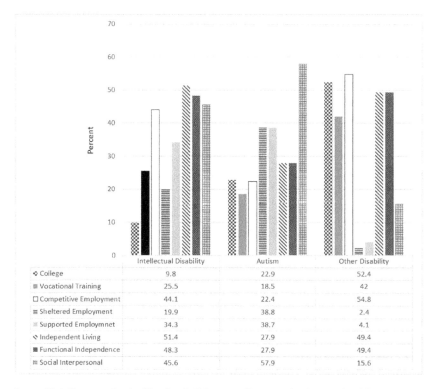

	Intellectual Disability	Autism	Other Disability
◇ College	9.8	22.9	52.4
▦ Vocational Training	25.5	18.5	42
☐ Competitive Employment	44.1	22.4	54.8
≡ Sheltered Employment	19.9	38.8	2.4
▦ Supported Employmnet	34.3	38.7	4.1
⬙ Independent Living	51.4	27.9	49.4
■ Functional Independence	48.3	27.9	49.4
▥ Social Interpersonal	45.6	57.9	15.6

Figure 12.1 Primary Goal of Student's Education Program for Post-school Preparation

supported employment, maximizing functional independence, and enhancing social/personal relationships.

Consider, then, what this means about the expectations for youth with ASD after high school. They are half as likely as youth with other disabilities (not including intellectual disability) to have goals pertaining to college, and less likely than all other students to have goals pertaining to vocational training. Somewhat amazingly, youth with ASD had sheltered employment-focused goals two times more than youth with intellectual disability. There were no statistical differences between students with ASD and intellectual disability on goals pertaining to supported employment. Again, surprisingly, youth with ASD were less likely than all other students to have independent living goals, and more likely than all other students to have goals focused on maximizing functional independence or enhancing social/interpersonal relationships. Having low expectations for college, vocational training, competitive employment, or independent living is hardly a recipe for high quality of life in adulthood.

With regard to student participation in the actual transition planning process, 67.3 percent of students with ASD either did not attend

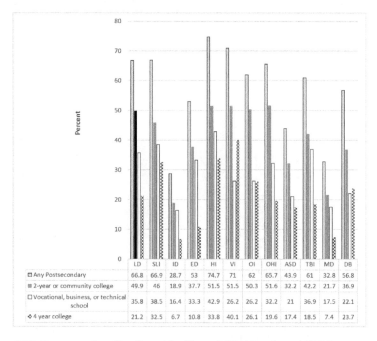

	LD	SLI	ID	ED	HI	VI	OI	OHI	ASD	TBI	MD	DB
☐ Any Postsecondary	66.8	66.9	28.7	53	74.7	71	62	65.7	43.9	61	32.8	56.8
▨ 2-year or community college	49.9	46	18.9	37.7	51.5	51.5	50.3	51.6	32.2	42.2	21.7	36.9
☐ Vocational, business, or technical school	35.8	38.5	16.4	33.3	42.9	26.2	26.2	32.2	21	36.9	17.5	22.1
◇ 4 year college	21.2	32.5	6.7	10.8	33.8	40.1	26.1	19.6	17.4	18.5	7.4	23.7

Figure 12.2 Postsecondary Enrollment by Type of Disability from NLTS2

Note:
LD = Learning Disabilities, SLI = Speech/Language Impairments, ID = Intellectual Disability, ED = Emotional Disturbance, HI = Hearing Impairment, VI = Visual Impairment, OI = Orthopedic Impairment, OHI = Other Health Impairment, ASD = Autism, TBI = Traumatic Brain Injury, MD = Multiple Disabilities, DB = Deafblindness

their planning meeting or attended but participated very little or not at all (Shogren & Plotner, 2012, p. 21). There were significant differences between students with ASD and students with intellectual disability and other disabilities in the "did not attend" category, with students with ASD having the highest percentage of students in that category. Of the remaining third of students with ASD, only 2.6 percent were identified as taking a leadership role in the meeting.

Now, if transition-related outcomes for students with ASD are fine, then these low expectations and low participation rates don't matter, really. But, of course, that is not the case. Take postsecondary education enrollment. As depicted in Figure 12.2, the low expectations reflected in the focus of goals youth with ASD had, seems fulfilled in postsecondary education enrollment for young adults with ASD. From all IDEA disability categorical areas, only young adults with multiple disabilities and intellectual disability had a lower percentage of enrollment in any type of postsecondary school. This same pattern held for every other type of postsecondary education setting (Newman et al., 2011).

Or, let's turn to employment status. From the same report from the NLTS2 (Newman *et al.*, 2011), Figure 12.3 provides data for paid employment outside the home after high school for young adults across

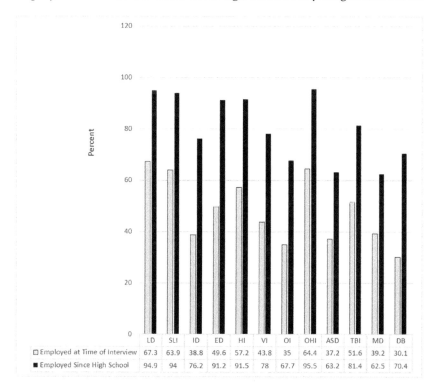

	LD	SLI	ID	ED	HI	VI	OI	OHI	ASD	TBI	MD	DB
☐ Employed at Time of Interview	67.3	63.9	38.8	49.6	57.2	43.8	35	64.4	37.2	51.6	39.2	30.1
■ Employed Since High School	94.9	94	76.2	91.2	91.5	78	67.7	95.5	63.2	81.4	62.5	70.4

Figure 12.3 Paid Employment after High School by Disability Category from NLTS2

disability categories. Once again, the low expectations reflected in goals set during transition planning play out in reality. From among young adults employed at the time that of the interview conducted by NLTS2 staff, only 37.2 percent of young adults with ASD were employed. Only young adults with Orthopedic Impairments or Deafblindness had lower levels of employment. Asked if the person had been employed any time since high school, only young adults with multiple disabilities had a lower percentage, and then only by 7/10ths of a percentage.

Finally, let's look at independent living. The NLTS2 dataset (Newman *et al.*, 2011) examined the percentage of young adults who lived independently, semi-independently, and their satisfaction with whichever living arrangement was in place. Figure 12.4 provides these data. No group had a lower rate of independent living than did young adults with ASD, and no group expressed a lower level of satisfaction than did young adults with ASD.

Clearly, youth with ASD are not leaving school to live high-quality lives, if such quality is determined by postsecondary education, employment, and independent living. Although the solution to this problem is

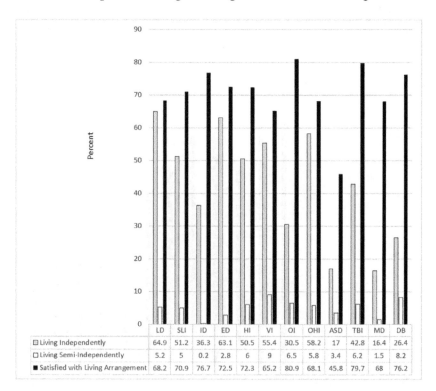

	LD	SLI	ID	ED	HI	VI	OI	OHI	ASD	TBI	MD	DB
▢ Living Independently	64.9	51.2	36.3	63.1	50.5	55.4	30.5	58.2	17	42.8	16.4	26.4
▢ Living Semi-Independently	5.2	5	0.2	2.8	6	9	6.5	5.8	3.4	6.2	1.5	8.2
■ Satisfied with Living Arrangement	68.2	70.9	76.7	72.5	72.3	65.2	80.9	68.1	45.8	79.7	68	76.2

Figure 12.4 Independent or Semi-independent Living Rates and Satisfaction with Living Arrangements across Disability Categories from NLTS2

multifaceted, we return to the low level of active involvement in transition planning and self-determination as one important area that needs attention. There is abundant evidence, discussed in the next section, that youth with disabilities who are more self-determined are more engaged in their transition planning process (Williams-Diehm, Wehmeyer, Palmer, Soukup, & Garner, 2008) and achieve more positive school (Shogren et al., 2012) and transition (Shogren et al., 2015) outcomes, including more positive employment and independent living outcomes. The following section introduces self-determination and student involvement and discusses what is known about the self-determination of students with ASD.

Self-determination and Youth and Young Adults with Autism Spectrum Disorders

Efforts to promote the self-determination of youth and young adults with disabilities were introduced in the early 1990s in response to data from studies in the mid-1980s that found that transition outcomes for youth with disabilities were, generally, less positive than anticipated (and, not coincidentally, these early studies provided impetus for the first National Longitudinal Transition Study to provide data to measure progress over time). The simple proposal forwarded at that time was that one of the reasons that students with disabilities were not succeeding after high school was that they were not aware of or engaged in their transition planning. The 1992 amendments to IDEA required, for the first, time that transition goals be discussed and that students with disabilities become involved in their transition planning.

What is Self-determination?

Self-determination is a general psychological construct within the organizing structure of theories of human agency which refers to self- (versus other-) caused action—to people acting volitionally, based on their own will. Human agency refers to the sense of personal empowerment involving both knowing and having what it takes to achieve goals. Human agentic theories share the view that people are active contributors to, or *authors* of their behavior, where behavior is self-regulated and goal-directed (Wehmeyer, Shogren, & Little, in press). A focus on self-determination in psychology (and, subsequently, education) grew out of philosophical discussions about determinism; the doctrine that all actions, including human behavior, are results of preceding causes. Self-determination, or self-determinism, refers fundamentally to self-caused versus other-caused action.

Shogren, Wehmeyer, Palmer, Forber-Pratt, Little and Lopez (in press) introduced Causal Agency Theory (an extension of a functional model of self-determination developed by Wehmeyer, 1992, 1999) to explain *how* people become self-determined; specifically, how they come to engage in self-caused, autonomous *actions*. Causal Agency Theory defines self-determination as a

> dispositional characteristic manifested as acting as the causal agent in one's life. Self-determined *people* (i.e., causal agents) act in service to freely chosen goals. Self-determined *actions* function to enable a person to be the causal agent is his or her life.
>
> (Shogren *et al.*, in press)

A *dispositional characteristic* is an enduring tendency used to characterize and describe differences between people; it refers to a tendency to act or think in a particular way, but presumes contextual variance (i.e. socio-contextual supports and opportunities, and threats and impediments). As a dispositional characteristic, self-determination can be measured, and variance will be observed across individuals and within individuals over time, particularly as the context changes (e.g. supports and opportunities are provided for self-determined action).

Broadly defined, *causal agency* implies that it is the person who makes or causes things to happen in his or her life. Causal agency implies more, however, than just causing action; it implies that the individual acts with an eye toward *causing* an effect to *accomplish* a *specific end* or to *cause* or *create change*. Self-determined actions enable a person to act as a causal agent.

Self-determined *action* is central to becoming self-determined, and self-determined actions are defined by three *essential characteristics—volitional action, agentic action*, and *action-control beliefs*. The essential characteristics refer not to specific actions, but to the *function* the action serves for the person; that is, whether the action enabled the person to act as a causal agent. Volitional actions are defined by self-initiation and autonomy; this involves making intentional, conscious choices based on one's preferences. Agentic actions are defined by self-regulation, self-direction, and pathways thinking; when acting agentically a person is working towards their goals, self-directing their actions, and identifying and navigating pathways to make progress. Action-control beliefs reflect each person's beliefs about the relationship between their actions and the outcomes they experience, or their control expectancies. When a person has adaptive action-control beliefs they can act with self-awareness and self-knowledge in an empowered, and goal-directed way.

The essential characteristics of self-determined action emerge across the lifespan as children and adolescents learn skills and develop attitudes and beliefs that enable them to be causal agents in their lives. These are the *component elements* of self-determined behavior, and include choice making, problem solving, decision making, goal setting and attainment, self-advocacy, and self-management skills.

Importance of Promoting Self-determination

Promoting the self-determination of youth and young adults with disabilities is important for several reasons. First, there is ample research to show that if provided adequate instruction, youth with disabilities can become more self-determined. Algozzine, Browder, Karvonen, Test, and Wood (2001) conducted single-subject design and group-design meta-analyses of studies focused on promoting component elements of self-determined behavior (e.g. problem-solving skills, decision-making skills, goal-setting and attainment skills, self-advocacy skills, self-management skills, and so forth) and found evidence for the efficacy of such instruction. Cobb, Lehmann, Newman-Gonchar, and Morgan (2009) conducted a narrative meta-synthesis—a narrative synthesis of multiple meta-analytic studies—covering seven existing meta-analyses examining self-determination and concluded that there is sufficient evidence to support the promotion of self-determination as effective.

Wehmeyer, Palmer, Shogren, Williams-Diehm, and Soukup (2012) conducted a randomized trial control group (RCT) study of the effect of interventions to promote self-determination on the self-determination of high school students with disabilities. Youth in the treatment group received instruction using a variety of instructional methods to promote self-determination and student involvement in educational planning meetings over three years, while youth in the control group did not. The self-determination of each student was measured using two instruments. Using latent growth curve analysis, Wehmeyer and colleagues found that youth with disabilities who participated in interventions to promote self-determination over a three-year period showed significantly more positive patterns of growth in their self-determination scores than did youth not exposed to interventions to promote self-determination, providing causal evidence that efforts to promote self-determination result in enhanced self-determination.

In another RCT study of the Self-Determined Learning Model of Instruction (SDLMI, Wehmeyer, Palmer, Agran, Mithaug, & Martin, 2000), described in detail in a subsequent section, Wehmeyer et al. (2012) examined the impact of instruction using the SDLMI on student self-determination, determining, again, that students who received instruction to promote self-determination became more self-determined.

Knowing that when provided instruction to promote self-determination, youth with disabilities become more self-determined, we turn to the evidence that enhanced self-determination results in more positive school and community outcomes. Research has found a relationship between enhanced self-determination and more positive academic (Fowler, Konrad, Walker, Test, & Wood, 2007), employment and independent living (Martorell, Gutierrez-Rechacha, Pereda, & Ayuso-Mateos, 2008; Wehmeyer & Schwartz, 1997; Wehmeyer & Palmer, 2003), and positive quality of life and life satisfaction outcomes (Nota et al., 2007; Shogren et al., 2006).

Again, however, several recent studies have found causal evidence of the impact of promoting self-determination on school and community outcomes, beginning with the latter. Shogren et al. (2015) conducted a follow-up study of the treatment and control group students from Wehmeyer et al. (2012), investigating adult outcomes one and two years after leaving school for young adults who had or had not received instruction to promote self-determination. The study measured employment, community access, financial independence, independent living, and life satisfaction outcomes. Results indicated that self-determination status at the end of high school predicted significantly more positive employment and community living outcomes. Additionally, a randomized trial study by Powers et al. (2012) provided causal evidence of the effect of promoting self-determination on community inclusion.

Two RCT studies of the implementation of the SDLMI with students with cognitive disabilities (intellectual disability, learning disabilities) provide causal evidence of the effect of intervention to promote self-determination on school-related outcomes. First, Lee, Wehmeyer, Palmer, Soukup and Little (2008) conducted a randomized trial, control group study implementing the SDLMI with students with learning disabilities and a few other disabilities (OHI, ED), including one student with Autism, and found that instruction using this model improved student access to the general education curriculum and enhanced student educational goal attainment. Second, Shogren et al. (2012) found that students with cognitive disabilities who received instruction to promote self-determination (and became more self-determined, e.g. Wehmeyer et al., 2012) performed better on education and transition-related goals and had greater access to the general education curriculum.

Importance of Promoting Student Involvement

The aforementioned 1992 amendments to IDEA required that students aged 14 and over receiving special education services (the federally required minimum age is now 16) must have access to transition services, including goals to promote the movement from school to college, vocational training, employment, independent living, and so forth. The 1992 amendments also required that if transition services are discussed at the IEP meeting, the student receiving special education services must be invited to the meeting. Since the IEP of every student aged 16 and over, now, must include transition services, then technically, every student aged 16 and over must be invited to the IEP meeting. Further, the transition services definition in IDEA indicated that such services should be based on student needs, taking into account student interests and preferences. These amendments, referred to as the student-involvement requirements in IDEA, established the importance of student involvement in transition planning.

Research since that time has documented a number of benefits of active student involvement in transition planning, including enhanced self-determination and student participation. Martin, Marshall, and Sale (2004) conducted a three-year study of middle, junior, and senior high school IEP meetings and found that the presence of students at IEP meetings had considerable benefits, including increasing parental involvement and improving the probability that a student's strengths, needs, and interests would be discussed. Test, Mason, Hughes, Konrad, Neale, and Wood (2004) conducted an extensive review of the literature pertaining to student involvement and determined that youth across disability categories can be successfully involved in transition planning and a number of programs, including several discussed subsequently, are effective in increasing student involvement.

The impact of some of these programs documents the importance of actively engaging youth in the transition planning process. For example, Martin, Van Dycke, Christensen, Greene, Gardner, and Lovett (2006) conducted a randomized trial control group study of an intervention called the *Self-Directed IEP* (SDIEP) and determined that students with disabilities who received instruction using the SDIEP (a) attended more IEP meetings; (b) increased their active participation in the meetings; (c) showed more leadership behaviors in the meetings; (d) expressed their interests, skills, and support needs across educational domains; (e) and remembered their IEP goals after the meeting at greater rates than did students in the control group, who received no such instruction. Wehmeyer, Palmer, Lee, Williams-Diehm and Shogren (2011) conducted a randomized trial, placebo control group design study of the impact of another student involvement intervention, *Whose Future is it Anyway?* (WFA; also discussed subsequently) on self-determination and transition knowledge and skills, finding that instruction using the WFA process resulted in significant, positive differences in self-determination when compared with a placebo-control group, and that students who received instruction gained transition knowledge and skills.

Promoting student involvement also has a beneficial effect on self-determination. Lee, Wehmeyer, Palmer, Williams-Diehm, Davies, and Stock (2011) conducted a randomized-trial study of the impact of the WFA process both with and without the use of technology, and determined significant gains in self-determination and transition knowledge and skills as a function of instruction with WFA. Seong, Wehmeyer,

Palmer, and Little (in press) conducted a randomized trial, placebo control group study of the SDIEP, finding that instruction using the process resulted in enhanced self-determination and transition knowledge. Finally, Williams-Diehm and colleagues (2008) studied the differences in level of self-determination between 276 youth with disabilities divided into groups that differed by level of student involvement in the IEP meeting. Multivariate analysis showed significant differences between self-determination scores using two different measures for students in a high involvement group versus students in a low involvement group, indicating that students who were more involved in their meetings were more self-determined. A second multivariate analysis found, though, that students who were more self-determined (two groups, high or low self-determination) were more likely to be involved in their IEP meeting, suggesting a reciprocal relationship between being self-determined and being involved with one's transition planning.

Self-determination and Students with Autism Spectrum Disorders

To begin with, it should be noted that there has been far too little research examining the self-determination of youth with ASD and the impact of interventions to promote self-determination on the self-determination of youth with ASD and outcomes for young adults with ASD. That said, there is no compelling reason to believe that promoting self-determination should not have the same positive outcomes for youth with ASD as for other students for whom more research is available. Further, although not represented at high levels, youth with ASD were included in a number of the studies referenced in the previous section.

The first step in determining both future research and intervention directions for the field, and for determining instructional needs and instruction efficacy for students, is an examination of the self-determination status of youth with ASD. To that end, Chou, Wehmeyer, Palmer, and Lee (2014) examined differences in self-determination among youth with ASD, youth with intellectual disability, and youth with learning disabilities. Using multivariate analysis of covariance, Chou and colleagues found that youth with ASD had the lowest mean total self-determination scores from among the three groups, with pairwise comparisons showing that the significant differences were in scores on the autonomous functioning section, with students with ASD scoring significantly lower than their peers with intellectual or learning disabilities.

When considering the unique needs of youth with ASD with regard to promoting self-determination, Wehmeyer, Shogren, Zager, Smith, and Simpson (2010) identified several areas of potential concentration. First, and perhaps foremost, self-determination, by its very nature, almost always has a social context. That is, self-determination is self-caused versus other-caused action, and the "other" in the latter is, most often, other people (Mithaug, 1998). Thus, issues pertaining to social interactions as they pertain to enabling youth and young adults with ASD to act in a self-determined manner will likely take on extra importance in interventions to promote self-determination. Further, a critical element of such social interactions, involving communication, and enabling youth and young adults with ASD to more effectively communicate preferences, interests, and values in ways that enable them to achieve goals, will also be critical in interventions to promote self-determination. Students, for example, who interpret communication literally and experience difficulty with abstract constructs will need support to better navigate the often complex social interactions associated with negotiation or self-advocacy communications (Hochhauser, Weiss, & Gal (2015).

Wehmeyer and Shogren (2008) reviewed the literature pertaining to component elements of self-determination and youth and young adults with ASD. Some of the intervention recommendations from this review will be included in the subsequent section, but we also identified several tendencies or characteristics of students with ASD that would impact the design and delivery of interventions to promote self-determination for this population. For one, the literature suggests that youth and young adults with ASD are more sequential in their goal-directed behavior and have difficulty addressing multiple goals at the same time (Ruble & Scott, 2002). Similarly, students with ASD may have difficulty solving problems, both because many problems are interpersonal and involve another person or persons, and because of difficulties reading social emotional cues.

We highlight some of these areas of particular focus not to identify limitations, specifically, but to identify specific types of interventions or elements of interventions that may be particularly salient to youth and young adults with ASD. A number of research-based interventions to promote self-determination are discussed in the next section, but we would note that given that Chou and colleagues found that youth with ASD were significantly lower in their autonomous functioning than youth with intellectual disability or learning disabilities, and given the NLTS2 data showing that youth and young adults with ASD are not involved in transition planning and are held to low expectations with regard to post-secondary education, employment, and independent living outcomes, it seems clear that among the most important things that need to happen don't involve changing the student but, instead, providing opportunities for students to become involved in a meaningful way in their transition planning, and for IEP teams to hold high expectations for youth and young adults with ASD with regard to employment, postsecondary education, and independent living.

To that end, Wehmeyer *et al.* (2010) recommended using a social-ecological approach to promoting the self-determination of youth and young adults with ASD. Social-ecological models of intervention emphasize the complex interactions that occur between person- and environment-specific variables and that account for significant changes in human behavior and enhanced human functioning. The emphasis in social-ecological models of interventions on enhancing both the capacity of the person and modifying the context or environment to enable success has particular relevance for students with ASD.

Promoting the Self-determination of Youth and Young Adults with Autism Spectrum Disorders

We have mentioned that the literature pertaining to interventions to promote the self-determination of students with ASD is limited. Although there are certain characteristics of youth and young adults with ASD that suggest particular areas of emphasis in interventions to promote self-determination, this is not to suggest that youth with ASD need substantially different interventions provided to them. They likely do not. All of the interventions detailed below included, even though at small numbers, students with ASD. As such, we have identified a number of research- or evidence-based methods, materials, and strategies that are logical places to begin with regard to promoting self-determination for students with ASD.

Assessing Self-determination

Educational interventions begin with assessment of areas of needed instruction. Chou, Wehmeyer, Shogren, Palmer, and Lee (2013) examined the reliability and validity, through confirmatory factor analysis, of two of the most used standardized assessments of self-determination: *The Arc's Self-Determination Scale* (Wehmeyer & Kelchner, 1995) and The AIR Self-Determination Scale (Wolman, Campeau, Dubois, Mithaug, & Stolarski, 1994). The factory analysis supported the measurement properties and factor structure of both instruments in a sample of adolescents with ASD. The Arc's Self-Determination Scale is a student-self report measure, and the AIR Self-Determination Scale has, as one of three versions, a student report version, so not only can these instruments be used for research and evaluation of the effect of intervention, but they can also be used to assist students in understanding their own self-determination and where they have strengths and areas of instructional need.

Promoting Component Elements of Self-determination

Perhaps the most straightforward action teachers can take to begin to promote the self-determination of youth and young adults with ASD is to provide instruction on the component elements of self-determined behavior, such as goal setting, problem solving, decision making, self-advocacy, self-regulation, and so forth, across the curriculum. At the heart of efforts to promote self-determination are efforts to teach students goal-setting and attainment skills. Instruction should focus on teaching students to set goals, develop objectives to achieve those goals, how to track progress toward goals, and then to self-monitor and self-evaluate their progress. Held, Thoma, and Thomas (2004) taught adolescents with ASD to set and achieve goals using the SDLMI (discussed subsequently in more detail).

Teaching students to solve problems is another important area of focus for intervention. Such instruction can be infused into just about any context or content area. Research to promote social problem-solving skills for people with ASD has tended to focus on youth with Asperger's syndrome, and to generally show that youth with ASD had difficulty generating solutions to social problems they encountered, but could judge the utility of alternate solutions when provided (Channon, Crawford, Orlowska, Parikh, & Thoma, 2014). Bauminger (2007a; 2007b) developed an intervention to promote social cognition and social interaction in students with ASD by teaching social and interpersonal problem-solving skills, using a cognitive-behavioral-ecological approach. After receiving intervention, students generated more appropriate solutions to problems faced in social situations and initiated more social interactions with peers.

Other important areas of instruction across the curriculum involve efforts to teach decision-making skills and, importantly, to maximally involve students with ASD in the decision-making process so as to provide opportunities for students to learn to overcome the emotions often associated with decisions that have to be made. Another important area of instruction involves promoting and supporting self-advocacy skills. Students need to be provided with instruction and opportunities to practice skills such as negotiation, leadership, and persuasion.

Of course, as intimated several times in this section, efforts to teach skills must be accompanied by efforts to promote opportunities for students to express preferences, communicate choices, advocate for themselves, demonstrate leadership, and so forth.

Student-directed Learning Strategies

One of the more robust areas with regard to interventions with proven efficacy for youth and young adults with ASD involves the use of student-directed learning strategies. These are instructional strategies that, as their name implies, are directed by—implemented by—the student, rather than the more traditional teacher-directed strategies. Such strategies are also often referred to as self-management strategies. These include self-monitoring (teaching students to track progress toward a goal or objectives), self-evaluation (teaching students to evaluate whether they have achieved a goal or objective based upon information gathered through self-monitoring), self-instruction (teaching students to instruct—verbally or otherwise—themselves through a task or process), antecedent cue regulation (teaching students to use images, pictures, or other visual or audio prompts to perform a multi-step task), and self-reinforcement (teaching students to provide their own reinforce based upon the outcome of self-monitoring/self-evaluation).

Lee, Simpson, and Shogren (2007) conducted a meta-analysis of single-subject design studies reporting the use of self-management strategies with students with ASD. This analysis found that "across subjects, settings, and particular conditions, self-management interventions generally resulted in improvements in socially desired behaviors" (p. 8). Self-monitoring was the most effective strategy evaluated. One of the benefits of implementing these student-directed learning strategies is that they can be combined into a multi-component intervention based upon the needs of the student and the focus of the intervention, and they can be applied to instruction on any topic area. Wehmeyer and Shogren (2008) documented evidence of the efficacy of such strategies across multiple school and community settings and activities, from improving school outcomes to promoting more positive employment outcomes.

Self-determined Learning Model of Instruction

Previous sections identified the Self-Determined Learning Model of Instruction (Wehmeyer et al., 2000) as having causal evidence with regard to its positive impact on student self-determination, as well as school- and community-based outcomes. The SDLMI is, essentially, a multi-component intervention to enable teachers to teach students to self-regulate problem solving in order to set a goal, create an action plan to achieve that goal, self-monitor and self-evaluate progress toward the goal, and revise the action plan or goal as needed so as to attain the goal. Wehmeyer and Palmer (1999) provided details with regard to the implementation of the SDLMI, as follows.

Implementation of the SDLMI consists of a three-phase instructional process. Each instructional phase presents a problem to be solved by the student. The student solves each problem by answering a series of four *Student Questions* per phase that students learn, modify to make their own, and apply to reach self-set goals. Each question is linked to a set of *Teacher Objectives*, and each instructional phase includes a list of *Educational Supports* teachers can use to teach or support students to self-direct learning.

The Student Questions are constructed to direct the student through a problem-solving sequence in each instructional phase. The four questions differ in each phase, but represent identical steps in the problem-solving sequence: (1) identify the problem, (2) identify potential solutions to the problem, (3) identify barriers to solving the problem, and (4) identify the consequences of each solution. These steps are the fundamental steps in any problem-solving process and they form the means–end problem-solving sequence represented by the Student Questions in each phase and enable the student to solve the problem posed in each instructional phase (*What is my goal? What is my plan? What have I learned?*). The Student Questions are written in first-person voice in a simple format, with the intention that they are the starting point for discussion between the teacher and the student. In essence, teachers use each Student Question as a teaching prompt to teach and support students to answer the question in ways that are indicated in the Teacher Objectives. Although some students will be able to become self-directed in posing and answering the questions, others will likely need ongoing support from teachers to answer each question. That is fine, in that the intent of the SDLMI is not that students become independent learners, necessarily, but that students remain at the center of the process and are actively engaging, to the greatest extent they are able to do so, in self-regulating problem solving to set and attain goals. The Educational Supports simply provide recommendations for teachers as to what instructional strategies they might use to enable students to answer questions.

We have already discussed multiple studies providing evidence of the efficacy of intervention using the SDLMI so will not repeat that in this section, other than to note that the SDLMI has been shown to be equally effective independent of the type of goal, whether academic or functional/transition. This process would enable teachers to focus on some of the issues raised previously that might have more salience for students with ASD than other populations. For example, since youth with ASD may have difficulty with complex goals, students could learn the SDLMI process as a means to narrow the scope of goals they have set. Social interaction and interpersonal problem solving could easily become areas in which students with ASD self-set goals to enhance their self-determination.

Promoting Student Involvement in Transition Planning

There are multiple programs or processes that have evidence with regard to their utility in enhancing student involvement in transition planning and enhancing self-determination. Two of these, The Self-Directed IEP (SDIEP; Martin & Marshall, 1995) and the Whose Future is it Anyway? (Wehmeyer et al., 2004) are described here.

The Self-Directed IEP (SDIEP; Martin & Marshall, 1995) is a process to teach students the leadership skills they need to direct their own IEP meeting. The SDIEP is part of a larger intervention, the ChoiceMaker series, focusing on teaching students goal setting and self-advocacy skills. Using the SDIEP, students learn 11 steps for leading their own planning meeting, including stating the purpose of the meeting, introducing meeting attendees, reviewing their past goals and progress, stating new transition goals, summarizing goals, and closing the meeting by thanking attendees. As noted previously, Martin and colleagues (2006) provided causal evidence of increased involvement in the IEP process by students who had participated and Seong and colleagues (in press) provided evidence of the positive effect of the SDIEP on student self-determination.

Whose Future is it Anway? (WFA; Wehmeyer *et al.*, 2003) is a student self-regulated process to promote more meaningful involvement in transition planning. Developed for students with intellectual and developmental disabilities, and appropriate for use with youth with ASD, the WFA process consists of 36 sessions enabling students to self-direct instruction related to (1) self- and disability-awareness; (2) making decisions about transition-related outcomes; (3) identifying and securing community resources to support transition services; (4) writing and evaluating transition goals and objectives; (5) communicating effectively in small groups; and (6) developing skills to become an effective team member, leader, or self-advocate. The materials are student-directed in that they are written for students as end-users. The level of support needed by students to complete activities varies greatly. Some students with difficulty reading or writing need one-to-one support to progress through the materials; others can complete the process independently. Wehmeyer *et al.* (2011) conducted a randomized trial study of the effect of the WFA on student self-determination, and transition knowledge and skills. The results indicated that instruction using the WFA process resulted in significant, positive differences in self-determination when compared with a control group and those students who received instruction gained transition knowledge and skills.

Conclusions

There is no reason to believe that promoting the self-determination of students with ASD is not as important to these youth and young adults as research has found to be the case for other students with disabilities. In fact, given the current status of transition planning opportunities and transition-related outcomes, one could argue that this is more important for this population because of the lack of focus in the past. The good news is that there are now validated assessments of self-determination that can be use for research, intervention evaluation, and individual student planning, and a number of research- and evidence-based practices to promote student-directed learning, self-determination, and active student involvement that can be implemented, evaluated, and, if necessary, refined. From the outcomes of the NLTS2, it is clear that such efforts need to begin as soon as possible, if youth and young adults are to achieve the school and community outcomes they desire, and that others desire for them.

References

Algozzine, B., Browder, D., Karvonen, M., Test, D. W., & Wood, W. M. (2001). Effects of interventions to promote self-determination for individuals with disabilities. *Review of Educational Research, 71*(2), 219–277.

Bauminger, N. (2007a). Brief report: Individual social-multi-modal intervention for HFASD. *Journal of Autism and Developmental Disorders, 37*, 1593–1604.

Bauminger, N. (2007b). Brief report. Group social-multi-modal intervention for HFASD. *Journal of Autism and Developmental Disorders, 37*, 1605–1615.

Channon, S., Crawford, S., Orlowska, D., Parikh, N., & Thoma, P. (2014). Mentalising and social problem solving in adults with Asperger's syndrome. *Cognitive Neuropsychiatry, 19*(2), 149–163.

Chou, Y.C., Wehmeyer, M.L., Shogren, KA., Palmer, S.B., & Lee, J.H. (2013). *Autism and self-determination: Factor analysis of two measures of self-determination.* Manuscript under review.

Chou, Y.C., Wehmeyer, M.L., Palmer, S.B., & Lee, J.H. (2014). *Comparisons of self-determination among students with autism, intellectual disability, and learning disabilities: A multivariate analysis.* Manuscript under review.

Cobb, B., Lehmann, J., Newman-Gonchar, R., & Morgan, A. (2009). Self-determination for students with disabilities: A narrative metasynthesis. Career Development for Exceptional Individuals, 32, 108–114.

Fowler, C.H., Konrad, M., Walker, A.R., Test, D.W., & Wood, W.M. (2007). Self-determination interventions' effects on the academic performance of students with developmental disabilities. *Education and Training in Developmental Disabilities, 42*(3), 270–285.

Held, M. F., Thoma, C. A., & Thomas, K. (2004). "The John Jones Show" How One Teacher Facilitated Self-Determined Transition Planning for a Young Man With Autism. *Focus on Autism and Other Developmental Disabilities, 19*(3), 177–188.

Hochhauser, M., Weiss, P.L., & Gal, E. (2015). Negotiation strategies of adolescents with high-functioning autism spectrum disorder during social conflicts. *Research in Autism Spectrum Disorders, 10*, 7–14.

Lee, S.H., Simpson, R.L., & Shogren, K.A. (2007). Effects and implications of self-management for students with autism: A meta-analysis. *Focus on Autism and Other Developmental Disabilities, 22*(1), 2–13.

Lee, S.H., Wehmeyer, M.L., Palmer, S.B., Soukup, J.H., & Little, T.D. (2008). Self-determination and access to the general education curriculum. *The Journal of Special Education, 42*(2), 91–107.

Lee, Y., Wehmeyer, M., Palmer, S., Williams-Diehm, K., Davies, D., & Stock, S. (2011). The effect of student-directed transition planning using a computer-based reading support program on the self-determination of students with disabilities. *Journal of Special Education, 45*, 104–117.

Martin, J. E., & Marshall, L. H. (1995). A Comprehensive self-determination transition program. *Intervention in School & Clinic*, *30*(3), 147–157.

Martin, J.E., Marshall, L.H., & Sale, P. (2004). A 3-year study of middle, junior high, and high school IEP meetings. *Exceptional Children*, *70*, 285–297.

Martin, J.E., Van Dycke, J.L., Christensen, W.R., Greene, B.A., Gardner, J.E., & Lovett, D.L. (2006). Increasing student participation in IEP meetings: Establishing the Self-Directed IEP as an evidenced-based practice. *Exceptional Children*, *72*(3), 299–316.

Martorell, A., Gutierrez-Recacha, P., Perda, A., & Ayuso-Mateos, J.L. (2008). Identification of personal factors that determine work outcome for adults with intellectual disability. *Journal of Intellectual Disability Research*, *52*(12), 1091–1101.

Mithaug, D. (1998). Your right, my obligation? *Journal of the Association for Persons with Severe Disabilities*, *23*, 41–43.

Newman, L., Wagner, M., Knokey, A.-M., Marder, C., Nagle, K., Shaver, D., . . . Schwarting, M. (2011). *The post-high school outcomes of young adults with disabilities up to 8 years after high school. A report from the National Longitudinal Transition Study-2 (NLTS2)* (NCSER 2011-3005). Menlo Park, CA: SRI International.

Nota, L., Ferrari, L., Soresi, S., & Wehmeyer, M.L. (2007). Self-determination, social abilities, and the quality of life of people with intellectual disabilities. *Journal of Intellectual Disability Research*, *51*, 850–865.

Powers, L. E., Geenen, S., Powers, J., Pommier-Satya, S., Turner, A., Dalton, L. D., . . . Swank, P. (2012). My life: Effects of a longitudinal, randomized study of self-determination enhancement on the transition outcomes of youth in foster care and special education. *Children and Youth Services Review*, *34*(11), 2179–2187.

Ruble, L.A., & Scott, M.M. (2002). Executive functions and the natural habitat behaviors of children with autism. *Autism*, *6*(4), 365–381.

Seong, Y., Wehmeyer, M.L., Palmer, S.B., & Little, T.D. (2015). Effects of *the Self-Directed IEP* on self-determination and transition of adolescents with disabilities. *Career Development and Transition for Exceptional* Individuals, *38*(4),132–141.

Shogren, K.A., Lopez, S.J., Wehmeyer, M.L., Little, T.D., & Pressgrove, C.L. (2006). The role of positive psychology constructs in predicting life satisfaction in adolescents with and without cognitive disabilities: An exploratory study. *Journal of Positive Psychology*, *1*, 37–52.

Shogren, K., Palmer, S., Wehmeyer, M.L., Williams-Diehm, K., & Little, T. (2012). Effect of intervention with the *Self-Determined Learning Model of Instruction* on access and goal attainment. *Remedial and Special Education*, *33*(5), 320–330.

Shogren, K.A., & Plotner, A.J. (2012). Transition planning for students with intellectual disability, autism, or other disabilities: Data from the National Longitudinal Transition Study-2. *Intellectual and Developmental Disabilities*, *50*(1), 16–30.

Shogren, K.A., Wehmeyer, M.L., Palmer, S.B., Forber-Pratt, A., Little, T., & Lopez, S. (2015). Causal Agency Theory: Reconceptualizing a functional model of self-determination. *Education and Training in Autism and Developmental Disabilities*, *50*(3), 251.

Shogren, K.A., Wehmeyer, M.L., Palmer, S.B., Rifenbark, G. & Little, T. (2015). Relationships between self-determination and postschool outcomes for youth with disabilities. *Journal of Special Education*, *48*(4), 256–267.

Test, D.W., Mason, C., Hughes, C., Konrad, M., Neale, M., & Wood, W. (2004). Student involvement in individualized education program meetings. *Exceptional Children*, *70*, 391–412.

Wehmeyer, M.L. (1992). Self-determination and the education of students with mental retardation. *Education and Training in Mental Retardation*, *27*, 302–314.

Wehmeyer, M.L. (1999). A functional model of self-determination: Describing development and implementing instruction. *Focus on Autism and Other Developmental Disabilities*, *14*, 53–61.

Wehmeyer, M.L., & Kelchner, K. (1995). *The Arc's self-determination scale*. Arlington, TX: The Arc National Headquarters.

Wehmeyer, M.L., Lawrence, M., Kelchner, K., Palmer, S., Soukup, J., & Garner, N. (2003). *Whose future is it anyway? A student-directed transition planning process* (2nd Ed.). Lawrence, KS: Beach Center on Disability.

Wehmeyer, M.L., & Palmer, S. (2003). Adult outcomes for students with cognitive disabilities three-years after high school: The impact of self-determination. *Education and Training in Developmental Disabilities*, *38*(2), 131–144.

Wehmeyer, M.L., & Palmer, S.B. (1999). *A teacher's guide to implementing the Self-Determined Learning Model of Instruction: Adolescent version*. Lawrence, KS: Beach Center on Disability.

Wehmeyer, M. L., Palmer, S. B., Agran, M., Mithaug, D. E., & Martin, J. E. (2000). Promoting causal agency: The self-determined learning model of instruction. *Exceptional Children*, *66*(4), 439–453.

Wehmeyer, M.L., Palmer, S.B., Lee, Y., Williams-Diehm, K., & Shogren, K.A. (2011). A randomized-trial evaluation of the effect of *Whose Future is it Anyway?* on self-determination. *Career Development for Exceptional Individuals*, *34*(1), 45–56.

Wehmeyer, M.L., Palmer, S., Shogren, K., Williams-Diehm, K., & Soukup, J. (2012). Establishing a causal relationship between interventions to promote self-determination and enhanced student self-determination. *Journal of Special Education*, *46*(4), 195–210.

Wehmeyer, M.L. & Schwartz, M. (1997). Self-determination and positive adult outcomes: A follow-up study of youth with mental retardation or learning disabilities. *Exceptional Children*, *63*, 245–255.

Wehmeyer, M.L., & Shogren, K. (2008). Self-determination and learners with autism spectrum disorders. In R. Simpson & B. Myles (Eds.), *Educating Children and Youth with Autism: Strategies for Effective Practice* (2nd Ed.) (pp. 433–476). Austin, TX: ProEd Publishers, Inc.

Wehmeyer, M., Shogren, K., & Little, T. (in press). Self-Determination. In S. Lopez (Ed.), *The Encyclopedia of Positive Psychology* (2nd Ed.). New York: Wiley Blackwell.

Wehmeyer, M.L., Shogren, K., Palmer, S., Williams-Diehm, K., Little, T., & Boulton, A. (2012). The impact of the *Self-Determined Learning Model of Instruction* on student self-determination. *Exceptional Children, 78*(2), 135–153.

Wehmeyer, M. L., Shogren, K. A., Zager, D., Smith, T. E., & Simpson, R. (2010). Research-based principles and practices for educating students with autism: Self-determination and social interactions. *Education and Training in Autism and Developmental Disabilities*, 475–486.

Williams-Diehm, K., Wehmeyer, M.L., Palmer, S., Soukup, J. H., & Garner, N. (2008). Self-determination and student involvement in transition planning: A multivariate analysis. *Journal on Developmental Disabilities, 14*, 25–36.

Wolman, J., Campeau, P., Dubois, P., Mithaug, D., & Stolarski, V. (1994). *AIR Self-Determination Scale and user guide*. Pola Alto, CA: American Institute for Research.

Chapter 13

Universal Design for Transition for Students on the Autism Spectrum

Linking Academic and Transition Education to Improve Postschool Outcomes

Colleen A. Thoma, Irina Cain, Andrew J. Wojcik, Kathryn Best, and LaRon A. Scott

Introduction

A few years ago I had a student named Gene. Gene had an encyclopedic knowledge of every movie he had ever watched, and he expressed a strong interest in working in a movie store. My school's administration was eager to match him with his preferred job. As the school-based case manager, I made arrangements with a local video rental store owner for Gene to test out different jobs. Gene adapted quickly to the steps necessary for restocking videos. He rewound the video tape, entered the video into the computer system, located the genre, and re-shelved the video. Gene worked during school hours, and after graduation the manager of the store hired him, and he worked for a number of years—until the store closed and the era of video rental stores was gone. Gene was unprepared for a new job search. Instead of preparing Gene for a variety of different jobs, we customized his high school experience to maximize his chances for getting his then dream job. Now, I wish we had developed a broader range of skills to prepare Gene for a variety of employment and education options. I wish we had helped him learn how to use transportation, how to enjoy community services, how to explore a multitude of employment and postsecondary education options, and hot to locate support systems outside the school. And I wish we had been able to find a way to do this without considering academic preparation as expendable. Like every other high school student, Gene needed that academic preparation to have the broadest range of postschool options available.

Gene's story, as told by his teacher, reflects the challenges that come from having a narrow focus on preparing students with disabilities for their transition to adult life. With increased participation of students with disabilities in the general education curriculum, teachers are finding that they now also struggle to address their need for transition-related education (Best, Scott, & Thoma, 2014). It is for this reason that a new framework for educational planning, instructional design, and assessment was developed: Universal Design for Transition (Thoma, Bartholomew, & Scott, 2009).

Universal Design for Transition (UDT) is a philosophy of instructional design that promotes successful transitional outcomes for students with disabilities by combining academic and transition education for all students. The system builds on the Universal Design philosophy, which embeds flexible and intuitive structures to increase the likelihood of access to different environments (Aslaksen, Bergh, Bringa, & Heggem, 1997). The UDT model also adopts strategies from the Universal Design from Learning model, which promotes student achievement with educational activities that employ: (a) multiple means of engagement, (b) multiple means of representation, and (c) multiple means of action and expression (Meyer, Rose, and Gordon, 2013). Most importantly, UDT focuses transitional development on improving the individual's ability to adapt to a variety of situations and environments. Instead of customizing services to the individual, UDT helps create a more adaptable individual who can find and utilize multiple natural supports. For example, instead of helping to develop transition supports for employment or postsecondary programs, the UDT method focuses on building the student's adaptability to a variety of different environments. To maximize the adaptability of the individual, UDT focuses on developing barrier-free transitional experiences in the areas of postschool life, self-advocacy, and academic skills. Specifically, UDT helps to improve the design, delivery, and assessment related to transition (Thoma, et al., 2009).

Traditionally, transitional services for individuals with autism spectrum disorder (ASD) have been set by a team of individuals (parents, teachers, the student, and school-based staff). The student's interests and goals were matched to what were thought to be *realistic* and available outcomes. In many cases services and instruction were customized to the individual student. For example, to help a student access postsecondary activities, the student might learn to sign up for recreational classes through a community education program. Academic lessons would be limited to the academic skills necessary to participate in the service. The student might be taught to read the course manual or to fill out a course request program. In the traditional approach, caregivers assumed that the transitional services would remain static across time. One of the limitations to the traditional approach is the narrow scope and vision of the planners. Teachers, parents, and students tend to customize the services based on prior experience. They focus on outcomes they believe were realistic and attainable for the student (Ayers et al., 2011, 2012), but too often what they believed to be realistic was, in fact, too restrictive. In the short run, the student might have access to community education services, for instance the home video class. In the long run, however, they might miss new opportunities (e.g. the computer class). In the traditional approach to transition, the focus on *realistic* outcomes can block many individuals with disabilities from participating in academics. UDT assumes that the *realistic* outcomes for students expand when academic and postsecondary skills participation takes place, and the UDT approach encourages the individual to develop a broad range of academic skills that can be applied flexibly to future situations.

Using a UDT framework, students with and without disabilities participating in a computer class would have the opportunity to learn to develop PowerPoint slides or a web-based blog. Students could individualize the content they wanted to incorporate into these files, and students with disabilities might use it to explore and identify specific goals for their transition planning meeting. All students would learn technology skills, and students with disabilities would specifically use them to support their transition educational goals as well.

UDT encourages the participation of all students in academic curriculums; the philosophy also includes and encourages the teaching of functional and vocational skills. In general, UDT encourages flexibility by embracing multiple teaching methodologies and practices to promote long-term outcomes. This chapter will review the principles of Universal Design for Transition, and provide examples and details of each component.

How does UDT Build on Research?

The current outcomes for individuals with significant disabilities, including those on the autism spectrum (ASD), are relatively dismal. Individuals with significant disabilities experience lower rates of employment, higher rates of poverty, and a greater degree of isolation than individuals with milder disabilities (Flexer, Daviso, Baer, Queen, & Mcindl, 2011). In academic postsecondary settings, individuals with ASD participate at lower rates than students with other disabilities (Newman et al., 2011). Similarly, individuals with ASD and intellectual disability are more likely to be isolated from the general education environment and curriculum (Kleinert et al., 2015). In the isolated environment, the three pedagogical approaches used: (a) community based instruction, (b) basic academic skills instruction, and (c) functional skills instruction have proven to be equally ineffective (Bouck, 2012). A different more robust academic approach is required (Courtade, Spooner, Browder, & Jiminez, 2012; Kleinert et al., 2015). UDT uses research to identify the conditions that create barriers or restrict flexibility for students. Also, UDT borrows the best evidence-based practices related to pedagogy, technology, and self-determination to help build new higher standards for students with ASD. As an open philosophy, UDT seeks out information from a diverse group of researchers and sources.

UDT aims to eliminate the obstacles preventing access for students with disabilities. Just as implementing a UDL framework provides an opportunity for teachers to design a curriculum that is accessible to all and eliminates the need to retro-fit a number of individual accommodations, the UDT framework infuses broad transition educational goals into academic lessons.

Outcomes and High Expectations

Faculty perceptions might be linked to a belief that students with ASD are unable to participate in academic situations. Low expectations create a barrier to success for students with significant disabilities. The research clearly documents low expectations as an obstacle to success for students with significant disabilities like autism. Many authors have noted an association between outcomes and expectations. Newman (2005) documented a link between parent expectations and student outcomes, and similar research has been conducted by other researchers (Grigal, Hart, & Weir, 2013). UDT builds on the research that encourages all students to meet high standards because they are provided with instruction designed to develop academic skills (Darling-Hammond, 2010) as well as meet their individual transition goals for the future (Best et al., 2015). UDT is a philosophy that embraces the best practices across all environments for a variety of students.

Evidence-based Practices

One of the greatest obstacles to successful postsecondary academic transition continues to be the lack of consistent evidence-based practices for students with autism across a variety of environments. Because researchers supporting students with ASD come from a variety of different disciplines (e.g. medicine, alternative communication science, psychology, rehabilitation science, and education), cross-field communication can sometimes be awkward if not confusing. Each field has different terms, different standards for evaluating evidence, and different goals. Because small samples of students are frequently studied, researchers will often cluster many studies together to get a bigger picture of the effectiveness of a strategy. For example, De Bruin, Deppeler, Moore, and Diamond (2013) found at least three approaches to be effective when they grouped single-subject studies into one of three categories: (a) Consequence-based Instruction (e.g. time delay, task analytic feedback,

TEACCH, Lovaas, and errorless learning), (b) self-management strategies (self-determination, self-monitoring, and self-reinforcement), and (c) video-based strategies (e.g. video modeling). Although the clustering practice can help to determine the relative effectiveness of a strategy, in the real world practitioners need to blend, mix, and match strategies together. Therefore, an effective practitioner might use a combination of strategies and approaches simultaneously. For example, Agran, Wehmeyer, Cavin, and Palmer (2010) encouraged the field of special education to recognize that approaches like self-determination and UDL overlap, blend, and blur together. The UDT model encourages the use of a variety of strategies and views this blending as an opportunity to link academic and transition skill development by building on the UDL framework. The next sections of this chapter will highlight the components of the UDT model: multiple means of representation; multiple means of expression; multiple means of engagement; multiple transition domains; multiple transition assessments; self-determination; and multiple sources of information (Thoma *et al.*, 2009).

Component 1: Multiple Means of Representation (UDL)

The most recognizable component of both UDL and UDT frameworks is multiple means of representation, which refers to presenting instruction in multiple ways so that students with a variety of learning support needs can participate (Thoma, Boyd, & Austin, 2013). In its simplest form, this would include having notes that go along with the teacher's lecture, and PowerPoint slides that highlight key information and include pictures to assist students in understanding the content and key points. The Center for Applied Special Technology's (CAST) research has found that multiple means of representation targets the recognition network of the brain; that it, is assists with learning ideas and concepts, or the "What" (CAST, from website: www.cast.org/our-work/about-udl.html - .VT0c1yFViko).

The CAST group has identified three different types of options to consider under multiple means of representation. They include: options for perception; language/mathematical expression and symbols; and comprehension. The use of instructional technology can assist with the implementation of multiple means of representation, as it provides individuals with ASD a variety of ways that material can be adapted. For example, electronic versions of text can be modified so that a student can "hear" the information, pictures can be added to assist with comprehension, or definitions and/or symbols for keywords can be embedded in the text. In addition, links can be added to web-based content that can provide a more concrete example of the concepts included in the text. These types of options can assist students with a range of learning challenges, including students on the autism spectrum. In addition, for students who need few distractions while learning, these options can be "turned off." For many students with ASD, hyperfocus is one of the characteristics that make transition between activities problematic. Technology can alleviate some of these issues by embedding prompts for transition within the content, or providing a tool for self-pacing.

The CAST group lists the following guidelines for providing instructional materials that use multiple means of representation to address the three different types of options: perception; language, mathematical expressions, and symbols; and comprehension (CAST, 2011). The first option for perception is that teachers consider ways of customizing the display of information. As previously stated, CAST recommends that multiple options be available and be flexible enough for students to choose which options best meet their needs for learning a particular academic lesson. This is important because learning needs can change, based on the type of information being shared and the goals for a specific lesson. Gene, the student described earlier, had no problem learning by reading text-based information for most academic content, particularly in math or science. However, when learning how to participate in a debate in his history class, Gene needed concrete examples of how to debate, and web-based links to video-taped debates provided an option to represent that information. Those links, however, were not required for all students in the class; they could be used if needed, or ignored if not. The CAST guidelines also include recommendations for alternatives for auditory and visual information (CAST, 2011).

In providing options for language, mathematical expressions, and symbols, CAST guidelines (2011) include five recommendations:

1   clarify vocabulary and symbols;
2   clarify syntax and structure;
3   support decoding of text, mathematical notation, and symbols;
4   promote understanding across languages; and
5   illustrate through multiple media.

These considerations each focus on providing clarification for terms and/or symbols that may be unfamiliar to the learner, and teachers can use a combination of visual, auditory, and/or links to definitions, video, or other online content that can help students decode, translate, and understand the new information. Many teachers report that higher academic expectations can result in fewer opportunities for community-based activities and the elimination of field trips. There are a number of virtual field trips that can be used to bring art, history, and science lessons to life for students. They also bring benefits to the education of students on the autism spectrum who may find actual field trips too overwhelming; students can participate in these virtual field trips over multiple and shorter time frames.

The final area teachers need to address under multiple means of representation is comprehension (CAST, 2011). Options to support students' comprehension can include providing background knowledge; highlighting patterns, relationships, critical features, and big ideas; guiding information processing, visualization, and manipulation; and maximizing transfer and generalization. These learning goals can be particularly important for a student like Gene, who may learn a vast array of factual information but struggles with applying that information in new situations. Gene was able to learn to calculate the area of a rectangle, but could he use that to determine the size of a room to be painted, and the amount of paint he needs to purchase to complete that task? Gene's teacher used multiple practical examples of tasks that required he determine the area of a rectangle in order to complete a project (i.e. painting, purchasing a rug for a room, determining whether furniture will fit in a room). Gene's teacher also used online resources to provide an opportunity for Gene to manipulate items to see if his calculations worked, and to find resources to learn about other projects that require learning to calculate area (including jobs that use this skill regularly).

Component 2: Multiple Means of Expression (UDL)

The second component of UDT, based on UDL characteristics, is the provision of multiple means of action and expression (CAST, 2011). This refers to providing multiple ways for students to communicate what they know or have learned. Students with ASD on the autism spectrum can face challenges in communication, so this component of a UDL approach provides a way to determine more accurately what they learned and how effectively a lesson reached a specific benchmark or learning goal. Done well, the use of multiple means of expression ensures that the strategic networks of the brain are activated, addressing the "how" of learning. In general terms, the strategic networks of the brain focus on how one organizes and expresses ideas and plans, and performs tasks. Examples of multiple means of action can include engaging in problem-solving activities, writing an essay, working collaboratively on a project, and/or building a model.

Guidelines for teachers from CAST (2011) recommend the following considerations that are part of providing multiple means of action and expression: provide options for physical action; provide options for expression and communication; and provide options for executive functions. Providing options for physical action includes not only opportunities to demonstrate through performance, but also varying the technology tools (including assistive technology) that can be used to access the lesson and demonstrate understanding. Technology also helps provide options for communication, from using an alternative communication system to using tools such as word prediction software to support efforts to communicate in writing. Lastly, there are a number of tools that can be used to support executive functions such as planning, goal setting, and monitoring of progress. Teachers use many of these tools as ways to provide multiple means of representation during lessons, but they also can be used to support the assessment process. For example, a flow chart used to help students take notes of the key concepts from a history lesson can also be used to help students organize their answers on a test of the material.

Students on the autism spectrum often struggle with communication and collaborative work. While that does not mean that they shouldn't have opportunities to engage in these activities, their performance in such activities should not be the only way that teachers assess progress in learning academic content or meeting individualized learning goals. Pairing these experiences with an opportunity to work independently in completing a more concrete assessment of their learning (a written test, writing an essay, or completing an online assessment) would be an effective way to provide multiple means of representation.

Component 3: Multiple Means of Engagement (UDL)

The third characteristic of UDL is that it provides multiple means of engagement (CAST, 2011), which centers on the affective networks of the brain and focuses on the "why of learning" (CAST, 2011). This emphasis helps students become purposeful, motivated learners. Teachers focus on increasing student interest in the learning activity; providing options for sustaining effort and persistence; and allowing students to self-regulate their own learning.

Typically, students with ASD have strengths when it comes to persistence in learning when the activity or content is highly motivating. In fact, "talking about preferred topics" and "seeking out objects or activities that offer desired stimulation to the exclusion of other activities" are listed as challenges students on the autism spectrum face (Schall, Targett, & Wehman, 2013, p. 452). The challenge comes in supporting students with ASD to be motivated when learning information that does not fall within an area of interest or preference.

A UDL approach provides a framework for scaffolding new content or new learning experiences by linking to those that are highly engaging. Strategies that overlap with components of self-determination are particularly relevant options for increasing student motivation to learn academic content. Students are less likely to be engaged in learning academic content that is difficult, particularly when they do not see how it is something they will need to use in the future. Finding ways for students to have a choice in how they engage with academic content, to solve problems, to assess and reward their progress, can all increase student motivation and engagement in learning.

Gene's history teacher could have increased student engagement in learning about the Civil War by having students explore what it was like to live in that era: what jobs were available, how people traveled to work or town, and how daily chores were done without many of our modern technologies. Students would still learn about the war itself, the timelines, and the key battles, but they could do so by also learning about the realities of life at the time, and comparing those to options available now (jobs, transportation, chores, technologies). This could provide information that could be used to not only learn about the civil war era, but could also help students explore options for their own lives.

Component 4: Multiple Transition Domains

Students with ASD, regardless of their level of support needs, have considerably more postsecondary options today than a few decades ago. Supports and programs specifically designed for people with disabilities have taken root in most major universities (Grigal, Hart, & Weir, 2013), while competitive integrated employment has become the standard in legislation (WIOA, 2014). However, when we design transition services for students with ASD, who all share deficits in communication, social skills, and the ability to generalize across settings, keeping in mind the variety of transition domains becomes essential.

"Multiple transition domains" refer to preparing students with disabilities for an adult lifestyle that reflects their goals, preferences, and interests. These include lifestyle options such as employment or postsecondary education, and the functional facets of life composed of community living, recreation, self-care, communication, self-determination, and transportation. These domains have been identified from the Transition Planning Inventory (TPI) and are generally accepted as covering both academic and functional skills (Carter, Trainor, Sun, & Owens, 2009).

UDT advocates for targeting an array of skills that enable youth to access all areas of life, not just academic skills. For example, a highly functioning high school student with ASD might be proficient in core academic skills, and therefore may not be seen as needing educational services for transition. However, the same student might need extensive supports to access transportation, live, communicate independently, and engage in meaningful relationships with peers. It is very likely for someone who does not have access to transportation to engage in solitary and sedentary leisure activities, such as watching TV, which would directly impact his ability to interact with same-aged youth or maintain a healthy weight.

The example in Figure 13.1 below is a one-page summary developed as part of the *I'm Determined* curriculum available through the Virginia Department of Education (www.imdetermined.org). This one-page summary provides a snapshot that a student can use to communicate his or her goals for an adult life with transition team members, as well as adult support

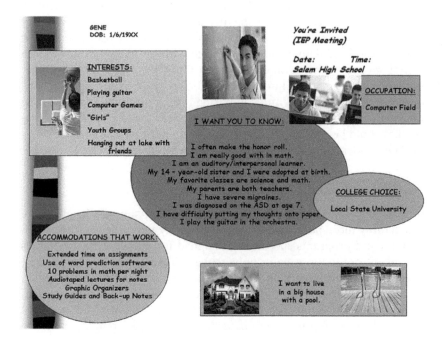

GENE
DOB: 1/6/19XX

You're Invited
(IEP Meeting)

Date: Time:
Salam High School

INTERESTS:
Basketball
Playing guitar
Computer Games
"Girls"
Youth Groups
Hanging out at lake with
        friends

OCCUPATION:
Computer Field

I WANT YOU TO KNOW:

I often make the honor roll.
I am really good with in math.
I am an auditory/interpersonal learner.
My 14 - year-old sister and I were adopted at birth.
My favorite classes are science and math.
My parents are both teachers.
I have severe migraines.
I was diagnosed on the ASD at age 7.
I have difficulty putting my thoughts onto paper.
I play the guitar in the orchestra.

COLLEGE CHOICE:
Local State University

ACCOMMODATIONS THAT WORK:
Extended time on assignments
Use of word prediction software
10 problems in math per night
Audiotaped lectures for notes
Graphic Organizers
Study Guides and Back-up Notes

I want to live
in a big house
with a pool.

Figure 13.1 Gene's one page transition IEP summary

providers. It demonstrates clearly that most individuals picture an adult life that includes more than just a job or going to college after high school.

Component 5: Multiple Means of Transition Assessment

Multiple means of transitional assessment means that the transitional support team for a student uses a variety of formal, informal, and alternative/performance-based transitional assessments to gather information about the student's interests, needs, and strengths. Formal assessments are often commercially produced or normed by researchers. Formal assessments are typically administered to all of the students within a school. The assessments might include career interest inventories (e.g. Career Opportunities Assessment (COPS), vocational placement tests (e.g. Armed Services Vocational Battery—ASVAB), the Brigance Transitional Skills Activities, or educational placement tests (e.g. Scholastic Aptitude Test—SAT). Formal transitional assessments might also be part of eligibility screening for government services like Social Security Disability Insurance (SSDI) or state or regional employment commissions. Informal assessments might include interviews with parents and students, observations of the student in the community, or teacher-made surveys. Importantly, assessments are given to students to identify the information that will help them connect with regional agencies.

There are some examples of accessible transition assessments. One option for students with communication or reading difficulties is the *Choose and Take Action* software package. This assessment shows the student short clips of individuals working in the community; two videos are shown consecutively and the student is asked choose the job they like best. Over a short period of time, the student will have narrowed his or her job choices. Similarly, the COPS picture inventory assesses a student's interest in a career after viewing images of individuals in different careers.

There are also a number of examples of informal transition assessments. Figure 13.2 presents a teacher-made informal survey to assess parental interest in postsecondary educational options. The assessment asks parents

---

**Informal Parent Inventory for Post
Secondary Education Options**

Directions

There are many college/university programs available for students with Autism. Please take a moment to answer the following questions. The questions will be used to direct you to future transitional support services.

Which educational options would you be interested in exploring?

❑   Adult continuing education programs
❑   Parks and retread on educational option
❑   Vocational opportunities
❑   2-year college programs
❑   4-year college programs
❑   I am rot sure.
❑   Other: [   ]

Have you ever taker a 'tour' of a post educational organization with your child?

❑   Yes
❑   No
❑   I am not sure.
❑   Other: [   ]

Which of the following post-secondary funding options would you like to explore?

❑   Federal Financial Aid
❑   Social Security/ (SSI/SSDI)
❑   Achieving a Better Life Experience (ABLE) account
❑   Apprentice programs
❑   Scholarship options
❑   Other: [   ]

Figure 13.2 An Example of an Informal Transitional Assessment. This particular teacher-made assessment is designed to measure a parent's interests in postsecondary educational options.

to choose options for postsecondary goals that the teacher uses to start conversations with the family. The first question invites the parents to explore a variety of postsecondary educational options, ranging from recreational educational programs to college programs designed for students with ASD. The second and third questions encourage the parents to explore different educational options with their child. The second part of the assessment, Figure 13.3, contains questions related to the admissions requirements for some of the local programs (e.g. transportation and a history of employment are sometimes stipulated by the college admissions teams).

Regardless of the accessibility, formal off-the-shelf assessments have significant weaknesses. First, commercial publications are based on the job market at the time of publication and they may not reflect recent changes in the economy and job market. Brick and mortar stores might still be described as viable job options within the formal assessments, despite the rapid movement towards an online marketplace. Jobs formerly considered viable might not be available in the near future. Similarly, commercial publications are not familiar with the local jobs market, and jobs

---

Check the statements which describe your child's transportation experiences.

☐   My child has a driver's license.
☐   My child has qualified for Para-transportation services?
☐   My child can use mass transit.
☐   My child can use/access a Van pooling or Carpooling service.
☐   My child can navigate independently on a campus.
☐   I am not sure.
☐   Other: [＿＿＿＿＿＿＿]

Check the statements which would describe your child's employment experiences.

☐   No experience.
☐   Some volunteer experience <100 hours.
☐   Extensive Volunteer Experience > 100 hours
☐   Part-time Summer employment
☐   Full-time Summer employment
☐   Supported employment (part or full time)
☐   Experience within a family business
☐   Other: [＿＿＿＿＿＿＿]

From Project BASE (Building Autism Supports with Evidence)

Created by A. Wojcik

Figure 13.3 The second half of the teacher-created assessment contains questions related to some of the obstacles that could prevent admission to a postsecondary education environment.

unique to localities will often be overlooked. For instance, oyster farmers might be needed in the maritime regions of Virginia, while gas attendants might be more readily employed in New Jersey. A third disadvantage to some of the off-the-shelf transitional assessments is that they might not focus on postsecondary educational options. A fourth disadvantage is that such formal assessments are typically inventory-like assessments that assume individuals have had sufficient experiences to identify their preferences; they are often only as accurate as the degree to which an individual has had these experiences and can identify preferences. For many students with disabilities, including students on the autism spectrum, their experiences are very limited, and the level of self-awareness necessary to make such inventories valid is often a challenge. Lastly, preferences for certain activities are often contextual. That is, what may be an undesirable activity could be acceptable if required as part of a larger picture that is highly preferred. For example, Gene answered that he preferred jobs that were done with minimal interaction. However, when working in the video store, he was able to interact with others in talking about movies, movie genres, and an early movie featuring a favorite actor.

Similar local issues can surface related to the postsecondary educational options located within each community. Each locality is likely to have unique educational and vocational options. For example, a large urban area might have multiple postsecondary education programs and adult support agencies that provide vocational and educational services for young adults with autism; this may be very different from rural and suburban areas that might have more limited agency support but whose communities might be more inclusive and supportive. Transition assessments must include a survey of the communities in which students plan to live, to identify the opportunities, supports, services, and barriers to their goals for adult life. A strategy known as community resource mapping (Crane & Mooney, 2005) provides a structure for investigating what is available in a specific community in terms of multiple transition domains. See the resource list at the end of this chapter for a link and a way to collect this important information.

Gathering information on student abilities should include assessments that observe their skills, strengths, and needs in real-world settings. These informal assessments can help to widen the transitional field for students and provide information that is more useful in planning supports and services needed for success in the new settings. Assessments should be used to start the conversation about transition, and the assessments should be used to help the team explore all available options. Teams should avoid using the results of transitional assessments to limit the postsecondary opportunities for students. If multiple transitional assessments are showing that a student has an academic need for support, then the transitional team can and should explore ways to support the student's self determination.

Component 6: Multiple Means to Support Student Self-determination

Student self-determination, a concept reflecting the belief that all individuals have the right to direct their own lives (Bremer, Kachgal, & Schoeller, 2003), lies at the heart of quality transition planning. A position statement on self-determination (Field, Martin, Miller, Ward, & Wehmeyer, 1998b) by the Council for Exceptional Children's Division on Career Development and Transition identified self-determination as a critically important component for improving education and the transition to adult life for students with disabilities. They further identified that focusing on supporting student self-determination can have a transformative impact on educational services for students with and without disabilities.

Research has supported these policy statements, particularly as related to improving post-school outcomes. This research demonstrates a link between enhanced self-determination and positive outcomes in employment (Field, 1996; Field, Martin, Miller, Ward, & Wehmeyer, 1998a; Wehmeyer, 1997; Wehmeyer & Schwartz, 1997, Wehmeyer & Palmer, 2003), quality of adult life and community living (Wehmeyer & Palmer, 2003; Wehmeyer & Schwartz, 1997), and postsecondary education (Brinckerhoff, 1994; Greenbaum, Graham, & Scales, 1995; Field, Sarver, & Shaw, 2003). In a literature review conducted by the National Secondary Transition Technical Assistance Center (NSTTAC), self-determination/ self-advocacy was identified as one of 16 predictors empirically linked to post-school success for students with disabilities (Test et al., 2009; Test, Mazzotti et al., 2009, Mazzotti, Test, & Mustian, 2012).

Self-determination is a key component of intrinsic motivation, self-regulation, and personal responsibility—traits that are crucial for success in both education and society (Deci, Vallerand, Pelletier, & Ryan, 1991)—and, according to Halloran (1993), it is education's ultimate goal. Using a UDT framework for instructional planning, students play a more active role in creating their own learning experiences than they would in a more traditional program. Students are encouraged to make and express choices based on their goals, learning styles, strengths and weaknesses, and preferences, fostering growth in understanding themselves and their own needs and predispositions. This approach not only supports improved academic achievement, it also prepares them to make decisions about their adult life (Best et al., 2015).

According to the principles of UDT, transition and planning services are designed to give students multiple ways to be engaged in the process, beginning with setting goals and working in a "backward-planning process" (Thoma et al., 2002, p. 86) to identify the skills, resources, needs, or modifications necessary for students to achieve those goals. Benz, Lindstrom, & Yovanoff (2000) found positive correlations between the completion of self-identified transition goals and competitive employment and enrolment in postsecondary education. There are many ways students can participate in this process, whether using a student-led or person-centered approach, depending on the student's level of comfort and the availability of supports (Thoma *et al.*, 2002). Self-determination involves the student's involvement in both the setting of goals and in the steps taken to achieve them (Landmark, Ju, & Zhang, 2010).

The Self-Determined Learning Model of Instruction (SDLMI; Wehmeyer, Lance, & Bashinski, 2002) provides a framework to foster self-determination through a problem-solving approach. The SDLMI involves three phases of questions to help students set a learning goal, construct a learning plan, and adjust behaviors (Wehmeyer et al., 2002). As noted by Thoma et al. (2002), the SDLMI is an effective organizational tool that facilitates students' roles as "the causal agent in their transition planning" (p. 36). While it teaches students to use a problem-solving strategy that increases their self-determination, it can be used to address multiple goals or problems, including academic learning, choosing transition goals, and/ or identifying options for dealing with a problem. See the example below Gene's use of SDLMI to organize his preparation for completing a book report for his American Literature class (Figure 13.4).

Component 7: Multiple Sources of Information

Transition planning requires teamwork, more so than any other type of educational planning process (Thoma, 1999). It is for this reason that stakeholders outside the school system are required to be invited to the transition IEP meeting, including a representative from any agency that will (or might) provide services to the student after graduation (Individuals with Disabilities Education Improvement Act (IDEA), 2004). One person alone cannot know the student's preferences, the postsecondary options available, and the means to make the connection between the two. Students and their families know how they envision their futures; teachers know the legal mandates and the steps to planning for transition; while other agency representatives are familiar with the types of postsecondary services available. For this very reason, interdisciplinary planning has been determined to be a critically important part of the transition planning process for youth with disabilities, including those on the autism spectrum (Noonan, Gaumer, Erickson, & Morningstar, 2012).

The UDT framework encourages transition teams to expand the network of individuals they consider including in the planning process and involving in instructional lessons. As Gene considered life after high school, he expressed an interest in working with technology. While his teachers had some knowledge of the different types of positions working in the field of technology, like software engineer or computer

Name: *Gene*	Date: *March 1, 2012*

Phase I: What is my goal?

Set a goal

1 What do I want to learn? *I want to be able to increase by English grade. More specifically, I want to improve my grades on the number of book reports I need to complete this term.*	3 What must change for me to learn what I don't know? *I need to develop a schedule for when the reports are due.* *I need to find ways to make reading more fun.* *I need to stop waiting until the last minute to read and do the reports.* *I need help with matching my strengths/preferences and needs with available supports.*
2 What do I know about it now? *I know that I struggle with reading.* *I know that I am easily distracted.* *I know that I usually wait until the last minute.*	4 What can I do to make this happen? *I can work with my teacher to identify steps to complete book reports and deadlines for completing each step.* *I can spend more time with the librarian identifying books that would be of greater interest to me, and on my reading level.*

Phase II: What is my plan?

Take action

1 What can I do to learn what I don't know? *I will meet with my teacher to develop a general book report plan with steps and timelines for completion.* *I will meet with the reading specialist in school to identify my reading level.* *I will develop a list of interests that I can use to choose books for specific assignments.*	3 What can I do to overcome these barriers? *I will meet with the school librarian to identify books that meet the criteria for class, are on my reading level, and better match my interests well in advance of when assignments are due.* *I will list the things that have distracted me from meeting deadlines in the past.* *I will use the general book report plan to identify concrete timelines and steps for each book report as they are assigned.* *I will find resources that the teacher and I can use to develop a book report timeline.* *I will request an evaluation of my reading level well in advance of book report deadlines.*
2 What could keep me from taking action? *I might not be able to follow the timeline that the teacher develops.* *The librarian might not have time to meet with me.* *The reading specialist might not be able to administer additional assessments.*	4 When will I take action? *I will use my study hall time this week to do the initial planning: scheduling meetings, developing a list of reading interests, and researching plans for completing book reports.* *I will get a list of the book report assignments and deadlines from my English teacher by the end of the week.* *I will schedule meetings with the reading specialist, the school librarian, and my teacher within the next 2 weeks.*

Figure 13.4 (continued)

Phase III: What have I learned?	
Adjust goal or plan	
1 What actions have I taken? I met with the reading specialist, who shared assessment information from previous years. He did not conduct additional assessments. I met with the librarian who provided a list of books on my reading level. I was able to identify books that would fit the requirements for my book report assignments. I found a template that I could use to complete the various steps of a book report (including scheduling time to read the book). Then my teacher and I sat down to modify it to meet the criteria for the class. I used this template to schedule my work in completing the book reports for the term.	3 What has changed about what I didn't know? I know additional resources that can help. I was able to complete all book reports with a grade of B or better. My English grade improved by using this approach
2 What barriers have been removed? I can talk about my learning style/ preferences.	4 Do I know what I want to know? I want to learn some of the technologies that were identified by the assistive technology specialist.

Figure 13.4 Student Worksheet for the Self-determined Learning Model of Instruction (from Thoma, C. A., Batholomew, C. C., & Scott, L. A. (2009). *Universal design for transition: A roadmap for planning and instruction* (pp. 37–39). Baltimore: Paul H. Brookes Publishing Co., adapted by permission)

programmer, they did not know all the types of jobs that are available. Gene's teacher invited a software engineer from a local firm to meet with the team to discuss a range of different positions in the field, as well as the educational requirements for each. This information provided guidance for high school course planning, as well as part-time jobs to gain valuable experience, and helped guide decisions about post-school options. Not only did this collaboration provide a way to improve the individual transition planning process, it also provided opportunities to improve educational lessons. This software engineer worked with teachers to identify computer skills that all students would need to enter the job market, and incorporated opportunities for students to work on those skills in academic courses. Using spreadsheets to present and analyze data, social media to communicate with the world, and the internet to research relevant information to guide decisions are all twenty-first century skills that students need to be competitive for employment. Teachers should be able to call on experts to help with lesson planning that incorporates useful strategies, and, when possible, to teach these hands-on practical aspects of the lesson. Skills like these would have prepared Gene for a specific job after graduation, but also would have helped him have other options for the future if he changed his mind, or if he wanted or needed to move on to other options later.

One of the barriers to inviting community resources into the transition planning process is the formality of the IEP process. Nevertheless, there are alternative meeting approaches that are designed to be more conducive to participation for a range of individuals, including the school personnel who are required to be there. To encourage the participation of students, parents, school and adult agency personnel, as well as community resources, one might consider using person-centered planning approaches (Mount, 1992) such as McGill Action Planning Systems (MAPS; Forest & Lusthaus, 1989); Planning Alternative Tomorrows with Hope (PATH; Pearpoint, O'Brien, & Forest, 1993); Group Action Planning (GAP; Turnbull & Turnbull, 1996), or a range of student-led planning processes (e.g. Thoma & Wehman, 2010). Research on the impact of these types of training processes found that not only did students and their parents interact more during IEP meetings that used these approaches, but teachers and school administrators also increased their communication during those meetings (Martin et al., 2006).

Incorporating a student-directed IEP approach can be viewed as a continuum of student involvement in the meeting (Thoma, Saddler, Purvis, & Scott, 2010), from student presence at the meeting through having the student lead all or part of the meeting. It is worthwhile considering the use of technology to support student involvement in the transition planning process and in academic assignments that facilitate goal setting, understanding the impact of a disability on strengths and needs, and developing self-advocacy skills. See Figure 13.5 below for a planning tool that can be used with students and their parents to improve the participation of student direction of the planning process.

Pulling It All Together

There are a number of resources available for teachers to help them incorporate a UDL framework in their lesson planning process, but how does a special educator expand that to include these critically important aspects of transition education and planning? Thoma et al. (2002) have developed a lesson-planning template that teachers can use to link transition and academic education for youth with disabilities (see Figure 13.6). It provides a way to consider all of the possible links that can and do exist between academic and transition education. It should be noted, of

Student: _____ **Date:** _____

PREPARING FOR THE MEETING

Please tell about how you think your child might participate in his/her IEP meeting.

What are some ways to be involved?	Readiness 1-Knows about or has done before 2-New skill or knowledge 3-Not this time	Support			Who will help?
		Would need lots of help	Would need some help	Could do on own	
Learn what the meeting is about					
Help decide who to invite to IEP meeting					
Make invitations for the meeting					
Send/deliver invitations					
Photocopy materials for the meeting					
Gather supplies, help set up and/or clean up the meeting room					
Make snacks for the meeting					
Serve snacks during the meeting					
Introduce people at the meeting					
Distribute papers during the meeting					
Write goals ahead of time to recommend					
Review goals from previous IEP and update them					
Read goals during the meeting (using voice, sign language, or assistive technology)					
Role play how to act and what to say					
Talk about likes/dislikes, best way to learn, what works/what doesn't (using preferred communication method)					
Prepare a notebook or portfolio about self					
Prepare a PowerPoint presentation about self					
Present information about self					
Share samples of work from class					
Show pictures of self in activities at home, job or in the community					

Figure 13.5 (continued)

Talk and ask questions during the meeting (using preferred communication method)					
Talk about and recommend accommodations					
Recommend goals					
Lead the IEP meeting					

Student: _____   **Date:** _____

THINKING ABOUT THE MEETING

How did it feel to have your child at the IEP meeting?

What did he/she say about it? or How do you think your child felt about it?

What surprised you most? Pleased you most? Concerned you most?

Compare this IEP meeting to others in which you have participated:

PREPARING FOR THE NEXT MEETING

What worked in your son's/daughter's meeting?

What did not work in your son's/daughter's meeting?

What would you like to see stay the same in terms of your son's/daughter's participation?

What would you like to see changed in terms of your son's/daughter's participation?

What suggestions do you have for increasing participation?

B. Purvis (2010)

Figure 13.5 IEP Meeting Schedule

UDT Template

Description of the learners, setting, and framework for lesson
1 2 3
Goals and standards
1 2 3
Transition links
1 2 3
Assessment methods (one or multiple)
1 2 3
Resources (one or multiple) – (technology, adaptive, etc.)
1 2 3
Reflection/evaluation
1 2 3

Figure 13.6 UDT Template

course, that not all lessons will incorporate all of the seven components of UDT. Instead, each of these should be considered for the most relevant links, with the ultimate goal of addressing each of these over time.

Of course, since goals for adult life are individual, there will come a time when the focus will be more individualized and less universal; however, the more that middle and early high school academic instruction infuses knowledge and skills that students will need to prepare for their future, the better the foundational preparation for life will be for all students. And that's ultimately the goal of education for all, isn't it? The following list of resources will help to identify the ways that academic and transition education can be linked for secondary school students.

Resources

Science & Social Science

1   The CAST Science Writer guides students through the steps of creating a science report. The following is the website: http://sciencewriter.cast.org/.
2   Building prior knowledge can be important, and virtual field trips can help students explore historic or scientific places of merit. The following is the website: www.middleweb.com/22188/virtual-field-trips-spice-up-learning/.

Math

CAST has created a number of resources to help students learn Algebra. This resource has developed a number of computer aided instructional tools for teaching Algebra skills to students. Website: http://iSolveIt.cast.org.

Reading/Language Arts

CAST has created a public library of UDL books. The books contain hyperlinks, read aloud, and prompting cues. The demonstration texts are available at the website and links to a library of electronic books are available at websites: http://udleditions.cast.org, and http://bookbuilder.cast.org.

Teacher Planning Tools

Graphic organizers can help students to structure information. There are a couple of free options available at the following websites: www.dailyteachingtools.com/free-graphic-organizers and www.dailyteachingtools.com/free-graphic-organizers-readerizer2.

Jigsaw reading assignments can help to strengthen comprehension skills. Teachers can use screenshots of text to create digital jigsaws using the following website: http: www.jigsawplanet.com.

Technology

Universal Design features are available on most computers. However, there are a number of free publicly available resources.

1   The Massachusetts Institute of Technology has created a Freedom Stick to help teachers and students activate different features like text-to-speech, speech-to-text, and visual contrast options. The

software can be stored on a USB drive or downloaded to the hard drive on a computer. The information is available at the following website: http://mits.cenmi.org/Resources/MITSFreedomStick. aspx.

2   The CAST website has developed a tool to help teachers and students to build UDL books. In addition, a library of free texts is available at the following website: http://bookbuilder.cast.org.

3   Natural Voice Reader is another option. The software recognizes text with optical character recognition and the software can read text aloud. The software is available at the following website: www. naturalreaders.com/.

4   Similar software is available for Mac computers at the following website: www.pure-mac.com/access.

5   A group of educators have created an interactive wiki to share UDL resources. The group collectively edits the resources using the following website: http://udltechtoolkit.wikispaces.com.

Self-determination Resources

1   The I'm Determined project promotes student self-advocacy. The program encourages students to advocate for services, promote policy reform, and participate in the individual's IEP. The following website provides more information: www.imdetermined.org/.

2   The National Gateway to Self-determination provides information about self-determination. The organization provides general information and resources for teachers and parents. The website is at: www. ngsd.org.

3   The Beach Center provides many resources for working with students with disabilities. The library provides a teacher's guide to self-determination. The resources are available at the following website: www.beachcenter.org.

4   The National Resource Center for Supported Decision-making provides state specific information related to issues for individuals with disabilities. The information is available at the following website: http://supporteddecisonmaking.org.

Transition Assessment

1   The National Secondary Transition Technical Assistance Center (NSTTAC) provides information related to the evidence-based practices in the world of transition and the organization has provided a toolkit for age-appropriate transition assessment. The website is at: http://nsttac.org/.

2   The Zarrow Center for Learning Enrichment has multiple transitional assessment resources including a preference assessment, a self-determination assessment, a curriculum, and a transitional goals generator. The information can be found at: http://tagg.ou.edu/tagg.

Information for Parents

Parents are important team members, and they often need support in the form of information. The PACER Center regularly publishes information for parents. Past publications have examined self-determination, issues associated with the age of majority, and other transition issues. The resources can be found at the following website: www.pacer.org/publications.

References

Agran, M., Wehmeyer, M., Cavin, M., & Palmer, S. (2010). Promoting active engagement in the general education classroom and access to the general education curriculum for students with cognitive disabilities. *Education and Training in Autism and Developmental Disabilities*, 163–174.

Aslaksen, F., Bergh, S., Bringa, O. R., & Heggem, E. K. (1997). Universal design: Planning and design for all. The Norwegian State Council on Disability. Retrieved March 10, 2015 from digitalcommons.ilr.cornell.edu.

Best, K., Scott, L., & Thoma, C. A. (2015). Starting with the end in mind: Inclusive education designed to prepare students for adult life. In E. Brown, R. G. Craven, & G. McLean (Eds.). *International Advances in Education: Global Initiatives for Equity and Social Justice: Vol. 9, Inclusive education for students with intellectual disabilities* (pp. 45–72). Charlotte, NC: Information Age Press.

Bouck, E. C. (2012). Secondary students with moderate/severe intellectual disability: Considerations of curriculum and post-school outcomes from the National Longitudinal Transition Study-2. *Journal of Intellectual Disability Research*, 56(12), 1175–1186.

Bremer, C., Kachgal, M., and Schoeller, K. (2003). Self-Determination: Supporting successful transition (National Center on Secondary Education and Transition Research to Practice Brief). *Improving Secondary Education and Transition Services through Research*, 2(1), 1–6.

Brinkerhoff, L. C. (1994). Developing effective self-advocacy skills in college-bound students with learning disabilities. *Intervention in School and Clinic*, 29(4), 229–237.

Carter, E. W., Trainor, A. A., Sun, Y., & Owens, L. (2009). Assessing the transition-related strengths and needs of adolescents with high-incidence disabilities. *Exceptional Children*, 76(1), 74–94.

CAST (2011). *Universal Design for Learning Guidelines version 2.0*. Wakefield, MA. Retrieved January 19, 2015 from www.udlcenter.org/aboutudl/udl-guidelines.

Courtade, G., Spooner, F., Browder, D., & Jimenez, B. (2012). Seven reasons to promote standards-based instruction for students with severe disabilities: A reply to Ayres, Lowrey, Douglas, & Sievers (2011). *Education and Training in Autism and Developmental Disabilities*, 3–13.

Crane, K. & Mooney, M. (2005). *Essential tools: Community resource mapping*. Retrieved February 22, 2015 from www.ncset.org/publications/essentialtools/mapping/default.asp.

Darling-Hammond, L. (2010). *The flat world and education: How America's commitment to equity will determine our future*. New York: Teachers College Press.

De Bruin, C. L., Deppeler, J. M., Moore, D. W., & Diamond, N. T. (2013). Public school–based interventions for adolescents and young adults with an Autism Spectrum Disorder: A meta-analysis. *Review of Educational Research*, *83*(4), 521–550.

Deci, E. L., Vallerand, R. J., Pelletier, L. G., & Ryan, R. M. (1991). Motivation and education: The self-determination perspective. *Educational psychologist*, *26*(3–4), 325–346.

Field, S., Martin, J., Miller, R., Ward, M., & Wehmeyer, M. (1998a). *A Practical Guide for Teaching Self-Determination*. Council for Exceptional Children, Reston, VA: CEC Publications.

Field, S., Martin, J., Miller, R., Ward, M., & Wehmeyer, M. (1998b). Self-determination in career and transition programming: A position statement of the Council for Exceptional Children. *Career Development for Exceptional Individuals*, *21*(2), 113–128.

Field, S., Sarver, M. D., & Shaw, S. F. (2003). Self-Determination a key to success in postsecondary education for students with learning disabilities. *Remedial and Special Education*, *24*(6), 339–349.

Flexer, R. W., Daviso, A. W., Baer, R. M., Queen, R. M., & Meindl, R. S. (2011). An epidemiological model of transition and postschool outcomes. *Career Development for Exceptional Individuals*, *34*(2), 83–94.

Forest, M., & Lusthaus, E. (1989). Promoting educational equality for all students: Circles and MAPS. In S. Stainback, W. Stainback, & M. Forest (Eds.), *Educational all students in the mainstream of regular education* (pp. 43–57). Baltimore, MD: Paul H. Brookes Publishing Co.

Greenbaum, B., Graham, S., & Scales, W. (1995). Adults with learning disabilities: Educational and social experiences during college. *Exceptional Children*, *61*(5), 460–471.

Grigal, M., Hart, D., & Weir, C. (2013). Postsecondary education for people with intellectual disability: Current issues and critical challenges. *Inclusion*, *1*(1), 50–63.

Halloran, W. D. (1993). Transition services requirement: Issues, implications, challenge. In R. C. Eaves & P.J. McLaughlin (Eds.), *Recent advances in special education and rehabilitation* (pp.210–224). Boston, MA: Andover Medical. Individuals with Disabilities Education Improvement Act of 2004, Pub. L. No. 108–446, 20 U.S.C. § 1400.

Kleinert, H., Towles-Reeves, E., Quenemoen, R., Thurlow, M., Fluegge, L., Weseman, L., . . . Kerbel, A. (2015). Where students with the most significant cognitive disabilities are taught: Implications for general curriculum access. *Exceptional Children*, *81*(3), 312–328. doi: 0014402914563697

Landmark, L. J., Ju, S., & Zhang, D. (2010). Substantiated best practices in transition: Fifteen plus years later. *Career Development for Exceptional Individuals*, *33*(3), 165–176.

Martin, J. E., Van Dycke, J. L., Christensen, W. R., Greene, B. A., Gardner, J. E., & Lovett, D. L. (2006). Increasing student participation in their transition IEP meetings: Establishing the *Self-Directed IEP* as an evidenced-based practice. *Exceptional Children, 72*(3), 299–316.

Mazzotti, V., Rowe, D., Kelley, K. R., Test, D. W., Fowler, C., Kohler, P., Kortering, L. (2009). Linking transition assessment and postsecondary goals: Key elements in the secondary transition planning process. *Teaching Exceptional Children, 42*(2), 44–51.

Mazzotti, V., Test, D., Mustian, A. (2012). Secondary transition evidence-based practices and predictors: Implications for policymakers. *Journal of Disability Policy Studies,* 1–14 doi: 1044207312460888.

Meyer, A., Rose, D. H., Gordon, D. (2013). *Universal Design for Learning: Theory and practice.* Wakefield, MA: Cast Professional Publishing.

Mount, B. (1992) *Person-centered planning: A sourcebook of values, ideas, and methods to encourage person-centered development.* New York: Graphic Futures.

Newman, L., (2005). *NLTS2 Data brief: Family expectations and involvement for youth with disabilities. A Report from the National Longitudinal Transition Study-2.* Retrieved February 22, 2015 from www.ncset.org/publications/viewdesc.asp?id=2473.

Newman, L., Wagner, M., Knokey, A. M., Marder, C., Nagle, K., Shaver, D., . . . Wei, X. (2011). *The post-high school outcomes of young adults with disabilities up to 8 years after high school: A report from the National Longitudinal Transition Study-2 (NLTS2)* (NCSER 2011-3005). Menlo Park, CA: SRI.

Noonan, P. M., Erickson, A. G., & Morningstar, M. E. (2012). Effects of community transition teams on interagency collaboration for school and adult agency staff. *Career Development and Transition for Exceptional Individuals, 36*(2), 96–104.

Pearpoint, J., O'Brien, J., & Forest, M. (1993). *PATH (Planning Alternative Tomorrows with Hope): A workbook for planning positive futures.* Toronto: Inclusion Press.

Schall, C., Targett, P., & Wehman, P. (2013). Applications for youth with autism spectrum disorders. In P. Wehman, *Life beyond the classroom: Transition strategies for young people with disabilities* (pp. 447–471). Baltimore, MD: Paul Brookes Publishing.

Test, D. W., Fowler, C. H., Richter, S. M., White, J., Mazzotti, V., Walker, A. R., . . . Kortering, L. (2009). Evidence-based practices in secondary transition. *Career Development for Exceptional Individuals, 32,* 115–128.

Test, D. W., Mazzotti, V. L., Mustian, A. L., Fowler, C. H., Kortering, L. J., & Kohler, P. H. (2009). Evidence-based secondary transition predictors for improving post-school outcomes for students with disabilities. *Career Development for Exceptional Individuals, 32,* 160–181.

Thoma, C. A., Bartholomew, C. C., & Scott, L. A. (2009). *Universal design for transition: A roadmap for planning and instruction.* Baltimore, MD: Paul H. Brookes Publishing.

Thoma, C. A., Boyd, K., & Austin, K. (2013). Teaching for Transition. In P. Wehman. *Life beyond the classroom: Transition strategies for young people with disabilities* (5th ed.) (pp. 201–236). Baltimore, MD: Paul H. Brookes Publishing.

Turnbull, A. & Turnbull, H. R. (1996). Group Action Planning as a strategy for providing comprehensive family support. In L. K. Koegel, R. L. Koegel, & G. Dunlap (Eds.), *Positive behavioral support: Including people with difficult behavior in the community* (pp. 99–114). Baltimore, MD: Paul H. Brookes Publishing.

Wehmeyer, M. L. (1997). Self-determination as an educational outcome: A definitional framework and implications for intervention. *Journal of Developmental and Physical Disabilities*, *9*, 175–209.

Wehmeyer, M. L., Lance, G. D., & Bashinski, S. (2002). Promoting access to the general education curriculum for students with mental retardation: A multilevel model. *Education and Training in Mental Retardation and Developmental Disabilities*, *37*(3), 223–234.

Wehmeyer, M. L., & Palmer, S. B. (2003). Adult outcomes for students with cognitive disabilities three-years after high school: The impact of self-determination. *Education and Training in Developmental Disabilities*, 131–144.

Wehmeyer, M. L., & Schwartz, M. (1997). Self-determination and positive adult outcomes: A follow-up study of youth with mental retardation or learning disabilities. *Exceptional Children*, *63*, 245–255.

Workforce Innovation and Improvement Act of 2014 Pub. L. *113-128* 128 USC § 1425 (2014).

Chapter 14

Positive Behavior Supports in Middle and Secondary School

Debra L. Cote and Shannon L. Sparks

Due to increased numbers of children with autism participating in inclusive settings, changes have occurred in school-wide expectations for these students and in corresponding supports needed. Middle- and secondary-age students with autism often struggle with maladaptive behaviors (e.g. communication, social interactions, stereotypic repetitive behaviors) and in managing their feelings and/or emotions (Li, 2009). Some students with autism spectrum disorders (ASD) may exhibit high levels of aggression, escape behaviors, and difficulties with transitions (Kern, Gallagher, Starosta, Hickman, & George, 2006). Inappropriate and challenging behaviors often prevent these students from making adequate academic progress, developing friendships, and learning basic skills.

Hence, students with ASD require educational supports that are scientifically sound, grounded in evidence-based practice (EBP), and based on research (Conley Downs & Downs, 2010). As a response to these special needs, teachers and parents need to adopt comprehensive and established teaching practices with histories that suggest they hold promise for preventing and managing the problematic behaviors. This chapter focuses on individualized behavioral supports, behavioral management strategies, positive learning environments in middle and high school, cognitive behavioral modification strategies, and intervention strategies that address culturally and linguistically diverse learners with ASD.

A comprehensive practice, positive behavior support (PBS), has strong evidence to support its use with students exhibiting challenging behaviors (Minke & Anderson, 2005):

> PBS is not a new intervention package or a new theory of behavior, but an application of a behaviorally based systems approach to enhance the capacity of schools, families, and communities to design effective environments that improve the fit or link between research-validated practices and environments in which teaching and learning occur.
>
> (Sugai et al., 2000, p. 133)

A PBS approach developed within the context of the student and his or her family directly impacts one's quality of life (Becker-Cottrill, McFarland, & Anderson, 2003).

Basic Concepts of Positive Behavior Supports

Positive behavior support strategies foster school and classroom environments that value and reinforce appropriate behaviors. An overall positive learning environment stimulates academic and behavioral achievement. PBS is an EBP that includes primary-, secondary-, and tertiary-level supports (Sugai et al., 2000): "The core values of PBS are derived from those expressed within the ABA community: prevention of inappropriate and nonfunctional behaviors, application of research/evidence-based practice to build behavior repertoires, and creating contexts and processes that are person centered and supportive" (Alberto & Troutman, 2013, p. 210). A PBS approach is a practice that decreases problem behaviors, since it reduces the negative impact often associated with consequences (Alberto & Troutman, 2013; Erbas, 2010). PBS extends the elements of applied behavioral analysis utilizing several key principles: (1) behaviors that are learned can be changed, (2) intervention follows a functional behavior assessment, (3) intervention targets prevention and teaching a communicative replacement behavior, (4) interventions are of social significance to the individual, and (5) multicomponent supports are involved (Janney & Snell, 2008). Two additional goals of PBS are: to improve one's quality of life and to make the challenging behavior ineffective by replacing it with a socially acceptable behavior (Alberto & Troutman, 2013; Carr et al., 2002)

While a PBS approach assessment and intervention strategies is best practice for supporting individual students and their behaviors, it can also be used within districts and schools for groups of students with ASD. The framework of PBS stresses prevention, a supportive environment with predictable routines, the teaching and reinforcing of positive behaviors and reliance on EBP (Scheuermann & Hall, 2016).

Philosophical Foundations and Research

The underlying philosophical foundation for PBS is applied behavior analysis (ABA), taken from Skinner's operant conditioning model. The model helps explain, predict and change human behavior (Alberto & Troutman, 2013). Some assumptions of ABA are that (a) behavior is learned; (b) behavior can be improved by altering antecedents and consequences and (c) systems of support can be put into place to increase/support appropriate behaviors and decrease undesirable behaviors (Storey & Post, 2012).

Thus, children with challenging behaviors may benefit from educational systems of support that utilize positive behavioral teaching principles (e.g. ABA, PBS, discrete trial training) in design and delivery of instruction. The use of positive behavioral practices/principles can facilitate student quality of life (Carr, 2007).

Ethical Issues and Laws That Address Behavior

Student behavior is addressed under federal law in the Individuals with Disabilities Education Act (IDEA, 1997). The act mandates that an IEP team identify strategies, supports, and positive behavior interventions when a child's challenging behavior impedes his or her learning (IDEA, 1997). Additionally, practitioners must address ethical issues when making decisions as to which method or intervention to use with a student. Ethical issues that can/may influence the practitioner's behavior include: one's personal history, cultural biases/and or religious rearing and the context in which the behavior occurs (Cooper, Heron, & Heward, 2007). Practitioners need to approach a student and his/her challenging behavior from an ethical perspective when deciding which practice or treatment to implement. This approach further connects the value and worth of the intervention to the student (Cooper et al., 2007).

Operant Principles

Principles of operant conditioning suggest that behavior is voluntary, measurable, discrete, and verifiable, and that functional relationships are formed between the behavior and its consequence (Alberto & Troutman, 2013). Practitioners should clearly define observable behaviors that give evidence of a functional relationship between treatment and the results (Alberto & Troutman, 2013).

Positive Reinforcement

A positive reinforcement system focuses on catching students when they display desired behaviors and reinforcing them, thereby increasing or maintaining these behaviors. Teachers should set up positive, class-wide reinforcing systems that teach and reinforce appropriate behaviors (Sayeski & Brown, 2014). "Positive, supportive teacher–student relationships are important for all students. However, they become critical for influencing the behavior and achievement of students who are experiencing academic and behavioral difficulties" (Jones & Jones, 2013, p. 89).

Negative Reinforcement

Negative reinforcement is the contingent removal of an aversive or negative stimulus following a response that leads to an increase in the future occurrence of the behavior (Alberto & Troutman, 2013; Cooper et al., 2007; Scheuermann & Hall, 2016). For example, a teacher tells students they will not be given homework if they finish the reading assignment by the end of the period (Shea & Bauer, 2012). Bob, a student with ASD, perceives homework as an aversive stimulus and finishes the reading assignment in class. Bob was negatively reinforced by the removal of the aversive stimuli (Shea & Bauer, 2012). While negative reinforcement may be effective, teachers should utilize positive reinforcement procedures to increase and teach appropriate behaviors (Simpson & Otten, 2005).

Punishment

Punishment is mistakenly confused with negative reinforcement. When educators utilize punitive methods, the behavior may decrease, however, punishment does not serve a child with ASD in the long term. It is a short-term solution that does not get at the function of a behavior (Janney & Snell, 2008). Yet without addressing the function, students are left without a communicative replacement behavior (Alberto & Troutman, 2013). In an attempt to avoid punishment, a student may stop performing the challenging target behavior and choose a replacement, one that is just as challenging as the original behavior (Chandler & Dahlquist, 2015).

Operational Definition of Behavior

When observing a student with ASD who displays challenging behaviors, it is crucial to provide a clear operational definition of the behavior prior to collecting data. Observations need to remain objective and include examples of what is being observed (Alberto & Troutman, 2013). For instance when defining talk outs, a concise description would be "When one student or a group of students makes an outward comment or begins talking to others about on-task or off-task topic. This would be considered as one talking out occurrence" (Gongola & Daddario, 2010, p.17). The success of data collection includes a well-defined description of the behavior so as to assist everyone (e.g. educator, paraeducator, parent, student) involved. Significant consideration should be given to clearly describing the operational definition of the behavior, as this enables data collection.

Methods for Observing and Recording Behavior

Practitioners must consider the data collection method they will use. They are encouraged to match the recording method to the type/characteristics of the desired or maladaptive behavior, while cognizant of time and staffing constraints. If the appropriate method is chosen, it will increase the likelihood that data collection is effective and remains consistent. Trustworthy recording methods include: event, interval, latency, and duration (Bicard & Bicard, 2012). When using an event recording method, practitioners can measure behaviors that have a clear beginning and end (Cooper et al., 2007). Interval recording (e.g. whole, partial) is best used during brief amounts of time (e.g. 15 seconds) to record whether or not a student exhibited a specific behavior. Latency recording assists teachers in noting how much time elapses from the presentation of the antecedent stimulus to the student initiating the corresponding behavior (Bicard & Bicard, 2012). Educators may find duration recording practical in identifying how long a student exhibits a behavior. For example, duration recording can reveal how long a student with ASD engages in a particular stereotypic behavior, remains in seat, or engages in independent reading.

Data Collection and Analysis

Routinely, teachers of students with ASD conduct formative assessments and collect/analyze data to assess the effectiveness of an instructional practice. Data collection is required by law to determine whether a student has made successful gains as a result of the academic or behavioral intervention (IDEA, 1997). As a result of regular analysis, teachers' responses to the data can be purposeful, in whether the intervention should be continued or stopped. Data analysis may reveal the following about an EBP: (a) treatment fidelity (i.e. instruction was not implemented as described by the researcher) was lacking, (b) adaptations should have been made based on the teacher's teaching style and/or student needs, and (c) the EBP did not match the context in which it was taught (Cook, Tankersley, & Harjusola-Webb, 2008).

Functional Assessment and Analysis

Educators may conduct functional assessments to gain insight as to the setting events, antecedents, activities, and consequences that directly impact behavior (O'Neil et al., 1997). Communication, learning styles, teacher/peer relationships, classroom environment, time of the day, delivery of instruction, and presence of certain individuals can set the stage for challenging behaviors to occur. Indirect and direct observations help educators determine the function(s) of a student's behavior (e.g. sensory, tangible, escape, attention) and form a hypothesis. For example, Billy hits the student next to him during a reading group activity. A hypothesis is that Billy hits to avoid reading words that are unfamiliar. To test the hypothesis, the teacher could pre-read the passage with Billy, to familiarize him with new vocabulary prior to the next day's group activity. O'Neil et al. note, "Functional analysis manipulations should not be carried out unless appropriate safeguards are available" (1997, p. 55). Given the serious challenging behaviors (e.g. aggression, head banging, biting, property destruction) that students with ASD may exhibit, expert teachers know that qualified staff must be present when conducting a functional behavior analysis (O'Neill, Albin, Storey, Horner, & Sprague, 2015; Wolfe & Wood, 2013). A qualified team that embraces a PBS approach is beneficial when creating a positive behavior support plan for those students who require tertiary (i.e. individual) supports.

Behavior Support Plans

As previously stated, goals and objectives are developed into a well-written behavior support plan (BSP) based on the results of a functional behavioral assessment and functional behavior analysis. Once developed, teachers continue to collect data, evaluate the results and make changes to the BSP. The BSP is fluid in that resources, student development, peers, staffing, and contexts are ever-changing (Wheeler & Richey, 2014). Within the BSP is a cohesive program that supports a student's quality of life. The program is based on information gathered by a functional assessment and details the intervention strategies to be used in addressing individual need (Wheeler & Richey, 2014).

Positive Behavior Support in Middle School

A PBS environment is especially important in middle school due to the size and sophistication of the students, as well as the social demands. The behaviors may occur in areas of the school where teachers have less influence and control (e.g. hallways, restrooms, cafeteria, during passing periods, gym, bus, lunch room) (Rusby, Crowley, Sprague, & Biglan, 2011). Positive behavior management practices need to occur at the middle school level, so that all students experience positive social interactions and feel supported and safe at school. Data suggests schools that implement PBS at the middle school level decrease the following: office discipline referrals, time spent sitting at the office, and school suspensions (Rusby et al., 2011). Students with ASD can and do benefit from school-wide PBS environments when IEP teams carefully design plans based on the components of a functional behavioral assessment and identify goals and objectives that focus on the problem behaviors (e.g. talk outs, disregard for personal space, out of seat) (Turnbull et al., 2002). In order for PBS to be effective, educators must create a positive learning environment for all students with ASD to thrive in, incorporate EBP into teaching, and utilize behavior reduction techniques.

Creating a Positive Learning Environment

Students thrive in positive learning environments, when they are reinforced to develop and apply needed skills. Therefore, practitioners
should reflect on how they can utilize direct instruction, modeling, role
play, positive classroom management, high expectations, teacher with-it-
ness, positive reinforcement contingent on student performance, guided
practice, explicit teaching practices, structured transitions, corrective
feedback, formative and summative assessments that guide instruction,
appropriate wait time/pacing, pre-corrects, task analysis, established routines and procedures to engage students (Alberto & Troutman, 2013;
Sayeski & Brown, 2014; Scheuermann & Hall, 2016; Smith & Yell,
2013). Middle school students make better academic and behavioral
gains when teachers engage in the following: address learning prefer-
ences/modality strengths, arrange the environment to decrease sensory
stimulation (e.g. provide a quiet area, soften the lighting), provide alter-
natives/choice (i.e. time of the day), assess students' physical needs and
encourage movement when working (Jones & Jones, 2013). Students
who struggle with change often exhibit challenging behaviors associated
with transitions. Teachers should prepare students with ASD for changes
in advance, signal upcoming events and incorporate the use of timers
(Chandler & Dahlquist, 2015). The following subsections list those elements that go into creating a positive learning environment.

Differential Reinforcement

Differential reinforcement is an EBP that adheres to the principles of the
Office of Special Education Programs (OSEP) and IDEA (1997) and is
used to decrease challenging target behaviors (Gongola & Daddario,
2010). Teachers can use differential reinforcement to reinforce appropriate behaviors that are already in students' repertoires, but are displayed inconsistently (Zirpoli, 2012). Using differential reinforcement of
other behavior (DRO), Tomi is reinforced for the absence of scream-
ing, exiting quietly, remaining quiet and putting away books when the
bell rings. Teachers can employ differential reinforcement of lower rates
of behavior, when students display appropriate behavior, however in
excess. For example, Bailey's teacher rewards her for finishing independent seat work, turning in homework, and asking to break four times
(i.e. lower rate), as an alternative of asking to break eight times (i.e. excess
rate) throughout the day (The IRIS Center for Training Enhancements,
2005). When substituting an undesired behavior with a topographically
incompatible behavior, teachers can use differential reinforcement of
incompatible behavior (Zirpoli, 2012). Reinforcement is provided when
Kevin walks to the homework basket with both hands by his side versus

high fiving the students as he walks by (The IRIS Center for Training Enhancements, 2005). Regardless of the differential reinforcement used, teachers must refrain from reinforcing a student's challenging behavior (i.e. extinction) (Chandler & Dahlquist, 2015).

Extinction

Extinction is an EBP shown to be successful in removing or reducing unwarranted behaviors in students with ASD (Aiken & Salzberg, 1984; Hagopian, Contrucci-Kuhn, Long, & Rush, 2005; Maag, Wolchik, Rutherford, & Parks, 1986; Rincover, 1978). Sullivan and Bogin (2010a) defined extinction as the act of withdrawing a positive reinforcement, one that is maintaining the behavior. Extinction helps eliminate an undesired behavior and is often used in conjunction with differential reinforcement to encourage appropriate behaviors in individuals with ASD from early childhood to middle school (Wong et al., 2013). In order to effectively extinguish challenging behaviors, educators must: (a) identify the behavior (i.e. outbursts, attention seeking, task avoidance, (b) identify data collection procedures to be used, and the method for obtaining baseline data, (c) identify the function of the behavior and what it looks like, (d) create an intervention plan or plan of action, (e) implement the intervention or plan of action, (f) compile the results of data, and (g) review the results of the intervention plan to see if it needs revision or modification (Sullivan & Bogin, 2010b).

A behavior that is put on extinction requires that the educator ignore the behavior that was previously reinforced (Zirpoli, 2012). Extinction can be effectively used with students with ASD when the behavior is extrinsically reinforced (e.g. teacher attention for escaping). However, teachers of students with ASD will find that extinction is not effective for behaviors that are intrinsically reinforcing to the student (e.g. rocking, humming, hand flapping). Severely aggressive behaviors should never be ignored (i.e. extinction) when they are harmful to the student or others (O'Neil et al., 1997; Zirpoli, 2012).

Functional Communication Training

Functional communication training (FCT) involves conducting a functional behavior assessment to identify the stimuli that reinforce the challenging/maladaptive behavior and teaching an appropriate communicative replacement behavior that meets the function (Cooper et al., 2007; Wheeler & Richey, 2014). The appropriate communicative replacement behavior may be an action, response or communication (e.g. place a picture in someone's hand, vocalize *break please*, gesture). For example, a high school student is reinforced with teacher attention when he or she raises a hand to answer/ask a question and ignored when talking out without permission (Wheeler & Richey, 2014; Zirpoli, 2012). Teachers may begin FCT once data are collected (i.e. following a functional behavior assessment) and the function has been determined. During FCT, teachers should use differential reinforcement with the new functionally equivalent behavior and extinction with the challenging behavior (Kuhn, Hardesty, & Sweeney, 2009).

Video Modeling

Video modeling has been found to be effective with students with ASD who struggle with generalizing skills across different settings (Bellini & Akullian, 2007; Franzone & Collet-Klingenberg, 2008). Video modeling allows students with ASD to view a task in its entirety, and then perform the skill set they previously viewed (Boutot & Myles, 2011; Cannella-Malone et al., 2006). There are a variety of video modeling methods: (a) basic modeling involves recording a video of someone modeling or performing a task or skill set, after which the learner watches the video at a later date, (b) video self-modeling involves the learner being recorded performing the desired task or skill, after which the video is viewed, (c) point-of-view modeling involves the task or skill set being recorded through the eyes of the learner, and (d) video prompting involves a skill or desired task being broken down into smaller chunks that allows the learner to view the video through a visual task analysis (Franzone & Collet-Klingenberg, 2008). Video modeling is used to teach students with ASD how to perform daily/functional life skills (Cardon, & Wilcox, 2011; Charlop-Christy & Daneshvar, 2003). The success of video modeling has been noted in the literature (Charlop & Milstein, 1989; Delano, 2007; Nikopoulos, & Keenan, 2004; Ogilvie, 2011). See Table 14.1 for an example of video modeling.

Table 14.1 Video Modeling (adapted from Ogilvie, 2011)

Example: Video Modeling
Parker is a 13-year-old middle school student with ASD who attends a public school. Data revealed Parker has difficulty responding to peers during typical conversations in the general education classroom. He struggles with conducting a conversation, understanding wait time or choosing appropriate topics to discuss. The teacher decides to implement video modeling by creating a short video with the help of two same-age peer mentors. Next the teacher introduces conversational steps to Parker and a classroom peer mentor. After viewing the video, Parker and the peer practice/review the steps for conducting a conversation.

Positive Behavior Support in High School

During the high school years, students must interact with increased staff and administrators, and with a larger population of students. In addition rules and behavioral expectations may vary from classroom to classroom (Flannery, Sugai, & Anderson, 2009). The dynamics of high school become more complex as students with ASD transition from middle to high school. PBS focuses on prevention, provides consistency for high school students with ASD, thus reducing problematic behaviors and preventing future reoccurrences (Carr et al., 2002).

High school students with ASD face many challenges when it comes to daily routines, environmental changes, mental health (i.e. anxiety), and the transition into adulthood (Test, Smith, & Carter, 2014). Since PBS enhances the capacity of a student, family, and community, practitioners should look beyond the constraints of the classroom, as the principles help meet the present and future needs of students and better prepare them for adult living and employment (Sugai et al., 2000; Test et al., 2014). In order to meet the needs, educators can help to: (a) build social and communication skills with peers and community members, (b) prepare others to work collaboratively in social settings with youth with ASD, and (c) foster supportive environments (Carter, Harvey, Taylor, & Gotham, 2013; Kolb & Hanley-Maxwell 2003). Research provides evidence that youth with ASD must play an active role in their individualized transition plan, have opportunities to explore postsecondary options, and receive ongoing instruction in the areas of self-management, decision making, problem solving, independent living, and functional skills (Carter et al., 2013). By preparing transition-age youth with ASD in high school for the real world, educators can help improve their overall quality of life (Lee & Carter, 2012; Test et al., 2014). What follows are aspects and or examples of PBS in high school.

Structured Learning Environments and Visual Supports

High school youth with ASD are best supported in structured learning environments with supports that include visual schedules, prompts and picture cues. Visual supports: (1) are a method of external control that some students require in order to access other environments, (2) help decrease errors, (3) promote maintenance and generalization of skills, and (4) serve as constant reminders (West, 2008). Noting the importance of structure and visual supports, Smith Myles and Southwick encourage teachers to secure visual prompts within student notebooks, to keep back-ups for those students who lose them, and to teach students how to organize their materials (2005). The challenge for educators is to provide only the support needed, while transferring that to more naturalistic methods.

Reinforcement in High School

It can be assumed that a student is positively reinforced when the behavior increases following reinforcement (e.g. tokens, praise, break) (Scheuermann & Hall, 2012). Yet, for reinforcement to be effective, educators must: (1) reinforce correct behaviors/responses, (2) vary the tone with delivery, (3) stay positive and upbeat, (4) deliver quickly with enthusiasm, and (5) plan to fade (Storey & Post, 2012). Due to the varied interests of students with ASD, it is important that high school teachers are thoughtful when selecting reinforcers. Reinforcement is more effective when it is highly favored. Since students may prefer computer time, class time to discuss sports scores, gaming, designing, movies, music or time to be alone, effective educators conduct reinforcement assessments. Perner and Delano (2013) note procedures educators can utilize for students with ASD who have limited communication (see Figure 14.1).

Behavior Reduction Techniques

Alberto and Troutman (2013) describe a behavior reduction procedural model. Included in Level 1 of their model are, Reinforcement-based strategies, such as differential reinforcement or non-contingent reinforcement; Level 2, Extinction; Level 3, Removal of the desired stimuli (i.e. time-out, response cost); and Level 4, Presentation of an aversive. Even so, punishment is never a first option. Only when a child's safety is in question or for serious behaviors, might physical or other aversive consequences be

---

Steps to Conducting a Reinforcer Preference Assessment for Students With ASD With Limited Verbal Skills

1   Start with a pool of items that may be reinforcing for the student. It is often easiest to observe the student to determine the sensory input she enjoys. For example if she seeks visual input, work with the OT to identify visually-based items that may serve as reinforces. Identify 10 to 20 objects in this category.
2   Organize two containers: (a) one for items selected and (b) one for items not selected. If an object will not fit into a container, place a picture in the container.
3   While sitting with the student, show her two items and give the direction, "Pick one."
4   Provide adequate wait time for the student to select an item using her form of communicator (e.g., visual orientation, reach, point, switch). Allow the student to interact with the item for a brief time period (i.e., 30 seconds using a visual/auditory timer to indicate start and end time).
5   Place items in the appropriate container (selected/not selected).
6   Continue the selection process until all items are presented to the student and placed in the proper container.
7   Place the container near the student's work area for reinforcement as appropriate.

Figure 14.1 Reinforcer Preference Assessment

From *A guide to teaching students with autism spectrum disorders* (p. 14), by D. Perner and M. E. Delano, 2013, Arlington, VA: Division on Autism and Developmental Disabilities of the Council for Exceptional Children. Copyright (2015) by Darlene Perner. Reprinted with permission.

acceptable (Alberto & Troutman, 2013). Limitations to behavior reduction options include parent/administrator/guardian consent, a detailed description of the plan (e.g. who will interact with the student, what will be done) and when the team will reconvene to examine the data (Simpson & Otten, 2005). High school teachers of students with ASD should use positive alternatives to decrease or eliminate inappropriate behavior. While teachers may feel students who exhibit inappropriate behavior should not be given choices, as it will increase the behavior, students can and do benefit from choice-making opportunities.

Choice-making

Researchers identified choice-making as one of the components of self-determined behavior (Shevin & Klein, 2004; Snell & Brown, 2011; Wehmeyer, Shogren, Zager, Smith, & Simpson, 2010). Extant literature supports teaching students with ASD to engage in choice-making opportunities (Carlson, Luiselli, Slyman, & Markowski, 2008; Graff, & Gibson, 2003; Hoch, McComas, Johnson, Faranda, & Guenther, 2002; Moes, 1998; Shevin & Klein, 2004; Snell, & Brown, 2011; Watanabe & Sturmey, 2003). Choice-making opportunities can begin by pointing, through the use of facial expressions or gestures, labeling an item and through the use of oral communication (Snell & Brown, 2011). Students with ASD can be taught a choice-making framework within the instructional setting, home environment and community (Shevin & Klein, 2004; Shrogen, Faggella-Luby, Bae, & Wehmeyer, 2004). Educators can encourage high school students to choose where they want to sit in the classroom, how they would like to complete a classroom assignment or activity or evaluate routines that occur naturally within their daily environment (Shevin & Klein, 2004; Van Tubbergen, Warshausky, Birnholz, & Baker, 2008; Wehmeyer et al., 2010).

Hidden Curriculum

In particular, the hidden curriculum is challenging for adolescents with ASD. The hidden curriculum refers to the unwritten principles, norms, rules or ethics adopted by most individuals and which are not specifically taught (Lee, 2011). An adolescent with ASD may inadvertently break one of the unwritten rules and suffer the negative consequences (Smith Myles, Trautman, & Schelvan, 2004). Sadly, this impacts the youth's social acceptance by same-age peers (Smith Myles et al., 2004). For example, a high school-age student with ASD may not grasp there are different rules that apply at home, at lunch, in the classroom and with friends. Thus, professionals play a critical role in identifying teachable moments when the hidden curriculum can/should be taught. The direct teaching of these unwritten rules is important at every grade level, as it can impact

of life outside of school and beyond graduation (Smith
... e Figure 14.2).

... Skills Training

The importance of social skills training for secondary students with
ASD cannot be overstated. High school students with ASD may experience difficulties forming or maintaining friendships, resulting in social
rejection or limited social interaction. They often become even more
isolated since they have not established positive reciprocal friendships,
the byproducts from the mutual interchanges among friends (Laugeson,
Frankel, Mogil, & Dilon, 2009). Instruction in social skills, as with the
hidden curriculum, requires direct instruction since students with ASD
do not learn these competencies through incidental observation. A few
research and/or evidence-based strategies that help promote students'
social skills include: (1) *Program for the education and enrichment of*

Sample Hidden Curriculum Items

- Treat all authority figures with respect (e.g., police, firefighters). You would not address a police officer like you would your brother.
- Not all people you are unfamiliar with are strangers you cannot trust. You may not know your bus driver or your police officer, but these are people who help you.
- What may be acceptable at your house may not be acceptable at a friend's house. For example, although it is acceptable to put your feel up on the table at home, your friend's mom may be upset if you do that in their home.
- People do not always want to know the honest truth even when they ask. Your best friend does not want to hear that she looks fat in a new dress she just bought for the high school dance.
- Teachers do not have all the same rules. One teacher may allow chewing gum in the classroom, while another gives out fines for chewing gum.
- Teachers assume certain expectations for their students. For example, students are expected to greet the teachers, sit down when the bell rings, and listen quietly to announcements.
- When a teacher gives you a warning, it means that she wants a given behavior to stop and that most likely there will be a consequence if the behavior continues or occurs again.
- It is impolite to interrupt someone talking, unless it is an emergency.
- Acceptable slang that may be used with your peers (e.g., dawg, phat) may not be acceptable when interacting with adults.
- When the teacher is scolding another student, it is not the best time to ask the teacher a question.
- When a teacher tells another student to stop talking, it is not an appropriate time for you to start talking to your neighbor.

Figure 14.2 Sample Hidden Curriculum

From *Asperger syndrome and difficult moments* (p. 89), by B. Smith Myles and J. Southwick, 2005, Shawnee, KS: Autism Asperger Publishing Co. Copyright (2015) by Kirsten McBride. Reprinted with permission.

relational skills (Laugeson, Frankel, Mogil, & Dillon, 2009); comic strip conversations (Pierson & Glaeser, 2007); social stories (Sargent, Perner, & Cook, 2012), power cards (Angell, Nicholson, Watts, & Blum, 2011), and *Building social relationships* (Bellini, 2008). It is recommended that educators take time every day to teach social skills and assess opportunities that lend themselves to instruction (e.g. those natural occurring situations) (Sargent, Perner, & Cook, 2012).

Social Communication

One major factor affecting youth with ASD in achieving positive peer social relationships is poor social communicative behaviors. Research suggests Pivotal Response Treatment (PRT), an EBP, improves students' communicative skills (Koegel & Koegel, 2012). For example, students with ASD may struggle with several pivotal behaviors (e.g. motivation, social initiation, self- management) that impact communication. However, the teaching of pivotal behaviors can improve high school-age students with ASD skills in other areas (e.g. social, affect, perseveration, academics) (Koegel & Frea, 1993; Koegel & Koegel, 2012).

Computer-aided Technology-based Instruction

There is strong consensus that computer-aided instruction is an important teaching tool for students with ASD academics, communication, and social skills (Odom, Collet-Klingenberg, Rogers, & Hatton, 2010). A variety of studies have involved the use of various forms of technology (e.g. iPad, portable electronic devices). For instance, adolescents with autism solved mathematical problems using video self-monitoring (VSM) and the iPad (Burton, Anderson, Prater, & Dyches, 2013). Data suggest (Mechling, Gast, & Seid, 2009; Mechling & Savidge, 2011) that middle and high school-age students with ASD can perform tasks independently with the support of technological devices (e.g. iPad, PDA, video). Technology-aided instruction is effective in that the device prompts responses and the level of prompt can be changed for the learner (e.g. visual, visual and audio, video) (Mechling & Savidge, 2011). Mechling et al. (2009) brings importance to teachers utilizing technology to assist students when first learning a task, to facilitate reaching criterion level and to assess for maintenance. Computer-aided instruction appears to be a natural addition when teaching behavioral and academic skills to students with ASD (Odom et al., 2010; Wong et al., 2013).

Cognitive Behavioral Modification Strategies

Cognitive behavioral interventions have proven helpful in enabling students with autism to regulate their emotions (e.g. anger, anxiety, frustrations)

(Sofronoff, Attwood, Hinton, & Levin, 2007). Cognitive behavioral interventions, such as self-determination, problem solving, social stories, cartooning, self-management, goal setting, self-instruction, self-evaluation and self-reinforcement can support students in managing their behaviors (Alberto & Troutman, 2013; Scheuermann & Hall, 2012; Simpson & Otten, 2005). One goal of a cognitive behavioral approach is to empower a student with ASD to understand feelings and how they affect the body (Sofronoff et al., 2007). Teachers can take advantage of cognitive behavioral methods to improve students' performance in (a) self-determination, (b) problem solving, (c) goal setting, (d) self-reinforcement, and (e) self-advocacy. They are presented in the following section.

Self-determination

Self-determination plays a critical role in the education of students with disabilities (Christiansen & Sitlington, 2008; Stang, Carter, Lane, & Pierson, 2009; Wehmeyer, 2005). Self-determination is a set of necessary component skills (e.g. decision making, goal setting) that individuals need to learn in order to exercise control over their lives (Haelewyck, Bara, & Lachapelle, 2005). Students who are self-determined express wants/ needs and make good or bad decisions as the causal agent in their lives (Wehmeyer, 2005). Therefore, self-determination is an important quality for a student with ASD to possess. Self-determination can help students with ASD to advocate for their direction in life (Boutot & Myles, 2011). The ability for one to advocate, necessitates that students with ASD are provided chances to exercise the skills that lead to self-determination (Boutot & Myles, 2011). Students with ASD must have equal access to and participate in the same activities as their typical peers. This means being encouraged to make decisions about one's own life, welfare, living arrangements, and job preference. Decision making entails making choices that may lead to success as well as disappointment (Taylor, 2006). Thus there is reason for students with ASD to utilize self-determined behaviors in everyday life situations (Simpson & Myles, 2008). However, instruction should be individualized to advance one's personal power and control over the future (Wehmeyer, 2005). During instruction, it is important to provide students opportunities for role play, self-advocacy, and personal preference (Thoma & Getzel, 2005).

Problem Solving

Students with disabilities need support in meeting/attaining their goals. Without the ability to problem solve, goals might be virtually unattainable (Gagne, 1959). Nevertheless, for students with ASD this process can be extremely difficult (Simpson & Myles, 2008). There is some evidence to support the use of teaching problem-solving skills to students with ASD to increase appropriate behaviors, and to facilitate meeting individualized education plan (IEP) goals (Agran, Cavin, Wehmeyer, & Palmer, 2006). Yet, problem-solving skills need to be taught specifically to students with ASD, modeled, and practice needs to be ongoing (Agran & Wehmeyer, 2005). In order to increase self-awareness and acquisition of personal efficacy, students with ASD need to be taught to recognize the supports and resources available to help them reach their goals (Wehmeyer, 1992). When students with ASD learn to find and locate answers to their own questions, they become more independent. Researchers suggest that educators and families provide occasions for developing problem-solving skills, and encouraging students to develop their own thinking (Glago, 2005; Kolb & Hanley-Maxwell, 2003; Simpson & Myles, 2008).

Goal Setting

Students with autism struggle with setting goals, another component of self-determination (Simpson & Myles 2008). Often, students with ASD have difficulty attending to multiple goals that contain complex steps. Yet, research has shown the benefits of the Self-Determination Model of Learning Instruction (SDMLI) in teaching middle school and high school students with autism to identify, set and achieve goals (Agran, Blanchard, Wehmeyer, & Hughes, 2002). However, goals need to be broken into smaller chunks or steps, making the goal attainable and not overwhelming the student with ASD (Simpson & Myles 2008).

Self-management

Self-management has come to be closely associated with increasing or reducing behavior and improving social, adaptive and communication skills in students with ASD (Simpson & Otten, 2005). Neitzel and Busick (2009) provide a step-by-step framework for implementing self-management as follows: (a) instruct students on how to monitor behavior, (b) teach students to record behavior (e.g. outburst, talking out, participation, social interaction), (c) show students ways to self-evaluate behavior and performance, and (d) determine a reward system for when meeting criterion. The goal of teaching self-management to students with ASD is for them to learn to be accountable for behavior(s) (Lee, Simpson, & Shrogen 2007). Not surprisingly, research has shown the benefits of self-management to be successful when implemented properly with students with ASD across age levels (i.e. elementary, middle school, secondary) (Carr, Moore, & Anderson, 2014; Koegel & Frea, 1993; Low, 2014; Morrison, Kamps, Garcia, & Parker, 2001; Newman, Buffington, & Hemmes, 1996; Newman et al., 1995; Odom et al., 2010; Soares, Vannest, & Harrison, 2009; Stahmer & Schreibman, 1992). The essence of teaching students to self-manage is to enhance their overall quality of life (Lee et al., 2007).

Self-advocacy

In order to display self-advocacy, students must be taught and given opportunities to communicate basic needs and wants. Additionally, they must have an understanding of those basic needs and wants and how to use that knowledge in an appropriate manner (Schreiner, 2007). Researchers identified a self-advocacy conceptual framework as knowledge of oneself and rights, and the ability to effectively communicate those needs or rights (Field, 1996; Furney, Carlson, Lisi, & Yuan, 1993; Test, Fowler, Wood, Brewer, & Eddy, 2005; Wehmeyer, 1992; Wehmeyer & Schwartz, 1997). Students can participate in their IEP using a self-advocacy strategy (Cook & Odom, 2013; Held, Thoma, & Thomas, 2004; Lee et al., 2011, Test et al., 2005; Test et al., 2014; Van Reusen, Bos, Schumaker, & Deshler, 1994; Wagner, Newman, Cameto, Javitz, & Valdes, 2012). Some of the resources listed in Table 14.2 are designed to aid student self-advocacy.

Comprehensive Autism Planning System (CAPS)

Due to the dynamics of school change, teachers and parents are rightly concerned when children with ASD transfer to secondary settings. Based on EBPs for students with ASD, the *Comprehensive Autism Planning System* (CAPS) was designed to support student success and facilitate smooth transitions from preschool into elementary, middle and high school (Henry & Smith Myles, 2007). Teachers of students with ASD have found CAPS a meaningful support throughout different times/periods of the day and when planning and setting goals (Smith Myles, Grossman, Aspy, & Henry, 2009). A student's schedule can be matched to the components

Table 14.2 Self-advocacy Models and Strategies

Self-advocacy Strategies, Curriculum, and Resources
Self-advocacy Strategy Student (Manual and CD)   www.edgeenterprisesinc.com
Whose Future Is It Anyway? (36 lesson sessions)   www.ou.edu
A Curriculum for Self-advocates (resource guide)   autismnow.org
It's My Choice (individual transition plan resource)   http://mn.gov
ME! Lessons for Teaching Self-Awareness and Self-Advocacy (lesson plans)   www.ou.edu
Stepping Forward: A Self-advocacy Guide for Middle and High School Students   (self-advocacy resource)   www.ct.gov

of CAPS: (a) time, (b) activity, (c) targeted skills to teach, (d) structure/modifications, (e) reinforcement, (f) sensory strategies, (g) communication/social skills, (h) data collection, and (i) generalization (Henry & Myles, 2007; Smith Myles et al., 2009).

Modified Comprehensive Autism Planning System (M-CAPS)

Middle and high school teachers may find the *Modified Comprehensive Autism Planning System* (M-CAPS) helpful in the transition (Smith Myles, Grossman, Aspy, Henry, & Coffin, 2007). M-CAPS focuses on individualizing specific activities for students with ASD, such as: (a) independent work, (b) group work, (c) tests, (d) lectures, and (e) homework (Smith Myles et al., 2007). This resource can be useful in providing documentation and just the right support students need as they transfer to various educational programs (see Figure 14.3).

Teacher, Parent, and Community Roles in the PBS Learning Environment

Teachers, parents, and community members all play a vital role in providing students with ASD positive behavior supports. It is important to keep in mind that there are many different roles each individual takes on. Families of children with ASD go through many adjustments. First, they have the everyday stressors that families typically face during child rearing as they go through the many transitions: birth to elementary school, elementary to middle school, middle school to high school, and high school to adulthood. Additionally, families of students with ASD have additional issues regarding the health and overall wellbeing of their children (Boutot & Smith Myles, 2011). It is important to bear in mind both student and family needs while being aware of the transitions all members of the family will face on graduation.

Culturally and Linguistically Diverse Behavioral Support

Attention must be given to the appreciation and respect of/for *all* students in the classrooms (Zirpoli, 2012). There is no question that family value systems, language and culture must be taken into account when discussing student behavior. The increasing numbers of students from culturally and linguistically diverse backgrounds necessitates that school cultures adapt to meet the needs of all (Boutot & Smith Myles, 2011; Simpson & Otten, 2005). For example, teachers may support students in a culturally responsive manner by: (a) becoming knowledgeable about other cultures (i.e. characteristics, belief systems, levels of acculturation, individualistic/collectivistic views), (b) researching one's own culture, (c) identifying cultural differences, (d) increasing cultural relevance, (e) ensuring

M-CAPS
Michael Thomas

Activity	Skills/STO	Structure/ Modifications	Reinforcement	Sensory Strategies	Social Skills Communication	Data Collection	Generalization
Independent Work	Task completion	– Task organizer – Organization calendar – Peer buddies	– Completing homework/ in-class work (from menu)	– Coping cards – Ear plugs – Stress thermometer	– Asking for help	– Task organizer – Organization calendar	– Homework completion
Group Work	Conversational rules	– Task organizer – Organization calendar – Peer buddies	– Completing homework/ in-class work (from menu)	– Relaxation techniques	– Cues for commenting and asking questions – Social Story™ about group work	– Task organizer	– Lunch conversation
Tests	Task completion	– Task organizer – Organization calendar	– Calming skills – Test completion (from menu)	– Relaxation techniques – Stress thermometer	– Cues for commenting and asking questions		– Turning in assignments
Lectures	Attention to task	– Task organizer – Organization calendar	– Appropriate conversation (from menu)	– Coping cards – Stress thermometer	– Conversation cues – Cues for commenting and asking questions	– Organization calendar	– Listening during group work
Homework	– Task completion – Materials and supplies needed	– Homework checklist (double-check with student)	– Homework turned in (from menu)	– Relaxation techniques – Stress thermometer	NA	– Homework turned in complete	– Turning in classwork

Figure 14.3 Sample M-CAPS

From *Planning a comprehensive program for students with autism spectrum disorders using evidence-based practices*, by B. Smith Myles, B. Grossman, R. Aspy, S. Henry, and A. B. Coffin, 2007, *Education and Training in Developmental Disabilities*, *42*, p. 407. Copyright (2015) by Stanley Zucker. Reprinted with permission.

that culturally valid measures are used, and (f) promoting cultural justice (Vincent, Randall, Cartledge, Tobin, & Swain-Bradway, 2011). Essentially critical is to be sensitive to students' feelings of alienation, to value all family members, to establish positive collaborative relationships between the school and family and to maintain high expectations (Zirpoli, 2012). Indeed, culturally responsive PBS involves data collection as evidence of the methods teachers, schools, districts and IEP teams use to improve cultural responsiveness (e.g. surveys, culturally responsive practice training, parent/community involvement, assessment for under-represented groups, adaptations/modifications made to resources) (Vincent et al., 2011).

Summary

It is important for educators and families to recognize that students with ASD experience many transitions throughout their lifetimes. Many times, students and youth with ASD exhibit stereotypical or problematic behaviors and need PBS in place in order to be successful across multiple settings. There are a variety of EBP strategies and resources described in detail throughout this chapter to support students with ASD at the secondary level. See Table 14.3 for a list of websites and professional organizations.

Using the evidence-based tools and resources provided will help educators and families as students with ASD transition into secondary school settings. A PBS approach emphasizes the supports needed to prepare adolescents for life's transitions. When comprehensive positive behavior supports are in place, adolescents with ASD are much better prepared to experience life to the fullest while offering support to family members throughout major life transitions.

Table 14.3 Websites and Professional Organizations

Websites and Professional Organizations
Autism internet modules
www.autisminternetmodules.org
Council for Exceptional Children
www.cec.sped.org
Division on Autism and Developmental Disabilities
http://daddcec.org
Positive behavioral interventions and supports
www.pbis.org
The National Professional Development Center on Autism Spectrum Disorders
http://autismpdc.fpg.unc.edu
What Works Clearinghouse
http://ies.ed.gov/ncee/wwc/

References

Agran, M., Blanchard, C., Wehmeyer, M. L., & Hughes, C. (2002). Increasing the problem-solving skills of students with developmental disabilities participating in general education. *Remedial and Special Education, 23*, 279–285.

Agran, M., Cavin, M., Wehmeyer, M. L., & Palmer, S. (2006). Participation of students with moderate to severe disabilities in the general curriculum: The effects of the self-determined learning model of instruction. *Research & Practice for Persons with Severe Disabilities, 31*, 230–241.

Agran, M., & Wehmeyer, M. (2005). Teaching problem solving to students with mental retardation. In M. L. Wehmeyer & M. Agran (Eds.), *Mental retardation and intellectual disabilities teaching students using innovative and research-based strategies* (pp. 255–271), Aukland: Pearson Education.

Aiken, J. M., & Salzberg, C. L. (1984). The effects of a sensory extinction procedure on stereotypic sounds of two autistic children. *Journal of Autism and Developmental Disorders, 14*(3), 291–299.

Alberto, P. A., & Troutman, A. C. (2013). *Applied behavior analysis for teachers* (9th ed.). Upper Saddle, NJ: Merrill Pearson Education, Inc.

Angell, M. E., Nicholson, J. K., Watts, E. H., & Blum, C. (2011). Using a multicomponent adapted power card strategy to decrease latency during interactivity transitions for three children with developmental disabilities. *Focus on Autism and Other Developmental Disabilities, 26*(4), 206–217.

Becker-Cottrill, B., McFarland, J., & Anderson, V. (2003). A model of positive behavioral support for individuals with autism and their families: The family focus process. *Focus on Autism and Other Developmental Disabilities, 18*(2), 110–120.

Bellini, S. (2008). *Building social relationships: A systematic approach to teaching social interaction skills to children and adolescents with autism spectrum disorders and other social difficulties.* Shawnee Mission, KS: Autism Asperger Publishing Co.

Bellini, S., & Akullian, J. (2007). A Meta-Analysis of Video Modeling and Video Self-Modeling Interventions for Children and Adolescents with Autism Spectrum Disorders. *Exceptional Children, 73*(3), 264–287.

Bicard, S. C., & Bicard, D. F. (2012). *Measuring behavior.* Retrieved March 21, 2015 from http://iris.peabody.vanderbilt.edu/case_studies/ ICS.pdf.

Boutot, E. A., & Smith Myles, B. (2011). *Autism spectrum disorders: Foundations, characteristics, and effective strategies.* Upper Saddle River, NJ: Pearson/ Prentice Hall.

Burton, C. E., Anderson, D. H., Prater, M. A., & Dyches, T. T. (2013). Video self-modeling on an iPad to teach functional math skills to adolescents with autism and intellectual disability. *Focus on Autism and Other Developmental Disabilities, 28*(2), 76–77.

Cannella-Malone, H., Sigaffoos, J., Reilly, M., De la Cruz, B., Edrisinha, C., & Lancioni, G. (2006). Comparing video prompting to video modeling for teaching daily living skills to six adults with developmental disabilities. *Journal of Education in Training in Developmental Disabilities, 41*(4), 344–356.

Cardon, T. A., & Wilcox, M. J. (2011). Promoting imitation in young children with autism: A comparison of reciprocal imitation training and video modeling. *Journal of Autism Developmental Disorders, 41*, 654–666.

Carlson, J., Luiselli, J., Slyman, A., & Markowski, A. (2008). Choice-making as intervention for public disrobing in children with developmental disabilities. *Journal of Positive Behavior Interventions*, 10(2), 86–90.

Carter, E. W., Harvey, M. N., Taylor, J. L., & Gotham, K. (2013). Connecting youth and young adults with autism spectrum disorders to community life. *Psychology in the Schools*, 50(9), 888–898.

Carr, E. G. (2007). The expanding vision of positive behavior support: Research perspectives on happiness, helpfulness, hopefulness. *Journal of Positive Behavior Interventions*, 9(1), 3–14.

Carr, E. G., Dunlap, G., Horner, R. H., Koegel, R., Turnbull, A. P., Sailor, W., . . . Fox, L. (2002). Positive behavior support: Evolution of an applied science. *Journal of Positive Behavior Interventions*, 4(1), 4–16.

Carr, M. E., Moore, D. W., & Anderson, A. (2014). Self-management interventions on students with autism: A meta-analysis of single subject research. *Exceptional Children*, 81(1), 28–44.

Chandler, L. K., & Dahlquist, C. M. (2015). *Functional assessment strategies to prevent and remediate challenging behavior in school settings* (4th ed.). Upper Saddle River, NJ: Pearson Education, Inc.

Charlop-Christy, M. H., & Daneshvar, S. (2003). Using video modeling to teach perspective taking to children with autism. *Journal of Positive Behavior Interventions*, 5,12–22.

Charlop-Christy, M. H., & Milstein, J. P. (1989). Teaching autistic children conversational speech using video modeling. *Journal of Applied Behavior Analysis*, 22(3), 275–285.

Christiansen, E., & Sitlington, P. (2008). Guardianship: Its role in the transition process for students with developmental disabilities. *Education and Training in Development Disabilities*, 43, 3–19.

Conley Downs, R., & Downs, A. (2010). Practices in early intervention for children with autism: A comparison with the national research council recommended practices. *Education and Training in Autism and Developmental Disabilities*, 45(1), 150–159.

Cook, B. G., & Odom, S. L. (2013). Evidence-based practices and implementation science in special education. *Exceptional Children*, 79,135–144.

Cook, B. G., Tankersley, M., & Harjusola-Webb, S. (2008). Evidence-based special education and professional wisdom: Putting it all together. *Intervention in School and Clinic*, 44(2), 105–111.

Cooper, J. O., Heron, T. E., & Heward, W. L. (2007). *Applied behavior analysis* (2nd ed.).Upper Saddle, NJ: Pearson Education, Inc.

Delano, M.E. (2007). Video modeling intervention for individuals with autism. *Remedial and Special Education*, 28(1), 33–42.

Erbas, D. (2010). A collaborative approach to implement positive behavior support plans for children with problem behaviors: A comparison of consultation versus consultation and feedback approach. *Education and Training in Autism and Developmental Disabilities*, 45(1), 94–107.

Field, S. (1996). Self-determination instructional strategies for youth with learning disabilities. *Journal of Learning Disabilities*, 29, 40–52.

Flannery, K. B., Sugai, G., & Anderson, C. M. (2009). School-wide positive behaviors support in high school. *Journal of Positive Behavior Interventions*, 11(3), 177–185.

Franzone, E., & Collet-Klingenberg, L. (2008). *Overview of video modeling.* Madison, WI: The National Professional Development Center on Autism Spectrum Disorders, Waisman Center, University of Wisconsin.

Furney, K., Carlson, N., Lisi, D., & Yuan, S. (1993). *Speak up for yourself and your future!* Burlington, VT: Enabling Futures Project.

Gagne, R. M. (1959). Problem solving and thinking. *Annual Review of Psychology, 10,* 147–172.

Glago, K. D. (2005). The effect of problem solving self-determination instruction on elementary students with learning disabilities and emotional disabilities (Doctoral dissertation, George Mason University, 2005). *Dissertation Abstracts International, 66*(02), 549.

Gongola, L. C., & Daddario, R. (2010). A practitioner's guide to implementing a differential reinforcement of other behaviors procedure. *Teaching Exceptional Children, 42*(6), 14–20.

Graff, R., & Gibson, L. (2003). Using pictures to assess reinforcers in individuals with developmental disabilities. *Behavior Modification, 27*(4), 470–483.

Haelewyck, M., Bara, M., & LaChapelle, Y. (2005). Facilitating self-determination in adolescents with intellectual disabilities. *Evaluation Review, 29,* 390–502.

Hagopian, L. P., Contrucci-Kuhn, S. A., Long, E. S., & Rush, K. S. (2005). Schedule thinning following communication training: Using competing stimuli to enhance tolerance to decrements in reinforcer density. *Journal of Applied Behavior Analysis, 38*(2), 177–193.

Held, M. F., Thoma, C. A., & Thomas, K. (2004). The John Jones show: How one teacher facilitated self-determined transition planning for a young man with autism. *Focus on Autism and Other Developmental Disabilities, 19,* 177–188.

Henry, S., & Smith Myles, B. (2007). *The comprehensive autism planning system (CAPS).* Shawnee Mission, KS: Autism Asperger Publishing Company.

Hoch, H., McComas, J., Johnson, L., Faranda, N., & Guenther, S. (2002). The effects of magnitude and quality on choice responding during play activities. *Journal of Applied Behavior Analysis, 35*(2), 171–181.

Individuals with Disabilities Education Act. (1997). 20 U.S.C. § 1400 et seq.

Janney, R., & Snell, M. E. (2008). *Behavioral support: Teachers' guides to inclusive practices.* Baltimore, MD: Paul H. Brookes Publishing Co.

Jones, V., & Jones, L. (2013). *Comprehensive classroom management.* Upper SaddleRiver, NJ: Pearson Education, Inc.

Kern, L., Gallagher, P., Starosta, K., Hickman, W. & George, M. (2006). Longitudinal outcomes of functional behavioral assessment-based intervention. *Journal of Positive Behavior Interventions, 8*(2), 67–78.

Koegel, R. L., & Frea, W. D. (1993). Treatment of social behavior in autism through the modification of pivotal social skills. *Journal of Applied Behavior Analysis, 26,* 369–377.

Koegel, R. L., & Koegel, L. K. (2012). *The PRT pocket guide.* Baltimore, MD: Paul H. Brookes Publishing Co.

Kolb, S, M., & Hanley-Maxwell, C. (2003). Critical social skills for adolescents with high incidence disabilities: Parental perspectives. *Exceptional Children, 69,* 163–179.

Kuhn, D. E., Hardesty, S. L., & Sweeney, N. M. (2009). Assessment and treatment of excessive straightening and destructive behavior in an adolescent diagnosed with autism. *Journal of Applied Behavior Analysis, 42*(2), 355–360.

Laugeson, E. A., Frankel, F., Mogil, C., & Dillon, A. R. (2009). Parent-assisted social skills training to improve friendships in teens with autism spectrum disorders. *Journal of Autism and Developmental Disorders, 39*, 596–606.

Lee, H. J. (2011). Cultural factors related to the hidden curriculum for students with autism and related curriculum. *Intervention in School and Clinic, 46*(3), 141–149.

Lee, G. K., & Carter, E. W. (2012). Preparing transition-age students with high functioning autism spectrum disorders for meaningful work. *Psychology in the Schools, 49*(10), 988–1000.

Lee, S. H., Simpson, R. L., & Shogren, K. A. (2007). Effects and implications of self-management for students with autism: A meta-analysis. *Focus on Autism and Other Developmental Disabilities, 22*, 2–13

Lee, Y., Wehmeyer, M. L., Palmer, S. B., Williams-Diehm, K., Davies, D. K., & Stock, S. E. (2011). The effect of student- directed transition planning using a computer-based reading support program on the self-determination of students with disabilities. *The Journal of Special Education, 45*, 104–117.

Li, A. (2009). Identification and intervention for students who are visually impaired and who have autism spectrum disorders. *Teaching Exceptional Children, 41*(4), 22–32.

Low, A. (2014). Utilizing the iPad to teach students with autism self-management (Masters Thesis). Retrieved March 21, 2015 from ProQuest Dissertations and Theses Database (1525271).

Maag, J. W., Wolchik, S. A., Rutherford, R. B., & Parks, B. T. (1986). Response covariation on self-stimulatory behaviors during sensory extinction procedures. *Journal of Autism and Developmental Disorders, 16*(2), 119–132.

Mechling, L. C., Gast, D. L., & Seid, N. H. (2009). Using a personal digital assistant to increase independent task completion by students with autism spectrum disorder. *Journal of Autism and Developmental Disorders, 39*, 1420–1434.

Mechling, L. C., & Savidge, E. J. (2011). Using a personal digital assistant to increase completion of novel task and independent transitioning by students with autism spectrum disorder. *Journal of Autism and Developmental Disorders, 39*, 1420–1434.

Minke, K. M., & Anderson, K. J. (2005). Family–school collaboration and positive behavior support. *Journal of Positive Behavior Interventions, 7*(3), 181–145.

Moes, D. R. (1998). Integrating choice-making opportunities within teacher-assigned academic tasks to facilitate the performance of children with autism. *The Association for Persons with Severe Handicaps, 23*, 319–328.

Morrison, L., Kamps, D., Garcia, J., & Parker, D. (2001). Peer mediation and monitoring strategies to improve initiations and social skills for students with autism. *Journal of Positive Behavior Interventions, 3*, 237–250.

Neitzel, J., & Busick, M. (2009). Overview of self-management. Chapel Hill, NC: National Professional Development Center on Autism Spectrum Disorders. Frank Porter Graham Child Development Institute, The University of North Carolina.

Newman, B., Buffington, D. M., & Hemmes, N. S. (1996). Self-reinforcement used to increase the appropriate conversation of autistic teenagers. *Education and Training in Mental Retardation and Developmental Disabilities, 31*, 304–309.

Newman, B., Buffington, D. M., O'Grady, M. A., McDonald, M. E., Poulson, C. L., & Hemmes, N. S. (1995). Self-management of schedule following in three teenagers with autism. *Behavioral Disorders, 20*, 190–196.

Nikopoulos, C. K., & Keenan, M. (2004). Effects of video modeling on social initiations by children with autism. *Journal of Applied Behavior Analysis, 37(1)*, 93–96.

Odom, S. L., Collet-Klingenberg, L., Rogers, S. J., & Hatton, D. D. (2010). Evidence-based practices in interventions for children and youth with autism spectrum disorders. *Preventing School Failure, 54(4)*, 275–282.

Ogilvie, C. R. (2011). Step by step social skills instruction for students with autism spectrum disorder using video models and peers mentors. *Teaching Exceptional Children, 43(6)*, 20–26.

O'Neill, R. E., Albin, R. W., Storey, K., Horner, R. H., & Sprague, J. R. (2015). *Functional assessment and program development for problem behavior.* Belmont, CA: Cengage.

O'Neill, R. E., Horner, R. H., Albin, R. W., Sprague, J. R., Storey, K., & Newton, J. S. (1997). *Functional assessment and program development for problem behavior.* Belmont, CA: Cengage.

Perner, D. E., & Delano, M. E. (2013). *A guide to teaching students with autism spectrum disorders.* Arlington, VA: Division on Autism and Developmental Disabilities of the Council for Exceptional Children.

Pierson, M. R., & Glaeser, B. C. (2007). Using comic strip conversations to increase social satisfaction and decrease loneliness in students with autism spectrum disorder. *Education and Training in Developmental Disabilities, 42(4)*, 460–466.

Rincover, A. (1978). Sensory Extinction: A procedure for eliminating self-stimulatory behavior in developmentally disabled children. *Journal of Abnormal Child Psychology, 6(3)*, 299– 310.

Rusby, J. C., Crowley, R., Sprague, J., & Biglan, A. (2011). Observations of the middle school environment: The context for student behavior beyond the classroom. *Psychology in the Schools, 48(40)*, 400–415.

Sargent, L. R., Perner, D., & Cook, T. (2012). *Social skills for students with autism spectrum disorders.* Arlington, VA: Council for Exceptional Children.

Sayeski, K. L., & Brown, M. R. (2014). Developing a classroom management plan using a tiered approach. *Teaching Exceptional Children, 47(2)*, 119–127.

Scheuermann, B.K., & Hall, J.A. (2012). *Positive Behavioral Supports for the Classroom*, A.C. Davis (Ed.). Upper Saddle River, NJ: Pearson Education.

Scheuermann, B. K. & Hall, J. A. (2016). *Positive behavior supports for the classroom.* Upper Saddle River, NJ: Pearson Education, Inc.

Screiner, M. B. (2007). Effective self-advocacy: What students and special educators need to know. *Intervention in School and Clinic, 42*, 300–304.

Shea, T. M., & Bauer, A. M. (2012). *Behavior management a practical approach for educators.* Upper Saddle River, NJ: Pearson.

Shevin, M., & Klein, N. (2004). The importance of choice-making skills with students with severe disabilities. *Research & Practice for Persons with Severe Disabilities, 29*, 161–168.

Shrogen, K., Fagella-Luby, M., Bae, Sung J., & Wehmeyer, M. (2004). The effect of choice-making as an intervention for problem behavior: A meta-analysis. *Journal of Positive Behavior Interventions, 6*, 228–237.

Simpson, R. L., & Myles, B. S. (2008) *Educating children and youth with autism: Strategies for effective practices.* Austin,TX: Pro Ed.

Simpson, R. L., & Otten, K. (2005). Structuring behavior management strategies and building social competence. In Dianne Zager (Ed.), *Autism Spectrum Disorders* (3rd ed.), (pp. 367–394). New York: Routledge.

Smith Myles, B., Grossmn, B. G., Aspy, R., & Henry. S. A. (2009). Planning a comprehensive program for young children with Autism Spectrum Disorder. *International Journal of Early Childhood and Special Education, 1*(2), 164–180.

Smith Myles, B., Grossman, B. G., Aspy, R., Henry. S. A., & Coffin, A. B. (2007). Planning a comprehensive program for students with Autism Spectrum Disorder using evidence-based practices. *Education and Training in Developmental Disabilities, 42*(4), 398–409.

Smith Myles, B., & Southwick, J. (2005). *Asperger syndrome and difficult moments practical solutions for tantrums, rage, and meltdowns.* Shawnee Mission, KS: Autism Asperger Publishing Co.

Smith Myles, B., Trautman, M. L., & Schelvan, R. L. (2004). *The hidden curriculum: Practical solutions for understanding unstated rules in social situations.* Shawnee Mission, KS: Autism Asperger Publishing Co.

Smith, S. W., & Yell, M. L. (2013). *A teacher's guide to preventing behavior problems in the elementary classroom.* Upper Saddle, NJ: Pearson Education, Inc.

Snell, M., & Brown, F. (2011). *Instruction for students with severe disabilities.* Boston, MA: Pearson.

Soares, D., Vannest, K., & Harrison, J. (2009). Computer aided self-monitoring to increase academic production and reduce self-injurious behavior in a child with autism. *Behavioral Interventions, 24,* 171–183.

Sofronoff, K., Attwood, T., Hinton, S., & Levin, I. (2007). A randomized controlled trial ofa cognitive behavioural intervention for anger management in children diagnosed with Asperger syndrome. *Journal of Autism and Developmental Disorders, 37,* 1203–1214.

Stahmer, A. C., & Schreibman, L. (1992). Teaching children with autism appropriate play in unsupervised environments using a self-management treatment package. *Journal of Applied Behavior Analysis, 25,* 447–459.

Stang, K., Carter, E., Lane, K., & Pierson, M. (2009). Perspectives of general and special educators on fostering self-determination in elementary and middle school. *Journal of Special Education, 43,* 94–106.

Storey, K., & Post, M. (2012). *Positive behavior supports in classrooms and schools.* Springfield, IL: Charles C. Thomas, LT.

Sugai, G., Horner, R. H., Dunlap, G., Hicneman, M., Nelson, C. M., Scott, T., . . . Ruef, M. (2000). Applying positive behavior support and functional behavioral assessment in schools. *Journal of Positive Behavior Interventions, 2*(3), 131–143.

Sullivan, L., & Bogin, J. (2010a). Overview of extinction. Sacramento: CA. National Professional Development Center on Autism Spectrum Disorders, M.I.N.D Institute. University of California at Davis Medical School.

Sullivan, L., & Bogin, J. (2010b). Steps for implementation: Extinction. Sacramento, CA: The National Professional Development Center on Autism Spectrum Disorders, M.I.N.D Institute, University of California at Davis School of Medicine.

Taylor, S. (2006). Christmas in purgatory: A retrospective look. *American Association of Mental Retardation, 44,* 145–149.

Test, D. W., Fowler, C. H., Wood, W. M., Brewer, D. M., & Eddy, S. (2005). A conceptual framework of self-advocacy for students with disabilities. *Remedial and Special Education, 26(1)*, 43–54.

Test, D. W., Smith, L. E., & Carter, E. W. (2014). Equipping youth with autism spectrum disorders for adulthood: Promoting rigor, relevance, and relationships. *Remedial and Special Education, 35(2)*, 80–90.

The IRIS Center for Training Enhancements. (2005). *Addressing disruptive and noncompliant behaviors (part 2): Behavioral interventions.* Retrieved March 21, 2015 from http://iris.peabody.vanderbilt.edu/module/bi2/#content.

Thoma, C., & Getzel, E. (2005). Self-determination is what it's all about: What post- secondary students with disabilities tell us are important considerations for success. *Education and Training in Developmental Disabilities, 40(3)*, 234–242.

Turnbull, A., Hank, E., Griggs, P., Wickham, D., Wayne, S., Freeman, R., . . . Warren, J. (2002). A blueprint for schoolwide positive behavior support: Implementation of three components. *Exceptional Children, 68(3)*, 377–402.

Van Reusen, A. K., Bos, C. S., Schumaker, J. B., & Deshler, D. D. (2007, January 1). Self-advocacy strategy student. Retrieved March 14, 2015 from www.edgeenter prisesinc.com/product_detail.php?product_id=87.

Van Tubbergen, M., Warshausky, S., Birnholz, J., & Baker, S. (2008). Choice beyond preference: Conceptualization and assessment of choice-making skills in children with significant impairments. *Rehabilitation Psychology, 53(1)*, 93–100.

Vincent, C. G., Randall, C., Cartledge, G., Tobin, T. J., & Swain-Braeway, J. (2011). Toward a conceptual integration of cultural responsiveness and school-wide positive behavior support. *Journal of Positive Behavior Interventions, 13(4)*, 219–229.

Wagner, M., Newman, L., Cameto, R., Javitz, H., & Valdes, K. (2012). A national picture of parent and youth participation in IEP and transition planning meeting. *Journal of Disability Policy Studies, 23*, 40–55.

Watanabe, M., & Sturmey, P. (2003). The effect of choice making opportunities during activity schedules on task engagement of adults with autism. *Journal of Autism and Developmental Disabilities, 33(5)*, 535–538.

Wehmeyer, M. (2005). Self-determination and individuals with severe disabilities: Re-examining meanings and misinterpretations. *The Association for Persons with Severe Disabilities, 30*, 113–120.

Wehmeyer, M. (1992). Self-determination: Critical skills for outcome-oriented transition services: Steps in transition that lead to self-determination. *The Journal for Vocational Special Needs Education, 15*, 3–7.

Wehmeyer, M., & Schwartz, M. (1997). The self-determination focus of transition goals for students with mental retardation. *Career Development for Exceptional Individuals, 21*, 75–86.

Wehmeyer, M., & Shogren, K., Zager, D., Smith, T., & Simpson, R. (2010). Research-based principles and practices for educating students with autism: Self-determination and social interactions. *Education and Training in Autism and Developmental Disabilities, 45(4)*, 475–486.

West, E. A. (2008). Effects of verbal cues versus pictorial cues on the transfer of stimulus control for children with autism. *Focus on Autism and Other Developmental Disabilities, 23(4)*, 229–241.

Wheeler, J. J., & Richey, D. D. (2014). *Behavior management: Principles and practices of positive behavior supports* (3rd ed.). Upper Saddle, NJ: Pearson Education, Inc.

Wolfe, A. M., & Wood, B. K. (2013). Use of functional assessment to address the fainting of an adolescent boy with traumatic brain injury: A case study. *Beyond Behavior*, 23(1), 46–58.

Wong, C., Odom, S. L., Hume, K., Cox, A. W., Fettig, A., Kucharczyk, S., . . . Schultz, T. R. (2013). *Evidence-based practices for children, youth, and young adults with Autism Spectrum Disorder.* Chapel Hill: The University of North Carolina, Frank Porter Graham Child Development Institute, Autism Evidence-Based Practice Review Group.

Zirpoli, T. J. (2012). *Behavior management: Positive applications for teachers* (6th ed.). Upper Saddle, NJ: Pearson Education, Inc.

Chapter 15

The Transition from High School to Higher Education

Inclusive Services and Supports

L. Lynn Stansberry-Brusnahan, Marc Ellison, and Dedra Hafner

By establishing that separate educational facilities were inherently unequal, the United States civil rights movement contributed to equal access and opportunity for minority populations previously segregated from society. Building off of this movement, the Individuals with Disabilities Education Act (IDEA, 2004) ensures that students with disabilities have the right to access a free appropriate public education (FAPE) that prepares them for further education, employment, and independent living. Public laws such as the Higher Education Opportunity Act (HEOA, 2008) improve access to appropriate education services for students with intellectual disabilities who wish to participate in education after high school. The HEOA, however, does not include an FAPE mandate like IDEA.

Postsecondary education (PSE) or higher education can be defined as all learning options available to students following high school (HS) (Grigal & Hart, 2010). PSE covers a broad range of educational options including vocational/technical schools and community colleges that teach a trade (e.g. childcare, food service, plumbing), short-term continuing education, credit and non-credit continuing academic coursework leading to a certificate, a license, or an associate degree, and institutes of higher education (IHE). In this chapter, IHE refers specifically to four-year colleges or universities offering higher education such as a bachelor's degree (Shaw, Madaus, & Dukes, 2010).

Unfortunately, a student who received special education support in HS will not automatically qualify for services in the PSE environment. When a student with a disability transitions to higher education environments, he or she moves from the mandates of the IDEA to the civil rights protections of Section 504 of the Rehabilitation Act (1973) and the Americans with Disabilities Act (ADA, 1990). Public and private universities and colleges that receive federal money must comply with Section 504 and ADA.

Section 504, subpart E stipulates that qualified individuals may not be denied or subjected to discrimination in admission or excluded from participation in activities such as academic, athletics, recreation, or other extracurricular activities in PSE on the basis of a disability (Zager & Smith, 2012). PSE programs must provide students with disabilities appropriate academic adjustments and auxiliary aids. The ADA also protects individuals with disabilities against discrimination in PSE settings. This act does not require IHEs to make modifications that would alter fundamental requirements of an academic course, but does protect qualified students with disabilities by requiring access to reasonable accommodations.

In this chapter, the focus is on individuals with autism spectrum disorders (ASD) with and without co-occurring intellectual disabilities (ID) and/or mental health challenges. Autism has been clearly defined in other chapters within this text. HEOA defines ID as a student who currently or formerly was eligible for a FAPE under the IDEA and has a cognitive impairment, characterized by significant limitations in (a) intellectual and cognitive functioning; and (b) adaptive behavior as expressed in conceptual, social, and practical adaptive skills.

A growing number of students with disabilities, who have been included in K-12 general education classes and experienced success, expect that inclusion will continue into PSE (Hart, Zimbrich, & Parker, 2005). Previously, low expectations coupled with minimal opportunities have prevented many students with disabilities from receiving the opportunity to acquire PSE contributing to poor outcomes. For example, over one in three young adults with ASD do not transition into either PSE or employment after HS, with 28 percent of these individuals not receiving any services (Roux, Shattuck, Rast, Rava, & Anderson, 2015). Typically, individuals with ID including those with ASD have had difficulty being accepted through the standard college admission procedures and accessing services in PSE (Grigal & Hart, 2010; Hartz, 2014). With support from the Office of Postsecondary Education (OPE), Transition and Postsecondary Programs for Students with Intellectual Disability (TPSIDs) have been created at a number of IHEs so that previously excluded individuals with disabilities can think about college (Grigal, et al., 2014). With many individuals with

Table 15.1 Legal Protections

Level	Legal Protection	Advocacy	Support
K-12	IDEA mandates free and appropriate education.	Student and parents advocate.	Adaptations, accommodations, and modifications included in IEP.
Postsecondary	Section 504 and ADA provides access.	Student advocates.	No IEP. Modifications are required only to provide access.

Source: Think College (n.d.). Differences between high school and college.

ASD having the academic ability to meet entrance criteria and initiatives to open higher education campuses to individuals with ID, increasing numbers of students with disabilities are expected to be present at colleges and universities.

Since 1987 there has been a 70 percent increase in youth with disabilities completing HS (Wagner, Newman, Cameto, & Levine, 2005), and the National Longitudinal Studies (NLTS) reveal that students with disabilities seeking PSE have almost doubled since 1990 (Newman, Wagner, Cameto, Knokey, & Shaver, 2010). In this chapter, we highlight effective practices for preparation for students with ASD transitioning from HS to PSE experiences. We then describe the benefits of continued education and a variety of higher education models of services and supports for students with ASD. We also provide benchmarks of campus readiness, along with challenges to success at both the institutional and ASD level. Lastly, we present effective practices at the PSE level to meet the needs of college and university students with ASD.

Effective Practices in High School

Research to date suggests that many students with disabilities lack PSE success because educational programs fail to offer comprehensive transition programming to help them succeed (Nietupski, McQuillen, Duncan Berg, Daugherty, & Hamre-Nietupski, 2001). Identification of factors that play a role in PSE success is essential to inform educational practices and interventions prior to HS graduation. When examining the secondary to postsecondary transition within the lens of practices that contribute to success and perseverance, factors that have been identified as critical include: (a) focusing on PSE during transition planning; (b) utilizing universal design for transition (UDT) principles; (c) creating a summary of performance (SoP); and (d) enhancing self-determination skills.

Transition Planning for Higher Education

For many years, public school educational programs have primarily focused on preparing individuals with disabilities for postsecondary transition to employment (Witte, 2001). Statistics reveal that only 11–12.6 percent of students with ASD and ID have an HS transition goal for preparation for PSE in the IEP (Grigal, Hart, & Migliore, 2011; Newman, Wagner, Cameto, & Knokey, 2009). The mindset that a student with a disability will not attend or succeed in higher education can ultimately set up barriers in regards to future employment. Thus, educators should create goals focused on PSE for the increasing number of students with disabilities who wish to continue their education to provide them the same opportunities as their peers.

IDEA (2004) requires that transition services begin at age 16 or younger and consist of a coordinated set of activities focused on improving the academic and functional achievement to facilitate movement from school to post-school activities, including PSE. Educators are required to develop postsecondary goals based upon transition assessments related to training, education, employment, and independent living skills when appropriate. From the beginning of the discussion on transition in HS, transition goals and activities that will prepare a student for PSE should be part of the conversation.

Ensuring opportunities for success in PSE requires careful planning to assure that coursework, supports, and accommodations are provided (Shaw et al., 2010). A person-centered planning process can identify individual goals and help students, families, and professionals create plans that support students as they strive to achieve their dreams. According to the National Center on Secondary and Education and Transition (NCSET, 2004), the person-centered planning process can strengthen the transition to postsecondary activities by:

- enhancing quality of assessments and planning;
- fostering positive collaborations, connections, and working relationships between student, families, school professionals, and outside agencies;
- providing better coordination of services and ensuring support for the student's goals;
- identifying and cultivating natural supports.

Many states start transition planning at age 14 to assure students are able to fulfill PSE goals. When planning a student's course of study, it is important not to waive HS courses that are needed in PSE, because this could limit access to higher education (Shaw et al., 2010). In addition to ensuring full academic access to HS courses, educators should teach independence, social, and interpersonal skills (Shaw et al., 2010).

Universal Design for Transition (UDT)

Universal design (UD) involves designing environments that can be accessed readily by the widest possible range of individuals (Rose, Harbour, Johnston, Daley, & Abarbanell, 2006). Universal design for learning (UDL) provides a framework to address instructional design and delivery to meet academic standards. Building off of UDL, an evidence-based practice available for preparing students for PSE is universal design for transition (UDT) (Scott et al., 2011). UDT addresses preparing students for a successful transition to adult life. The framework for UDL focuses on three specific principles: (a) representation of information, (b) expression of knowledge, and (c) engagement in learning.

UDT adds transition domains to this framework to link academic standards to transition domains. Planning should additionally involve: (a) transition domains, (b) transition assessments, (c) self-determination, and (d) transition resources (Thoma, Bartholomew, & Scott, 2009).

Summary of Performance (SoP)

Over a student's K-12 experience, schools accumulate a wealth of information including: functional and academic strengths; needed accommodations; successful strategies; and preferences. Previously, much of this important information did not exit with the student. IDEA (2004) requires schools to create a summary of performance (SoP), which is an exit from secondary school document focused on meeting the needs of a student in his or her post-HS environment. This exit document includes: (a) background information, (b) postsecondary goals, and (c) summary of academic achievement and functional performance along with recommendations on how to meet PSE goals. Table 15.2 highlights suggested contents to include in the SoP (National Transition Documentation Summit, 2005).

To capture a student's functional performance, it is important to conduct dynamic and collaborative transition assessments to assess the individual's strengths, interests, and preferences (Sitlington & Clark, 2007). Schools should utilize direct and indirect methods of assessment to gather information such as: (a) interviews, (b) observations, (c) standardized tests, (d) curriculum-based assessments, (e) performance samples, and (f) situational assessments (Koehler, 2013). When planning assessments for the student who will be attending a college or university, it is helpful

---

Table 15.2 Summary of Performance Contents

Background information

- Student name, birth date, graduation date
- Disability information
- Individualized education program (IEP) or Section 504 plan information
- Most recent copy of diagnostic and functional assessments

Postsecondary goals

- Goal(s) focused on the postsecondary environment(s) the student intends to transition to upon completion of HS

Summary of performance

- Academic, cognitive, and functional levels of performance
- Adaptations (e.g. accommodations, modifications, assistive technology) utilized to assist the student in achieving progress
- Recommendations to assist the student in meeting postsecondary goals

Source: National Transition Documentation Summit, 2005

to determine PSE support needs in areas such as: (a) academics, (b) independent living skills, (c) socialization, (d) safety, (e) sexuality, (f) stress, and (g) self-determination.

The SoP is viewed as a powerful tool that can provide a seamless transition and bridge the gap as students shift from the secondary to post-secondary environment (Sopko, 2008; Shaw, Dukes, & Madaus, 2012). Local education agencies (LEAs) are required to create an SoP when a student's special education eligibility terminates due to exceeding the state's maximum age eligibility for a FAPE or due to graduation with an HS diploma or certificate. The SoP is to be completed no later than the final year of a student's HS education. The intent of the SoP is to provide information to those who may assist the individual in the future, thus providing that information when it is most timely makes the most sense. Some LEAs wait until spring of a student's final year to provide the most up-to-date information on performance. LEAs could choose to prepare an SOP earlier for students who are meeting with an accessibility and disability services professional at a college or university.

The SoP can be linked with the IEP transition planning process. While the SoP is connected to information contained in the IEP, it should be a separate document which condenses, summarizes, and organizes key information to provide the student's next location with information to help them get to know the individual. The document should be written in a clear non-jargon manner so that personnel without backgrounds in disability and/or special education can interpret the information and to assure that the student understands the contents. The SoP should include information about life goals.

Higher education programs set their own standards in relation to required documentation to establish that an individual has a disability and is eligible for support (Shaw et al., 2012). Prior to the ADA Amendments Act of 2008 (ADAAA) being enacted into law, colleges and universities required students to prove that they had a disability by presenting a statement of the disability, usually by a health care or educational professional. This documentation needed to be submitted to the Disability Services Office before accommodations would be put in place. Students who didn't have the proper documentation of their condition incurred additional expenses for psychological or other testing, or the accommodations were delayed while the college waited for medical records. Amendments and revisions have made it easier to obtain protection under the ADA by helping clarify (a) who has a disability entitled to protection under the ADA and Section 504, (b) who is entitled to accommodations, and (c) how those determinations are made and by whom. There is no legislation, nor are there regulations, that require documentation of the disability in order to receive reasonable accommodations from a college or university. Colleges and universities may not withhold accommodations based on waiting for proof-of-disability documentation. Congress stated that the ADA establishes the "floor" not the "ceiling" of protection (AHEAD, 2012).

The Association of Higher Education and Disability provides guidelines for disability service offices to identify acceptable sources for disability disclosure and substantiating a student's disabilities (AHEAD, 2012). First, the disability service professional should consider the student's self-disclosure as the primary source to document a student's disability and their need for accommodations. The student can provide their own narrative of their history, barriers, and effective accommodations. Second, the higher education disability professionals can also gather their own impressions through a process of interactions with and observations of the student. Third, even though submission of documents is not required, students can provide to colleges and universities documentation from external, third-party sources such as the Individual Education Program (IEP) or a Summary of Performance (SOP) from a school district. Thus the SoP may assist in determining eligibility for PSE disability support services and/or accommodations and provide information on how to best support a student in the higher education environment.

Educators should ensure student involvement in the development of the SoP as the greater the involvement, the greater the likelihood of the individual understanding their disability and corresponding needs (Gil, 2007). In PSE, students must be able to self-disclose their disability in order to receive accommodations. Getting a student involved in the SoP process is an excellent way to facilitate a deeper understanding of his or her disability (Kochhar-Bryant & Izzo, 2006).

Self-determination Skills

A powerful predictor of positive postsecondary outcomes is self-determination skills (Kohler & Field, 2003; Landmark, Ju, & Zhang, 2010). Self-determination skills enable individuals to problem-solve, self-advocate, self-manage, set goals, and make choices and decisions that impact their lives (Agran & Krupp, 2011; Rowe, Mazzotti, & Sinclair, 2015; Wehmeyer, Shogren, Smith, Zager, & Simpson, 2010; Zhang & Benz, 2006). Teaching self-determination is important because as students transition from HS to PSE, the responsibility for advocacy shifts from relying on accommodations to be arranged by school personnel or parents directly to the individual with the disability. To contribute to more positive PSE outcomes, schools should focus transition planning on the development of key self-determination skills (Test, Fowler, Wood, Brewer, & Eddy, 2005). Self-determination skills are critical, yet, it is estimated that only 50 percent of public schools implement curricula to teach these skills to secondary students with disabilities

(Kochhar-Bryant & Izzo, 2006). Recommendations to ensure that students graduate HS with self-determination skills include: (a) embed self-determination skills in IEP goals; (b) teach self-determination skills; and (c) teach self-advocacy and goal-setting skills.

Embed Skills in IEP Goals

Schools should embed self-determination in student's IEP goals, as there is a positive correlation between the degree of self-determination and quality of life for individuals with disabilities (Wehmeyer & Schwartz, 1998). Research suggests educators know the importance of providing instruction in self-determination, yet few address these skills in IEP goals (Wehmeyer, Agran, & Hughes, 2000; Wehmeyer & Schwartz, 1998). Educators play a vital role in promoting the acquisition of self-determined behaviors and must work collaboratively with students, families, and the community to find opportunities to expose and support students in instruction that facilitates the growth of self-determination skills (Rowe et al., 2015; Wehmeyer et al., 2010). Embedding self-determination in IEP goals promotes educators working on teaching these important life skills.

Teach Self-disclosure Skills

Schools should help students understand their disability and rights in regards to self-disclosure. Students who are unable to articulate their disability or needs may be unable to initiate or request needed accommodations (Gil, 2007). Thus, transition programming should provide the student with an understanding of his/her disability, including its effect on the individual in school and work environments. Students should leave HS knowing how, when, and where to request needed accommodations.

In PSE settings, students with disabilities must disclose or inform the disability services on campus of their disability. Disclosure can be defined as the individual telling the college, university or an individual professor about a documented disability and requesting accommodations. Educators should teach a student his or her rights and best ways in which to self-advocate for assistance and disclose disability. Educators should teach students to access, accept, and use individually needed supports and accommodations. Students with disabilities can first begin to apply their self-advocacy skills within the context of HS IEP meetings when the multidisciplinary team discusses the student's educational program (Field & Hoffman, 2007). IDEA (2004) requires the individual with a disability be invited to attend the IEP team meeting if a purpose of the meeting will be the consideration of the postsecondary goals and the transition services needed to assist in reaching those goals. Students' participation in the development of the SoP is another opportunity for students to practice self-advocacy and decision-making skills as well as better understand their disability (Kochhar-Bryant & Izzo, 2006).

Teach Self-advocacy and Goal-setting Skills

It is important for students with disabilities to develop self-determination skills for the transition to postsecondary settings so they can self-advocate for the supports and services they need for success (Eckes & Ochoa, 2005; Field & Hoffman, 2007; Gil, 2007; Kochhar-Bryant & Izzo, 2006; Madaus, 2005; Test et al., 2005; Wehmeyer & Schwartz, 1997). Once a student understands their disability and rights, educators should teach them strategies to solve problems and reach goals (Agran, Blanchard, & Wehmeyer, 2000; Agran, Cavin, Wehmeyer, & Palmer, 2006; Wehmeyer et al., 2010). Individuals with disabilities who possess self-determination skills can self-advocate for their needs (Test et al., 2005; Wehmeyer et al., 2010).

Higher Education Benefits for Individuals with Disabilities

The College Board (Baum, Ma, & Payea, 2013) reports that PSE benefits include higher quality of life such as increased health, longevity, and happiness. IHEs offer coursework and subjects that individuals with disabilities may not have access to in HS (Grigal, Neubert, & Moon, 2002) allowing an individual to gain additional knowledge and skills (Hartz, 2014; Moon, Grigal, & Neubert, 2001; Uditsky & Hughson, 2012). This section highlights some benefits of participation in higher education for individuals with disabilities which include: (a) economic and employment, (b) inclusive and social, (c) self-determination, and (d) independent living.

Economic and Employment Benefits

Higher education can lead to financial benefits, such as a successful career path and enhanced lifetime earnings (Carnevale, Rose, & Cheah, 2011). More specifically, the College Board (Baum et al., 2013) reports PSE benefits include more stable and meaningful employment and greater job satisfaction. The U.S. Bureau of Labor national statistics (2011) reveals that education pays in higher earnings. Many of today's jobs require training and PSE can prepare individuals for high-growth employment opportunities. According to the U.S. Department of Education, approximately 90 percent of the fastest growing job areas require PSE. Since 2000, there has been a pattern of higher unemployment rates corresponding with lower levels of educational attainment (U.S. Department of Education, 2013). The median annual earnings of individuals' aged

25–34 years with an associate or bachelor's degree are greater than individuals who only complete HS (U.S. Department of Education, 2013).

Even with some college attendance but no degree, individuals earn 14 percent more than high school graduates working full time, with their median after-tax earnings 13 percent higher (Baum et al., 2013). When comparing peers with and without disabilities, youth with disabilities have significantly lower PSE, lower earnings, limited employment options, higher rates of poverty, and are disproportionately represented in low-skilled jobs (Hart et al., 2005).

One predictor of a greater likelihood of employment for students with disabilities is having a PSE transition goal (Grigal et al., 2011). Access to opportunities afforded by PSE can make a difference in employability of individuals with disabilities (Gilmore, Schuster, Zafft, & Hart, 2001). Youth with disabilities who complete PSE are likely to have more opportunities and be competitively employed and obtain higher earnings than peers who do not further their education (Gilmore, et. al., 2001; Lindstrom, Doren, & Miesch, 2011). Findings show that individuals with disabilities who have taken even some amount of PSE are employed at double the rate of those with just an HS diploma (Gilmore, Bose, & Hart, 2001). As a result of employment outcomes, more vocational agencies have begun to recognize PSE as a path to employment for students with disabilities (Thacker & Sheppard-Jones, 2011). In this increasingly competitive workforce, individuals need every bit of education and training they can get, especially with the positive relationships found between levels of education, employment, and disability (Wehman, 2002).

Inclusive and Social Benefits

There are many advantages to higher education inclusion and numerous social benefits for students with disabilities. In addition to PSE providing the opportunity to develop students as lifelong learners (Hart et al., 2005), it provides a unique opportunity for young adults with disabilities to develop a sense of community and belonging (Hafner, 2008). Participating in higher education can improve integration and provide increased opportunities for socialization and friendships with typical peers (Hartz, 2014; Moon et al., 2001; Uditsky & Hughson, 2012). The college campus provides students with disabilities opportunities to have inclusive and social contact (Hartz, 2014) with socially appropriate role models that they can observe and imitate (Alper, 2003). Through social interactions, individuals can build their social communication skills (Alper, 2003). IHEs provide individuals with disability social outlets through campus organizations such as fraternities, sororities, clubs, and athletics. These outlets provide access for individuals with disabilities to engage in non-academic activities (Grigal et al., 2002) and can expand social networks and involvement with people without disabilities (Hart et al., 2005). This involvement increases the probability that students with disabilities will continue to participate in a variety of integrated settings throughout their lives (Alper, 2003).

Self-determination Benefits

Self-determination is an important element of both special education and transition services for youth with disabilities (Hartz, 2014). There is evidence to support the importance and impact of promoting self-determination in the lives of students with disabilities (Cobb, Lehmann, Newman-Gonchar, & Alwell, 2009; Wehmeyer et al., 2011). The demands of living and learning on campus create an ideal place to gain self-advocacy skills (Lindstrom et al., 2011). Participating in higher education allows an individual to build self-confidence (Hartz, 2014; Moon et al., 2001; Uditsky & Hughson, 2012). PSE provides a unique opportunity for young adults with disabilities to develop a sense of identity (Hafner, 2008). Students with disabilities report acting and viewing themselves differently after the opportunity to learn in a PSE-inclusive setting (Folk, Yamamoto, & Stodden, 2012). In addition, students report that PSE at an IHE influenced them to learn more, reach their own potential, and show other people what they could do (Folk et al., 2012).

Independent Living Skills Benefits

Going to college or a university is a natural stepping stone, as independent living skills are an important part of learning for all PSE students with and without disabilities (Hartz, 2014). Leaving home and moving to a campus can increase critical life skills that contribute to the successful, independent functioning of an individual in adulthood (Alwell & Cobb, 2009; Bouck, 2004). To be successful after HS, students with disabilities are likely to have better adult outcomes if they are able to master functional independent living skills (Bouck, 2010). Thus, it is important to provide students with opportunities to develop and learn life skills, which may require repeated instruction in different settings (Carothers & Taylor, 2004). The demands of living and learning on campus create an ideal place to gain independence (Lindstrom et al., 2011). When students with disabilities live in integrated settings, this can contribute to positive outcomes and enhance their academic performance, personal, and social development (De Araujo & Murray, 2010). From typical peers, students with disabilities can learn about responsibility, self-discipline, and increased independence by becoming part of the college community (Hafner & Moffatt, 2012).

Higher Education Participation

Inclusion in higher education is a term with varying definitions, both in the literature and in descriptions of inclusive programs. This section highlights some of the different higher education service delivery approaches for the inclusion of students with disabilities on the college or university campus. Some students with disabilities are able to access higher education through traditional disability support services and/or dual enrollment while in HS. Additional identified approaches include: (a) inclusive individual, (b) substantially separate, and (c) mixed hybrid (Hart, Grigal, Sax, Martinez, & Will, 2006). Table 15.3 provides an overview of these models. The following sections describe some of the distinguishing features of each approach.

Disability Support Services Model

This model incorporates a traditional disability services support approach for the student who meets the traditional admissions process and is

Table 15.3 Higher Education Participation for Individuals with Disabilities

Models	Student Participation	Admission
Traditional disability services	Students participate in courses, certificate programs, and degree programs through the use of disability support services for qualified individuals with disabilities (Graham-Smith & LaFayette, 2004).	Traditional with qualified disability.
Dual enrollment: High school transition partnership	Students participate in courses, certificate programs, and degree programs through transition partnerships using dual enrollment with school districts (Moon et al., 2001).	Student is still in high school and not officially a college or university student.
Inclusive individual	Students participate in courses, certificate programs, and degree programs and receive individual services and supports guided by their personal vision and career goals (Hart et al., 2006).	Traditional.
Substantially separate	Students participate in courses primarily with other students with disabilities. They may participate in social activities on campus and have employment experiences.	Alternative.
Mixed hybrid	Students participate in academic courses and/or social activities with peers with and without disabilities.	Traditional or alternative.

Source: Grigal & Hart, 2010; Hart et al., 2006

deemed qualified to take courses towards earning a degree. This model relies on the college or university disability services office providing equal access and reasonable accommodations to qualified individuals with disabilities to support academic access (Duffy & Gugerty, 2005). With this model, a student is responsible for self-disclosure and providing documentation of his or her disability. If qualified, the student can request accommodations be made for his or her disability to provide access to academic programs (Schutz, 2002). Accommodations typically originate from recommendations from a professional (e.g. psychologist, psychiatrist, counselor, educational diagnostician) and may be based on a student's educational SoP. Research has found that students who frequently use available disability support services have better self-advocacy skills and higher grade point averages (GPA) compared to students who use the supports infrequently (Getzel, McManus, & Briel, 2004). Common characteristics of this approach include (Graham-Smith & LaFayette, 2004):

- Tutor and provide academic support.
- Permit test accommodations (extra test time or an alternative testing site).
- Provide comprehensive orientation and early registration.
- Assist or provide additional training focused on life skills (time management).
- Allow utilization of auxiliary aids and needed assistive technology.

Dual Enrollment: Transition Partnership Model

The dual enrollment or transition partnership program model *bridges* the transition from HS to PSE. This process begins with transition goals, designed through person-centered planning, to meet the needs, preferences, and interests of an individual student (Grigal, Neubert, Moon, & Graham, 2003). An IEP higher education goal sets the stage for a student with a disability to participate in PSE with transition preparation, assistance, and supports or services provided by partnerships with school programs, adult agency services, and natural supports in the community (Whetstone & Browning, 2002). As a result of IDEA, a HS student, through the utilization of an IEP, may gain access to higher education through dual enrollment in HS and a PSE program (Hart et al., 2006). In this model, students may receive transition services through a local school district while participating in activities on an IHE campus. Providing services in the PSE settings gives students with disabilities between the ages of 18 and 21 an age-appropriate environment for their public education and transition experiences. The types of transition programs on college campuses within this model are often initiated by parents, school districts, and community service providers using a method of blended funding from the local school district, the state vocational rehabilitation agency, community service providers, and parents to pay for tuition, housing and program support agency (Neubert, Moon, Grigal, & Redd, 2002). With this model, an IHE and LEA partner to offer a program where transition-aged students enroll as special students and audit or take credit-bearing or non-credit continuing education courses and/or activities with typical students without disabilities. This model might offer a menu of individualized supports and services (Hart et al., 2005). Common characteristics of this model include:

- Provide dual enrollment in the K-12 educational system and PSE for students between the ages of 18 and 21 with disabilities.
- Fund through the LEA's postsecondary program. This can be accomplished in two ways. The first approach is that the school district can consider the IHE as a community environment for teaching functional and foundational skills and provide all the staff support and student accommodations. The program remains under the auspices of the local school district with support staff employed by the school district. A second approach is the IHE can provide a transition program for students and build costs of specialized supports into tuition with the LEA financing this model. Students have access to IHE facilities and may audit courses while they are still technically HS students (Neubert et al., 2002). In some cases, professors and/or departments are contracted to provide special course sessions designed to include transition students (Moon *et al.*, 2001).

Inclusive Individual Model

An inclusive individual support model strives to meet the true intent of full inclusion and offers a menu of areas of study and activities, as well as individual services and adequate supports (Hart et al., 2006). This model incorporates a person-centered approach and a plan of study is created and guided by the student's personal vision and career goals. Students can audit or take classes for credit working towards a possible certificate, internship or degree (Stodden & Whelley, 2004). In this model, academic classes and non-academic activities are not separate, so there are no special programs or specially designated classes for the students with disabilities. Value is placed on the beneficial experience of inclusion to both students with disabilities and to the greater community (Weinkauf, 2002). These inclusive programs try to reflect natural proportions. This type of model provides opportunities to engage in extracurricular activities, facilitates relationships through natural activities and interests, and does not seek out students to volunteer to be *buddies* in prearranged relationships (Greenholtz, Mosoff, & Hurtado, 2005). In this model, students might engage in meaningful paid employment.

Common characteristics of an inclusive individualized model include:

- Provide access to students with disabilities.
- Provide an inclusive environment that mirrors a typical undergraduate IHE experience to students with disabilities.
- Ensure that students with disabilities have socially valued roles through participation in the same activities and environments as peers.
- View IHEs as a natural transition and pathway to the world of work and community involvement.
- View all students as adult learners.
- Extend education beyond the classroom and do not limit student's education to just classroom learning.
- Plan for success utilizing a person-centered planning focus, which might include support services based on student choices and preferences.
- Provide opportunities for students to establish friendships and relationships.
- Provide individualized services, accommodations, and supports to ensure access and participation.
- Matriculate students to work towards completion of a course of study resulting in employment.
- Provide job training and/or opportunities for internships.
- Design a student-centered program of inclusion where the student's disability is not their defining characteristic.
- Fund through a collaboration by the college, local public school district, and the family.

Substantially Separate Model

A substantially separate model provides individuals with disabilities a college-like experience that may take place on a college campus but offers a separate academic program from the traditional college students. This model provides a college atmosphere in a self-contained program for students with disabilities on a campus. Referred to as life skills or transition programs, the program may be based on a college campus but students do not have sustained interaction with others in the general student body. In this model, students participate only in life skills and transition classes with other students with disabilities. This model does not generally provide the option of taking standard college courses with peers who do not have disabilities. In some of the programs utilizing this model there may be a small percentage of students taking college credit courses, with this accomplished through online distance learning and/or cooperative partnerships with the IHEs. But generally, the students have a presence on campus without the typical academic component of the experience. PSE programs with separate programs tend to serve a larger number of students than the mixed/hybrid or independently inclusive programs (Hart et al., 2005). This model's curriculum generally emphasizes vocational training, independent living, developmental growth, and leisure time activities. This model may provide opportunities for students with disabilities to participate in generic social activities on campus and employment experiences through pre-established employment slots (Hart et al., 2006). In this model, students may have access to campus cafeterias, unions, libraries, and exercise facilities. Common characteristics of this model include:

- Participate in a separate program from the matriculated course of study provided to other students.
- Provide housing in separate dorm-like settings or large apartments.
- Participate in a schedule that does not follow a typical college routine.
- Participation may not result in recognized certificates, licenses, or degrees.
- Participate in limited to no interaction with peers without disabilities.
- Focus on the life skills curriculum.
- Staff with special education teachers and adult service providers, not by college faculty.
- Provide job training
- Fund through the local public education school districts or by the family.

There are also programs offering life skills or transition programs that utilize the term "college" in their name or description of their program, but they are not actually based on or linked in any way to an IHE campus.

Mixed and Hybrid Models

In a review of inclusion in PSE, more than half of the programs use an approach that has a mixed or hybrid combination of inclusive and non-inclusive features (Hart *et al.*, 2005). A mixed or hybrid program model incorporates a combination of integrated campus courses of study, as well as substantially separate life skills programs on the IHE campus (Stodden & Whelley, 2004). A National Survey on Postsecondary Programs for Youth with Intellectual Disabilities findings indicate over that 50 percent offer a combination of separate settings or segregated classrooms (Hart et al., 2005). In this model, students are supported to take standard academic courses and to participate in campus-wide recreational and social activities while also providing a focus on functional life skills. Thus, students with disabilities are supported, on a limited basis, in taking typical college courses, as well as providing separate life skill courses. Some of these programs are designed to admit a small number of students per year between the typical ages of 18 and 25. Programs utilizing this model generally provide an individualized, student-centered plan of study that might include objectives in areas such as: (a) general studies, (b) vocational development, (c) independent life, and (d) socialization. Students may work to possibly earn a certificate or matriculate into an accredited degree program. Programs utilizing this model might provide students with trained college peer mentors who assist in tutoring and social inclusion. These programs might provide on-campus residency, meaning students are housed on campus. This model provides interaction with the general student body through campus events. Common characteristics of this model include:

- Participate in college academic courses (audit or modified courses).
- Participate in separate classes, such as life skills or transition classes.
- Participate in social activities with students with and without disabilities.
- Provide employment experiences on and off campus.
- Fund through a collaboration of college, local public school districts, and families.

Challenges Related to Higher Education of Students with ASD

Research to date suggests that effectively meeting the challenges related to the PSE of students with ASD requires a combination of services and supports such as those embedded in the models just discussed. In addition to an array of evidence-based strategies being necessary to meet the needs of students with disabilities, holistic supports that address all areas of campus living—including mental health—may be necessary. Ellison, Clark, Cunningham, and Hansen (2013) employed a Delphi survey of experts on the topic of ASD in higher education to identify the support needs of IHE students on the autism spectrum. Some of these findings include:

- *Finances and resources* dedicated to non-academic needs, such as needs associated with social and independent living-skill challenges common to ASD, are important for success.
- Assistance with *social interaction, independent living*, and *cognitive organization* needs are potentially more important for this student population than *academic* supports. Resources dedicated to *social challenges* are integral to successful outcomes for students with ASD.
- *Campus-based knowledge about ASD* is integral to the provision of successful support services. Dedicated staff with specialized ASD training, a campus community that is well informed about the autism spectrum, and a well-staffed support program that employs ASD specialists foster success. This knowledge can influence positive *faculty and staff attitudes* about ASD, which may be fundamental to success for IHE students with autism.

Unfortunately, faculty and staff within higher education are often puzzled by students on the autism spectrum. Recognizing and understanding ASD can be difficult for college personnel because of the continuum of how individual students experience characteristics of the disorder, which may range from mild to profound (Ellison, Hovatter, & Nelson, 2013; Farrell, 2004; VanBergeijk, Klin, & Volkmar, 2008). As a result, faculty may be unsure of how to recognize challenges in the classroom, and disability service staff may be unsure of how to design appropriate services. Understanding challenges related to ASD, as well as overcoming institutional barriers, appears integral to proper supports (Ellison et al., 2013). Campus readiness, institutional attitudes, and characteristics of ASD can all serve as barriers that prevent students with ASD from experiencing success on a college campus.

Campus Readiness

Ellison et al. (2013) created benchmarks of effective supports for PSE students with ASD from research. The benchmarks are organized into three support areas: (a) campus living, (b) academic, and (d) non-academic. The benchmarks outline the holistic services and institutional culture necessary to best support PSE students with ASD (see Table 15.4).

Institutional Barriers

There are many institutional barriers that can stand in the way of an individual with ASD experiencing success in the PSE setting. These barriers include breaking down the perception of who the higher education student is and the attitudinal bias that accompanies this historical perspective. Another institutional barrier includes a lack of holistic supports.

History and Tradition

Higher education is noted for having a long, historical resistance to change. In 1973, fewer than 3 percent of all college students in the United States disclosed a disability (Madeus, 2011). Change appears to be especially difficult when it involves the enrollment of what was once considered *non-traditional students*. Wechsler (2007, p. 442) wrote:

> The arrival of a new constituency on a college campus has rarely been an occasion for unmitigated joy. Perhaps such students brought with them much needed tuition dollars. In that case, their presence was accepted and tolerated. Yet higher education officials, and often students from traditional constituencies, usually perceived the arrival of new groups not as a time for rejoicing, but as a problem: a threat to an institution's stated mission (official fear) or to its social life (student fear).

Table 15.4 Benchmarks of Effective Supports for Higher Education for ASD

Campus living supports	• Dedicated finances and on-campus resources for supporting students with ASD. • On-campus expertise regarding ASD and the supports necessary for an effective college experience. • Professionals who assist with the development of on-campus social networks. • Professionals who assess and teach independent living skills. • Mentoring services that support organizational needs, such as: goal setting, meeting deadlines, completing assignments, and planning. • Mentoring services that assist students in recognizing a need for self-advocacy, and to support skill development for carrying out the activity. • Professionals who facilitate social learning and skill development.
Academic supports	• Access to basic academic adjustments and reasonable accommodations (extended time on tests, note-taking services) necessary for success in the classroom. • Professionals available to provide information, support, and assistance to faculty and academic staff. • Existing systems dedicated to teaching self-advocacy and disclosure skills necessary for positive academic outcomes. • Professionals available to provide assistance with academic organization, guidance, and mentoring. • Existing systems that provide specialized assistance to educators, staff, and other college personnel to aid or improve academic outcomes. • An on-campus support program that provides traditional academic accommodations, but recognizes the importance of delivering supports for identified non-academic needs.
Non-academic supports	• Professionals available to teach skills necessary for social networking. • Professionals available to teach and mentor the development of social communication skills. • Professionals available to provide assistance with identifying available on-campus and off-campus resources. • Professionals available to provide assistance with learning or improving independent living skills. • Mental health professionals trained to provide assessment, counseling and other therapeutic services to students with ASD.

Note:
Used with permission: Ellison et al., 2013

Non-traditional students with disabilities require a university to have to interpret the government's broad instructions on the delivery of support services within higher education (Dillon, 2007; Hughes, 2009). The broadness of the instructions results in various interpretations as to how disability support services within higher education must be carried out to provide equal opportunity for individuals with disabilities. Some of the interpretations about what is considered discrimination on the basis of disability are played out in the United States Courts. For example, there have been court decisions that have centered on testing accommodations.

Examinations are meant to be a fair assessment of a student's knowledge and skills. Several cases, to date, provide clarification of the requirements for testing accommodations to accurately reflect individual achievement. In the 2011 case of *Enyart v. National Conference of Bar Examiners Inc.*, the courts required the provision of a laptop equipped with an individual's "specified" screen reader to complete an examination instead of one of the options on the Examiners "prescribed" list of auxiliary aids (2011). The provisions of ADA that govern testing entities provides the following:

> Any person that offers examinations or courses related to applications, licensing, certification, or credentialing for secondary or post-secondary education, professional, or trade purposes shall offer such examinations or courses in a place and manner accessible to persons with disabilities or offer alternative accessible arrangements for such individuals.
>
> (ADA Title III, 42 U.S.Code § 12189)

The regulations governing testing do not use the term "reasonable." After the *Enyart* case, a U.S. Department of Justice (DOJ) brief interpreted the intent of the law and explicitly stated that examinations must be administered so as to "best ensure" that they measure an individual's achievement (ADA, 28 C.F.R. § 36.309(b)(1)(i)). The "best ensure" requirement is a more stringent standard than "reasonableness." The DOJ brief also noted that it was Congress' intent that the auxiliary aids and services provided to individuals with disabilities would keep pace with the rapidly changing technology of the times. According to the Courts, one reasonable reading of the requirements is that entities must make exams "accessible" and provide people with disabilities an equal opportunity to demonstrate their knowledge or abilities to the same degree as individuals without disabilities. In other words, the exam must be administered so as to "best ensure" that the results accurately reflect aptitude rather than disabilities. This requires schools to think beyond traditional methods currently in place for the delivery of services and may require changes in how things have been traditionally accomplished on the university campus.

Attitudinal Bias

Research to date suggests strongly that on-campus attitudinal bias may play an integral role in the effective support of students with ASD. Ellison et al. (2013, p.70) concluded from a survey of experts on the topic:

> The tradition within higher education is to admit, instruct, and support students who exhibit the academic and social leadership skills necessary to transition into the workforce. Panel members in this study suggest [students with ASD] may suffer an on-campus attitudinal bias: attitudes about the disorder may create unwillingness to provide intensive supports, and a general lack of understanding about the disorder may lead to the development of a deeper bias.

Lack of Holistic Supports

PSE students with ASD typically require specialized assistance to have what is considered by many to be a full IHE experience—living in campus housing, developing and maintaining social networks, utilizing self-advocacy skills, interacting effectively with faculty, and using independent living skills on a day-to-day basis. Research to date (Dillon, 2007; Ellison et al., 2013; Hughes, 2009; Smith, 2007) suggests that holistic services are needed to effectively meet the needs of PSE students with ASD. Campus disability services are traditionally focused on academic support and generally lack the expertise and financial resources necessary to effectively and holistically support this student population (Ellison et al., 2013).

Supports to address the social and independent living needs of PSE students with ASD are as essential as the academic supports traditionally provided (Ellison et al., 2013). Still, those supports appear to be lacking within higher education. In a survey of public colleges and universities in the United States, only 4.8 percent of institutions that responded to the survey item related to *independent living skills* ($n = 186$) employ staff fully dedicated to assisting students with ASD in learning about, and improving upon, their independent living skills (Ellison, 2013). Nearly one-third of those responding to the survey item related to social-related services ($n = 187$) reported that no staff were employed to teach skills related to *social networking* (32.1 percent) and *social communication* needs (32.1 percent). Findings from the survey suggest that if those services are provided on IHE campuses to students with ASD, they are carried out only through traditional disability service programs (Ellison, 2013).

ASD-specific Barriers

Other barriers to PSE success for students are related specifically to ASD characteristics. Although individuals with ASD experience characteristics of the disorder to varying degrees of difficulty, each presents with clinically significant challenges in social communication, social interaction, and restricted interests or repetitive patterns of behavior (APA, 2013). Characteristics such as theory of mind (ToM), comorbidity, and executive function can impact a student with ASD's PSE success. Most IHEs require students to meet minimum academic achievement prior to admission unless they are participating in a non-matriculated program. Success in higher education requires more than intellectual ability. Social networking, planning for, and carrying out self-advocacy, personal flexibility, and the ability to structure free time are all important skills needed for college success. A well-formed plan should be developed to address individual characteristics and assist with the transition from HS to PSE (Wolf, Brown, & Bork Kuikiela, 2009). An assessment can be used to help determine an individual with ASD's college readiness and identify areas of need. The assessment, outlined in Table 15.5, considers seven domains of campus living. Individuals with ASD, family members, and professionals supporting the transition to college can score each criterion on a 1 (Never without support), 2 (With frequent support), 3 (With some support), 4 (With infrequent support), to 5 (Always without support) scale.

Theory of Mind

Challenges related to theory of mind (ToM) may present one of the most pervasive needs for intensive supports for college students with ASD (Ellison et al., 2013). The development of a ToM allows humans to predict the behavior of others (Colle, Baron-Cohen, & Hill, 2007), and is a skill necessary for social communication and understanding. ToM helps one recognize and understand that others have thoughts, feelings, and beliefs different than one's own. A poorly developed ToM may create significant difficulties related to social communication and social networking; social interest in sharing observations and events with other people; joint attention skills; and the ability to connect emotionally with others.

Comorbidity

Research to date suggests that in addition to diagnostic criteria, some individuals identified on the autism spectrum may also experience comorbid psychiatric conditions (de Bruin, Ferdinand, Meester, de Nijs, & Verheij, 2007). The Center for Disease Control and Prevention (CDC, 2014) reports that 83 percent of individuals with ASD live with a co-existing developmental disorder not related to ASD, and that 10 percent live with a co-existing psychiatric disorder. Anxiety disorders appear common to the autism spectrum (de Bruin, et al., 2007; Tureck, Matson, May, Whiting, & Davis, 2014). This comorbidity often results in "reduced functioning

Table 15.5 Assessment

Academics	• Attends class or tutoring sessions regularly
	• Alerts professors or tutors if absence is necessary
	• Listens, participates, and learns in the classroom
	• Engages in commonly understood and appropriate classroom etiquette
	• Reads educational texts carefully, understands key concepts, and rephrases those concepts into his or her own words
	• Captures notes while listening to a class lecture
	• Completes all assigned homework, and out-of-class assignments
	• Understands and practices appropriate classroom behavior
	• Respects debate and the opinions of others while still being able to express individual opinion
	• Accepts academic evaluations from professors and tutors
	• Possesses study habits that can contribute to academic success
	• Possesses a high level of academic curiosity
Independent living	• Leads efforts to plan for, and carry out his or her educational experience
	• Expresses his or her need for additional academic help to professors, tutors or other students
	• Manages his or her time effectively
	• Recognizes when reasonable accommodations are needed and alerts an authority to that need
	• Manages small amounts of money on a day-to-day basis
	• Manages large amounts of money (such as regular bills) on a periodic and routine basis
	• Plans and follows a personal menu that meets dietary needs or identified dietary restrictions
	• Self-medicates, including the ability to refill prescriptions
	• Travels independently through the local community, including planning for and using public transportation
	• Seeks out and participates in activities that promote career or vocational exploration
Socialization	• Joins and attends campus-based groups, clubs, and other recreational activities
	• Joins and attends community-based social and recreational activities
	• Plans social activities, including making appropriate accommodations and preparations
	• Enjoys the company of others and is able to seek out friendships
	• Possesses wide and varied interests

Safety	• Recognizes when he or she is being taken advantage of by others
	• Walks safely through traffic and crosses public streets of all designs
	• Recognizes personal illness or injury that will require medical treatment and alerts an authority to that need
	• Recognizes situations that are of an urgent, emergency, or crisis level and takes appropriate action
	• Engages in activities that promote physical, emotional, and psychological wellness
Sexuality	• Demonstrates a mature understanding of his or her sexual values
	• Possesses a mature understanding of sexuality, including sexual intercourse, sexually transmitted diseases, birth control, and the practice of safe sex
	• Respects the views of others regarding sexuality
	• Recognizes the private nature of sexual interest and activity
	• Distinguishes between friendship and romance
Stress	• Recognizes distress and makes adjustments to alleviate symptoms
	• Participates in activities designed to reduce stress in a healthy manner, including activities such as: physical exercise, improved time management, relaxation techniques, and other wellness activities
	• Responds calmly and is resilient in a crisis, urgent situation or personal setback
	• Accepts assistance from others and values collaborative teamwork
	• Responds well in competitive environments and situations
Self-determination	• Sets personal goals and designs a plan to reach those goals
	• Chooses a field of study or major
	• Seeks out new and challenging experiences
	• Accommodates when sudden change occurs and remains flexible
	• Accepts a high level of personal responsibility
	• Articulates knowledge of his or her specific ASD

Note:
Used with permission: West Virginia Autism Training Center at Marshall University

and quality of life" (Selles & Storch, 2013, p. 410) for individuals with ASD. The symptoms associated with ASD, combined with comorbid psychiatric conditions recognized as common to the autism spectrum, may create significant challenges to a successful transition from HS to PSE. Research on the transition for first year IHE students with ASD found those who live with higher levels of internalizing symptoms (e.g. anxiety, depression) make poorer adjustments in PSE (Emmons, McCurry, Ellison, Klinger, & Klinger, 2010).

Executive Dysfunction

The CDC (2014) reported that 46 percent of individuals with ASD have average to above average intellectual ability. While some students with ASD have the cognitive ability to achieve academically, difficulties related to executive functioning may create academic challenges (Gibbons & Goins, 2008). Difficulties related to regulating emotions, remembering classroom etiquette, solving problems, and coping with the transitions that occur in a school setting can create significant challenges for the education of individuals with ASD. Difficulty predicting and integrating sensory-based information such as light, sound, and smells commonly creates challenges in the classroom for students with ASD. These cognitive difficulties can create significant challenges in the classroom.

Effective Practices in Higher Education

Many of the PSE students with ASD have the intellectual ability to succeed in a college classroom (Ellison et al., 2013). Experts agree, however, that faculty and staff must understand how best to prepare the environment and provide support for the academic, social, and independent living needs of this student population. The strategies discussed in this section include: (a) universal design, (b) academic supports, and (c) social and independent living supports.

Universal Design for Learning (UDL)

Universal design (UD) involves designing environments that can be accessed readily by the widest possible range of individuals anticipating in advance the need for alternatives, options, and adaptations to meet the challenge of diversity (Rose et al., 2006). More specifically, universal design for learning (UDL) focuses on learning environments and the design of accessible teaching and learning opportunities. As previously stated, the framework for UDL consists of three specific principles: (a) representation of information, (b) expression of knowledge, and (c) engagement in learning. Universal Design for Transition (UDT) adds transition domains to the UDL framework to link academic standards to transition domains.

Multiple Means of Representation

This principle of UDL applies to the methods and techniques for teaching. Students differ in the ways that they perceive and comprehend information. Students with ASD, because of their cognitive strengths and challenges, may face barriers in accessing information when presented in a manner that assumes students all share a common background. Faculty in higher education should consider, in advance, how to provide instruction in a manner optimal for a diverse student population. Instruction should highlight critical features, emphasize big ideas, and connect new information to background knowledge to make instruction accessible to the different types of learners on an IHE campus (Rose et al., 2006). Multiple means of presenting information is key to ensuring an effective transference of knowledge to diverse learners.

Multiple Means of Expression

This principle of UDL applies to students' expression of knowledge. Students differ in the ways they express what they know, with many students able to express themselves more skillfully in one medium than another. Students with ASD may lack the organizational skill to integrate knowledge into application or the executive functioning skills required to complete long-term projects. Faculty in higher education should consider providing alternatives for students' means of expression to assess learning. Scaffolds and supports at the PSE level to support learning can include review sessions, feedback on projects before submitted, and readings to address different levels of prior knowledge (Rose et al., 2006). There is not one means of expression optimal for all students nor one kind of support, so multiple means are essential.

Multiple Means of Engagement

This principle of UDL applies to the methods of engagement in course material. Students differ in ways in which they engage in learning, as not all students are motivated by the same extrinsic rewards or classroom conditions. Students with ASD may be highly engaged by topics that are of special interest to them and may be unmotivated by novel or unfamiliar topics. Faculty should consider that students with ASD might engage better in environments that are static or unchanging, or opposed to dynamic social forms of learning. There is not one means of engaging students that will be optimal across the diversity that exists, so alternative means of engagement are essential.

Academic Supports

It is known that specialized classroom instruction is most useful for students with ASD (Donaldson & Zager, 2010; Simpson, Gaus, Biggs, & Williams, 2010). Research recommends that academic supports be designed to meet the individualized needs of IHE students with ASD (Dillon, 2007; Smith, 2007). The most effective supports occur when educators understand characteristics associated with ASD (Smith, 2007) and modify their instructional style (Hughes, 2009). Effective supports may include non-traditional classroom supports and the use of technology.

Non-traditional Classroom Supports

While traditional disability services within higher education—extended testing time, note-taking assistance, and alternative test formats, for example—can offer assistance, evidence shows that the needs of students with ASD may extend beyond the scope of traditional disability services (Dillon, 2007; Ellison et al., 2013; Hughes, 2009). Because individuals with ASD experience characteristics to varying degrees, it is considered best practice to design academic supports to meet the unique needs of each student (Dillon, 2007). Research suggests that faculty be thoughtful of their instructional style as a means to accommodate the needs of students with ASD. Suggestions for educators include: (a) provide detailed instructions; (b) provide clear deadlines for assignments; (c) offer students a summary of key lecture points at the start and conclusion of each class; (d) share visual forms of information (PowerPoints); (e) break down assignments into smaller, manageable chunks; and (f) use peer mentors to clarify assignments and answer basic questions for students with ASD (Hughes, 2009).

Technology

Technology may provide for effective academic supports for IHE students with ASD. When planning utilizing universal design, consider assistive technology (AT) as this can increase access and support by limiting or overcoming barriers in the environment for individuals with disabilities. Relatively "low-tech" (e.g. highlighters) to "high-tech" (e.g. computer technology) AT can provide an impact on PSE experiences for students with disabilities. Students can compensate for organizational challenges, caused by executive dysfunction, by using simple tools such as online calendars and technology with alarms (Dillon, 2007). Laptop computers or other electronic devices may help students overcome motor challenges that otherwise may impede notes and test taking (Hughes, 2009).

Social and Independent Living Supports

Services designed to support social needs are essential to success for students with ASD in higher education. Research suggests that social supports may be even more critical for postsecondary success than academic supports, as students with ASD admitted into a matriculated college program are generally "intellectually capable of performing in the classroom but struggle with the social and organizational aspects of the college lifestyle" (Ellison et al., 2013, p. 70). Traditional disability services, due to a lack of resources and expertise, may be lacking in the ability to support the social needs of this student population (Ellison et al., 2013). Some areas in which supports may be necessary include: (a) campus housing, (b) social skills, (c) independent living, and (d) mental health.

Campus Housing Support

Navigating the community that is a college or university campus may be daunting to students on the autism spectrum (Dillon, 2007; Ellison et al., 2013; Hughes, 2009). The social networking inherent within campus housing may pose significant challenges for this student population (Hughes, 2009). Research suggests that challenges related to social skills and social communication may prevent students from fully advocating for their on-campus needs, including making appropriate and timely decisions regarding self-disclosure (Ellison *et al.*, 2013). A well-informed community appears to be important to the social support of this student population.

Social Support

Anticipating the social needs of students with ASD affords disability service professionals the opportunity to develop basic systemic supports that may reduce social anxiety. Examples include providing students with an early and detailed schedule of orientation, and identifying quiet, less populated cafeteria spaces in which students with ASD may eat meals (Hughes, 2009). Research highlights the importance of assessing social skill challenges of students with ASD, and formalizing individual and group activities that promote the development of social skills training to meet identified needs (Dillon, 2007; Ellison et al., 2013). The use of peer mentors can facilitate the development of social relationships while providing advice and support for organizational needs (Dillon, 2007).

Independent Living Support

Research suggests that college students with ASD are often challenged by having under-developed independent living skills (Ellison et al., 2013).

Students within this population tend to struggle with transition, flexibility, free time, and self-advocacy (Wolf et al., 2009). A college campus is a complex society with rules, protocols, and customs that can overwhelm a student with ASD (VanBergeijk et al., 2008). Regularly scheduled psychoeducational group meetings may be beneficial to students with ASD to improve social and independent living skills and provide an opportunity for social networking. Table 15.6 illustrates possible topics discussed during a semester (Kiss, 2015).

Mental Health Support

Access to appropriate on-campus mental health services appears to be important to the success of PSE students with ASD. The mental health of students with ASD must be carefully considered when designing non-academic disability services (VanBergeijk et al., 2008). Comorbidity is common. Students with ASD may experience characteristics of anxiety disorders, obsessive compulsive disorder (OCD), Tourette's syndrome, and depressive disorders (VanBergeijk et al., 2008). Due to challenges related to executive dysfunction, ToM, and social communication, students with ASD who need mental health services may not attempt to access them. This highlights the need for a campus community that is well informed about ASD (Ellison et al., 2013). Students with ASD may need to rely on faculty, staff, and peers to provide unsolicited advice about seeking mental health services.

There is concern that on-campus mental health services may be generally ineffective in meeting the needs of this student population. For example, insight development as a goal of traditional psychotherapy may be ineffective due to the communication and cognitive challenges common to the autism spectrum (VanBergeilk et al., 2008). The micro-counseling skills used traditionally by therapists to establish rapport, assess progress, and guide therapy may be less helpful with this population due to challenges specific to social communication, ToM, and speech pragmatics (Ellison et al., 2013). Researchers agree that a more directive, psychoeducational approach that emphasizes skill building is most helpful to individuals with ASD involved in mental health counseling (Ellison et al., 2013; Vanbergeijk et al., 2008).

Summary

In response to the growing numbers of students with ASD who wish to continue their education beyond high school, colleges and universities have begun to provide opportunities for inclusive PSE experiences (Neubert, Moon, Grigal, & Redd, 2001). In this chapter, we have highlighted effective practices for the preparation of students with ASD transitioning

Table 15.6 Session Topics Examples

Topic	Points for Discussion
Orientation	• Who are we and what do we want to learn? • Conduct introductions. • Create group rules and expectations. • Complete *Me, myself, and I* lesson to explore likes, beliefs, and personal values. • Identify topics to explore, understand, or learn more about.
Developing time management skills and smart goals	• What is executive functioning and what do we need to know about time management, scheduling, organizing, and prioritizing? • Complete *Academic Success* time budget lesson to learn about time management. • Set *Smart Goals* utilizing a step-by-step approach. • Learn organization and planning strategies.
Developing a social radar	• What is the difference between talking and having a conversation? • Complete *All about me, All about you* lesson and learn the difference between dialog versus monolog. • Learn about under sharing versus over sharing and the importance of finding the balance. • What is theory of mind and how does it affect social communication and relationship building?
Building relationships and communication skills	• Learn that people have their own thoughts, motivations, and intentions. • What does the early phases of relationship building look like? • Complete *Enough about me, Tell me about you!* lesson. • Learn when and how to start, maintain, repair, and end a conversation. • Read body language during a conversation. • Learn how shared interests can impact relationships. • Engage in small talk to learn how it's done.

(continued)

Table 15.6 (continued)

Topic	Points for Discussion
Building healthy relationships	• What does a healthy relationship look like? • Learn how to approach someone to talk. • Practice reading body language and learn what subtle movements and expressions really mean. • Complete *Yes, I'm interested!* (Now, what does that look like?) lesson. • *I hope you're interested!* (Now, what does that look like?) lesson.
Building a positive campus Reputation	• What is my reputation and am I happy with it? • Learn about the influence of actions and words on how you're perceived. • Learn the difference between how you talk to professors versus talking to friends. • Reflect on previous role models and the impact of their influence.
Making decisions and resolving conflicts	• What questions should I ask (myself) before making an important decision? • Engage in independent decision making. • Experience consequences of a wrong decision. • Learn to analyze conflict situations to understand the other party involved. • Learn how to disagree and tell someone you think they're wrong and not get into a fight doing it!
Coping with stress and anxiety	• What does it feel and look like to be stressed? • Learn to recognize personal triggers. • Assess sensory sensitivity and stress and learn possible links. • Learn prevention strategies and how to cope with stress.
Managing anger	• How can I appropriately express my frustration and have control over my thoughts and feelings! • Learn to take criticism but avoid being hurt. • Practice recognizing and understanding your own feelings.

Note:
Used with permission: West Virginia Autism Training Center at Marshall University

from HS to PSE. We described the benefits of participation in higher education for students with disabilities. We presented a variety of higher education models and programs of services and supports to facilitate the inclusion of students with disabilities. We discussed benchmarks of readiness for success in higher education and challenges, both institutional and those directly related to ASD characteristics. Most importantly, we highlighted effective practices at the PSE level to meet the needs of students with ASD.

References

Agran, M., Blanchard, C., & Wehmeyer, M. L. (2000). Promoting transition goals and self-determination through student-directed learning: The self-determined learning model of instruction. *Education and Training in Mental Retardation and Developmental Disabilities*, 35, 351–364.

Agran, M., Cavin, M., Wehmeyer, M., & Palmer, S. (2006). Participation of students with moderate to severe disabilities in the general curriculum: The effects of the self-determined learning model of instruction. *Research and Practice for Persons with Severe Disabilities*, 31, 230–241.

Agran, M., & Krupp, M. (2011). Providing choice making in employment programs: The beginning or end of self-determination? *Education and Training in Autism and Developmental Disabilities*, 45, 565–575.

Alper, S. (2003). The relationship between inclusion and other trends in education. In D. Ryndak, & S. Alper (Eds.), *Curriculum and instruction for students with significant disabilities in inclusive setting* (2nd ed.), 13–30. Boston, MA: Allyn and Bacon.

Alwell, M., & Cobb, B. (2009). Functional life skills curricular interventions for youth with disabilities: A systematic review. *Career Development for Exceptional Individuals*, 32(2), 82–93.

Americans with Disabilities Act of 1990 (ADA). (1990). Public Law No. 101-336, 42 U.S.C. 12101 et seq. Retrieved February 15, 2015 from www.ada.gov/pubs/ada.htm.

Americans with Disabilities Act (ADA). (1990). 42 U.S. Code § 12189. Examinations and courses. Retrieved February 15, 2015 from http://uscode.regstoday.com/42USC_CHAPTER126.aspx#42USC12189.

Americans with Disabilities Act Amendments Act of 2008 (ADAAA). (2008). Public Law No. 110-325, 42 U.S.C. 12101 et seq. Retrieved February 15, 2015 from www.ada.gov/pubs/ada.htm.

Americans with Disabilities Act Regulation (ADA). (2011). 28 C.F.R. § 36.309(b)(1)(i). Examinations and courses. Retrieved February 15, 2015 from www.ada.gov/reg3a.html.

American Psychiatric Association. (2013). *Diagnostic and statistical manual of mental disorders* (5th ed.). Washington, DC: Author.

Association on Higher Education And Disability (AHEAD). (2012). Supporting *accommodations requests: Guidance on documentation practices*. Huntersville, NC: AHEAD.

Baum, S., Ma, J., & Payea, K., (2013). Education pays: The benefits of higher education for individuals and society. *College Board*. Retrieved March 13, 2015 from www.rilin.state.ri.us/Special/ses15/commdocs/Education%20Pays,%20 The%20College%20Board.pdf.

Bouck, E. C. (2004). The state of curriculum for secondary students with mild mental retardation. *Education and Training in Developmental Disabilities*, *39*, 169–176.

Bouck, E. C. (2010). Reports of life skill training for students with intellectual disabilities in and out of school. *Journal of Intellectual Disability Research*, *54*, 1093–1103.

Carnevale, A. P., Rose, S. J. & Cheah, B. (2011). The college payoff: Education, occupations, lifetime earnings. *The Georgetown University Center on Education and the Workforce.*

Carothers, D. E., & Taylor, R. L. (2004). How teachers and parents can work together to teach independent living skills to children with autism. *Focus on Autism and Other Developmental Disabilities*, *19*(2), 102–104.

Center for Disease Control and Prevention (CDC). (2014). *Autism spectrum disorders data and statistics.* Retrieved February 15, 2015 from www.cdc.gov/ ncbddd/autism/facts.html.

Cobb, B., Lehmann, J., Newman-Gonchar, R., & Alwell, M. (2009). Self-determination for students with disabilities: A narrative metasynthesis. *Career Development and Transition for Exceptional Individuals*, *32*(2), 108–114.

Colle, L., Baron-Cohen, S., & Hill, J. (2007). Do children with autism have a theory of mind? A non-verbal test of autism vs. specific language impairment. *Journal of Autism and Developmental Disorders*, *37*(4), 716–723.

De Araujo, P., & Murray, J. M. (2010). Channels for improved performance – From living on campus. *American Journal of Business Education*, *3*(12), 5764.

de Bruin, E. I., Ferdinand, R. F., Meester, S., de Nijs, P. A., & Verheij, F. (2007). High rates of psychiatric co-morbidity in PDD-NOS. *Journal of Autism and Developmental Disorders*, *37*(5), 877–886.

Dillon, M. R. (2007). Creating supports for college students with Asperger syndrome through collaboration. *College Student Journal*, *41*(2), 499–504.

Donaldson, J. B., & Zager, D. (2010). Mathematics interventions for students with high functioning autism/Asperger's syndrome. *Teaching Exceptional Children*, *42*(6), 40–46.

Duffy, J. T., & Gugerty, J. (2005). The role of disability support services. In E. E. Getzel and P. Wehman (Eds.), *Going to College: Expanding Opportunities for People with Disabilities*, 89–115. Baltimore, MD: Brookes Publishing.

Eckes, S. E., & Ochoa, T. A. (2005). Students with disabilities: Transitioning from high school to higher education. *American Secondary Education*, 6–20.

Ellison, L. M. (2013). Assessing the readiness of higher education to instruct and support students with Asperger's Disorder. *Theses, Dissertations and Capstones*, 428, Marshall University, Huntington, WV.

Ellison, M., Clark, J., Cunningham, M. & Hansen, R. (2013). *Academic and Campus Accommodations that Foster Success for College Students with Asperger's Disorder.* Southern Regional Council on Educational Administration.

Ellison, M., Hovatter, P., & Nelson, A. (2013). *Asperger's disorder: Developing a therapeutic relationship.* Pittsburgh, PA: *Autism Society of America.*

Emmons, J., McCurry, S., Ellison, M., Klinger, M.R., & Klinger, L.G. (2010). College programs for students with ASD: Predictors of successful college transition. *International Meeting for Autism Research* Poster session, Philadelphia, PA.

Enyart v. National Conference of Bar Examiners Inc. (2011). United States Court of Appeals, Ninth Circuit. Retrieved February 15, 2015 from http://caselaw.findlaw.com/us-9th-circuit/1551247.html.

Farrell, E. F. (2004). Asperger's confounds colleges. *Chronicle of Higher Education, 51*(7), 35–36.

Field, S., & Hoffman, A. (2007). Self-determination in secondary transition assessment. *Assessment for Effective Instruction, 32*(3), 181–190.

Folk, E. D. R., Yamamoto, K. K., & Stodden, R. A. (2012). Implementing inclusion and collaborative teaming in a model program of postsecondary education for young adults with intellectual disabilities. *Journal of Policy and Practice in Intellectual Disabilities, 9*(4), 257–269.

Getzel, E. E., McManus, S., & Briel, L. W. (2004). An effective model for college students with learning disabilities and attention deficit hyperactivity disorders. *Research to Practice, 3*(1).

Gibbons, M. M., & Goins, S. (2008). Getting to know the child with Asperger syndrome. *Professional School Counseling, 11* (5), 347–352.

Gil, L. A. (2007). Bridging the transition gap from high school to college: Preparing students with disabilities for a successful postsecondary experience. *Exceptional Children, 40*(2), 12–15.

Gilmore, D., Schuster, J., Zafft, C., & Hart, D. (2001). Postsecondary education services and employment outcomes within the vocational rehabilitation system. *Disability Studies Quarterly, 21*(1).

Gilmore, S., Bose, J., & Hart, D. (2001). Postsecondary education as a critical step toward meaningful employment: Vocational rehabilitation's role. *Research to Practice, 7*(4), 1–4.

Graham-Smith, S. & LaFayette, S. (2004). Quality disability support for promoting belonging and academic success within the college community. *College Student Journal, 38*(1), 90–99.

Greenholtz, J., Mosoff, J., & Hurtado, T. (2007). STEPS forward: Inclusive postsecondary education for young adults with intellectual disabilities. *Society for Research into Higher Education*. Retrieved Match 15, 2015 from www.steps-forward.org/research.

Grigal, M., & Hart, D. (2010). *Think college! Postsecondary education options for students with intellectual disabilities*. Baltimore, MD: Brookes.

Grigal, M., Hart, D., & Migliore, A. (2011). Comparing transition planning, postsecondary education, and employment outcomes of students with intellectual disabilities. *Career Development for Exceptional Individuals, 34*(1), 4.

Grigal, M., Neubert, D. A., & Moon, S. M. (2002). Postsecondary options for students with significant disabilities. *Teaching Exceptional Children, 35*(2), 68.

Grigal, M., Neubert, D. A., Moon, M.S., & Graham, S. (2003). Self-determination for students with disabilities: Views of parents and teachers. *Exceptional Children, 70*, 97–112.

Grigal, M., Hart, D., Smith, F. A., Domin, D., Sulewski, J., & Weir, C. (2014). *Think college national coordinating center: Annual report on the transition and postsecondary programs for students with intellectual disabilities (2012–2013)*. Boston, MA: University of Massachusetts, Institute for Community Inclusion.

Hafner, D. (2008). *Inclusion in postsecondary education: Phenomenological study on identifying and addressing barriers to inclusion of individuals with significant disabilities as a four-year liberal arts college*. Doctoral Dissertation.

Hafner, D., & Moffatt, C. (2012). *Cutting-Edge Report 2007–2012*, Edgewood College.

Hart, D., Grigal, M., Sax, C., Martinez, D., & Will, M. (2006). Postsecondary education options for students with intellectual disabilities. *Research to Practice-Issue #45*. Retrieved February 15, 2015 from www.communityinclusion.org/article_id=178&style=print.

Hart, D., Zimbrich, K., & Parker, D. (2005). Dual enrollment as a postsecondary education option for students with intellectual disabilities. In E. Getzel & P. Wehman (Eds.), *Going to college: Expanding opportunities for people with disabilities*, 253–266, Baltimore, MD: Brookes.

Hartz, E. J. (2014). *Outcomes of inclusive postsecondary education for students with intellectual disabilities at Edgewood College*. Dissertation.

Higher Education Opportunity Act of 2008 (HEOA). (2008). Public Law No. 110–315 § 122 Stat. 3078.

Hughes, J. (2009). Higher education and Asperger's syndrome. *Chronicle of Higher Education*, *55*(40), 21.

Individuals with Disabilities Education Act, 20 U.S.C. § 1400. (2004). Public Law No. 108-446.

Kiss, E. (2015) Skill Building Group Topic Examples. *West Virginia Autism Training Center*: Marshall University, WV.

Kochhar-Bryant, C., & Izzo, M. (2006). Access to post-high school services: Transition assessment and the summary of performance. *Career Development for Exceptional Individuals*, *29*, 70–89.

Kohler, P. D., & Field, S. (2003). Transition-focused education foundation for the future. *The Journal of Special Education*, *37*(3), 174–183.

Landmark, L. J., Ju, S., & Zhang, D. (2010). Substantiated best practices in transition: Fifteen plus years later. *Career Development for Exceptional Individuals*, *33*(3), 165–176.

Lindstrom, L., Doren, B., & Miesch, J. (2011). Waging a living: Career development and long- term employment outcomes for young adults with disabilities. *Exceptional Children*, *77*(4), 423–434.

Madaus, J. W. (2005). Navigating the college transition maze: A guide for students with learning disabilities: *Teaching Exceptional Children*, *37*(3), 32–37.

Madaus, J. W. (2011). The history of disability services in higher education. *New Directions For Higher Education*, *154*, 5–15.

Moon, M. S., Grigal, M., & Neubert, D. (2001). High school and beyond. *The Exceptional Parent*, *31*(7), 52–57.

National Center on Secondary and Education and Transition (NCSET). (2004). *Person-centered planning: A tool for transition*. Retrieved from www.ncset.org/publications/viewdesc.asp?id=1431.

National Survey on Postsecondary Programs for Youth with Intellectual Disabilities. (2005).

National Transition Documentation Summit. (2005). Summary of performance model template. *Council for Exceptional Children. Council for Educational Diagnostic Services.* Retrieved February 15, 2015 from http://community.cec.sped.org/ceds/home.

Neubert, D. A., Moon, M. S., Grigal, M., & Redd, V. (2001). Post-secondary educational practices for individuals with mental retardation and other significant disabilities: A review of the literature. *Journal of Vocational Rehabilitation, 16*(3/4), 155–168.

Neubert, D. A., Moon, M. S., Grigal, M., & Redd, V. (2002). Post-secondary education and transition services for students age 18–21 with significant disabilities. *Focus on Exceptional Children, 34*(8), 1–11.

Newman, L., Wagner, M., Cameto, R., & Knokey, A. M. (2009). *The post-high school outcomes of youth with disabilities up to 4 years after high school. A Report of findings from the National Longitudinal Transition Study-2 (NLTS2) (SRI Project P11182).* Retrieved February 15, 2015 from www.nlts2.org/reports/2009_04/ntlts2_report_2009_04_complete.pdf.

Newman, L., Wagner, M., Cameto, R., Knokey, A. M., & Shaver, D. (2010). *Comparisons across time of the outcomes of youth with disabilities up to 4 Years after high school. A report of findings from the National Longitudinal Transition Study-2 (NLTS2).* Menlo Park, CA: SRI International.

Nietupski, J., McQuillen, D., Berg, D., Daughtery, V., & Hamre-Nietupski, S. (2001). Preparing students with mild disabilities for careers in technology: A process and recommendations from Iowa's High School High Tech program. *Journal of Vocational Rehabilitation, 16,* 179–188.

Rose, D. H., Harbour, W. S., Johnston, C. S., Daley, S. G., & Abarbanell, L. (2006). Universal design for learning in postsecondary education: Reflections on principles and their application. *Journal of Postsecondary Education and Disability, 19*(2), 135–151.

Roux, A. M., Shattuck, P. T., Rast, J. E., Rava, J. A., & Anderson, K. A. (2015). *National autism indicators report: Transition into young adulthood.* Philadelphia, PA: Life Course Outcomes Research Program, A. J. Drexel Autism Institute.

Rowe, D., Mazzotti, V., & Sinclair, J. (2015). Strategies for teaching self-determination skills in conjunction with the common core. *Intervention in School and Clinic, 5*(3), 131–141.

Schutz, P. F. (2002). Transition from secondary to postsecondary education for students with disabilities: An exploration of the phenomenon. *Journal of College Reading and Learning, 33*(1), 46–61.

Scott, L. A., Thoma, C. A., Saddler, S., Bartholomew, C. A., Alder, N., & Tamura, R. (2011). Universal design for transition: A single subject research study on the impact of UDT on student achievement, engagement and interest. *Journal on Educational Psychology, 4*(4), 21–31.

Section 504 of the Rehabilitation Act of 1973. (1973). Public Law No. 93-112, 29 U.S.C. § 701 et seq.

Selles, R., & Storch, E. (2013). Translation of anxiety treatment to youth with autism spectrum disorders. *Journal of Child and Family Studies, 22*(3), 405–413.

Shaw, S. F. (2005). IDEA will change the face of post-secondary disability documentation. *Disability Compliance for Higher Education*, *11*(1), 7.

Shaw, S. F., Dukes, L. L., & Madaus, J. W. (2012). Beyond compliance: Using the summary of performance to enhance transition planning. *Teaching Exceptional Children*, *44*(5), 6–12.

Shaw, S. F., Madaus, J. W., & Dukes, L. L. (2010). *Preparing students with disabilities for college success: A practical guide for transition planning*. Baltimore, MD: Brookes.

Simpson, C. G., Gaus, M. D., Biggs, M., & Williams Jr., J. (2010). Physical education and implications for students with Asperger's syndrome. *Teaching Exceptional Children*, *42*(6), 48–56.

Sitlington, P. L., & Clark, G. M. (2007). The transition assessment process and IDEIA 2004. *Assessment for Effective Intervention*, *32*, 133–142.

Smith, C. P. (2007). Support services for students with Asperger's syndrome in higher education. *College Student Journal*, *41*(3), 515–531.

Sopko, K. (2008). Summary of performance. Project Forum at NASDSE. *In forum Brief Policy Analysis*. Retrieved from www.nasdse.org/Portals/0/SummaryofPerformance.pdf.

Stodden, R. A., & Whelley, T. (2004). Postsecondary education and persons with intellectual disabilities: An introduction. *Education and Training in Developmental Disabilities*, *39*(1), 6–15.

Test, D., Fowler, C., Wood, W., Brewer, D., & Eddy, S. (2005). A conceptual framework of self-advocacy for students with disabilities. *Remedial and Special Education*, *26*(1), 43–54.

Thacker, J., & Sheppard-Jones, K. (2011). *Research brief: Higher education for students with intellectual disabilities. A study of KY OVR counselors*. Lexington, KY: University of Kentucky, Human Development Institute.

Think College (n.d.). Differences between high school and college. Retrieved February 15, 2015 from www.thinkcollege.net/topics/highschool-college-differences.

Thoma, C. A., Bartholomew, C. C., & Scott, L. A. (2009). *Universal design for transition: A roadmap for planning and instruction*. Baltimore, MD: Brookes.

Tureck, K., Matson, J., May, A., Whiting, S., & Davis, T. (2014). Comorbid symptoms in children with anxiety disorders compared to children with autism spectrum disorders. *Journal of Developmental and Physical Disabilities*, *26*(1), 23–33.

Uditsky, B., & Hughson, E. (2012). Inclusive postsecondary education – an evidence-based moral imperative. *Journal of Policy and Practice in Intellectual Disabilities*, *9*(4), 298– 302.

U.S. Bureau of Labor Statistics. (2011). *United States Department of Labor*. Retrieved February 15, 2015 from www.bls.gov/.

U.S. Department of Education, National Center for Education Statistics. (2013). *The Condition of Education 2013 (NCES 2013–037)*, *Annual Earnings of Young Adults*. Retrieved February 15, 2015 from http://nces.ed.gov/fastfacts/display.asp?id=77.

VanBergeijk, E., Klin, A., & Volkmar, F. (2008). Supporting more able students on the autism spectrum: College and beyond. *Journal of Autism and Developmental Disorders*, *38*(7), 1359–1370.

Wagner, M., Newman, L., Cameto, R., & Levine, P. (2005). *Changes over time in the early post-school outcomes of youth with disabilities.* National Longitudinal Transition Study 2, SRI Project P11182.

Wechsler, H. (2007). An academic Gresham's Law: Group repulsion as a theme in American higher education. In L. Foster (Ed.), *The History of Higher Education,* 442–456. Boston, MA: Pearson.

Wehman, P. (2002). *Testimony to President's Commission on Excellence in Special Education Transition Task Force Meeting, 4/30/02.* Retrieved February 15, 2015 from www.beachcenter.org/Books%5CFullPublications%5CPDF%5CPresidentReport.pdf.

Wehmeyer, M. L., Abery, B. H., Zhang, D., Ward, K., Willis, D., Hossain, W. A., . . . Walker, H. M. (2011). Personal self-determination and moderating variables that impact efforts to promote self-determination. *Exceptionality, 19*(1), 19–30.

Wehmeyer, M. L., Agran, M., & Hughes, C. (2000). A national survey of teachers' promotion of self-determination and student-directed learning. *Journal of Special Education, 34,* 58–68.

Wehmeyer, M. L., & Schwartz, M. (1997). Self-determination and positive adult outcomes: A follow-up study of youth with mental retardation or learning disabilities. *Exceptional Children, 63,* 245–255.

Wehmeyer, M. L., & Schwartz, M. (1998). The relationship between self-determination and quality of life for adults with mental retardation. *Education and Training in Mental Retardation and Developmental Disabilities, 33,* 3–12.

Wehmeyer, M. L., Shogren, K., Smith, T., Zager, D., & Simpson, R. (2010). Research-based principles and practices for educating students with autism: Self-determination and social interactions. *Education and Training in Autism and Developmental Disabilities, 45*(4) 475–486.

Weinkauf, T. (2002). College and university? You've got to be kidding: Inclusive post-secondary education for adults with intellectual disabilities. *Crossing Boundaries –An Interdisciplinary Journal, 1*(2), 28–37.

Whetstone, M., & Browning, P. (2002). Transition: A frame of reference. *Alabama Federation on Council for Exceptional Children On-Line Journal,* 1, 1–9.

Witte, R. H. *(2001).* College graduates with learning disabilities and the Americans with Disabilities Act (ADA): Do they know their employment rights? *Learning Disabilities: A Multidisciplinary Journal,* 11, 27–30.

Wolf, L., Brown, J., & Bork Kukicla, R. (2009). *Students with Asperger Syndrome: A Guide for College Personnel.* Shawnee Mission, KS: Autism Asperger Publishing Company.

Zager, D., & Smith, T. (2012). Inclusion at the postsecondary level for students with autism spectrum disorders. *Division on Autism and Developmental Disabilities*: Position Paper.

Zhang, D., & Benz, M. R. (2006). Enhancing self-determination of culturally diverse students with disabilities: Current status and future directions. *Focus on Exceptional Children, 38*(9), 1.

Chapter 16

Promoting Integrated Employment Options

Dianne Zager and Francine L. Dreyfus

This chapter addresses preparation for integrated employment and community living for people with autism spectrum disorders. In order to provide a picture of the state-of-the-art, the chapter begins with an overview of pertinent literature and legislation related to transition services and employment framed by historical perspectives. Implicit challenges in autism spectrum disorders (ASD) that may impact individuals' transition to employment (e.g., problems with executive functioning and social communication) are covered to help readers gain awareness of services that may be needed to enhance transition outcomes. Necessary components of person-centered secondary and postsecondary education programs are discussed, with a focus on (a) collaborative models that include personnel from varied disciplines, (b) family involvement, and (c) experiences and supports needed to enhance the likelihood of successful outcomes. Models for employment preparation, intervention, and ongoing support are presented.

Employment Outcomes for People with ASD: Historical Overview

Despite decades of federal regulations mandating implementation of transition services that are connected to school-to-work initiatives, competitive employment outcomes remain poor for individuals with disabilities, especially those with ASD. Unemployment rates for individuals with autism are significantly higher than for other disability categories (Shattuck et al., 2012). The U.S. Department of Labor (2014) reported unemployment for people without disabilities in 2013 at 6.3 percent and unemployment for people with disabilities at 11.9 percent, with labor force participation for people with disabilities at 18.7 percent. Generally, research studies indicate that between 50 percent and 75 percent of adults with autism are not employed in competitive work or that they are underemployed, and 86 percent of youth with ASD leaving high school are unemployed (Autism Society, 2011; Chiang, Cheung, Li, & Tsai,

2013; Van Laarhoven, Winiarski, Blood, & Chan 2012; Wagner, Newman, Cameto, Garza, & Levine, 2005). College graduates with ASD experience significant underemployment and frequent loss of employment (Barnhill, 2007; Hendricks & Wehman, 2009; Henninger & Taylor, 2013; Hurlbutt & Chalmers, 2004). Underemployed adults with ASD work fewer hours and earn lower wages compared to other individuals with disabilities (Burgess & Cimera, 2014; Cimera & Cowan, 2009). The annual cost for caring for the 1.5 million people in the U.S. with autism has been estimated from $35 billion to $60 billion (Autism Society, 2013), with the lifetime expense of caring for a person with autism at $3.2 million, a substantial cost to society. Two-thirds of these costs occur after the age of 18 (Ganz, 2006) and are directly related to unemployment.

Limited employment opportunities for individuals with ASD may be related to unique cognitive, communication, and behavior challenges of the disorder, often resulting in difficulty navigating work situations (Hendricks & Wehman, 2009; Walsh, Lyndon, & Healy, 2014). Stereotypic behaviors associated with ASD, including motor movements and vocalizations, insistence on rigidity and sameness, and sensory issues are associated specifically with the disorder (Schall & McDonough, 2010; Taylor & Seltzer, 2011). Demands in work environments and the ability to comprehend communication methods and materials used by employers (e.g., verbal directions, written handbooks with abstract concepts) present critical difficulties for individuals with ASD. Adapting to social and cultural norms of workplace environments tends to be difficult, as well. These challenges may prevent individuals with autism, including individuals with Asperger syndrome, from succeeding at work (Chiang et al., 2013; Schall & McDonough, 2010; Shattuck et al., 2012; Walsh, Lyndon, & Healy, 2013).

Generally, the existing literature related to employment outcomes for persons with ASD has focused on the characteristics associated with autism, difficulty accessing services to facilitate employment or community participation, and poor outcomes for individuals affecting the quality of their adult life (Burgess & Cimera, 2014; Cimera & Cowan, 2009; Hendricks, 2010; Shattack et al., 2011, 2012; Wehman et al., 2014). In reviewing the scientific interventions and practices for young adults with ASD, Chen, Leader, Sung, and Leahy (2014) found a scarcity of empirical research to identify specific models to promote successful employment outcomes. Most research that has been conducted consists of experimental designs with small numbers of participants or qualitative studies (Chen et al., 2014). As a result, there has been an emphasis on utilizing correlation research to identify evidence-based predictors associated with employment outcomes (Gerhardt & Lainer, 2011; Test et al., 2009; Wehman et al., 2014).

The majority of studies on outcomes of adults with ASD originate from follow-up studies and analyses of data from the National Longitudinal Transition Study-2 (NLTS2) conducted in the United States from 2001 to 2009, including 11,000 individuals with disabilities. Specifically, the NLTS2 data includes 922 youth and adults with ASD from 13 to 26 years old (Burgess & Cimera, 2014). Shattuck et al. (2011), in analyzing the NTLS2 data, reported that in the eight years after exiting high school, only 53 percent of individuals with autism had worked for pay and only 6 percent of young adults were employed in competitive jobs. Similarly, in reviewing the NTLS2 data, Roux et al. (2013) found that only 53 percent of adults with ASD aged 21–25 had ever worked for a salary outside of the home, the lowest rate among all the disability groups. Shattuck et al. (2012) reported that the employment outcomes, for 500 individuals with ASD were poor particularly in the first two years after leaving high school; young adults with ASD were not working or attending school. Studies analyzing the NTLS2 data reported that individuals with ASD from lower-income families and those individuals with more significant functional impairments were more likely to be disengaged from employment (Chiang et al., 2013; Roux et al., 2013; Shattuck et al. 2012).

Several studies of employment outcomes revealed limited opportunities for adults with ASD. Howlin, Goode, Hutton, and Rutter (2004) studied the employment outcomes for 68 adults (21–48 years old) in the United Kingdom; approximately 34 percent of the adults were employed and approximately 13 percent were in competitive employment. Taylor and Seltzer (2011) conducted a longitudinal ten-year study of 66 adults (19–26 years old), who graduated from high school between 2004 and 2008; 6 percent were in competitive employment, 12 percent in supported employment, a majority of the young adults (56 percent) were in sheltered workshops or day center (adult habilitation) activities, and 12 percent did not participate regularly in any activities in adulthood.

Similarly, in a longitudinal study of employment outcomes by Billstedt, Gillberg, and Gillberg (2005), 78 percent of the sample of 120 young adults with autism were unemployed and not living independently. Due to their cognitive ability, it is assumed that adults with higher functioning autism and Asperger's syndrome would have more success in being employed and sustaining employment; however, existing studies do not support this conclusion (Chen et al., 2014). Although, a number of adults with higher functioning autism and Asperger's syndrome were employed, from 11 percent to 55 percent, (Farley et al. 2009; Howlin, 2000; Hurlbutt & Chalmers, 2004; Mawhood & Howlin, 1999) generally individuals were underemployed. Adults with Asperger's syndrome and higher functioning autism who had completed high school and attended postsecondary education (and also obtained college degrees) were employed in unskilled jobs, paid below the minimum wage, and often unemployed for extended periods (Chen et al., 2014; Hurlbutt & Chalmers, 2004; Wilczynski, Trammell, & Clarke, 2013).

According to self-reports from individuals with ASD, maintaining employment success was related to social interaction and communication skills rather than their specific job responsibilities (Barnhill, 2007; Hurlbutt & Chalmers, 2004). Many young adults with ASD who graduate from high school are not prepared for competitive employment. Shattuck *et al.* (2012) reported that youth with ASD have the highest risk of being disengaged from employment; the risk was greater than 50 percent for the first two years following high school graduation. Burgess and Cimera (2014) studied the employment outcomes of 34,501 transition-aged young adults from 2002 to 2011 throughout the United States who were served by vocational rehabilitation services. Of the 34,413 individuals receiving transition services, more than 20,000 individuals did not achieve successful employment. Similarly, youth with ASD who were employed were underemployed; they worked fewer hours (17–30 hours per week) and their overall yearly wages were below the poverty level for a single wage earner (Burgess & Cimera, 2014).

There are critical components that define the quality of life for all adults: residential living, employment, and social relationships (Walsh, Lyndon, & Healy, 2014). Employment enables people to earn sufficient wages and support themselves in the community, pursue social relationships, and interests (Hendricks, 2010). According to Hendricks (2010), "employment provides a forum that promotes personal dignity and has been demonstrated to improve the quality of life of individuals with ASD" (p. 126).

The lack of gainful employment has a considerable impact on residential options and participation by individuals in the community. Although Hendricks and Wehman (2009) showed that with appropriate training and supports, individuals with ASD could participate successfully in competitive work, generally youths and adults with ASD live at home with only a small percentage living independently. Wagner, Newman, Cameto, Garza, and Levine (2005) surveyed young adults with ASD and found that only 4 percent were living independently. Wagner, Newman, Cameto, Levine, and Marder (2007), surveyed young adults with ASD who participated in the NTLS2 study to determine their perception and expectations in community activities. The study indicated that 22 percent of the young adults did not expect to live independently and approximately 25 percent did not expect to be financially independent.

Based on a correlational review of the literature and several studies, the National Secondary Transition Technical Assistance Center (NSTTAC) has identified transition planning as an evidenced-based practice for increasing the probability of young adults with ASD securing competitive employment. Roux, Shattuck, Rast, Rava, and Anderson (2015), using the NTLS2 data, found that only 58 percent of youth with ASD had a transition plan developed by the age of 14, the federally required age. Furthermore, according to Wagner et al. (2007) in their survey of young adults with ASD, transition plans included 20 percent of goals for competitive employment, 25 percent of goals for supported employment, and 15 percent for sheltered workshop. Generally, transition plans do not include paid employment during high school in preparation for competitive employment. Roux et al. (2015) reported that only 58 percent of young adults worked for a salary between high school and their early twenties, a significantly lower rate that young adults with other disabilities.

Generally, studies focusing on transition planning have been descriptive and have made global recommendations for improving the transition process (Landmark, Ju & Zhang, 2010; Papay & Bambara, 2014; Wehman et al., 2014). Using NLTS2 data, Shogren & Plotner (2012) concluded that young adults with ASD had significantly less transition goals related to competitive employment compared to other disability groups. The study indicated that the majority of students with ASD did not assume a leadership role in planning their own transition, although young adults with ASD have more postsecondary support needs. According to Hagner et al. (2012), poor adult outcomes for individuals with ASD are associated with a transition process that is professionally controlled and does not include active participation by the student or family.

Transition Legislation and Federal Initiatives

The Individuals with Disabilities Act (2004) defines the process of transition planning as a coordinated array of activities to ensure that every student with a disability has individualized goals on their IEP in the areas of postsecondary options, including employment or vocational training and community living. For high school students with ASD, the IEP should detail a course of study linked to transition goals. According to the Individuals with Disabilities Education Improvement Act (IDEIA, 2004), postsecondary goals indicated on the student's IEP should frame the trajectory of skills that students need to learn to function as adults, including career and vocational skills (Hendricks & Wehman, 2009).

Since the 1980s, the need for comprehensive transition services (and transition education) has been the focus of mandated disability regulations encompassing, employment, adult services, and independent living options. Federal initiatives were created to improve transition services for youth with disabilities based on their needs, preferences, and abilities (Morningstar & Liss, 2008). Transition services were mandated with the Individuals with Disabilities Education Act of 1990, the subsequent re-authorization of the Act in 1997, and the last re-authorization entitled the Individuals with Disabilities Education Improvement Act, IDEIA (2004).

The Americans with Disabilities Act (1990) required schools to prepare students with disabilities to transition to post-school options by including a statement of services needed into the student's Individualized Education Program (IEP) by the age of 16 and to update the IEP annually. According to IDEA, post-school activities may include postsecondary education, vocational training, integrated (including supported) employment, adult education and services, and independent living and community participation (Morningstar & Liss, 2008).

The last revision of IDEIA mandated that schools must address the transition needs and services for the student not later than the first IEP to be in effect when the child turns 16, or younger if determined appropriate by the IEP Team; however, states may choose to continue beginning the IEP transition requirement at age 14. [34 CFR 300.320(b) and (c)] [20 U.S.C. 1414 (d)(1)(A)(i)(VIII)]. The re-authorization of IDEIA, in 2004, delineated the schools accountability for students' progress functionally, as well as in academic achievement. According to IDEIA, transition goals must be measureable and results oriented, based on an age-appropriate transition assessment, and include areas related to postsecondary goals such as training, education, employment, and, if appropriate, independent living skills (Etscheidt, 2006; Morningstar & Liss, 2008; Wehman, 2013a).

In conjunction with mandates for transition services and education, federal legislation has focused on improving access and support for all youth successfully from school to work. In 1990, The Americans with Disabilities Act (ADA) banned discrimination in employment for individuals with disabilities and ensured accessibility to workplaces, public services, and accommodations. The School-To-Work Opportunities Act of 1994 (Public Law 103-239) was similar to IDEA in its purpose to create results-oriented, performance-based education and training programs statewide to prepare all youth for competitive employment. The regulation addressed opportunities for students to participate in career exploration and counseling, work experiences during high school, and standards-based instruction that focused on achievement in occupational and academic skills. The Workforce Investment Act (1998) created federally funded demonstration projects for job training and employment services. This Act included mandates for state and local governments to include accommodations for the needs of individuals with disabilities (Hardman & Dawson, 2010).

Components of Transition Preparation

Current research studies have identified evidence-based practices in transition planning for young adults with ASD. Test et al. (2009), using the National Secondary Transition Technical Assistance Center (NSTTAC) database, concluded that student participation in the transition process, specifically teaching students *self-advocacy* and *self-determination* skills, were evidence-based practices. Self-determination involves the individual assuming an active, self-directed role in changing his or her life by making plans, implementing, and adjusting those plans as necessary. Self-determination includes effectuating choice-making skills, decision-making skills, problem-solving skills, goal-setting and self-evaluation skills, independence, self-awareness skills, and self-advocacy and leadership skills (Wehman et al., 2014; Wehmeyer, Shogren, Smith, Zager, & Simpson, 2010). Specifically teaching high school students with ASD to participate and lead in their transition planning is a strategy to enhance their self-advocacy and self-determination skills (Test, Smith, & Carter, 2014).

Ideally, participation in the transition process will assist young adults with ASD to enhance their ability to perceive their skills and preferences in context with the postsecondary environment, participate in career exploration to collect information, and subsequently make informed decisions (Hagner et al., 2012). For young adults with ASD, *person-centered planning* is an essential process to effectively plan for adult life. The plan focuses on the wants, hopes, concerns, and needs of individuals with disabilities and their families. It includes a long-term vision and descriptive statement of the desired outcomes for the young adult in 3–5 years and is the blueprint for learning experiences, supports, and services for the individual and the family (Meadan, Sheldon, Appel, & DeGrazia, 2010).

Family Involvement

Given the important role of family involvement in providing support to a young adult with ASD, including advocacy, linkages with the community and service providers, and developing postsecondary supports, family participation in the transition process is a critical predictor of positive postsecondary outcomes (Hagner et al., 2012; Landmark, Ju, & Zhang, 2010; Schall, Wehman, & McDonough, 2012). Utilizing the NLTS2 data, including 830 youth with ASD, Shorgren and Plotner (2012) found that only 67 percent of families received information about postsecondary services. Transition programs that result in positive outcomes for young adults with ASD continually involve families throughout the school years (Schall, Wehman, & McDonough, 2012).

A study conducted by Hagner et al. (2012) focused on families with young adults with ASD, 16–19 years old, who participated in training on strategies for person-centered planning and utilized adult service options to create postsecondary opportunities. As a result, the families reported higher student and family expectations for the future, improvement in the young adults' self-determination skills, and appropriate future career decision-making plans.

State Vocational Rehabilitation Services

The Rehabilitation Act of 1973, as amended and re-authorized in 1998 under the Workforce Investment Act of 1998, provides federal grants to states to coordinate transition planning and vocational rehabilitation (VR) services to individuals. Services for individuals can include: assessments to determine eligibility of services, counseling, job placement, supported employment, and vocational training. Although the VR system is a core resource for individuals with disabilities, it has not been prepared to meet the needs of youth and adults with ASD (Chen et al., 2014; Hendricks, 2010). Lawer, Brusilovskiy, Salzer, and Mandell (2009) examined the experiences of individuals with ASD in the VR system. The subjects included 382,221 adults ages 18–65 served by VR, whose cases were closed in 2005; 1,707 of these were adults with ASD. The study revealed that adults with ASD were more likely than adults with other disabilities to be denied services due to the severity of their disability. Furthermore, VR services did not provide job coaching and other on-site supports that met the unique needs of individuals with ASD.

The need for services for adults with ASD has considerably increased. From 2002 to 2011, the numbers of adults with ASD seeking VR services increased by 792 percent (Burgess & Cimera, 2014). Schaller and Yang (2005), analyzing the employment outcomes of 1,323 adults with ASD, found that 62 percent received VR services for supportive or competitive employment services and, as a result, 66 percent were successfully employed. The costs of providing VR services for individuals with ASD are expensive and they mostly costly compared to other disability groups (Cimera & Cowan, 2009). However, it is less cost effective to support adults with ASD who leave VR services and earn lower wages and work fewer hours. Burgess and Cimera concluded that transition-age adults (under 22 years old) with ASD were more likely to become successfully employed as a result of receiving VR services than other disability groups served by VR.

The recently enacted Workforce Innovation and Opportunity Act of 2014 places new requirements on state VR agencies transitioning youth with disabilities, and the most significant disabilities, to employment options. This act mandates that VR services increase their role in transition through coordination between VR and other agencies, extending services for VR in supported employment from 18 to 24 months, and modification in eligibility to promote access to individuals with the most significant disabilities. Each state's VR program will have a larger role in assisting young adults with disabilities transition from school to adult life. Services will include job exploration counseling, work-based learning experiences, workplace readiness training, and training on self-advocacy (Hoff, 2014). Hopefully, more individuals with ASD will be placed in supported employment and other employment options.

Key Players

Special educators and vocational rehabilitation counselors play critical roles in preparing students to obtain employment and to live within their community. Lack of educators' knowledge about transition programming, as well as about support services and systems, contributes to inadequate career development and has resulted in underemployment of people with autism and developmental disabilities (Müller, Schuler, Burton, & Yates, 2003; Standifer, 2009). Effective secondary education to prepare students for employment that builds skills to enable all individuals to live, work, and recreate within their communities has the potential to improve the current low rates of unemployment (Chiang et al., 2013) and to help individuals succeed in integrated community living. Unfortunately, although federal policy has focused on transition to employment initiatives for people with disabilities for over two decades, a clear effective pathway to successful employment has yet to be proven (Luecking & Luecking, 2015).

Challenges Related to Employment

Transition to employment for people with autism spectrum disorders has been, and continues to be, a pressing problem (Carter, Austin, & Trainer, 2012; Hendricks & Wehman, 2009). Despite evidence of the potential of people with autism to perform competitive jobs and reports that work preparation programs can improve adult outcomes (Wehman et al., 2012), success rates in employment and community integration for this population remain extremely poor (Allen, Wallace, Greene, Bowen, & Burke, 2010a; Cimera & Cowan, 2009). There has been limited research and insufficient evidence to support the effectiveness of any particular transition approach for adults with autism (Schall, Targett, & Wehman, 2013), resulting in service delivery that is fraught with widespread lack of understanding of the employment support needs of this population. Today, far too many students with autism are leaving high school without the skills, experiences, supports, and linkages that will enable them to enter college or the workplace (Kucharczyk et al., 2015). Yet, on a positive note, as surveys and research studies (e.g. Carter et al., 2012; Shattuck et al., 2012), continue to draw attention to the inadequacy of prevailing secondary education programs, there is growing momentum in the field to improve transition programs.

Individuals with autism have markedly different service needs than individuals with other disabilities. Cimera and Cowan (2009) reported that adults with autism were likely to be denied services because of the magnitude of their needs, which often require intensive services. Lack of knowledge of characteristics of autism spectrum disorders, especially unfamiliarity with strengths and abilities that may exist in individuals on the spectrum, has contributed heavily to this problem. In addition, a lack of effective secondary education to prepare students with ASD for careers continues to result in a low employment rate (Chiang et al., 2013). While it is true that communication, cognitive, behavioral, sensory, and social characteristics inherent in this disorder may necessitate ongoing services, appropriate supports can increase success rates and enable individuals with autism make significant contributions to the workplace and their communities.

Widespread lack of understanding within special education and vocational rehabilitation of the needs of individuals with autism in adulthood, along with the current lack of knowledge about available options to accommodate and support them (McEathron, Beuhring, Maynard, & Mavis, 2013), has negatively impacted employment outcomes (Müller et al., 2003; Standifer, 2009). In fact, limited expertise in helping individuals with autism find and maintain work in the face of their unique challenges has led to persistent high rates of unemployment (Lawer et al., 2009).

The juxtaposition of evidence that people with autism can successfully sustain employment when provided with adequate support and reports showing the inadequacy of employment support, points directly to a need for improved systems that will enable individuals with autism to be employed (Zager, Thoma, & Fleisher, 2014). The following section discusses three key areas of difficulty (interpersonal interaction, executive functioning, and sensory processing), each of which is an implicit challenge in autism that may significantly impact employment and community living outcomes. Later in the chapter, strategies for improving competence in these areas, as well as options to accommodate people with autism in community workplaces, are presented.

Interpersonal Interaction Differences

Success in the workplace is dependent, in large measure, on the ability to navigate the social terrain of the job site. Social communication and interpersonal interaction can be difficult for people with autism, affecting transition to new environments. Problems understanding the behaviors and feelings of others, referred to as *Theory of Mind* can result in verbal, as well as behavioral responses that may be deemed inappropriate (Baron-Cohen, Leslie, & Frith, 1985). In short, interacting appropriately with co-workers, employers, and patrons is critical to maintaining employment. While people with autism may lose their job due to problems in productivity or accuracy (Smith & Philippen, 2005), jobs are more likely to be lost because of behaviors that do not fit in the workplace. An employee may be expected to solve problems, work collaboratively, and comply with appropriate etiquette and varied other non-work skills referred to as soft skills.

According to the U.S. Department of Labor's Office of Disability Employment Policy, some key skills needed on the job are (a) communicating effectively, (b) managing time, (c) taking initiative, (d) responding to the needs of others, (e) maintaining a positive attitude, (f) participating on collaborative teams, and (g) thinking critically to solve problems (Zager, Alpern, McKeon, Maxam, & Mulvey, 2013). A lack of proficiency in these soft skills, which are particularly challenging for individuals on the spectrum, is more likely to cause job loss, than is difficulty with specific job-related skills.

Executive Functioning Challenges

Executive functions serve to enable individuals to manage themselves, engage in activities, and complete tasks in order to reach their goals. These abilities have been compared to a Global Positioning System that guides the brain to keep individuals focused and headed in the right direction during tasks (Azano & Tuckwiller, 2011). Executive function is neurologically based and serves to control emotions and self-regulatory behavior. The numerous definitions of executive functioning have a basic commonality in that they describe a set of skills needed to accomplish everyday tasks, such as planning, organizing, prioritizing, and multi-tasking (Hughes, Russell, & Robbins, 1994; Russell, Jarrold, & Hood, 1999). Executive functions are critical in goal-directed behavior and for directing one's performance, especially guiding the planning processes required in task completion, organizing, strategizing, sustaining attention to and remembering details, along with management of time and space.

Executive dysfunction may interfere with an individual's work performance in a variety of ways. Some examples of challenges related to executive dysfunction include following multi-step instructions, coordinating sets of activities, attending to pertinent details in assigned tasks, etc. Such abilities are necessary to be able to follow a morning routine to get to work on time, or to complete tasks according to a designated time frame (Zager et al., 2013).

The degree of executive competence individuals possess in organization and management affects their behavior. As anxiety resulting from problems caused by executive dysfunction escalates and individuals feel overwhelmed by task complexity, self-regulation of behavior becomes increasingly difficult. The good news is that executive function relies on modifiable and teachable skills (Thoma, Gentry, Boyd, & Streagle, 2013). Special educators, vocational counselors, and family members can be instrumental in fostering the development of employment-related and independent living skills that will lead to improved executive functioning. By providing concrete literal instruction in relevant real-life training opportunities (Zager & Feinman, 2013), it is possible to improve the skills influenced by an individual's executive functioning system.

Sensory Integration Issues

Sensory integration refers to the ability to process external and internal stimuli simultaneously. Humans are continually confronted with oncoming stimuli, which our senses are expected to perceive and interpret, leading to some form of response. Intact sensory processing enables people to adapt their behavior in order to participate in community life. For instance, in a loud bar, people tend to raise their voices to be heard; or while driving in the city, drivers must be responsive to oncoming traffic from different directions, traffic signals, pedestrians, and weather conditions.

People with autism may be hyper- or hypo-sensitive to stimuli, either over-reacting or under-reacting to visual, tactile, or auditory stimuli. Some individuals find themselves unsure as to where another person's space begins and ends. When external stimuli are coming from more than one source—such as smell, sound, and touch—a person with ASD may become overwhelmed (Miller & Lane, 2000). It is much easier to avoid or prepare for overwhelming situations than it is to rectify the resultant issues and behaviors. Some ways to prepare for situations are to desensitize the individual to a particular environment, step by step, to build tolerance. Other possibilities include accommodations, such as headphones to block noise. Needed supports should be determined on an individual basis and should be situation specific.

Considerations in Educational Planning for Transition

The goal of education for all individuals is to expand their knowledge and skills so that they can achieve personal independence upon graduation from school (Hendricks & Wehman, 2009). The transition from school to options including postsecondary education and paid employment improves the possibilities that all individuals will become independent, productive, and participating members of their community (Hendricks, 2010; Hendricks & Wehman, 2009; Wehman et al., 2014). Research studies conducted in the 1980s reported that adult outcomes including employment, integration into the community, and independent living were, at that time, usually unattainable for young adults with disabilities (Hasazi, Gordon, & Roe, 1985; Landmark et al., 2010; Mithaung, Horiuchi, & Fanning, 1985).

In response to the failure of schools to provide systematic training and education to ensure the transition of individuals with disabilities into the workforce, the U.S. Department of Education's Office of Special Education and Rehabilitation created a school-to-work model. The Bridges from School to Working Life Model focused exclusively on the transition from school-to-work. The model was created for students with disabilities aged 16 and above and extended the length of service and support that would be needed to attain the goal of sustained paid employment (Will, 1984). However, other research studies in the 1990s that examined the efficacy of special education revealed that students with disabilities graduating from special education programs had a considerably different quality of life compared to their non-disabled peers (Johnson & Halloran, 1997; Landmark et al., 2010; Shattuck et al., 2012; Wehman, 2013). The majority of graduates of special education programs remained underemployed or unemployed and did not have access to community participation (Landmark et al., 2010).

Transition Goals for Secondary and Postsecondary Students

Inherent characteristics of autism, as they affect behavior and learning *for each individual*, should influence educational planning. By respecting underlying characteristics of autism and building on student strengths while accommodating cognitive, sensory and social challenges, practitioners can improve transition outcomes. Talents, interests and preferences are key factors in designing programs for students with autism. Personal interests, as well as challenges and educational needs, change over time as individuals with ASD progress though different stages of development (Zager et al., 2013).

Approaches for instructing students with ASD have varying degrees of empirical support. It is useful to consider how various approaches might be adapted and combined on an individual basis to facilitate the transition process, and how data could be collected throughout implementation of selected practices to facilitate learning and enhance transition to employment and independent living. While during the childhood years education may be provided through approaches, such as Applied Behavior Analysis (ABA), Structured teaching of the TEACCH (Treatment and Education of Autistic and Related Communication-Handicapped Children) Program, or the Developmental Individual Difference Relationship Model (DIR, FloorTime), secondary school programs tend to combine approaches, adding more emphasis on the development of functional academics, independence and self-determination, and with attention directed toward longitudinal goal setting and life-long planning.

The research and literature base in the field of autism have shown that instructional effectiveness is improved through the application of behavioral techniques (e.g., providing and fading prompts and utilizing positive reinforcement techniques) (see, for example, Baer, Wolf, & Risely, 1968; Duker & Didder, 2004; Hundert, 2009; Iovannone, Dunlap, Huber, & Kincaid, 2003). There is also abundant research and written material promoting the TEACCH method (Marcus, Lansing, Andrews, & Schopler, 1978; Mesibov, Browder, & Kirkland, 2002; Mesibov & Shea, 2010). Regardless of the level of functioning of students on the spectrum, these techniques can provide a much-needed framework for learning. In recent years, another approach, the DIR Model, has garnered supportive data, as well (Greenspan, 1999; Greenspan & Wieder, 2006; Mahoney & Perales, 2005; Wieder & Greenspan, 2003).

For adolescents and young adults who have benefited from years of behavioral intervention, transition instruction at this stage should be presented through a broader behavioral framework. Such behavioral programming can increase age-appropriate behaviors required in inclusive community settings, where naturally occurring reinforcement is a powerful tool. Relating new concepts to actual experiences can enhance meaning and facilitate learning new knowledge. Because individuals with ASD and other developmental disabilities often have difficulty generalizing learned information to new situations (Wacker, Berg, Berrie, & Swatta, 1985), it is incumbent upon teachers at the secondary level to conduct a large portion of instruction in settings beyond their classroom walls, utilizing community-based learning strategies for transition. Research studies have noted the importance of community-based instruction in the preparation of youth with autism and other education severe disabilities (Berkell, 1992; Wacker, Berg, Berrie, & Swatta, 1985).

In selecting transition preparation settings, environmental factors should be considered. Research informs us of the interplay between environmental factors and sensory issues (Ben-Sasson, Fluss, Cermak, Engel-Yeger, & Gal, 2008). Noise, lighting, smells, crowds, animals, etc. may pose sensory discomfort for individuals with ASD. By taking into account these considerations, agitation and maladaptive behaviors may be reduced, therein increasing the likelihood of successful transition. Instructional approaches to prepare students with autism to be successful in work and adult living should focus on (a) building on strengths and interests, rather than on a deficit-based model; (b) presenting opportunities to learn in varied ways to accommodate challenges associated with autism, such as sensory issues (e.g. hyper-sensitivity to noise, smell, or touch), distractibility, restricted interests, repetitive behaviors; and (c) turning behaviors that could be perceived negatively into work-related assets (e.g. over-attention to detail, persistent attraction to specific activities).

Universal Design for Transition

The promotion of integrated community-based work for people with ASD requires creation of effective sustainable models of employment intervention. One model that has been shown to be effective in transition programming for secondary school students with intellectual disabilities and that shows promise for students with ASD is Universal Design for Transition (UDT) (Thoma, Bartholomew, & Scott, 2009). Universal Design for Transition offers evidence-based practices for preparing adults with autism for employment. Universal Design for Transition practices have been demonstrated to be highly effective in preparing persons for disabilities for the transition to work, by providing the framework for employment preparation and serving as a guide to move individuals toward attainment of their goals.

This model is founded on the principles of Universal Design for Learning: (1) multiple means of representation, (2) multiple means of expression, and (3) multiple means of participation and engagement. Universal Design for Learning (UDL) builds on individuals' strengths and interests rather than using a deficit-based model. As with UDL, the goal of UDT is to enable all individuals to sustain competitive/supported employment by ensuring maneuverable and accessible work environments. In UDT, tasks are scaffolded into sequential segments, permitting participants to enter the task at their level. Assistive technology is utilized to provide options for information presentation and task completion. Knowledge and skills are presented concretely, aligned with individual talents and interests, and taught in a meaningful way through real-life experiences. For example, a person who wants to work in a restaurant would benefit from experiential instruction on-site in a restaurant or simulated restaurant. Skills taught might include sorting silverware and dishes, setting tables, following directions for job tasks, and conversing with co-workers and patrons.

Self-determination is a critical component of UDT employment training. A clear connection between self-determination competence and improved outcomes in employment has been demonstrated (Wehmeyer & Palmer, 2003). Self-determination instruction utilizes person-centered planning and is based on a problem-solving approach that encourages individuals to bridge the gap between current situations and targeted goals. Instruction should guide learning through a series of questions that help steer future planning, and interface with person-centered planning to include (a) goal setting, (b) constructing learning plans, and (c) adjusting behaviors. Utilization of UDT with emphasis on self-determination competence has been shown to enhance work-related learning (Thoma et al., 2009) and to improve employment outcomes (Wehmeyer, Lattimore, et al., 2003).

Multiple avenues for service delivery are helpful in identifying and using strengths to meet employment goals. Essential elements in successful programming are: (a) varied work experiences in multiple employment settings that take into account students' strengths as well as challenges often associated with autism, such as executive dysfunction, concrete thinking, rigidity, sensory issues, and social communication challenges; (b) self-determination competence instruction identifies opportunities that take into account special talents and skills that may have been developed and honed to high levels through over-selective interests in specific topics (e.g. trains, cars, animals, theater, food, mathematics); (c) multiple representations of learning tasks, such as modeling and video presentations that take into account unique learning and behavior characteristics associated with autism (e.g. difficulty with abstract concepts, trouble with fast-paced or language, preference for well-organized visual presentation); (d) multiple engagement in varied work activities, such as individual work, cooperative tasks, and technology driven activities that take into account learning and behavior needs (e.g. difficulty with generalization of learned information to new situations, desire to have friends but inability to take initiative or act reciprocally, difficulty understanding expectations in cooperative group situations); (e) multiple expressions of knowledge such as role playing, drawing, and writing that take advantage of skills and strengths that can be used to demonstrate competence; and (f) reflection and evaluation of learned knowledge through self-assessment, involving the need to look objectively at the consequences of one's actions and considering the interpretation of, and response to, one's acts by others.

Employment intervention should include (a) work experiences in settings that consider the learner's strengths as well as challenges (e.g., sensory issues, rigidity social communication issues); (b) person-centered planning that focuses on development of self-determination competence; (c) modeling, role playing, and videos to illustrate critical job components; (d) technology-assisted instruction that accommodates unique learner characteristics; (e) participation in cooperative activities as appropriate; (f) self-assessment and reflection to look at the consequences of one's actions, understand the response of others to these actions, and proactively plan more appropriate actions.

Role of Educators

It is the responsibility of educators to deliver transition curricula that incorporate person-centered planning, targeted academic instruction for job readiness, real-life work experiences, family involvement, and employer support into their transition programs. Educators involved in transition programs need to be familiar with their state agencies and systems in order to help families obtain services and make a seamless transition to adult services. Family involvement is essential to successful employment outcomes. Engaging and supporting parents/families in the employment process involves ongoing communication with families. Family members may need assistance in accessing necessary services, resolving obstacles to job attainment, and navigating the bureaucracy of agencies. It is important to listen to the concerns of individuals and their families, to help them obtain needed services, navigate agencies' bureaucracies, and resolve problems and obstacles.

It is also critical to include work supervisors who will be interacting with individuals with ASD at the jobsite. Supervisors will benefit from information about the core challenges associated with autism, such as the difficulty that persons with autism have in understanding abstract language and concepts (Zager & Alpern, 2010). As supervision responsibilities are transferred from the job coach to on-site personnel, communication channels between all key stakeholders should remain open so that difficult situations that arise may be handled swiftly and seamlessly.

It is the educators' primary job to deliver evidence-based instructional activities that utilize strategies that enable all students to progress. As with all instruction, transition programs should provide appropriate accommodations and supports, including technology to meet specific needs associated with autism (e.g., communication difficulty, sensory issues, restricted interests, repetitive behaviors). They should utilize ongoing assessment to evaluate their programs' effectiveness, reflect on progress, adapt and modify programs as necessary, manage pertinent data, and communicate with other stakeholders in the employment support process. Programs should build on individuals' strengths and interests rather than using a deficit-based model. A major focus should center on enhancing self-determination for employment, including identifying employment goals, working toward goals, and adjusting plans or goals as needed (Wehmeyer & Shogren, 2014). Teachers need to engage in person-centered planning to facilitate choice-making, goal setting, and self-advocacy. It is helpful to channel students' behaviors that could be perceived negatively, such as over-attention to detail and persistent attraction to specific activities, into work-related assets.

Instructional strategies should build on strengths, respect individual interests and preferences, and accommodate challenges inherent in autism. During the school years, students should be guided to identify jobs that utilize abilities and talents and maximize human potential. Generic skills and behaviors that are vital for success in community-based employment settings should be taught, such as helping students plan and implement strategies so they can self-regulate, attend to and complete tasks, follow directions, organize activities, manage time efficiently, and work cooperatively with others. Students should learn how to request assistance, appropriately converse with co-workers, be active listeners, and engage in appropriate social etiquette. Challenging behaviors should be handled in a manner that can be generalized to the workplace, incorporating behavior management strategies, positive behavior supports, and relationship-based approaches for building positive behavior and resolving behavior issues in community-based settings. Curricula must address living skills related to job success, guiding students as they learn to manage tasks related to bill paying, financial budgeting, laundry, personal hygiene, time management, meal preparation, getting to work on time, and home cleanliness.

Integrated Supported Employment Options

Employment First, enacted in 2012, is based on the premise that all citizens, including youth and adults with significant disabilities, are capable of full inclusion in integrated employment and community life, and that individuals with disabilities secure employment that offers least minimum or customary benefits and wages (U.S. Department of Labor, Office of Disability Employment Policy, n.d.). Subsequently, in July 2014, the federal government re-authorized the Workforce Investment Act of 1998, now titled the Workforce Innovation and Opportunity Act (WIOA). The Act further defines supported employment as integrative competitive employment including ongoing support services for individuals with the most severe disabilities for whom competitive employment has not occurred or has been intermittent due to a severe disability. Supported employment is a viable option for individuals who need intensive supported services due to the severity of their disabilities and extended services.

The Act further delineates that youth with disabilities aged 24 and younger would be prohibited from working for subminimum wages, which are generally positions in sheltered workshops or enclaves (Diament, 2015; Hoff, 2014). For young adults with ASD, in relation to their needs for support in behavioral, job-related skills, and social communication skills, supported employment is a critical phase in the transition to competitive employment.

Individuals with ASD must have equal employment rights to competitive employment as their neurotypical peers and peers with other disabilities (Chen et al., 2014; Walsh et al., 2014). A key component in achieving employment equality may be focusing on changing employers' and co-workers' attitudes regarding the employability of individuals with ASD (Chappel & Sommers, 2010; Gerhardt & Lainer, 2011; Hendricks, 2010; Morgan & Alexander, 2005). Studies focused on employers' attitudes indicate that a lack of understanding or awareness of autism spectrum disorders is the most significant challenge to successful employment for individuals with ASD (Chen et al., 2014; Hendricks, 2010; Morgan & Alexander 2005; Nesbitt, 2000; Wilczynski et al., 2013). Studies identifying advantages to employing individuals with ASD included consistent attendance and high productivity, as well as employers' compliance with workforce diversity policies (Hagner & Cooney, 2005; Henderson & Cone, 2014; Morgan & Alexander, 2005).

Supported Employment

According to Griffin, Hammis, Keeton, and Sullivan (2014), enrollment in sheltered workshops increased during the 1990s, despite one of the strongest economies in the history of the United States. Historically, employment options for individuals with ASD have been sheltered workshops, in which individuals with disabilities have been paid less than minimum wages, or voluntary, unpaid work experiences (Hendricks, 2010; Nicholas, Attridge, Zwaigenbaum, & Clarke, 2015). Community-based competitive employment that offers work options for a minimum wage remains a limited possibility for individuals with ASD. Müller and Cannon (2014) conducted research focusing on the quality of life for 22 young adults with ASD and cognitive impairments. The study revealed that only 26 percent were employed in competitive employment while the majority of individuals, 65 percent, were volunteers in an organization.

Supported employment is another option that recognizes the capacity of an individual to be employed while ongoing supports are provided (Gerhardt & Lainer, 2011). Supported employment includes structured support services that are necessary for an individual to gain and maintain paid employment in an integrative environment (Hendricks, 2010; Nicholas et al., 2015). Hendricks (2010) examined the research focusing on successful supported employment programs and case studies of adults with ASD. Vocational supports for individuals with ASD may be grouped into five areas: job placement, supervisors and co-workers, on-the-job training, work place modification, and long-term support. The range of supports includes: job assessment based on the individual's goals and interests; job development in relation to career searches and job site training when the individual finds employment; support strategies including the use of technology; and long-term supports to ensure job retention (Wehman et al., 2012; Wilczynski et al., 2013). Westbrook et al. (2012), identified additional effective supports for individuals with ASD, including the use of functional behavioral assessments, positive reinforcement, social skills training, task analyses for facilitating training in specific job duties, and task preference assessments.

Job-site training facilitated by a job coach is often necessary for individuals with ASD to learn job-specific tasks and assimilate successfully into culture of the workplace. Specifically, the job coach assists the employee to identify the workplace's natural supports (including identifying supports from co-workers and supervisors), compensatory strategies, self-management skills, and specific instruction in job skills (Nicholas et al., 2015; Wehman et al., 2014; Wilczynski et al., 2013). Holmes (2007) concluded that failure to adequately assess and provide necessary supports results in unemployment, underemployment, and continual job loss for individuals with ASD. Although there has been limited research conducted focusing on teaching skills to individuals with ASD in workplace environments (Hendricks (2010), supported work programs that included on the-job training by a job coach with effective supports have been shown to result in increased employment rates, wages, and job retention rates for individuals with ASD.

Westbrook et al. (2012), in their extensive study of the current literature analyzing the efficacy of interventions with supported employment, identified only two quasi-experimental studies conducted by Mawhood and Howlin (1999) and Garcia-Villamisar, Ross, and Wehman (2000) that demonstrated the advantages of individuals with ASD in supported employment work programs or who were not in programs compared to individuals who attended in a sheltered workshop program. The Mawhood and Howlin two-year study specifically compared employment outcomes of 50 individuals with Asperger's syndrome. The experimental group of 30 adults received assistance from a job coach and a control group of 20 individuals matched by age, intellectual ability, and education. During the two-year period, more participants in the experimental group found paid employment, worked for longer periods of time, earned higher wages, and were employed in higher-level jobs (e.g. technical and administrative positions), compared to the individuals in the control group.

As a follow-up to the 1999 study, Howlin, Alcock, and Burkin (2005) examined employment outcomes for adults with Asperger's syndrome who participated in a supported employment program over an eight-year period. The program components included employment preparation, job finding assistance particularly focused on the individual's needs and abilities, and job coaching. The eight-year follow-up study revealed the same results as the earlier study; individuals had successfully secured and maintained employment; salaries and job types were higher; and the employees were employed longer than the individuals in the control group. Although the study conducted by Garcia-Villamisar, Ross and Wehman (2000) did not indicate a definitive correlation between the effectiveness of interventions and outcomes, the research had significant implications for individuals with ASD participating in supportive employment. The study compared employment outcomes of 51 young adults with ASD who participated in supported and sheltered employment groups in relation to the clinical symptomology of autism, demonstrating that individuals in the sheltered workshop group exhibited increased symptoms and a deterioration of their skills, while subjects in the supported employment group showed fewer symptoms than the other group and were more likely to maintain employment.

Hillier et al. (2007) evaluated the impact of a vocational support program that provided on-site job coaching and other workplace supports for nine high school students and recent high school graduates with ASD. At the conclusion of the program, the majority of participants had retained their initial job placements and their income increased. Wehman, et al., (2012) collected data from 33 adults with ASD enrolled in a supported employment program working individually with an on-site employment specialist. As a result of implementing a highly individualized program of supports, including long-term supports to foster job retention, of the 33 individuals participating in the program, 27 successfully obtained competitive employment jobs. Wehman et al., (2013b) documented the results of a randomized clinical trial of Project SEARCH (an intensive internship program for high school-age students in a hospital environment) providing vocational training and supports (e.g. specialized structure and schedules, intensive social skills instruction). Of the 24 young adults, 18–21 years old, in the treatment group, 21 (approximately 88 percent) acquired employment with higher than minimum wages. Of the 16 participants in the control group, only one participant gained employment.

These qualitative studies indicate the efficacy of supported employment in increasing the rates of employment, wages, and the ability of individuals with ASD to retain employment. For individuals who were employed for longer periods of time and received higher wages, the quality of their life substantially improved. For adults with ASD who were employed for at least six months, there were significant improvements in their behavior in relation to independent functioning and socialization skills with co-workers (Westbrook et al., 2012).

Additionally, supported employment may be correlated with increasing the cognitive performance of individuals with ASD. Garcia-Villamisar and Hughes (2007) studied 44 adults with ASD engaged in supported employment and a group of adults who were unemployed. Adults in the supported employment program scored significantly higher on executive functioning skills, such as working memory and problem solving, in comparison to the unemployed groups who exhibited no change in cognitive functioning.

Customized Employment

Customized employment is defined as individualizing the relationship between an individual job seeker and an employer in a way that meets the needs of both (Citron et al., 2008; U.S. Department of Labor, Office of Disability Employment Policy, 2005). According to the National Center on Workforce and Disability (n.d.), customized employment results in jobs designed for the individual and have the potential for advancement for individuals with significant disabilities who have been chronically unemployed or underemployed.

According to Griffin et al. (2014), the success in individuals acquiring community-based employment was the result of a paradigm shift that focused on an economic development approach to creating job opportunities for individuals with significant disabilities. Compared to supported employment, which generally matches individuals to existing jobs, customized employment focuses on creating an individualized job for the employee through employer negotiations resulting in a highly customized job description (Gerhardt & Lainer, 2011). It may include other employment strategies such as supported employment, supported entrepreneurial initiatives, and individualized job development, or other strategies that result in job responsibilities customized to meet the needs of an individual with ASD.

Customized employment begins with an exploration process in collaboration with a personal representative to identify the individual's interests, strengths, and need for supports. Generally, the personal representative is a vocational rehabilitation specialist or other public or private disability service providers. The representative identifies potential employers and approaches them with the possibility of creating and negotiating a specific job description to meet the unique skills of the job seeker and the employer's business needs. The negotiation process addresses areas such as job duties and terms of employment. Other components in this process are creating a system of job supports, if necessary, (e.g. job coaching, technology, transportation) that is individualized and meets the needs of the job seeker. The job seeker confers with the employer and if the job description and responsibilities mutually meet the needs of both, the job seeker is hired.

In conjunction with the process and principles of customized and supportive employment, Condon and Callahan (2008) advocate for implementation of the Individualized Career Planning Model for young adults attending high school (14–21 years old) to plan for transition to competitive employment, including self-employment options. Key steps in this model include: working with the individual to identify interests, strengths, and support needs included in a Vocational Profile, creating a Representational Portfolio to negotiate a job with an employer, and the utilization of Social Security Work Incentives and linkages to promote collaborative funding and choices of services.

Business Partnership Models

As a result of federal legislation to initiate equal opportunities for transition-age youth and adults with ASD to acquire competitive and integrated employment opportunities, business partnerships have been expanded. The legislation and resultant partnerships are enabling more individuals to enter the workforce (Carter et al., 2009; Henderson & Cone, 2014).

Sustaining business partnerships will be critical in supporting individuals who will be entering the labor force. Presently, there are some large business corporations that have been recognized for promoting employment of individuals with disabilities including ASD. Marriott Bridges School to Work program was established in 1990 and has assisted more than 15,000 young adults, 17–22 years old with disabilities including autism, to successfully transition to customized employment (Marriott Foundation for People with Disabilities, 2012). The Bridges program is a 15–24-month internship program for young adults and includes the components of skill assessment, career planning, job development, job placement, evaluation, and follow-up. According to the Bridges from School to Work Progress report, during 2012, 813 young adults with disabilities were placed in employment and 539 remained employed for at least 180 days in 358 participating businesses. The National Secondary Transition Technical Assistance Center identified students' completion of the Bridges from School to Work Program as a moderate, evidenced-based indicator in predicting post-school employment for transition-age youth with disabilities, including individuals with ASD.

Similarly, Walgreens, the retail pharmacy chain, has been at the forefront of creating inclusive work environments and embedded job supports for individuals with ASD. In 2007, Walgreens pioneered hiring individuals with ASD in its distribution center located in South Carolina and it has extended this hiring practice throughout its facilities with the intention of hiring 20 percent of its workforce from people with disabilities (Walgreens, 2011). Walgreens provides accommodations using assistive technology for employees with ASD; visual prompting systems using pictures are used to provide instructions to employees in task completion and computers with icon-based touch screens. Additionally, to assist individuals with ASD with sensory challenges, Walgreens has equipped its facility with special chairs and other materials to appropriately meet their employees' needs in the workplace.

A unique business partnership concept that was launched in 2013 involved Specialisterne U.S.A, and its collaboration with Computer Aid, Inc. (CAI). Computer Aid, Inc. hires individuals with ASD, in collaboration with Specialisterne for information technology projects with the intent of hiring individuals with ASD (to constitute 3 percent of its workforce) throughout the United States (Autism Speaks, 2012). Specialisterne was originally founded in Denmark in 2004 to create jobs for individuals with high-functioning ASD and Asperger syndrome thorough entrepreneurships and customized employment models in technology; specifically in the areas of software management, testing and registration, and data logistics (Ozretic, 2013). Specialisterne provides assessment of the individual's abilities and needs for supports as well as training in software testing, data handling, and social interaction skills such as working with colleagues.

Employer and Co-worker Supports

Employees with ASD often need extended support to prevent a deterioration of acquired job and interpersonal skills that may occur if their support services are removed, and which then can result in the loss of employment (Hendricks, 2010). Personal accounts from adults with ASD highlight the need for long-term supports to assist them mediate the daily challenges they experience at work (Hurlbutt & Chalmers, 2004; Müller, Schuler, Burton, & Yates, 2003). However, employment models that rely on individualized on-site job training and sustained coaching are costly to maintain. Furthermore, this intensive level of support may be detrimental to the individual with ASD in assimilating into the work culture and maintaining adherence to routines and job responsibilities (Autism Speaks, 2012; Targett & Wehman, 2009).

As on-site support from the job coach fades and is ultimately eliminated, relationships and support strategies are transferred to supervisors and co-workers to continue to provide support in the workplace. Existing support structures in businesses may be utilized and include human resource personnel and employee assistance programs, trade associations, and unions (Wilczynski et al., 2013). According to Hagner and Cooney (2004), the key components of supervising employees with ASD are ensuring that communication is direct and comprehended, assisting the individual to learn social communication cues (and the interpretation of cues) in the workplace, and explaining changes and supporting the individual to cope with them (e.g. schedule). Similarly, co-workers can function as mentors and trainers of employees of ASD and provide supports that include prompting and modeling job responsibilities, performance feedback, and social interactions. Wilczynski et al. (2013) concluded that the support of co-workers is critical in assisting the employee with ASD to cope with their communication challenges and increase social interactions.

Assistive Technology Supports

To facilitate employment success, research suggests the use of strategies that include applied behavior analysis, video modeling, structured reward systems, errorless learning, prompt systems, and use of computers and hand held personal digital assistant devices (PDAs) (Chen et al., 2014; Nicholas et al., 2015; Test et al., 2014; Wilczynski et al., 2013; Walsh et al., 2014). Technology is an evidence-based practice that is effective in teaching work-related skills and increasing the ability for employees with ADS to perform job tasks independently (Odom, Collet-Klingenberg, Rogers, & Hattan, 2010). During the past several decades, technologies such as video modeling, audio cueing, video prompting, computer instruction, and virtual reality have been utilized for different training purposes with individuals with ASD.

Allen, Wallace, Renes, Bowen, and Burke (2010b) investigated the efficacy of using video modeling and positive behavior reinforcement with three young adults (17–22 years old) with ASD. The study focused on the employees who received video instruction that presented video-taped demonstrations of skills necessary to promote products in a retail environment while wearing an air-inflated mascot costume. The employees were observed during a four-month period before and after watching a video. The participants were able to correctly implement the skills modeled in the video in the workplace.

Similarly, Van Laarhoven et al. (2012) demonstrated the effectiveness of the use of video modeling on the maintenance of vocational tasks with six young adults, 15–17 years old, with ASD and developmental disabilities. Two tasks were assigned to each individual and their independence in completing the task was measured before and after a two-week period. One task was assigned to the video modeling intervention and the other was a control for each participant. The individuals reviewed the videos during the two-week period. As a result of viewing the videos, all students increased their independence with both tasks. Both of these studies indicate that by modeling behaviors on videotape, young adults have the ability to learn, memorize, and generalize the behaviors effectively in the workplace. Studies have determined that video modeling resulted in expediting the rate of skill acquisition for individuals with ASD. Additionally, videos can be used repeatedly and ensure that training is delivered in a standardized manner (Kellems & Morningstar, 2012).

Other studies have reported on young adults with ASD being trained to use iPhones and Apple video iPods, and PDA devices to prompt the completion of tasks. Burke, Anderson, Bowen, Howard, and Allen (2010) designed a prompt system using an adapted iPhone application to teach six young adults work-related, social-vocational skills. The young adults were employed to assist in conducting a fire safety training session and to complete 63 scripted behaviors necessary to facilitate the training. One study focused on the participant completing the company's training program and using the iPhone and the performance cue system to meet performance criteria. The other study involved different participants who used only the iPhone to learn the same work behaviors. The results of the study indicated that five of the six participants attained the task criteria only after using the iPhone and the performance cue system. The iPhone technology was effective in providing prompts to enable individuals to learn and execute complex tasks. Similarly, Kellems and Morningstar (2012) evaluated the efficacy of using video modeling through an Apple video iPod to teach job-related tasks (e.g. facility maintenance skills, recycling materials, and refilling vending machines and inventory) to four young adults, aged 20–22, in community workplaces. Observational data revealed that the participants improved the percentage of the steps they independently completed in each task using the iPod. The study also indicated—based on informal interviews of the participant, employers, and job coaches—that the use of the iPod was helpful, the participants enjoyed using the device, and it was socially acceptable to use the iPod at work.

A technological intervention, virtual reality, is promising in facilitating the development of work-related social skills that are relevant to acquiring and maintaining employment. Strickland, Coles, and Southern (2013), developed an internet-based training program with an embedded virtual reality environment to teach young adults with high functioning ASD job interview skills. The study revealed that the young adults who completed the training sessions using virtual reality practice demonstrated more effective interview skills that the young adults who did not.

Another promising use of virtual technology, specifically Google Glass, is its potential to assist individuals with ASD to identify the emotions of others (Autism Speaks, 2013). Google Glass, an eye-glass wearable computer, displays information in a smartphone prototype hands-free format and permits the user to communicate with the internet using voice commands (Fichten, Asuncion, & Scapin, 2014). Applications for Google Glass are presently being developed and tested to teach individuals with ASD social interaction skills, including improving eye contact and understanding non-verbal social cues. Specifically for individuals with ASD who, due to the nature of the disorder, are challenged by social interactions and interpersonal communication, using Google Glass could significantly assist them in learning these essential work-related skills.

Self-employment

According to Griffin et al. (2014), there are an estimated 700,000 new businesses launched in the United States annually. The self-employment rate is increasing by more than 20 percent annually, with micro-enterprises (businesses employing one to five employees) generating 64 percent of all new jobs. Historically, self-employment has not been a widely used option for individuals with ASD but it is now evolving into a viable reality as an option for some people on the spectrum as an employment model that is. As of 2013, with the implementation of the Employment First legislation, self-employment and business ownership are recognized in revised state VR policies and through the policies of the U.S. Department of Labor's Office of Disability Employment Policy (Griffin et al., 2014).

The Rehabilitation Act of 1973 and the Workforce Investment Act of 1998 (WIA) direct vocational rehabilitation programs to assist individuals with disabilities purchase equipment, training, and other supports. Griffin, Brooks-Lane, Hammis and Crandell, 2007, advocate that individuals with significant disabilities develop resource ownership (i.e., a skill or resource) that the individual can supply to meet the needs of the prospective employer. The resource belongs to the individual (e.g., repairing computers) and may provide the trajectory of employment opportunities from customized employment to self-employment and, possibly, business ownership.

Conclusion

In summary, effective employment intervention can enable and empower individuals with autism to use their unique talents and interests to attain and sustain employment through building on their strengths; recognizing and accommodating cognitive, sensory, and social challenges; and respecting preferences and interests. Ideally, transition preparation occurring in the secondary school years should ready adolescents to move on to postsecondary education or employment, so that they may live, work, and recreate within their community.

Through research-based knowledge combined with person-centered planning, it is possible to create an intervention model that will improve the likelihood of successful employment. In preparing students for the transition to work through the use of strategies based on the principles of Universal Design for Transition, secondary and postsecondary programs will significantly enhance their effectiveness. Further, by infusing this intervention with strategies that have been designed to build self-determination competence, educators will be able to identify, target, and meet employment goals that they develop with their students.

In order to utilize diverse talents and strengths of individuals with ASD, varied employment models may be necessary. Supported employment and customized employment are currently among the most widely used models. Employer and co-worker supports, along with assistive technology, can significantly enhance success in the workplace. These options recognize the capacity of individuals with significant disabilities to be gainfully employed when they are provided with ongoing supports, and when job descriptions are tailored to enable them to succeed in the workplace.

References

Allen, K.D., Wallace, D.P., Greene, D., J., Bowen, S.L., & Burke, R.V. (2010a). Community-based vocational instruction using video-taped modeling for young adults with autism spectrum disorders performing in air-inflated mascots. *Focus on Autism and Other Developmental Disabilities*, 25(3), 186–192.

Allen, K.D., Wallace, D.P., Renes, D. Bowen S.L., & Burke, R.V. (2010b). Use of video modeling to teach vocational skills to adolescent with autism spectrum disorders. *Education and Treatment of Children, 33*(3), 339–349.

Americans With Disabilities Act of 1990, Pub. L. No. 101-336, 104 Stat. 328 (1990).

Autism Society. (2011). *Facts and statistics.* Retrieved February 23, 2015, from www.autism-society.org/about-autism/fact.

Autism Speaks. (2012). Employment think tank report. Retrieved March 1, 2015, from www.autismspeaks.org/sites/default/files/as_think_tank_exec_.

Autism Speaks. (2013, Oct. 23). Google Glass shows promise improving lives of people with autism. Retrieved from http://autismspeaks.org/news-item-google-glass-shows-promise-improving-lives.

Azano, A., & Tuckwiller, E.D. (2011). GPS for the English classroom: Understanding executive dysfunction in secondary students. *Teaching Exceptional Children, 43*, 38–44.

Baer, D.M., Wolf, M.M., & Risley, T.R. (1968). Some current dimensions of applied behavior analysis, *Journal of Applied Behavior Analysis, 1*(1), 91–97.

Barnhill, G.P. (2007). Outcomes in adults with Asperger syndrome. *Focus on Autism and other Developmental Disabilities, 22*(2), 116–126.

Baron-Cohen, S., Leslie, A.M., & Frith, U. (1985). Does the autistic child have a theory of mind? *Cognition, 21*, 37–46.

Billstedt, E., Gillberg, I.C., & Gillberg, C. (2011) Aspects of quality of life in adults diagnosed with autism in childhood: A population-based study. *Autism, 25*(1), 720. doi: 10.1177/1362361309346066

Burgess, S., & Cimera, R.E. (2014). Employment outcomes of transition-aged adults with autism spectrum disorders: A state of the states report. *American Journal of Intellectual and Developmental Disabilities, 119* (1), 63–84. doi: 10.1352/1944-7558-119.1.64

Burke, R.V., Anderson, M.N., Bowen, S.L., Howard, M.R., & Allen, K.D. (2010). Evaluation of two instruction methods to increase employment options for young adults with autism spectrum disorders. *Research in Developmental Disabilities, 31*(6), 1223–1233.

Carter, E.W., Austin, D., & Trainer, A.A. (2012). Predictors of postschool employment for young adults with severe disabilities. *Journal of Disability Policy Studies, 23*(1), 50–63.

Carter, E.W., Trainor, A.A., Cakiroglu, O., Cole, O., Swedeen, B., Ditchman, N., . . . Owen, L. (2009). Exploring school-employer partnerships to expand career development and early work experiences for youth with disabilities. *Career Development for Exceptional Individuals, 32*(3), 145–159.

Chappel, S.L. & Somers, B.C. (2010). Employing persons with autism spectrum disorders: A collaborative effort. *Journal of Vocational Rehabilitation, 32*, 117–124. doi: 10.3233/JVR-2010-0501

Chen, J.L., Leader, G., Sung, C., & Leahy, M. (2014). Trends in employment for individuals with autism spectrum disorder: A review of the research literature. *Review Journal of Autism and Developmental Disorders.* Retrieved from http://link.spinger.com/article/10.1007/s40489-014-0041-6

Chiang, H.M., Cheung, Y.K., Li, H., & Tsai, L.Y. (2013). Factors associated with participation in employment for high school leavers with autism. *Journal* of *Autism and Developmental Disorders, 43,* 1832–1842. doi: 10.1007/ s10803-012-1734-2

Cimera, R.E., & Cowan, R.J. (2009). The costs of services and employment outcomes achieved by adults with autism in the US. *Autism, 13*(3), 285–302. doi: 10.1177/1362361309103791

Citron, T., Brooks-Lane, N., Crandell, D., Brady, K., Cooper, M., & Grant, R. (2008). A revolution in the employment process of individuals with disabilities: Customized employment as the catalyst for system change. *Journal of Vocational Rehabilitation, 28,* 169–179.

Condon, E. & Callahan, M. (2008). Individualized career planning for students with significant support needs utilizing the discovery and vocational profile process, cross-agency collaboration funding and Social Security work incentives. *Journal of Vocational Rehabilitation, 28,* 85–96.

Diament, M. (2015, April 14). Feds take aim at sheltered workshops. *Disability Scoop.* Retrieved April 2, 2015, from http://disabilityscoop.com/2015/04/14/ feds-aim-sheltered-workshops/20216/.

Etscheidt, S. (2006). Issues in transition planning: Legal decisions. *Career Development for Exceptional Individuals, 29*(1), 28–47.

Farley, M.A., McMahon, W.M., Fombonne, E., Jenson, W.R., Miller, J., Gardner, . . . Coon, H. (2009). Twenty-year outcome for individuals with autism and average or near-average cognitive abilities. *Autism Research, 2*(2), 109–118.

Fichten, C.S., Asuncion, J., & Scapin, R. (2014). Digital technology, learning, and postsecondary students with disabilities: Where we've been and where we're going. *Journal of Postsecondary Education and Disability, 27*(4), 369–379.

Ganz, M.L. (2006). The costs of autism. In S.O. Moldin, & J.R.L. Rubenstein (Eds.), *Understanding Autism: From Basic Neuroscience to Treatment* (pp. 476–498). Boca Raton, FL: Taylor & Francis.

Garcia-Villamisar, D., & Hughes, C. (2007). Supported employment improves cognitive performance in adults with autism. *Journal of Intellectual Disability Research, 51*(2), 142–150. doi: 10/1111/j.1365-2788.2006.00854.x

Garcia-Villamisar, D., Ross, D., & Wehman, P. (2000). Clinical differential analysis of persons with autism: A follow-up study. *Journal of Vocational Rehabilitation, 14,* 183–185.

Gerhardt, P.F., & Lainer, I. (2011). Addressing the need of adolescents and adults with autism: A crisis on the horizon. *Journal of Contemporary Psychotherapy, 41,* 37–45. doi: 10.1007/s10879-010-9160-2

Greenspan, S. (1999). *Building healthy minds: The six experiences that create emotional growth in babies and young children.* Cambridge, MA: Perseus Books.

Greenspan, S.I., & Wieder, S. (2006). *Engaging autism: Using the Floortime approach to help children relate, communicate, and think.* Cambridge, MA: DaCapo.

Griffin, C., Brookes-Lane, N., Hammis D.C., & Crandell, D. (2007). Self-employment: Owning the American dream. In P. Wehman, K.J. Inge, W.G. Revell Jr., & V.A. Brooks (Eds.), *Real Work for Real Pay: Inclusive Employment for People with Disabilities* (pp. 215–235). Baltimore, MD: Paul H. Brookes Publishing Co.

Griffin, C., Hammis, D., Keeton, B., & Sullivan, M. (2014). *Making self employment work for people with disabilities* (2nd ed.) Baltimore, MD: Paul H. Brooks Publishing.

Hagner, D., & Cooney, B.F. (2005). "I do that for everybody": Supervising employees with autism. *Focus on Autism and Other Disabilities, 20*(2), 91–97.

Hagner, D., Kurtz, A., Cloutier, H., Arakelian, C., Brucker, D.L., May, J. (2012). Outcomes of a family-centered transition process for students with autism spectrum disorders. *Focus on Autism and Other Developmental Disabilities, 27*(1), 43–50. doi: 10.1177/1088357611430841

Hardman, M. L., & Dawson, S.A. (2010). *Historical and legislative foundations.* Thousand Oaks, CA: Sage Publications, Inc.

Hasazi, S.B., Gordon, L., & Roe, C.A. (1985). Factors associated with the employment status of handicapped youth exiting high school from 1979–1983. *Exceptional Children, 20*, 141–164.

Henderson, L., & Cone, A.A. (2014). Answering employers' questions about hiring people with significant disabilities. *TASH Connections, 40*(1), 35–40.

Hendricks, D. (2010). Employment and adults with autism spectrum disorders: Challenges and strategies for success. *Journal of Vocational Rehabilitation, 32*, 125–134. doi: 10.3233/JVR-2010-0502

Hendricks, D., & Wehman, P. (2009). Transition from school to adulthood for youth with autism spectrum disorders: Review and recommendations. *Focus on Autism and Other Developmental Disabilities, 24*(2), 77–88.

Henninger, N.A., & Taylor, J.L. (2013). Outcomes in adults with autism spectrum disorders: A historical perspective. *Autism, 17*(1), 103–116. doi: 10.1177/1362361312441266

Hillier, A., Campbell, H., Mastriani, K., Izzo, M.V., Tucker-Kool, A.K., Cherry, A., & Beversdorf, D.Q. (2007). Two-year evaluation of a vocational support program for adults on the autism spectrum. *Career Development for Exceptional Individuals, 30*(1), 35–47.

Hoff, D. (2014). WIA is now WIOA: What the new bill means for people with disabilities. *Institute for Community Inclusion.* Retrieved March 1, 2015 from www.communityinclusion.org.

Holmes, D. (2007). When the school bus stops coming: The employment dilemma for adults with autism. *Autism Advocate, 46*(1), 16–21.

Howlin, P. (2000). Outcome in adult life for more able individuals or Asperger syndrome. *Autism, 4*(1), 63–81.

Howlin, P., Alcock, J. & Burkin, C. (2005). An 8-year follow-up of a specialist supported employment service for high-ability adults with autism or Asperger syndrome. *Autism, 9*(5), 533–549.

Howlin, P., Goode, S., Hutton, J., & Rutter, M. (2004). Adult outcomes for children with autism. *Journal of Child Psychology and Psychiatry, 45*(2), 212–229.

Hughes, C., Russell, J., & Robbins, T.W. (1994). Evidence for executive dysfunction in autism. *Neuropsychologia, 32*(4), 477–492.

Hundert, J. (2009). *Inclusion of students with autism: Using ABA-based supports in general education.* Austin, TX: Pro-Ed.

Hurlbutt, K., & Chalmers, L. (2005). Employment and adults with Asperger syndrome. *Focus on Autism and other Developmental Disorders, 19(4),* 215–222.

Individuals with Disabilities Education Improvement Act (2004). Pub. L. 108–466.

Iovannone, R., Dunlap, G., Huber, H., & Kincaid, D. (2003). Effective educational practices for students with autism spectrum disorder. *Focus on Autism and Other Developmental Disabilities, 18(3),* 150–165.

Johnson, D., & Halloran, W.H. (1997). The federal legislature context and goals of the state systems change initiative on transition for youth and disabilities. *Career Development for Exceptional Individuals, 20,* 109–121.

Kellems, R.O., & Morningstar, M.E. (2012). Using video modeling delivered through iPods to teach vocational tasks to young adults with autism spectrum disorders. *Career Development and Transition for Exceptional Individuals, 35(3),* 155–167. doi: 10.1177/0885728812443082

Kucharczyk, S., Reutebuch, C.K., Carter, E.W., Hedges, S.E.L., Zein, F., Fan, H., . . . Gustafson, J.R. (2015). Addressing the needs of adolescents with autism spectrum disorder: Considerations and complexities for high school interventions, *Exceptional Children, 8(3),* 329–349.

Landmark, L.J., Ju, S., & Zhang, D. (2010). Substantiated best practices in transition: Fifteen plus years later. *Career Development for Exceptional Individuals, 3,* 165–176.

Lawer, L., Brusilovkiy, E., Salzer, M.S., Mandell, D.S. (2009). Use of vocational rehabilitative services among adults with autism. *Journal of Autism and Developmental Disorders, 39(3),* 487–494.

Luecking, D.M., & Luecking, R.G. (2015). Translating research into a seamless transition model. *Career Development and Transition for Exceptional Individuals, 38(1),* 4–13.

McEathron, M.A., Beuhring, T., Maynard, A., & Mavis, A. (2013). Understanding the diversity: A taxonomy for postsecondary education programs and services for students with intellectual and developmental disabilities. *Journal of Postsecondary Education and Disability, 26(40),* 303–320.

Mahoney, G., & Perales, F. (2005). A comparison of the impact of relationship-focused intervention on young children with pervasive developmental disorders and other disabilities. *Journal of Developmental and Behavioral Pediatrics, 26,* 77–85.

Marcus, L.M., Lansing, M., Andrews, C.E., & Schopler, E. (1978). Improvement of teaching effectiveness in parents of autistic children. *Journal of the American Academy of Child Psychiatry, 17,* 625–639.

Marriott Foundation for People with Disabilities. (2013). *Bridges from School to Work Progress Report.* Retrieved on March 25, 2015, from www.bridgesto work.org.

Martin, J.E., & Williams-Diehm, K. (2013). Student engagement and leadership in the transition planning process. *Career Development and Transition for Exceptional Individuals, 36(1),* 43–50.

Mawhood, L., & Howlin, P. (1999). The outcome of a supported employment scheme for high functioning adults with autism or Asperger syndrome. *Autism, 3(3),* 229–254. doi: 10.1177/1362361399003003003

Meadan, H., Shelden, D.L., Appel, K., & DeGrazia, R.L. (2010). Developing a long-term vision: A road map for students' futures. *Exceptional Children*, 43(2), 8–13.

Mesibov, G.B., Browder, D.M., & Kirkland, C. (2002). Using individual schedules as a component of positive behavioral support for students with developmental disabilities, *Journal of Positive Behavioral Interventions*, 4, 73–79.

Mesibov, G.B., & Shea, V. (2010). The TEACCH program in the era of evidence-based practice. *Journal of Autism and Developmental Disorders*, 40(5), 570–579.

Miller, E.K., & Lane, S.(2000). Toward consensus in terminology in sensory integration theory and practice. Part 1: Taxonomy of neuropsychological processes. *Sensory Integration Special Interest Section*, 23(1), 1–4.

Mithaung, D.E., Horiuchi, C.N., & Fanning, P.N. (1985). A report on the Colorado statewide follow-up survey of special education students. *Exceptional Children*, 51(5), 397–404.

Morgan, R.L., & Alexander, M. (2005). The employer's perception: Employment of individuals with developmental disabilities. *Journal of Vocational Rehabilitation*, 23, 39–49.

Morningstar, M.E., & Liss, J.M. (2008). A preliminary investigation of how states are responding to the transition assessment requirements under IDEIA 2004. *Career Development for Exceptional Individuals*, 31(1), 48–55. doi: 10.1177/0885728807313776

Müller, E., & Cannon, L. (2014). Parent perspectives on outcomes and satisfaction levels of young adults with autism and cognitive impairments. *Focus on Autism and Other Developmental Disabilities*, 1–12. doi: 10.1177/1088357614528800

Müller, E., Schuler, A., Burton, B.A., & Yates, G.B. (2003). Meeting the vocational support needs of individuals with Asperger syndrome and other autism spectrum disabilities, *Journal of Vocational Rehabilitation*, 18(3), 163–175.

Nesbitt, S. (2009). Why and why not? Factors influencing employment for individuals with Asperger syndrome. *Autism*, 4(4), 357–369. doi: 10.1177/1362361300004004002

National Center on Workforce and Disability (n.d.). *Customized Employment: Principles and Indicators*. Retrieved on February 17, 2015, from www.onestops.info/article.php?article_id=254&subcat_id=101.

Nicholas, D.B., Attridge, M., Zwaigenbaum, & Clarke, M. (2015). Vocational support approaches in autism spectrum disorder: A synthesis review of the literature. *Autism*, 19(2), 235–245. doi: 10.1177/1362361313516548

Odom, S.L., Collet-Klingenberg, L., Rodgers, S.J. & Hatton, D.D. (2010). Evidence-based practices in intervention for children and youth for children and youth with autism spectrum disorders. *Preventing School Failure, 54*, 275–282. doi: 10.1080/10459881003785506

Ozretic, A. (2013, Oct. 22). Creating great employees (who happen to be autistic). *Techonomy Exclusive*. Retrieved on March 30, 2015 from http://techonomy.com/2013/10/creating-great-employees-happen-autistic/.

Papay, C.K., & Bambara, L.M. (2014). Best practices in transition to adult life for youth with intellectual disabilities. *Career Development and Transition for Exceptional Individuals*, 37(3), 136–148.

Roux, A.M., Shattuck, P.T., Cooper, B.P., Anderson, K.A., Wagner, M., & Narendorf, S.C. (2013). Postsecondary employment experiences among young adults with autism with an autism spectrum disorder RH: Employment in young adults with autism. *Journal of the American Academy of Child and Adolescent Psychiatry, 52*(9), 931–939. doi: 10.1016/jaac.2013.05.019

Roux, A.M., Shattuck, P.T., Rast, J.E., Rava, J.A., & Anderson, K.A. (2015). *National autism indicators report: Transition into young adulthood.* Life Course Outcomes Research Program, A.J. Drexel Autism Institute. Philadelphia: PA. Retrieved on March 1, 2015 from Drexel.edu/autisminstitute/research-projects/research/ResearchPrograminLifeCourseOutcomes.

Russell, J., Jarrold, C., & Hood, B. (1999). Two intact executive functions in autism: Implications for the nature of the disorder. *Journal of Autism and Developmental Disorders, 29*, 103–285.

Schall, C.M. (2010). Positive behavior support: Supporting adults with autism spectrum disorders in the workplace. *Journal of Vocational Rehabilitation, 32*, 109–115. doi: 10.3233/JVR-2010-0500&

Schall, C.M. & McDonough,T.J., (2010). Autism spectrum disorders in adolescence and early adulthood: Characteristics and issues. *Journal of Vocational Rehabilitation, 32*, 81–88. doi: 10.3233/JVR-2010-0503

Schall, C., Targett, P., & Wehman, P. (2013). Applications for youth with autism spectrum disorders. In P. Wehman (Ed.), *Life beyond the classroom*, 5th ed. (pp. 447–472). Baltimore, MD: Paul H. Brookes Publishing.

Schall, C., Wehman, P. & McDonough, J. L. (2012). Transition from school to work for students with autism spectrum disorders: Understanding the process and achieving better outcomes. *Pediatric Clinics, 59*(1), 189–202. doi: http://dx.org/10.1016/j.pcl.2011.10.009

Schaller, J., & Yang, N.K. (2005). Competitive employment for people with autism: Correlates of successful closure in competitive and supported employment. *Rehabilitation Counseling Bulletin, 49*(1), 4–16. doi: 10.1177/00343552050490010201

Shattuck, P.T., Narendorf, S.C., Cooper, B., Sterzing, P.R., Wagner, M., & Taylor, J.L. (2012). Postsecondary education and employment among youth with an autism spectrum disorder. *Pediatrics, 129*(2), 1042–1049. doi: 10.1542/peds.2011-2864

Shattuck P.T., Wagner, M., Narendorf, S., Sterzing, P., Hensley, M. (2011). Post high school service use among young adults with autism spectrum disorder. *Archives of Pediatric Medicine, 165*(2), 141–146. doi: 10.1001archpediatrics.2010.279

Shogren, K.A. & Plotner, A.J. (2012). Transition planning for students with intellectual disability, autism, or other disabilities: Data from the national longitudinal transition study-2. *Intellectual and Developmental Disabilities, 50*(1), 16–30. doi: 10.1352/1934-9556-50.1.16

Smith, M.D., & Philippen, L.R. (2005). Community integration and supported employment. In D. Zager (Ed.). *Autism spectrum disorders: Identification, education, and treatment (3rd ed.)*, (pp. 493–5140. Mahwah, NJ: Lawrence Erlbaum Associates.

Standifer, S. (2009). *Adult autism and employment: A guide for vocational rehabilitation professionals.* Disability Policy Studies, School of Health Professions,

University of Missouri. Retrieved February 10, 2014, www.dps.missouri.edu/Autism/Adults.

Strickland, D.C., Coles, C.D. & Southern, L.B. (2014) JobTIPS: A transition to employment program for individuals with autism spectrum disorders. *Journal of Autism and Developmental Disorders, 43*(10), 2472–2483. doi: 10.1007/s10803-013-1800-4

Targett, P.S., & Wehman, P. (2009). Integrated Employment. In P. Wehman, M.D., & C. Schall (Eds.), *Autism & the transition to adulthood: Success beyond the classroom.* Baltimore, MD: Paul H. Brooks Publishing Co.

Taylor, J.L. & Seltzer, M.M. (2011). Employment and post-secondary educational activities for young adults with autism spectrum disorders during the transition to adulthood. *Journal of Autism and Developmental Disorders, 41*(5), 566–574. doi: 10.1007/s10803-010-1070-3

Test, D.W., Fowler, C.H., Richter, S.M., White, J., Mazzotti, Walker, A.R., . . . Kortering, L. (2009). Evidence-based practice in secondary transition. *Career Development for Exceptional Individuals, 32*(2), 115–128.

Test, D.W., Smith, L.E. & Carter, E.W. (2014). Equipping youth with autism spectrum disorders for adulthood: Promoting rigor, relevance, and relationships. *Remedial and Special Education, 35*(2), 80–90.

Thoma, C.A., Bartholomew, C.C., & Scott, L.A. (2009). *Universal design for transition: A roadmap for planning and instruction.* Baltimore: Paul H. Brookes Publishing Co.

Thoma, C.A., Gentry, R., Boyd, K., & Streagle, K. (2013). Academic assessment in transition planning in C.A. Thoma & R. Tamura (Eds.). *Demystifying transition assessment.* Baltimore: Paul H. Brookes Publishing Co.

U.S. Department of Education (November, 2009). *State of the science conference on postsecondary education for students with intellectual disabilities.* Fairfax, VA.

U.S. Department of Labor, Office of Disability Employment Policy. (2005). *Customized employment: Practical solutions for employment success.* Retrieved March 10, 2015, from www.dol.gov/odep/categories/workforce/Customized Employment.

U.S. Department of Labor, Office of Disability Employment Policy. (n.d.). *Employment First.* Retrieved January 20, 2015 from www.dol.gov/odep/topics/EmploymentFirst.

Van Laarhoven, T., Winiarskii, L., Blood, E., & Chan, J.M. (2012), Maintaining vocational skill of individuals with autism an developmental disabilities through video modeling. *Education and Training in Autism and Developmental Disabilities, 47*(4), 447–461.

Wacker, D.P., Berg, W.K., Berrie, P., & Swatta, P. (1985). Generalization and maintenance of complex skills by severely handicapped adolescents following picture prompt training. *Journal of Applied Behavior Analysis, 18*, 329–336.

Wagner, M., Newman, L., Cameto, R., Garza, N., & Levine, P. (2005). *After high school: A first look at the postschool experiences of youth with disabilities. A report from the National Longitudinal Transition Study-2 (NTLS-2).* Menlo Park, CA: SRI International. Retrieved March 1, 2015 from http://eric.ed.gov/?id=ED494935.

Wagner, M., Newman, L., Cameto, R., Levine, P., & Marder, C. (2007). *Perceptions of youth with disabilities: A special topic report of findings with the National Longitudinal Transition Study-2 (NTLS)* (NSCER 2007-3006). Menlo Park: CA SRI International. Retrieved March 1, 2015 from http://eric. ed.gov/?id=ED498185.

Walgreens. *Aim Hire* (2011, October). Retrieved February 28, 2015 from, www. walgreens.com/topic/sr/sr_disabiity_inclusions_awards_recognition.

Walsh, L., Lyndon, S., & Healy, O. (2014). Employment and vocational skill among individuals with autism spectrum disorder: Predictors, impact, and interventions. *Review Journal of Autism and Developmental Disorders, 1,* 266–275. Retrieved from http://link.springer.com/article 10.1007/s40489-014-0024-7.

Wehman, P. (2013a). Transition from school to work: Where are we and where do we need to go? *Career Development and Transition for Exceptional Individuals, 36* (1), 58–66. doi: 10.1177/2165143413483137

Wehman, P., Lau, S., Molinelli, A., Brooke, A., Thompson, V., Moore, C., & West, M. (2012). Supported employment for young adults with autism spectrum disorder: Preliminary data. *Research and Practice for Persons with Severe Disabilities, 37*(10), 160–169.

Wehman, P., Schall, C., Carr, S., Targett, P., West, T. & Cifu, G. (2014). Transition from school to adulthood for youth with autism spectrum disorder: What we know and what we need to know. *Journal of Disability Policy Studies, 25*(1), 30–40. doi: 10.1177/1044207313518071

Wehman, P., Schall, C.M., McDonough, J., Kregel, J., Brooke, V., Molinelli, A., Ham, W., . . . Thiss, W. (2013b). Competitive employment for youth with autism spectrum disorders: Early results from a randomized clinical trial. *Journal of Autism and Developmental Disorders, 44*(3), 487–500. doi: 10.1177/1098300712459760

Wehman, P., Schall, C., McDonough, J., Molinelli, A., Riehle, E., Ham, W., Thiss, W.R. (2012). Project SEARCH for youth with autism spectrum disorders: Increasing competitive employment on transition from high school. *Journal of Positive Behavior Interventions, 20*(10), 1–12.

Wehmeyer, M.L., & Shogren, K. (2014, January). *Evidence-based practices to promote self-determination on postschool outcomes.* Paper presented at conference of the Division on Autism and Developmental Disabilities, Clearwater, FL.

Wehmeyer, M., Shogren, K.A., Smith, T.E.C., Zager, D., & Simpson, R. (2010). Research-based principals and practices for educating students with autism: Self-determination and social interactions. *Education and Training in Autism and Developmental Disabilities, 45*(4), 475–486.

Westbrook, J.D., Nye, C., Fong, C.J., Wan, J.T., Cortopassi, T., & Martin, F.H. (2012). Adult employment assistance services for persons with autism spectrum disorders: Effects on employment outcomes. *Campbell Systematic Reviews.* Retrieved from http://ideas.repec.org/p/mpr/mprres/7398.html

Wieder, S., & Greenspan, S. (2003). Climbing the symbolic ladder in the DIR model through floortime/interactive play, *Autism, 7,* 425–436.

Wilczynski, S.M., Trammell, B. & Clarke, L.S. (2013). Improving employment outcomes among adolescents and adults on the autism spectrum. *Psychology in the Schools, 50*(9), 876–887. doi: 10.1002/pits.21718

Will, M. (1984). OSERS programming for the transition of youths with disabilities. Bridges from school to working life. Washington, DC: United States Department of Education, Office of Special Education and Rehabilitative Services.

Zager, D., Alpern, C., McKeon, B., Maxam, S., & Mulvey, J. (2013). *Educating college students with autism spectrum disorders*. New York: Routledge.

Zager, D., & Feinman, S. (2013, Winter). Employing evidence-based practices in high school to enhance accessibility to learning and to build executive competence. *Autism Spectrum News*, *5(3)*, 8, 34.

Zager, D., Thoma, C.A., & Fleisher, S.M. (2014, Spring). Employment for persons on the autism spectrum: Examination of the state of the field and the path to pursue. *Autism Spectrum News, (6)*4, 1, 18, 42.

Chapter 17

Collaboration to Improve Education and Treatment Outcomes

Emily C. Bouck, Gauri S. Joshi, and Pei-Lin Weng

Interdisciplinary collaboration is an important component in the education of students with disabilities (Friend & Cook, 2013). Although collaboration can mean different things to different individuals, for the purposes of this chapter we subscribe to Friend and Cook's definition of collaboration as "a style for direct interaction between at least two coequal parties voluntarily engaged in shared decision-making as they work towards a common goal" (p. 6). In other words, those engaged in collaboration need to agree to collaborate, have equal voice within the collaborative decision-making, understand they are striving for at least one mutual goal, and share in the responsibility for the outcome of the decision (Friend & Cook).

Collaboration and Students with ASD

While collaboration is an essential ingredient in the education of all children, it is especially important in the education of students with autism spectrum disorders (ASD). Given that ASD is characterized by impairments in communication, social interaction, and restricted interests that impact a child's educational attainment, it seems intuitive that an interdisciplinary method is the best way to approach the education of students with ASD (Donaldson & Stahmer, 2014; Gargiulo, 2015; Individuals with Disabilities Education Act [IDEA], 2004; Simpson, Mundschenk, & Heflin, 2011; Tincani, 2007). Positive and effective interdisciplinary collaboration—meaning multiple service providers and/or other individuals (e.g. parents) working and making decisions together—improves the education and treatment outcomes of students with ASD (Kelly & Tincani, 2013; Simpson et al., 2011). Throughout this chapter, we discuss key players involved in interdisciplinary collaboration and what that collaboration involves across the different age-spans of educating students with ASD—from early childhood experiences through transition. We also consider the research and practical aspects of collaboration to improve the education and treatment outcomes for students with ASD. Finally, while we acknowledge the provision of education and treatment to students with ASD outside of formal PK-12 educational settings, the focus of our discussion primarily involves formal education structures provided through IDEA.

In special education—inclusive of PK-12 education, as well as early intervention services (i.e., birth through two years of age)—interdisciplinary collaboration occurs among educators who are providing direct and related services or supplementary services (Gargiulo, 2015; Simpson *et al.*, 2011). Aside from general and special education teachers, other professionals collaborating to provide services to students with disabilities include—but are not limited to—audiologists, interpreters, medical providers (e.g. school nurses), occupational therapists, orientation and mobility specialists, physical therapists, counselors, social workers, school psychologists, recreational therapists (e.g., music or art therapists), speech-language pathologists, behavioral specialists, transition specialists, and assistive technology specialists (Gargiulo, 2015; see Table 17.1 for more information regarding different service providers and their roles). Paraprofessionals (i.e. aides working one-on-one or with multiple students in a classroom) also collaborate with other service providers. In addition, parents are key collaborators with all service providers and educational teams in the education of students with disabilities, including students with ASD (Barnhill, Polloway, Sumutka, 2011; Taber-Doughty & Bouck, 2012).

Table 17.1 Service Providers Involved in Interdisciplinary Collaboration and Their Roles

General education teacher	• Provides instruction in general education setting
Special education teacher	• Provides or supports instruction in special education setting • Consults, collaborates, or co-teaches with general education teachers • Provides case management services
Speech-language pathologist	• Identifies students with speech or language impairments • Provides speech and language services
Occupational therapist	• Provides therapy to promote independent functioning, including in areas of motor skills, play, and perceptual abilities
Physical therapist	• Provides physical therapy relative to movement or other gross motor functions
Social worker	• Assesses students for special education eligibility • Provides individual or group counseling and support to students
Behavior analyst	• Provides applied behavior analysis (ABA) therapy • Consults with teachers regarding behavior strategies
School psychologist	• Assesses students for special education eligibility • Consults or manages counseling services for families

(continued)

Table 17.1 (continued)

Recreational therapist	• Provides recreational therapy, such as music or art therapy
Assistive technology specialist	• Assesses students for assistive technology needs • Provides assistive technology services and maintains assistive technology devices
Transition specialist	• Provides or supports transition services (i.e. coordinated activities to promote post-school success)
Rehabilitation counselor	• Provides services focused on employment, community integration, and/or independence
Counseling services	• Provides parent counseling or training
Paraprofessional	• Provides one-on-one or group support to students in a variety of settings
Audiologist	• Identifies students with hearing loss • Provides audiology services to eligible students • Consults with other educators regarding educational programming
Interpreter	• Provides interpretation services, such as sign language transliteration or oral transliteration
Medical provider (e.g. school nurse)	• Provides medical services as needed for student to receive a free appropriate public education (FAPE)
Orientation and mobility specialist	• Provides services to help students with visual impairments orient and move within their environments

Note:
Adapted from Roles of related services personnel in inclusive schools. In R. Villa & J. Thousand, (Eds.), *Restructuring for caring and effective education: Piecing the puzzle together* (2nd ed.) by M. F. Giangreco, P. Prelock, R. Reid, R. Dennis, and S. Edelman, (pp. 360–388). Copyright 2000 by Paul H. Brookes. Adapted from *The law and special education* (3rd ed.) by M. Yell, 2012. Copyright 2012 by Pearson. Adapted from the Individuals with Disabilities Education Improvement Act. Copyright 2004.

Legal and Practical Aspects of Collaboration

Legally, collaboration is implied for the provision of services for students with disabilities (Friend & Cook, 2013). In other words, collaboration is supported in IDEA (2004) through the provision of related services and the multidisciplinary—or interdisciplinary—nature of decision- making in the educational planning of students with disabilities. For example, to determine the eligibility of a student with ASD, a multidisciplinary team conducts the pre-referral process and the evaluation. The team consists of school personnel, including participants such as a school psychologist, school social worker, and a speech-language pathologist. However, the team can also consider the evaluation of professionals, such as pediatricians (Ritzema, Sladeczek, Ghosh, Karagiannakis, & Manay-Quian, 2014). Parents can also be active collaborators during the referral and evaluation process (Chen & Gregory, 2011). Once eligibility is determined, collaboration continues among the different educators to determine a student's educational programming. During an individualized education program

(IEP) meeting, educators—including teachers and related service providers (e.g. social worker)—along with parents determine appropriate services, goals, and supplementary aids to provide a student with ASD with a free appropriate public education (FAPE) (Tincani, 2007; Yell, 2012).

Ideally, educational programming of students with ASD continues along a collaborative path. In other words, given the nature of ASD, educators must work together to provide services. Such collaboration can occur through the provision of services in concert (e.g. co-teaching) or through consultation (Dettmer, Knackendoffel, & Thurston, 2013; Kelly & Tincani, 2013; Simpson et al., 2011; Tincani, 2007). For example, collaboration can occur through a special education teacher and a general education teacher co-teaching together. Collaboration can also occur through a speech-language pathologist or a social worker delivering the therapy or intervention in a general education setting rather than pulling out the student with ASD to work one-on-one in a separate setting (Kelly & Tincani, 2013). When service providers consult with other educators, such as a behavior analyst consulting with a general or special education teacher, they also engage in collaborative practices (Dettmer et al., 2013; Friend & Cook, 2013; Kelly & Tincani, 2013).

From a legal stance, students with ASD are eligible to receive services from any direct or related service providers (IDEA, 2004; Yell, 2012; refer to Table 17.1 for a non-exhaustive list). However, from a practical stance, certain providers are more likely to work together to improve the educational and treatment outcomes of students with ASD. Common service providers for students with ASD, outside of general education and special education teachers, include speech-language pathologists and occupational therapists (Hume, Bellini, & Pratt, 2005; Wei, Wagner, Christiano, Shattuck, & Yu, 2014). Recently, researchers suggested that services received by students with ASD differ based on a student's age (Wei et al., 2014) such as increases in behavioral support, paraprofessionals, and social work for students with ASD as they transition from elementary to secondary education (Kurth & Mastergeorge, 2010; Wei et al., 2014). In addition to services changing as students age, they are likely to receive fewer services (Kurth & Mastergeorge, 2010; McConachie & Robinson, 2006; Wei et al., 2014; White, Scahill, Klin, Koenig, & Volkmar, 2007).

Collaboration During the Early Years

Collaboration during the early years can set the foundation for the education and outcomes of students with ASD. The education of students with ASD during the early years can include services provided to students from birth through two years of age, which are covered under Part C of the Individuals with Disabilities Education Act (IDEA, 2004) and referred to as early intervention, as well as services provided to students between ages three and eight, referred to as early childhood education, which are covered under Part B of IDEA (Gargiulo & Kilgo, 2013; Yell, 2012). A major shift occurs as children transition from receipt of Part C services, if eligible, to Part B services, as Part C services focus on the family and are often provided in the home or natural community settings. Part B services, on the other hand, focus on the individual child and most generally are provided in school settings, including inclusive or self-contained pre-school classes (Podvey, Hinojosa, & Koening, 2013). In this chapter, we focus more on early childhood services rather than the early intervention services for students from birth through age two years.

Research and Practice Issues

Researchers suggest that preschool-aged children with ASD receive more services than students with other types of disabilities. Yet, parents of students with ASD reported feeling their child needed more services than they were receiving (Bitterman, Daley, Misra, Carlson, & Markowitz, 2008). Wei et al. (2014) found that preschool-aged students with ASD received, on average, 4.7 services across such categories as communication, behavioral health and life skills, learning supports, technology, and other services (e.g. transportation). Other studies, focused more on parental reporting, as well as considering outside school services and occurring on the Internet, reported a higher average number of interventions received per child (i.e. seven), with ranges from 0 to 47 (Goin-Kochel, Myers, & Mackintosh, 2007; Green, Pituch, Itchon, Choi, O'Reilly, & Sigafoos, 2006). The most frequently reported service in the Wei et al. (2014) study was speech and language therapy (85.2 percent), followed by occupational therapy (65.3 percent) and then behavior management (44.6 percent). Early services, such as those offered through early intervention or early childhood special education has been shown to benefit students with ASD, with documented improvements in social, communication and academic outcomes (Dawson et al., 2010; Schertz & Odom, 2007).

Key Collaborators

It is during the early years that most children with ASD are identified. Hence, much collaboration occurs during the early years in terms of both identification and then providing services (Pizur-Barnekow, Muusz, McKenna, O'Connor, & Cutler, 2012). Both Part C and Part B of IDEA allow a variety of individuals to refer students for evaluation, including parents and physicians (Pizur-Barnekow et al., 2012). Young children with ASD receive services from a variety of individuals during the early intervention and early childhood years (Wei et al., 2014) including related services professionals (e.g. speech-language pathologists), parents, and even outside service providers.

Parents

Given the focus on families—and families as recipients of services—in Part C of IDEA, parents are large collaborators in early intervention services for students with ASD (Brown, 2009). Parents can struggle with the transition to Part B early childhood special education services when their child turns three, given the perception of less collaboration (Podvey et al., 2013). Parents report a decrease in input, including in their child's IEP development, as well as communication with the child's service providers once they begin formal schooling (Podvey et al., 2013).

Beyond general parent involvement in identification, evaluation, and program decisions addressed in IDEA (2004), certain autism-specific interventions actively use parents as collaborators or co-therapists. For example, with the Treatment and Education of Autistic and related Communications handicapped Children (TEACCH) Program, parents are active collaborators and often co-therapists (Karst & Vaughan Van Hecke, 2012; Schopler & Reichler, 1981). The TEACCH Program was determined to be an evidence-supported approach for students with ASD (Odom, Boyd, Hall, & Hume, 2010).

Speech-language Pathologists

Given that communication is one of the main challenges associated with ASD, many professionals work with students with ASD on communication (Koegel, Matos-Freden, Lang, & Koegel, 2012). The professional responsible for overseeing or leading the development of communication skills is typically a speech-language pathologist. Speech-language pathologists can work with young children with disabilities in school settings—including preschool, early intervention settings (e.g. home), and in private settings (e.g. clinic) (American Speech-Language-Hearing Association [ASHA], 2006; 2015). Speech-language pathologists address areas such as speech sound production, voice, fluency, language, pragmatic communication, augmentative and alternative communication, and swallowing (Causton & Tracy-Bronson, 2014). Speech-language pathologists can also help young children with ASD address social skills or social interaction (ASHA, n.d.). Speech-language pathologists not only provide individual or small-group therapy, but also collaborate with other educators and parents to support communication in various settings outside of the therapy time (Causton & Tracy-Bronson, 2014).

When appropriate, speech-language pathologists may assess, train, and support young children with ASD for use of augmentative and alternative communication (AAC; ASHA, n.d.). AAC "includes all forms of communication (other than oral speech) that are used to express thoughts, needs, wants, and ideas" (ASHA, n.d.). AAC involves unaided approaches (e.g. sign language) or aided approaches (i.e. assistive technology) to support students with complex communication needs, including some students with ASD. Common AAC for young children includes gestures, aided communication books or boards, Picture Exchange Communication System (PECS; ASHA; n.d.), and simple electronic devices with digitized speech (Binger & Light, 2006; Hustad et al., 2005). Regardless of the type of AAC, speech-language pathologists collaborate with educators, other service providers, and parents for assessment, training, implementation, and maintenance of the AAC to improve opportunities for communication and outcomes for young children with ASD.

Center-based or In-home Providers

In addition to receiving school-based services from birth through age 21, under federal law, parents or caregivers of children with ASD sometimes take advantage of private or outside service providers, such as clinics or centers (e.g. autism clinic located within a university or non-profit autism centers) or in-home therapy (e.g. Applied Behavior Analysis [ABA]) (Irvin, McBee, Boyd, Hume, & Odom, 2012). These centers or clinics can support provide evaluations as well as services or interventions. Often it is parents of higher socioeconomic status that are able to take advantage of private services (Irvin et al. 2012; Patten, Baranek, Watson, & Schulz, 2011). However, Medicaid does pay for services for young children with ASD as well (e.g. behavior modification, home health aide, speech-language therapy) (Cidav, Lawer, Marcus, & Mandell, 2013).

Often in center-based programs or clinics, young children can receive more intense therapies or services, with greater frequency and longer duration than are typically available in general preschool or school settings. Researchers have found that participation in intensive interventions can lead to significant early improvements, but that these changes are not always long lasting (Cohen, Amerine-Dickens, & Smith, 2006; Howard, Sparkman, Cohen, Green, & Stanislaw, 2005; Reed, Osborne, & Corness, 2007).

Collaboration During the School Years

Collaboration during the school years should build upon a strong foundation of collaboration established during the early years of education for students with ASD. Typically, collaboration during the school years continues to involve many of the same individuals who fill the same roles as during early childhood special education (e.g. teachers, speech-language pathologists, occupational therapists, social workers, behavioral therapists). However, the nature of services received by students with ASD during the school years may vary depending on their age, as well as the severity and unique characteristics of their disability (Wei et al., 2014).

Research and Practice Issues

Today, higher rates of inclusion of students with disabilities, including students with ASD, are occurring than in the past (Tincani, 2007). According to the most recent IDEA data available, from 2012, 41.3 percent of students with ASD aged 6–11 spend 80 percent or more of their school day in a general education setting; an additional 16.6 percent spend 40–79 percent of their school day in a general education setting. The frequency rates are similar for students aged 12–17: 41.3 percent for 80 v of their day in a general education setting and 20.6 percent for 40–79 percent of their day in a general education setting (IDEA Data Center, 2012). Conversely, 36.1 percent of students with ASD aged 6–11 and 28.1 percent of students between the ages of 12 and 17 spend less than 40 percent of their day in a general education classroom. These data represent a lower percentage of students with ASD who are served in separate settings during the preschool years (aged 3–5): 43.9 percent in a separate class and 4.8 percent in a separate school (IDEA Data Center, 2012).

During the school years, students with disabilities are also experiencing a range of services by professionals. Wei, Wagner, Christiano, and colleagues (2014) reported a variety of related services received by students with ASD in grades K-6 and then 7–10. For students with ASD in elementary school, the most frequently reported related service was speech and language therapy (84.6 percent), followed by occupational therapy (50 percent), special transportation (44.7 percent), and behavioral support (43.8 percent). For secondary students with ASD, the most frequently received related service was also speech and language therapy (66.8 percent), followed by special transportation (54 percent), adaptive physical education (50.9 percent), and behavioral support (34.6 percent). Other services received by students with ASD included adaptive physical education, social work services, and counseling to the family. Given that students with ASD in elementary and secondary schools received, on average, 3.7 and 3.9 services, a lot of collaboration is—or should be—occurring around the education of students with ASD (Wei et al., 2014).

The need for collaboration among general education teachers, special education teachers, and related service providers increases with higher rates of inclusion and becomes increasingly critical as more related ser-vices are provided for students with ASD (Loiacono & Valenti, 2010; Rodriguez, Saldana, & Moreno, 2012). Related, the need for teacher and related service provider preparation or professional development intensifies for all regarding how to educate and support students with disabilities as well as *how to collaborate* (Rodriguez *et al.*, 2012; Simpson et al., 2011).

Key Collaborators

During the school years, students with ASD receive services from various professionals (Wei et al., 2014). These service providers include special and general educators, as well as related service providers who provide required services as described in the IEP for a student with ASD (refer to Table 17.1). While all of the collaborators contribute to the education of students with ASD, we highlight the following: parents, paraprofessionals, and behavior specialists.

Parents

During the school years, as with all years of education, collaboration with parents is key. Parental participation was one of the six main mandates of the Education for All Handicapped Children Act in 1975 (PL-94-142), the precursor to the Individuals with Disabilities Education Act (IDEA, 2004). According to IDEA, parents must be given notice and consent to both their child's evaluation and special education ser-vices as well as receive reports on their child's progress on IEP goals (Yell, 2012). In addition, parents are to be active members of the IEP development, including providing input on goals and services (Tucker & Schwartz, 2013; Yell, 2012).

A recent survey by Tucker and Schwartz (2013) indicated that par-ents of students with ASD report several barriers to collaborating with school personnel. These barriers involve communication challenges and negative perceptions of school personnel, including a perceived lack of knowledge regarding ASD. In a parental survey, 60 percent of parents indicated that the school asked for their input on the draft of the IEP, but only 31 percent reported that their suggestions for goals and objectives were included in the IEP (Tucker & Schwartz, 2013). Increasing paren-tal involvement should be a goal for schools, as parental involvement is associated with greater satisfaction of their child's education (Renty & Roeyers, 2006).

Beyond parental perceptions, effective parent–school collaboration can be hindered because of the adversarial role that can exist when parents acting as advocates for their child are pitted against schools (Bacon & Causton-Theoharis, 2013). Bacon and Causton-Theoharis (2013) suggested that understanding of each group's perspective could help foster collaboration. In other words, collaboration can be improved when parents recognize that, most often, school personnel do want the best for each student, and educators recognize that parents would prefer collaboration to an adversarial relationship.

Paraprofessionals

Paraprofessionals are aides that work one-on-one with students with disabilities or support multiple students and/or a general or special teacher in a classroom with a licensed professional (e.g. teacher) supervising them in their responsibilities (Shyman, 2010). In recent years, the United States Department of Education (2012) reported that more paraprofessionals were employed in schools than teachers, and the majority of paraprofessionals work to support students with ASD (Carter, O'Rourke, Sisco, & Pelsue, 2009). Hence, these individuals play an increasingly important role in the education of students with ASD and are fundamental players in interdisciplinary collaboration (Giangreco & Broer, 2005; Suter & Giangreco, 2009).

The involvement of paraprofessionals in the education of students with disabilities, in general, and students with ASD, specifically, is controversial (Brock & Carter, 2013). Concerns exist that paraprofessionals are often teaching students most in need of high-quality teachers (Brock & Carter, 2013). The vast majority of paraprofessionals report providing one-on-one instruction (Carter et al., 2009). Other roles include providing behavioral or social support (Fisher & Pleasants, 2012), which is also controversial over concerns that paraprofessionals limit peer interactions, especially in inclusive settings (Carter, Sisco, Brown, Brickham, & Al-Khabbaz, 2008; Giangreco, 2010).

In general, paraprofessionals may perform various tasks such as individualized instruction, providing instructional support to small groups, fostering social relationships, assisting with behavior management programs, and clerical work for students with disabilities (Carter et al., 2009). Paraprofessionals assisting students with ASD perform similar roles. They provide support with academic, social, and behavior issues, collect data, and collaborate with educators to inform educational programming for these students (Rosetti & Goessling, 2010). It is imperative that teachers and other service providers work collaboratively with paraprofessionals to ensure the high quality of education, as well as create opportunities for independence for students with ASD across the grade spans (Brock & Carter, 2013).

Behavior Specialists

Wei, Wagner, Christiano, and colleagues (2014) found that over 40 percent of elementary-aged students with ASD receive behavior support. While behavior support can arise from multiple individuals (e.g. school social workers), behavior analysts, specifically Applied Behavior Analysts, are professionals whose primary function is to provide behavioral support to students with ASD. One type of behavioral support is referred to Applied Behavior Analysis (ABA). ABA techniques are supported by research and are used to teach students with ASD a variety of skills, including communication, social interaction, play, task engagement, self-help skills, and regulating problem behavior (Vismara & Rogers, 2010; Smith, 2012). Often behavior analysts provide ABA therapy in homes, clinics, centers, or private schools; they can also collaborate on behavioral interventions for students with ASD in traditional school settings (Axelrod, McElrath, & Wine, 2012; Kamau, 2014; Kelly & Tincani, 2013).

Behavior analysts are increasingly collaborating with school professionals to support students with ASD (Boutot & Hume, 2012), and such collaboration and inclusion of ABA in school settings benefits students. For example, Eikeseth, Smith, Jahr, and Eldevik (2002) found that elementary-aged students with ASD who received ABA in general education settings made more progress than those who received eclectic special education interventions. More recently, Grindle et al. (2012) found that elementary students with ASD educated in an ABA classroom in a typical school made growth over two years that was larger than students with ASD who received their typical educational interventions.

Collaboration During Transition and Beyond

Along with the service personnel involved in the education of students with ASD during the school years, transition specialists and vocational rehabilitation counselors may play a major role during a student's transition from school to adult life. Given the complexity of transition services, it is imperative that personnel from diverse agencies and organizations are involved in transition planning to help students achieve their post-school goals (Test, Aspel, & Everson, 2006). Such involvement and collaboration is also mandated by special education law, which defines transition services as a "coordinated set of activities for a child with a disability" ([34 CFR 300.43 (a)] [20 U.S.C. 1401(34)]). In other words, planning and providing transition services is a multi-faceted process involving teachers, related services personnel from the school district, the student, family members, and frequently adult service agencies (Steere, Rose, & Cavaiuolo, 2007). An important consideration from the collaboration perspective is that facilitating a student's transition from school to life post school is not exclusively the school's responsibility, but also involves adult agencies and organizations to support students during this process by providing funding and/or services (Steere et al., 2007).

Research and Practice Issues

Fundamental differences exist between services that students receive during high school and those after school exit, including a lack of a single point of service coordination as well as the change from services provided by entitlement under IDEA to ones determined by eligibility under Section 504 of the 1973 Rehabilitation Act or the Americans with Disabilities Act Amendments Act of 2008 (Brooke, Revell, McDonough, & Green, 2013; Getzel & Briel, 2013; Revell & Miller, 2009). The shift from public education to adult service agencies or post-secondary entities encountered during the transition process necessitates understanding new resources, organizations, and agencies along with their eligibility requirements, procedures, and policies (Revell & Miller, 2009). Students and their families must navigate through a maze of unfamiliar agencies and service providers to learn about the services available and to obtain the desired ones (Brooke et al, 2013; Revell & Miller, 2009). The transition from a school system to the adult service system is often by accompanied by decreased services and limited support for accessing such services (Lubetsky, Handen, Lubetsky, & McGonigle, 2014). Given the challenges in obtaining post-school services that meet the unique and varied needs of students with ASD, Test, Smith, and Carter (2014) recommended that natural community supports of family, friends, and the local community be considered as part of their comprehensive transition planning.

Historically, students with ASD have not experienced the same degree of positive post-school outcomes (e.g., employment, independent living, post-secondary attendance) as students with other disabilities or students without disabilities (Chiang, Cheung, Hickson, Xiang, & Tsai, 2012; Shattuck, Narendorf, Cooper, Sterzing, Wagner, & Taylor, 2012). For example, in a study of young adults with ASD who had exited high school, 56.1 percent participated in sheltered employment or day activity centers, 13.6 percent attended a college or university, 12.1 percent reported no regular activities, and 6.1 percent were competitively employed (Taylor & Seltzer, 2011). The results were divided between students with ASD with (almost 75 percent) and without an intellectual disability. Students with ASD with an intellectual disability were more likely to participate in sheltered employment or day activities (73.5 percent), while students with ASD without an intellectual disability were more likely to attend college or university (47.1 percent of the sample) or have no regular activities (23.5 percent) (Taylor & Seltzer, 2011). In their research, Cimera and

Cowan (2009) reported that while individuals with ASD were employed with higher frequency than many other disability categories examined (e.g. intellectual disability), they worked for fewer hours and earned lower wages. Data from the National Longitudinal Transition Study-2 (NLTS2) also documented poor post-school outcomes for students with ASD, including low rates of employment, independent living, and completion of post-secondary education (Newman et al., 2011; Wagner, Newman, Cameto, Levine, & Marder, 2007).

Based on the unique and diverse characteristics of students with ASD, interagency collaboration is beneficial throughout the transition process— assessment, training, provision of specific supports and services as well as follow-up (Westbrook et al., 2015). In practice, however, external agency participation in transition planning is limited for students with ASD and these individuals may not receive their required services after exiting school (Shattuck, Wagner, Narendorf, Sterzing, & Hensley, 2011; Shogren & Plotner, 2012). Lawer, Brusilovskiy, Salzer, and Mandell (2009) reported that adults with ASD were more likely to not receive vocational rehabilitation services due to severity of their disability, as compared to individuals with other disabilities. Vocational rehabilitation services received by adults with ASD may also be more expensive than those received by individuals with other disabilities (Cimera & Cowan, 2009; Lawer et al., 2009). Beyond assistance for employment, collaborative efforts need to support students with ASD in post-secondary educational settings. Data from the NLTS2 suggest that students with ASD do not always inform their school about their disability, which is a necessary first step in receiving services and accommodations in postsecondary environments (Newman et al., 2011; Wei et al., 2014).

Key Collaborators

Students with ASD require thorough and personalized transition planning, given their unique characteristics including strengths, needs, and desired post-school outcomes (Test et al., 2014). Needless to say, such transition programming requires the involvement of a variety of service providers at the school, district, and community level (Test et al., 2014). While several collaborators contribute to the transition of students with ASD, we highlight the following: transition specialists, vocational rehabilitation counselors, and college support programs or disability service offices (Please see Table 17.2 for a non-exhaustive list of external agency service providers).

Transition Specialist

The Council for Exceptional Children's Division on Career Development and Transition defines a transition specialist as "an individual who plans,

Table 17.2 External Agency Service Providers Involved in Transition Collaboration

Agency	Role
Developmental disability administration	Provide wide range of services such as vocational service programs, housing and social services
Social security administration	Provide financial support through programs such as Supplemental Security Income (SSI), Medicaid and Medicare
Community rehabilitation programs	Assist in providing assessments, job placement, and follow-up services
Centers for independent living	Provide information on community resources and provide training in such areas as socialization, financial management, and other aspects of independent living
One stop career centers	Provide information and referral services to available community resources, job listings for potential opportunities, career guidance, and competitive employment services including skills training, placement, and follow-up
Community colleges and vocational-technical institutions	Provide support and information on applications, financial aid, and accessibility
Disability support services at institutions of higher education	Determine eligibility to receive services and address specialized support or accommodation requests such as scribes, extra time on tests, distraction-free testing environment, and organizational help

Note:
Adapted from Postsecondary options for students with autism. In P. Wehman, M. D. Smith, & C. Schall (Eds.) (2009), *Autism and the transition to adulthood: Success beyond the classroom* by L. W. Briel and E. E. Getzel, pp. 189–207. Copyright 2008 by Paul H. Brookes; Transition planning and community resources: Bringing it all together. In P. Wehman (Ed.), *Life beyond classroom: Transition strategies for young people with disabilities* by V. Brooke, W. G. Revell, J. McDonnough, and H. Green, p. 143–171. Copyright 2013 by Paul H. Brookes; Pursuing postsecondary education opportunities for individuals with disabilities. In P. Wehman (Ed.), *Life beyond classroom: Transition strategies for young people with disabilities* by E. E. Getzel and L. W. Briel, p. 363–376. Copyright 2013 by Paul H. Brookes; Navigating the world of adult services and benefits planning. In P. Wehman, M. D. Smith, & C. Schall (Fds.), *Autism and transition to adulthood: Success beyond the classroom* by G. Revell and L. A. Miller, p. 139–162. Copyright 2009 by Paul H. Brookes; *Growing up: Transition for adult life for students with disabilities* by D. E. Steere, E. Rose, and D. Cavaiuolo. Copyright 2007 by Allyn and Bacon; Supporting more able students on the autism spectrum: College and beyond by E. VanBergeijk, A. Klin, and F. Volkmar, 2008, *Journal of Autism and Developmental Disorders*, *38*, p. 1379. Copyright 2008 by Springer; Educational supports for high functioning youth with ASD: The postsecondary pathway to college, by S. M. Zeedyk, L. A. Tipton, and J. Blacher, 2014, *Focus on Autism and Other Developmental Disabilities*, Advanced Online Publication. Copyright 2014 by Sage.

coordinates, delivers, and evaluates transition education and services at the school or system level, in conjunction with other educators, families, students, and representatives of community organizations" (Council for

Exceptional Children, 2000, p.1). A transition specialist is a school or district employee responsible for service coordination, as well as assembling transition teams, executing activities identified by the team, and ensuring effective functioning of the team (Test et al., 2006). Transition specialists also play the role of a liaison between various stakeholders in the transition process, such as students, parents, and staff, to connect transition goals with educational programming (Morningstar & Claveanna-Deane, 2014). Although all schools may not have a designated transition specialist position, oftentimes several staff members, such as guidance counselors, work-study coordinators, special education teachers, and supervisors may jointly perform the role of a transition specialist (Baer & Flexer, 2013).

Vocational Rehabilitation

Vocational rehabilitation is a cooperative program between state and federal governments that provides a variety of resources and supports focused on employment, as well as other services such as assessment, vocational counseling, training, personal assistant services, rehabilitation technology services, job placement, and supported employment services (McDonough & Revell, 2010; Revell & Miller, 2009). Applicants for vocational rehabilitation services are assigned to a counselor who determines their eligibility (Brooke et al., 2013). Once eligibility is determined, the vocational rehabilitation counselor creates an individualized plan for employment with input from the student, their family, and the transition team that includes the student's employment goals and identifies services required to achieve those goals (McDonough & Revell, 2010; Revell & Miller, 2009). Vocational rehabilitation can also provide funding to support students with ASD in postsecondary education, provided the student's employment goals warrant advanced education (Brooke et al., 2013; McDonough & Revell, 2010; Revell & Miller, 2009). Vocational rehabilitation counselors are extremely useful resources, since they can provide information on other funding and community resources and case management services, and can even coordinate services through widespread contacts with employers and other agencies such as supported employment (Brooke et al., 2013; McDonough & Revell, 2010; Revell & Miller, 2009).

College Support Programs

Increasingly, students with ASD are attending post-secondary education at institutions of higher education (Smith, 2007). Typically, institutions of higher education support the educational needs of their students with

ASD through the disability services office (Briel & Getzel, 2009; Getzel & Briel, 2013). However, over the last decade college support programs at institutions of higher education have been developed to specifically support students with ASD and students with intellectual disability to attend and succeed at college (Briel & Getzel, 2009; Wehmeyer & Patton, 2012). These specialized programs range from substantially separate entities to truly immersive and inclusive programs (Briel & Getzel, 2009; Getzel & Briel, 2013; Hart, Grigal, Sax, Martinez, & Will, 2006; Wehmeyer & Patton, 2012). While the research focused on students with ASD in postsecondary settings is limited (Gelbar, Smith, & Reichow, 2014), key factors or considerations for supporting students with ASD in college settings include: the student's communication needs, self-regulation, technology, self-determination, and attention to academic and social supports (Adreon & Durocher, 2007; Alpern & Zager, 2007; Briel & Getzel, 2009; Hart et al., 2006).

Conclusion

Collaborative problem solving is key to solving difficult problems (i.e. difficult to solve problems) and challenging situations (Friend & Cook, 2013). The education of students with ASD, like the education of all students, can be viewed in a difficult problem or challenging situation. Hence, collaboration is key to meeting the challenges inherent in educating students on the autism spectrum and delivering programs that will improve their educational outcomes. To fully embrace collaborative problem solving, we need to ensure that all key players have the training and resources to engage in collaboration (Blacher, Linn, & Zeedyk, 2015).

As stated throughout this chapter, collaboration should occur for students with ASD at all stages of their educational career: early childhood, school years, and transition to adult life. Through well-planned and implemented collaboration among educators, related service providers, and parents, educational outcomes for students with ASD can be improved.

References

Adreon, D., & Durocher, J. S. (2007). Evaluating the college transition needs of individuals with high-functioning autism spectrum disorders. *Intervention in School and Clinic, 45*, 271–279.

Alpern, C., & Zager, D. (2007). Addressing communication needs of young adults with autism in a college-based inclusion program. *Education and Training in Developmental Disabilities, 42*, 428–436.

American Speech-Language-Hearing Association. (2006). *Guidelines for speech-language pathologists in diagnosis, assessment, and treatment of autism spectrum disorders across the life span* [Guidelines]. Retrieved February 12, 2015 from www.asha.org/policy/GL2006-00049/#sec1.12.

American Speech-Language-Hearing Association (ASHA). (2015). *Autism (Autism Spectrum Disorder)*. Retrieved February 17, 2015, from www.asha.org/public/speech/disorders/Autism/#two.

American Speech-Language-Hearing Association (ASHA). (n.d.). *Augmentative and alternative communication (AAC)*. Retrieved September 4, 2014, from, www.asha.org/public/speech/disorders/AAC/.

Americans with Disabilities Act Amendments Act (ADAAA) of 2008, Pub. L. No. 110-325, 42 U.S.C. §§ 12101 et seq.

Axelrod, S., McElrath, K. K., & Wine, B. (2012). Applied behavior analysis: Autism and beyond. *Behavioral Interventions, 27*, 1–15. DOI: 10.1002/bin.1335

Bacon, J. K., & Causton-Theoharis, J. (2013). "It should be teamwork": A critical investigation of school practices and parent advocacy in special education. *International Journal of Inclusive Education, 17*, 682–699. doi: 10.1080/13603116.2012.708060

Baer, R., & Flexer, R. (2013). Coordinating transition services. In R. W. Flexer, R. M. Baer, P. Luft, & T. J. Simmons (Eds.), *Transition planning for secondary students with disabilities* (pp. 227–250). Upper Saddle River, NJ: Pearson.

Barnhill, G. P., Polloway, E. A., & Sumutka, B. M. (2011). A survey of personnel preparation practices in autism spectrum disorders. *Focus on Autism and Other Developmental Disabilities, 26*, 75–86. doi: 10.1177/1088357 610378292

Binger, C., & Light, J. (2006). Demographics of preschoolers who require AAC. *Language, Speech, and Hearing Services in Schools, 37*, 200–208.

Bitterman, A., Daley, T., Misra, S., Carlson, E., & Markowitz, J. (2008). A national sample of preschoolers with autism spectrum disorders: Special education services and parent satisfaction. *Journal of Autism and Developmental Disorders, 38*, 1509–1517. doi:10.1007/s10803-007-0531-9

Blacher, J., Linn, R. H., & Zeedyk, S. M. (2015). The role of graduates schools of education in training autism professionals to work with diverse families. In D. E. Mitchell, & R. K. Reem (Eds.), *Professional responsibility: The fundamental issue in education and health care reform* (pp. 231–246). New York: Springer. doi: 10.1007/978-3-319-02603-0_14

Boutot, E. A., & Hume, K. (2012). Beyond time out and table time: Today's applied behavior analysis for students with autism. *Education and Training in Autism and Developmental Disabilities, 47*, 23–28.

Briel, L. W., & Getzel, E. E. (2009). Postsecondary options for students with autism. In P. Wehman, M. D. Smith, & C. Schall (Eds.), *Autism and the transition to adulthood: Success beyond the classroom* (pp. 189–207). Baltimore, MD: Brookes.

Brock, M. E., & Carter, E. W. (2013). A systematic review of paraprofessional-delivered educational practices to improve outcomes for students with intellectual and developmental disabilities. *Research & Practice for Persons with Severe Disabilities, 38*, 211–221. doi: 10.1177/154079691303800401

Brooke, V., Revell, W. G., McDonnough, J., & Green, H. (2013). Transition planning and community resources: Bringing it all together. In P. Wehman (Ed.), *Life beyond classroom: Transition strategies for young people with disabilities* (pp. 143 –171). Baltimore, MD: Paul H. Brookes Publishing Co.

Brown, M. (2009). Perspectives on outcome: What disability insiders and outsiders each bring to the assessment table. *Archives of Physical Medicine and Rehabilitation, 90*(11, Suppl. 1), S36–S40.

Carter, E. W., O'Rourke, L., Sisco, L. G., & Pelsue, D. (2009). Knowledge, responsibilities, and training needs of paraprofessionals in elementary and secondary schools. *Remedial and Special Education, 30,* 344–359. doi: 10.1177/0741932508324399

Carter, E. W., Sisco, L. G., Brown, L., Brickham, D., & Al-Khabbaz, Z. A. (2008). Peer interactions and academic engagement of youth with developmental disabilities in inclusive middle and high school classrooms. *American Journal on Mental Retardation, 113,* 479–494.

Causton, J., & Tracy-Bronson, C. P. (2014). *The speech-language pathologist's handbook for inclusive school practices.* Baltimore, MD: Brookes Publishing.

Chen, W.-B., & Gregory, A. (2011). Parental involvement in the prereferral process: Implications for schools. *Remedial and Special Education, 32,* 447–457. doi: 10.1177/0741932410362490

Chiang, H., Cheung, Y. K., Hickson, L., Xiang, R., & Tsai, L. Y. (2012). Predictive factors of participation in postsecondary education for high school leavers with autism. *Journal of Autism and Developmental Disabilities, 42,* 685–696. doi: 10.1007/s10803-011-1297-7.

Cidav, Z., Lawer, L., Marcus, S. C., & Mandell, D. S. (2013). Age-related variation in health service use and associated expenditures among children with autism. *Journal of Autism and Developmental Disorders, 43,* 924–931. doi: 10.1007/s10803-012-1637-2

Cimera, R. E., & Cowan, R. J. (2009). The cost of services and employment outcomes achieved by adults with autism in the US. *Autism, 13,* 285–302.

Cohen, H., Amerine-Dickens, M., & Smith T. (2006). Early intensive behavioral treatment: Replication of the UCLA model in a community setting. *Journal of Developmental & Behavioral Pediatrics, 27*(2 suppl), S145–S155

Council for Exceptional Children, Division on Career Development and Transition. (2000). *Transition Specialist Competencies (Fact Sheet).* Retrieved February 12, 2015 from www.nsttac.org/sites/default/files/assets/pdf/DCDT FactSheeCompentencies.pdf.

Dawson, G., Rogers, S., Munson, J., Smith, M., Winter, J., Greenson, J., . . . Varley, J. (2010). Randomized, controlled trial of an intervention for toddlers with autism: The Early Start Denver Model. *Pediatrics, 125*(1), 17–23. doi: 10.1542/peds.2009-0958

Dettmer, P., Knackendoffel, A., & Thurston, L. P. (2013). *Collaboration, consultation, and teamwork for students with special needs* (7th ed.). Boston, MA: Pearson.

Donaldson, A. L., & Stahmer, A. C. (2014). Team collaboration: The use of behavior principles for serving students with ASD. *Language, Speech, and Hearing Services in Schools, 45,* 261–276.

Eikeseth, S., Smith, T., Jahr, E., & Eldevik, S. (2002). Intensive behavioral treatment at school for 4- to 7-year-old children with autism: A 1-year comparison controlled study. *Behavior Modification, 26,* 49–68. doi: 10.1177/0145445502026001004

Fisher, M., & Pleasants, S. L. (2012). Roles, responsibilities, and concerns of paraeducators: Findings from a statewide survey. *Remedial and Special Education, 33*, 287–297. DOI: 10.1177/0741932510397762

Friend, M., & Cook, L. (2013). *Interactions: Collaboration skills for school professionals* (7th ed.). Boston, MA: Pearson.

Gargiulo, R. (2015). *Special education in contemporary society: An introduction to exceptionality* (5th ed.). Thousand Oaks, CA: Sage.

Gargiulo, R. M., & Kilgo, J. (2013). *An introduction to young children with special needs: Birth though age eight*. Belmont, CA: Wadsworth Cengage Learning.

Gelbar, N. W., Smith, I., & Reichow, B. (2014). Systematic review of articles describing experience and supports of individuals with autism enrolled in college and university programs. *Journal of Autism and Developmental Disorders, 44*, 2593–2601.

Getzel, E. E., & Briel, L.W. (2013). Pursuing postsecondary education opportunities for individuals with disabilities. In P. Wehman (Ed.), *Life beyond classroom: Transition strategies for young people with disabilities* (pp. 363–376). Baltimore, MD: Paul H. Brookes Publishing Co.

Giangreco, M. F. (2010). One-to-one paraprofessionals for students with disabilities in inclusive classrooms: Is conventional wisdom wrong? *Intellectual and Developmental Disabilities, 48(1)*, 1–13.

Giangreco, M. F., & Broer, S. M. (2005). Questionable utilization of paraprofessionals in inclusive schools: Are we addressing symptoms or root causes? *Focus on Autism and Other Developmental Disabilities, 20*, 10–26.

Goin-Kochel, R. P., Myers, B. J., & Mackintosh, V. H. (2007). Parental reports on the use of treatments and therapies for children with autism spectrum disorders. *Research in Autism Spectrum Disorders, 1*, 195–209.

Green, V. A., Pituch, K. A., Itchon, J., Choi, A., O'Reilly, M., & Sigafoos, J. (2006). Internet survey of treatments used by parents of children with autism. *Research in Developmental Disabilities, 27*, 70–84.

Grindle, C. R., Hastings, R. P., Saville, M., Hughes, J. C., Huxley, K., Kovshoff, H, ... Remington, B. (2012). Outcomes of a behavioral education model for children in autism in a mainstream school setting. *Behavior Modification, 36*, 298–319. DOI: 10.1177/0145445512441199

Hart, D., Grigal, M., Sax, C., Martinez, D., & Will, M. (2006). Postsecondary education options for students with intellectual disabilities. *Research to Practice, 45*, 1–4.

Howard, J. S., Sparkman, C. R., Cohen, H. G., Green, G., & Stanislaw, H. (2005). A comparison of intensive behavior analytic and eclectic treatments for young children with autism. *Research in Developmental Disabilities, 26(4)*, 359–383.

Hume, K., Bellini, S., & Pratt, C. (2005). The usage and perceived outcomes of early intervention and early childhood programs for young children with autism spectrum disorder. *Topics in Early Childhood Special Education, 25*, 195–207.

Hustad, K., Berg, A., Bauer, D., Keppner, K., Schanz, A., & Gamradt, J. (2005). *AAC interventions for toddlers and preschoolers: Who, what, when, why*. Mini-seminar presented at the annual convention of the American Speech Language Hearing Association, San Diego, CA.

Individuals with Disabilities Education Improvement Act of 2004, Pub. L. No. 108-446, 20 U.S.C. §§ 1400 *et seq*. IDEA Data Center. (2012). *2012*

Part B Data. Retrieved February 12, 2015 from, https://inventory.data.gov/dataset/8715a3e8-bf48-4eef-9deb-fd9bb76a196e/resource/a68a23f3-3981-47db-ac75-98a167b65259/download/userssharedsdf2012ideapartbchildcounteducenvrmnts.csv.

Irvin, D. W., McBee, M., Boyd, B. A., Hume, K., & Odom, S. L. (2012). Child and family factors associated with the use of services for preschoolers with autism spectrum disorder. *Research in Autism Spectrum Disorders, 6,* 565–572. doi: 10.1016/j.rasd.2011.07.018

Kamau, L. Z. (2014). *Applied behavior analysis based interventions in public schools: Understanding factors that hinder adoption, implementation, and maintenance.* (Unpublished doctoral dissertation). Northeastern University, Boston, MA.

Karst, J., & Vaughan Van Hecke, A. (2012). Parent and family impact of autism spectrum disorders: A review and proposed model for intervention evaluation. *Clinical Child and Family Psychological Review, 15,* 247–277.

Kelly, A., & Tincani, M. (2013). Collaborative training and practice among applied behavior analysts who support individuals with autism spectrum disorder. *Education and Training in Autism and Developmental Disabilities, 48,* 120–131.

Koegel, L., Matos-Freden, R., Lang, R., & Koegel, R. (2012). Interventions for children with autism spectrum disorders in inclusive school settings. *Cognitive and Behavioral Practice, 19,* 401–412.

Kurth, J., & Mastergeorge, A. M. (2010). Individual education plan goals and services for adolescents with autism: Impact of age and educational setting. *Journal of Special Education, 44,* 146–160. doi: 10.1177/0022466908329825

Lawer, L., Brusilovskiy, E., Salzer, M. S., & Mandell, D. S. (2009). Use of vocational rehabilitative services among adults with autism. *Journal of Autism and Developmental Disabilities, 39,* 487–494. doi: 10.1007/s10803-008-0649-4

Loiacono, V. & Valenti, V. (2010). General education teachers need to be prepared to co-teach the increasing number of children with autism in inclusive settings. *International Journal of Special Education, 25*(3), 24–32.

Lubetsky, M. J., Handen, B. L., Lubetsky, M., & McGonigle, J. J. (2014). Systems of care for individuals with autism spectrum disorder and serious behavioral disturbance through the lifespan. *Child and Adolescent Psychiatric Clinics of North America, 23,* 97–110. doi: 10.1016/j.chc.2013.08.004

McConachie, H., & Robinson, G. (2006). What services do young children with autism spectrum disorder receive? *Child Care, Health and Development, 32,* 553–557. doi: 10.1111/j.1365-2214.2006.00672

McDonough, J. T., & Revell G. (2010). Accessing employment supports in the adult system for transitioning youth with autism spectrum disorders. *Journal of Vocational Rehabilitation, 32,* 89–100. doi: 10.3233/JVR-2010-0498

Morningstar, M. E., & Clavenna-Deane, B. (2014). Preparing secondary special educators and transition specialists. In P. T. Sindelar, E. D., McCray, M. T. Brownell, & B. Lignugaris/Kraft (Eds.), *Handbook of research on special education teacher preparation* (pp. 405–419). New York: Routledge

Newman, L., Wagner, M., Knokey, A. M., Marder, C., Nagle, K., Shaver, D., . . . Schwarting, M. (2011). *The post-high school outcomes of young adults with disabilities up to 8 years after high school. A report from the National Longitudinal Transition Study-2 (NLTS2).* (NCSER 2011–3005). Menlo Park, CA: SRI International.

Odom, S. L., Boyd, B. A., Hall, L. J., & Hume, K. (2010). Evaluation of comprehensive treatment models for individuals with autism spectrum disorders. *Journal of Autism and Developmental Disorders, 40*, 425–436. doi: 10.1007/s10803-009-0825-1

Patten, E., Baranek, G. T., Watson, L. R., & Schulz, B. (2011). Child and family characteristics influencing intervention choices in autism spectrum disorders. *Focus on Autism and Other Developmental Disabilities, 28*, 138–146. doi: 10.1177/1088357612468028

Pizur-Barnekow, K., Muusz, M., McKenna, C., O'Connor, E., & Cutler, A. (2012). Service coordinators' perceptions of autism-specific screening and referral practices in early intervention. *Topics in Early Childhood Special Education, 33*, 153-161. doi: 10.1177/0271121412463086

Podvey, M. C., Hinojosa, J., & Koening, K. P. (2013). Reconsidering insider status for families during the transition from early intervention to preschool special education. *The Journal of Special Education, 46*, 211–222. doi: 10.1177/0022466911407074

Reed, P., Osborne, L. A., & Corness, M. (2007). Brief report: Relative effectiveness of different home-based behavioral approaches to early teaching intervention. *Journal of Autism and Developmental Disorders, 37(9)*, 1815–1821.

Renty, J., & Roeyers, H. (2006). Satisfaction with formal support and education for children with autism spectrum disorder: The voices of parents. *Child: Care, Health, and Development, 32*, 371–385.

Revell, G., & Miller, L. A. (2009). Navigating the world of adult services and benefits planning. In P. Wehman, M. D. Smith, & C. Schall (Eds.), *Autism and transition to adulthood: Success beyond the classroom* (pp. 139–162). Baltimore, MD: Paul H. Brookes Publishing Co.

Ritzema, A. M., Sladeczek, I. E., Ghosh, S., Karagiannakis, A., & Manay-Quian, N. (2014). Improving outcomes for children with developmental disabilities through enhanced communication and collaboration between school psychologists and physicians. *Canadian Journal of School Psychology, 29*, 317–337. doi: 10.1177/0829573514536529

Rodriguez, I. R., Saldana, D., & Moreno, F. J. (2012). Support, inclusion, and special education teachers' attitudes towards the education of students with autism spectrum disorders. *Autism Research and Treatment, 2012*, 1–9. doi: 10.1155/2012/259468

Rossetti, Z. S., & Goessling, D. P. (2010). Facilitating friendships between secondary students with and without autism spectrum disorders or developmental disabilities. *Teaching Exceptional Children, 42*, 64–70.

Schertz, H. H., & Odom, S. L. (2007). Promoting joint attention in toddlers with autism: A parent-mediated developmental model. *Journal of Autism and Developmental Disorders, 37*, 1562–1575.

Schopler, E., & Reichler, R. (1981). Parents as co-therapists in the treatment of psychotic children. *Journal of Autism and Childhood Schizophrenia, 1(1)*, 87–102.

Shattuck, P. T., Narendorf, S. C., Cooper, B., Sterzing, P. R., Wagner, M., & Taylor, J. L. (2012). Postsecondary education and employment among youth with autism spectrum disorder. *Pediatrics, 12*, 1042–1049. doi: 10.1542/peds.2011.2864

Shattuck, P. T., Wagner, M., Narendorf, S., Sterzing, P., & Hensley, M. (2011). Post-high school service usage among young adults with an autism spectrum disorder. *Archives of Pediatrics and Adolescent Medicine, 165,* 141–146. doi: 10.1001/archpediatrics.2010.279.

Shogren, K. A., & Plotner, A. J. (2012). Transition planning for students with intellectual disability, autism, and other disabilities: Data from the National Longitudinal Transition Study -2. *Intellectual and Developmental Disabilities, 50,* 16–30. doi: 10.1352/1934-9556-50.1.16

Shyman, E. (2010), Identifying predictors of emotional exhaustion among special education paraeducators: A preliminary investigation, *Psychology in the Schools, 47,* 828–841.

Simpson, R. L., Mundschenk, N. A., & Heflin, L. J. (2011). Issues, policies, and recommendations for improving the education of learners with autism spectrum disorders. *Journal of Disability Policy Studies, 22,* 3–17. doi: 10.1177/1044207310394850

Smith, C. P. (2007). Support services for students with asperger's syndrome in higher education. *College Student Journal, 41*(3), 515–531.

Smith, T. (2012). Evolution of research on intervention for individuals with autism spectrum disorder: Implications for behavior analysts. The *Behavior Analyst, 35*(1), 101–113.

Steere, D. E., Rose, E., & Cavaiuolo, D. (2007). *Growing up: Transition for adult life for students with disabilities.* Boston, MA: Allyn and Bacon.

Suter, J. C., & Giangreco M. F. (2009). Numbers that count: Exploring special education and paraprofessional service delivery in inclusion-oriented schools. *Journal of Special Education, 43,* 81–93.

Taber-Doughty, T., & Bouck, E. C. (2012). Family support and involvement throughout the school years. In D. Zager, M. Wehmeyer, & R. Simpson (Eds.), *Educating students with autism spectrum disorders: Research-based principles and practices* (pp. 262–277). New York: Routledge.

Taylor, J. L., & Seltzer, M. M. (2011). Employment and postsecondary educational activities for young adults with autism spectrum disorders during the transition to adulthood. *Journal of Autism and Developmental Disorders, 41,* 566–574. doi: 10.1007/s10803-010-1070-3.

Test, D. W., Aspel, N. P., & Everson, J. M. (2006). *Transition methods for youth with disabilities.* Upper Saddle River, NJ: Pearson Education, Inc.

Test, D. W., Smith, L. E., Carter, E. W. (2014). Equipping youth with autism spectrum disorders for adulthood: Promoting rigor, relevance, and relationships. *Remedial and Special Education, 35,* 80–90. doi: 10.1177/0741932513514857

Tincani, M. (2007). Beyond consumer advocacy: Autism spectrum disorders, effective instruction, and public schools. *Intervention in School and Clinic, 43,* 47–51. doi: 10.1177/10534512070430010601

Tucker, V., & Schwartz, I. (2013). Parents' perspectives of collaboration with school professional: Barriers and facilitators to successful partnerships in planning for students with ASD. *School Mental Health, 5,* 3–14. doi: 10.1007/s12310-012-9102-0.

U.S. Department of Education. (2012). *Paraprofessionals employed (FTE) to provide special education and related services to children ages 6 through 21 under IDEA, Part B, by qualifications and state: Fall 2010* [Data file]. Retrieved March 1, 2015 from www.ideadata.org.

VanBergeijk, E., Klin, A., & Volkmar, F. (2008). Supporting more able students on the autism spectrum: College and beyond. *Journal of Autism and Developmental Disorders, 38,* 1359–1370. doi: 10.1007/s10803-007-0524-8

Villa, R. & Thousand, J. Roles of related services personnel in inclusive schools. In *Restructuring for caring and effective education: Piecing the puzzle together* (2nd ed.), M. F. Giangreco, P. Prelock, R. Reid, R. Dennis, and S. Edelman (Eds.), *Restructuring for caring and effective education: Piecing the puzzle together* (pp. 360–388). Baltimore, MO: Paul H. Brookes.

Vismara, L. A., & Rogers, S. J. (2010). Behavioral treatments in autism spectrum disorders: What do we know? *Annual Review of Clinical Psychology, 6,* 447–468. Doi: 10.1146/annurev.clinpsy.121208.131151

Wagner, M., Newman, L., Cameto, R., Levine, P., & Marder, C. (2007). *Perceptions and expectations of youth with disabilities. A special topic report of findings from the National Longitudinal Transition Study-2 (NLTS2)* (NCSER 2007-3006). Washington, DC: National Center for Special Education Research.

Wei, X., Wagner, M., Christiano, E. R. A., Shattuck, P., & Yu, J. W. (2014). Special education services received by students with autism spectrum disorders from preschool through high school. *The Journal of Special Education, 48,* 167–179. doi: 10.1177/0022466913483576

Wei, X., Wagner, M., Hudson, L., Yu, J. W., & Shattuck, P. (2014). Transition to adulthood: Education and disengagement in individuals with autism spectrum disorders. *Emerging Adulthood.* Advance online publication. doi: 10.1177/2167696814534417

Wehman, P., Smith, M., & Schall, C. (2009). *Autism and the transition to adulthood: Success beyond the classroom.* Baltimore, MD: Paul Brookes.

Wehmeyer, M. L., & Patton, J. R. D. (2012). Transition to postsecondary education, employment, and adult living. In D. Zager, M. L. Wehmeyer, & R. L. Simpson (Eds.), *Educating students with autism spectrum disorder: Research-based principles and practices.* New York: Routledge.

Westbrook, J. D., Fong, C. J., Nye, C., Williams, A., Wendt, O., & Cortopassi, T. (2015). Transition services for youth with autism: A systematic review. *Research on Social Work Practice, 25,* 10–20, doi: 10.1177/1049731514524836

White, S. W., Scahill, L., Klin, A., Koenig, K., & Volkmar, F. R. (2007). Educational placements and service patterns of individuals with autism spectrum disorder. *Journal of Autism and Developmental Disorders, 37,* 1403–1412. doi: 10.1007/s10803-006-0281-0

Yell, M. (2012). *The law and special education* (3rd ed.). Boston, MA: Pearson.

Zeedyk, S. M., Tipton, L. A., & Blacher, J. (2014). Educational supports for high functioning youth with ASD: The postsecondary pathway to college. *Focus on Autism and Other Developmental Disabilities.* Advanced online publication]. doi: 10.1177/1088257614525435

Index

Note: page numbers referring to a table are followed by a *t*.